The Drama Scholars' Index
To Plays and Filmscripts:

A Guide to Plays and Filmscripts in Selected
Anthologies, Series and Periodicals

Volume 2

by
GORDON SAMPLES

The Scarecrow Press, Inc.
Metuchen, N. J., & London
1980

v.2

Library of Congress Cataloging in Publication Data   (Revised)

Samples, Gordon.
    The drama scholars' index to plays and filmscripts.

        1. Drama--Indexes.   I.   Title.
    Z5781. S17   [PN1655]   016. 80882   73-22165
    ISBN 0-8108-1249-5

For

JANICE

CONTENTS

INTRODUCTION

The second volume of The Drama Scholars' Index to Plays and Filmscripts continues in much the same vein as the first, that of providing the serious drama student an advantage in finding plays and filmscripts in anthologies, series, and periodicals in their original languages, or in various translations. The work is designed to reflect the richness, scope, and diversity of all dramatic endeavor. The standard is here, but so is the unusual, and coverage is balanced both historically and ethnically. In addition to the standard, emphasis is placed on indexing those items not covered by other indexes.

Fragments and condensations have not been included, except in some cases where only an excerpt is available, and such fragment would enrich the bibliographic research of the user. Occasionally, separate complete acts of plays have been included if deemed important enough to stand alone from the complete work.

Fewer filmscripts seem to have been published in the last several years. A substitute designed for a wider, general coverage has come into being, called the "film novel," or the "cinenovel." Instead of publishing the exact script, it is novelized by different authors from the original script. Publishers, probably believing in the old theory that filmscripts make poor reading and that tricked-up novelized versions gain more sales, have gone more heavily toward the substitution. This is unfortunate, for most all "film novels" end up poor imitations of the original screenplays, and are of little value to the film scholar. Another popular treatment of films is to write a book about the making of the film, including some scenes from the original screenplay. Neither this type of film book nor the "film novels" are included in this index.

Because of letters from users of the first volume who offered suggestions for additions to a second work, it has been decided to call it Volume 2 instead of a supplement. Indexing for the second volume goes back to the beginning of recorded dramatic literature and continues through 1977. Both volumes are designed to be used separately, or for broader coverage, of course, in conjunction with each other.

An author list of anthologies indexed in Volume 2 has been included as was done in Volume 1. In addition, a cumulative title list of anthologies indexed in Volumes 1 and 2 has been included. This is in response to users who wish both listings of the anthologies.

vii

As in Volume 1, complete information is given under the author, indicating whether the work is a play, filmscript, television script, or radio script. In addition, film, television, and radio scripts are so designated under title as well for added clarification from play titles. Added "see" references are included for titles, joint authors, adapters, authors upon whose work the script is based, and historical names of people upon which a biographical script is based.

Since the early 60s, the film director has been generally considered to be the author of his film, with all other members of his crew under him contributing toward the joint effort of a translation to the screen. Because of this, one will find filmscripts entered interchangeably under the director and the scriptwriter, with cross references to both.

There are also cross references to variant spellings of names. Translators, while given in the main entries, are not given added entries unless they also contributed as adapters, or offered major different versions from the original. There are also considerable added entries for pseudonyms, title variations, and other related information which should further enhance the work's usefulness as a reference book in addition to its being an index.

Every effort has been made to index complete sets or continuations. In cases where only certain volumes contain scripts, the entry would indicate only such volumes, e.g., Vols. 2-4, or Vol. 5, 9. The same would hold true in volumes of sets not yet published, e.g., Vols. 1, 5, 10. Plays and films about historical characters are indicated by an asterisk at the beginning of the title. Those scripts adapted from another author's work are indicated by a double asterisk. All source references are to titles of anthologies, periodicals, and series.

The author wishes to express his appreciation to the following persons at San Diego State University Library: to Ann Wright and Karen Hogarth for Inter-Library Loan services; to Dolores Woods for computerized catalog information service; and to Ian Elliott for typing the manuscript.

In addition, appreciation is extended to many others who wrote letters expressing interest and offering suggestions, and to those who forwarded items and ideas for possible inclusion.

It has been the author's intent to unearth and group the titles of plays and filmscripts in a meaningful way, remembering the comment from Alistair Cooke, who called anthologies "famous graveyards of literature," because so many works are "buried" without indexes.

Gordon Samples

San Diego State University
California
July 1978

ERRATA TO VOLUME 1

(Changes or additions are underlined)

page 39, line 8:   should read, Enrico, Robert.
page 42, line 40:   should read, Boleyn, Anne, Consort of Henry
VIII, King of England, 1507-1536.
page 76, line 39:   should read, The Clandestine Marriage.
page 91, line 2:   should read, D'AVENANT, Sir William, 1606-1668.
page 117, after line 26 add: Eternal Return (see Cocteau, Jean).
page 149, line 32:   should read, GOGOL, Nikolai Vasil'evich, 1809-
1852.
page 158, line 8:   should read, Lady Jane Grey (see ROWE, Nicholas).
page 165, line 39:   should read, HARRIGAN, Edward, 1845-1911.
page 195, line 25:   should read,
Iwasaki, Yozan T.
Nari-kin
(In Three Modern Japanese Plays).
page 217, after line 40 add: Lady Jane Grey (see ROWE, Nicholas).
page 273, line 37:   should read, MURRIETA, Joaquin, 1828/9-1853.
page 301, line 1:   PIEXERECOURT, M. add: spelling as in Cumberland's British Theatre, see Piexerecourt, Rene Charles Guilbert
de (Library of Congress spelling).   Lines 2-4:   delete.
page 303, after line 48 add:
PIXERECOURT, Rene Charles Guilbert de, 1773-1844
Le Pelerin Blanc; translated and adapted as "The Wandering
Boys: A Melodrama," with music by Mr. Nicholson
(In Cumberland's British Theatre, Vol. 30, no. 2)
page 326, lines 8-12:   delete.
page 329, after line 36:   should read,
Lady Jane Grey
(In Bell's British Theatre, 1797, Vol. 15)
The Royal Convert
(In Bell's British Theatre, 1797, Vol. 27)
page 330, line 24:   should read, The Royal Convert (see ROWE,
Nicholas).
page 348, line 11:   should read, Seymour, Jane, 2nd wife of Henry
VIII, King of England, 1509?-1537.
page 365, line 42:   should read, Squatter Sovereignty (see HARRI-
GAN, Edward).
page 394, line 14:   should read, UDALL, Nicholas, 1505-1556.
page 431, line 2:   add Vol. 2.
page 432, line 35:   should read, Buitenen, Johannes Adrianus Ber-
nardus van.
page 440, line 25:   should read, Litto, Frederic M.

Life's moving pictures, well-wrought plays,
To others' grief attention raise:
Here, while the tragic fictions glow,
We borrow joy by pitying woe;
There gaily comic scenes delight,
And hold true mirrors to our sight.

--Matthew Green, from The Spleen, 1804.

ABC--A Cinema Scenario for Reading (see Rozov, Victor)
AC/DC (see Williams, Heathcote)
A. E. (pseud.) (see Russell, George W.)
A³ (see Bridges, James)
A Bomba (see Souto, Alexandrino de)
A Cada Caul Segun Su Apetito (see Mogin, Jean)
A Favor de la Corriente (see Adamov, Arthur)
A la Salida de la Luna (see Gregory, Isabella A.)
A l'Est d'Eden screenplay (see Kazan, Elia)
A Media Luz los Tres (see Mihura, Miguel)
A Quelque Chose Hasard Est Bon (see Hugo, Victor M.)
A-A-America! (see Bond, Edward)
El Abanderado (see Heiremans, Luis A.)
ABBENSETTS, Michael
    Sweet Talk
        (In Plays and Players, Vol. 20, no. 11, Aug. 1973)
ABBOTT, George, 1887-
    Fiorello! (see Bock, Jerry)
    New Girl in Town (see Merrill, Bob)
Abbott and Costello radio script (see Smith, Kate)
'ABD AL-SABUR, Salah
    Murder in Baghdad (Ma'sat al-Hallaj)
        (In Arabic Translation Series of The Journal of Arabic Liter-
        ature, Vol. 1, 1972)
Abdelazer; or, The Moor's Revenge (see Behn, Mrs. Aphra)
ABE, Kobo, 1924-
    Aquí está el Fantasma
        (In Teatro Japonés Contemporaneo)
    Friends
        (In Evergreen Plays Series, 1969)
  **Woman in the Dunes; screenplay (see Teshigahara, Hiroshi)
Abe Lincoln in Illinois (see Sherwood, Robert E.)
ABEL, Lionel, 1910-
    The Death of Odysseus
        (In Playbook: Five Plays for a New Theatre)
Abelard and Heloise (see Millar, Ronald)
ABELARDO, Victoria
    World Peace--a Dream; adapted from "The Voice of Peace"
        by Ricardo C. Galang and "A Dream" by Nani Zaballero.
        (In Philippine Harvest)
Abele (see Alfieri, Vittorio)
ABELL, Kjeld, 1901-1961
    Anna Sophie Hedvig
        (In Masterpieces of the Modern Scandinavian Theatre)

1

(In <u>Scandinavian Plays of the 20th Century</u>, Series 2)
Aben Humeya (see Martinez de la Rosa, Francisco)
Abendlicht (see Arbusow, Alexej)
Der Abenteurer und die Sängerin (see Hofmannsthal, Hugo von H.)
Abide with Me (see Keeffe, Barrie)
ABLEMAN, Paul
    Hank's Night: A Sea-Blue Comedy, from "Blue Comedy. "
        (In <u>Methuen Playscripts</u>, 1968)
    Madly in Love: A Sky-Blue Comedy, from "Blue Comedy. "
        (In <u>Methuen Playscripts</u>, 1968)
    Tests
        (In <u>Methuen Playscripts</u>, 1966)
Abortion (see O'Neill, Eugene)
About Mortin (see Pinget, Robert)
Abraham and Isaac (Anon.)
    (In <u>A Book of Short Plays</u>, XV-XX Centuries)
Abraham et Samuel (see Haim, Victor)
Abraham, L'Ami de Dieu (see Lamarche, Gustave)
Abraham Lincoln (see Drinkwater, John)
Abraham Sacrifiant (see Bèze, Théodore de)
Abroad and at Home (see Holman, Joseph G.)
Absalom, 3rd son of David
    *The Brief and Violent Reign of Absalom (see Pendleton, James
    D.)
ABSE, Dannie
    Gone
        (In <u>Gambit</u>, no. 1)
        (In his <u>Three Questor Plays</u>)
    House of Cowards
        (In his <u>Three Questor Plays</u>)
    In the Cage
        (In his <u>Three Questor Plays</u>)
Absent Friends (see Ayckbourn, Alan)
The Absent Man (see Bickerstaff, Isaac)
Les Absents (see Daudet, Alphonse)
Abstraction (Anon.)
    (In <u>World Drama</u>, Vol. 1)
Absurd Person Singular (see Ayckbourn, Alan)
The Academy (see Fratti, Mario)
Acapulco Madame (see Jamaique, Yves)
Accidents Will Happen (see Langner, Lawrence)
L'Accoppiamento (see Bona, Giampiero)
Ace of Clubs (see Coward, Noël)
ACHARD, Marcel, 1899-
    Le Corsaire
        (In his <u>Histoires d'Amour</u>)
    Jean de la Lune
        (In his <u>Histoires d'Amour</u>)
    Marlborough s'en Va-t-en Guerre
        (In his <u>Histoires d'Amour</u>)
    Voulez-vous Jouer avec Môa?
        (In his <u>Histoires d'Amour</u>)
Achilles (see Gay, John)

Achtung des Kriegers (see Kaiser, Georg)
Acis and Galatea (see Gay, John)
ACKLAND, Rodney, 1906-
    After October
        (In Famous Plays of 1935-36)
    Before the Party, based on a short story by W. Somerset Maugham.
        (In Plays of the Year, Vol. 2, 1949)
    The Old Ladies
        (In Famous Plays of 1934-35)
Acrobats (see Horovitz, Israel)
Across the Continent; or, Scenes from New York Life and the Pacific
    Railroad (see McCloskey, James J.)
Across the Everglades; a play for the screen (see Schulberg, Budd)
Act the Second: The Norwich Incident (see Levitt, Paul M.)
Les Acteurs de Bonne Foi (see Marivaux, Pierre C.)
Actor from Vienna (see Molnar, Ferenc)
Actors (see Bromberg, Conrad)
Adam and Eve (see Bulgakov, Mikhail)
Adam the Creator (see Capek, Karel)
Adam (The Mystery of Adam) (Anon.)
        (In World Drama, Vol. 1)
ADAMOV, Arthur, 1908-
    A Favor de la Corriente
        (In his Teatro, Vol. 2)
    All Against All
        (In Themes of Drama)
    La Grande y la Pequeña Maniobra
        (In his Teatro, Vol. 1)
    L'Invasion. Text in French.
        (In Le Théâtre d'Aujourd'hui)
    La Invasion. Text in Spanish.
        (In his Teatro, Vol. 1)
    Monsieur le Modere
        (In Le Théâtre d'Aujourd'hui)
    Paolo Paoli
        (In Teatro Francés de Vanguardia)
    Le Parodia
        (In his Teatro, Vol. 1)
    Ping Pong
        (In his Two Plays)
    Le Ping-Pong. Text in French.
        (In Le Théâtre d'Aujourd'hui)
    El Ping-Pong. Text in Spanish.
        (In his Teatro, Vol. 2)
    El Profesor Taranne. Text in Spanish.
        (In his Teatro, Vol. 1)
    Professor Taranne
        (In Four Modern French Comedies)
        (In his Two Plays)
    El Reencuentro
        (In his Teatro, Vol. 2)
    Todos Contra Todos
        (In his Teatro, Vol. 1)

Adams, John, Pres. , U. S. , 1735-1826
  *1776 (see Edwards, Sherman)
ADAMS, Lee, 1924-
  Applause (see Strouse, Charles)
ADAMSON, Hans Christian
  New Horizons; radio script from the series, Apr. 26, 1939.
    (In Best Broadcasts of 1938-39)
The Adding Machine (see Rice, Elmer L.)
Addio (see Young, Stark)
ADDISON, Joseph, 1672-1719
  Cato
    (In Five Restoration Tragedies)
    (In Plays of the Restoration and 18th Century)
  **The Upholsterer; or, What News? (see Murphy, Arthur)
ADE, George, 1866-1944
  Aunt Fanny from Chautauqua
    (In One-Act Plays for Stage and Study, 10th Series)
  The Mayor and the Manicure
    (In One-Act Plays for Stage and Study, 1st Series)
L'Ade d'Or (see Feydeau, Georges)
ADELLACH, Alberto, 1933-
  March
    (In The Orgy)
Adieu Philippine (see Rozier, Jacques, 1926-)
The Admirable Bashville; or, Constancy Unrewarded (see Shaw,
  George Bernard)
The Admirable Crichton (see Barrie, James M.)
The Admiral (see Kennedy, Charles R.)
Adrea (see Belasco, David)
Adrienne Ambrossat (see Kaiser, Georg)
Advent (see Strindberg, August)
The Adventures of Covent-Garden (see Farquhar, George)
The Advertisement (see Ginzburg, Natalia)
AESCHYLUS, 525-456 B. C.
  Agamemnon; adapted by Herwig Hensen
    (In Teatro Flamenco Contemporaneo)
  Agamemnon; adapted by Paul Claudel
    (In Claudel's Théâtre I)
  Agamemnon; adapted by Steven Berkoff
    (In East and Other Plays)
  Agamemnone; text in Italian adapted by Vittorio Alfieri
    (In Alfieri's Tragedie, Vol. 1)
  Les Choephores; adapted by Paul Claudel
    (In Claudel's Théâtre I)
  Eumenides
    (In The Drama, Vol. 1)
  Les Eumenides; adapted by Paul Claudel
    (In Claudel's Théâtre I)
  The House of Atreus, adapted from the "Oresteia" of Aeschylus
    by John Lewin
    (In Minnesota Drama Editions, no. 2)
  Introit; from "Supplices, " translated by J. Lembke
    (In Arion, n. s. , Vol. 1, nos. 5-6, Spring 1973)

Prometheus Bound
    (In World Drama, Vol. 1)
Aesop, c. 620-c. 560 B. C.
    *Aesop, pts. 1 & 2 (see Vanbrugh, Sir John)
An Affair (see Kovak, Primož)
L'Affair de la Rue de Lourcine (see Labiche, Eugéne)
L'Affair Edouard (see Feydeau, Georges)
Affair of Honor (see Kunert, Günter)
The Affair of the Lone Banana (see Milligan, Spike)
Affairs of State (see Verneuil, Louis)
The Affected Ladies (Les Précieuses Ridicules) (see Molière, Jean
    B.)
L'Affiche Rouge (see Cassenti, Frank)
The Affidavit (see Golden, David T.)
L'Affranchie (see Donnay, Maurice C.)
AFINOGENOV, Alexander Nikolayevich, 1904-1941
    Far Taiga
        (In Soviet Scene)
    Fear
        (In Six Soviet Plays)
    On the Eve
        (In Seven Soviet Plays)
Afore Night Came (see Rudkin, David)
After Haggerty (see Mercer, David. Dopo Haggerty; text in French)
After Lydia; or, In Priase of Love (see Rattigan, Sir Terence M.)
After Midnight; radio script (see Kirkpatrick, John A.)
After October (see Ackland, Rodney)
After the Fall (selection) (see Miller, Arthur)
After the Funeral; television script (see Owen, Alun)
After the Tempest (see Trease, Geoffrey)
An Afternoon at the Festival (see Mercer, David)
Afternoon Tea (see Perr, Harvey)
Agamemnon (see Aeschylus)
Agamennone (see Aeschylus)
Ages Ago (see Gilbert, William S.)
Agesilas (see Corneille, Pierre)
Aggression (see Michel, Georges)
Agide (see Alfieri, Vittorio)
Aglavaine et Selysette (see Maeterlinck, Maurice)
Agnes Bernauer (see Kroetz, Franz X.)
Agnete (see Kaiser, Georg)
El Agua (see Hoorink, Eduardo)
Agua en las Manos (see Pico, Pedro E.)
Aguas Estancadas (see Usigli, Rudolfo)
AGUILERA-MALTA, Demetrio
    Black Hell
        (In Modern International Drama, Vol. 10, no. 2, Spring 1977)
    Infierno Negro
        (In El Teatro Actual Latinoamericano)
    El Tigre
        (In El Teatro Hispanoamericano Contemporaneo, Vol. 2)
AGUIRRE, Isadora
    Los Papeleros
        (In El Teatro Actual Latinoamericano)

Die Agyptische Helena (see Hofmannsthal, Hugo von H.)
Ah Kiou (see Chartreux, Bernard)
Ah, Wilderness! (see O'Neill, Eugene)
Ahab, 7th King of Samaria, ?-c. 853 B.C.
    *A King's Daughter (see Masefield, John)
Ahasuerus (see Xerxes)
Ahora Que la Aldea ya no Existe (see Brulin, Tone)
L'Ai Compromis Ma Femme (see Labiche, Eugene)
Aida (see Verdi, Giuseppe)
L'Aiguillage (see Dube, Marcel)
AIKEN, Conrad Potter, 1889-
    **Silent Snow, Secret Snow (see Kearney, Gene)
AIKEN, George L., 1830-1876
    Uncle Tom's Cabin, based on the book by Harriet Beecher Stowe
        (In Dramas from the American Theatre, 1762-1909)
        (In 50 Best Plays of the American Theatre, Vol. 1)
        (In Representative Plays by American Dramatists, Vol. 2)
L'Air des Bijoux (see Tholy, René)
L'Air du Temps (see Vildrac, Charles)
Air Raid: A Verse Play for Radio (see MacLeish, Archibald)
Akara (see Weingarten, Romain)
AKINS, Zoë, 1886-1958
    Such a Charming Young Man
        (In Five Plays from the Other Side)
        (In One-Act Plays for Stage and Study, 1st Series)
AKSYONOV, Vasilii, 1932-
    Your Murderer: An Antialcoholic Comedy
        (In Performing Arts Journal, Vol. 2, no. 1, Spring 1977)
Al Fin Mujer (see Lozano Garcia, Lazaro)
AL HAKIM, Tawfik, 1902-
    The Death of Mohammed
        (In New Directions, Vol. 15, 1955)
    Fate of a Cockroach
        (In Fate of a Cockroach: Four Plays of Freedom)
    Not a Thing Out of Place
        (In Fate of a Cockroach: Four Plays of Freedom)
    The Song of Death
        (In Fate of a Cockroach)
    The Sultan's Dilemma
        (In Fate of a Cockroach: Four Plays of Freedom)
    The Tree Climber
        (An Oxford Three Crowns Book, 1966)
AL KHONSARI, Aboul-Kass im-Mohamed
    Le Martyre de Hourh-Ibn-Iazid
        (In Le Théâtre et la Danse en Iran)
Al Otro Dia (see Ocampo, Maria L.)
Alabama Fables (see Browne, Theodore)
Alain und Elise (see Kaiser, Georg)
ALARCON, Pedro Antonio de, 1833-1891
    Sainete Nuevo
        (In Clásicos Castellanos, Vol. 200)
Las Alas del Pez (see Sanchez Mayans, Fernando)
Alas, Poor Fred (see Saunders, James)

ALBAN GOMEZ, Ernesto
    Jeuves
        (In Teatro Ecuatoriano Contemporaneo, Vol. 2)
Los Albaniles (see Lenero, Vicente)
The Albany Depot (see Howells, William Dean)
ALBEE, Edward, 1928-
    All Over
        (In Best American Plays, 7th Series, 1967-1973)
    Box
        (In This Is My Best in the Third Quarter Century)
    Who's Afraid of Virginia Woolf?
        (In 50 Best Plays of the American Theatre, Vol. 4)
ALBERTI, Rafael
    Night and War in the Prado Museum
        (In Modern Spanish Theatre)
ALBERTO, Raimundo
    Os Mansos da Terra
        (In Revista de Teatro, no. 406, July/Aug. 1975)
Albert's Bridge (see Stoppard, Tom)
ALBERY, Peter
    Anne Boleyn
        (In Plays of the Year, Vol. 14, 1955/56)
Albion and Albanius (see Dryden, John)
Albovine (see D'Avenant, Sir William)
ALBRIGHT, Hardie, 1903-
    The Final Word
        (In One-Act Plays for Stage and Study, 10th Series)
The Album (see James, Henry)
El Alcalde de Zalamea (see Calderón de la Barca, Pedro)
Alceste (see Wieland, Christoph M.)
Alceste Seconda (see Alfieri Vittoria)
Alcestes (see Usigli, Rudolfo)
Alcestis (see Euripides)
The Alchemist (see Fath'Ali, Akhund-Zādah)
The Alchemist (see Jonson, Ben)
The Alchemist; a Persian drama (Anon.)
        (In The Drama, Vol. 3)
ALCOCK, Fred
    The Ides of March (see Bennett, Arnold)
ALDIS, Mrs. Mary (Reynolds), 1872-
    The Drama Class
        (In her Plays for Small Stages)
    Extreme Unction
        (In her Plays for Small Stages)
    The Letter
        (In her Plays for Small Stages)
    Mrs. Pat and the Law
        (In her Plays for Small Stages)
    Temperament
        (In her Plays for Small Stages)
ALDRICH, Thomas Bailey, 1836-1907
    The Set of Turquoise
        (In The Knickerbocker, Vol. 52, no. 6, Dec. 1858)

The Aldrich Family radio scripts
  A Halloween Story (see Goldsmith, Clifford)
ALDRIDGE, Ira, 1807-1867
  Christmas 1938 (see Smith, Kate)
  The Black Doctor
    (In Black Theater U. S. A. , 1847-1974)
Aleichem, Sholom (pseud.) (see Rabinowitz, Shalom)
ALEKSIN, Anatoly
  The Young Guard; lyrics by Robert Rozhdestvensky and music by
    Oscar Feltzman. (Molodaya Gvardia)
    (In Russian Plays for Young Audiences)
ALENCAR PIMENTEL, Altimar de
  A Ultima Lingada
    (In Revista de Teatro, no. 415, Jan/Feb 1977)
ALEXANDER, Hartley Burr, 1873-1939
  Carved Woman
    (In More One-Act Plays by Modern Authors)
Alexander I (Aleksandr Pavlovich), Emperor of Russia, 1777-1825
  *Field Marshall Kutuzov (see Solovyov, Vladimir A.)
Alexander II (Aleksandr Nikolaevich), Russian Emperor, 1818-1881
  *Bismarck; oder, Warum Stecht der Soldat Da? (see Unruh,
    Fritz von)
Alexander III, known as "Alexander the Great, " 356-323 B. C.
  *Alexander the Great (see Racine, Jean Baptiste)
  *Amintas (see Rolt, Richard)
  *The Rival Queens; or, The Death of Alexander the Great (see
    Lee, Nathaniel)
Alexander VI (Rodrigo Lanzoly Borja), Pope, 1431?-1503
  *The Duke of Gandia (see Swinburne, Algernon Charles)
Alexander Nevsky; screenplay (see Eisenstein, Sergei M.)
Alexander the Great (see Racine, Jean Baptiste)
ALFIERI, Vittorio, 1749-1803
  Abele; text in Italian
    (In his Tragedie, Vol. 3)
  *Agamennone; text in Italian (see Aeschylus)
  Agide; text in Italian
    (In his Tragedie, Vol. 2)
  Alceste Seconda; text in Italian
    (In his Tragedie, Vol. 3)
  Antigone; text in Italian
    (In his Tragedie, Vol. 1)
  Antonio e Cleopatra; text in Italian
    (In his Tragedie, Vol. 3)
  Bruto Primo; text in Italian
    (In his Tragedie, Vol. 3)
  Bruto Secondo; text in Italian
    (In his Tragedie, Vol. 3)
  La Congiura de' Pazzi; text in Italian
    (In his Tragedie, Vol. 2)
  Don Garzia; text in Italian
    (In his Tragedie, Vol. 2)
  Filippo; text in Italian
    (In his Tragedie, Vol. 1)

Maria Stuarda; text in Italian
    (In his Tragedie, Vol. 2)
Merope; text in Italian
    (In his Tragedie, Vol. 2)
Mirra; text in Italian
    (In his Tragedie, Vol. 3)
Myrrha
    (In The Drama, Vol. 5)
Oreste; text in Italian
    (In his Tragedie, Vol. 1)
Ottavia; text in Italian
    (In his Tragedie, Vol. 2)
Polinice; text in Italian
    (In his Tragedie, Vol. 1)
Rosamunda; text in Italian
    (In his Tragedie, Vol. 1)
Saul; text in English
    (In World Drama, Vol. 2)
Saul; text in Italian
    (In his Tragedie, Vol. 2)
Sofonisba; text in Italian
    (In his Tragedie, Vol. 3)
Timoleone; text in Italian
    (In his Tragedie, Vol. 2)
Virginia; text in Italian
    (In his Tragedie, Vol. 1)
Un Alfiler en los Ojos (see Baez, Edmundo)
ALFON, Estrella D., 1917-
    Rice
        (In Philippine Harvest)
Alfonso II, King of Naples, 1448-1495
    *The Guardian (see Massinger, Philip)
    *The History of Charles the Eighth of France; or, The Invasion
        of Naples by the French (see Crowne, John)
Alfonso V, el Magnanimo, King of Aragon, 1416-1458
    *The Comicall Historie of Alphonsus, King of Aragon (see Greene,
        Robert)
Alfonso VII, King of Leon & Castile, called El Emperador, d. 1157
    *The King, the Greatest Alcalde (see Vega Carpio, Lope F.)
Alfonso X, "Alphonso the Wise," King of Castile & Leon, 1221-1284
    *The Tragedy of Alphonsus Emperor of Germany (see Chapman,
        George)
Alfonso XII, King of Spain, 1857-1885
    *Donde Vas, Alfonso XII? (see Luca de Tena, Juan I.)
    *Donde Vas, Triste De Ti? (see Luca de Tena, Juan I.)
ALFONSO MILLAN, José Juan
    Mayores Con Reparos
        (In Teatro Español, 1964-65)
ALFRED, William, 1922-
    Hogan's Goat
        (In Eight American Ethnic Plays)
ALFRIEND, Edward M.
    The Great Diamond Robbery, by Edward M. Alfriend and A. C.
        Wheeler

(In Favorite American Plays of the 19th Century)
Algo Mas Que Dos Sueños (see Canas, Alberto)
ALGYER, Harold C.
    These Honored Dead
        (In 100 Non-Royalty Radio Plays)
Alice in Wonderland (see Manhattan Project)
Alice in Wonderland; radio script (see Wicker, Irene)
Alice-sit-by-the-fire (see Barrie, James M.)
Alison Mary Fagan (see Selbourne, David)
Alison's House (see Glaspell, Susan)
Alive Forever (see Rozov, Victor S.)
Alkestis des Euripides (see Hofmannsthal, Hugo von H.)
All About Eve; screenplay (see Mankiewicz, Joseph L.)
All Against All (see Adamov, Arthur)
The All-American Boy; screenplay (see Eastman, Charles)
All Fools (see Chapman, George)
All for Love; or, The World Well Lost (see Dryden, John)
All God's Chillun Got Wings (O'Neill, Eugene)
All in the Family television scripts
    Archie and the Computer (see Turner, Lloyd)
    Archie and the Editorial (see Bloom, George)
    Archie in the Hospital (see Nicholl, Don)
    Gloria Poses in the Nude (see Ross, Michael)
    Mike's Appendix (see Ross Michael)
All My Sons (see Miller, Arthur)
All Over (see Albee, Edward)
All the World's a Stage (see Jackman, Isaac)
All White Caste (see Caldwell, Ben)
All You Need Is One Good Break; radio script (see Manoff, Arnold)
Alladine and Palomides (see Maeterlinck, Maurice)
Allegro (see Rodgers, Richard)
ALLEN, Fred (John Florence Sullivan), 1894-1956
    The Fred Allen Show; radio scripts for Apr. 24, and May 1,
    1940
        (In Best Broadcasts of 1939-40)
    Town Hall Tonight; a radio script, Dec. 7, 1938
        (In Best Broadcasts of 1938-39)
ALLEN, Gracie, 1906-1964
    Burns and Allen; radio script (see Burns, George)
ALLEN, Woody, 1935-
    Annie Hall; text in French
        (In L'Avant-Scène Cinéma, no. 198, Dec. 15, 1977)
    Play It Again, Sam
        (In Best American Plays, 7th Series, 1967-1973)
    Play It Again, Sam; screenplay and frame enlargements of the
    film directed by Herbert Ross; screenplay by Woody Allen
    from his play
        (In Woody Allen's "Play It Again, Sam")
Alligator Man (see Kaplan, Jack A.)
ALLIO, René
    Moi, Pierre Rivière, Ayant Egorgé Ma Mère, Ma Soeur et Mon
    Frère ...
        (In L'Avant-Scène Cinéma, no. 183, Mar. 1, 1977)

Rude Journee pour la Reine
    (In L'Avant-Scène Cinéma, no. 143-144)
ALLOM, Mikhail
    The Girl in the Tube
    (In Best One-Act Plays of 1941, London)
All'uscita (see Pirandello, Luigi)
El Alma Buena de Sechuan (see Brecht, Bertolt)
Alma Mater (see Green, Paul)
Almanzor, Caliph of Arabia (see Mansur, Al-, "Abdullah Al-Mansur")
ALMEIDA, Lyad de
    A Cigarra e a Formiga; peca infantil de Lyad de Almeida e Luiz
    Maria
    (In Revista de Teatro, no. 395, Sept./Oct. 1973)
Almo Guajira (see Salinas, Marcelo)
Almost Like Being (see Van Itallie, Jean-Claude)
ALONSO MILLAN, Juan José
    El Dia de la Madre
    (In Teatro Español, 1969-70)
    Juegos de Sociedad
    (In Teatro Español, 1970-71)
L'Alouette (see Anouilh, Jean)
Alphonsus, Emperor of Germany (see Alfonso X, "Alphonso the
    Wise," King of Castile & Leon)
Als der Krieg zu Ende War (see Frisch, Max)
ALSON, Lawrence
    Plaster
    (In Collision Course)
Alta Austria (see Kroetz, Franz X.)
Alta Fidelidad (see Neville, Edgar)
Altman, Robert
    Buffalo Bill and the Indians (see Rudolph, Alan)
    Nashville (see Tewkesbury, Joan)
Altri Tempi (see Pinter, Harold)
L'Altro Figlio (see Pirandello, Luigi)
ALURISTA
    Dawn
    (In Contemporary Chicano Theatre)
ALVAREZ QUINTERO, Joaquin, 1873-1944
    Concha La Limpia (see Alvarez Quintero, Serafin)
    Doña Clarines (see Alvarez Quintero, Serafin)
    Las Flores (see Alvarez Quintero, Serafin)
    Fortunato (see Alvarez Quintero, Serafin)
    Los Galeotes (see Alvarez Quintero, Serafin)
    A Hundred Years Old (see Alvarez Quintero, Serafin)
    The Lady from Alfaqueque (see Alvarez Quintero, Serafin)
    La Patria Chica (see Alvarez Quintero, Serafin)
    Sangre Gorda (see Alvarez Quintero, Serafin)
    Solico en el Mundo (see Alvarez Quintero, Serafin)
    Ventolera (see Alvarez Quintero, Serafin)
    The Women Have Their Way (see Alvarez Quintero, Serafin)
ALVAREZ QUINTERO, Serafin, 1871-1938
    Concha La Limpia by Hermanos Alvarez Quintero
    (In their Teatro Selecto)

Doña Clarines, by Serafin and Joaquin Alvarez Quintero
   (In 20th Century Plays)
Las Flores, by Hermanos Alvarez Quintero
   (In their Teatro Selecto)
Fortunato, by Serafin and Joaquin Alvarez Quintero, in English
   version by Helen and Harley Granville-Barker
   (In their Four Plays)
Los Galeotes by Hermanos Alvarez Quintero
   (In their Teatro Selecto)
A Hundred Years Old, by Serafin and Joaquin Quintero, in Eng-
   lish version by Helen and Harley Granville-Barker
   (In their Four Plays)
The Lady from Alfaqueque, by Serafin and Joaquin Alvarez
   Quintero, in English version by Helen and Harley Granville-
   Barker
   (In their Four Plays)
La Patria Chica by Hermanos Alvarez Quintero
   (In their Teatro Selecto)
Sangre Gorda by Hermanos Alvarez Quintero
   (In their Teatro Selecto)
Solico en el Mundo by Hermanos Alvarez Quintero
   (In their Teatro Selecto)
Ventolera by Hermanos Alvarez Quintero
   (In their Teatro Selecto)
The Women Have Their Way, by Serafin and Joaquin Alvarez
   Quintero, in English version by Helen and Harley Granville-
   Barker
   (In their Four Plays)
Alyuma (see Murphy, Arthur)
Alzaire (see Voltaire, François M.)
Alzira Power (see Bivar, Antonio)
AMADO, João Jorge
   Oncilda e Zé Buscapé
   (In Revista de Teatro, no. 416, Mar/Apr 1977)
Amahl and the Night Visitors (see Menotti, Gian-Carlo)
AMALRIK, Andrei, 1938-
   East-West A Dialogue in Suzdal
   (In Methuen's New Theatrescripts, no. 4, 1976)
   (In Nose! Nose? No-se! & Other Plays)
   The Fourteen Lovers of Ugly Mary-Ann
   (In Nose! Nose? No-se! & Other Plays)
   Is Uncle Jack a Conformist?
   (In Methuen's New Theatrescripts, no. 4, 1976)
   (In Nose! Nose? No-se! & Other Plays)
   My Aunt Is Living in Volokolamsk
   (In Nose! Nose? No-se! & Other Plays)
   Nose! Nose? No-se! Adapted from the story "The Nose," by
   Nikolai Gogol
   (In Nose! Nose? No-se! & Other Plays)
   The Story of the Little White Bull
   (In Nose! Nose? No-se! & Other Plays)
L'Amant Militaire (see San Francisco Mime Troup)
La Amante (see Calvo Sotelo, Joaquin)

Amants (see Donnay, Maurice C.)
Amarcord; screenplay (see Fellini, Federico)
The Amazed Evangelist (see Mavor, Osborne Henry)
The Ambitious Statesman; or, The Loyal Favourite (see Crowne,
    John)
Amboyna; or, The Cruelties of the Dutch (see Dryden, John)
Ambush at Tether's End (see Walker, George F.)
L'Ame en Foile (see Curel, François)
L'Ame et la Danse (see Valéry, Paul)
Amédée (see Ionesco, Eugene)
Amédée et les Messieurs en Rang (see Romains, Jules)
Amédée ou Comment s'en Debarrasser (see Ionesco, Eugene)
Amelia (see Voltaire, François M.)
The Amen Corner (see Baldwin, James)
A-A-America! (see Bond, Edward)
The American (see James, Henry)
American Graffiti; screenplay (see Lucas, George)
American Hurrah (see Van Itallie, Jean-Claude)
American Night Cry Trilogy (see Dean, Phillip H.)
THE AMERICAN PLAYGROUND
    Kites
        (In Guerilla Street Theater)
An American Sunset (see Prideaux, James)
An American Tragedy; screenplay (see Eisenstein, Sergei)
The "America's" Cup (see Higley, Philo)
L'Ami de la Maison (see Beaumarchais, Pierre A.)
L'Ami des Femmes (see Dumas, Alexandre, Fils)
L'Amica delle Mogli (see Pirandello, Luigi)
An Amicable Settlement (see Turgenev, Ivan S.)
Le Amiche; screenplay (see Antonioni, Michelangelo)
AMIEL, Denys, 1884-
    Le Femme en Fleur
        (In his Théâtre)
    Ma Liberté
        (In his Théâtre)
Amitas (see Rolt, Richard)
Amleto Principe di Danimarca (see Brecht, Bertolt)
Among the Paths to Eden (see Capote, Truman)
Among Thieves (see Gullette, William H.)
El Amor es un Potro Descobado (see Escobar, Luis)
Amor sin Pasaporte (see Laiglesia, Alvaro de)
Amor Vincit Omnia ad Nauseam (see Updike, John)
Amore de Don Perlimplin con Belisa en su Jardin (see Garcia Lorca,
    Federico)
El Amore de los Cuatro Coroneles (see Ustinov, Peter)
Amore e Magia Nella Cucina di Manna (see Wertmüller, Lina)
The Amorous Bigotte, with the second part of Tegue O Divelly (see
    Shadwell, Thomas)
The Amorous Prawn (see Kimmins, Anthony)
The Amorous Prince (see Behn, Mrs. Aphra)
The Amorous Quarrel (Depit Amoureux) (see Molière, Jean B.)
L'Amour Africain (see Mérimée, Prosper)
L'Amour en Visites (see Jarry, Alfred)

L'Amour et la Vérité (see Marivaux, Pierre C.)
Amour et Piano (see Feydeau, Georges)
L'Amour Fou; ou, La Première Surprise (see Roussin, André)
El Amour Médico (see Téllez, Gabriel)
Amoureuse (see Porto-Riche, Georges de)
Les Amours Impossibles (see Arrabal, Fernando)
Les Amours Tragique de Pyrame et Thisbé (see Vian, Théophile de)
L'Ampelour (see Audiberti, Jacques)
Amphion (see Valéry, Paul)
Amphion; text in French (see Valéry, Paul)
Amphitruo (see Plautus, Titus M.)
Amphitryon (see Kleist, Heinrich von)
Amphitryon (see Molière, Jean B.)
Amphitryon; or, Jupiter in Disguise (see Plautus, Titus M.)
Amphitryon; or, The Two Socias (see Dryden, John)
Amphitryon; or, The Two Socias (see Molière, Jean B.)
Amphitryon 38 (see Giraudoux, Jean)
Amy Robsart (see Hugo, Victor M.)
Amy Robsart; text in French (see Hugo, Victor M.)
Amyntas; or, The Impossible Dowry (see Randolph, Thomas)
Ana Kleiber (see Sastre, Alfonso)
Anastacio (see Camargo, Joracy)
Anastasia (see Marcelle-Maurette)
Anastasia Nikolaevna, Grand Duchess of Russia, 1901-1913
    *Anastasia, adapted by Guy Bolton (see Marcelle-Maurette)
Anatol; text in German (see Schnitzler, Arthur)
The Anatomist (see Mavor, Osborne Henry)
The Anatomist; or, The Sham Doctor (see Ravenscroft, Edward)
Ancestral 66 (see Icaza, Alberto)
Ancey, George (pseud.) (see Curnieu, Georges de)
Ancre, Marquis d' (Concino Concini), d. 1617
    *La Maréchale d'Ancre (see Vigny, Alfred V.)
And Did Those Feet; television script (see Merver, David)
And So Ad Infinitum (see Capek, Karel)
And Suddenly There Came a Bang! (see Obaldia, René de)
And the Big Men Fly (see Hopgood, Alan)
And the Gods Play; radio script (see Monroe, Robert A.)
And There Was Light (see Kennedy, Charles O'Brien)
And They Put Handcuffs on the Flowers (see Arrabal, Fernando)
"... And Things That Go Bump in the Night" (see McNally, Terrence)
ANDERSEN, Hans Christian, 1805-1875
    **The Red Shoes (see Powell, Michael)
    **The Swineherd (see Smith, Moyne R.)
ANDERSON, Garland, 1886-1939
    Appearances
        (In Black Theater U.S.A., 1847-1974)
ANDERSON, Harold L.
    It's Really Quite Simple; television script
        (In New Fields for the Writer)
ANDERSON, Lindsay, 1923-
    O Lucky Man! screenplay by Lindsay Anderson and David Sherwin
        (In Evergreen Filmscript Series, 1973)

ANDERSON, Maxwell, 1888-1959
   The Bad Seed; dramatized from William March's novel
     (In Best Mystery and Suspense Plays of the Modern Theatre)
   The Feast of Ortolans
     (In 10 Short Plays)
   High Tor
     (In 50 Best Plays of the American Theatre, Vol. 2)
   Lost in the Stars (see Weill, Kurt)
   The Masque of Kings
     (In Representative American Dramas)
   What Price Glory? by Maxwell Anderson and Lawrence Stallings
     (In 20th Century Plays)
   Winterset
     (In The Disinherited: Plays)
     (In Representative American Plays, 1792-1949)
   Winterset (selection)
     (In This Is My Best)
ANDERSON, Robert Woodruff, 1917-
   Double Solitaire
     (In The Best Short Plays 1973)
   Tea and Sympathy
     (In 50 Best Plays of the American Theatre, Vol. 4)
ANDERSON, Sherwood, 1876-1941
   The Triumph of the Egg
     (In 10 Short Plays)
Andorra (see Frisch, Max)
ANDRADE, Euclides Marques
   Cao com Gato
     (In Revista de Teatro, no. 391, Jan/Feb 1973)
ANDRADE RIVERA, Gustavo, 1921-
   Remington 22
     (In Teatro Breve Hispanoamericano Contemporaneo)
Andre (see Dunlap, William)
André del Sarto (see Musset, Alfred de)
ANDREEV, Leonid Nikolaevich, 1871-1919
   The Black Maskers
     (In his Plays, 1915)
   He Who Gets Slapped
     (In Dramas of Modernism)
     (In 20th Century Russian Plays)
   The Life of Man
     (In his Plays, 1915)
     (In Representative Continental Dramas)
   Professor Storitsyn
     (In Masterpieces of the Russian Drama, Vol. 2)
   The Sabine Women
     (In his Plays, 1915)
ANDREU IGLESIAS, César
   El Inciso Hache
     (In Teatro Puertorriqueño: Quino Festival)
Andrew (see Goss, Clay)
ANDREWS, Charlton
   The Purloined Letter; a radio script adapted from the story by
   Edgar Allan Poe

(In On the Air: 15 Plays for Broadcast)
ANDREWS, Miles Peter, d. 1814
Better Late than Never
(In The London Stage, Vol. 3)
Andreyeff, Leonid (see Andreev, Leonid N.)
Andreyev, Leonid Nikolayevich (see Andreev, Leonid N.)
Androcles and the Lion (see Harris, Aurand)
Androcles and the Lion: A Fable Play (see Shaw, George B.)
Andromache (see Racine, Jean B.)
Andromède (see Corneille, Pierre)
Andronic (Andronicus) (see Campistron, Jean-Galbert de)
Andronicus Comnenius (see Wilson, John)
Andronicus I Comnenus, 1110?-1185
*Andronicus Comnenius (see Wilson, John)
L'Ane et le Ruisseau (see Musset, Alfred de)
Angel Street (see Hamilton, Patrick)
Angela (see Tamayo y Baus, Manuel)
Angela Is Happening (see Moore, Elvie A.)
Angelface (see Foreman, Richard)
Angelica (see Hughes, Babette)
Angelina o el Honor de un Brigadier (see Jardiel Poncela, Enrique)
Angelita (see Martinez Ruiz, Azorin, José)
Angelo (see Hugo, Victor M.)
Angelo; text in Italian (see Jacquemard, Yves)
Angelo, Tyran de Padoue (see Hugo, Victor M.)
ANGELOPOULOS, Theo
    Le Voyage des Comediens; titre original: "O Thiassos"; musique,
        Loukianos Kilaidonis
        (In L'Avant-Scène Cinéma, no. 164, Dec. 1975)
Angelus (see Taylor, Helen L.)
Anger (see Ionesco, Eugene)
Anillos Para una Dama (see Gala, Antonio)
Animal (see Hailey, Oliver)
Animal Crackers; screenplay (see Ryskind, Morris)
The Animal Kingdom (see Barry, Philip)
Animal Magnetism (see Inchbald, Mrs. Elizabeth)
Animas de Día Claro (see Sieveking, Alejandro)
Ann Veronica (see Gow, Ronald)
"Anna Christie" (see O'Neill, Eugene)
Anna Laub (see Lind, Jakov)
Anna-Luse (see Mowat, David)
Anna Sophie Hedvig (see Abell, Kjeld)
Annajanska, the Bolshevik Empress: A Revolutionary Romancelet
    (see Shaw, George Bernard)
Anne Boleyn (see Albery, Peter)
Anne Boleyn (see Boker, George H.)
Anne et les Loups; screenplay (see Saura, Carlos)
L'Annee Dernière à Marienbad; screenplay (see Robbe-Grillet, Alain)
L'Annee Nouvelle (see Mace, Jean)
Annibal (see Marivaux, Pierre C.)
Annie Hall; text in French (see Allen, Woody)
The Anniversary (see Chekhov, Anton)
Anniversary Dinner (see Molnar, Ferenc)

Anniversary on Weedy Hill (see Joseph, Allen)
L'Annonce Faite à Marie (see Claudel, Paul)
ANNUNZIO, Gabriel d', 1863-1938
    The Daughter of Jorio
      (In Representative Continental Dramas)
The Anonymous Work (see Witkiewicz, Stanislaw I.)
Another "Lay of Ancient Rome, " not by Macauley
      (In The Knickerbocker, Vol. 21, no. 5, May 1843)
Another Part of the Forest (see Hellman, Lillian)
Another Sunday and Sweet F. A. ; television script (see Rosenthal,
    Jack)
ANOUILH, Jean, 1910-
    L'Alouette
      (In his Pièces Costumées)
      (In Théâtre de la Table Ronde, 1953)
    Antigone
      (In his Collected Plays, Vol. 2)
    Antigone; text in French
      (In his Nouvelle Pieces Noires)
      (In Théâtre de la Table Ronde, 1947)
    Ardèle; ou, La Marguerite
      (In his Pieces Grinçantes)
      (In Théâtre de la Table Ronde, 1949)
    Becket; or, The Honor of God
      (In Introduction to Literature: Plays)
    Becket; ou, l'Honneur de Dieu
      (In Théâtre de la Table Ronde, 1959)
    Le Boulanger, la Boulandère et le Petit Mitron
      (In Théâtre de la Table Ronde, 1969)
    The Cavern
      (In Methuen's Modern Plays Series, 1966)
    Cecile; ou, L'Ecole des Pères
      (In Théâtre de la Table Ronde, 1962)
    Cher Antoine; ou, l'Amour Raté
      (In Théâtre de la Table Ronde, 1969)
    Chers Zoiseaux
      (In L'Avant-Scène Théâtre, no. 620, Dec. 15, 1977)
    La Cita en Senlis
      (In his Teatro: Piezas Rosas)
    Colombe
      (In his Pièces Brillantes)
    Columbe
      (In Théâtre de la Table Ronde, 1965)
    Dear Antoine; or, The Love That Failed
      (In Hill & Wang Spotlight Drama Series, 1971)
    Dinner with the Family
      (In his Collected Plays, Vol. 1)
      (In Methuen's Modern Plays Series, 1958)
    Le Directeur de l'Opéra
      (In Théâtre de la Table Ronde, 1972)
    Director of the Opera
      (In Methuen's Modern Plays Series, 1973)

L'Ecole des Pères
   (In his Pièces Brillantes)
Episode in the Life of an Author
   (In Best Short Plays of the World Theatre, 1968-1973)
The Ermine
   (In his Collected Plays, VoL 1)
The Ermine, translated by Miriam John
   (In Plays of the Year, VoL 13, 1955
Eurydice (Legend of Lovers)
   (In Masterpieces of the Modern French Theatre)
The Fighting Cock
   (In Methuen's Modern Plays Series, 1967)
La Foire d'Empoigne
   (In his Pièces Costumées)
   (In Théâtre de la Table Ronde, 1962)
La Grotte
   (In Théâtre de la Table Ronde, 1961)
Humulus the Mute, by Jean Anouilh and Jean Aurenche
   (In Modern French Theatre)
L'Hurluberlu; ou, Le Reactionnaire Amoureux
   (In Théâtre de la Table Ronde, 1959)
L'Invitation au Chateau
   (In his Pièces Brillantes)
   (In Théâtre de la Table Ronde, 1948)
Jezabel
   (In his Nouvelles Pièces Noires)
The Lark, adapted by Lillian Hellman
   (In Hellman's Collected Plays)
Leocadia; text in French
   (In his Pièces Roses)
Leocadia; text in Spanish
   (In his Teatro: Piezas Roses)
Medea
   (In his Collected Plays, VoL 2)
Medea, translated by Lothian Small
   (In Plays of the Year, VoL 15, 1956)
Médée
   (In his Nouvelles Pièces Noires)
   (In Théâtre de la Table Ronde, 1967)
Monsieur Barnett
   (In L'Avant-Scène Théâtre, no. 559, Mar. 1, 1975)
Ne Reveillez pas Madame
   (In Théâtre de la Table Ronde, 1970)
Ornifle
   (In Hill & Wang Spotlight Drama Series, 1970)
Ornifle; ou, Le Courant d'Air
   (In Théâtre de la Table Ronde, 1956)
   (In his Pièces Grinçantes)
Pauvre Bitos; ou, Le Dîner de Têtes
   (In his Pièces Grinçantes)
   (In Théâtre de la Table Ronde, 1958)
Point of Departure
   (In his Collected Plays, VoL 2)

Les Poissons Rouges; ou, Mon Père, ce Héros
   (In Théâtre de la Table Ronde, 1970)
Le Rendez-vous de Senlis
   (In his Pièces Roses)
La Repetition; ou, L'Amour Puni
   (In his Pièces Brillantes)
Restless Heart
   (In his Collected Plays, Vol. 1)
Ring Round the Moon
   (In Three European Plays)
Romeo and Jeanette
   (In his Collected Plays, Vol. 2)
Romeo et Jeanette
   (In his Nouvelle Pièces Noires)
Le Scenario
   (In L'Avant-Scène Théâtre, no. 614, Sept. 1, 1977)
Thieves' Carnival
   (In his Collected Plays, Vol. 1)
Time Remembered
   (In his Collected Plays, Vol. 2)
Traveler Without Luggage
   (In his Collected Plays, Vol. 1)
La Valse des Toréadors
   (In L'Avant Scène du Théâtre, no. 541, May 1974)
   (In his Pièces Grinçantes)
   (In Théâtre de la Table Ronde, 1952)
Le Voyageur sans Bagage
   (In The French Theater Since 1930)
Waltz of the Toreadors, adapted by Lucienne Hill
   (In Plays of the Year, Vol. 8, 1952/53)
Anski, S. (pseud.) (see Rappoport, Shloyme Z.)
Anstey, Frank (pseud.) (see Guthrie, Thomas A.)
Antar of Araby (see Cuney-Hare, Maud)
The Anthem Sprinters (see Bradbury, Ray)
Anthony, C. L. (pseud.) (see Smith, Dorothy G.)
ANTHONY, Joseph, 1912-
   The Rainmaker (see Nash, N. Richard)
Antigone (see Anouilh, Jean)
Antigone (see Hasenclever, Walter)
Antigone (see Sophocles)
Antigone; text in French (see Anouilh, Jean)
Antigone; text in Italian (see Alfieri, Vittorio)
The Antipodes (see Brome, Richard)
The Antiquary (see Marmion, Shakerly)
Antoninus, Marcus Aurelius (see Caracalla)
Antonio and Mellida (see Marston, John)
Antonio e Cleopatra; text in Italian (see Alfieri, Vittorio)
Antonio von Elba (see Mainardi, Renato)
ANTONIONI, Michelangelo, 1912-
   Le Amiche
   (In Sei Film)
   L'Avventura
   (In Dal Soggetto al Film Series, no. 15, 1960)

(In <u>Sei Film</u>)
Blow-Up; film directed by Michelangelo Antonioni, with script
by Antonioni and Edward Bond
(In <u>Lorrimer Screenplay Series</u>, 1971)
(In <u>Modern Film Scripts Series</u>, 1971)
I Cortometraggi
(In <u>Dal Soggetto al Film Series Retrospettiva</u>, no. 3)
Cronaca di un Amore
(In <u>Dal Soggetto al Film Series Retrospettiva</u>, no. 3)
Desert Rosso
(In <u>Sei Film</u>)
Il Deserto Rosso
(In <u>Dal Soggetto al Film Series</u>, no. 32, 1964)
L'Eclisse
(In <u>Dal Soggetto al Film Series</u>, no. 23, 1962)
(In <u>Sei Film</u>)
Il Grido
(In <u>Dal Soggetto al Film Series</u>, no. 8, 1958)
(In <u>Sei Film</u>)
La Notte
(In <u>Sei Film</u>)
The Passenger; script by Mark Peploe, Peter Wollen, and
Michelangelo Antonioni
(An <u>Evergreen Black Cat</u> Filmscript, 1975)
La Signora Senza Camelie
(In <u>Dal Soggetto al Film Series Retrospettiva</u>, no. 3)
Tentato Suicidio
(In <u>Dal Soggetto al Film Series Retrospettiva</u>, no. 3)
I Vinti
(In <u>Dal Soggetto al Film Series Retrospettiva</u>, no. 3)
Zabriskie Point
(In <u>Dal Soggetto al Film Series</u>, no. 40, 1970)
Antonio's Revenge (see Marston, John)
Antonius in Athen (see Heym, Georg)
Antonius, Marcus, 83?-30 B. C.
   *Antonio e Cleopatra; text in Italian (see Alfieri, Vittorio)
   *Bruto Secondo; text in Italian (see Alfieri, Vittorio)
   *Caesar (see Voltaire)
   *Herod the King (see Munk, Kaj H.)
   *Pompee (see Corneille, Pierre)
Antony and Cleopatra (see Shakespeare, William)
ANTROBUS, John
   An Apple a Day
      (In <u>Calder & Boyars Playscript</u> Series no. 7)
   The Missing Links
      (In <u>Calder & Boyars Playscript</u> Series no. 7)
   Trixie & Baba
      (In <u>Calder & Boyars Playscript</u> Series no. 22)
   Why Bournemouth?
      (In <u>Calder & Boyars Playscript</u> Series no. 7)
Any Time You're Ready, I'll Sparkle (see Hopkins, John R.)
Anything for a Quiet Life (see Middleton, Thomas)
Apaga a Luz e Faz de Conta que Estamos Bebados (see Radde,
Ronald)

El Apartamiento (see Marques, Rene)
The Apartment; filmscript (see Wilder, Billy)
Apenas de Este Mundo (see Ulises, Estrella)
API 2967 (see Gurik, Robert)
APOLINAR, Danny
    Your Own Thing (see Driver, Donald)
APOLLINAIRE, Guillaume, 1880-1918
    The Beasts of Tiresias
        (In Calder & Boyars Playscript Series no. 26)
        (In Modern French Theatre)
L'Apollon de Bellac (see Giraudoux, Jean)
El Apostol (see Usigli, Rudolpho)
The Apothecary (see Wells, Charles F.)
La Appassionata (see Azar, Hector)
Appearance Is Against Them (see Inchbald, Mrs. Elizabeth)
Appearances (see Anderson, Garland)
Appius Claudius Crassus, Roman Consul, 471-451 B. C.
    *Appius and Virginia (see Webster, John)
    *Virginia (see Alfieri, Vittorio)
    *Virginia (see Tamayo y Baus, Manuel)
    *Virginius (see Knowles, Ames S.)
Applause (see Strouse, Charles)
An Apple a Day (see Antrobus, John)
The Apple Bit; a Vaudeville for Two Players (see Dietz, Norman D.)
The Apple Cart: A Political Extravaganza (see Shaw, George Bernard)
Apprenez à Conduire par Correspondance (see Fortuno, Claude)
The Apprentice (see Murphy, Arthur)
Apricots (see Griffiths, Trevor)
APSTEIN, Theodore Emanuel, 1903-
    Wetback Run
        (In Eight American, Ethnic Plays)
Una Apuesta (see Tamayo y Baus, Manuel)
El Apuntador (see Maggi, Carlos)
The Aquarium (see Conn, Stewart)
Aquarium 2 (see Gruza, Jerzy)
Aquí Está el Fantasma (see Abe, Kobo)
Arabella (see Hofmannsthal, Hugo von H.)
The Arabian Powder (see Holberg, Ludvig von)
ARAGON, Louis, 1897-
    Au Pied du Mur (Backs to the Wall)
        (In The Drama Review, Vol. 18, no. 4, Dec. 1974)
    The Mirror-Wardrobe One Fine Evening
        (In Modern French Theatre)
ARAUJO, Alcione, 1945-
    Ha Vagas Para Mocas de Fino Trato
        (In Revista de Teatro, no. 417, May/June 1977)
ARAUZ, Alvaro
    Entre Medina y Olmedo
        (In 12 Obras en un Acto)
Los Arboles Mueren de Pie (see Rodriguez Alvarez, Alejandro)
ARBUSOW, Alexej
    Abendlicht
        (In Theater der Zeit, no. 5, 1975)

ARBUTHNOT, John, 1667-1735
  Three Hours After Marriage (see Gay, John)
L'Arc de Triomphe (see Mithois, Marcel)
A Arca de Noe Nao Parte Hoje (see Pongetti, Henrique)
The Arcadia, a Pastoral (see Shirley, James)
The Archbishop (see Zieglemaier, Gregory)
ARCHER, William, 1856-1924
  A Doll's House, translated by William Archer (see Ibsen, Henrik)
  Ghosts, translated by William Archer (see Ibsen, Henrik)
Archer; The Feast at Solhough (see Ibsen, Henrik)
ARCHIBALD, William, 1924-1970
  The Innocents, based on the novel by Henry James
    (In 10 Classic Mystery and Suspense Plays of the Modern
    Theatre)
The Architect and the Emperor of Assyria (see Arrabal, Fernando)
L'Architecte et l'Empereur d'Assyrie (see Arrabal, Fernando)
Architruc (see Pinget, Robert)
Ardèle; ou, l'Honneur de Dieu (see Anouilh, Jean)
Ardele; ou, La Marguerite (see Anouilh, Jean)
ARDEN, John, 1930-
  Armstrong's Last Goodnight
    (In Evergreen Playscripts Series, 1965)
  The Bagman; or, The Impromptu of Muswell Hill; an autobio-
    graphical play
    (In Methuen's Modern Plays Series, 1971)
  The Business of Good Government a Christmas Play
    (In Methuen's Modern Plays Series, 1963)
    (In Evergreen Playscripts Series, 1967)
  Friday's Hiding
    (In Soldier, Soldier and Other Plays)
  The Island of the Mighty, by John Arden with Margaretta D'Arcy.
    Part I: Two Wild Young Noblemen, II: "Oh the Cruel Winter, "
    III: A Handful of Watercress
    (In Performance, Vol. 2, no. 1, Fall 1973)
    (In Plays and Players, Vol. 20, nos. 5 & 6, Feb. & Mar.,
    1973)
  Left-handed Liberty; a play about Magna Carta
    (In Methuen's Modern Plays Series, 1965)
    (In Evergreen Playscripts Series, 1966)
  Soldier, Soldier
    (In Soldier, Soldier and Other Plays)
  The True History of Squire Jonathan and His Unfortunate Treas-
    ure; an autobiographical play
    (In Methuen's Modern Plays Series, 1971)
  Wet Fish
    (In Soldier, Soldier and Other Plays)
  Where Is a Door Not a Door?
    (In Soldier, Soldier and Other Plays)
  The Workhouse Donkey; a Vulgar Melodrama
    (In Methuen's Modern Plays Series, 1964)
    (In Evergreen Playscripts Series, 1965)
Arden, of Feversham (Anon.)
    (In Disputed Plays of William Shakespeare)

Arden of Feversham (see Lillo, George)
ARDREY, Robert, 1908-
    Jeb
        (In his Plays of Three Decades)
    Shadow of Heroes; a play in five acts from the Hungarian
    Passion
        (In his Plays of Three Decades)
    Thunder Rock
        (In his Plays of Three Decades)
Are Men Superior? (see Ford, Harriet)
The Area Belle (see Brough, William)
ARELLANO GUERRA, Fausto E.
    La Creacion
        (In Teatro Ecuatoriano Contemporanco, Vol. 2)
Arena (see Flanagan, Hallie)
ARENT, Arthur
    Power; a Living Newspaper
        (In Federal Theatre Plays)
L'Areopage (see Lamarche, Gustave)
Aretha in the Ice Palace (see Eyen, Tom)
AREVALO MARTINEZ, Rafael, 1884-
    Los Duques de Endor
        (In Teatro Guatemalteco Contemporaneo)
ARGELANDER, Ron
    Havana Jo Jo, by Studio Scarabee and Ron Argelander
        (In Drama Review, Vol. 21, no. 3, Sept. 1977)
ARGUELLES, Hugo, 1932-
    La Ronda de la Hechizada
        (In Teatro Méxicano del Siglo XX, Vol. 5)
The Argument (see Moore, Mavor)
Ariadne (see Marcel, Gabriel)
Ariane (Ariadne) (see Corneille, Thomas)
Ariane et Barbe-Bleue (see Maeterlinck, Maurice)
ARIOSTO, Lodovico, 1474-1533
    The Coffer (La Cassaria); both prose and verse versions are in-
    cluded
        (In his Comedies)
    **The Historie of Orlando Furioso (see Greene, Robert)
    Lena (La Lena)
        (In his Comedies)
    The Necromancer (Il Negromante)
        (In his Comedies)
    The Pretenders (I Suppositi)
        (In his Comedies)
    The Scholastics (La Scholastica)
        (In his Comedies)
    The Students (I Studenti)
        (In his Comedies)
Aristippus; or, The Jovial Philosopher (see Randolph, Thomas)
ARISTOPHANES, c. 450-c. 385 B.C.
    The Birds
        (In his Four Comedies, 1962)
        (In his Five Comedies, 1955)

The Clouds
   (In The Drama, VoL 2)
   (In his Five Comedies, 1955)
The Ecclesiazusae; or, Women in Council
   (In The Drama, VoL 21)
The Frogs
   (In his Four Comedies, 1962)
   (In his Five Comedies, 1955)
Ladies' Day
   (In his Four Comedies, 1962)
Lysistrata
   (In his Four Comedies, 1962)
   (In his Five Comedies, 1955)
   (In Themes of Drama)
The Wasps
   (In his Five Comedies, 1955)
Aristotle's Bellows (see Gregory, Isabella A.)
Arlequin-Deucalion (see Prion, Alexis)
Arlequin Poli par l'Amour (see Marivaux, Pierre C.)
Arlequin Roi de Serendib (see Lesage, Alain-Rene)
Arlequin Sauvage (see La Drevetiere, Louis F.)
L'Arlesienne (see Daudet, Alphonse)
ARLETT, Vera Isabel, 1896-
   Interlude to Diplomacy
   (In Best One-Act Plays of 1939, London)
   Nocturne
   (In Best One-Act Plays of 1938, London)
ARLEY, Catherine
   La Femme de Paille
   (In L'Avant-Scène Théâtre, no. 591, July 15, 1976)
Der Arme Vetter (see Barlach, Ernst)
L'Armoire Classique (see Audiberti, Jacques)
Arms and the Man (see Shaw, George Bernard)
ARMSTRONG, Louise Van Voorhis
   The Late Captain Crow
   (In One-Act Plays for Stage and Study, 5th Series)
Armstrong's Last Goodnight (see Arden, John)
Armut, Reichtum, Mensch und Tier (see Jahnn, Hans H.)
The Army with Banners (see Kennedy, Charles R.)
L'Arnacoeur (see Bruno, Pierrette)
ARNE, Thomas Augustine, 1710-1778
   The Cooper
   (In A Collection of the Most Esteemed Farces ..., VoL 6)
   Thomas and Sally; or, The Sailor's Return (see Bickerstaff, Isaac)
Arno Prinz von Wolkenstein Oder Kader Entscheiden Allen (see Strakl, Rudi)
The Arnold Bliss Show (see Patrick, Robert)
Arnold von Brescia (see Heym, Georg)
ARNSTEIN, Marc
   The Eternal Song
   (In One-Act Plays from the Yiddish)
AROUT, Gabriel
   La Passion d'Anna Karénini; tirée du roman de Léon Tolstoi

(In L'Avant-Scène Théâtre, no. 592, Aug. 1976)
ARRABAL, Fernando, 1932-
  Les Amours Impossibles
    (In his Théâtre V)
  And They Put Handcuffs on the Flowers
    (In Evergreen Plays Series, 1974)
  The Architect and the Emperor of Assyria
    (In Evergreen Plays Series, 1969)
    (In his Plays, Vol. 3)
  L'Architecte et l'Empereur d'Assyrie
    (In Le Théâtre d'Aujourd'hui)
    (In his Théâtre V)
  Ars Amandi
    (In his Plays, Vol. 4)
    (In his Théâtre VIII)
  L'Aurore Rouge et Noire
    (In his Théâtre VIII)
  The Automobile Graveyard
    (In his The Automobile Graveyard and The Two Executioners)
  Bestial ité Erotique
    (In his Théâtre VI)
  La Bicyclette du Condamne
    (In his Théâtre II)
  The Car Cemetery
    (In his Plays, Vol. 1)
  Ceremonie pour un Noir Assassine
    (In his Théâtre III)
  Ceremony for a Murdered Black
    (In his Plays, Vol. 4)
  Une Chevre sur un Nuage
    (In his Théâtre V)
  Le Ciel et la Merde
    (In his Théâtre IX)
  Le Cimetière des Voitures
    (In Le Théâtre d'Aujourd'hui)
    (In his Théâtre I)
  La Communion Solennelle
    (In his Théâtre V)
  Concert dans un Oeuf
    (In his Théâtre IV)
  The Condemned Man's Bicycle
    (In his Plays, Vol. 2)
  Les Deux Bourreaux
    (In his Théâtre I)
  Dieu est-il Devenu Fou?
    (In his Théâtre V)
  Dieu Tente par les Mathématiques
    (In his Théâtre VIII)
  ... Et ils Passerent des Menottes aux Fleurs
    (In his Théâtre VII)
  Fando and Lis
    (In his Plays, Vol. 1)
  Fando et Lis

(In his <u>Théâtre I</u>)
First Communion
    (In <u>Modern Spanish Theatre</u>)
Garden of Delights
    (In <u>Evergreen Plays Series</u>, 1974)
Le Grand Ceremonial
    (In <u>Le Théâtre d'Aujourd'hui</u>)
    (In <u>his Théâtre III</u>)
The Grand Ceremonial
    (In his <u>Plays</u>, Vol. 3)
La Grande Revue du XX Siècle; ou, "Marie Satanas c'est pas
    Degueulasse"
    (In his <u>Théâtre IX</u>)
Guernica
    (In his <u>Guernica and Other Plays</u>)
    (In his <u>Plays</u>, Vol. 2)
    (In his <u>Théâtre II</u>)
Le Jardin des Delices
    (In his <u>Théâtre VI</u>)
La Jeunesse Illustree
    (In his <u>Théâtre V</u>)
The Labyrinth
    (In his <u>Guernica and Other Plays</u>)
    (In his <u>Plays</u>, Vol. 2)
Le Labyrinthe le Tricycle
    (In his <u>Théâtre II</u>)
Le Lai de Barabbas
    (In his <u>Théâtre IV</u>)
Oraison
    (In his <u>Théâtre I</u>)
An Orange on the Mount of Venus
    (In <u>Gambit</u>, Vol. 8, no. 30, 1977)
Orison
    (In his <u>Plays</u>, Vol. 1)
Picnic on the Battlefield
    (In his <u>Guernica and Other Plays</u>)
    (In his <u>Plays</u>, Vol. 2)
Pique-nique en Campagne
    (In his <u>Théâtre II</u>)
Les Quatre Cubes
    (In his <u>Théâtre V</u>)
The Solemn Communion
    (In <u>Gambit</u>, Vol. 3, no. 12)
    (In his <u>Plays</u>, Vol. 3)
Strip-tease de la Jalousie
    (In his <u>Théâtre V</u>)
Une Tortue Nommee Dostoievsky
    (In his <u>Théâtre VI</u>)
The Tricycle
    (In his <u>Guernica and Other Plays</u>)
    (In <u>Modern International Drama</u>, Vol. 9, no. 2)
    (In his <u>Plays</u>, Vol. 2)
The Two Executioners

(In his The Automobile Graveyard and The Two Execution-
ers)
(In his Plays, VoL 1)
L'Arret (see Voulet, Jacqueline)
The Arrival (see Zemme, Oskar)
ARRIVI, Francisco, 1915-
   Un Cuento de Hadas
      (In Teatro Breve Hispanoamericano Contemporaneo)
L'Arriviste; screenplay (see Bernol, Marc)
ARRUFAT, Anton, 1935-
   La Repeticion
      (In El Teatro Actual Latinoamericano)
Ars Amandi (see Arrabal, Fernando)
Arsaces I, King of Parthia, c. 250-248 B. C.
   *Tiridate (Tiridates) (see Campistron, Jean-Galbert de)
Arsenic and Old Lace (see Kesselring, Joseph)
Arson (see Taylor, Peter H.)
Art and Mrs. Palmer (see Hughes, Glenn)
The Art of Making Friends (see Valdrac, Charles M.)
Artaud, Antonin, 1896-1948
   *Baptism (see Tembeck, Robert)
   Der Blutstrahl
      (In Theater Heute, no. 12; Dec. 1977)
   The Cenci
      (In Calder & Boyars Playscript Series no. 18)
      (In Evergreen Plays Series, 1970)
   Jet of Blood
      (In Modern French Theatre)
Arthur (see Molnar, Ferenc)
Arthur, King of the Britons, d. 537?
   *Camelot (see Loewe, Frederick)
   *King Arthur; or, The British Worthy (see Dryden, John)
   *Lancelot (see Mavor, Osborne H.)
Arthur and Emmeline (see Garrick, David)
Arthur and the Acetone (see Shaw, George Bernard)
Article 330 (see Moinaux, Georges)
L'Article 330 (see Moinaux, Georges)
The Artist (see Milne, A. A.)
Artist Descending a Staircase (see Stoppard, Tom)
Artistes and Admirers (see Ostrovskii, Alexander N.)
Der Arzt, sein Weib, sein Sohn (see Jahnn, Hans H.)
As Husbands Go (see Crothers, Rachel)
As Long as They're Happy (see Sylvaine, Vernon)
As the Crow Flies (see Clarke, Austin)
As the Limb Is Bent (see Kirby, Rollin)
As the Tumbrils Pass (see Van der Veer, Ethel)
As You Find It (see Mansfield, Richard)
The Ascent of F6 (see Auden, W. H.)
ASCH, Sholem, 1880-1957
   God of Vengeance
      (In The Great Jewish Plays)
Ashes, parts 1-3 (see Rudkin, David)
Ashes in the Wind (see Shoub, Mac)

AHSTON, Winifred, 1891?-1965
 **Cousin Muriel (see Shaw, George Bernard)
 Wild Decembers, by Clemence Dane, pseud.
   (In Six Plays)
Asi Es La Vida (see Llanderas, Nicolas de las)
Asi Pasan ... (see Davalos, Marcelino)
Asi Que Pasen Cinco Años (see Garcia Lorca, Federico)
Ask Aunt Mary (see Woodward, Helen R.)
Asmodee (see Mauriac, François)
The Aspern Papers (see Redgrave, Sir Michael)
Assassino Speranza Delle Donne (see Kokoschka, Oscar)
The Assignation; or, Love in a Nunnery (see Dryden, John)
Astrate (Astrates) (see Quinault, Philippe)
Astrologers (see Brighouse, Harold)
Astucia Femenina (see Perez Rey, Lupe)
ASTURIAS, Miguel Angel
 La Audiencia de los Confines
   (In his Teatro I)
 Chantaje
   (In his Teatro I)
 Dique Seco
   (In his Teatro I)
 Soluna
   (In Teatro Guatemalteco Contemporaneo)
   (In his Teatro I)
Astyages, Last King of Media, fl. 584-550 B.C.
 *Cyrus (see Chénier, Marie J.)
ASUNCION REQUENA, Maria
 Ayayema
   (In Teatro Contemporaneo Chileño)
At the Exit (see Pirandello, Luigi)
At the Gates of the Righteous (see Davies, William R.)
At the Hawk's Well (see Yeats, William Butler)
At the Jumping Bean (see Bowles, Jane A.)
At the Mitre (see Turnbull, Margaret)
At the Telephone (see Lorde, Andre de)
Atalanta in Calydon (see Swinburne, Algernon Charles)
Athaliah (see Racine, Jean Baptiste)
ATHAYDE, Roberto, 1949-
 Madame Marguerite, de Roberto Athayde, adaptation de Jean-
 Loup Dabadie
   (In L'Avant-Scène Théâtre, no. 561, April 1, 1975)
Athelie; ou, Les Scandinaves (see Hugo, Victor)
Atlanima (see Audiberti, Jacques)
ATLAS, Leopold
 A Matter of Life and Death
   (In 100 Non-Royalty Radio Plays)
 So Long
   (In One-Act Plays for Stage and Study, 8th Series)
Atlas-Hotel (see Salacrou, Armand)
The Atonement (see Broch, Hermann)
Atree et Thyeste (see Crebillon, Prosper J.)
ATTENBOROUGH, Richard, 1923-

Young Winston; screenplay (see Foreman, Carl)
Attila, King of the Huns, 433?-453
  *Attila (see Corneille, Pierre)
Attuned (see Gerstenberg, Alice)
Au Pied du Mur (Backs to the Wall) (see Aragon, Louis)
Au Retour des Oies Blanches (see Dubé, Marcel)
AUB, Max, 1902-
  Espejo de Avarica
    (In Teatro Inquieto Español)
AUDEN, Wystan Hugh, 1907-1973
  The Ascent of F6, by W. H. Auden and Christopher Isherwood
    (In their Two Great Plays)
  The Dark Valley; radio script, June 2, 1940
    (In Best Broadcasts of 1939-40)
  The Dog Beneath the Skin, by W. H. Auden and Christopher
    Isherwood
    (In their Two Great Plays)
AUDIBERTI, Jacques 1899-1965
  L'Ampelour
    (In his Théâtre I)
  L'Armoire Classique
    (In his Théâtre IV)
  Atlanima
    (In his Théâtre III)
  Baton et Ruban
    (In his Théâtre V)
  Un Bel Enfant
    (In his Théâtre IV)
  Boutique Fermee
    (In his Théâtre V)
  La Brigitta
    (In his Théâtre V)
  La Cavalier Seul
    (In L'Avant-Scène du Théâtre, no. 533, Jan., 1974)
  Coeur à Cuire
    (In his Théâtre IV)
  Les Femmes du Boeuf
    (In his Théâtre I)
  La Fête Noire
    (In his Théâtre II)
  La Fourmi dans le Corps
    (In his Théâtre IV)
  La Logeuse
    (In his Théâtre III)
  Le Mal Court
    (In his Théâtre I)
    (In Le Théâtre d'Aujourd'hui)
  Les Naturels du Bordelais
    (In his Théâtre II)
    (In Le Théâtre d'Aujourd'hui)
  Opéra Parle
    (In his Théâtre III)
  Le Ouallou

Auto de los Reyes Magos (see Vicente, Gill)
Auto de San Martin (see Vicente, Gill)
Auto Pastoril Castellano (see Vicente, Gill)
Auto Sacramental (see Mira de Amescua, Antonio)
L'Autobus (see Pillement, Georges)
The Automobile Graveyard (see Arrabal, Fernando)
L'Autre Danger (see Donnay, Maurice C.)
L'Autre Valse (see Dorin, Françoise)
AUTREAU, Jacques, 1657?-1745
    Le Naufrage au Port-a-l'Anglais ou les Nouvelles Dabarquees
        (In Théâtre du XVIII Siècle, Vol. 1)
An Autumn Afternoon; filmscript (excerpt) (see Ozu, Yasujiro)
The Autumn Garden (see Hellman, Lillian)
Autumn in Han Palace (see Ma Chih-yüan)
The Autumn Ladies and Their Lovers' Lovers (see Nanus, Susan)
Avant de T'En Aller (see Dubé, Marcel)
L'Avare en Gants Jaunes (see Labiche, Eugène)
Avatar (see Grisolli, Paulo A.)
L'Avenir (see Ionesco, Eugene)
Averígüello Vargas (see Tellez, Gabriel)
Les Aveugles (see Maeterlinck, Maurice)
AVILDSEN, John G.
    Joe; screenplay (see Wexler, Norman)
    Rocky; screenplay (see Stallone, Sylvester)
L'Avventura; filmscript (see Antonioni, Michelangelo)
Awake and Sing! (see Odets, Clifford)
Awakening (see Stramm, August)
Away from It All (see Ward, Monica)
The Axe (see Curnow, Allen)
Axel og Valborg (see Oehlenschläger, Adam G.)
AXELROD, George, 1922-
    The Seven Year Itch
        (In 50 Best Plays of the American Theatre, Vol. 4)
AXENFELD, Israel, 1787-1866
    Recruits, by Israel Axenfeld and Lipe Reznik
        (In Epic and Folk Plays of the Yiddish Theatre)
Ayar Manko (see Rios, Juan)
Ayayemo (see Asuncion Requena, Maria)
AYCKBOURN, Alan, 1939-
    Absent Friends
        (In his Three Plays)
    Absurd Person Singular
        (In his Three Plays)
    Bedroom Farce
        (In his Three Plays)
Ayer ... Sera Mañana (see Soriano de Andia, Vincente)
AYKROYD, Dan, and others
    Saturday Night Live; television script directed by Dave Wilson
        and produced by Lorne Michaels for Above Average Productions
        (An Avon Books script, 1977)
AYME, Marcel, 1902-1967
    Clerambard
        (In Four Modern French Comedies)

Clerambard; text in French
(In Le Théâtre d'Aujourd'hui)
Lucienne et le Boucher
(In L'Avant-Scène Théâtre, no. 606, May 1, 1977)
(In Le Théâtre d'Aujourd'hui)
La Tête des Autres
(In Le Théâtre d'Aujourd'hui)
AYRER, Jacob, 1540-1605
**Tragedia, von dem Griegischen Keyser zu Constantinopel und
Seiner Tochter Pelimperia mit dem Ghengten Horatio (see Kyd,
Thomas)
Azalea Mountain (see China Peking Opera Troupe)
AZAR, Hector, 1930-
La Appassionata
(In Teatro Méxicano del Siglo XX, Vol. 5)
Corrido de Pablo Damian
(In 12 Obras en un Acto)
Olimpica
(In Teatro Méxicano, 1964)
Azémire (see Chénier, Marie-Joseph B.)
Azorin (see Martinez Ruiz, José)

Ba-Ra-Ka (see Jones, LeRoi)
Baal (see Brecht, Bertolt)
Baal (see Pisemskii, Aleksei F.)
Babbitt's Boy (see Hughes, Glenn)
BABEL, Isaac, 1894-1941
Marie; adaptation Française de Lily Denis, mise en scène
Bernard Sobel
(In L'Avant-Scène Théâtre, no. 576, Dec. 1, 1975)
Babes in the Wood (see Mavor, Osborne H.)
BABO, Joseph Marius, 1756-1822
Dagobert, King of the Franks
(In The Drama, Vol. 12)
Babouscka (see Van der Veer, Ethel)
The Baby (see Mankowitz, Wolf)
The Baby Austin; vaudeville script (see Fields, W. C.)
The Babysitter (see Obaldia, Rene de)
The Bacchae (see Euripides)
The Bacchae of Euripides (see Soyinka, Wole)
The Bachelor (see Turgenev, Ivan S.)
Back Door to Heaven (see Bright, John)
Back There (see Serling, Rod)
Back to Back (see Spielberg, Peter)
Back to Methuselah: A Metabiological Pentateuch (see Shaw, George
Bernard)
Back to 1960! (see Moore, Eugene)
Background (see Chetham-Strode, Warren)
BACON, Nathaniel, 1642-1676
**The Widow Ranter; or, The History of Bacon in Virginia (see
Behn, Mrs. Aphra)
Bad Habits (see McNally, Terrence)

Bad Man (see Edmonds, Randolph)
The Bad Penny (see Field, Rachel L.)
The Bad Seed (see Anderson, Maxwell)
The Bad Sleep Well; screenplay (see Kurosawa, Akira)
Badger's Green (see Sherriff, Robert C.)
Badin the Bold (see Moinaux, Georges)
BAEZ, Edmundo, 1914-
    Un Alfiler en los Ojos
        (In Teatro Méxicano del Siglo XX, Vol. 2)
BAGG, Helen
    The Left Overs
        (In Prize Plays of 1927-28, Vol. 1)
The Bagman; or, The Impromptu of Muswell Hill (see Arden, John)
BAGNOLD, Enid
    Call Me Jacky
        (In her Four Plays)
    The Chalk Garden
        (In her Four Plays)
    The Chinese Prime Minister
        (In her Four Plays)
    The Last Joke
        (In her Four Plays)
    Lottie Dundass
        (In her Theatre)
    Poor Judas
        (In her Theatre)
La Bague de l'Oubli (see Rotrou, Jean)
BAIERL, Helmut
    Die Lachtaube
        (In Theater der Zeit, no. 9, 1974)
    Die Sommerbürger
        (In Theater der Zeit, no. 5, 1976)
    ... stolz auf 18 Stunden
        (In Theater der Zeit, Vol. 29, no. 1, Jan. , 1974)
El Baile (see Neville, Edgar)
El Baile de los Ladrones (see Anouilh, Jean)
BAILEY, Paul
    A Worthy Guest
        (In Plays and Players, Vol. 21, no. 10, July 1974)
BAILLON, Jacques, 1944-
    Le Paradoxe sur le Comédien; texte de Diderot, adaptation
    Jacques Baillon
        (In L'Avant-Scène Théâtre, no. 612, June 15, 1977)
Un Bain de Ménage (see Feydeau, Georges)
Bajazet (see Racine, Jean Baptiste)
BAKAITIS, Helmut
    The Incredible Mind-Blowing Trial of Jack Smith
        (In Australian Theatre Workshop no. 7, 1973)
BAKER, Elizabeth
    Cupid in Clapham
        (In One-Act Plays for Stage and Study, 3rd Series)
BAKER, Fred
    Events, 1968-1969; a film

(In <u>Evergreen Filmscripts Series</u>, 1970)
BAKER, George Melville, 1832-1890
  Bread on the Waters
    (In his <u>The Mimic Stage</u>)
  Capuletta; or, Romeo and Juliet Restored; an operatic burlesque
    (In his <u>The Mimic Stage</u>)
  A Close Shave
    (In his <u>The Mimic Stage</u>)
  Down by the Sea
    (In his <u>The Mimic Stage</u>)
  The Great Elixir
    (In his <u>The Mimic Stage</u>)
  Humors of the Strike
    (In his <u>The Mimic Stage</u>)
  The Man with the Demijohn; a temperance sketch
    (In his <u>The Mimic Stage</u>)
  "My Uncle, the Captain"
    (In his <u>The Mimic Stage</u>)
  No Cure, No Pay
    (In his <u>The Mimic Stage</u>)
  An Original Idea; a duologue for a lady and gentleman
    (In his <u>The Mimic Stage</u>)
Le Bal des Vampires (see Polanski, Roman)
Le Bal des Voleurs (see Anouilh, Jean)
The Balachites (see Eveling, Stanley)
La Balance (see Reichman, Claude)
Les Balances (see Moinaux, Georges)
Balboa, Vasco Nunez de, 1475-1519
  *Vasco Nuñez de Balboa (see Gonzalez Bocanegra, Francisco)
  *Vasco Nuñez de Balboa (see Tapia y Rivera, Alejandro)
Le Balcon (see Genet, Jean)
The Bald Primadonna (see Ionesco, Eugene)
BALDERSTON, John Lloyd, 1889-
  Dracula (see Deane, Hamilton)
  Frankenstein (see Whale, James)
BALDUCCI, Alfredo, 1920-
  Le Nuova Isola
    (In <u>Sipario</u>, no. 337, June 1974)
Baldur hiin Gode (see Oehlenschläger, Adam G.)
BALDWIN, James, 1924-
  The Amen Corner
    (In <u>Black Theater</u>)
    (In <u>Black Theater U.S.A.</u>, 1847-1974)
  One Day, When I Was Lost
    (A Dial Press Play, 1972)
The Ball (see Chapman, George)
BALL, David
  Woyzeck (see Büchner, Georg)
Ballad of a Soldier; screenplay; text in Russian (see Chukrai, Grigori)
The Ballad of the Seven Sleeping Brothers of China (see Micinski, Tadeusz)
Ballad of Youth (see Kreymborg, Alfred)

Ballade vom Schönen Mädchen (see Kaiser, Georg)
BALLARD, Fred
    Young America, by Fred Ballard and Pearl Franklin
        (In One-Act Plays for Stage and Study, 2nd Series)
Balls (see Foster, Paul)
Balo (see Toomer, Jean)
BALZAC, Honoré de, 1799-1850
    L'Ecole des Manages
        (In his Oeuvres Completes: Théâtre II, Vol. 35)
    Le Faiseur
        (In his Oeuvres Completes: Théâtre II, Vol. 35)
  **Le Faiseur (see Franck, Pierre)
    La Maratre
        (In his Oeuvres Completes: Théâtre II, Vol. 35)
    Mercadet
        (In his Plays)
        (In his Works, Vol. 35-36, pt. 1)
    Pamela Giraud
        (In his Plays)
        (In his Works, Vol. 33-34, pt. 2)
    Pamela Giraud; text in French
        (In his Oeuvres Completes: Théâtre I, Vol. 34)
    The Resources of Quinola
        (In his Plays)
        (In his Works, Vol. 33-34, pt. 2)
    Les Ressources de Quinola
        (In his Oeuvres Completes: Théâtre I, Vol. 34)
   *Les Secrets de la Comedie Humaine (see Marceau, Felicien)
    The Stepmother
        (In his Plays)
        (In his Works, Vol. 35-36, pt. 1)
    Vautrin
        (In his Plays)
        (In his Works, Vol. 33-34, pt. 2)
    Vautrin; text in French
        (In his Oeuvres Completes: Théâtre I, Vol. 34)
BAMBER, George
    Return to Dust: Suspense radio script
        (In On the Air)
The Banana Box (see Chappell, Eric)
La Banda Casaroli (see Vancini, Florestano)
The Bandit Queen (see Valdivielso, José de)
The Bank Dick; screenplay (see Fields, W. C.)
The Banker's Daughter (see Howard, Bronson)
Ein Bankrott (see Bjørnson, Bjørnstjerne)
The Bankrupt (see Bjørnson, Bjørnstjerne)
The Bankrupt (see Foote, Samuel)
The Bankrupt (see Mercer, David)
Banting, Sir Frederick Grant, 1891-1941
    *Banting: Discoverer of Insulin, a drama of science (see Del-
        ston, Vernon)
Baptism (see Tembeck, Robert)
Barabbas (see Ghelderode, Michel de)

La Baracca dei Saltimbanchi (see Blok, Aleksàndr)
Baraka, Imamu Amiri (see Jones, LeRoi)
BARALT, Luis A., 1892-
    Tragedia Indiana
        (In Teatro Cubano Contemporaneo)
BARANGA, Aurel, 1913-
    Die Öffentliche Meinung
        (In Theater der Zeit, no. 9, 1976)
Barbara Fritchie (see Fitch, Clyde)
Barbara's Wedding (see Barrie, James M.)
Barbarians (see Gor'kii, Maksim)
The Barber of Seville (see Beaumarchais, Pierre)
The Barber Shop; filmscript (see Fields, W. C.)
Barberine (see Musset, Alfred de)
Le Barbier de Seville; text in French (see Beaumarchais, Pierre)
Barca, Pedro Calderón de la (see Calderón de la Barca, Pedro)
La Barca Sin Prescador (see Rodriguez Alvarez, Alejandro)
BARILLET, Pierre, 1923-
    Peau de Vache; piece de Barillet et Gredy
        (In L'Avant-Scène Théâtre, no. 577, Dec. 15, 1975)
    Une Rose au Petit Dejeuner, une comedie de Pierre Barillet et
    Jean-Pierre Gredy.   Mise en scène de Rene Clermont
        (In L'Avant-Scène du Théâtre, no. 532, Jan. 1974)
BARING, Maurice, 1874-1945
    Catherine Parr; or, Alexander's Horse
        (In A Book of Short Plays, XV-XX Centuries)
    Jason and Medea
        (In Parodies)
    The Rehearsal
        (In Parodies)
BARKER, Albert, 1900-
    Portrait by Proxy
        (In One-Act Plays for Stage and Study, 8th Series)
Barker, Harley Granville (see Granville-Barker, Harley Granville)
BARKER, Howard
    Cheek
        (In New Short Plays: 3)
    Claw
        (In his Stripwell and Claw)
    Heroes of Labour; a play for television
        (In Gambit, Vol. 8, no. 29, 1976)
    Stripwell
        (In Plays and Players, Vol. 23, nos. 2-3, Nov.-Dec. 1975)
        (In his Stripwell and Claw)
    That Good Between Us
        (In Gambit, Vol. 8, no. 31, 1977)
BARKER, James Nelson, 1784-1858
    The Indian Princess; or, La Belle Sauvage
        (In Representative Plays by American Dramatists, Vol. 1)
    Superstition
        (In Representative American Plays, 1792-1949)
BARLACH, Ernst, 1870-1938
    Der Arme Vetter

(In his Das Dichterische Werk 1, Die Dramen)
Der Blaue Boll
    (In his Das Dichterische Werk 1, Die Dramen)
The Blue Boll
    (In his Three Plays)
Die Echten Sedemunds
    (In his Das Dichterische Werk 1, Die Dramen)
Der Findling
    (In his Das Dichterische Werk 1, Die Dramen)
The Flood
    (In his Three Plays)
The Genuine Sedemunds
    (In his Three Plays)
Der Graf von Ratzeburg
    (In his Das Dichterische Werk 1, Die Dramen)
Die Gute Zeit
    (In his Das Dichterische Werk 1, Die Dramen)
Squire Blue Boll
    (In Seven Expressionist Plays)
Die Sündflut
    (In his Das Dichterische Werk 1, Die Dramen)
Der Tote Tag
    (In his Das Dichterische Werk 1, Die Dramen)
Barnaby Brittle; or, A Wife at Her Wits End (see Betterton, Thomas)
BARNES, Peter, 1931-
    Honni soit qui mal y pense; titre original: "The Ruling Class,"
    adaptation Française de Claude Roy
    (In L'Avant-Scène du Théâtre, no. 517, May 1, 1973)
    The Purging (see Feydeau, Georges)
    The Ruling Class; a baroque comedy
    (In Evergreen Playscripts Series, 1969)
    The Singer (see Wedekind, Frank)
BARNOUW, Erik
    The Pursuit of Happiness; radio script, by Erik Barnouw, John
    Tucker
    Battle, Carl Carmer, Norman Corwin, Jan. 7, 1940
    (In Best Broadcasts of 1939-40)
Barnum, Phineas Taylor, 1810-1891
    *The Mighty Barnum (see Fowler, Gene)
BAROJA Y NESSI, Pio, 1872-1956
    El Horroroso Crimen de Penaranda del Campo
    (In his Obras Completas, Vol. 6)
    La Leyenda de Juan de Alzate
    (In his Obras Completas, Vol. 6)
    El "Nocturno" del Harmano Beltran
    (In his Obras Completas, Vol. 6)
    Todo Acaba Bien ... a Veces
    (In his Obras Completas, Vol. 6)
Le Baron de Fourchevif (see Labiche, Eugene)
Le Baron Fantome; screenplay (see Cocteau, Jean)
The Baron's Will (see Bergman, Hjalmar F.)
BARR, Betty
    The Good and Obedient Young Man, by Betty Barr and Gould

Stevens; a play in the Japanese manner, suggested by Grace
James' story "Reflection."
    (In One-Act Plays for Stage and Study, 7th Series)
Barranco Abajo (see Sanchez, Florencio, 1875-1910)
BARRAULT, Jean-Louis, 1910-
    Rabelais: A Dramatic Game in Two Parts Taken from the Five
    Books of François Rabelais
    (In Faber & Faber Plays Series, 1971)
    (In Hill & Wang Spotlight Drama Series, 1971)
    Thus Spake Zarathustra (see Nietzsche, Friedrich W.)
BARRIE, Sir James Matthew, bart., 1860-1937
    The Admirable Crichton
    (In his Plays)
    Alice-sit-by-the-fire
    (In his Plays)
    Barbara's Wedding
    (In his Plays)
    Dear Brutus
    (In Masterpieces of the Modern English Theatre)
    (In his Plays)
    Half an Hour
    (In his Plays)
    A Kiss for Cinderella
    (In his Plays)
  **A Kiss for Cinderella; filmscript (see Goldbeck, Willis)
    Mary Rose
    (In his Plays)
    The New World
    (In his Plays)
    Old Friends
    (In his Plays)
    The Old Lady Shows Her Medals
    (In his Plays)
    Pantaloon
    (In his Plays)
  **Peter Pan; text in German (see Kästner, Erich)
    Peter Pan; or, The Boy Who Would Not Grow Up
    (In his Plays)
    Quality Street
    (In his Plays)
    Rosalind
    (In his Plays)
    Seven Women
    (In his Plays)
    Shall We Join the Ladies?
    (In A Book of Short Plays, XV-XX Centuries)
    (In his Plays)
    The Twelve-Pound Look
    (In his Plays)
    A Well-remembered Voice
    (In his Plays)
    What Every Woman Knows
    (In his Plays)

The Will
   (In his Plays)
BARRY, Christiane
   C'Est Pitie Qu'elle Soite une Putain (see Ford, John)
BARRY, Julian
   Lenny; a play based on the life and works of Lenny Bruce
    (In Evergreen Playscripts Series, 1971)
BARRY, Philip, 1896-1949
   The Animal Kingdom
    (In States of Grace)
   Here Come the Clowns
    (In States of Grace)
   Holiday
    (In Representative American Dramas)
    (In States of Grace)
   Hotel Universe
    (In States of Grace)
   Paris Bound
    (In Representative American Plays, 1792-1949)
   The Philadelphia Story
    (In 50 Best Plays of the American Theatre, Vol. 2)
    (In States of Grace)
   Second Threshold
    (In States of Grace)
   White Wings
    (In States of Grace)
   You and I
    (In States of Grace)
BARRY, Spranger
   A Blot on the Landscape
    (In 100 Non-Royalty Radio Plays)
   What's Your Name, Dear?
    (In 100 Non-Royalty Radio Plays)
BARSHA, Anthony Richard, 1938-
   The Hawk (see Mednick, Murray)
BARSTOW, Stan
   An Enemy of the People (see Ibsen, Henrik)
BART, Lionel
   Fings Ain't Wot They Used T' Be, a play by Frank Norman and
   lyrics by Lionel Bart
    (In Evergreen Playscripts Series, 1960)
Bartholomew Fair (see Jonson, Ben)
Bartolomé de Torres Naharro (see Torres Naharro, Bartolomé de)
BARTSCH, Kurt
   Der Bauch
    (In Theater der Zeit, no. 6, 1977)
   Die Goldgräber
    (In Theater der Zeit, no. 6, 1977)
   Der Strick
    (In Theater der Zeit, no. 6, 1977)
La Bascule (see Donnay, Maurice C.)
The Bashful Lover (see Massinger, Philip)
The Bashful Man (see Moncrieff, William T.)

The Basic Training of Pavlo Hummel (see Rabe, David W.)
BASS, George Houston
   Games
     (In Break Out!)
BASSHE, Emjo, 1900-
   Doomsday Circus (selection)
     (In The New Caravan)
   Invitation
     (In One-Act Plays for Stage and Study, 4th Series)
BASURTO, Luis G. , 1920-
   Cada Quien Su Vida
     (In Teatro Méxicano Contemporaneo)
     (In Teatro Méxicano del Siglo XX, Vol. 2)
   Los Reyes del Mundo
     (In Teatro Méxicano, 1959)
Bate, Henry (see Dudley, Sir Henry Bate, bart.)
BATEMAN, Mrs. Sidney Frances (Cowell), 1823-1881
   Self
     (In Representative Plays by American Dramatists, Vol. 2)
Bathsheba, 2nd Wife of David and Mother of Solomon
   *King David and His Wives (see Pinski, David)
   *The Love of King David and Fair Bethsaba (see Peele, George)
Les Batisseurs d'Empire (see Vian, Boris)
Baton et Ruban (see Audiberti, Jacques)
Battering Ram (see Freeman, David)
Battle at Tematangi (see Curteis, Ian)
The Battle of Alcazar (see Peele, George)
Battle of Angels (see Williams, Tennessee)
The Battle of Bunkershill (see Brackenridge, Hugh H.)
Battleship Potemkin; screenplay (see Eisenstein, Sergei M.)
Der Bauch (see Bartsch, Kurt)
BAUER, Wolfgang, 1941-
   Change
     (In Change and Other Plays)
   Magic Afternoon
     (In Change and Other Plays)
   Microdramas: Ramses, The Three Musketeers, William Tell,
     Caligula, Columbus, Romeo and Juliet. Both German and
     English texts are given
     (In Dimension, Vol. 5, no. 1, 1972)
   Party for Six
     (In Change and Other Plays)
El Baul de los Disfraces (see Salom, Jaime)
BAUM, Lyman Frank, 1856-1919
   The King of Gee-Whiz
     (In The Musical Fantasies of L. Frank Baum)
   The Maid of Athens
     (In The Musical Fantasies of L. Frank Baum)
   The Pipes o' Pan
     (In The Musical Fantasies of L. Frank Baum)
BAUMER, Marie, 1905-
   It's an Ill Wind
     (In One-Act Plays for Stage and Study, 5th Series)

Der Baurenknecht Will Zwo Frauen Haben (see Sachs, Hans)
BAX, Clifford, 1886-
    Silly Willy
       (In A Book of Short Plays, XV-XX Centuries)
    Socrates
       (In Six Plays: Famous Plays Series, 1930)
    Square Pegs
       (In his Polite Satires)
    The Unknown Hand
       (In his Polite Satires)
    The Volcanic Island
       (In his Polite Satires)
Be Good, Sweet Maid (see Webber, C. E.)
The Bear (see Chekhov, Anton)
The Beast (see Wilson, Snoo)
Beau Brummell (see Fitch, Clyde)
BEAUMARCHAIS, Pierre Augustin Caron de, 1732-1799
    L'Ami de la Maison
       (In his Théâtre Complet, Vol. 2)
    The Barber of Seville
       (In Three Popular French Comedies)
       (In World Drama, Vol. 2)
    Le Barbier de Seville
       (In his Théâtre Complet)
   *Beaumarchais (see Guitry, Sacha)
    Les Deux Amis
       (In his Théâtre Complet, Vol. 1)
    Eugenie
       (In his Théâtre Complet, Vol. 1)
    La Folle Journee; ou, Le Mariage de Figaro
       (In his Théâtre Complet, Vol. 3)
    La Mère Coupable
       (In his Théâtre Complet, Vol. 4)
    Tarare
       (In his Théâtre Complet, Vol. 4)
BEAUMONT, Francis, 1584-1616
    Beggars Bush (see Fletcher, John)
    The Bloody Brother; or, Rollo (see Fletcher, John)
    Bonduca (see Fletcher, John)
    The Captain, by Beaumont and Fletcher
       (In their Works, Vol. 5)
    The Chances (see Fletcher, John)
    The Coronation, by Beaumont and Fletcher
       (In their Works, Vol. 8)
    The Coxcomb, by Beaumont and Fletcher
       (In their Works, Vol. 8)
    Cupid's Revenge, by Beaumont and Fletcher
       (In their Works, Vol. 9)
    The Custom of the Country (see Fletcher, John)
    The Double Marriage (see Fletcher, John)
    The Elder Brother, by Beaumont and Fletcher
       (In their Works, Vol. 2)
    The Faithful Shepherdess, by Beaumont and Fletcher

(In their Works, Vol. 2)
The False One, by Beaumont and Fletcher
  (In their Works, Vol. 3)
Four Plays; or, Moral Representations in One, by Beaumont
and Fletcher
  (In their Works, Vol. 10)
The Honest Man's Fortune, by Beaumont and Fletcher
  (In their Works, Vol. 10)
The Humorous Lieutenant, by Beaumont and Fletcher
  (In their Works, Vol. 2)
The Island Princess (see Fletcher, John)
A King, and No King, by Beaumont and Fletcher
  (In their Works, Vol. 1)
The Knight of Malta, by Beaumont and Fletcher
  (In their Works, Vol. 7)
The Knight of the Burning Pestle, by Beaumont and Fletcher
  (In The Drama, Vol. 14)
  (In their Works, Vol. 6)
The Laws of Candy, by Beaumont and Fletcher
  (In their Works, Vol. 3)
The Little France Lawyer, by Beaumont and Fletcher
  (In their Works, Vol. 3)
Love Cure; or, The Martial Maid, by Beaumont and Fletcher;
sometimes attributed to Philip Massinger.
  (In their Works, Vol. 7)
Lover's Pilgrimage, by Beaumont and Fletcher
  (In their Works, Vol. 6)
The Lover's Progress, by Beaumont and Fletcher
  (In their Works, Vol. 5)
The Loyal Subject (see Fletcher, John)
The Mad Lover, by Beaumont and Fletcher
  (In their Works, Vol. 3)
The Maid in the Mill (see Fletcher, John)
The Maid's Tragedy, by Beaumont and Fletcher
  (In their Works, Vol. 1)
  (In World Drama, Vol. 1)
The Masque of the Gentlemen of Grays-Inne and the Inner-Temple
  (In Works, Vol. 10)
Monsieur Thomas, by Beaumont and Fletcher
  (In their Works, Vol. 4)
The Nice Valour; or, The Passionate Mad-Man, by Beaumont
and Fletcher
  (In their Works, Vol. 10)
The Night-Walker; or, The Little Thief, by Beaumont and
Fletcher
  (In their Works, Vol. 7)
The Noble Gentleman, by Beaumont and Fletcher
  (In their Works, Vol. 8)
Philaster; or, Love Lies Bleeding, by Beaumont and Fletcher
  (In their Works, Vol. 1)
The Pilgrim, by Beaumont and Fletcher
  (In their Works, Vol. 5)
The Prophetess, by Beaumont and Fletcher

(In their Works, Vol. 5)
The Queen of Corinth, by Beaumont and Fletcher
    (In their Works, Vol. 6)
Rule a Wife, and Have a Wife (see Fletcher, John)
The Scornful Lady, by Beaumont and Fletcher
    (In their Works, Vol. 1)
The Sea Voyage, by Beaumont and Fletcher
    (In their Works, Vol. 9)
The Spanish Curate, by Beaumont and Fletcher
    (In their Works, Vol. 2)
Thierry and Theodoret, by Beaumont and Fletcher
    (In their Works, Vol. 10)
The Two Noble Kinsmen, by Beaumont and Fletcher
    (In their Works, Vol. 9)
Valentinian (see Fletcher, John)
A Wife for a Month, by Beaumont and Fletcher
    (In their Works, Vol. 5)
The Wild-Goose Chase (see Fletcher, John)
Wit at Several Weapons, by Beaumont and Fletcher
    (In their Works, Vol. 9)
Wit Without Money (see Fletcher, John)
The Woman-Hater, by Beaumont and Fletcher
    (In their Works, Vol. 10)
The Woman's Prize; or, The Tamer Tam'd, by Beaumont and
    Fletcher
    (In their Works, Vol. 8)
Women Pleas'd, by Beaumont and Fletcher
    (In their Works, Vol. 7)
A Beautiful Day (see Krauss, Ruth I.)
Beauty and the Beast (see Weyl, Fernand)
Beauty and the Beast; screenplay (see Cocteau, Jean. La Belle et
    la Bête)
Beauty and the Jacobin (see Tarkington, Booth)
Beauty is Fled (see Carroll, Paul Vincent)
Beauty's Duty (see Shaw, George Bernard)
Les Beaux Dimanches (see Dubé, Marcel)
The Beaux Stratagem (see Farquhar, George)
Because I Love You (see Brieux, Eugene)
BECHER, Ulrich, 1910-
    Mademoiselle Löwenzorn
        (In Teatro Aleman Contemporaneo)
Becket (see Tennyson, Alfred Lord)
Becket; ou, l'Honneur de Dieu (see Anouilh, Jean)
BECKETT, Samuel, 1906-
    Breath
        (In his First Love and Other Shorts)
        (In Gambit, Vol. 4, no. 16)
    Come and Go; a Dramaticule
        (In Modern Drama, Vol. 19, no. 3, Scpt. 1976)
    Damals; text in German
        (In Theater Heute, no. 11, Nov. 1976)
    En Attendant Godot
        (In Le Théâtre d'Aujourd'hui)

Esperando a Godot (En Attendant Godot)
    (In Teatro Frances de Vanguardia)
Fin de Partie
    (In Le Théâtre d'Aujourd'hui)
Footfalls
    (In his Ends and Odds)
Ghost Trio; a television play
    (In his Ends and Odds)
    (In Journal of Beckett Studies, no. 1, Winter 1976)
Mercier and Camier
    (In Evergreen Playscripts Series, 1975)
Not I
    (In his Ends and Odds)
    (In his First Love and Other Shorts)
... Nur Noch Gewölk ...
    (In Theater Heute, no. 12, Dec. 1977)
The Old Tune (see Pinget, Robert)
Radio I & Radio II
    (In his Ends and Odds)
That Time
    (In his Ends and Odds)
Theatre I & Theatre II
    (In his Ends and Odds)
Tritte; text in German
    (In Theater Heute, no. 11, Nov. 1976)
BECQUE, Henri, 1837-1899
Les Corbeaux
    (In his Théâtre Complet II)
L'Enfant Prodique
    (In his Théâtre Complet I)
Les Honnêtes Femmes
    (In his Théâtre Complet II)
Michel Pauper
    (In his Théâtre Complet I)
La Navette
    (In his Théâtre Complet I)
The Parisian Woman
    (In Masterpieces of the Modern French Theatre)
La Parisienne
    (In his Théâtre Complet II)
Sardanapale; opéra imité de Lord Byron
    (In his Théâtre Complet I)
Bed and Board; filmscript (see Truffaut, François)
The Bed Was Full (see Drexler, Rosalyn)
The Bedbug (see Mayakovsky, Vladimir V.)
Bedroom Farce (see Ayckbourn, Alan)
Bedroom Suite (see Morley, Christopher D.)
Bedtime Story (see O'Casey, Sean)
Beerbohm, Sir Max, 1872-1956
    *The Incomparable Max Beerbohm (see Lawrence, Jerome)
Bees on the Boat Deck (see Priestley, John B.)
BEETHOVEN, Ludwin van, 1770-1827
    Fidelio; opéra en deux actes, livret de Joseph Sonnleithner et
        Georg Friedrich Treitschke, d'aprés le mélodrame de Jean-

Nicolas Bouilly, "Léonore ou l'Amour Conjugal"
(In L'Avant-Scène Opéra, no. 10, May/June 1977)
Der Befehl (see Hochwälder, Fritz)
Before Breakfast (see O'Neill, Eugene)
Before Cannae (see Munk, Kaj H.)
Before the Party (see Ackland, Rodney)
Before the Unamerican Committee (see Bentley, Eric R.)
The Beggar; or, The Dead Dog (see Brecht, Bertolt)
Beggars Bush (see Fletcher, John)
Beggar's Gift (see Kennedy, Charles R.)
The Beggar's Opera (see Gay, John)
The Begging Machine (see Ruibal, José)
BEHAN, Brendan, 1923-
    La Grande Casa
        (In Sipario, no. 337, June 1974)
    Richard Gamba di Sughero; text in Italian
        (In Sipario, no. 323, April 1973)
    Richard's Cork Leg
        (In Methuen's Modern Plays Series, 1973)
BEHN, Mrs. Aphra (Amis), 1640-1689
    Abdelazer; or, The Moor's Revenge; altered from "Lust's Do-
    minion; or, The Lascivious Queen, " by Dekker, Marlowe, and
    Day.
        (In her Works, Vol. 2)
    The Amorous Prince, founded on Robert Davenport's "The City
    Night-Cap"
        (In her Works, Vol. 4)
    The City Heiress; or, Sir Timothy Treat-All, based on Massin-
    ger's "The Guardian" and Middleton's "A Mad World, My
    Masters. "
        (In her Works, Vol. 2)
    The Dutch Lover; founded upon "The History of Don Fenise, "
    by Francisco de Las Coveras
        (In her Works, Vol. 1)
    The Emperor of the Moon, founded on "Arlequin Empereur dans
    la Lune" of the Commedia dell'Arte all'Improviso
        (In her Works, Vol. 3)
    The False Count; or, A New Way to Play an Old Game, founded
    on Molière's "Les Precieuses Ridicules"
        (In her Works, Vol. 3)
    The Feign'd Curtezans; or, A Night's Intrigue
        (In her Works, Vol. 2)
    The Forc'd Marriage; or, The Jealous Bridegroom
        (In her Works, Vol. 3)
    The Lucky Chance; or, An Alderman's Bargain, founded in part
    on Shirley's "The Lady of Pleasure"
        (In Restoration Comedy, Vol. 3)
        (In her Works, Vol. 3)
    The Roundheads; or, The Good Old Cause; founded on John
    Tatham's "The Rump; or, The Mirror of the Late Times"
        (In her Works, Vol. 1)
    The Rover; or, The Banished Cavaliers, pts. 1 and 2; based on
    Thomas Killigrew's "Thomaso; or, The Wanderer"
        (In Restoration Comedy, Vol. 2)

(In her Works, Vol. 1)
Sir Patient Fancy; founded on Molière's "Le Malade Imaginaire"
  and Brome's "The Damoiselle; or, The New Ordinary"
  (In her Works, Vol. 4)
The Town-Fop; or, Sir Timothy Tawdrey, founded upon George
  Wilkins' "The Miseries of Enforced Marriage"
  (In her Works, Vol. 3)
The Widow Ranter; or, The History of Bacon in Virginia
  (In her Works, Vol. 4)
The Young King; or, The Mistake, based on the eighth part of
  La Calprèn dé's "Cléopâtre"
  (In her Works, Vol. 2)
The Younger Brother; or, The Amorous Jilt
  (In her Works, Vol. 4)
BEHRMAN, Samuel Nathaniel, 1893-
  The Second Man
    (In Representative American Dramas)
Bekannte Gesichter, Gemischte Gefühle (see Strauss, Botho)
Un Bel Di (see Patrick, Robert)
Un Bel Enfant (see Audiberti, Jacques)
BELASCO, David, 1853-1931
  Adrea, by David Belasco and John Luther Long
    (In his Six Plays)
  The Darling of the Gods; by David Belasco and John Luther Long
    (In his Six Plays)
  Du Barry
    (In his Six Plays)
  The Girl of the Golden West
    (In Representative American Dramas)
    (In his Six Plays)
  The Heart of Maryland
    (In Favorite American Plays of the 19th Century)
  Madam Butterfly; a tragedy of Japan, from the story by John
    Luther Long
    (In Representative American Plays, 1792-1949)
    (In his Six Plays)
  Mima (see Molnar, Ferenc)
  The Return of Peter Grimm
    (In Representative Plays by American Dramatists, Vol. 3)
    (In his Six Plays)
BELAVAL, Emilio S.
  Circe; o, El Amor
    (In Teatro Puertorriqueño: Quinto Festival)
Belcher's Luck (see Mercer, David)
La Bella Dorotea (see Mihura, Miguel)
La Bella Durmiente (see Brulez, Raymond)
Bellamira Her Dream (see Killigrew, Thomas)
BELLAN, José Pedro
  Dios Te Salve!
    (In Teatro Uruguayo Contemporaneo)
Bellavita (see Pirandello, Luigi)
La Belle Aphrede (see Rotrou, Jean)
La Belle et la Bête; screenplay (see Cocteau, Jean)

Bellerophon (see Kaiser, Georg)
Les Belles Soeurs (see Tremblay, Michel)
The Belle's Stratagem (see Cowley, Mrs. Hannah)
BELLIDO, José Maria
    Bread and Rice; or, Geometry in Yellow
        (In The New Wave Spanish Drama)
    Fantastic Suite
        (In Modern International Drama, Vol. 6, no. 2, Spring 1973)
    Football
        (In Modern Spanish Theatre)
    The Scorpion
        (In Drama and Theatre, Vol. 11, no. 3, Spring 1973)
    Train to H ...
        (In The New Wave Spanish Drama)
Bellissima; screenplay (see Visconti, Luchino)
BELLOCCHIO, Marco, 1940-
    La Cina è Vicina
        (In Dal Soggetto al Film Series, no. 36, 1967)
    I Pugni in Tasca
        (In Garzanti Filmscript Series, 1967)
    Nel Nome del Padre
        (In Dal Soggetto al Film Series, no. 44, 1971)
BELLON, Loleh
    Les Dames du Jeudi
        (In L'Avant-Scène Théâtre, no. 607, Apr. 1, 1977)
BELLOW, Saul, 1915-
    Orange Souffle
        (In Best Short Plays of the World Theatre, 1968-1973)
Belphegor; or, The Marriage of the Devil (see Wilson, John)
Belshazzar's Feast (see Calderón de la Barca, Pedro)
BENAVENTE Y MARTINEZ, Jacinto, 1866-1954
    The Bonds of Interest
        (In Representative Continental Dramas)
    The Witches' Sabbath
        (In Masterpieces of the Modern Spanish Theatre)
BENCO, Silvio, 1874-1949
    L'Uomo Malato
        (In Sipario, no. 333, Feb. 1974)
The Bending of the Bough (see Moore, George)
BENE, Carmelo, 1937-
    Un Hamlet de Moins; titre original: "Un Amleto Meno, " d'après
        Shakespeare et Jules Laforgue
        (In L'Avant-Scène Cinéma, no. 178, Dec. 1976)
BENEDETTI, Mario, 1920-
    Ida y Vuelta
        (In El Teatro Hispanoamericano Contemporaneo, Vol. 1)
BENEDIX, Roderich, 1811-1873
    Obstinacy
        (In The Drama, Vol. 11)
BENEKE, Walter, 1928-
    Funeral Home
        (In El Teatro Hispanoamericano Contemporaneo, Vol. 2)
BENET, Stephen Vincent, 1898-1943
  **Blood of the Martyrs (see Macfarlane, Donald)

BENET I JORNET, Josep
  The Ship
    (In Modern International Drama, Vol. 8, no. 1, 1974)
    (In 3 Catalan Dramatists)
Benito Cereno (see Lowell, Robert)
BENJAMIN, James
  No Man Is an Island; television script by James Benjamin and
  Don Kellerman, based on an original story by Helen Kroner,
  broadcast July 21, 1957 on the "Look Up and Live" series,
  CBS
    (In The Seeking Years)
BENNETT, Alan, 1934-
  Habeas Corpus
    (In Faber & Faber Plays Series, 1973)
BENNETT, Arnold, 1867-1931
  The Ides of March, by Arnold Bennett and Fred Alcock
    (In One-Act Plays for Stage and Study, 8th Series)
  The Snake Charmer
    (In One-Act Plays for Stage and Study, 6th Series)
BENNETT, Gordon C.
  Meet Noah Smith
    (In his From Nineveh to Now)
  On the Plain of Dura
    (In his From Nineveh to Now)
  So Why Does That Weirdo Prophet Keep Watching the Water?
    (In his From Nineveh to Now)
BENNETT, John
  **Kidnapped in London (see Mason, Timothy)
BENNY, Jack (Benjamin Kubelsky), 1894-1974
  The Edgar Bergen Show (see Rose, Si)
  The Jack Benny Show; radio script of March 3, 1940
    (In Best Broadcasts of 1939-40)
BENTLEY, Eric Russell, 1916-
  Before the Unamerican Committee
    (In Break Out!)
  Larry Parks' Day in Court
    (In Best Short Plays of the World Theatre, 1968-1973)
  Madman's Diary (see Gogol, Nikolai V.)
  Roaring All Day Long; an epilogue
    (In New Directions, Vol. 16, 1957)
  A Time to Die
    (In Evergreen Playscripts Series, 1970)
  A Time to Live
    (In Evergreen Playscripts Series, 1970)
BENTON, Rita, 1881-
  The Children Who Work and the Children Who Play
    (In The Elf of Discontent and Other Plays)
  The Elf of Discontent
    (In The Elf of Discontent and Other Plays)
  The Happy Prince; from the story by Oscar Wilde
    (In The Elf of Discontent and Other Plays)
  Ivan the Fool; from the story by Leo Tolstoy
    (In The Elf of Discontent and Other Plays)

The Liberty Bell
    (In The Elf of Discontent and Other Plays)
Old Gentleman Gay; adapted from "A Good Thanksgiving" by
    Marian Douglas
    (In The Elf of Discontent and Other Plays)
Queen Cross-Patch and the Scullery Wench
    (In The Elf of Discontent and Other Plays)
The Silver Arrow of Robin Hood
    (In The Elf of Discontent and Other Plays)
What Men Live By; from the story by Leo Tolstoy
    (In The Elf of Discontent and Other Plays)
BEOLCO, Angelo, called Il Ruzzante, c. 1502-1542
    Bilora, the Second Rustic Play, translated by Babette and Glenn
    Hughes
        (In World Drama, Vol. 2)
    **Les Vilains (see Gille, Andre)
Beorhtnoth, son of Beorhthelm, Duke of Essex, d. 991
    *The Homecoming of Beorhtnoth, Beorhthelm's Son (see Tolkien,
    J. R. R.)
Beppo and Beth (see Wilson, Edmund)
Berenice, Queen of Palestine, 28?-75 A.D.
    *Berenice (see Racine, Jean Baptiste)
BERG, Barry
    Kindly Observe the People
        (In Modern International Drama, Vol. 7, no. 1B, Spring 1976)
Die Bergbahn (see Horvath, Odön von)
BERGEN, Edgar John, 1903-1978
    The Edgar Bergen Show (see Rose, Si)
Les Bergeries (see Racan, Honorat de Bueil)
BERGMAN, Hjalmar Fredrik Elgerus, 1883-1931
    The Baron's Will
        (In his Four Plays)
    La Familia Swedenhielm
        (In Teatro Sueco Contemporaneo)
    Markurells of Wadköping
        (In his Four Plays)
    Mr. Sleeman is Coming
        (In his Four Plays)
        (In Scandinavian Plays of the 20th Century, Series 1)
    Swedenhielms
        (In his Four Plays)
        (In Scandinavian Plays of the 20th Century, Series 3)
BERGMAN, Ingmar, 1918-
    Cris et Chuchotements
        (In L'Avant-Scène du Cinéma, no. 142, Dec. 1973)
    Face to Face
        (A Pantheon Books Screenplay, 1976)
    A Little Night Music (see Sondheim, Stephen)
    The Magician (The Face)
        (In his Four Screenplays)
    Persona
        (In Persona and Shame)
    Scenes from a Marriage

(A <u>Pantheon Books Screenplay</u>, 1974)
(A <u>Bantam Books Screenplay</u>, 1974)
The Serpent's Egg; screenplay for film produced by Dino De
    Laurentis
(A <u>Bantam Books Screenplay</u>, 1978)
(A <u>Pantheon Books Screenplay</u>, 1977)
The Seventh Seal
    (In his <u>Four Screenplays</u>)
Shame
    (In <u>Persona and Shame</u>)
Smiles of a Summer Night
    (In his <u>Four Screenplays</u>)
The Snakeskin
    (In <u>Persona and Shame</u>)
Wild Strawberries
    (In his <u>Four Screenplays</u>)
BERGMANN, Alfred
Nina + Georg: When the Music's Over
    (In <u>Theater Heute</u>, no. 6, June, 1976)
Das Bergwerk zu Falun; texts in English and German (see Hofmann-
    sthal, Hugo von H.)
BERKELEY, Reginald, 1890-
The Dweller in the Darkness
    (In <u>Types of Modern Dramatic Composition</u>)
BERKOFF, Steven
Agamemnon (see Aeschylus)
East
    (In his <u>East and Other Plays</u>)
The Fall of the House of Usher, based on the work of Edgar
    Allan Poe
    (In his <u>East and Other Plays</u>)
BERLIN, Nathan
Frontier Fighters, a historical adventure. I: Wyatt Earp; II:
    Wild Bill Hickok, by Nathan Berlin and Richard Pack
    (In <u>100 Non-Royalty Radio Plays</u>)
What's in a Word? by Nathan Berlin and Richard Pack
    (In <u>100 Non-Royalty Radio Plays</u>)
Les Berlingots (see Rene-Georges)
BERMANGE, Barry, 1933-
Nathan and Tabileth
    (A <u>Methuen Playscript</u>, 1967)
BERMEL, Albert
The Work Out
    (In <u>Gambit</u>, no. 3)
Bermondsey (see Mortimer, John C.)
Bernabé (see Valdez, Luis M.)
BERNARD, Jean Jacques, 1888-
Glamour
    (In <u>Eight European Plays</u>)
Martine
    (In <u>Eight European Plays</u>)
The Poet's Secret
    (In <u>Modern One-Act Plays from the French</u>)

BERNARD, Kenneth, 1930-
    The Giants in the Earth
        (In his Night Club and Other Plays)
    The Lovers
        (In his Night Club and Other Plays)
    Mary Jane
        (In his Night Club and Other Plays)
    The Moke-eater
        (In his Night Club and Other Plays)
    The Monkeys in the Organ Grinder
        (In his Night Club and Other Plays)
    Night Club (Bubi's Hide-Away)
        (In his Night Club and Other Plays)
    The Unknown Chinaman
        (In Playwrights for Tomorrow, Vol. 10)
BERNARD, Tristan, 1866-1947
    Free Treat
        (In Modern One-Act Plays from the French)
Bernardo do Palissy (see Tapia y Rivera, Alejandro)
BERNEY, William Claibourne, 1920-
    Dark of the Moon (see Richardson, Howard)
BERNHARD, Thomas
    Die Macht der Gewohnheit
        (In Theater Heute, Vol. 15, no. 9, Sept. 1974)
    Minetti
        (In Theater Heute, no. 10, Oct. 1976)
Bernice (see Masefield, John)
BERNIER, François, d. 1688
  **Aureng-Zebe (see Dryden, John)
BERNOL, Marc
    L'Arriviste
        (In L'Avant-Scène du Cinéma, no. 137, June 1973)
BERNSTEIN, Leonard, 1918-
    Candide (see Hellman, Lillian)
    West Side Story; book by Arthur Laurents; music by Leonard
      Bernstein; lyrics by Stephen Sondheim; based on a conception
      of Jerome Robbins
        (In Ten Great Musicals of the American Theatre)
    Wonderful Town. Book by Joseph Fields and Jerome Chodorov,
      based upon their play "My Sister Eileen," and the stories of
      Ruth McKenney; music by Leonard Bernstein; lyrics by Betty
      Comden and Adolph Green
        (A Random House Play, 1953)
        (In Ten Great Musicals of the American Theatre, Vol. 2)
BERREBY, Georges
    Hors Service
        (In L'Avant-Scène Théâtre, no. 620, Dec. 15, 1977)
Il Berretto a Sonagli (see Pirandello, Luigi)
BERTOLUCCI, Bernardo, 1941-
    Last Tango in Paris
        (In Delta Screenplays Series, 1973)
The Bespoke Overcoat (see Mankowitz, Wolf)
The Best Man; filmscript (see Vidal, Gore)

BHAVABHUTI, 8th Century A. D.
    The Later Story of Rama
        (In Great Sanskrit Plays)
    Rama's Later History
        (In Six Sanskrit Plays)
BIBLE, O. T.
    Meet Noah Smith (see Bennett, Gordon C.)
    On the Plain of Dura (see Bennett, Gordon C.)
    So Why Does That Weirdo Prophet Keep Watching the Water?
    (see Bennett, Gordon C.)
BICAT, Tony
    Devil's Island
        (In Plays and Players, Vol. 24, nos. 5-6, Feb. -Mar. 1977)
BICKERSTAFF, Isaac, 1735?-1812?
    The Absent Man; hint taken from Menalcas in "Les Caracteres"
    of La Bruyère
        (In A Collection of the Most Esteemed Farces ..., Vol. 6)
    Daphne and Amintor, altered from "The Oracle" of Monsieur St.
    Foix and Mrs. Cibber
        (In A Collection of the Most Esteemed Farces ..., Vol. 5)
    Dr. Last in His Chariot, from Molière's "Malade Imaginaire"
        (In A Collection of the Most Esteemed Farces ..., Vol. 5)
    The Ephesian Matron, with music by Mr. Dibdin
        (In A Collection of the Most Esteemed Farces ..., Vol. 6)
    He Wou'd If He Cou'd; or, An Old Fool Worse than Any, with
    music by Mr. Dibdin
        (In A Collection of the Most Esteemed Farces ..., Vol. 5)
    The Hypocrite
        (In The London Stage, Vol. 1)
    Lionel and Clarissa
        (In The London Stage, Vol. 1)
    Love in a Village
        (In The London Stage, Vol. 1)
    The Maid of the Mill
        (In The London Stage, Vol. 1)
    The Padlock
        (In The London Stage, Vol. 1)
    The Recruiting Serjeant, with music composed by C. Dibdin
        (In A Collection of the Most Esteemed Farces ..., Vol. 6)
        (In The London Stage, Vol. 3)
    The Romp, altered from "Love in the City" by Mr. Bickerstaff
    and music by Mr. Dibdin
        (In A Collection of the Most Esteemed Farces ..., Vol. 6)
        (In The London Stage, Vol. 4)
    The Spoiled Child
        (In The London Stage, Vol. 4)
    The Sultan; or, A Peep into the Seraglio, founded on "Solomon
    II, " one of Marmontel's Contes Moraux
        (In A Collection of the Most Esteemed Farces ..., Vol. 1)
        (In The London Stage, Vol. 3)
    Thomas and Sally; or, The Sailor's Return; with music by Arne
        (In A Collection of the Most Esteemed Farces ..., Vol. 2)
        (In The London Stage, Vol. 4)

La Bicyclette du Condamne (see Arrabal, Fernando)
Il Bidone; screenplay (see Fellini, Federico)
Biedermann et les Incendiaires (see Frisch, Max)
Biedermann und die Brandstifter (see Frisch, Max)
BIEL, Nicholas, 1912-
    Gone for a Soldier
        (In Gambit, Vol. 3, no. 10)
BIELER, Manfred
    Jerome; a radio play; both German and English texts are given
        (In Dimension, Vol. 4, no. 1, 1971)
Bienvenido Don Goyito (see Méndez Ballester, Manuel)
BIERCE, Ambrose, 1842-1914?
    **An Occurrence at Owl Creek Bridge; screenplay (see Vidor,
      Charles)
    **On Owl Creek; film adaptation (see Enrico, Robert)
    Two Administrations
        (In his Collected Works, Vol. 12)
Bierce Takes on the Railroad! (see Bosakowski, Philip A.)
BIETTE, Jean-Claude, 1942-
    La Soeur du Cadre
        (In L'Avant-Scène Cinéma, no. 147, May 1974)
The Big Day (see Gorelik, Mordecai)
The Big Deal; television script (see Chayefsky, Paddy)
Big Deal in Laredo; television script (see Carroll, Sidney)
Big Mother (see Dizenzo, Charles)
The Big Scene (see Schnitzler, Arthur)
Big Soft Nellie (see Livings, Henry)
Big Time Buck White (see Tuotti, Joseph D.)
Big White Fog (see Ward, Theodore)
BIGELOW, Franklyn
    As the Tumbrils Pass (see Van der Veer, Ethel)
    The Emperor's Doll (see Van der Veer, Ethel)
BIGGERS, Earl Derr, 1884-
    **Seven Keys to Baldpate (see Cohan, George M.)
La Bigote (see Renard, Jules)
Le Bijou de la Reine (see Dumas, Alexandre, Fils)
Bilan (see Dubé, Marcel)
BILLETDOUX, François Paul, 1927-
    Il Faut Passer par les Nuages
        (In Le Théâtre d'Aujourd'hui)
    Tchin-Tchin
        (In Le Théâtre d'Aujourd'hui)
    Les Veuves
        (In L'Avant-Scène Théâtre, no. 571, 1975)
The Billy-Club Puppets (see Garcia Lorca, Federico)
Billy the Kid (see Bonney, William H.)
Bilora (see Beolco, Angelo)
THE BIM-BOM TROUPE AND THE AFANASJEFF FAMILY CIRCUS
    Joy in Earnest
        (In Twentieth-Century Polish Avant-Garde Drama)
BINAZZI, Massimo
    La Favola d'Orfeo
        (In Sipario, no. 379, Dec. 1977)

La Paura; text in Italian
        (In Sipario, no. 360, 1976)
Bingo: Scenes of Money and Death (see Bond, Edward)
The Bird (see Obrenović, Aleksandar)
BIRD, Robert Montgomery, 1806-1854
    The Broker of Bogotá
        (In Representative American Plays, 1792-1949)
    The Gladiator
        (In Dramas from the American Theatre, 1762-1909
The Bird in a Cage (see Shirley, James)
Birdbath (see Melfi, Leonard)
The Birds (see Aristophanes)
Birdwatchers (see Hite, Barbara A.)
BIRO, Lajos, 1880-
    The Heart of Kings
        (In Gods and Kings)
    Midsummer Night
        (In Gods and Kings)
    The Private Life of Henry VIII; screenplay by Lajos Biro and
      Arthur Wimperis, for the film directed by Alexander Korda
        (In Garland Classics of Film Literature Series)
    Revision
        (In Gods and Kings)
    Revolt
        (In Gods and Kings)
    Scandal in the House of Zeus
        (In Gods and Kings)
    Sorcery
        (In Gods and Kings)
Biron, Charles de Gontaut, duc de, 1562-1602
    *The Conspiracy of Charles Duke of Byron (see Chapman, George)
    *The Tragedy of Charles Duke of Byron (see Chapman, George)
The Birth of Merlin; or, The Child Hath Found His Father (Anon.)
        (In Disputed Plays of William Shakespeare)
The Birth of a Private Man (see Mercer, David)
Birthday Honours (see Jones, Paul)
The Birthday Party (see Pinter, Harold)
Bishop Jon Arason (see Sveinbjörnsson, Tryggvi)
The Bishop's Candlesticks (see McKinnel, Norman)
Bismarck (see Unruh, Fritz von)
Bismarck, Otto Eduard von, 1815-1898
    *Bismarck; oder, Warum Steht des Soldat Da?
BISSON, Jean-Pierre
    The Red Morning
        (In Break Out!)
Bits and Pieces (see Jacker, Corinne)
A Bitter Fate (see Pisemskii, Aleksei F.)
Bitter Sweet (see Coward, Noël)
DIVAR, Antônio
    Alzira Power
        (In Revista de Teatro, no. 401, Sept./Oct. 1974)
    Cordélia Brasíl
        (In Revista de Teatro, no. 413, Sept./Oct. 1976)

Visitation (see Kanigher, Robert)
BLACK, Stephen
    The Horse Latitudes
        (In Best Short Plays, 1976)
Black and White (see Pinter, Harold)
Black Bog Beast Bait (see Shepard, Sam)
The Black Book (see Middleton, Thomas)
The Black Bottle (see O'Brien, Seuman)
Black Chiffon (see Storm, Lesley)
Black Comedy (see Staffer, Peter)
Black Cycle (see Charles, Martie)
The Black Death (see Cunningham, Frank)
The Black Doctor (see Aldridge, Ira)
Black Dreams (see Ravel, Aviva)
The Black Eye (see Mavor, Osborne Henry)
Black-Eyed Susan; or, All in the Downs (see Jerrold, Douglas)
Black Fast (see Clarke, Austin)
Black Hell (see Aguilera-Malta, Demetrio)
The Black Horseman (see Richardson, Willis)
Black-Ice (see Patterson, Charles)
Black Light (see Desleal, Alvaro M.)
The Black Maskers (see Andreev, Leonid N.)
Black Mass (see Edward Bond)
Black Oliver (see Guinan, John)
Black Opera (see Cousin, Gabriel)
The Black Suitcase (see Riley, Mrs. Alice C. D.)
Black Terror (see Wesley, Richard)
Blackberrying; a Minstrel Show (Anon.)
        (In Dramas from the American Theatre, 1762-1909)
Blacklist; television script (see Kinoy, Ernest)
BLADES, William, 1824-1890
    Ceremony of the Printer's Apprentice
        (In The Drama, Vol. 4)
BLAND, Mrs. Edith (Nesbit), 1858-1924
    **Long and Short Division (see Smith, Moyne Rice)
BLANK, Franklin
    Department of Interesting Authors: Struggle for an Unknown
        Cause
        (In The Journal of Irish Literature, Vol. 5, no. 2, May 1976)
Blank Pages (see Marcus, Frank)
Der Blaue Boll (see Barlach, Ernst)
The Blaumilch Canal (see Kishon, Ephraim)
The Bleaching Yard (see Vesaas, Tarjei)
BLECHMAN, Burt
    **My Mother, My Father and Me (see Hellman, Lillian)
Bleeding Hearts (see Edmonds, Randolph)
Blessing (see Landon, Joseph)
The Blind (see Maeterlinck, Maurice)
The Blind Beggar of Alexandria (see Chapman, George)
The Blind Man (see Flavin, Martin)
The Blind Men (see Ghelderode, Michel de)
Der Blind Mesner mit dem Pfarrer und Seim Weib (see Sachs, Hans)
The Blind Warrior (see Rellán, Miguel A.)

The Blindfold (see Lopez Rubio, José)
BLINN, William
 Brian's Song
  (A Bantom Books Screenplay, 1972)
Blithe Spirit (see Coward, Noël)
BLITZSTEIN, Marc, 1905-1964
 The Cradle Will Rock (selection)
  (In The American Writer and the Great Depression)
Blk Love Song #1 (see Ferdinand, Val)
BLOCH, Pedro
 Karla, Valeu a Pena?
  (In Revista de Teatro, no. 414, Nov./Dec. 1976)
BLOK, Aleksàndr Aleksandrovich, 1880-1921
 La Baracca dei Saltimbanchi
  (In Sipario, no. 375-376, Aug./Sept. 1977)
 The Puppet Show
  (In 20th Century Russian Plays)
 La Sconosciuta; l'epigrate è romanzo "L'Idiota," di Dostoeskij
  (In Sipario, no. 377, Oct. 1977)
 The Unknown Woman
  (In Transition, Vol. 1, nos. 2-4, May-July, 1927)
The Blood Knot (see Fugard, Athol)
The Blood of the Bambergs (see Osborne, John)
Blood of the Martyrs (see Macfarlane, Donald)
Blood Wedding (see Garcia Lorca, Federico)
Bloodrites (see Jones, LeRoi)
The Bloody Brother; or, Rollo (see Fletcher, John)
The Bloody Poplar (see Turkish Theatre. Karagöz)
BLOOM, George
 Archie and the Editorial; television script for an episode in "All
  in the Family," by George Bloom and Don Nicholl
  (In Samuel French's Tandem Library Series)
The Bloomers (see Sternheim, Carl
A Blot in the 'Scutcheon (see Browning, Robert)
A Blot on the Landscape (see Barry, Spranger)
Blow-Up; screenplay (see Antonioni, Michelangelo)
The Blue Boll (see Barlach, Ernst)
The Blue Dahlia; filmscript (see Chandler, Raymond)
Blue Danube (see Molnar, Ferenc)
Blue Movie; filmscript (see Warhol, Andy)
The Blue Prince (see Riley, Mrs. Alice C. D.)
Blue Sea and Red Rose (see Hughes, Glenn)
Blue Thunder (see Green, Paul)
The Blue Vase (see Williams, Frayne)
Bluebeard (see Ludlam, Charles)
Blues for Mister Charlie (see Jones, LeRoi)
Blurt, Master-Constable (see Middleton, Thomas)
Der Blutstrahl (see Artaud, Antonin)
Boabdil (Abu-Abdullah), Moorish King of Granada, Mohamed XI,
 d. 1533 or 1534
 *The Conquest of Granada by the Spaniards, pts. 1&2 (see Dryden,
  John)
BOAL, Augusto, 1930-
 Zio Paperone

(In Sipario, no. 315-316, Aug./Sept. 1972)
The Boarding School (see Coffey, Charles)
BOARDMAN, True
    Expert Opinion; radio script from "The Silver Theatre"
      (In Best Broadcasts of 1838-39)
    For Richer--For Richer; a radio script, Dec. 10, 1939
      (In Best Broadcasts of 1939-40)
The Boat in the Forest (see Haitov, Nicolai)
The Boat Without a Fisherman (see Rodriguez Alvarez, Alejandro)
The Bob Hope Show radio script (see Hope, Bob)
BOBB, Ralph
    A Hundred Fires
      (In Drama and Theatre, Vol. 10, no. 2, Winter 1971-72)
BOCCACCIO, Giovanni, 1313-1375
    **The Falcon (see Tennyson, Alfred, Lord)
    Boccaccio '70; filmscript (see Fellini, Federico)
BOCK, Jerry, 1928-
    Fiddler on the Roof; book by Joseph Stein; music by Jerry Bock;
    lyrics by Sheldon Harnick; based on Sholom Aleichem's stories
      (In Best Plays of the Sixties)
      (In 50 Best Plays of the American Theatre, Vol. 4)
      (In Ten Great Musicals of the American Theatre)
    Fiorello! Book by Jerome Weidman and George Abbott; lyrics
    by Sheldon Harnick; music by Jerry Bock. A musical celebra-
    tion of the life and times of Mayor Fiorello H. La Guardia
      (In Ten Great Musicals of the American Theatre, Vol. 2)
Bodas de Sangre (see Garcia Lorca, Federico)
BODEL, Jean, fl. 12th Century
    Le Jeu de Saint Nicolas; text in English
      (In Medieval French Plays)
    The Play of Saint Nicholas (Le Jeu de Saint Nicholas)
      (In Five Comedies of Medieval France)
Body (see Rezvani)
The Bodybuilders (see Weller, Michael)
Boesman and Lena (see Fugard, Athol)
The Bogie Men (see Gregory, Isabella A.)
BOHANON, Mary
    Find the Girl
      (In A Galaxy of Black Writing)
BOITO, Camillo, 1836-1914
    **Senso; screenplay (see Visconti, Luchino)
BOKER, George Henry, 1823-1890
    Anne Boleyn
      (In his Plays & Poems, Vol. 1)
    The Betrothal
      (In his Plays & Poems, Vol. 2)
    Calaynos
      (In his Plays & Poems, Vol. 1)
    Francesca da Rimini
      (In Dramas from the American Theatre, 1762-1909)
      (In his Plays & Poems, Vol. 1)
      (In Representative American Plays, 1792-1949)
      (In Representative Plays by American Dramatists, Vol. 3)

Leonor de Guzman
(In his Plays & Poems, Vol. 1)
The Widow's Marriage
(In his Plays & Poems, Vol. 2)
La Bola de Nieve (see Tamayo y Baus, Manuel)
BOLAND, Bridget
Cockpit
(In Plays of the Year, Vol. 1, 1948-49)
The Prisoner
(In Plays of the Year, Vol. 10, 1953/54)
The Return
(In Plays of the Year, Vol. 9, 1953)
A Bold Stroke for a Husband (see Cowley, Mrs. Hannah)
Boleyn, Anne, Consort of Henry VIII, King of England, 1507-1536
*Anne Boleyn (see Albery, Peter)
*Anne Boleyn (see Boker, George Henry)
*Cant; a play of Henry III and Anne Boleyn (see Munk, Kaj H.)
*Henri VIII (see Chenier, Marie J.)
BOLOGNINI, Mauro, 1923-
La Viaccia
(In Dal Soggetto al Film Series, no. 18, 1961)
La Bolsa Negra (see Ramirez, Frank)
BOLT, Carol
Maurice
(In Performing Arts in Canada, Vol. 11, no. 4, Winter 1974)
BOLT, Robert, 1924-
Doctor Zhivago; screenplay of David Lean's film based on the
novel by Boris Pasternak
(A Random House Screenplay, 1965)
Gentle Jack
(A Random House Play, 1965)
A Man for All Seasons
(In Heineman Drama Library Series, 1960)
(In Random House Play, 1962)
The Thwarting of Baron Bollingrew
(In All the World's a Stage)
(In Heineman Drama Library Series, 1966)
Vivat! Vivat Regina!
(In Heineman Drama Library Series, 1971)
BOLTON, Guy, 1884-
Anastasia (see Marcelle-Maurette)
Don't Listen Ladies! (see Guitry, Sacha)
Bolzoni, Francesco
I Misteri de Roma (Rocca San Casciano); filmscript based on
the work of Cesare Zavattini
(In Dal Soggetto al Film Series, no. 26, 1963)
Bomen, John, 1924-
The Waiting Room
(In Best Short Plays of the World Theatre, 1968-1973)
Bompiani, Valentino
Miedo de si Mismo
(In Teatro Italian Contemporaneo)
Bon Ton; or, High Life Above Stairs (see Garrick, David)

BONA, Giampiero, 1926-
    L'Accoppiamento
        (In Sipario, no. 326, July 1973)
Bonaparte (see Unruh, Fritz von)
Bonaventure (see Hastings, Charlotte)
The Bond (see Strindberg, August)
BOND, Edward, 1934-
    A-A-America!
        (In his A-A-America! and Stone)
        (In Methuen's New Theatrescripts, no. 2, 1976)
    Bingo: Scenes of Money and Death
        (In his Bingo & The Sea)
    Black Mass
        (In Gambit, Vol. 5, no. 17)
    Blow-Up (see Antonioni, Michelangelo)
    Early Morning
        (In Calder & Boyars Playscript Series, no. 18)
    Grandma Faust
        (In his A-A-America! and Stone)
        (In Fireweed, Vol. 5, June 1976)
    Die Hochzeit des Papstes
        (In Theater: Chronik und Bilanz des Bühenjahres, 1970)
    Der Irre
        (In Theater Heute, no. 5, May 1977)
    Lear
        (In Hill & Wang's Spotlight Drama Series, 1972)
    Lear; text in German
        (In Theater: Chronik und Bilanz des Bühenjahres, 1972)
    Lear; text in Italian
        (In Sipario, no. 317, Oct. 1972)
    Il Mare; text in Italian
        (In Sipario, no. 335, April 1974)
    Narrow Road to the Deep North
        (In Hill & Wang's Spotlight Drama Series, 1969)
    The Pope's Wedding
        (In Methuen Modern Plays Series, 1971)
    Saved
        (In Hill & Wang's Spotlight Drama Series, 1966)
        (In New Theatre of Europe, Vol. 4)
    The Sea
        (In his Bingo & The Sea)
        (In Methuen's Modern Plays Series, 1973)
    Die See; text in German
        (In Theater Heute, no. 11, Nov. 1973)
    Stone
        (In his A-A-America! and Stone)
        (In Performing Arts Journal, Vol. 2, no. 2, Fall 1977)
    The Swing
        (In his A-A-America! and Stone)
The Bondman (see Massinger, Philip)
The Bonds of Interest (see Benavente y Martinez, Jacinto)
Bonduca (see Fletcher, John)
Bonjour la Bonjour (see Tremblay, Michel)

BONN, John E.
    15-Minute Red Revue, an Agit-Prop Play
       (In The Drama Review, Vol. 17, no. 4, Dec. 1973)
BONNEAU, Jean-Pierre
    Le Premier Combat
       (In L'Avant-Scène Cinéma, no. 159, June 1975)
BONNER, Marita, 1905-
    The Purple Flower
       (In Black Theater U.S.A., 1847-1974)
Les Bonnes (see Genet, Jean)
Bonney, William H.
    *Le Gaucher; screenplay, text in French (see Penn, Arthur)
BONNIN ARMSTRONG, Ana Inés
    La Dificil Esperanza
       (In Teatro Puertorriqueño: Octavo Festival)
BONTEMPS, Arna Wendell, 1902-
    St. Louis Woman, by Arna Bontemps and Countee Cullen; from
    the novel "God Sends Sunday." Lyrics by Johnny Mercer,
    music by Harold Arlen
       (In Black Theater)
The Book of Job (see Rogers, Merrill)
The Bookseller Cannot Sleep (see Olsen, Ernst B.)
The Boor (see Chekhov, Anton)
Booth, John Wilkes, 1838-1865
    *J. Wilkes Booth; or, The National Tragedy (see Luby, William
    A.)
    *Madame Surratt (see Rogers, James W.)
    *The Story of Mrs. Surratt (see Goggan, John P.)
BORCHERT, Wolfgang, 1921-
    La Calle sin Puertas
       (In Teatro Alemán Contemporaneo)
    The Outsider
       (In Postwar German Theatre)
BORDEAUX, Henry, 1870-1963
    Shattered
       (In Modern One-Act Plays from the French)
BORDON, Furio
    Giochi di Mano
       (In Sipario, no. 370, Mar. 1977)
BORG, Sonia
    Lament the Days That Are Gone By; an episode from the Rush
    television series
       (In Australian Theatre Workshop no. 13)
BORGEN, Johan, 1902-
    The House
       (In Modern Nordic Plays: Norway)
Borgia, Caesar, 1476-1507
    *Caesar Borgia; Son of Pope Alexander the Sixth (see Lee,
    Nathaniel)
    *The Duke of Gandia (see Swinburne, Algernon Charles)
Borgia, Lucretia, 1480-1519
    *The Duke of Gandia (see Swinburne, Algernon Charles)
    *Lucrece Borgia; text in French (see Hugo, Victor)

*Lucretia Borgia; text in English (see Hugo, Victor)
Boris Godunov (see Pushkin, Aleksandr)
Born Yesterday (see Kanin, Garson)
BOSAKOWSKI, Philip A.
    Bierce Takes on the Railroad!
        (In Playwrights for Tomorrow, Vol. 11)
The Boss (see Sheldon, Edward)
A Bosses' Christmas Carol (see Radical Arts Troup, University of
    Connecticut)
BOSTON, Stewart
    Counsellor Extraordinary
        (In A Collection of Canadian Plays, Vol. 1)
Both Ends Meet (see MacRae, Arthur)
Bothwell, 4th Earl of, James Hepburn, 1536-1578
*Bothwell (see Swinburne, Algernon Charles)
Botticelli (see McNally, Terrence)
The Bottle Imp (see Koopman, Romance C.)
Boubourche (see Moinaux, Georges)
Boubourche; text in French (see Moinaux, Georges)
BOUCHET, Pierre
    Tout un dimanche ensemble ...
        (In L'Avant-Scène du Théâtre, no. 511, Feb. 1, 1973)
BOUCICAULT, Dionysius Lardner, 1820 or 1822-1890
    The Corsican Brothers
        (In English Plays of the 19th Century, Vol. 11: Dramas
        1850-1900)
        (In Victorian Melodramas)
    Flying Scud
        (In Favorite American Plays of the 19th Century)
    London Assurance
        (In The Drama, Vol. 22)
        (In Representative British Dramas)
    The Octoroon; or, Life in Louisiana
        (In Representative American Plays, 1792-1949)
    The Shaughraun
        (In English Plays of the 19th Century, Vol. II: Dramas
        1850-1900)
BOUILLY, Jean-Nicolas, 1792-1842
    **Fidelio (see Beethoven, Ludwig van)
Le Boulanger, la Boulandere et le Petit Mitron (see Anouilh, Jean)
Les Boulingrin (see Moinaux, Georges)
Bound East for Cardiff (see O'Neill, Eugene)
BOURDET, Edouard, 1887-
    La Cage Ouverete
        (In his Théâtre I)
    La Fleur des Pois
        (In his Théâtre III)
    Fric-Frac
        (In his Théâtre IV)
    L'Heure du Berger
        (In his Théâtre I)
    L'Homme Enchaine
        (In his Théâtre I bis)

Hymenee
  (In his Théâtre IV)
Margot
  (In his Théâtre III)
Mimsy
  (In his Théâtre IV)
Pére
  (In his Théâtre IV)
La Prisonniere
  (In his Théâtre I bis)
Le Rubicon
  (In his Théâtre I)
Le Sexe Faible
  (In his Théâtre II)
Les Temps Difficiles
  (In his Théâtre III)
Vient de Paraitre
  (In his Théâtre II)
BOURGEADE, Pierre
  Etoiles Rouges
    (In L'Avant-Scène Théâtre, no. 604, Feb. 15, 1977)
Le Bourgeon (see Feydeau, Georges)
BOUTEILLE, Romain
  Le Soir des Diplomates
    (In L'Avant-Scène du Théâtre, no. 511, Feb. 1, 1973)
La Boutique (see Worms, Jeannine)
Boutique Fermee (see Audiberti, Jacques)
Le Bouton de Rose (see Zola, Emile)
BOUTRON, Pierre
  Le Portrait de Dorian Gray; une adaptation de Pierre Boutron
  d'aprés le roman d'Oscar Wilde
    (In L'Avant-Scène Théatre, no. 602, Jan. 15, 1977)
BOVASSO, Julie, 1930-
  Gloria and Esperanza
    (In The Off Off Broadway Book)
  Schubert's Last Serenade
    (In Spontaneous Combustion; The Winter Repertory Vol. 6)
  Standard Safety
    (In Best Short Plays, 1976)
BOWEN, John, 1924-
  The Corsican Brothers; a play with music in two acts, based
  on the nouvelle by Alexandre Dumas; lyrics by John Holmstrom
  and John Bowen
    (In Methuen Playscripts Series, 1970)
  Little Boxes: The Coffee Lace and Trevor
    (In Methuen Modern Plays Series, 1968)
  Robin Redbreast
    (In The Television Dramatist)
  Roger
    (In London Magazine, Vol. 16, no. 4, Oct./Nov. 1976)
BOWERING, George, 1935-
  The Home for Heroes
    (In Ten Canadian Short Plays)

BOWLES, Jane Aver
    At the Jumping Bean
       (In her Feminine Wiles)
BOWLES, Paul Frederic, 1911-
    Senso; screenplay (see Visconti, Luchino)
Box (see Albee, Edward)
Box and Cox (see Morton, John Maddison)
Boxes (see Yankowitz, Susan)
Boxing for One (see Ronild, Peter)
Boy-Children (see Peterkin, Julia)
Boy Waiting; radio script (see Pooler, James)
The Boy Will (see Rogers, Robert Emmons)
BOYCE, William, 1710-1779
    The Chaplet (see Mendez, Moses)
BOYER, L'Abbe Claude, 1618-1698
    Oropaste (Oropastes)
       (In More Plays by Rivals of Corneille and Racine)
BOYLE, Robert, 1st Earl of Orrery, 1627-1691
    The Tragedy of Mustapha
       (In Five Heroic Plays)
BOYLSTON, Helen Dore
    The Key, a drama for women, adapted for radio by Edward
      Goldberger
       (In 100 Non-Royalty Radio Plays)
The Boys in the Band (see Crowley, Mart)
BRACCO, Robert, 1862-1943
    Don Pietro Caruso
       (In Modern Italian One-Act Plays)
    The Little Saint
       (In Gambit, no. 6)
BRACH, Gerard
    Cul-de-Sac (see Polanski, Roman)
    Repulsion (see Polanski, Roman)
BRACKENRIDGE, Hugh Henry, 1748-1816
    The Battle of Bunkershill
       (In Representative Plays by American Dramatists, Vol. 3)
BRACKETT, Charles, 1892-1969
    Ninotchka (see Lubitsch, Ernst)
BRADBURY, Ray, 1920-
    The Anthem Sprinters
       (In his The Anthem Sprinters and Other Antics)
    A Clear View of an Irish Mist
       (In his The Anthem Sprinters and Other Antics)
    Dandelion Wine
       (In Readers Theatre Handbook)
    The First Night of Lent
       (In his The Anthem Sprinters and Other Antics)
    The Great Collision of Monday Last
       (In his The Anthem Sprinters and Other Antics)
    To the Chicago Abyss
       (In The Wonderful Ice Cream Suit and Other Plays)
    The Veldt
       (In The Wonderful Ice Cream Suit and Other Plays)

The Wonderful Ice Cream Suit and Other Plays
    (In The Wonderful Ice Cream Suit and Other Plays)
BRADFORD, Roark, 1896-1948
**The Green Pastures; a fable (see Connelly, Marcus C.)
BRADFORD ART COLLEGE THEATRE GROUP
    John Ford's Cuban Missile Crisis
        (In Methuen Young Drama Series, 1972)
BRAGA, J. Alberto
    O Misterioso Caso de Queijo Desaparecido
        (In Revista de Teatro, no. 394, July/Aug. 1973)
Braganza (see Jepherson, Robert)
BRAID, Angus
    Outport
        (In Performing Arts in Canada, Vol. 8, no. 4, Winter 1971)
Brains (see Flavin, Martin)
BRANCH, William, 1927-
    A Medal for Willie
        (In Black Drama Anthology)
    In Splendid Error
        (In Black Theater)
        (In Black Theater U. S. A., 1847-1974)
Brand (see Ibsen, Henrik)
Der Brand im Opernhaus (see Kaiser, Georg)
Brandane, John, pseud. (see MacIntyre, John)
BRANDAO, Raúl, 1878-1930
    El Loco y la Muerte
        (In Teatro Portugues Contemporaneo)
Brandywine (see Torphy, William)
BRANNER, H. C., 1903-1960
    El Juez
        (In Teatro Danes Contemporaneo)
    Thermopylae
        (In Modern Nordic Plays: Denmark)
BRASCH, Thomas
    Lovely Rita; text in German
        (In Theater Heute, no. 2, Feb. 1977)
    Rotter
        (In Theater: Chronik und Bilanz des Bühenjahres, 1977)
BRASILLACH, Robert, 1909-
    La Reine de Cesaree
        (In L'Avant-Scène du Théâtre, no. 523, Aug. 1973)
BRAUN, Volker
    Hinze und Kunze
        (In Theater der Zeit, no. 2, 1973)
    Tinka
        (In Theater Heute, no. 6, June 1977)
The Brazen Age (see Heywood, Thomas)
Bread (see Eastman, Fred)
Bread (see Kirshon, Vladimir)
BREAD AND PUPPET THEATER
    Johnny Comes Marching Home
        (In Guerilla Street Theater)
    Mississippi

(In Guerilla Street Theater)
Bread and Rice (see Bellido, José Maria)
Bread on the Waters (see Baker, George M.)
The Breadshop (see Brecht, Bertolt)
The Bread-Winner (see Maugham, William Somerset)
Breakdown (see Werry, Wilfred)
The Breaking of the Calm (see Totheroh, Dan)
The Breakout (see Gordon, Charles)
BREAL, Pierre-Aristide, 1905-
    La Grande Oreille
        (In Le Théâtre d'Aujourd'hui)
    Les Hussards
        (In Le Théâtre d'Aujourd'hui)
The Breasts of Tiresias (see Apollinaire, Guillaume)
Breath (see Beckett, Samuel)
A Brebis Tondue Dieu Mesure le Vent (see Mace, Jean)
BRECHT, Bertolt, 1898-1956
    El Alma Buena de Sechuan
        (In Teatro Aleman Contemporaneo)
    Amleto Principe di Danimarca, di autori vari: Bertolt Brecht,
        Friedrich Dürrenmatt, Erich Fried, Günther Grass, Peter
        Hacks, Peter Handke, Karl Hoche, Rolf Hochhuth, Franz X.
        Kroetz, Heinar Müller, Martin Sperr, Martin Walser, Peter
        Weiss
        (In Sipario, no. 325, June 1973)
    Baal
        (In his Collected Plays, Vol. 1)
    The Beggar; or, The Dead Dog
        (In his Collected Plays, Vol. 1)
    The Breadshop
        (In The New Review, Vol. 3, no. 33, Dec. 1976)
    The Catch
        (In his Collected Plays, Vol. 1)
    The Caucasian Chalk Circle)
        (In his Collected Plays, Vol. 7)
        (In Contemporary Drama: 13 Plays)
        (In Masterpieces of the Modern German Theatre)
        (In his Seven Plays)
    Coriolanus, adapted from the work of Shakespeare
        (In his Collected Plays, Vol. 9)
    Don Juan, adapted from the work of Molière
        (In his Collected Plays, Vol. 9)
    Drums in the Night
        (In his Collected Plays, Vol. 1)
    The Duchess of Malfi, adapted from the work of John Webster
        (In his Collected Plays, Vol. 7)
    The Elephant Calf
        (In his The Jewish Wife and Other Short Plays)
    The Exception and the Rule
        (In his The Jewish Wife and Other Short Plays)
        (In New Directions, Vol. 15, 1955)
    Galileo
        (In his Seven Plays)

The Good Woman of Sitzuan
  (In his Seven Plays)
He Drives Out a Devil
  (In his Collected Plays, Vol. 1)
He Who Says Yes and He Who Says No; two plays based on
  "Taniko," the Japanese Noh play; music by Kurt Weill
  (In All the World's a Stage)
In Search of Justice
  (In his The Jewish Wife and Other Short Plays)
In the Jungle of Cities
  (In his Collected Plays, Vol. 1)
In the Swamp
  (In his Seven Plays)
The Informer
  (In his The Jewish Wife and Other Short Plays)
Der Jasager; a school opera in two acts, text by Bertolt Brecht,
  music by Kurt Weill, based on the Japanese Noh play "Taniko"
  (In Yale/Theatre, Vol. 6, no. 2, Winter 1975)
The Jewish Wife
  (In his The Jewish Wife and Other Short Plays)
The Life of Edward II of England
  (In his Collected Plays, Vol. 1)
Life of Galileo
  (In his Collected Plays, Vol. 5)
Lux in Tenebris
  (In his Collected Plays, Vol. 1)
A Man's a Man
  (In his Seven Plays)
The Measures Taken
  (In his The Jewish Wife and Other Short Plays)
The Mother; adapted by the San Francisco Mime Troup
  (In Ramparts, Vol. 13, Aug. 1974)
Mother Courage
  (In New Directions, Vol. 6, 1941)
  (In his Seven Plays)
Mother Courage and Her Children
  (In his Collected Plays, Vol. 5)
L'Opéra de Quat'sous (Die Dreigroschenoper) (see Pabst, Georg
W.)
Saint Joan of the Stockyards
  (In his Seven Plays)
Schweyk in the Second World War
  (In his Collected Plays, Vol. 7)
The Threepenny Opera; screenplay (see Lania, Leo)
The Trial of Joan of Arc at Rouen, 1431; after a radio play by
  Anna Seghers
  (In his Collected Plays, Vol. 9)
The Trial of Lucullus
  (In his Collected Plays, Vol. 5)
Trumpets and Drums; adapted from George Farquhar's "The
  Recruiting Officer"
  (In his Collected Plays, Vol. 9)
The Tutor, adapted from the work of Jakob Michael Reinhold
  Lenz

(In his Collected Plays, Vol. 9)
Der Untergang des Egoisten Fatzer
(In Theater Heute, no. 4, Apr. 1976)
The Visions of Simone Marchard, by Bertolt Brecht and Lion
  Feuchtwanger
(In his Collected Plays, Vol. 7)
The Wedding
(In his Collected Plays, Vol. 1)
Breeders (see Edmonds, Randolph)
BRENON, Herbert, 1880-1958
   A Kiss for Cinderella; script adapted for the film (see Goldbeck,
   Willis)
BRENTON, Howard, 1942-
   Christie in Love
     (In his Christie in Love and Other Plays)
   The Education of Skinny Spew
     (In his Christie in Love and Other Plays)
   Gum and Goo
     (In Plays for Public Places)
   Heads
     (In his Christie in Love and Other Plays)
   Revenge
     (In Methuen Playscript Series, 1970)
   The Salvia Milkshake
     (In New Plays, First Series, no. 4, 1977)
   Scott and the Antarctic
     (In Plays for Public Places)
   Wesley
     (In Plays for Public Places)
Bresci, Gaetano
   *Il 29 Luglio del 1900, di Sergio Liberovici ed Emilio Jona; vita
   e morte di Gaetano Bresci
     (In Sipario, no. 321, Feb. 1973)
BRESSON, Robert
   Les Dames du Bois de Boulogne; screenplay
     (In L'Avant-Scène Cinéma, no. 196, Nov. 15, 1977)
BRETON, André, 1896-1966
   If You Please, by André Breton and Philippe Soupault
     (In Modern French Theatre)
Brewster McCloud (see Cannon, Doran W.)
Brian's Song (see Blinn, William)
BRICAIRE, Jean-Jacques
   Les Deux Viérges; de Jean-Jacques Bricaire et Maurice Lasay-
   gues
     (In L'Avant-Scène Théâtre, no. 579, Jan. 15, 1976)
Brice, Fanny (Fanny Borach), 1891-1951
   *Funny Girl (see Styne, Jule)
BRICKENDEN, Catherine
   Zanorin
     (In Canada on Stage)
The Bridal Chamber (see Quiles, Eduardo)
A Bride for the Unicorn (see Johnston, Denis)
The Bride of Messina (see Schiller, Johann)

Bride Roses (see Howells, William Dean)
BRIDGES, James
  A³
      (In New Theatre in America, Vol. 2)
Bridges (see Kummer, Mrs. Clare)
Bridget's House (see Hull Truck Theatre Company)
Bridie, James (pseud.) (see Mavor, Osborne Henry)
The Brief and Violent Reign of Absolom (see Pendleton, James D.)
Brief Encounter; screenplay (see Lean, David)
BRIEUX, Eugene, 1858-1932
  Because I Love You
      (In Modern One-Act Plays from the French)
The Brigadier (see Fonvizin, Denis I.)
Brigadoon (see Loewe, Frederick)
BRIGHOUSE, Harold, 1882-
  Astrologers, by Olive Conway, pseud.
      (In Best One-Act Plays of 1939, London)
  British Passport
      (In Best One-Act Plays of 1939, London)
  The Funk-hole
      (In Best One-Act Plays of 1938, London)
  The Ghosts of Windsor Park
      (In One-Act Plays for Stage and Study, 6th Series)
  Hallowed Ground
      (In Best One-Act Plays of 1941, London)
  Lonesome-Like
      (In One-Act Plays for Stage and Study, 1st Series)
  Maid of France
      (In One-Act Plays by Modern Authors)
  The Night of "Mr. H."
      (In More One-Act Plays by Modern Authors)
  One of Those Letters, by Olive Conway, pseud.
      (In Best One-Act Plays of 1938, London)
  The Price of Coal
      (In Scottish Repertory Plays Series, no. 3, 1911)
  Smoke-Screens
      (In One-Act Plays for Stage and Study, 7th Series)
  The Stoker
      (In One-Act Plays for Stage and Study, 5th Series)
  Under the Pylon
      (In One-Act Plays for Stage and Study, 9th Series)
  When Did They Meet Again?
      (In One-Act Plays for Stage and Study, 3rd Series)
  The Witch's Daughter
      (In One-Act Plays for Stage and Study, 4th Series)
BRIGHT, John
  Back Door to Heaven; screenplay by John Bright and Robert
      Tasker, from an original story by William K. Howard, directed
      by William K. Howard. (Complete final scene of the film.)
      (In New Fields for the Writer)
La Brigitta (see Audiberti, Jacques)
Bring It All Back Home (see McNally, Terrence)
Bring on the Angels; television script (see Sloane, Allen)

Brion, Philippe de Chabot, amiral de, 1492-1543
  *The Tragedy of Chabot Admiral of France (see Chapman, George)
Britannia Triumphans (see D'Avenant, Sir William)
Britannicus (Claudius Tiberius Germanicus), 41-55 A. D.
  *Britannicus (see Racine, Jean Baptiste)
British Passport (see Brighouse, Harold)
Brocéliande (see Montherlant, Henry de)
BROCH, Hermann, 1886-
  The Atonement
    (In German Drama Between the Wars)
BROGGER, Frederick
  David Copperfield; screenplay (see Pulman, Jack)
Broke (see Turgenev, Ivan S.)
The Broken Banjo (see Richardson, Willis)
The Broken Jug (see Kleist, Heinrich von)
The Broker of Bogotá (see Bird, Robert M.)
BROMBERG, Conrad
  Actors
    (In Best Short Plays, 1976)
BROME, Richard, d. 1652?
  The Antipodes
    (In his Dramatic Works, Vol. 3)
    (In Six Caroline Plays)
  The City Wit; or, The Woman Wears the Breeches
    (In his Dramatic Works, Vol. 1)
  The Court Beggar
    (In his Dramatic Works, Vol. 1)
  The Damiselle; or, The New Ordinary
    (In his Dramatic Works, Vol. 1)
  The English Moor; or, The Mock-marriage
    (In his Dramatic Works, Vol. 2)
  A Joviall Crew; or, The Merry Beggars
    (In his Dramatic Works, Vol. 3)
  The Lovesick Count; or, The Ambitious Politique
    (In his Dramatic Works, Vol. 2)
  A Mad Couple Well Matched; edited by A. S. Knowland
    (In Six Caroline Plays)
  Madd Couple Well Matcht
    (In his Dramatic Works, Vol. 1)
  The New Academy; or, The New Exchange
    (In his Dramatic Works, Vol. 2)
  The Northern Lasse
    (In his Dramatic Works, Vol. 3)
  The Nouvella
    (In his Dramatic Works, Vol. 1)
  The Queen and Concubine
    (In his Dramatic Works, Vol. 2)
  The Queen's Exchange
    (In his Dramatic Works, Vol. 3)
  Sir Patient Fancy (see Behn, Mrs. Aphra)
  The Sparagus Garden
    (In his Dramatic Works, Vol. 3)
  The Wedding of the Covent-Garden; or, The Middlesex-justice of
    Peace

(In his Dramatic Works, Vol. 2)
The Bronx Is Next (see Sanchez, Sonia)
The Bronze Lady and the Crystal Gentleman (see Duvernois, Henri)
BROOK, Peter
    US; the Book of the Royal Shakespeare Theatre Production, by
    Peter Brook, Denis Cannan and others (Filmed under title:
    "Tell Me Lies")
    (In Calder & Boyars Playscript Series, no. 9)
BROOKE, Henry, 1703-1783
    Gustavus Vasa
    (In The London Stage, Vol. 3)
BROOKS, George S., 1895-
    Fortinbras in Plain Clothes
    (In One-Act Plays for Stage and Study, 4th Series)
BROOKS, Harry, 1891-
    Six Men of Dorset (see Malleson, Miles)
BROOKS, Mel
    Silent Movie; screenplay by Mel Brooks, Ron Clark, Rudy De-
    Luca and Barry Levinson, story by Ron Clark
    (A Ballantine Books Screenplay, 1976)
BROOKS, Richard, 1912-
    Sweet Bird of Youth; screenplay, written for the screen and
    directed by Richard Brooks, from the play by Tennessee
    Williams
    (A Signet Film Series Screenplay, 1962)
Brother Bill (see Kreymborg, Alfred)
Brother Carl (see Sontag, Susan)
Brotherhood (see Ward, Douglas T.)
The Brothers (see Shirley, James)
BROUGH, William, 1826-1870
    The Area Belle, by William Brough and Andrew Halliday
    (In English Plays of the 19th Century, Vol. IV: Farces)
BROUGHAM, John, 1810-1880
    Po-ca-hon-tas; or, The Gentle Savage
    (In The Drama, Vol. 20)
    (In Dramas from the American Theatre, 1762-1909)
BROWN, Alan
    Brown Ale with Gertie
    (In his Wheelchair Willie and Other Plays)
    O'Connor
    (In his Wheelchair Willie and Other Plays)
    Wheelchair Willie
    (In his Wheelchair Willie and Other Plays)
BROWN, Beverly S.
    Snake Chief
    (In Negro History Bulletin, Vol. 34, March 1971)
BROWN, David Paul, 1795-1875
    Sertorius; or, The Roman Patriot
    (In Representative Plays by American Dramatists, Vol. 2)
BROWN, Ivor
    Down on the Farm
    (In Best One-Act Plays of 1939, London)
BROWN, Lennox
    Devil Mas'

(In Kuntu Drama)
BROWN, William Wells, 1814-1884
    The Escape; or, A Leap for Freedom
        (In Black Theater U.S.A., 1847-1974)
        (In The Disinherited: Plays)
        (In Early Black American Prose)
Brown Ale with Gertie (see Brown, Alan)
The Brown Overcoat (see Sejour, Victor)
BROWNE, Maurice
    Wings over Europe (see Nichols, Robert)
BROWNE, Theodore, 1910-
    Alabama Fables, I: Jonah and the Whale; 2: Little Red Riding
    Hood
        (In 100 Non-Royalty Radio Plays)
    Natural Man
        (In Black Theater U.S.A., 1847-1974)
BROWNE, William, 1591-c.1643
    The Inner Temple Masque
        (In A Book of Short Plays, XV-XX Centuries)
BROWNE, Wynyard
    The Holly and the Ivy
        (In Plays of the Year, Vol. 3, 1949-50)
BROWNING, Robert, 1812-1899
    A Blot in the 'Scutcheon
        (In Representative British Dramas)
        (In his Works, Vol. 2)
    Colombe's Birthday
        (In his Works, Vol. 2)
  **The Duke's Miracle (see Curnow, Allen)
    Fust and His Friends
        (In his Works, Vol. 10)
    In a Balcony
        (In his Works, Vol. 4)
    King Victor and King Charles
        (In his Works, Vol. 2)
    Luira
        (In his Works, Vol. 3)
    Paracelsus
        (In his Works, Vol. 1)
    Pippa Passes
        (In his Works, Vol. 2)
    The Return of the Druses
        (In his Works, Vol. 2)
    A Soul's Tragedy
        (In his Works, Vol. 3)
    Strafford
        (In his Works, Vol. 2)
BROWNING, Tod, 1882-1962
    Freaks; titre français "La Monstrueuse Parade"; scenario Willis
    Goldbeck, d'après le roman "Spurs" de Clarence Tod Robbins
        (In L'Avant-Scène Cinéma, no. 160-161, July/Sept. 1975)
The Browning Version (see Rattigan, Sir Terence M.)
BROWNJOHN, Alan
    A Love Song

(In The New Review, Vol. 2, no. 16, July 1975)
Bruce, Lenny (Leonard Alfred Schneider), 1926-1966
*Lenny (see Barry, Julian)
BRUCKMAN, Clyde, 1895-1955
    The Fatal Glass of Beer (see Fields, W. C.)
Brudder Bone's Love Scrape; a Minstrel Show (Anon.)
    (In Dramas from the American Theatre, 1762-1909)
Brujerías (see Duarte Clark, Rodrigo)
BRULE, Claude
    Le Siècle des Lumières
    (In L'Avant-Scène Théâtre, no. 559, Mar. 1, 1975)
    Les Liaisons Dangereuses; screenplay (see Vialland, Roger)
BRULEZ, Raymond, 1895-
    La Bella Durmiente
    (In Teatro Flamenco Contemporaneo)
BRULIN, Tone, 1926-
    Ahora Que la Aldea ya no Existe
    (In Teatro Flamenco Contemporaneo)
BRUNO, Pierrette
    L'Arnacoeur
    (In L'Avant-Scène du Théâtre, no. 545, July 15, 1974)
Brussels Sprouts (see Kardish, Larry)
BRUST, Alfred, 1891-1934
    Dan Spiel Jenseits
    (In his Dramen, 1917-1924)
    Das Indische Spiel
    (In his Dramen, 1917-1924)
    Das Spiel Christa vom Schmerz der Schönheit des Weibes
    (In his Dramen, 1917-1924)
    Ein Bauspiel
    (In his Dramen, 1917-1924)
    Der Ewige Mensch
    (In his Dramen, 1917-1924)
    Frühlingsspiel
    (In his Dramen, 1917-1924)
    Heiligung
    (In his Dramen, 1917-1924)
    Höllenspiil
    (In his Dramen, 1917-1924)
    Leäna
    (In his Dramen, 1917-1924)
    Ostrom
    (In his Dramen, 1917-1924)
    Die Schlacht der Heilande
    (In his Dramen, 1917-1924)
    Der Singende Fisch
    (In his Dramen, 1917-1924)
    Südseespiel
    (In his Dramen, 1917-1924)
    Der Tag des Zorns
    (In his Dramen, 1917-1924)
    Tolkening
    (In his Dramen, 1917-1924)

The Wolves
(In Seven Expressionists Plays)
BRUSTEIN, Robert
Oedipus Nix; A Mythical Tragedy
(In Yale/Theatre, Vol. 5, no. 1, Fall 1973)
Bruto Primo (see Alfieri, Vittorio)
Bruto Secondo (see Alfieri, Vittorio)
Brutus (see Payne, John H.)
Brutus (see Voltaire)
Brutus, Lucius Junius, fl. 500 B.C.
  *Brutus; or, The Fall of Tarquin (see Payne, John H.)
  *Lucius Junius Brutus, Father of His Country (see Lee, Nathaniel)
Brutus, Marcus Junius, 85?-42 B.C.
  *Brutus (see Voltaire)
  *Brutus et Cassius, ou Les Derniers Romains (see Chénier,
    Marie Joseph)
  *Caesar (see Voltaire)
  *Marcus Brutus (see Foster, Paul)
BRYDEN, Bill
  Old Movies
    (A National Theatre Play, 1977)
  Willie Rough
    (In Plays of the Year, Vol. 43, 1972-73)
BRYKS, Rachmil
  **The Windows of Heaven (see Wincelberg, Shimon)
BUCHANAN, George, 1506-1582
  Jephté ou Le Voeu
    (In Four Renaissance Tragedies)
Des Buches Erstes und Letztes Blatt (see Jahnn, Hans H.)
BUCHWALD, Art, 1925-
  Sheep on the Runway
    (In his Counting Sheep)
  What Is It, Mrs. Perkins?
    (In Readers Theatre Handbook)
BUCKINGHAM, George Villiers, 2nd Duke of, 1626-1687
  **The Meeting of the Company (see Garrick, David)
  The Rehearsal
    (In British Plays from the Restoration to 1820, Vol. 1)
    (In A Collection of the Most Esteemed Farces ..., Vol. 6)
    (In Plays of the Restoration and 18th Century)
Das Bucklige Pferdchen (see Endler, Adolf)
Bucks, Have At Ye All (see Garrick, David)
BUECHNER, Georg, 1813-1837
  Woyzeck
    (In Gambit, Vol. 6, no. 23)
    (In Masterpieces of the Modern German Theatre)
    (In New Directions, Vol. 12, 1950)
    (In Themes of Drama)
  Woyzeck, adapted by David Ball
    (In Minnesota Showcase: Four Plays, Minnesota Drama Edi-
    tions, no. 9)
BUENAFE, Manuel E., ?-1963
  The Return of the Warrior

(In Philippine Harvest)
BUENAVENTURA, Enrique, 1925-
En la Diestra de Dois Padre
(In El Teatro Hispanoamericano Contemporaneo, Vol. 1)
El Menu
(In El Teatro Actual Latinoamericano)
The Orgy
(In The Orgy)
The Schoolteacher
(In The Orgy)
Los Buenos Días Perdidos (see Gala, Antonio)
Buenos Días, Señor Presidente! (see Usigli, Rudolfo)
Die Bürger von Calais (see Kaiser, Georg)
BUERO VALLEJO, Antonio, 1916-
Las Cartas Boca Abajo
(In Teatro Español, 1957-58)
(In Teatro Selecto de Antonio Buero Vallejo)
The Concert at Saint Ovide
(In The Modern Spanish Stage: Four Plays)
El Concierto de San Ovidio
(In Teatro Selecto de Antonio Buero Vallejo)
El Concierto de San Ovidio; musica de Rafael Rodriguez Albert
(In Teatro Español, 1962-63)
The Dream Weaver
(In Masterpieces of the Modern Spanish Theatre)
En la Ardiente Oscuridad
(In Teatro Español, 1950-51)
La Fundación
(In Teatro Español, 1973-74)
Historia de una Escalera
(In Teatro Español, 1949-50)
(In Teatro Selecto de Antonio Buero Vallejo)
Hoy es Fiesta
(In Teatro Español, 1956-57)
Irene; o, El Tesoro
(In Teatro Español, 1954-55)
Madrugada
(In Teatro Español, 1953-54)
Las Meninas
(In Teatro Español, 1960-61)
(In Teatro Selecto de Antonio Buero Vallejo)
Un Sonador Para un Pueblo
(In Teatro Español, 1958-59)
(In Teatro Selecto de Antonio Buero Vallejo)
El Sueño de la Razón
(In Teatro Español, 1969-70)
La Tejedora de Sueños
(In Teatro Español, 1951-52)
El Tragaluz
(In Teatro Español, 1967-68)
Buffalmacco's Jest (see Jagendorf, Moritz A.)
Buffalo Bill (see Cody, William Frederick)
Buffalo Bill and the Indians; or, Sitting Bull's History Lesson; screen-
play (see Rudolph, Alan)

The Buffer (see Gerstenberg, Alice)
BUKOVCAN, Ivan
    Ehe der Hahn Kräht
        (In Theater der Zeit, no. 4, 1977)
BULGAKOV, Mikhail Afanasevich, 1891-1940
    Adam and Eve
        (In Russian Literature Triquarterly, no. 1, Fall 1971)
    A Cabal of Hypocrites
        (In his Early Plays)
    The Crimson Island
        (In his Early Plays)
    The Days of the Turbins
        (In his Early Plays)
        (In Six Soviet Plays)
        (In 20th Century Russian Plays)
    Flight A Play in Eight Dreams and Four Acts
        (In his Early Plays)
        (In Evergreen Playscript Series, 1969)
    Ivan Vasilievich
        (In Modern International Drama, Vol. 7, no. 2, Spring 1974)
    Zoya's Apartment
        (In his Early Plays)
BULLINS, Edward Artri, 1935-
    Clara's Ole Man
        (In The Off Off Broadway Book)
    The Corner
        (In Black Drama Anthology)
        (In The Theme Is Blackness)
    Death List
        (In Four Dynamite Plays)
    Dialect Determinism; or, The Rally
        (In Spontaneous Combustion; The Winter Repertory, Vol. 6)
        (In The Theme is Blackness)
    The Fabulous Miss Marie
        (In The New Lafayette Theatre Presents)
    The Gentleman Caller
        (In A Black Quartet)
        (In Contemporary Black Drama)
    Goin' a Buffalo
        (In Black Theater U.S.A., 1847-1974)
    The Helper
        (In The Theme Is Blackness)
    How Do You Do
        (In Black Fire)
    In the Wine Time
        (In Black Theater)
        (In The Great American Life Show)
    It Bees Dat Way
        (In Four Dynamite Plays)
    It Has No Choice
        (In The Theme Is Blackness)
    The Man Who Dug Fish
        (In The Theme Is Blackness)

A Minor Scene
(In The Theme Is Blackness)
Night of the Beast
(In Four Dynamite Plays)
The Pig Pen
(In Four Dynamite Plays)
A Son, Come Home
(In Contemporary Drama: 13 Plays)
Street Sounds
(In The Theme Is Blackness)
Bulwer-Lytton, Edward (see Lytton, Edward George Lytton Bulwer-
Lytton, 1st baron, 1803-1873)
BUNCE, Oliver Bell, 1828-1890
Love in '76
(In Representative Plays by American Dramatists, Vol. 3)
A Bunch of the Gods Were Sitting Around One Day (see Spencer,
James)
Bunker-Hill; or, The Death of General Warren (see Burk, John D.)
BUNSHO, Kuruwa
Love Letter from the Licensed Quarter
(In Kabuki: Five Classic Plays)
BUÑUEL, Luis, 1900-
Le Charme Discret de la Bourgeoisie
(In L'Avant-Scène du Cinéma, no. 135, April 1973)
The Exterminating Angel
(In Modern Filmscripts Series, 1972)
Le Fantôme de la Liberté; un film de Luis Buñel, avec la
collaboration de Jean-Claude Carriere
(In L'Avant-Scène du Cinéma, no. 151, Oct. 1974)
Nazarin
(In Modern Filmscripts Series, 1972)
Los Olvidados; screenplay, English release title "The Young and
the Damned"
(In Modern Filmscripts Series, 1972)
Los Olvidados; screenplay, text in French
(In L'Avant-Scène du Cinéma, no. 137, June 1973)
Bouyant Billions: A Comedy of No Manners (see Shaw, George
Bernard)
Ein Burger, Bauer und Edelmann, die Holen Krapfen (see Sachs,
Hans)
BURGESS, Katharine Stanbery
Duetto
(In One-Act Plays for Stage and Study, 3rd Series)
The Burghers of Calais (see Kaiser, Georg)
The Burghers of Calais (see White, Edgar)
The Burglar Who Failed (see Hankin, St. John)
BURGOYNE, John, 1722-1792
The Heiress
(In The London Stage, Vol. 3)
The Maid of the Oakes
(In A Collection of the Most Esteemed Farces ..., Vol. 6)
(In The London Stage, Vol. 3)
The Burgraves (see Hugo, Victor)

The Burial Mound (see Ibsen, Henrik)
BURK, John Daly, ?-1808
    Bunker-Hill; or, The Death of General Warren
        (In Dramas from the American Theatre, 1762-1909)
BURKE, Charles St. Thomas, 1822-1854
    Rip Van Winkle, a Legend of the Catskills, based on Washington
    Irving's "Sketch Book." This version first produced in Phila-
    delphia in 1850
        (In The Drama, Vol. 19)
        (In Representative Plays by American Dramatists, Vol. 3)
BURKE, Inez M.
    Two Races
        (In Plays and Pageants from the Life of the Negro)
Burke's Company (see Reed, Bill)
The Burlador (see Lilar, Suzanne)
El Burlador de la Pampa (see Silva Valdés, Fernan)
El Burlador de Sevilla (see Téllez, Gabriel)
El Burlador o El Angel del Demonio (see Lilar, Suzanne)
BURN, David, 1798-1875
    The Bushrangers, edited and arranged for production by W. &
    J. E. Hiener
        (In Australian Theatre Workshop no. 6, 1971)
The Burned House (see Strindberg, August)
BURNETT, Murray
  **Casablanca (see Epstein, Julius J.)
BURNETT, Whit
    Sherrill, adapted for radio by Edward Goldberger
        (In 100 Non-Royalty Radio Plays)
The Burning (see Conn, Stewart)
BURNING CITY THEATER, NEW YORK
    The People's Park in Berkeley
        (In Guerilla Street Theater)
BURNS, George (Nathan Birnbaum), 1896-
    Burns and Allen; radio script
        (In Best Broadcasts of 1939-40)
    George and Gracie's First Act at the Palace Theatre; vaudeville
    script (excerpts)
        (In his Living It Up)
    The George Burns and Gracie Allen Show, television script no.
    125, "Carnations," 1955
        (In his I Love Her, That's Why!)
    The George Burns-Carol Channing Show; vaudeville script (ex-
    cerpts)
        (In his Living It Up)
The Burnt Flower-Bed (see Betti, Ugo)
BURRILL, Mary
    They That Sit in Darkness
        (In Black Theater U.S.A., 1847-1974)
BURROUGHS, William S., 1914-
    The Last Words of Dutch Schultz; a film
        (A Cape Goliard Press Filmscript, 1970)
BURROWS, John
    The Golden Pathway Annual (see Harding, John)

The Bursting of the Bubble (see Hyde, Douglas)
Bury the Dead (see Shaw, Irwin)
Bury-Fair (see Shadwell, Thomas)
BUS-GEKETE, Ladislaus
  **Ladies and Gentlemen (see Hecht, Ben)
BUSH, Stephen
  Once a Giant; an Idealistic Parable in Dramatic Form for Young
    and Not-So-Young People
    (In Performing Arts in Canada, Vol. 11, no. 2, Summer
    1974)
The Bushrangers (see Burn, David)
The Business of Good Government (see Arden, John)
Bussy d'Amboise, Louis de Clermont d'Amboise, sieur de Bussy,
  called, 1549-1579
  *Bussy d'Ambois (see Chapman, George)
  *The Revenge of Bussy d'Ambois (see Chapman, George)
Buster Keaton Rides Again: A Sequel (see Garcia Lorca, Federico)
Buster Keaton's Ride (see Garcia Lorca, Federico)
BUSTILLO ORO, Juan, 1904-
  San Miguel de las Espinas
    (In Teatro Méxicano del Siglo XX, Vol. 2)
BUTCHER, James W., Jr., 1909-
  The Seer
    (In The Negro Caravan)
Butley (see Gray, Simon J.)
Button Your Lip (see Neiman, Irving G.)
BYRNE, John
  Writer's Cramp
    (In Plays and Players, Vol. 25, no. 3, Dec. 1977)
BYRNE, Muriel St. Clare
  Busman's Honeymoon (see Sayers, Dorothy L.)
BYRNE, Seamus, 1904-
  Design for a Headstone
    (In 7 Irish Plays)
Byron, Charles, Duke of (see Biron, Charles de Gontaut, duc de)
Byron, George Gordon Noël Byron, 6th Baron, 1788-1824
  *Camino Real (see Williams, Tennessee)
  *Lord Byron's Love Letter (see Williams, Tennessee)
  *Sardanapale; opéra imité de Lord Byron (see Becque, Henri)
A Byzantine Afternoon (see Weyl, Fernand)

A Cabal of Hypocrites (see Bulgakov, Mikhail A.)
El Caballero de las Espuelas de Oro (see Rodriguez Alvarez, Alejan-
  dro)
Los Caballos (see Rosencof, Mauricio)
Cabaret (see Kander, John)
Cabbages and Kings (see Fyleman, Rose)
Le Cabinet du Docteur Caligari; screenplay (see Wiene, Robert)
Cabiria; screenplay (see Fellini, Federico. Le Notti di Cabiria)
La Caccia al Lupo (see Verga, Giovanni)
La Cachemire X. B. T. (see Labiche, Eugene)
Cada Quien Su Vida (see Basurto, Luis G.)

La Caduta Degli Dei (Götterdämmerung); screenplay (see Visconti, Luchino)
Caesar, Gaius Julius, 100-44 B. C.
  *Bruto Secondo (see Alfieri, Vittorio)
  *Caesar (see Voltaire)
  *Caesar and Cleopatra: a History (see Shaw, George Bernard)
  *Catiline (see Voltaire)
  *Julius Caesar (see Shakespeare, William)
  *La Morte de Pompee (The Death of Pompey) (see Corneille, Pierre)
  *Pompee (see Corneille, Pierre)
  *The Tragedy of Caesar and Pompey (see Chapman, George)
Caesar Borgia; Son of Pope Alexander the Sixth (see Lee, Nathaniel)
Caesar's Wife (see Maugham, William Somerset)
La Cage aux Folles (see Poiret, Jean)
La Cage Ouverte (see Bourdet, Edouard)
CAGLI, Bruno
  Crudele Intromissione; text in Italian
    (In Sipario, no. 344, Jan. 1975)
  L'Ombra di Banquo ossia La Lezione di Potere
    (In Sipario, no. 363-364, Aug. -Sept. 1976)
La Cagnotte (see Labiche, Eugene)
CAHOON, Herbert
  Three Verse Plays: Three Wars, The Market, The Removal of the Academy
    (In New Directions, Vol. 9, 1946)
CAIN, James Mallahan, 1892-
  **Ossessione; screenplay (see Visconti, Luchino)
Caius Gracchus (see Chénier, Marie Joseph B.)
CALAFERTE, Louis, 1928-
  Chez les Titch Trafic
    (In L'Avant-Scène Théâtre, no. 557, Feb. 1, 1975)
Calas, Jean, 1698-1762
  *Jean Calas, ou L'Ecole des Juges (see Chénier, Marie Joseph B.)
Calaynos (see Boker, George H.)
CALDERON, George, 1868-1915
  The Fountain
    (In Scottish Repertory Plays Series, no. 2, 1911)
CALDERON DE LA BARCA, Pedro, 1600-1681
  El Alcalde de Zalamea
    (In Clásicos Castellanos, Vol. 138)
  Belshazzar's Feast
    (In The Drama, Vol. 4)
  The Constant Prince
    (In World Drama, Vol. 2)
  La Dama Duende
    (In Clásicos Castellanos, Vol. 137)
  La Devoción de la Cruz
    (In Clásicos Castellanos, Vol. 106)
  **An Evening's Love; or, The Mock Astrologer (see Dryden, John)
  The Great Stage of the World, translated by George W. Brandt
    (In Classics of Drama in English Translation Series, 1976)

King Belshazzar's Feast
(In Three Spanish Sacramental Plays)
El Magico Prodigioso
(In Clásicos Castellanos, Vol. 106)
**Mais Qu'est-ce Qui Fait Courir les Femmes, la Nuit a Madrid? ... (see Ceccaldi, Daniel)
El Médico de Su Honra
(In Clásicos Castellanos, Vol. 142)
No Hay Cosa Como Callar
(In Clásicos Castellanos, Vol. 141)
El Pintor de Su Deshonra
(In Clásicos Castellanos, Vol. 142)
El Principe Constante
(In Clásicos Castellanos, Vol. 204)
A Secreto Agravio, Secreta Venganza
(In Clásicos Castellanos, Vol. 141)
La Vida Es Sueño
(In Clásicos Castellanos, Vol. 138)
CALDWELL, Ben, 1937-
All White Caste
(In Black Drama Anthology)
The Job
(In A Gathering of Ghetto Writers)
The King of Soul; or, The Devil and Otis Redding
(In The Disinherited: Plays)
Prayer Meeting; or, The First Militant Minister
(In Black Fire)
(In A Black Quartet)
CALDWELL, Erskine, 1903-
**Tobacco Road (see Kirkland, Jack)
Caleb Stone's Death Watch (see Flavin, Martin)
Caleb the Degenerate (see Cotter, Joseph S., Sr.)
The Caledonian Express; filmscript (see Fields, W. C.)
CALEFFI, Fabrizio, 1952-
I Tagliatori di Teste
(In Sipario, no. 332, Jan. 1974)
Caligula, Emperor of Rome (Gaius Caesar), 12-41 A.D.
*Caligula (see Camus, Albert)
*Caligula (see Crowne, John)
Calisto; or, The Chaste Nimph (see Crowne, John)
Call It a Day (see Smith, Dorothy G.)
Call Me a Liar (see Mortimer, John C.)
Call Me Jacky (see Bagnold, Enid)
The Call of the Whippoorwill (see Dufrense, Guy)
Callados Como Muertos (see Peman, José M.)
CALLAGHAN, Barry
Politics of Passion
(In Performing Arts in Canada, Vol. 9, no. 2, Summer 1972)
La Calle del Pecado (see Salmon, Raul)
La Calle Sin Puertas (see Borchert, Wolfgang)
CALLEGARI, Gian Paolo
Cristo Ha Matado
(In Teatro Italiano Contemporaneo)

Calling for Help (see Handke, Peter)
Calm Down Mother (see Terry, Megan)
Calvary (see Yeats, William Butler)
CALVET, Aldo
    Casa de Ninguem
        (In his Teatro)
    Dr. Judas
        (In his Teatro)
    Exaustacao
        (In his Teatro)
    Trompette
        (In his Teatro)
CALVO SOTELO, Joaquin, 1905-
    La Amante
        (In Teatro Español, 1967-68)
    Criminal de Guerra
        (In Teatro Español, 1950-51)
    La Herencia
        (In Teatro Español, 1957-58)
    Historia de un Resentido
        (In Teatro Español, 1955-56)
    Un Hombre Puro
        (In Teatro Español, 1973-74)
    El Jefe
        (In Teatro Español, 1952-53)
    Micaela
        (In Teatro Español, 1962-63)
    Milagro en la Plaza del Progreso
        (In Teatro Español, 1953-54)
    Una Muchachita de Valladolid
        (In Teatro Español, 1956-57)
    La Muralla
        (In Teatro Español, 1954-55)
    El Poder
        (In Teatro Español, 1965-66)
    El Proceso del Arzobispo Carranza
        (In Teatro Español, 1963-64)
    La Vista Que No Toco el Timbre
        (In Teatro Español, 1949-50)
Il Calzolajo Inglese in Roma (see Rossi, Gherardo de)
CAMARA, Isabel, 1940-
    As Mocas: O Beijo Final
        (In Revista de Teatro, no. 395, Sept. /Oct. 1973)
CAMARGO, Joracy
    Anastacio
        (In Revista de Teatro, no. 392, Mar. /Apr. 1973)
Cambises (see Preston, Thomas)
Camelot (see Loewe, Frederick)
Camera Obscura (see Patrick, Robert)
Camille (La Dame aux Camelias) (see Dumas, Alexandre, fils)
Camille: A Minstrel Show (see Griffin, G. W. H.)
O Caminho de Volta (see Castro, Consuelo de)
Camino Real (see Williams, Tennessee)

La Camisa (see Olmo, Lauro)
Camoens (see Tapia y Rivera, Alejandro)
The Camp (see Sheridan, Richard B.)
Le Camp de Grande-Pre; ou, Le Triomphe de la République (see
  Chénier, Marie-Joseph B.)
The Camp of Wallenstein (see Schiller, Johann)
La Campana (see Ortega, Julio)
Campanella und der Kommandeur (see Schatrow, Michail)
CAMPBELL, Alistair
  The Suicide: a Radio Play
    (In Landfall, Vol. 28, no. 4, December 1974)
CAMPBELL, Bartley Theodore, 1843-1888
  My Partner
    (In Favorite American Plays of the 19th Century)
CAMPBELL, Ken
  The Great Caper: A Visionary Drama
    (In Plays and Players, Vol. 22, nos. 1 & 2, Oct. & Nov.
    1974)
The Campden Wonder (see Masefield, John)
Il Campiello (see Goldoni, Carlo)
Camping in the Snow (see Chang, Feng-chao)
CAMPISTRON, Jean-Galbert de, 1656-1723
  Andronic (Andronicus)
    (In The Chief Rivals of Corneille and Racine)
  Tiridate (Tiridates)
    (In More Plays by Rivals of Corneille and Racine)
CAMPOS GARCIA, Jesus
  The Marriage of Drama and Censorship
    (In Modern International Drama, Vol. 8, no. 1, 1974)
CAMUS, Albert, 1913-1960
  Caligula
    (In The Collected Plays of Albert Camus)
  Cross Purpose
    (In The Collected Plays of Albert Camus)
  The Just
    (In The Collected Plays of Albert Camus)
  Le Malentendu
    (In The French Theater Since 1930)
  The Possessed; based on the novel by Fyodor Dostoievsky
    (In The Collected Plays of Albert Camus)
Can Long Endure (see Tazewell, Charles)
La Cana de Pescar (see Torre, Claudio de la)
The Canal (see Milligan, Spike)
CANALE, Raymond
  The Jingo Ring
    (In The Factory Lab Anthology)
CANAS, Alberto, 1920-
  Algo Mas Que Dos Sueños
    (In Teatro Breve Hispanoamericano Contemporaneo)
    (In El Teatro de Hoy en Costa Rica)
  El Heroe
    (In Obras Breves del Teatro Costarricense, Vol. 2)
The Canavans (see Gregory, Isabella A.)

Candida (see Shaw, George Bernard)
The Candidates; or, The Humours of a Virginia Election (see Munford, Colonel Robert)
Candide; text in French (see Ganzl, Serge)
Candide; comic operetta (see Hellman, Lillian)
CANKAR, Ivan
   I Servi; versione Italiana di Furio Bordon
     (In Sipario, no. 378, Nov. 1977)
CANNAC, Genia
   Le Triangle Immortel (see Evreinoff, Nicolas)
CANNAN, Denis, 1919-
   Dear Daddy
     (In Plays and Players, Vol. 24, nos. 1 & 2, Oct. & Nov. 1976)
   US; the Book of the Royal Shakespeare Theatre Production (see Brook, Peter)
CANNON, Doran William
   Brewster McCloud
     (In On Making a Movie: "Brewster McCloud")
CANOY, Reuben R., 1929-
   Let the People Speak
     (In Philippine Harvest)
Cant (see Munk, Kaj H.)
Cantate du Narcisse (see Valèry, Paul)
La Cantatrice Chauve (see Ionesco, Eugene)
CANTILLION, Arthur
   Pierrot Before the Seven Doors
     (In Types of Modern Dramatic Composition)
Cantique des Cantiques (see Giraudoux, Jean)
CANTON, Wilberto, 1923-
     (In 12 Obras en un Acto)
   Malditos
     (In Teatro Méxicano, 1958)
   We Are God
     (In Drama and Theatre, vol. 10, no. 3, Spring 1972)
CANTOR, Eli
   Murder Among the Psychologists
     (In 100 Non-Royalty Radio Plays)
Canvas (see Roszkowski, David)
Cão com Gato (see Andrade, Euclides M.)
CAPEK, Josef, 1887-1945
   Adam the Creator (see Capek, Karel)
   And So Ad Infinitum (see Capek, Karel)
CAPEK, Karel, 1890-1938
   Adam the Creator, by Karel and Josef Capek
     (In Dramas of Modernism)
   And So Ad Infinitum, by Karel and Josef Capek
     (In 20th Century Plays)
   R. U. R.
     (In Masterpieces of the Modern Central European Theatre)
Capitan Despues de Dios (see Hartog, Jan de)
Capitane Bada (see Vauthier, Jean)

CAPOTE, Truman, 1924-

Among the Paths to Eden; television script by Truman Capote, Eleanor and Frank Perry, based on Capote's story (In Trilogy)

A Christmas Memory; television script by Truman Capote, Eleanor and Frank Perry, based on Capote's story (In Trilogy)

Miriam; television script by Truman Capote, Eleanor and Frank Perry, based on Capote's story (In Trilogy)

A Caprice (see Musset, Alfred de)

Un Caprice (see Musset, Alfred de)

Les Caprices de Marianne (see Musset, Alfred de)

The Captain (see Beaumont, Francis)

Captain Bassbound's Conversion: an Adventure (see Shaw, George Bernard)

Captain Jinks of the Horse Marines (see Fitch, Clyde)

Captain O'Blunder (see Sheridan, Thomas)

The Captain of Köpenick (see Zuckmayer, Carl)

The Captives (see Gay, John)

The Captives (see Plautus, Titus M.)

Captives of the Faceless Drummer (see Ryga, George)

The Capuchin (see Foote, Samuel)

Capuletta; or, Romeo and Juliet Restored (see Baker, George M.)

The Car Cemetery (see Arrabal, Fernando)

Les Carabiniers; screenplay (see Godard, Jean-Luc)

Caracalla, Marcus Aurelius Antoninus, Roman emperor, 188-217 A. D.

*Geta (see Pechantre)

CARAGIALE, Ion Luca

Mr. Leonida Face to Face with the Reaction (In Drama and Theatre, Vol. 10, no. 2, Winter 1971-72)

CARB, David

Grandma Pulls the String (see Delano, Edith B.)

CARBALLIDO, Emilio, 1925-

El Censo (In 12 Obras en un Acto)

The Clockmaker from Cordova (In his The Golden Thread and Other Plays)

La Danza Que Sueña la Tortuga (In Teatro Méxicano del Siglo XX, Vol. 3)

The Golden Thread (In his The Golden Thread and Other Plays)

The Intermediate Zone (In his The Golden Thread and Other Plays)

The Mirror (In his The Golden Thread and Other Plays)

Silencio, Pollos Pelones, Ya les Van a Echar Su Maíz! (In Teatro Méxicano, 1963)

Theseus (In his The Golden Thread and Other Plays)

The Time and the Place: Dead Love, The Glacier, The Wine Cellar

(In Contemporary Drama Service, Comedy Kit A-2, no. 3)
Gone with the Breeze; a parody of the film "Gone with the Wind"
(In Contemporary Drama Service, Comedy Kit A-6, no. 1)
Guess What's Coming to Dinner; a parody of the film "Guess
Who's Coming to Dinner"
(In Contemporary Drama Service, Comedy Kit A-5, no. 2)
High School Classmates
(In Contemporary Drama Service, Comedy Kit A-4, no. 1)
Hospital Nudge
(In Contemporary Drama Service, Comedy Kit A-3, no. 5)
Insurance Adjuster
(In Contemporary Drama Service, Comedy Kit A-4, no. 2)
The Late Date
(In Contemporary Drama Service, Comedy Kit A-3, no. 4)
Lovely Story; a parody of the film "Love Story"
(In Contemporary Drama Service, Comedy Kit A-2, no. 1)
The Most Happy Stella; a parody of the play "Most Happy Fellow"
(In Contemporary Drama Service, Comedy Kit A-2, no. 2)
Old Folks #1
(In Contemporary Drama Service, Comedy Kit A-1, no. 5)
The Old Folks #2
(In Contemporary Drama Service, Comedy Kit A-4, no. 5)
The Old Folks #3
(In Contemporary Drama Service, Comedy Kit A-6, no. 4)
Passion on 10th Avenue
(In Contemporary Drama Service, Comedy Kit A-6, no. 2)
Prison Nudge
(In Contemporary Drama Service, Comedy Kit A-5, no. 4)
Red Dust; a parody of MGM jungle movies
(In Contemporary Drama Service, Comedy Kit A-1, no. 1)
Return to Andy Hardy; a parody of the Hardy Family movies
(In Contemporary Drama Service, Comedy Kit A-1, no. 2)
The Rolls Royce
(In Contemporary Drama Service, Comedy Kit A-4, no. 3)
So Proudly We Heal; a parody of the film "So Proudly We Hail"
(In Contemporary Drama Service, Comedy Kit A-5, no. 1)
The Wallflowers
(In Contemporary Drama Service, Comedy Kit A-3, no. 3)
The Welfare Worker
(In Contemporary Drama Service, Comedy Kit A-6, no. 3)
Carola (see Renoir, Jean)
Carona de Amor y Muerte (see Rodriguez Alvarez, Alejandro)
Carousel (see Rodgers, Richard)
CARPENTER, Edward Childs, 1872-1950
(In One-Act Plays for Stage and Study, 2nd Series)
CARPENTER, S. D.
The Irrepressible Conflict; or, The Rise, Progress and Decline
of "One Idea," including the principal acts in the life of Abra-
ham the First
(In Magazine of History, Vol. 9, Extra no. 34, 1914)
Carr, Henry Wilfred, 1894-1962
*Travesties (see Stoppard, Tom)
CARRIERE, Albert
He Who Gets Hooked

(In One-Act Plays for Stage and Study, 10th Series)
CARRIERE, Jean-Claude
    Le Fantome de la Liberté; un film (see Buñuel, Luis)
CARRINGTON, Elaine Sterne
    Pepper Young's family; radio script, episode no. 1031: "Back
      in the Old House," Dec. 25, 1939
      (In Best Broadcasts of 1939-40)
CARROLL, Ellison, pseud.
    Teacher, Teacher; television script, NBC, Feb. 5, 1969
      (In Electronic Drama)
Carroll, Lewis (pseud.) (see Dodgson, Charles L.)
CARROLL, Paul Vincent, 1900-1968
    Beauty Is Fled
      (In his Irish Stories and Plays)
    Coggerers
      (In The White Steed and Coggerers)
    The Conspirators
      (In his Irish Stories and Plays)
    The Devil Came from Dublin
      (In his Irish Stories and Plays)
    Farewell to Greatness! based on the life of Dean Jonathan Swift
      (In The "Lost Play" Series, no. 3)
    Goodbye to the Summer
      (In The "Lost Play" Series, no. 8)
    Interlude
      (In his Irish Stories and Plays)
    The Strings, My Lord, Are False
      (In his Three Plays)
    Things That Are Caesar's
      (In his Three Plays)
    The White Steed
      (In his Three Plays)
      (In The White Steed and Coggerers)
CARROLL, Sidney
    Big Deal in Laredo; television script, NBC, Oct. 7, 1962
      (In Electronic Drama)
CARROLL, Robert F. (Dean Carroll)
    Time Is a Thief
      (In One-Act Plays for Stage and Study, 10th Series)
Le Carrosse du Saint-Sacrement (see Mérimée, Prosper)
El Carrusell (see Ruiz Iriarte, Victor)
The Carrying of X from A to Z (see Howard, Roger)
La Carta de Don Juan (see Treves, Luisa)
Las Cartas Boca Abajo (see Buero Vallejo, Antonio)
CARTER, Lonnie
    The Sovereign State of Boogedy Boogedy; formerly known as
      "Trade-Offs"
      (In Yale/Theatre, Vol. 7, no. 3, Spring 1976)
CARTER-HARRISON, Paul
    The Great MacDaddy
      (In Kuntu Drama)
CARTWRIGHT, William, 1611-1643
    The Lady-Errant

(In his Plays & Poems)
The Ordinary
(In his Plays & Poems)
The Royall Slave
(In his Plays & Poems)
The Siedge; or, Love's Convert
(In his Plays & Poems)
Carved Woman (see Alexander, Hartley B.)
CARY, Falkland
Sailor, Beware! (see King, Philip)
La Casa (see Peman, José Maria)
La Casa de Bernarda Alba (see Garcia Lorca, Federico)
La Casa de las Chivas (see Salom, Jaime)
La Casa de los Siete Balcones (see Rodriguez Alvarez, Alejandro)
Casa de Ninguem (see Calvet, Aldo)
La Casa de To de la Luna de Agosto (see Goggan, John P.)
La Casa sin Reloj (see Marques, René)
Casablanca (see Curtiz, Michael)
CASALE, Michael
Slowly Comes the Wind
(In Guthrie New Theater, Vol. 1)
The Case (see Sukhovo-Kobylin, Aleksandr)
Case for a Rebel (see Robles, Emmanuel)
The Case Is Altered (see Jonson, Ben)
The Case of Astrolabe (see Hutchins, Maude P.)
The Case of the Crushed Petunias (see Williams, Tennessee)
CASEY, Warren
Grease, a new 50's Rock 'n Roll musical; music, book and
lyrics by Jim Jacobs and Warren Casey
(In Winter Repertory Special Number)
Cask of Amontillado; adapted for radio (see Newman, Ellis)
El Caso de Don Juan Manuel (see Lazo, Agustin)
Un Caso Fortunato (see Mrozek, Slawomir)
Casona, Alejandro (see Rodriguez Alvarez, Alejandro)
Cassander, King of Macedonia, 316-297 B. C.
*Olympia (see Voltaire)
CASSAVETES, John, 1929-
Minnie and Moskowitz; screenplay
(A Black Sparrow Press Screenplay)
Shadows; text in French
(In L'Avant-Scène Cinéma, no. 197, Dec. 1, 1977)
CASSENTI, Frank
L'Affiche Rouge
(In L'Avant-Scène Cinéma, no. 174, Oct. 15, 1976)
Le Casseur d'Assiettes (see Salacrou, Armand)
La Cassica Alla Volpe (see Verga, Giovanni)
Cassidy, Butch (see Parker, Robert)
CASSIERI, Giuseppe, 1926-
L'Orecchio di Dionisio
(In Sipario, no. 319, Dec. 1972)
The Cassilis Engagement (see Hankin, St. John E.)
Cassius (Gaius Cassius Longinus) d. 42 B. C.
*Brutus et Cassius, ou Les Derniers Romains (see Chénier,
Marie-Joseph B.)

The Cassone (see Shaw, George Bernard)
Caste (see Robertson, Thomas W.)
CASTELLANI, Renato, 1913-
    Giulietta e Romeo
        (In Dal Soggetto al Film Series, No. 1, 1956)
CASTELOT, André, 1911-
    Napoleon III a la Barre de l'Histoire
        (In L'Avant-Scène Théatre, no. 568, July 15, 1975)
Castle in the Air (see Caverhill, William M.)
The Castle of Sorrento (see Heartwell, Henry)
The Castle Spectre (see Lewis, Matthew G.)
Castle Wetterstein (see Wedekind, Frank)
CASTRI, Massimo
    E' Arrivato Pietro Gori, di Massimo Castri, Emilio Jona, Ser-
        gio Liberovici
        (In Sipario, no. 346, Mar. 1975)
    Per Uso di Memoria, di Massimo Castri, Emilio Jona e Sergio
        Liberovici
        (In Sipario, no. 359, April 1976)
CASTRO, Consuelo de, 1946-
    O Caminho de Volta
        (In Revista de Teatro, no. 410, Mar./Apr. 1976)
CASTRO, Felipe
    Los Pelados
        (In El Teatro de la Esperanza)
CASTRO, H. Alfredo, 1889-1966
    Juego Limpio
        (In Obras Breves del Teatro Costarricense, Vol. 1)
Castro, Inez de, 1320?-1355
    *Ines de Castro (see Houdar de la Motte, Antoine)
    *Inez de Castro (see Hugo, Victor)
    *Queen After Death (see Montherlant, Henri de)
Casualties (see Flavin, Martin)
CASULE, Kole, 1921-
    Darkness
        (In Five Modern Yugoslav Plays)
The Cat (see Walter, Otto F.)
The Cat and the Moon (see Yeats, William Butler)
Cat on a Hot Tin Roof (see Williams, Tennessee)
The Catch (see Brecht, Bertolt)
Caterina delle Midericordie (see Cuomo, Franco)
Catherine II, Empress of Russia, 1729-1796
    *Great Catherine (Whom Glory Still Adores) (see Shaw, George
        Bernard)
Catherine and Petruchio (see Garrick, David)
Catherine de Medici, 1519-1589
    *Charles IX, or La Saint-Barthelemi (see Chénier, Marie-Joseph
        B.)
    *The Queen-Mother (see Swinburne, Algernon Charles)
Catherine Parr; or, Alexander's Horse (see Baring, Maurice)
Cathleen Ni Houlihan (see Yeats, William Butler)
Catilina, Lucius Sergius, 108?-62 B. C.
    *Catilina (see Crebillion, Prosper)

*Catiline (see Voltaire)
*Catiline; 1st and 2nd versions (see Ibsen, Henrik)
*Catiline His Conspiracy (see Jonson, Ben)
*Lucius Sergius Catilina (see Heym, Georg)
Cato, Marcus Porcius (Cato the Younger), 95-46 B.C.
    *Catiline (see Voltaire)
CATS, Jacob, 1577-1660
    Pleasant Dialogues and Dramas (see Heywood, Thomas)
Cats of Egypt (see Morris, Thomas B.)
The Caucasian Chalk Circle (see Brecht, Bertolt)
Le Cauchemar de Dracula; screenplay (see Fisher, Terence)
The Cause of It All (see Tolstoi, Lev N.)
Cavalcade (see Coward, Noël)
The Cavalier of the Rose (see Hofmannsthal, Hugo von H.)
Le Cavalier Seul (see Audiberti, Jacques)
Cavalleria Rusticana (see Verga, Giovanni)
CAVANI, Liliana
    Francesco e Galileo
        (In Gribaudi Piero Filmscript Series, 1970)
    Milarepa
        (In Dal Soggetto al Film Series, no. 49, 1974)
The Cave of Salamanca (see Cervantes Saavedra, Miguel de)
CAVERHILL, William Melville, 1910-
    Castle in the Air, by Alan Melville, pseud.
        (In Plays of the Year, Vol. 3, 1949/50)
    Dear Charles (Les Enfants d'Edouard) (see Sauvajon, Marc-
        Gilbert)
The Cavern (see Anouilh, Jean)
Ce Formidable Bordel! (see Ionesco, Eugene)
CECCALDI, Daniel, 1927-
    Mais Qu'est-ce Qui Fait Courir les Femmes, la Nuit a Ma-
        drid? ... d'après Calderon de la Barca
        (In L'Avant-Scène du Théâtre, no. 528, Nov. 1, 1973)
Cece (see Pirandello, Luigi)
Cecile; ou, L'Ecole des Peres (see Anouilh, Jean)
Celebration (see Jones, Tom)
La Celestine (see Laville, Pierre)
Celimare le Bien-aimé (see Labiche, Eugene)
CELINE, Louis-Ferdinand, 1894-
    Entretiens avec le Professeur Y, adaptation theatrâle de Jean
        Rougerie
        (In L'Avant-Scène Théâtre, no. 584, April 1, 1976)
The Cellar and the Almond Tree (see Mercer, David)
Celles Qu'on Prend dans ses Bras (see Montherlant, Henry de)
CELLI, Giorgio, 1935-
    Il Sonno dei Carnefici
        (In Sipario, no. 332, Jan. 1974)
La Cellule (see Dubé, Marcel)
Celos del Aire (see López Rubio, José)
The Cenci (see Artaud, Antonin)
Cenci (see Heym, Georg)
The Cenci (see Shelley, Percy Bysshe)
CENDRARS, Blaise, 1887-1961
  **Sutter's Gold; film scenario (see Eisenstein, Sergei M.)

La Cenente (see Mihura, Miguel)
El Censo (see Carbillido, Emilio)
Censored Scenes from King Kong (see Shuman, Howard)
Cent Millions Qui Tombent (see Feydeau, Georges)
CENTLIVRE, Mrs. Susanna, 1667?-1723
    The Man's Bewitch'd; or, The Devil to Do About Her
        (In A Collection of the Most Esteemed Farces ..., Vol. 6)
Le 120 Giornate di Sodoma (see Vasilico, Giuliano)
El Cepillo de Dientes (see Diáz, Jorge)
Ceremonie pour un Noir Assassine (see Arrabal, Fernando)
Ceremonies in Dark Old Men (see Elder, Lonnie, III)
Ceremony for a Murdered Black (see Arrabal, Fernando)
Ceremony of the Printer's Apprentice (see Blades, William)
Le Cerimonie (see Maffei, Francesco S.)
CERVANTES SAAVEDRA, Miguel de, 1547-1616
    The Cave of Salamanca
        (In World Drama, Vol. 2)
    Don Quixote in England (see Fielding, Henry)
    Man of La Mancha (see Leigh, Mitch)
    Sancho's Master (see Gregory, Isabella A.)
Cervantes Saavedra, Miguel de, 1547-1616
    *El Ultimo Capitulo (see Othon, Manuel J.)
CESAIRE, Aime
    A Season in the Congo
        (In Calder & Boyars Playscript Series, no. 21, 1968)
        (In Evergreen Plays Series, 1968)
        (In Kuntu Drama)
César-Antechrist (see Jarry, Alfred)
C'Est Beau (see Sarraute, Nathalie)
C'Est Pitié Qu'elle Soit une Putain (see Ford, John)
C'Est une Femme du Monde (see Feydeau, Georges)
Chabot, Philip, Admiral of France (see Brion Philippe de Chabot,
    amiral de)
Chafed Elbows; screenplay (see Downey, Robert)
The Chairs (see Ionesco, Eugene)
Les Chaises (see Ionesco, Eugene)
CHALBAUD, Roman, 1931-
    Las Pinzas
        (In Teatro Breve Hispanoamericano Contemporaneo)
CHALFI, Raquel
    Felicidad; a Play for Dolls, Dummies, Manequins, Masks,
        Puppets and People
        (In Drama & Theatre, Vol. 12, no. 1, Fall 1974)
The Chalk Circle, translated by Ethel Van der Veer (Anon.)
        (In World Drama, Vol. 1)
The Chalk Garden (see Bagnold, Enid)
A Challenge for Beautie (see Heywood, Thomas)
Chamber Piece (see O'Keefe, John)
CHAMBERS, Charles Haddon, 1860-1921
    The Tyranny of Tears
        (In English Plays of the 19th Century, Vol. III: Comedies)
La Chambre Mandarine (see Thomas, Robert)
Champagne (see Perez, Isaac Loeb)

The Champagne Pool (see O'Hara, John)
Champignol Malgre Lui (see Feydeau, Georges)
Championship of the Universal Class Struggle (see Maiakovskii, Vladimir V.)
Chan Wan-ch'eng (The Battle of Wan-ch'eng)
     (In Famous Chinese Plays)
La Chance de François (see Porto-Riche, Georges de)
The Chances (see Fletcher, John)
The Chandelier (see Musset, Alfred de)
Le Chandelier (see Musset, Alfred de)
The Chandler (see Musset, Alfred de)
CHANDLER, Raymond, 1888-1959
     The Blue Dahlia; a screenplay for the film directed by George Marshall
     (In The Blue Dahlia)
Chang, Feng-chao
     Camping in the Snow, a comic dialogue by Feng-chao and Cheng-kuo Tiao
     (In Chinese Literature, no. 2, 1973)
Chang Boils the Sea (see Li Hao-ku)
Ch'ang-pan P'o (The Battle of Ch'ang-pan P'o)
     (In Famous Chinese Plays)
Change (see Bauer, Wolfgang)
A Change of Heart (see James, Henry)
A Change of Mind (see Speirs, Russell)
Change of Pace (see Pomerantz, Edward)
The Changed Bridegroom (see Holberg, Ludvig von)
The Changeling (see Middleton, Thomas)
Changes; or, Love in a Maze (see Shirley, James)
Changing Places (see Ehrlich, Mrs. Ida L.)
The Changing Room (see Storey, David)
CHANSLOR, Roy
     **Johnny Guitar; screenplay; text in French (see Ray, Nicholas)
Chant du la Veille des Armes (see Lamartine, Alphonse)
Chantaje (see Asturias, Miguel A.)
CHANTEL, Lucien, 1887-
     Who Killed Me?
     (In Modern One-Act Plays from the French)
Un Chapeau de Paille d'Italie (see Labiche, Eugene)
The Chaperon (see James, Henry)
CHAPIN, Harold, 1886-1915
     Augustus in Search of a Father
     (In Scottish Repertory Plays Series, no. 4, 1911)
The Chaplet (see Mendez, Moses)
CHAPLIN, Sid
     **Close the Coalhouse Door (see Plater, Alan)
CHAPMAN, George, 1559?-1634
     All Fools
     (In his Comedies, Vol. 1)
     An Humorous Day's Mirth
     (In his Comedies, Vol. 1)
     The Ball, by George Chapman and James Shirley
     (In his Comedies, Vol. 2)

(In Shirley's <u>Dramatic Works & Poems</u>, Vol. 3)
The Blind Beggar of Alexandria
    (In his <u>Comedies</u>, Vol. 1)
Bussy d'Ambois
    (In his <u>Tragedies</u>, Vol. 1)
The Conspiracy of Charles Duke of Byron
    (In his <u>Tragedies</u>, Vol. 1)
Eastward Ho, by George Chapman, Ben Jonson, and John Marston
    (In his <u>Comedies</u>, Vol. 2)
    (In Marston's <u>Plays</u>, Vol. 3)
The Gentleman Usher
    (In his <u>Comedies</u>, Vol. 1)
Hero and Leander (see Marlowe, Christopher)
The Masque of the Middle Temple and Lincoln's Inn
    (In his <u>Comedies</u>, Vol. 2)
May-Day
    (In his <u>Comedies</u>, Vol. 1)
Monsieur D'Olive
    (In his <u>Comedies</u>, Vol. 1)
Revenge for Honour
    (In his <u>Tragedies</u>, Vol. 2)
The Revenge of Bussy d'Ambois
    (In his <u>Tragedies</u>, Vol. 1)
Sir Giles Goosecap, Knight
    (In his <u>Comedies</u>, Vol. 2)
The Tragedy of Alphonsus Emperor of Germany
    (In his <u>Tragedies</u>, Vol. 2)
The Tragedy of Caesar and Pompey
    (In his <u>Tragedies</u>, Vol. 2)
The Tragedy of Chabot Admiral of France, by George Chapman
  and James Shirley
    (In his <u>Tragedies</u>, Vol. 1)
    (In Shirley's <u>Dramatic Works & Poems</u>, Vol. 6)
The Tragedy of Charles Duke of Byron
    (In his <u>Tragedies</u>, Vol. 1)
The Widow's Tears
    (In his <u>Comedies</u>, Vol. 1)
CHAPPELL, Eric
    The Banana Box
        (In <u>Plays and Players</u>, Vol. 20 no. 9, June 1973)
The Character Against Himself (see Vauthier, Jean)
Charade; filmscript (see Stone, Peter)
Charades on East Fourth Street (see Elder, Lonne)
The Charge-House (see MacIntyre, John)
Charity in Two Keys (see Shearer, Marjorie)
The Charity That Began at Home (see Hankin, St. John)
El Charlatan (see Rodriguez Buded, Ricardo)
CHARLES, Martie
    Black Cycle
        (In <u>Black Drama Anthology</u>)
    Job Security
        (In <u>Black Theater U.S.A.</u>, 1847-1974)
Charles I, King of Great Britain, 1600-1649
  *Strafford (see Browning, Robert)

Charles II, King of Great Britain, 1660-1685
  *Charles the Second (see Payne, John H.)
  *"In Good King Charles's Golden Days": a True History That
    Never Happened (see Shaw, George Bernard)
Charles V, Roman Emperor and as Charles I, King of Spain, 1500-
  1558
  *Corona de Luz: La Virgen (see Usigli, Rudolfo)
Charles VII, King of France, 1403-1461
  *The Maid of Orleans (see Schiller, Johann)
  *Saint Joan: a Chronicle Play in Six Scenes and an Epilogue
    (see Shaw, George Bernard)
  *The Visions of Simone Marchard (see Brecht, Bertolt)
Charles VIII, King of France, 1470-1498
  *The History of Charles the Eighth of France; or, The Invasion
    of Naples by the French (see Crowne, John)
Charles IX, King of France, 1550-1574
  *Charles IX, or La Saint-Barthélemi (see Chénier, Marie-Joseph)
  *The Massacre of Paris (see Lee, Nathaniel)
  *The Queen-Mother (see Swinburne, Algernon Charles)
Charlie (see Mrozek, Slawomir)
Charlie McCarthy radio scripts (see Fields, W. C.)
Charlie Who? (see French, Helen)
CHARLOT, Jean, 1898-
  Moa a Mo'i, Chicken into King
    (In his Three Plays about Ancient Hawaii)
  Na'auao, The Light Within
    (In his Three Plays about Ancient Hawaii)
  Snare-That-Lures-a-Far-Flung-Bird; bilingual play in Hawaiian
    and English
    (In his Two Hawaiian Plays)
  Two Lonos; bilingual play in Hawaiian and English
    (In his Two Hawaiian Plays)
  Ul' a U'i, Beauty Meets Beauty
    (In his Three Plays about Ancient Hawaii)
Charlotte, Empress consort of Maximilian, Emperor of México,
  1840-1927
  *Corona de Sombra; pieza antihistorica (see Usigli, Rodolfo)
Le Charme Discret de la Bourgeoisie; filmscript (see Buñuel, Luis)
CHARTREUX, Bernard
  Ah Kiou, pièce de Bernard Chartreux et Jean Jourdheuil, trage-
    die Chinoise d'après Lou Sin, pseud. ("The True Story of Ah
    Q," by Shu-jen Chou)
    (In L'Avant-Scène Théâtre, no. 581, Jan. 15, 1976)
The Chase (see Foote, Horton)
CHASE, Mary (Coyle), 1907-
  Harvey
    (In 50 Best Plays of the American Theatre, Vol. 3)
Chaslelard (see Swinburne, Algernon Charles)
La Chasse au Dahut (see Hamon, Franck)
La Chasse aux Corbeaux (see Labiche, Eugene)
La Chasseur Français (see Vian, Boris)
La Chaste Isabelle (see Gueullette, Thomas S.)
A Chaste Maid in Cheapside (see Middleton, Thomas)

The Chastening (see Kennedy, Charles Rann)
Chat en Poche (see Feydeau, Georges)
Le Chateau du Diable (see Hugo, Victor)
Chatterton, Thomas, 1752-1770
    *Chatterton (see Vigny, Alfred V.)
    *Thomas Chatterton (see Jahnn, Hans H.)
LA CHAUSSEE, Pierre-Claude Nivelle de, 1692-1754
    Mélanide
        (In Théâtre de XVIII Siécle, VoL 1)
Chauvelin, oder Lang Lebe der König! (see Kästner, Erich)
CHAYEFSKY, Paddy, 1923-
    The Big Deal
        (In Great Television Plays)
    The Mother
        (In The Mentor Book of Short Plays)
    The Tenth Man
        (In Eight American Ethnic Plays)
The Cheats (see Wilson, John)
The Cheats of Scapin (see Otway, Thomas)
The Cheats of Scapin (Les Fourberies de Scapin) (see Molière, Jean
    Baptiste)
Chee-Chee (see Pirandello, Luigi)
Cheek (see Barker, Howard)
CHEESEMAN, Peter
    Fight for Shelton Bar
        (In Methuen's New Theatrescripts, no. 10, 1977)
    The Knotty
        (In Methuen Playscript Series, 1970)
CHEEVER, John
    **Children (see Gurney, A. R. , Jr.)
CHEKHOV, Anton Pavlovich, 1860-1904
    The Anniversary
        (In The Oxford Chekhov, VoL 1)
    **The Baby (see Mankowitz, Wolf)
    The Bear
        (In The Oxford Chekhov, VoL 1)
    The Boor
        (In The Play Book)
    The Cherry Orchard
        (In Dramas of Modernism)
        (In Masterpieces of the Modern Russian Theatre)
        (In Masterpieces of the Russian Drama, VoL 2)
        (In The Moscow Art Theatre Series of Russian Plays)
        (In The Oxford Chekhov, VoL 3)
    The Impure Tragedians and the Leprous Playwrights; a dread-
        fully-terribly-shockingly-desperate trrragedy, by my brother's
        brother, pseud.
        (In 20th Century Russian Plays)
    Ivanov
        (In The Oxford Chekhov, VoL 2)
    **The Last of the Cheesecake (see Mankowitz, Wolf)
    A Marriage Proposal
        (In The Drama, VoL 18)

  (In The Mentor Book of Short Plays)
The Night Before the Trial
  (In The Oxford Chekhov, Vol. 1)
On the High Road
  (In The Oxford Chekhov, Vol. 1)
Platonov
  (In The Oxford Chekhov, Vol. 2)
The Proposal
  (In The Oxford Chekhov, Vol. 1)
The Seagull
  (In The Oxford Chekhov, Vol. 2)
  (In Representative Continental Dramas)
  (In 20th Century Russian Plays)
Smoking Is Bad for You
  (In The Oxford Chekhov, Vol. 1)
Swan Song
  (In The Oxford Chekhov, Vol. 1)
Tatyana Repin
  (In The Oxford Chekhov, Vol. 1)
The Three Sisters
  (In The Moscow Art Theatre Series of Russian Plays)
  (In The Oxford Chekhov, Vol. 3)
A Tragic Role
  (In The Oxford Chekhov, Vol. 1)
Uncle Vanya
  (In Contemporary Drama: 13 Plays)
  (In Masterpieces of the Modern Russian Theatre)
  (In The Moscow Art Theatre Series of Russian Plays)
  (In The Oxford Chekhov, Vol. 3)
  (In The Storm and Other Russian Plays)
Uncle Vanya, translated by Tyrone Guthrie and Leonid Kipnis
  (In Minnesota Drama Editions, no. 5)
Uncle Vanya, a new version by Christopher Hampton
  (In Plays of the Year, Vol. 39, 1969/70)
The Wedding
  (In The Oxford Chekhov, Vol. 1)
The Wood-Demon
  (In The Oxford Chekhov, Vol. 3)
Le Chemin de la Fortune (see Marivaux, Pierre C.)
CHENG TEH-HUI, early 14th Century
  The Soul of Ch'ien-nü Leaves Her Body
    (In Six Yüan Plays)
CHENIER, Marie-Joseph Blaise, 1764-1811
  Azemire
    (In his Théâtre, Vol. 1)
  Brutus et Cassius, ou Les Derniers Romains
    (In his Théâtre, Vol. 2)
  Caius Gracchus
    (In his Théâtre, Vol. 1)
  Le Camp de Grand-Pré, ou Le Triomphe de la République
    (In his Théâtre, Vol. 2)
  Charles IX, or Le Saint-Barthélemi
    (In his Théâtre, Vol. 1)

Cyrus
    (In his Théâtre, Vol. 2)
De Ninon
    (In his Théâtre, Vol. 3)
Electre
    (In his Théâtre, Vol. 3)
Fénélon
    (In his Théâtre, Vol. 2)
Henri VIII
    (In his Théâtre, Vol. 1)
Jean Calas, ou L'Ecole des Juges
    (In his Théâtre, Vol. 1)
Nathan le Sage
    (In his Théâtre, Vol. 3)
Oedipe à Colone
    (In his Théâtre, Vol. 3)
Oedipe-Roi
    (In his Théâtre, Vol. 3)
Philippe II
    (In his Théâtre, Vol. 2)
Portraits de Famille
    (In his Théâtre, Vol. 3)
Tibère
    (In his Théâtre, Vol. 3)
Timoléon
    (In his Théâtre, Vol. 2)
Cher Antoine (see Anouilh, Jean)
CHERRY, Andrew
    The Soldier's Daughter
      (In The London Stage, Vol. 1)
The Cherry Orchard (see Chekhov, Anton)
Chers Zoiseau (see Anouilh, Jean)
Chestnuts from the Fire (see Musset, Alfred de)
CHETHAM-STRODE, Warren, 1899-
    Background
      (In Plays of the Year, Vol. 4, 1950)
CHEVIGNY, Hector
    Daniel Webster
      (In Best Television Plays, 1954)
Une Chevre sur un Nuage (see Arrabal, Fernando)
Chez les Tich Trafic (see Calaferte, Louis)
CHI CHUN-HSIANG, late 13th Century
    The Orphan of Chao
      (In Six Yüan Plays)
Chi ku Ma Ts'ao (Beating the Drum and Cursing Ts'ao)
    (In Famous Chinese Plays)
Ch'i Shuang Hui (An Extraordinary Twin Meeting)
    (In Famous Chinese Plays)
Ch'i Tang T'ung O Pao (A Wife and Her Wicked Relations Reap
    Their Reward)
      (In Famous Chinese Plays)
CHIANG, Ching
    The Red Detachment of Women

(In Five Chinese Communist Plays)
CHIARA, Ghigo de
     Itaca, Itaca!
     (In Sipario, no. 336, May 1974)
Chickadee (see Conkle, Ellsworth P.)
Chicago (see Shepard, Sam)
The Chicken Pie and the Chocolate Cake (Le Pâte et la Tarte) (Anon.)
     (In Five Comedies of Medieval France)
Chicken Soup with Barley (see Wesker, Arnold)
The Chickencoop Chinaman (see Chin, Frank)
The Chief's Bride (see Phiri, Desmond D.)
La Chienne; screenplay (see Renoir, Jean)
CHIKAMATSU MONZAEMON
     Fair Ladies at a Game of Poem-Cards
     (In World Drama, Vol. 1)
Childhood (see Wilder, Thornton)
The Children (see Edson, Russell)
Children (see Gurney, A. R., Jr.)
Children of the Kingdom (see Opper, Don K.)
The Children Who Work and the Children Who Play (see Benton, Rita)
The Children's Hour (see Hellman, Lillian)
CHILDRESS, Alice
     Mojo
     (In Best Short Plays of the World Theatre, 1968-1973)
     Trouble in Mind
     (In Black Theater)
     Wine in the Wilderness
     (In Black Theater U.S.A., 1847-1974)
     (In Plays by and About Women)
Child's Play (see Marasco, Robert)
The Chimes of the Kremlin (see Pogodin, Nikolai F.)
CHIN, Frank, 1940-
     The Chickencoop Chinaman
     (In Aiiieeeee!)
Chin So Chi (The Golden Locket Plot)
     (In Famous Chinese Plays)
CHINA. PEKING OPERA TROUP
     Azalea Mountain; written by Wang Shu-yan and others
     (In Five Chinese Communist Plays)
     (In Chinese Literature, no. 1, 1974)
     Fighting on the Plain, written by Chang Yung-mei and others
     (In Chinese Literature, no. 5, 1974)
     The Red Lantern
     (In Five Chinese Communist Plays)
     Taking the Bandits' Stronghold
     (In Five Chinese Communist Plays)
     The White-Haired Girl
     (In Five Chinese Communist Plays)
CHINA. SHANTUNG PROVINCIAL PEKING OPERA TROUPE
     Raid on the White Tiger Regiment (Sept. 1972 script)
     (In Chinese Literature, no. 3, 1973)
Chinamen (see Frayn, Michael)
La Chinche (see Maiakovski, Vladimir V.)

Chinchills ... Figures in a Classical Landscape with Ruins (see
    MacDonald, Robert D.)
The Chinese (see Schisgal, Murray)
The Chinese Icebox (see Laszlo, Carl)
The Chinese Prime Minister (see Bagnold, Enid)
The Chinese Water Wheel (see Strachan, Edna H.)
Die Chinesische Mauer (see Frisch, Max)
Ch'ing Ting Chu (The Lucky Pearl)
    (In Famous Chinese Plays)
El Chino de los Winslow (see Rattigan, Sir Terence M.)
The Chip Woman's Fortune (see Richardson, Willis)
CHIPMAN, Karyl Kanet
    What Men Live By; adapted for radio from the story by Leo
    Tolstoy
        (In 100 Non-Royalty Radio Plays)
CHIPP, Elinor
    The Honor and the Glory
        (In One-Act Plays for Stage and Study, 10th Series)
Chips with Everything (see Wesker, Arnold)
Chiu Keng T'ien (The Day of Nine Watches)
    (In Famous Chinese Plays)
CHLUMBERG, Hans, 1897-1930
    The Miracle at Verdun
        (In 20th Century Plays)
Cho Fang Ts'ao (The Capture and Release of Ts'ao)
    (In Famous Chinese Plays)
CHODOROV, Edward, 1904-
    Kind Lady
        (In 10 Classic Mystery and Suspense Plays of the Modern
        Theatre)
CHODOROV, Jerome, 1911-
    Wonderful Town (see Bernstein, Leonard)
Les Choephores (see Aeschylus)
Le Choix d'un Gendre (see Labiche, Eugene)
Chop-Chin and the Golden Dragon (see Smith, Moyne R.)
CHORELL, Walentin, 1912-
    The Sisters
        (In Five Modern Scandinavian Plays)
CHOU, Shu-jen, 1881-1936
    **Ah Kiou (see Chartreux, Bernard)
CHRISTIANSEN, Sigurd, 1891-1947
    Un Viaje en la Noche
        (In Teatro Noruego Contemporaneo)
CHRISTIE, Agatha (Miller), 1891-1975
    Ten Little Indians, based on the author's novel "And Then There
    Were None"
        (In 10 Classic Mystery and Suspense Plays of the Modern
        Theatre)
    Witness for the Prosecution
        (In Best Mystery and Suspense Plays of the Modern Theatre)
CHRISTIE, Dorothy
    His Excellency, by Dorothy and Campbell Christie
        (In Plays of the Year, Vol. 4, 1950)

Christie in Love (see Brenton, Howard)
Christmas at the Ivanovs' (see Vvedensky, Alexander)
A Christmas Carol (see Gaines, Frederick)
Christmas Eve (see O'Brien, Seumas)
A Christmas Memory (see Capote, Truman)
The Christmas Party (see Holberg, Ludvig von)
The Christmas Story (see Folprecht, William)
Christopher Columbus (see Ghelderode, Michel de)
Christopher Columbus (see Tucholsky, Kurt)
The Chronicle of King Edward I (see Peele, George)
Chronicle of the Battle of Ichinotani (see Sōsuke, Namiki)
Chronicles of Hell (see Ghelderode, Michel de)
Chrononhotonthologos (see Carey, Henry)
Chu Lien Chai (Pearly Screen Castle)
     (In Famous Chinese Plays)
Chu Sha Chih (The Cinnabar Mole)
     (In Famous Chinese Plays)
Chuang Yuan P'u (A Chuang Yuan's Record)
     (In Famous Chinese Plays)
Chuck (see Larson, Jack)
CHUKRAI, Grigori, 1921-
     Ballad of a Soldier; screenplay by Grigory Chukrai and Valentin
        Yoshov for the film directed by Grigori Chukrai; text in Rus-
        sian
        (In Ballada o Soldate)
Ch'un Ying Hui (The Meeting of the League of Heroes)
     (In Famous Chinese Plays)
The Church Fight (see Gaines-Shelton, Ruth)
CHURCHILL, Caryl
     Owners
        (In Methuen Playscripts Series, 1973)
        (In Plays and Players, Vol. 20, no. 4, Jan. 1973)
Churchill, Sir Winston (Leonard Spencer), British Prime Minister,
     1874-1965
     *Young Winston; screenplay (see Foreman, Carl)
A Chuva de Sorrisos (see Lourenco, Pasqual)
CIARDI, John, 1916-
     A Year-End Dialogue with Outer Space
        (In Readers Theatre Handbook)
Ciascuno a Suo Modo (see Pirandello, Luigi)
CIBBER, Colley, 1671-1757
     The Careless Husband
        (In British Plays from the Restoration to 1820, Vol. 1)
        (In Colley Cibber: Three Sentimental Comedies)
        (In The London Stage, Vol. 3)
        (In Restoration Comedy, Vol. 4)
     Damon and Phillida
        (In A Collection of the Most Esteemed Farces ..., Vol. 5)
     Flora; or, Hob in the Well
        (In A Collection of the Most Esteemed Farces ..., Vol. 4)
     The History of King Richard III, based on the work of Shake-
        speare
        (In Five Restoration Adaptations of Shakespeare)

The Lady's Last Stake: or, The Wife's Resentment
  (In Colley Cibber: Three Sentimental Comedies)
Love Makes a Man
  (In The London Stage, Vol. 3)
Love's Last Shift, or, The Fool in Fashion
  (In Colley Cibber: Three Sentimental Comedies)
  (In Plays of the Restoration and 18th Century)
  (In Restoration Comedy, Vol. 3)
She Would and She Would Not
  (In The London Stage, Vol. 3)
The Non-juror, adapted from Molière's "Tartuffe"
  (In Plays from Molière)
The Provoked Husband (see Vanbrugh, Sir John)
Cicero, Marcus Tullius, 106-43 B. C.
  *Catiline (see Voltaire)
Cicilia & Clorinda; or, Love in Arms (see Killigrew, Thomas)
Cid, El, Campeador, 1043-1099
  *The Cid (see Corneille, Pierre)
  *Le Cid (see Corneille, Pierre)
CID PEREZ, José, 1906-
  Hombres de los Mundos
    (In Teatro Cubano Contemporaneo)
Le Ciel et la Merde (see Arrabal, Fernando)
Le Ciel et l'Enfer (see Mérimée, Prosper)
La Cigale Chez Fourmis (see Labiche, Eugene)
A Cigarra e a Formiga (see Almeida, Lyad de)
Le Cimetiére des Voitures (see Arrabal, Fernando)
La Cina e Vincina (see Bellocchio, Marco)
Cinema of the Year Zero (see Hauptman, Ira)
Cinna, Lucius Cornelius, d. 84 B. C.
  *Cinna (see Corneille, Pierre)
  *Cinna; text in French (see Corneille, Pierre)
Cinq-Mars, Marquis de (Henri Coiffier de Ruze), 1620-1642
  *Marion de Lorme (see Hugo, Victor)
La Cinquantaine (see Moinaux, Georges)
Cinque (see Melfi, Leonard)
Circe o El Amor (see Belaval, Emilio S.)
The Circle (see Maugham, William Somerset)
El Circo (see Menen Desleal, Alvaro)
Le Circuit (see Feydeau, Georges)
Circus Lady (see Miller, Jason)
A Circus Story (see Salacrou, Armand)
Cisco Pike; screenplay (see Norton, Bill L.)
Les Ciseauz d'Anastasie (see Kraemer, Jacques)
CISNEROS, José Antonio
  Diego el Mulato
    (In Teatro Méxicano del Siglo XIX, Vol. 1)
The Cit Turned Gentleman (see Molière, Jean Baptiste)
La Cita en Senlis (see Anouilh, Jean)
La Cité du Soleil (see Petresco, Julia)
Cities in Bezique: The Owl Answers and A Beast Story (see Kennedy, Adrienne)
The Citizen (see Murphy, Arthur)

The Citizens of Calais (see Nicol, Eric)
Citta Aperta; filmscript (see Rossellini, Roberto)
The City (see Fitch, Clyde)
The City Heiress; or, Sir Timothy Treat-All (see Behn, Mrs. Aphra)
The City Madam (see Massinger, Philip)
City on the Edge of Forever; television script (see Ellison, Harlan)
City Politicks (see Crowne, John)
City Sugar (see Poliakoff, Stephen)
The City Wit; or, The Woman Wears the Breeches (see Brome, Richard)
The City Without Love (see Ustinov, Lev)
Una Ciudad Para Vivir (see Retes, Ignacio)
CIXOUS, Helene
    Portrait of Dora
        (In Gambit, Vol. 8, no. 30, 1977)
CLAIR, Rene, 1898-
    The Italian Straw Hat; direction and scenario by Rene Clair, from the play by Eugene Labiche
        (In Masterworks of the French Cinema)
The Clandestine Marriage (see Colman, George)
La Claque (see Roussin, André)
Claracilla (see Killigrew, Thomas)
Clara's Ole Man (see Bullins, Edward A.)
CLARK, John Pepper, 1935-
    The Masquerade
        (In his Three Plays)
    Ozidi
        (An Oxford Three Crowns Book, 1966)
    The Raft
        (In his Three Plays)
    Song of a Goat
        (In his Three Plays)
    The Song of a Goat; excerpt
        (In African English Literature)
CLARK, Sylvia
    How to Train a Dog; a radio monologue
        (In On the Air: 15 Plays for Broadcast)
    Rosie at the Train; a radio monologue
        (In On the Air: 15 Plays for Broadcast)
CLARKE, Austin, 1896-
    As the Crow Flies
        (In his Collected Plays)
    Black Fast
        (In his Collected Plays)
    The Flame
        (In his Collected Plays)
    The Kiss
        (In his Collected Plays)
    The Moment Next to Nothing
        (In his Collected Plays)
    The Plot Is Ready
        (In his Collected Plays)
    The Plot Succeeds

(In his Collected Plays)
The Second Kiss
(In his Collected Plays)
Sister Eucharia
(In his Collected Plays)
The Son of Learning
(In his Collected Plays)
The Viscount of Blarney
(In his Collected Plays)
Classical Therapy or A Week Under the Influence ... (see Foreman,
  Richard)
Claude (see Ould, Hermon)
CLAUDEL, Paul, 1868-1955
  Agamemnon (see Aeschylus)
  L'Annonce Faite a Marie
    (In his Théâtre II)
  Les Choéphores (see Aeschylus)
  L'Echange
    (In his Théâtre I)
  L'Endormie
    (In his Théâtre I)
  Les Euménides (see Aeschylus)
  La Femme et Son Ombre
    (In his Théâtre II)
  L'Histoire de Todie et de Sara
    (In his Théâtre II)
  L'Homme et Son Désir
    (In his Théâtre II)
  Jeanne d'Arc au Bûcher
    (In his Théâtre II)
  Le Jet de Pierre
    (In his Théâtre II)
  La Jeune Fille Violaine
    (In his Théâtre I)
  Le Livre de Christophe Colomb
    (In his Théâtre II)
  La Lune a la Recherche d'Elle-même
    (In his Théâtre II)
  La Nuit de Noël 1914
    (In his Théâtre II)
  L'Otage
    (In his Théâtre II)
  L'Ours et la Lune
    (In his Théâtre II)
  Le Pain Dur
    (In his Théâtre II)
  La Parabole du Festin
    (In his Théâtre II)
  Partage de Midi
    (In his Théâtre I)
  Le Pere Humillié
    (In his Théâtre II)
  Protée

    (In his Théâtre II)
La Ravissement de Scapin
    (In his Théâtre II)
Le Repos du Septième Jour
    (In his Théâtre I)
La Sagesse; ou, La Parabole du Festin
    (In his Théâtre II)
Le Soulier de Satin
    (In his Théâtre II)
Sous le Rempart d'Athénes
    (In his Théâtre II)
Tête d'Or
    (In his Théâtre I)
Tobias and Sara (L'Histoire de Tobie et de Sara)
    (In Port-Royal)
La Ville
    (In his Théâtre I)
Claudius (see Kaiser, Georg)
CLAUS, Hugo, 1929-
Una Novia en la Mañana
    (In Teatro Flamenco Contemporaneo)
CLAVEL, Maurice, 1920-
Les Incendiaires
    (In Le Théâtre d'Aujourd'hui)
La Terrasse de Midi
    (In Le Théâtre d'Aujourd'hui)
Claw (see Barker, Howard)
CLAY, Frederic
Ages Ago (see Gilbert, William S.)
Eyes and No Eyes (see Gilbert, William S.)
Happy Arcadia (see Gilbert, William S.)
No Cards (see Gilbert, William S.)
Our Island Home (see Gilbert, William S.)
A Sensational Novel (see Gilbert, William S.)
Clay, Henry, 1777-1852
*Daniel Webster (see Chevigny, Hector)
A Clean Kill (see Gilbert, Michael)
A Clear View of an Irish Mist (see Bradbury, Ray)
Clearway (see Welburn, Vivienne C.)
CLEARY, Beverly
Henry and Ribsy
    (In Readers Theatre Handbook)
Clemençeau, Georges, French Premier, 1841-1929
*Wilson (see Greanias, George)
CLEMENS, Samuel Langhorne, 1835-1910
Colonel Sellers as a Scientist (see Howells, William Dean)
The Diaries of Adam and Eve; by Mark Twain, pseud.
    (In Readers Theatre Handbook)
CLEMENT, Rene, 1913-
La Diga Sul Pacifico
    (In Dal Soggetto al Film Series, no. 7, 1958)
Clementina (see Kelly, Hugh)
CLEMENTS, Colin Campbell, 1894-
Hot Lemonade (see Ryerson, Florence)

Love in a French Kitchen, by Colin Clements and John Monk
    Saunders
        (In One-Act Plays for Stage and Study, 4th Series)
    The Siege
        (In More One-Act Plays by Modern Authors)
    The Willow Plate (see Ryerson, Florence)
Clemo Uti - "The Water Lilies" (see Lardner, Ring)
Cleomenes III, King of Sparta, d. c. 219 B. C.
    *Cleomenes, The Spartan Heroe (see Dryden, John)
Cleopatra, Queen of Egypt, 69-30 B. C.
    *Antonio e Cléopâtra (see Alfieri, Vittorio)
    *Herod the King (see Munk, Kaj H.)
    *Pompee (see Corneille, Pierre)
    *Caesar and Cleopatra: a History (see Shaw, George Bernard)
    *La Mort de Pompee (The Death of Pompey) (see Corneille,
        Pierre)
Cleopatra Thea, Queen of Syria, d. 121 B. C.
    *Rodogune (see Corneille, Pierre)
Clerambard (see Ayme, Marcel)
CLERMONT, Rene
    Une Rose au Petit Dejeuner (see Barillet, Pierre)
Clever Gretel (see Grimm, Jakob L.)
Clevinger's Trial (see Heller, Joseph)
Un Client Serieux (see Moinaux, Georges)
Clifford, Rosamund "Fair Rosamund, " mistress of King Henry II,
        d. 1176?
    *Rosamond (see Swinburne, Algernon Charles)
    *Rosamund, Queen of the Lombards (see Swinburne, Algernon
        Charles)
A Climate of Fear (see Mercer, David)
The Climbers (see Fitch, Clyde)
CLINE, Edward, 1892-1961
    The Bank Dick (see Fields, W. C.)
The Clinic; radio script (see Key, Ted)
CLISHAM, Stephen
    The University Today, 1: The Rise of the University
        (In 100 Non-Royalty Radio Plays)
Clitandre (see Corneille, Pierre)
The Clock (see Robles, Emmanuel)
The Clockmaker from Cordova (see Carballido, Emilio)
Clope (see Pinget, Robert)
CLOQUEMIN, Paul
    The Lighthouse Keepers; a radio script, Sept. 12, 1938
        (In Best Broadcasts of 1938-39)
Close the Coalhouse Door (see Plater, Alan)
Closely Observed Trains; screenplay (see Menzel, Jiri)
The Closet (see Halman, Doris F.)
CLOSSON, Herman, 1901-
    Los Cuatro Aymon
        (In Teatro Belga Contemporaneo)
Clotilde en Su Casa (see Ibargüengoitia, Jorge)
Le Clou aux Maris (see Labiche, Eugene)
The Clouds (see Aristophanes)

CLOUZOT, Henri-Georges, 1907-
  Le Corbeau
    (In L'Avant-Scène Cinéma, no. 186, Apr. 15, 1977)
  The Wages of War; directed by Henri-Georges Clouzot, scenario
  and dialogue by Henri-Georges Clouzot and J. Geronimi
    (In Masterworks of the French Cinema)
I Clowns (see Fellini, Federico)
Le Club Champenois (see Labiche, Eugene)
The Clue of the Wrong Thing (see Sartoris, Ramón)
Coats (see Gregory, Isabella A.)
COBB, James, 1756-1818
  The First Floor
    (In The London Stage, Vol. 3)
  Paul and Virginia
    (In The London Stage, Vol. 4)
  The Siege of Belgrade
    (In The London Stage, Vol. 4)
Cobbler, Stick to Thy Last (see Hill, Kay)
The Cobbler's Den (see O'Brien, Seumas)
Cobweb Kings (see Davies, Mary Carolyn)
Cock-a-Doodle Dandy (see O'Casey, Sean)
Cockpit (see Boland, Bridget)
Cockroaches (see Witkiewicz, Stanislaw I.)
Cocktail Party (see Eliot, T. S.)
Coconut Folk-Singer (see Owens, Rochelle)
COCTEAU, Jean, 1889-1963
  Le Baron Fantome; d'aprés le conte de Mme. Leprince de
  Beaumont
    (In L'Avant-Scène du Cinéma, no. 138-139, July/Sept. 1973)
  La Belle et la Bête
    (In L'Avant-Scène du Cinéma, no. 138-139, July/Sept. 1973)
  La Machine Infernal
    (In The French Theater Since 1930)
  Les Maries de la Tour Eiffel; text in English
    (In New Directions, Vol. 2, 1937)
  Over the Wire
    (In Atlantic Harvest)
  Les Parents Terribles
    (In L'Avant-Scène Théâtre, no. 608, Apr. 15, 1977)
  The Wedding on the Eiffel Tower
    (In Modern French Theatre)
Coda (see Wymark, Olwen)
Cody, William Frederick "Buffalo Bill, " 1846-1917
  *Buffalo Bill and the Indians; or, Sitting Bull's History Lesson
  (see Rudolph, Alan)
  *Indians (see Kopit, Arthur K.)
COES, George H.
  Sublime and Ridiculous; a minstrel show
    (In Dramas from the American Theatre, 1762-1909
Coeur a Cuire (see Audiberti, Jacques)
COFFEE, Lenore
  Family Portrait, by Lenore Coffee and W. Joyce Cowan
    (In Plays of the Year, Vol. 1, 1948-49)

The Coffer (La Cassaria) (see Ariosto, Lodovico)
COFFEY, Charles, d. 1747
   The Boarding School
     (In A Collection of the Most Esteemed Farces ..., Vol. 5)
   The Devil to Pay; or, The Wives Metamorphosed
     (In A Collection of the Most Esteemed Farces ..., Vol. 2)
Coggerrers (see Carroll, Paul Vincent)
COGSWELL, T. R.
   Contact Point, by T. R. and G. R. Cogswell
     (In Six Science Fiction Plays)
COHAN, George Michael, 1878-1942
   The Farewell Case
     (In One-Act Plays for Stage and Study, 10th Series)
   Seven Keys to Baldpate, based on the novel by Earl Derr Biggers
     (In 10 Classic Mystery and Suspense Plays of the Modern
      Theatre)
Cohn of Arc (see Feiffer, Jules)
Cokain, Sir Aston (see Cokayne, Sir Aston)
COKAYNE, Sir Aston, bart., 1608-1684
   **Duke or No Duke; or, Trapolin's Vagaries (see Tate, Nahum)
   A Masque
     (In his Dramatic Works)
   The Obstinate Lady
     (In his Dramatic Works)
   The Tragedy of Ovid
     (In his Dramatic Works)
   Trappolin
     (In his Dramatic Works)
La Cola de la Sirena (see Nale Roxlo, Conrado)
La Colere (see Ionesco, Eugene)
Colickie Meg (see Smith, Sydney G.)
La Colina (see Gallegos, Daniel)
Collacocha (see Solari Swayne, Enrique)
Collect Your Hand Baggage (see Mortimer, John C.)
The Collection (see Pinter, Harold)
COLLIER, John, 1901-
   Milton's Paradise Lost. Screenplay for Cinema of the Mind
     (A Borzoi Book Screenplay, 1973)
COLLINS, Margaret
   Love Is a Daisy
     (In Theatre Wagon Plays)
   3 Filosofers in a Firetower
     (In Theatre Wagon Plays)
COLMAN, George, The Elder, 1732-1794
   The Clandestine Marriage, by George Colman and David Garrick
     (In British Plays from the Restoration to 1820, Vol. 2)
     (In The Drama, Vol. 15)
     (In Garrick's Dramatic Works, Vol. 3)
     (In The London Stage, Vol. 1)
     (In Plays of the Restoration and 18th Century)
   Comus (see Milton, John)
   The Deuce Is in Him
     (In A Collection of the Most Esteemed Farces ..., Vol. 1)

(In The London Stage, Vol. 3)
The Musical Lady
(In A Collection of the Most Esteemed Farces ..., Vol. 2)
Polly Honeycombe
(In A Collection of the Most Esteemed Farces ..., Vol. 3)
(In 18th Century Drama: Afterpieces)
COLMAN, George, The Younger, 1762-1836
The Iron Chest
(In 18th Century Tragedy)
John Bull; or, The Englishman's Fireside
(In English Plays of the 19th Century, Vol. III: Comedies)
Ways and Means
(In The London Stage, Vol. 4)
Colman & Guaire (see Gregory, Isabella A.)
Colombe (see Anouilh, Jean)
Colombe's Birthday (see Browning, Robert)
Colombyre; ou, Le Brasier de la Paix (see Marcel, Gabriel)
Colonel Sellers as a Scientist (see Howells, William Dean)
Colonel Wotherspoon (see Mavor, Osborne Henry)
The Colonial Dudes (see Duberman, Martin)
La Colonie (see Maribaux, Pierre C.)
El Color de Nuestra Piel (see Gorostiza, Celestino)
Colour the Flesh the Colour of Dust (see Cook, Michael)
Colours in the Dark (see Reaney, James)
COLQUHON, Donald
Jean
(In Scottish Repertory Plays Series, no. 7, 1914)
COLTON, John, 1889-1946
Rain, by John Colton and Clemence Randolph, founded on Wil-
liam Somerset Maugham's story "Miss Thompson."
(In 50 Best Plays of the American Theatre, Vol. 1)
COLUM, Padraic, 1881-
The Betrayal
(In One-Act Plays for Stage and Study, 3rd Series)
The Fiddler's House
(In his Three Plays)
The Land
(In his Three Plays)
Thomas Muskerry
(In Representative British Dramas)
(In his Three Plays)
Columbe (see Anouilh, Jean)
Columbus, Christopher, 1451-1506
*Christopher Columbus; a dramatic fairy tale in three scenes
(see Ghelderode, Michel de)
*Christopher Columbus (see Tucholsky, Kurt)
*Le Vivre de Christophe Colomb (see Claudel, Paul)
Com a Rainha e Assim (see Pongetti, Henrique)
Comanche Cafe (see Hauptman, William)
COMDEN, Betty, 1919-
Applause (see Strouse, Charles)
Wonderful Town (see Bernstein, Leonard)
Come and Be Killed (see Eveling, Stanley)

Come and Go: A Dramaticule (see Beckett, Samuel)
Come Back, Little Sheba (see Inge, William M.)
Come into the Garden Maude (see Coward, Noël)
Come Prima, Meglio di Prima (see Pirandello, Luigi)
Come to the Front (see Whiskin, Nigel)
Come Tu Mi Vuoi (see Pirandello, Luigi)
The Comeback (see Hanson, Meyer)
Comedia Armelina (see Rueda, Lope de)
Comedia del Viudo (see Vicente, Gill)
Comedia Eufemia (see Rueda, Lope de)
La Comedia Nueva (see Moratin, Leandro F.)
La Comédie sans Titre; ou, La Régénération (see Svevo, Italo)
Une Comedie sous le Gegne de Louis XV (see Musset, Alfred de)
Comedies of Family Life (see Witkiewicz, Stanislaw I.)
The Comicall Historie of Alphonsus, King of Aragon (see Greene,
    Robert)
Coming Through the Rye (see Saroyan, William)
Command Decision (see Haines, William W.)
Comme il Signor Mockinpott Fu Liberato Dai Suoi Tormenti (see
    Weiss, Peter)
COMMEDIA DELL' ARTE
    The Emperor of the Moon (see Behn, Mrs. Aphra)
    Peter's Banquet; or, The Criminal Son, by Dorimon and Villiers;
        three scenes
        (In The Theatre of Don Juan)
Comment Harponner le Requin (see Haim, Victor)
Comment les Chose Arrivent (see Danaud, Jean-Claude)
Le Commissaire est Bon Enfant (see Moinaux, Georges)
The Commissary (see Foote, Samuel)
The Commissioner (see Moinaux, Georges)
The Commissioner Has a Big Heart (see Moinaux, Georges)
La Commode de Victorine (see Labiche, Eugene)
Common Man (see Prelovsky, Anatoly)
La Communion Solennelle (see Arrabal, Fernando)
La Communion Solennelle (see Féret, René)
Como Se Llama Esta Flor? (see Rechani Agrait, Luis)
I Compagni (The Organizer); screenplay (see Monicelli, Mario)
Company (see Sondheim, Stephen)
A Competitive Examination for Charenton (see Daudet, Alphonse)
Los Complices (see Croiset, Max)
La Composition d'Histoire (see Mace, Jean)
COMPTON-BURNETT, Ivy
    A Family and a Fortune (see Mitchell, Julian)
Le Comte d'Essex (The Earl of Essex) (see Corneille, Thomas)
Comus (see Milton, John)
Con Gusto a Muerte (see Davila Vazquez, Jorge)
The Conceited Peddler (see Randolph, Thomas)
The Concert at Saint Ovide (see Buero Vallejo, Antonio)
Concert dans un Oeuf (see Arrabal, Fernando)
Concha, La Limpia (see Alvarez Quintero, Joaquin)
El Concierto de San Ovidio (see Buero Vallejo, Antonio)
Il Concilio d'Amore (see Panizza, Oscar)
The Condemned (see Dagerman, Stig)

The Condemned Man's Bicycle (see Arrabal, Fernando)
Condemned Squad (see Sastre, Alfonso)
El Condenado a Muerte (see Dagerman, Stig)
La Condesa Catalina (see Yeats, William Butler)
Conditions of Agreement (see Whiting, John)
El Condor sin Alas (see Luca de Tena, Juan I.)
CONE, Thomas
    Veils
        (In Performing Arts in Canada, Vol. 11, no. 1, Spring 1974)
The Confederacy (see Vanbrugh, Sir John)
Confessional (see Wilde, Percival)
Confessional (see Williams, Tennessee)
Confidences (see Lamartine, Alphonse)
La Congiura de' Pazzi (see Alfieri, Vittorio)
I Congiurati del Sud (see Doplicher, Fabio)
CONGREVE, William, 1670-1729
    The Double Dealer
        (In his Complete Plays)
        (In The London Stage, Vol. 4)
    Love for Love
        (In his Complete Plays)
        (In The London Stage, Vol. 3)
        (In Restoration Comedy, Vol. 3)
    The Mourning Bride
        (In his Complete Plays)
        (In The London Stage, Vol. 4)
    The Old Batchelour
        (In his Complete Plays)
    The Way of the World
        (In British Plays from the Restoration to 1820)
        (In his Complete Plays)
        (In The London Stage, Vol. 4)
        (In Plays of the Restoration and 18th Century)
        (In Restoration Comedy, Vol. 4)
La Conjuración de Venecia (see Martinez de la Rosa, Francisco)
CONKLE, Ellsworth Prouty, 1899-
    Chickadee
        (In One-Act Plays for Stage and Study, 9th Series)
    Incident at Eureka Bumps
        (In One-Act Plays for Stage and Study, 10th Series)
    Lavender Gloves
        (In Canada on Stage)
    Th' Feller from Omaha
        (In One-Act Plays for Stage and Study, 8th Series)
    Things Is That-a-Way
        (In One-Act Plays for Stage and Study, 4th Series)
CONN, Stewart
    The Aquarium
        (In his The Aquarium and Other Plays)
    The Burning
        (In Calder & Boyars Scottish Library Series, 1973)
    I Didn't Always Live Here
        (In his The Aquarium and Other Plays)

The Man in the Green Muffler
  (In his The Aquarium and Other Plays)
Connais-Toi (see Hervieu, Paul E.)
CONNELLY, Marcus Cook, 1890-
  Dulcy (see Kaufman, George S.)
  The Green Pastures, a fable, suggested by Roark Bradford's
    southern sketches, "Ol' Man Adam an' His Chillun."
    (In Famous Plays: Six Plays, 1930)
    (In 50 Best Plays of the American Theatre, Vol. 1)
    (In The Great American Parade)
    (In Representative American Dramas)
    (In 20th Century Plays)
The Conquest of Granada by the Spaniards (see Dryden, John)
La Conquista (see Ortiz Guerrero, Manuel)
La Conquista de México (see Valdez, Luis)
CONRAD, Joseph, 1857-1924
  Laughing Anne
    (In his Three Plays)
  One Day More
    (In his Three Plays)
  The Secret Agent
    (In his Three Plays)
CONRAD, Robert Taylor, 1810-1858
  Jack Cade, the Captain of the Commons
    (In Representative Plays by American Dramatists, Vol. 2)
Conscience (see Iffland, August W.)
The Conscious Lovers (see Steele, Sir Richard)
Conserto pour un Exil (see Ecare, Desire)
The Conspiracy of Charles Duke of Byron (see Chapman, George)
The Conspirators (see Carroll, Paul Vincent)
The Constant Couple; or, A Trip to the Jubilee (see Farquhar,
  George)
The Constant Lover (see Hankin, St. John)
The Constant Maid (see Shirley, James)
The Constant Prince (see Calderon de la Barca, Pedro)
The Constant Wife (see Maugham, William Somerset)
Constantine I, called "The Great," (Flavius Valerius Aurelius Con-
  stantinus), Roman emperor, 280?-337
  *Constantine the Great (see Lee, Nathaniel)
  *Maximian (see Corneille, Thomas)
Contact Point (see Cogswell, T. R.)
A Contention for Honor and Riches (see Shirley, James)
The Contention of Ajax and Ulysses for the Armour of Achilles
  (see Shirley, James)
Les Contes de la Lune Vague après le Pluie; screenplay (see
  Mizoguchi, Kenji)
Contigo Pan y Cebolla (see Gorostiza, Manuel Eduardo de)
The Contractor (see Storey, David)
The Contrast (see Tyler, Royall)
The Contrivances (see Carey, Henry)
A Conversation on the Highway (see Turgenev, Ivan S.)
Conversation Piece (see Coward, Noël)
Conversation Piece; screenplay (see Visconti, Luchino. Violence et
  Passion)

La Conversion d'Alceste (see Moinaux, Georges)
The Conversion of St. Paul (anon.)
    (In Medieval Church Music-Dramas)
Cook, Captain James, 1728-1779
    *Two Lonos (see Charlot, Jean)
COOK, Michael
    Colour the Flesh the Colour of Dust
        (In A Collection of Canadian Plays, Vol. 1)
    Jacob's Wake
        (In Talonplays Series, 1975)
The Cookie Jar (see Donahue, John Clark)
Coolus, Romain (pseud.) (see Weil, Rene)
The Cooper (see Arne, Thomas A.)
COOPER, James Fenimore, 1789-1851
    **Wept of the Wish-Ton-Wish, anonymous playscript from the
    novel by James Fenimore Cooper
        (In The Drama, Vol. 19)
COOPER, Merian C. , 1893-1973
    King Kong; screenplay (see Simple, Lorenzo, Jr.)
COOVER, Robert
    The Kid
        (In The Great American Life Show)
Cop-Out (see Guare, John Edward)
COPEAU, Jacques, 1879-1945
    The Little Poor Man (Le Petit Pauvre)
        (In Port-Royal)
Cophetua (see Drinkwater, John)
COPI (Raul Damonte), 1939-
    Eva Peron
        (In his Plays, Vol. 1)
    The Four Twins
        (In his Plays, Vol. 1)
    The Homosexual; or, The Difficulty of Expressing Oneself
        (In his Plays, Vol. 1)
    Loretta Strong
        (In his Plays, Vol. 1)
    L'Omosessuale o la Difficolta di Esprimersi
        (In Sipario, no. 315-316, Aug. /Sept. 1972)
Copperfaced Jack (see O'Donovan, John)
La Coquette de Village ou le Lot Suppose (see Dufresny, Charles R.)
The Coral (see Kaiser, Georg)
La Corbata (see Paso, Alfonso)
Le Corbeau; screenplay (see Clouzot, Henri-Georges)
Le Corbeau et la Grue (see Thomas, Robert)
Les Corbeaux (see Becque, Henri)
Corbett, James J. , 1866-1933
    *Gentleman Jim; scenario; text in French (see Walsh, Raoul)
Cordelia! (see Inclán, Federico S.)
Cordélia Brasíl (see Bivar, Antônio)
CORDERO C. , Gustavo
    Paralelo al Sueño
        (In Teatro Ecuatoriano Contemporaneo, Vol. 2)
Coriolanus (see Brecht, Bertolt)

Coriolanus (see Shakespeare, William)
The Corn Is Green (see Williams, Emlyn)
La Cornada (see Sastre, Alfonso)
CORNEILLE, Pierre, 1606-1684
    Agesilas; text in French
       (In his Théâtre Complet, Vol. 3)
    Andromede; text in French
       (In his Théâtre Complet, Vol. 2)
    Attila
       (In Moot Plays of Corneille)
    Attila; text in French
       (In his Théâtre Complet, Vol. 3)
    The Cid
       (In Chief Plays of Corneille)
       (In World Drama, Vol. 2)
    Le Cid; text in French
       (In his Théâtre Complet, Vol. 1)
    Cinna
       (In Chief Plays of Corneille)
    Cinna; text in French
       (In his Théâtre Complet, Vol. 1)
    Clitandre; text in French
       (In his Théâtre Complet, Vol. 1)
    *Corneille (see Hugo, Victor)
    Don Sanche d'Aragon; text in French
       (In his Théâtre Complet, Vol. 2)
    Don Sancho of Aragon (Don Sanche d'Aragon)
       (In Moot Plays of Corneille)
    La Galerie du Palais; text in French
       (In his Théâtre Complet, Vol. 1)
    Heraclius
       (In Moot Plays of Corneille)
    Heraclius; text in French
       (In his Théâtre Complet, Vol. 2)
    Horace (The Horatii)
       (In Chief Plays of Corneille)
    Horace; text in French
       (In his Théâtre Complet, Vol. 1)
    L'Illusion; text in French
       (In his Théâtre Complet, Vol. 1)
    Itie et Berenice; text in French
       (In his Théâtre Complet, Vol. 3)
    Médée; text in French
       (In his Théâtre Complet, Vol. 1)
    Melite; text in French
       (In his Théâtre Complet, Vol. 1)
    Le Menteur; text in French
       (In his Théâtre Complet, Vol. 2)
    La Morte de Pompee (The Death of Pompey)
       (In Moot Plays of Corneille)
    Nicomede (Nicomedes)
       (In Chief Plays of Corneille)
    Nicomède; text in French

(In his <u>Théâtre Complet</u>, VoL 2)
Oedipe; text in French
(In his <u>Théâtre Complet</u>, VoL 3)
Oedipus (see Dryden, John)
Othon (Otho)
(In <u>Moot Plays of Corneille</u>)
Othon; text in French
(In his <u>Théâtre Complet</u>, VoL 3)
Pertharite; text in French
(In his <u>Théâtre Complet</u>, VoL 2)
The Philosopher Duped by Love
(In <u>The Drama</u>, VoL 7)
La Place Royale; text in French
(In his <u>Théâtre Complet</u>, VoL 1)
Polyeucte
(In <u>Chief Plays of Corneille</u>)
Polyeucte; text in French
(In his <u>Théâtre Complet</u>, VoL 2)
Pompee; text in French
(In his <u>Théâtre Complet</u>, VoL 2)
Psyche (see Shadwell, Thomas)
Psyche; text in French
(In his <u>Théâtre Complet</u>, VoL 3)
Pulcheria
(In <u>Moot Plays of Corneille</u>)
Pulchérie; text in French
(In his <u>Théatre Complet</u>, VoL 3)
Rodogune
(In <u>Chief Plays of Corneille</u>)
Rodogune; text in French
(In his <u>Théâtre Complet</u>, VoL 2)
Sertorius
(In <u>Moot Plays of Corneille</u>)
Sertorius; text in French
(In his <u>Théâtre Complet</u>, VoL 3)
Sophonisbe; text in French
(In his <u>Théâtre Complet</u>, VoL 3)
La Suite du Menteur; text in French
(In his <u>Théâtre Complet</u>, VoL 2)
La Suivante; text in French
(In his <u>Théâtre Complet</u>, VoL 1)
Suréna; text in French
(In his <u>Théâtre Complet</u>, VoL 3)
Surenas
(In <u>Moot Plays of Corneille</u>)
Theodore, Vierge et Martyre; text in French
(In his <u>Théâtre Complet</u>, VoL 2)
La Toison d'Or; text in French
(In his <u>Théâtre Complet</u>, VoL 3)
La Veuve; text in French
(In his <u>Théâtre Complet</u>, VoL 1)
CORNEILLE, Thomas, 1625-1700
Ariane (Ariadne)

(In More Plays by Rivals of Corneille and Racine)
Le Comte d'Essex (The Earl of Essex)
  (In The Chief Rivals of Corneille and Racine)
Laodice
  (In The Chief Rivals of Corneille and Racine)
Maximian
  (In More Plays by Rivals of Corneille and Racine)
Timocrate (Timocrates)
  (In More Plays by Rivals of Corneille and Racine)
Corneille (see Hugo, Victor)
Cornelia (see Kyd, Thomas)
Cornelius (see Priestley, John B.)
The Corner (see Bullins, Ed)
Cornered (see Patrick, Robert)
CORNISH, Roger N.
 Open Twenty-Four Hours
  (In Contact with Drama)
  (In Themes of Drama)
Corona de Amor y Muerte (see Rodriguez Alvarez, Alejandro)
Corona de Fuego (see Usigli, Rudolfo)
Corona de Luz (see Usigli, Rudolfo)
Corona de Sombra (see Usigli, Rudolfo)
The Coronation (see Shirley, James)
The Coronation (see Beaumont, Francis)
Correggio (see Oehlenschläger, Adam G.)
Corrido de Pablo Damian (see Azar, Hector)
CORRIE, Joe
 Home Ain't So Sweet
  (In Best One-Act Plays of 1941, London)
 Nicodemus
  (In Best One-Act Plays of 1938, London)
 Old Verily
  (In The Best One-Act Plays of 1958-59, London)
Corrupcion en el Palacio de Justicia (see Betti, Ugo)
Le Corsaire (see Achard, Marcel)
The Corsican Brothers (see Boucicault, Dion)
The Corsican Brothers; a play with music in two acts (see Bowen,
 John)
The Corsican Lieutenant (see Housum, Robert)
CORSO, Gregory
 In This Hung-Up Age
  (In New Directions in Prose and Poetry, Vol. 18, 1964)
La Corte delle Stalle (see Kroetz, Franz Xaver)
Cortez, or Cortes, Hernando, 1485-1547
 *Corona de Fuego; tragedia antihistórica Americana (see Usigli,
  Rudolfo)
CORTEZ, Alfredo, 1880-1946
 "Rouge!"
  (In Teatro Portuges Contemporaneo)
I Cortometraggi; filmscript (see Antonioni, Michelangelo)
CORWIN, Norman Lewis, 1910-
 My Client, Curley, by Norman Corwin and Lucille Fletcher
  Herrmann; a radio script, Mar. 7, 1940

(In Best Broadcasts of 1939-40)
(In 10 Short Plays)
Seems Radio Is Here to Stay; radio script, Apr. 24, 1939
(In Best Broadcasts of 1938-39)
Cosas de Papá y Mamá (see Paso, Alfonso)
Las Cosas Simples (see Mendoza, Hector)
Cosi e (Se Vi Pare) (see Pirandello, Luigi)
Cosroès (Chosroes) (see Rotrou, Jean)
Cosroes (Chosroes) King of Persia (see Khosrau)
COSTA-GRAVAS, 1933-
State of Siege; screenplay (see Solinas, Franco)
COSTINE, Jacques
Le Prestige Mâle
(In L'Avant-Scène du Théâtre, no. 532, Jan. 1974)
COTTER, Joseph S., Sr., 1861-194?
Caleb the Degenerate
(In Black Theater U.S.A., 1847-1974)
COTTERELL, A. F.
Social Service; or, All Creatures Great and Small
(In Gambit, Vol. 4, no. 16)
Les Coulisses de l'Ame (see Evreinov, Nicolas)
COULTER, John
The Drums Are Out
(In Irish Drama Series, Vol. 6)
Counsellor-at-Law (see Rice, Elmer L.)
Counsellor Extraordinary (see Boston, Stewart)
Counsel's Opinion (see Pertwee, Roland)
Count Oederland (see Frisch, Max)
The Count of Narbonne (see Jepherson, Robert)
Count Your Bellings (see Jeans, Ronald)
A Counterfeit Presentment (see Howells, William Dean)
The Countess Cathleen (see Yeats, William Butler)
The Countess of Escarbagnas (see Molière, Jean Baptiste)
The Country Girl (see Odets, Clifford)
The Country House (see Vanbrugh, Sir John)
Country Music (see Smith, Michael Townsend)
The Country Wife (see Wycherley, William)
The Country Wit (see Crowne, John)
The Country Woman (see Turgenev, Ivan S.)
Le Coup d'Aile (see Curel, François)
Le Coup de Grace; un film (see Schlondorff, Volder)
Le Coup de l'Etrier (see Dubé, Marcel)
Courageous Princess (see Witkiewicz, Stanislaw I.)
La Course du Flambeau (see Hervieu, Paul Ernest)
The Court Begger (see Brome, Richard)
The Court Secret (see Shirley, James)
Courteline, Georges (pseud.) (see Moinaux, Georges)
The Courtesan (see Lenz, Jakob M.)
The Courting of Marie Jenvrin (see Ringwood, Gwen P.)
Courtois d'Arras; text in English (Anon.)
(In Medieval French Plays)
COUSIN, Gabriel
Black Opera
(In Calder & Boyars Playscripts Series, no. 35)

The Girl Who Barks Like a Dog
   (In Calder & Boyars Playscripts Series, no. 35)
Cousin, Cousine (see Tacchella, Jean-Charles)
La Cousin de Rose (see Renard, Jules)
Cousin Muriel (see Shaw, George Bernard)
COUSINS, James, 1874-1956
  The Sleep of the King
   (In Irish Drama Series, Vol. 8)
  The Sword of Dermot
   (In Irish Drama Series, Vol. 8)
COUSINS, Norman
  The Pursuit of Happiness; radio script (see Barnouw, Erik)
Le Couter des Generaux (see Vian, Boris)
The Covent-Garden Tragedy (see Fielding, Henry)
The Covetous Knight (see Pushkin, Aleksandr)
The Coward (see Lenormand, Henri R.)
COWARD, Noël Pierce, 1899-1973
  Ace of Clubs
   (In his Play Parade, Vol. 6)
  Bitter Sweet
   (In his Play Parade, Vol. 1)
  Blithe Spirit
   (In his Play Parade, Vol. 5)
  Brief Encounter (see Lean, David)
  Cavalcade
   (In his Play Parade, Vol. 1)
  Come into the Garden Maude
   (In his Suite in Three Keys)
  Conversation Piece
   (In his Play Parade, Vol. 2)
  Design for Living
   (In his Play Parade, Vol. 1)
   (In Six Plays)
  Easy Virtue
   (In his Play Parade, Vol. 2)
  Un Espiritu Burlon
   (In Teatro Ingles Contemporaneo)
  Fallen Angels
   (In his Play Parade, Vol. 2)
  Hay Fever
   (In his Play Parade, Vol. 1)
  Home Chat
   (In his Play Parade, Vol. 3)
  "I'll Leave It to You"
   (In his Play Parade, Vol. 3)
  Look After Lulu! Based on "Occupe-toi d'Amelie," by Georges
  Feydeau
   (In Heineman Drama Library, 1959)
  The Marquise
   (In his Play Parade, Vol. 3)
  Nude with Violin
   (In Heineman Drama Library, 1956)
   (In his Play Parade, Vol. 6)

Operette
    (In his Play Parade, Vol. 2)
Pacific 1860
    (In his Play Parade, Vol. 5)
"Peace in Our Time"
    (In his Play Parade, Vol. 5)
Point Valaine
    (In his Play Parade, Vol. 6)
Post-Mortem
    (In his Play Parade, Vol. 1)
Present Laughter
    (In his Play Parade, Vol. 4)
Private Lives
    (In his Play Parade, Vol. 1)
    (In 20th Century Plays)
Quadrille
    (In his Play Parade, Vol. 5)
The Queen Was in the Parlour
    (In his Play Parade, Vol. 3)
The Rat Trap
    (In his Play Parade, Vol. 3)
Relative Values
    (In Heineman Drama Library, 1952)
    (In his Play Parade, Vol. 5)
Shadows of the Evening
    (In his Suite in Three Keys)
Sirocco
    (In his Play Parade, Vol. 3)
A Song at Twilight
    (In Best Short Plays of the World Theatre, 1968-1973)
    (In his Suite in Three Keys)
South Sea Bubble
    (In Heineman Drama Library, 1956)
    (In his Play Parade, Vol. 6)
This Happy Breed
    (In his Play Parade, Vol. 4)
"This Was a Man"
    (In his Play Parade, Vol. 3)
This Year of Grace
    (In his Play Parade, Vol. 2)
Tonight at 8:30
    (In his Play Parade, Vol. 4)
The Vortex
    (In his Play Parade, Vol. 1)
Waiting in the Wings
    (In his Play Parade, Vol. 6)
Words and Music
    (In his Play Parade, Vol. 2)
The Young Idea
    (In his Play Parade, Vol. 3)
Cowboy Mouth (see Shepard, Samuel)
Cowboys #2 (see Shepard, Samuel)
COWLES, Albert
    The Killer

(In <u>Types of Modern Dramatic Composition</u>)
COWLEY, Mrs. Hannah (Parkhouse), 1743-1809
    The Belle's Stratagem
        (In <u>The Drama</u>, Vol. 15)
    A Bold Stroke for a Husband
        (In <u>The London Stage</u>, Vol. 3)
The Coxcomb (see Beaumont, Francis)
COYLE, McCarthy
    The Root
        (In <u>Playwrights for Tomorrow</u>, Vol. 12)
COYNE, Joseph Stirling, 1803-1868
    How to Settle Accounts with Your Laundress
        (In <u>English Plays of the 19th Century</u>, Vol. IV: Farces)
The Cozeners (see Foote, Samuel)
CRABBE, Kerry Lee
    The Last Romantic
        (In <u>Plays of the Year</u>, Vol. 45, 1976)
Crabdance (see Simons, Beverly)
The Cradle Song (see Martinez-Sierra, Gregorio)
The Cradle Will Rock (see Blitzstein, Marc)
Craig's Wife (see Kelly, George Edward)
CRAVEN, Frank, 1875-1945
    The Little Stranger
        (In <u>One-Act Plays for Stage and Study</u>, 10th Series)
CRAVEN, Margaret
  **I Heard the Owl Call My Name (see Di Pego, Gerald)
The Crawlers (see Edson, Russell)
The Crazy Locomotive (see Witkiewicz, Stanislaw I.)
The Crazy World of Advertising (see Hopkinson, Simon)
La Creación (see Arellano Guerra, Fausto E.)
CREAN, Robert
    My Father and My Mother
        (In <u>Great Television Plays</u>, Vol. 2)
La Creation du Monde et Autres Bisness (see Miller, Arthur)
CREBILLON, Prosper Jolyot de, 1674-1762
    Atree et Thyeste
        (In his <u>Théâtre Complet</u>)
        (In <u>Théâtre du XVIII Siécle</u>, Vol. 1)
    Catilina
        (In his <u>Théâtre Complet</u>)
    Electre
        (In his <u>Théâtre Complet</u>)
    Idomenee
        (In his <u>Théâtre Complet</u>)
  **The Orphan of China (see Murphy, Arthur)
    Pyrrhus
        (In his <u>Théâtre Complet</u>)
    Rhadamiste et Zenobie
        (In his <u>Théâtre Complet</u>)
        (In <u>Chief Rivals of Corneille and Racine</u>)
    Semiramis
        (In his <u>Théâtre Complet</u>)
    Le Triumvirat

(In his <u>Théâtre Complet</u>)
Xerxes
    (In his <u>Théâtre Complet</u>)
Creditors (see Strindberg, August)
CREGAN, David, 1931-
    The Dancers
        (In his <u>Transcending and The Dancers</u>)
    George Reborn
        (In his <u>The Land of the Palms & Other Plays</u>)
    The Houses by the Green
        (In <u>Methuen Playscripts</u>, 1969)
    If You Don't Laugh You Cry
        (In his <u>The Land of the Palms & Other Plays</u>)
    Jack in the Box
        (In his <u>The Land of the Palms & Other Plays</u>)
    The Land of the Palms
        (In his <u>The Land of the Palms & Other Plays</u>)
    Liebestraum
        (In his <u>The Land of the Palms & Other Plays</u>)
    Miniatures
        (In <u>Methuen Playscripts Series</u>, 1970)
    Poor Tom
        (In <u>Methuen's New Theatrescripts</u>, no. 5, 1976)
        (In his <u>Poor Tom/Tina</u>)
    The Problem
        (In his <u>The Land of the Palms & Other Plays</u>)
    Three Men for Colverton
        (In <u>Methuen Playscript Series</u>, 1967)
    Tina
        (In <u>Methuen's New Theatrescripts</u>, no. 5, 1976)
        (In his <u>Poor Tom/Tina</u>)
    Transcending
        (In his <u>Transcending and The Dancers</u>)
CRIADO, Eduardo
    Cuando las Nubes Cambian de Nariz
        (In <u>Teatro Español</u>, 1960-61)
O Crime de Cabra (see Pallottini, Renata)
The Crime in the Whistler Room (see Wilson, Edmund)
Crime on Goat Island (see Betti, Ugo)
O Crime Roubado (see Bethencourt, Joao)
El Crimen de Tintalia (see Ortiz Guerrero, Manuel)
Criminal de Guerra (see Calvo-Sotelo, Joaquin)
"A Criminosa, Grotesca, Sofrida e Sempre Gloriosa Caminhada de
    Alqui Caba la Silva em Busca da Grande Luz" (see Levi, Clovis)
The Crimson Island (see Bulgakov, Mikhail A.)
Cripple Play (see Richards, Max)
Cripure (see Guilloux, Louis)
Cris et Chuchotements; screenplay (see Bergman, Ingmar)
Crispin, Rival of His Master (see Le Sage, Alain-Rene)
Crispin Rival de Son Maître (see Le Sage, Alain-Rene)
Cristo Ha Matado (see Callegari, Gian Paolo)
The Critic (see Sheridan, Richard Brinsley)
La Critica de "La Mujer No Hace Milagros" (see Usigli, Rudolfo)

CROCKER, Bosworth, pseud.
    Josephine, by Bosworth Crocker, pseud. Real name, Mary
      Arnold (Crocker) Lewisohn, Mrs. Ludwig Lewisohn
      (In One-Act Plays for Stage and Study, 6th Series)
CROISET, Max
    Los Complices
      (In Teatro Neerlandes Contemporaneo)
Croisset, Francis de (pseud.) (see Wiener, Frantz)
CROMMELYNECK, Fernand, 1888-
    The Magnificent Cuckold
      (In Two Great Belgian Plays About Love)
Cromwell, Oliver, 1599-1658
    *Cromwell (see Storey, David)
Cromwell, Richard, 1626-1712
    *Cromwell (see Hugo, Victor)
    *Cromwell; text in French (see Hugo, Victor)
Cromwell, Thomas, Earl of Essex, 1485-1540
    *The Life and Death of Thomas, Lord Cromwell; anonymously
      written
      (In Disputed Plays of William Shakespeare)
Cronaca di un Amore; filmscript (see Antonioni, Michelangelo)
CROSS, James C., d. 1810?
    The Purse
      (In The London Stage, Vol. 4)
Cross Purpose (see Camus, Albert)
Cross Purposes (see O'Brien, William)
CROTHERS, Rachel, 1878-1958
    As Husbands Go
      (In 20th Century Plays)
    Expressing Willie
      (In her Three Plays, 1924)
    He and She
      (In Representative American Plays, 1792-1949)
    The Importance of Being a Woman
      (In her Six One-Act Plays)
    The Importance of Being Clothed
      (In her Six One-Act Plays)
    The Importance of Being Married
      (In her Six One-Act Plays)
    The Importance of Being Nice
      (In her Six One-Act Plays)
    A Little Journey
      (In her Three Plays, 1923)
    Mary the Third
      (In her Three Plays, 1923)
    Nice People
      (In Representative American Dramas)
      (In her Three Plays, 1924)
    "Old Lady 31"
      (In her Three Plays, 1923)
    Peggy
      (In her Six One-Act Plays)
      (In Types of Modern Dramatic Composition)

The Rector
    (In One-Act Plays for Stage and Study, 1st Series)
39 East
    (In her Three Plays, 1924)
What They Think
    (In her Six One-Act Plays)
CROUSE, Russel, 1893-1966
    Life with Father (see Lindsay, Howard)
    State of the Union (see Lindsay, Howard)
CROWLEY, Mart, 1935-
    The Boys in the Band
        (In Best American Plays, 7th Series, 1967-1973)
        (In Best Plays of the Sixties)
Crown Matrimonial (see Ryton, Royse)
Crown of Light (see Usigli, Rudolfo)
Crown of Shadows (see Usigli, Rudolfo)
CROWNE, John, 1640?-1712
    The Ambitious Statesman; or, The Loyal Favourite
        (In his Dramatic Works, Vol. 3)
    Caligula
        (In his Dramatic Works, Vol. 4)
    Calisto; or, The Chaste Nimph
        (In his Dramatic Works, Vol. 1)
    City Politicks
        (In his Dramatic Works, Vol. 2)
    The Country Wit
        (In his Dramatic Works, Vol. 3)
    Darius, King of Persia
        (In his Dramatic Works, Vol. 3)
    The Destruction of Jerusalem, pts. 1 & 2
        (In his Dramatic Works, Vol. 2)
    The Destruction of Jerusalem, pt. 2
        (In Five Heroic Plays)
    The English Friar; or, The Town Sparks
        (In his Dramatic Works, Vol. 4)
    The History of Charles the Eighth of France; or, The Invasion
        of Naples by the French
        (In his Dramatic Works, Vol. 1)
    Juliana; or, The Princess of Poland
        (In his Dramatic Works, Vol. 1)
    The Married Beau; or, The Curious Impertinent
        (In his Dramatic Works, Vol. 4)
    Regulus
        (In his Dramatic Works, Vol. 4)
    Sir Courtly Nice; or, It Cannot Be
        (In his Dramatic Works, Vol. 3)
        (In Restoration Comedy, Vol. 2)
Cruce de Vias (see Solórzano, Carlos)
La Cruche (see Moinaux, Georges)
The Crucible (see Miller, Arthur)
The Crucificado (see White, Edgar)
The Crucifixion (see Solórzano, Carlos)
Crudd Boys; radio script (see Fields, W. C.)

Crudele Intromissione (see Cagli, Bruno)
CRUDEN, Thomas
 Life of Hercules: Page One
  (In The Best One-Act Plays of 1958-59, London)
The Cruel Brother (see D'Avenant, Sir William)
'Cruiter (see Matheus, John)
Cruma (see Pedrolo, Manuel de)
Crumbs (see Kennedy, Charles Rann)
The Crumbs That Fall (see Hubbard, Philip)
Cry of the Cassowary (see Kaniku, John W.)
Cry on My Shoulders (see Parker, Kenneth T.)
Crystal and Fox (see Friel, Brian)
Cuando las Nubes Cambian de Nariz (see Criado, Eduardo)
La Cuadratura del Circulo (see Kataiev, Valentin P.)
CUARDA, Pablo Antonio, 1912-
 Por los Caminos Van los Campesinos
  (In El Teatro Hispanoamericano Contemporaneo, Vol. 2)
La Cuarterona (see Tapia y Rivera, Alejandro)
Los Cuatro Aymon (see Closson, Herman)
Cuatro Cuadras de Tierra (see Viana, Oduvaldo)
Cuauhtémoc, Aztec Emperor (see Guatemotzin)
Un Cuento de Hadas (see Arrivi, Francisco)
El Cuerpo (see Olmo, Lauro)
Cuestion de Narices (see Vilalta, Maruxa)
Cul-de-Sac (see Polanski, Roman)
CULLEN, Countee, 1903-1946
 St. Louis Woman (see Bontemps, Arna)
La Culta Dama (see Novo, Salvador)
CUMBERLAND, Richard, 1732-1811
 The Carmelite
  (In The London Stage, Vol. 4)
 False Impressions
  (In The London Stage, Vol. 4)
 The Fashionable Lover
  (In British Plays from the Restoration to 1820, Vol. 2)
 First Love
  (In The London Stage, Vol. 3)
 The Mysterious Husband
  (In The London Stage, Vol. 3)
 The West Indian
  (In Plays of the Restoration and 18th Century)
CUNEY-HARE, Maud
 Antar of Araby
  (In Plays and Pageants from the Life of the Negro)
CUNNINGHAM, Frank
 The Black Death
  (In 100 Non-Royalty Radio Plays)
 The Devil's Flower
  (In 100 Non-Royalty Radio Plays)
CUOMO, Franco, 1938-
 Caterina delle Misericordie
  (In Sipario, no. 308, Jan. 1972)
 Storia di Giovanna

(In Sipario, nos. 351-352, Aug./Sept. 1975)
The Cup (see Tennyson, Alfred Lord)
A Cup of Tea (see Parker, Kenneth T.)
The Cup of the Lip (see Musset, Alfred de)
Cupid and Death (see Shirley, James)
Cupid in Clapham (see Baker, Elizabeth)
Cupid's Revenge (see Beaumont, Francis)
El Curato en Que Se Vive (see Greene, Graham)
A Cure for a Cuckold (see Webster, John)
Cured (see Ehrlich, Mrs. Ida L.)
CUREL, François, vicomte de, 1854-1928
    L'Ame en Foile
      (In his Théâtre Complet, Vol. 5)
    Le Coup d'Aile
      (In his Théâtre Complet, Vol. 5)
    La Danse Devant le Miroir
      (In his Théâtre Complet, Vol. 1)
    L'Envers d'une Sainte
      (In his Théâtre Complet, Vol. 2)
    La Figurante
      (In his Théâtre Complet, Vol. 1)
    La Fille Sauvage
      (In his Théâtre Complet, Vol. 4)
    Les Fossiles
      (In his Théâtre Complet, Vol. 2)
    The Fossils
      (In Four Plays of the Free Theater)
    L'Invitée
      (In his Théâtre Complet, Vol. 3)
    La Nouvelle Idole
      (In his Théâtre Complet, Vol. 3)
    Le Repas du Lion
      (In his Théâtre Complet, Vol. 4)
The Curfew (see Tobin, John)
Un Curioso Accidente (see Goldoni, Carlo)
CURNIEU, Georges de, 1860-1917
    The Dupe, by Georges Ancey, pseud.
      (In Four Plays of the Free Theater)
CURNOW, Allen
    The Axe
      (In Four Plays)
    The Duke's Miracle, a play for radio from Browning's "My
      Last Duchess"
      (In Four Plays)
    The Overseas Expert
      (In Four Plays)
    Resident of Nowhere
      (In Four Plays)
CURRIMBHOY, Asif
    "Darjeeling Tea?"
      (In Asif Currimbhoy's Plays)
    The Doldrummers
      (In Asif Currimbhoy's Plays)

Goa
  (In Asif Currimbhoy's Plays)
Inquilab
  (In Asif Currimbhoy's Plays)
The Refugee
  (In Asif Currimbhoy's Plays)
Sonar Bangla
  (In Asif Currimbhoy's Plays)
Curtains (see Gonzales, Gloria)
CURTEIS, Ian
  Battle at Tematangi
    (In Playscript 54:   Long Voyage Out of War)
  The Gentle Invasion
    (In Playscript 54:   Long Voyage Out of War)
  The Last Enemy
    (In Playscript 54:   Long Voyage Out of War)
CURTIS, George Washington Parke, 1781-1857
  Pocahontas; or, The Settlers of Virginia
    (In Representative American Plays, 1792-1949)
CURTIZ, Michael, 1888-1962
  Casablanca; screenplay by Julius and Philip G. Epstein and
  Howard Koch from the play "Everybody Goes [sic.] to Rick's, "
  by Murray Burnett and Joan Alison, directed by Michael Curtiz.
  Pictures and complete dialogue edited by Richard J. Anobile
    (In The Film Classics Library, 1974)
  Casablanca; script by Julius J. Epstein, Philip G. Epstein and
  Howard Koch; film directed by Michael Curtis; based on the
  play "Everybody Comes to Rick's, " by Murray Burnett and
  Joan Alison
    (In Casablanca, Script and Legend)
Curve (see Dorst, Tankred)
The Custom of the Country (see Fletcher, John)
CUZZANI, Agustin, 1924-
  Sempronio
    (In El Teatro Hispanoamericano Contemporaneo, Vol. 1)
Cymbeline (see Garrick, David)
Cymbeline Refinished (see Shaw, George Bernard)
Cymon (see Garrick, David)
Cynthia's Revels (see Jonson, Ben)
Cyprian's Prayer (see Wilson, Edmund)
Cyrano de Bergerac (see Rostand, Edmond)
Cyrus, "The Great, " or "The Elder, " King of Persia, 600?-529
  B. C.
  *Cyrus (see Chénier, Marie-Joseph B.)

DA (see Leonard, Hugh)
DABADIE, Jean-Loup, 1938-
  Madame Marguerite (see Alhayde, Roberto)
DABRIL, Lucien
  De Zéro à Vingt, par Lucien Dabril et Leone Dietrich
    (In L'Avant-Scène Théâtre, no. 580, Feb. 1, 1976)
Daceapo (see Lopez, Sabatino)

DA COSTA, Bernard, 1942-
    Pourquoi le Robe d'Anna Ne Veut Pas Redescendre adaptation
    française de Bernard Da Costa
        (In L'Avant-Scène Théâtre, no. 549, Oct. 1, 1974)
DAGERMAN, Stig, 1923-
    The Condemned
        (In Scandinavian Plays of the 20th Century, Series 3)
    El Condenado a Muerte
        (In Teatro Sueco Contemporaneo)
Daggers and Diamonds (see Moseley, Katharine P.)
Dagobert, King of the Franks, fl. 628-639
    *Dagobert, King of the Franks (see Babo, Joseph M.)
Daisy Miller (see James, Henry)
La Dama Duende (see Calderon de la Barca, Pedro)
Damals (see Beckett, Samuel)
La Dame aux Camelias (see Dumas, Alexandre, Fils)
La Dame de Chez Maxim (see Feydeau, Georges)
La Dame de la Mer (see Ibsen, Henrik)
Damer's Gold (see Gregory, Isabella A.)
Les Dames du Bois de Boulogne; screenplay (see Bresson, Robert)
Les Dames du Jeudi (see Bellon, Loleh)
The Damiselle; or, The New Ordinary (see Brome, Richard)
The Damned (see Selbourne, David)
Damon and Phillida (see Cibber, Colley)
Dan Spiel Jenseits (see Brust, Alfred)
DANAUD, Jean-Claude
    Comment les Chose Arrivent
        (In L'Avant-Scène du Théâtre, no. 523, Aug. 1973)
    Dimanche
        (In L'Avant-Scène Théâtre, no. 553, Dec. 1, 1974)
    Les Observateurs
        (In L'Avant-Scène Théâtre, no. 602, Jan. 15, 1977)
    Un Ouvrage de Dames
        (In L'Avant-Scène Théâtre, no. 612, June 15, 1977)
The Dance of Death I and II (see Strindberg, August)
A Dance of the Forests (see Soyinka, Wole)
The Dancers (see Cregan, David)
The Dancing Bear (see Mavor, Osborne Henry)
DANCOURT, Florent Carton sieur, 1661-1725
    **Miss in Her Teens; or, The Medley of Lovers (see Garrick,
      David)
    Woman's Craze for Titles
        (In The Drama, Vol. 8)
Dandelion Wine (see Bradbury, Ray)
Dane, Clemence (pseud.) (see Ashton, Winifred)
DANEK, Oldřich, 1927-
    Der Krieg Bricht Nach der Pause Aus
        (In Theater der Zeit, no. 9, 1977)
Dangerous Corner (see Priestley, John B.)
Daniel Webster (see Chevigny, Hector)
Daniel Webster: Eighteen in America (see Stein, Gertrude)
The Danites in the Sierras (see Miller, Joaquin)
D'Annunzio, Gabriel (see Annunzio, Gabriel d')

La Danse Devant le Miroir (see Curel, François)
La Danza Que Sueña la Tortuga (see Carballido, Emilio)
Daphne and Amintor (see Bickerstaff, Isaac)
DA PONTE, Lorenzo, 1749-1838
    The Punished Libertine; or, Don Giovanni
        (In The Theatre of Don Juan)
D'ARCY, Margaretta
    The Island of the Mighty (see Arden, John)
DARION, Joe
    Man of La Mancha (see Leigh, Mitch)
Darius III, King of Persia, d. 330 B.C.
    *Darius, King of Persia (see Crowne, John)
"Darjeeling Tea?" (see Currimbhoy, Asif)
Dark Comet (see Totheroh, Dan)
Dark Harvest (see Ringwood, Gwen P.)
The Dark Lady of the Sonnets (see Shaw, George Bernard)
The Dark Moon and the Full; a chamber play (see Hart, Joseph)
Dark of the Moon (see Richardson, Howard)
The Dark Valley; radio script (see Auden, W. H.)
Darkness (see Casūle, Kole)
Darling; filmscript (see Raphael, Frederick)
The Darling of the Gods (see Belasco, David)
Darwin, Charles Robert, 1809-1882
    *Darwins Reise (see Loepelmann, Götz)
DAS, K., 1929-
    Lela Mayang, based on a translation by Adibah Amin of an ori-
        ginal television play by Y. A. M. Raja Ismail Iskandar
        (In New Drama One: Oxford in Asia Modern Authors)
DASSIN, Jules, 1912-
    La Legge
        (In Dal Soggette al Film Series, no. 11, 1959)
Dat's What's de Matter (see Poole, John F.)
DAUDET, Alphonse, 1840-1897
    Les Absents
        (In his Théâtre I)
    L'Arlesienne
        (In his Théâtre I)
    A Competitive Examination for Charenton
        (In his Works, Vol. 12)
    La Dernier Idole
        (In his Théâtre I)
    The Eight Mrs. Blue-Beards
        (In his Works, Vol. 12)
    La Frère Aine
        (In his Théâtre I)
    Fromont Jeune et Risler Aine
        (In his Théâtre IV)
    Jack
        (In his Théâtre III)
    Lise Tavernier
        (In his Théâtre IV)
    La Lutte pour la Vie
        (In his Théâtre II)

La Menteuse
    (In his Théâtre IV)
Le Nabab
    (In his Théâtre III)
The Nightingale of the Cemetery
    (In his Works, Vol. 12)
Numa Roumestan
    (In his Théâtre II)
L'Obstacle
    (In his Théâtre II)
L'Oeillet Blanc
    (In his Théâtre I)
La Petite Paroisse
    (In his Théâtre IV)
The Romance of Red-Riding-Hood
    (In his Works, Vol. 12)
Le Sacrifice
    (In his Théâtre I)
Sapho
    (In his Théâtre III)
The Souls of Paradise
    (In his Works, Vol. 12)
The Struggle for Life
    (In his Works, Vol. 15)
The Trumpet and the Trumpeter
    (In his Works, Vol. 12)
Der Dauerklavierspieler (see Laube, Horst)
The Daughter of Jorio (see Annunzio, Gabriel d')
DAUMAL, Rene, 1908-1944
En Ggarrrde!
    (In Modern French Theatre)
DAVALOS, Marcelino, 1871-1923
  Asi Pasan ...
    (In Teatro Méxicano del Siglo XX, Vol. 1)
Dave, (see Gregory, Isabella A.)
D'AVENANT, Sir William, 1608-1668
Albovine
    (In his Dramatic Works, Vol. 1)
Britannia Triumphans
    (In his Dramatic Works, Vol. 2)
The Cruel Brother
    (In his Dramatic Works, Vol. 1)
The Distress
    (In his Dramatic Works, Vol. 4)
Entertainment at Rutland House
    (In his Dramatic Works, Vol. 3)
The Fair Favourite
    (In his Dramatic Works, Vol. 4)
The Just Italian
    (In his Dramatic Works, Vol. 1)
The Law Against Lovers
    (In his Dramatic Works, Vol. 5)
Love and Honour

(In his Dramatic Works, Vol. 3)
Macbeth, adapted from the work of Shakespeare
    (In his Dramatic Works, Vol. 5)
    (In Five Restoration Adaptations of Shakespeare)
The Man's the Master
    (In his Dramatic Works, Vol. 5)
News from Plymouth
    (In his Dramatic Works, Vol. 4)
The Platonic Lovers
    (In his Dramatic Works, Vol. 2)
The Playhouse to Be Let
    (In his Dramatic Works, Vol. 4)
The Prince d'Amour
    (In his Dramatic Works, Vol. 1)
The Rivals
    (In his Dramatic Works, Vol. 5)
Salmacida Spolia
    (In his Dramatic Works, Vol. 2)
The Siege
    (In his Dramatic Works, Vol. 4)
The Siege of Rhodes
    (In his Dramatic Works, Vol. 3)
    (In Plays of the Restoration and 18th Century)
The Tempest; or, The Enchanted Island (see Dryden, John)
The Temple of Love
    (In his Dramatic Works, Vol. 1)
The Unfortunate Lovers
    (In his Dramatic Works, Vol. 3)
The Wits
    (In his Dramatic Works, Vol. 2)
    (In Six Caroline Plays)
DAVENPORT, Robert, fl. 1623
**The Amorous Prince (see Behn, Mrs. Aphra)
David, King of Judah & Israel, 1013?-973 B. C.
    *The Brief and Violent Reign of Absalom (see Pendleton, James
      D.)
    *King David and His Wives (see Pinski, David)
    *The Love of King David and Fair Bethsaba (see Peele, George)
    *The Procession of the Prophets (Anon.)
        (In Medieval Church Music-Dramas)
    *Saul (see Lamartine, Alphonse M.)
DAVID, Michael Robert
    The Justice Box
        (In Drama and Theatre, Vol. 11, no. 1, Fall 1972)
David and Broccoli; a play for television (see Mortimer, John C.)
David & Goliath (see Kaiser, Georg)
David Copperfield; screenplay (see Pulman, Jack)
David und Goliath (see Kaiser, Georg)
DAVIES, Mary Carolyn
    Cobweb Kings
        (In One-Act Plays for Stage and Study, 4th Series)
    Tables and Chairs
        (In One-Act Plays for Stage and Study, 5th Series)

DAVIES, William Robertson, 1913-
    At the Gates of the Righteous
        (In his Four Favourite Plays)
    Eros at Breakfast
        (In his Four Favourite Plays)
    Fortune, My Foe
        (In his Four Favourite Plays)
    General Confession
        (In his Hunting Stuart and Other Plays, New Drama 3, 1972)
    Hunting Stuart
        (In his Hunting Stuart and Other Plays, New Drama 3, 1972)
    King Phoenix
        (In his Hunting Stuart and Other Plays, New Drama 3, 1972)
    Overlaid
        (In Canada on Stage)
        (In Ten Canadian Short Plays)
    The Voice of the People
        (In his Four Favourite Plays)
DAVILA VAZQUEZ, Jorge
    Con Gusto a Muerte
        (In Teatro Ecuatoriano Contemporaneo, Vol. 2)
Daviot, Gordon (pseud.) (see Mackintosh, Elizabeth)
DAVIS, Donald, 1902-
    Knock Three Times
        (In One-Act Plays for Stage and Study, 7th Series)
DAVIS, Ossie, 1917-
    Purlie Victorious
        (In Black Theater)
        (In Cavalcade)
        (In Contemporary Black Drama)
DAVIS; Owen, 1874-1956
    The Detour
        (In Representative American Dramas)
    Ethan Frome, by Owen and Donald Davis
        (In 50 Best Plays of the American Theatre, Vol. 2)
DAVIS, Richard Harding, 1864-1916
    Peace Manoeuvres
        (In One-Act Plays for Stage and Study, 1st Series)
Davy Crockett; or, Be Sure You're Right, Then Go Ahead (see Murdoch, Frank)
Dawn (see Alurista)
The Dawn (see Verhaeren, Emile)
Dawn (see Wilde, Percival)
Dawn, Day, Night (see Niccodemi, Dario)
DAY, Frederic Lansing
    Heaven Is Deep
        (In Drama & Theatre, Vol. 12, no. 1, Fall 1974)
DAY, John, 1574-1640?
  **Abdelazer; or, The Moore's Revenge (see Behn, Mrs. Aphra)
The Day After the Fair (see Harvey, Frank)
Day for Night; filmscript (see Truffaut, François)
The Day I Drank the Glass of Water; radio script (see Fields, W. C.)
A Day in October (see Kaiser, Georg)

Day of Absence (see Ward, Douglas T.)
The Day of the Swallows (see Portillo, Estela)
The Day They All Came Back (see Finch, Robert V.)
Days Ahead (see Wilson, Lanford)
The Days of the Turbins (see Bulgakov, Mikhail A.)
Days to Come (see Hellman, Lillian)
Days Without End (see O'Neill, Eugene)
De la Jura del Principe (see Mira de Amescua, Antonio)
De la Mañana a la Medianoche (see Kaiser, Georg)
De l'Autre Côte du Mur (see Dubé, Marcel)
De Ninon (see Chénier, Marie-Joseph B.)
De Zero a Vingt (see Dabril, Lucien)
Dead (see Khaminwa, Charles)
The Dead Are Free (see Kreymborg, Alfred)
Dead Letter (see Pinget, Robert)
Dead on Nine (see Popplewell, Jack)
The Dead Poet (see Young, Stark)
The Dead Lover (see Pilon, Frederick)
DEAN, Phillip Hayes
    American Night Cry Trilogy
        (In his The Sty of the Blind Pig and Other Plays)
    Minstrel Boy, from the trilogy "American Night Cry"
        (In his The Sty of the Blind Pig and Other Plays)
    The Owl Killer
        (In Best Short Plays, 1974)
        (In Black Drama Anthology)
    The Sty of the Blind Pig
        (In his The Sty of the Blind Pig and Other Plays)
    This Bird of Dawning Singeth All Night Long, from the trilogy
        "American Night Cry"
        (In his The Sty of the Blind Pig and Other Plays)
    Thunder in the Night, from the trilogy "American Night Cry"
        (In his The Sty of the Blind Pig and Other Plays)
DeANDA, Peter
    Ladies in Waiting
        (In Black Drama Anthology)
DEANE, Hamilton
    Dracula, dramatized from Bram Stoker's novel, by Hamilton
        Deane and J. L. Balderston
        (In Best Mystery and Suspense Plays of the Modern Theatre)
Dear Antoine; or, The Love That Failed (see Anouilh, Jean)
Dear Brutus (see Barrie, Sir James M.)
Dear Charles (Les Enfants d'Edouard) (see Sauvajon, Marc-Gilbert)
Dear Daddy (see Cannan, Denis)
The Dear Departed (see Houghton, Stanley)
Death (see Fineberg, Larry)
Death and Devil (see Wedekind, Frank)
Death List (see Bullins, Ed)
Death of a Salesman (see Miller, Arthur)
The Death of Cuchulain (see Yeats, William Butler)
The Death of Doctor Faust (see Ghelderode, Michel de)
The Death of Ivan the Terrible (see Tolstoy, Alexey K.)
The Death of Mohammed (see Al Hakim, Tawfiq)

The Death of Odysseus (see Abel, Lionel)
The Death of Off-Broadway, a street play (see Eyen, Tom)
The Death of Tarelkin (see Sukhovo-Kobylin, Aleksandr V.)
The Death of Tintagiles (see Maeterlinck, Maurice)
The Death of Wallenstein (see Schiller, Johann C.)
Death Sends for the Doctor (see Heltai, Eugene)
The Death-Stone; a Nō drama (Anon.)
   (In The Drama, Vol. 3)
Death Thrust (see Sastre, Alfonso)
Death's Mistake: The Thirteenth Guest (see Khlebnikov, Velimir)
The Debauchees; or, The Jesuit Caught (see Fielding, Henry)
Debiera Haber Obispas (see Solana, Rafael)
DEBUSSY, Claude Achille, 1862-1918
   Pelléas et Mélisande, de Maurice Maeterlinck, musique de
   Claude Debussy
   (In L'Avant-Scène Opéra, no. 9, Mar./Apr. 1977)
The Debutante (see Fitzgerald, F. Scott)
DE CASALIS, Jeanne
   St. Helena (see Sherriff, Robert C.)
DECAUX, Alain
   Dumas le Magnifique
   (In L'Avant-Scène du Théâtre, no. 518, May 15, 1973)
Deceivers (see De Mille, William C.)
Decision for Freedom; NBC Radio documentary (see Greene, Robert
   S.)
Le Dedale (see Hervieu, Paul Ernest)
DEEVY, Teresa
   Katie Roche
   (In Famous Plays of 1935-36)
The Defeat: A Play About the Paris Commune (see Grieg, Nordahl)
The Defenders television script, "Blacklist" (see Kinoy, Ernest)
DEFRESNE, Augusto
   La Isla Desierta
   (In Teatro Neerlandes Contemporaneo)
DEICKE, Günther
   Meister Röchle; oper (see Werzlau, Joachim)
Deirdre (see Russell, George W.)
Deirdre (see Yeats, William Butler)
Deirdre of the Sorrows (see Synge, John M.)
Le Dejeuner Marocain (see Romaines, Jules)
DEKKER, Thomas, 1570?-1641
   **Abdelazer; or, The Moore's Revenge (see Behn, Mrs. Aphra)
   The Roaring Girl (see Middleton, Thomas)
DE LAURENTIIS, Dino, 1919-
   King Kong; screenplay (see Simple, Lorenzo, Jr.)
   Notti de Cabiria; screenplay (see Fellini, Federico)
   The Serpent's Egg; screenplay (see Bergman, Ingmar)
Del Dicho el Hecho (see Tamayo y Baus, Manuel)
DELANEY, Shelagh, 1939-
   The Lion in Love
   (In Evergreen Playscripts Series, 1961)
DELANO, Edith Bernard
   Grandma Pulls the String, by Edith Barnard Delano and David
   Carb

(In <u>Types of Modern Dramatic Composition</u>)
Delayed Glory (see Vining, Donald)
El Deleitoso (see Rueda, Lope de)
DELGADO BENAVENTE, Luis
    Media Hora Antés
        (In <u>Teatro Español</u>, 1955-56)
Delire a Deux (see Ionesco, Eugene)
Delisle de la Drevetiere (see La Drevetiere, Delisle de, Louis
    François)
The Deliverer (see Gregory, Isabella A.)
Della Notte (see Doplicher, Fabio)
De Lorme, Marion, 1611-1650?
    *Marion de Lorme (see Hugo, Victor)
DELSTON, Vernon
    Banting: Discoverer of Insulin, a drama of science
        (In <u>100 Non-Royalty Radio Plays</u>)
    Give Me Wings, Brother
        (In <u>100 Non-Royalty Radio Plays</u>)
    Three Strikes You're Out, a comedy-romance of a piano tuner
        (In <u>100 Non-Royalty Radio Plays</u>)
DELTEIL, Joseph, 1894-
    **Jésus II (see Liger, Christian)
Demain il Fera Jour (see Montherlant, Henry de)
La Demande (see Renard, Jules)
La Demarieuse (see Dupoyet, Pierrette)
Demetria (see Hillhouse, James A.)
Démétrios (see Romaines, Jules)
Demetrius I (Pseudo-Demetrius) Czar of Russia, 1581-1606
    *Demetrius; text in German (see Hebbel, Friedrich)
    *Demetrius; or, The Blood Wedding in Moscow (see Schiller,
        Johann C.)
    *Dimitrii the Impostor (see Sumarokov, Alexandr P.)
The Demi-Gods (see Stephens, James)
DE MILLE, William Churchill, 1878-1955
    Deceivers
        (In <u>One-Act Plays for Stage and Study</u>, 1st Series)
The Demi-Monde (see Dumas, Alexandre, Fils)
DEMPSTER, Curt
    Mimosa Pudica
        (In <u>Best Short Plays</u>, 1977)
Den Lille Hyrdedreng (see Oehlenschläger, Adam G.)
DENEVI, Marco, 1922-
    Romeo Before the Corpse of Juliet
        (In <u>The Orgy</u>)
    You Don't Have to Complicate Happiness
        (In <u>The Orgy</u>)
DENHAM, Reginald, 1894-
    Ladies in Retirement (see Smith, Edward P.)
Denise (see Dumas, Alexandre, Fils)
DENISON, Merrill
    Marsh Hay
        (In <u>A Collection of Canadian Plays</u>, Vol. 3)
DENNIS, Nigel, 1912-
    Cards of Identity

(In <u>Themes of Drama</u>)
Le Dénouement Imprevu (see Marivaux, Pierre C.)
La Dente Rouge (see Lenormand, Henri R.)
The Dentist (see Fields, W. C.)
Department of Interesting Authors: Struggle for an Unknown Cause
    (see Blank, Franklin)
The Departures (see Languirand, Jacques)
DE PRINS, Peter
    The Ear of Malchus
        (In <u>Gambit</u>, Vol. 4, no. 13)
DERBES, Claude
    The Last Refuge
        (In <u>One-Act Plays for Stage and Study</u>, 7th Series)
DERMAN, Lou
    Junior the Senior; television script for an episode in "Good
    Times, " by Lou Derman and Bill Davenport, and Lloyd Garver
    and Ken Hecht
        (In <u>Samuel French's Tandem Library Series</u>)
Le Dernier des Hommes; filmscript (see Mayer, Carl)
Le Dernier des Métiers (see Vian, Boris)
La Dernier Idole (see Daudet, Alphonse)
Le Dernier Nabab; screenplay (see Pinter, Harold)
Le Dernier Train (see Houweninge, Chiem van)
Les Derniers (see Gor'kii, Maksim)
Derricks on a Hill (see Whitehand, Robert)
La Derrota (see Grieg, Nordhal)
Dervorgilla (see Gregory, Isabella A.)
Des Souris et des Hommes (see Steinbeck, John)
Los Desarraigados (see Robles, J. Humberto)
La Desconocida de Arras (see Salacrou, Armand)
Desde Isabel, Con Amor (see Paso, Alfonso)
The Desert Island (see Murphy, Arthur)
Desert Rosso; screenplay (see Antonioni, Michelangelo)
The Desert Shall Rejoice; radio script (see Finch, Robert)
The Deserted Daughter (see Holcroft, Thomas)
The Deserter (see Dibdin, Charles)
Il Deserto Rosso (see Antonioni, Michelangelo)
DE SICA, Vittorio, 1901-
    La Riffa
        (In <u>Dal Soggetto al Film</u>, no. 22, 1962)
    Il Tetto
        (In <u>Dal Soggetto al Film</u>, no. 4, 1959)
Design for a Headstone (see Byrne, Seamus)
Design for Living (see Coward, Noël)
Desire Caught by the Tail (see Picasso, Pablo)
Desire Under the Elms (see O'Neill, Eugene)
DESLEAL, Alvaro Menen (Alvaro Menendez Leal), 1931-
    Black Light
        (In <u>Drama and Theatre</u>, Vol. 10, no. 2, Winter 1971/72)
        (In <u>The Orgy</u>)
DESNOS, Robert, 1900-1945
    La Place de l'Etoile
        (In <u>Modern French Theatre</u>)

(In <u>Modern International Drama</u>, Vol. 9, no. 1, Fall 1975)
DIAMOND, Dick
   Reedy River
     (In <u>Australian Theatre Workshop</u> no. 5, 1970)
DIAMOND, I. A. L.
   The Apartment; filmscript (see Wilder, Billy)
DIAMOND, Muni
   My Mother
     (In <u>100 Non-Royalty Radio Plays</u>)
Diamond Cut Diamond (see Murray, William Henry)
Diamond Cut Diamond (see Williamson, Hugh Ross)
Diana e la Tuda (see Pirandello, Luigi)
Diana Está Comunicando (see Lopez Rubio, José)
Diane de Lys (see Dumas, Alexandre, Fils)
The Diaries of Adam and Eve (see Clemens, Samuel Langhorne)
The Diary of Anne Frank (see Goodrich, Frances)
Dias Gomes, Alfredo (see Gomes, Alfredo Dias)
DIAZ, Gregor, 1933-
   Los del Cuatro
     (In <u>Teatro Contemporaneo Hispanoamericano</u>, Vol. 1)
DIAZ, Jorge, 1930-
   El Cepillo de Dientes
     (In <u>Teatro Contemporaneo Chileno</u>)
   The Eve of the Execution; or, Genesis Was Tomorrow
     (In <u>The Orgy</u>)
DIAZ DUFOO, Carlos, 1861-1941
   Padre Mercader
     (In <u>Teatro Méxicano del Siglo XX</u>, Vol. 1)
DIBDIN, Charles, The Elder, 1745-1814
   The Deserter
     (In <u>A Collection of the Most Esteemed Farces ...</u>, Vol. 4)
   The Ephesian Matron (see Bickerstaff, Isaac)
   He Wou'd If he Cou'd; or, An Old Fool Worse than Any (see
     Bickerstaff, Isaac)
   The Recruiting Serjeant (see Bickerstaff, Isaac)
   The Romp (see Bickerstaff, Isaac)
   The Waterman
     (In <u>A Collection of the Most Esteemed Farces ...</u>, Vol. 6)
     (In <u>The London Stage</u>, Vol. 4)
DIBDIN, Charles, The Younger, 1768-1833
   The Farmer's Wife
     (In <u>The London Stage</u>, Vol. 4)
   My Spouse and I
     (In <u>The London Stage</u>, Vol. 4)
DIBDIN, Thomas Frognall, 1776-1847
   What Next?
     (In <u>The London Stage</u>, Vol. 4)
DICENTA, José Fernando
   La Jaula
     (In <u>Teatro Español</u>, 1972-73)
Dick and Jane (see Feiffer, Jules)
DICKENS, Charles, 1912-1870
  **A Christmas Carol (see Gaines, Frederick)

**David Copperfield; screenplay (see Pulman, Jack)
The Dickey Bird (see O'Higgins, Harvey)
Diderich the Terrible (see Holberg, Ludvig von)
DIDEROT, Denis, 1713-1783
**Le Paradoxe sur le Comédien (see Baillon, Jacques)
Dido, Queen of Carthage (see Marlowe, Christopher)
Didon Se Sacrifiant (see Jodelle, Etienne)
Diego el Mulato (see Cisneros, José A.)
DIETZ, Norman D.
    The Apple Bit; a Vaudeville for Two Players
        (In Fables & Vaudevilles & Plays)
    Deus Ex Machinist; a Play for Two Players
        (In Fables & Vaudevilles & Plays)
    Harry and the Angel; a Vaudeville for Two Players
        (In Fables & Vaudevilles & Plays)
    O to Be Living, O to Be Dying; Two Short Plays for Two
        Players
        (In Fables & Vaudevilles & Plays)
    Old Ymir's Clay Pot; a Fable for Three Players
        (In Fables & Vaudevilles & Plays)
    Tilly Tutweiler's Silly Trip to the Moon
        (In Fables & Vaudevilles & Plays)
Dieu est-il Devenu Fou? (see Arrabal, Fernando)
Dieu Tente par les Mathématiques (see Arrabal, Fernando)
DIEZ BARROSO, Victor Manuel, 1890-1930
    Vencente a Ti Mismo
        (In Teatro Méxicano del Siglo XX, Vol. 1)
The Difficult Hour (see Lagerkvist, Pär F.)
The Difficult Man (see Hofmannsthal, Hugo von H.)
Diff'rent (see O'Neill, Eugene)
La Dificil Esperanza (see Bonnin Armstrong, Ana I.)
La Diga Sul Pacifico; screenplay (see Clement, Rene)
DIGHTON, John
    The Happiest Days of Your Life
        (In Plays of the Year, Vol. 1, 1948-49)
Dimanche (see Danaud, Jean-Claude)
Dimitrii the Impostor (see Sumarokov, Aleksandr P.)
Dina (see Oehlenschläger, Adam G.)
Le Dindon (see Feydeau, Georges)
Diner au Champagne (see Millaud, Fernand)
Dingo (see Wood, Charles)
DINNER, William
    The Late Edwina Black, written by William Dinner and William
        Morum
        (In Plays of the Year, Vol. 2, 1949)
Dinner at Eight (see Kaufman, George S.)
Dinner Bridge (see Lardner, Ring)
Dinner for Two (see Hughes, Glenn)
Dinner Party (see Sarossy, Via)
Dinner with the Family (see Anouilh, Jean)
Dino (see Rose, Reginald)
Diocletian, Gaius Aurelius Valerius Diocletian, Emperor of Rome,
    245-313
    *Saint Genest (Saint Genesius)

Diogenes, 412?-323 B. C.
   *Das Gespräch Alexandri Magni mit dem Philosoph Diogeni
      (In his Werke in Zwei Bänden, VoL 2)
DION, Jean-François, 1948-
   Les Machins de l'Existence
      (In L'Avant-Scène du Cinéma, no. 141, Nov. 1973)
Dione (see Gay, John)
Dios, Batidillo y la Mujer (see Usigli, Rudolfo)
Dios Te Salve! (see Bellan, José P.)
DIOSDADO, Ana
   El Ikapi
      (In Teatro Español, 1972-73)
   Olivada los Tambores
      (In Teatro Español, 1970-71)
   Usted También Podra Disfrutar de Ella
      (In Teatro Español, 1973-74)
DI PEGO, Gerald
   I Heard the Owl Call My Name, based on the book by Margaret
      Craven
         (In Great Television Plays, VoL 2)
Dique Seco (see Asturias, Miguel A.)
Le Directeur de l'Opéra (see Anouilh, Jean)
Director of the Opera (see Annouilh, Jean)
Diritti dell'Anima (see Giacosa, Giuseppe)
Dirty Hands (see Sartre, Jean-Paul)
Dirty Hearts (see Sanchez, Sonia)
Dirty Linen (see Stoppard, Tom)
Dis (see Howard, Roger)
Discourse on Vietnam (see Weiss, Peter)
Disengaged (see James, Henry)
The Dispensary (see Gregory, Isabella A.)
The Dispossessed (see John, Errol)
Dispossessed (see Ravel, Aviva)
La Dispute (see Marivaux, Pierre C.)
The Distracted State (see Tatham, John)
The Distress (see D'Avenant, Sir William)
The Distress'd Wife (fragment) (see Gay, John)
The Distrest Mother (see Philips, Ambrose)
The Distrest Mother (see Racine, Jean)
District of Columbia (see Richards, Stanley)
Le Divertissement Posthume (see Marcel, Gabriel)
Divinas Palabras (see Valle-Inclan, Ramón del)
Divine Comedy (see Dodson, Owen)
Divine Comedy; three choruses from a verse drama (see Dodson,
   Owen)
The Divine Tragedy (see Longfellow, Henry Wadsworth)
Divine Words (see Valle-Inclan, Ramón M.)
El Divino Impaciente (see Peman, José M.)
DIZENZO, Charles
   Big Mother
      (In Big Mother and Other Plays)
   The Drapes Come
      (In Off-Broadway Plays, VoL 1)

An Evening for Merlin Finch
    (In Big Mother and Other Plays)
    (In Off-Broadway Plays, Vol. 1)
The Last Straw
    (In Big Mother and Other Plays)
Do Not Go Gentle into That Good Night; television script (see Mandel,
    Loring)
Do Not Pass Go (see Nolte, Charles M.)
Do You Like Me? Say You Like Me (see Rizzo, Frank)
Doc; screenplay (see Hamill, Pete)
Doce y Una, Trece (see Garcia Ponce, Juan)
The Dock Brief (see Mortimer, John C.)
The Doctor and the Devil (see Thomas, Dylan)
Dr. Fausto Da Silva (see Pontes, Paulo)
Doctor Faustus (see Marlowe, Christopher)
The Doctor in Spite of Himself (see Molière, Jean Baptiste)
The Doctor in Spite of Himself (see also The Forced Physician)
Dr. Jekyll and Mr. Hyde; screenplay (see Mamoulian, Rouben)
Dr. Judas (see Calvet, Aldo)
Dr. Kheal (see Fornes, Maria I.)
Dr. Korczak and the Children (see Sylvanus, Erwin)
Dr. Last in His Chariot (see Bickerstaff, Isaac)
Doctor W. C. Fields; radio script (see Fields, W. C.)
Doctor Zhivago; screenplay (see Bolt, Robert)
Doctor's Delight (see Molière, Jean Baptiste)
The Doctor's Dilemma (see Shaw, George Bernard)
The Doctor's Duty (see Pirandello, Luigi)
Documents: The Dear Queen (see Ganly, Andrew)
Dodesukaden; filmscript (see Kurosawa, Akira)
DODGSON, Charles Lutwidge, 1832-1898
    **Alice in Wonderland (see Manhattan Project Theatre Company)
    **Alice in Wonderland; radio script (see Wicker, Irene)
The Dodo Bird (see Fried, Emanuel)
DODSLEY, Robert, 1703-1764
    The Miller of Mansfield
        (In A Collection of the Most Esteemed Farces ..., Vol. 3)
        (In The London Stage, Vol. 4)
    The Toy-Shop
        (In A Collection of the Most Esteemed Farces ..., Vol. 3)
DODSON, Owen, 1914-
    Divine Comedy; three choruses from a verse drama
        (In Black Theater U.S.A., 1847-1974)
        (In Blackamerican Literature 1760-Present)
    Divine Comedy (selection)
        (In The Negro Caravan)
The Dog Beneath the Skin (see Auden, W.H.)
Dog Days (see Gray, Simon)
The Dog in the Manger (see Vega Carpio, Lope F.)
The Dogs of Salonika; texts in English and German (see Federspiel,
    Jürg)
Les Doigts dans la Tête; screenplay (see Doillon, Jacques)
DOILLON, Jacques
    Les Doigts dans la Tête

(In <u>L'Avant-Scène Cinéma,</u> no. 157, Apr. 1975)
Doing a Good One for the Red Man (see Medoff, Mark)
Dois Primos ... Do Outro Mundo (see Pongetti, Henrique)
Doit-on le Dire? (see Labiche, Eugene)
Der Doktor mit der Grossen Nasen (see Sachs, Hans)
La Dolce Vita (see Fellini, Federico)
The Doldrummers (see Currimbhoy, Asif)
A Doll's House (see Ibsen, Henrik)
Dolls No More (see Fratti, Mario)
Dolly Reforming Herself (see Jones, Henry Arthur)
Dolly's Little Bills (see Jones, Henry Arthur)
A Domestic Picture (see Ostrovskii, Alexandr N.)
The Dominant Sex (see Egan, Michael)
DOMINGOS, Anselmo
    Maria de Fé
        (In <u>Revista de Teatro,</u> no. 393, May/June 1973)
Domino Courts (see Hauptman, William)
Don Alvaro (see Rivas, Angel Perez)
Don Alvaro o La Fuerza del Sino (see Rivas, Angel Perez)
Don Bernard de Cabere (see Rotrou, Jean)
Don Carlos: A Dramatic History (see Schiller, Johann C.)
Don Cesar de Bazan (see Hugo, Victor)
Don Garcia of Navarre; or, The Jealous Prince (see Molière, Jean
    Baptiste)
Don Garzia (see Alfieri, Vittorio)
Don John; or, The Libertine (see Molière, Jean Baptiste)
Don Juan (see Brecht, Bertolt)
Don Juan (see Maraini, Dacia)
Don Juan; or, The Love of Geometry; Acts IV and V (see Frisch,
    Max)
Don Juan; Act II (see Montherlant, Henry de)
Don Juan and Don Pietro; or, The Dead Stone's Banquet. A puppet
    play from Augsburg (Anon.)
        (In <u>The Theatre of Don Juan</u>)
Don Juan and Faust (see Grabbe, Christian D.)
Don Juan in Hell (see Man and Superman)
Don Juan Kommt aus dem Krieg (see Horvath, Odön von)
Don Juan oder Die Lieber zur Geometrie (see Frisch, Max)
Don Juan; or, The Libertine (see Molière, Jean Baptiste)
Don Juan Tenorio (see Zorrilla y Moral, José)
Don Pietro Caruso (see Bracco, Roberto)
Don Quijote de Todo el Mundo (see Garcia Guerra, Ivan)
Don Quixote in England (see Fielding, Henry)
Don Sanche d'Aragon (see Corneille, Pierre)
Don Sancho of Aragon (Don Sanche d'Aragon) (see Corneille, Pierre)
Don Sebastian, King of Portugal (See Dryden, John)
Doña Beatriz (La Sin Ventura) (see Solórzano, Carlos)
Doña Clarines (see Alvarez Quintero, Serafin)
Doña Rosita la Soltera; o, El Lenguaje de las Flores (see Garcia
    Lorca, Federico)
Donadieu (see Hochwälder, Fritz)
DONAHUE, John Clark
    The Cookie Jar

(In his The Cookie Jar and Other Plays)
(In Minnesota Showcase: Four Plays, Minnesota Drama Edi-
     tions, no. 9)
How Could You?
     (In his The Cookie Jar and Other Plays)
Old Kieg of Malfi
     (In his The Cookie Jar and Other Plays)
DONAHUE, Patricia M.
     Up She Rises
     (In Best One-Act Plays of 1939, London)
DONATI, Paolo Luca
     Robinson, Venerdi e Domenica
     (In Sipario, no. 345, Feb. 1975)
La Doncella, el Marinero y el Estudiante (see Garcia Lorca,
     Federico)
Donde Vas, Alfonso XII? (see Luca de Tena, Juan I.)
Donde Vas, Triste de Ti? (see Luca de Tena, Juan I.)
DONDO, Mathurin
     The Miracle of Saint Martin
     (In One-Act Plays for Stage and Study, 4th Series)
DONEN, Stanley, 1924-
     Charade; screenplay (see Stone, Peter)
     Two for the Road; screenplay (see Raphael, Frederic)
The Donkey and the Stream (see Musset, Alfred de)
DONLEAVY, James Patrick, 1926-
     Fairy Tales of New York
     (In his Plays)
     The Ginger Man
     (In his Plays)
     The Saddest Summer of Samuel S
     (In his Plays)
     A Singular Man
     (In his Plays)
DONNAY, Maurice Charles, 1859-1945
     L'Affranchie
     (In his Théâtre, Vol. 2)
     Amants
     (In his Théâtre, Vol. 2)
     L'Autre Danger
     (In his Théâtre, Vol. 4)
     La Bascule
     (In his Théâtre, Vol. 3)
     La Douloureuse
     (In his Théâtre, Vol. 2)
     Education de Prince
     (In his Théâtre, Vol. 1)
     Eix!
     (In his Théâtre, Vol. 1)
     Folle Entreprise
     (In his Théâtre, Vol. 1)
     Georgette Lemeunier
     (In his Théâtre, Vol. 3)
     Lovers

(In Representative Continental Dramas)
Lysistrata
    (In his Théâtre, Vol. 1)
Le Retour de Jerusalem
    (In his Théâtre, Vol. 4)
Le Torrent
    (In his Théâtre, Vol. 3)
Don't Crush That Dwarf, Hand Me the Pliers (see The Firesign
    Theatre)
Don't Leave Me Alone (see Johnson, Wallace)
Don't Listen Ladies! (see Guitry, Sacha)
Don't Walk Around Stark Naked (see Feydeau, Georges)
Don't You Want to Be Free? (see Hughes, Langston)
Doomsday (see Unt, Mati)
Doomsday Circus (see Basshe, Emjo)
A Door Must Be Either Open or Shut (see Musset, Alfred de)
Doors That Slam; radio script (see Sievers, Wieder D.)
DOPLICHER, Fabio
    I Congiurati del Sud
       (In Sipario, no. 371, Apr. 1977)
    Della Notte
       (In Sipario, no. 357, Feb. 1976)
Dopo Haggerty (see Mercer, David)
Dopo una Giornata di Lavoro Chiunque Può Essere Brutale (see
    Xardo, Franco)
Dorabella (see Selbourne, David)
DORALL, Edward, 1936-
    The Hour of the Dog
       (In New Drama Two: Oxford in Asia Modern Authors)
    A Tiger Is Loose in Our Community
       (In New Drama One: Oxford in Asia Modern Authors)
Dorimon and Villiers (see Commedia dell'Arte)
DORIN, Françoise
    L'Autre Valse
       (In L'Avant-Scène Théâtre, no. 583, Mar. 15, 1976)
    Le Tournant
       (In L'Avant-Scène Théâtre, no. 555, Jan. 1, 1975)
Dormez, Je le Veux! (see Feydeau, Georges)
Die Dornfelds (see Kaiser, Georg)
DORSET, Thomas Sackville, 1st Earl of, 1536-1608
    Gorboduc; or, Ferrex and Porrex (see Norton, Thomas)
DORST, Tankred
    Auf dem Chimborazo
       (In Theater Heute, no. 3, Mar. 1975)
    Curve
       (In New Theatre in Europe, Vol. 3)
    Eiszeit
       (In Theater Heute, Vol. 14, no. 5, May 1973)
    Freedom for Clemens
       (In Postwar German Theatre)
Dos Brasas (see Eighelbaum, Samuel)
Las Dos Caras del Patroncito (see Valdez, Luis)
Dos Mujeres a las Nueve (see Luca de Tena, Juan I.)

Dos Ranchos; or, The Purification (see Williams, Tennessee)
Dostigaeff and the Others (see Gor'kii, Maksim)
DOSTOEVSKII, Fedor Mikhailovich, 1821-1881
  **The Idiot; screenplay (see Kurosawa, Akira)
  **Le Notti Bianche; screenplay (see Visconti, Luchino)
  **The Possessed (see Camus, Albert)
  **La Sconosciuta (see Blok, Aleksàndr)
  **Subject to Fits (see Montgomery, Robert)
  *Une Tortue Nommée Dostoievsky (see Arrabal, Fernando)
  **The Wedding Feast (see Wesker, Arnold)
The Double Dealer (see Congreve, William)
The Double Dutch Act; a vaudeville skit
     (In The Disinherited: Plays)
La Double Expertise (see Marcel, Gabriel)
Double Identity (see Parker, Kenneth T.)
La Double Inconstance (see Marivaux, Pierre C.)
Double Infidelity (see Marivaux, Pierre C.)
The Double Marriage (see Fletcher, John)
Double Solitaire (see Anderson, Robert)
The Double Wop Act; a vaudeville skit
     (In The Disinherited: Plays)
Double Yolk (see Williams, Hugh)
The Doubtful Heir (see Shirley, James)
Douglas (see Home, John)
DOUGLAS, James, 1929-
    The Ice Goddess
      (In 7 Irish Plays)
DOUGLAS, Marian (Mrs. Annie Douglas G. Robinson)
  **Old Gentleman Gay (see Benton, Rita)
Douglass, Frederick, 1817?-1895
  *In Splendid Error (see Branch, William)
La Douloureuse (see Donnay, Maurice C.)
Il Dovere del Medico (see Pirandello, Luigi)
DOVZHENKO, Oleksandr Petrovych, 1894-1956
    Earth
      (In Lorrimer Screenplay Series, 1973)
      (In Two Russian Film Classics)
Dowling, Jennette (see Letton, Jennette Dowling)
DOWN, Oliphant, 1885-1917
    The Idealist
      (In One-Act Plays for Stage and Study, 2nd Series)
    The Maker of Dreams
      (In One-Act Plays by Modern Authors)
    Wealth and Wisdom
      (In One-Act Plays for Stage and Study, 1st Series)
Down and Out (see Gor'kii, Maksim)
Down by the Sea (see Baker, George Melville)
Down on the Farm (see Brown, Ivor)
Down Our Street (see Wise, Ernest G.)
DOWNEY, Robert, 1936-
    Chafed Elbows; screenplay, written, directed and produced by
    Robert Downey
      (A Lancer Books Screenplay, 1967)

DOWNING, Henry Francis, 1861-1925?
  Lord Eldred's Other Daughter
    (In Early Black American Prose)
DOWSON, Ernest Christopher, 1867-1900
    The Pierrot of the Present
      (In On the High Road)
    The Pierrot of the Minute
      (In One-Act Plays by Modern Authors)
DOYLE, Sir Arthur Conan, 1859-1930
    **The Great Speckled Band; a radio script (see Hardwick, Michael)
    **Sherlock Holmes (see Gillette, William H.)
Dracula (see Deane, Hamilton)
Dracula: Sabbat (see Katz, Leon)
The Drag (see Welburn, Vivienne C.)
DRAGHI, Giovanni Battista, 17th Century
    Psyche (see Shadwell, Thomas)
The Dragon (see Gregory, Isabella A.)
The Dragon and the Dove (see Mavor, Osborne Henry)
Dragon of Wantley (see Carey, Henry)
DRAGUN, Oswaldo, 1929-
    Historia del Hombre Que Se Convirtio en Perro
      (In Teatro Breve Hispanoamericano Contemporaneo)
    The Story of Panchito Gonzalez
      (In The Orgy)
    The Story of the Man Who Turned into a Dog
      (In The Orgy)
The Drama Class (see Aldis, Mrs. Mary Reynolds)
A Drama de Copas e o Rei de Cuba (see Wehbi, Timochenco)
Un Drama Nuevo (see Tamayo y Baus, Manuel)
The Drapes Come (see Dizenzo, Charles)
DRAYTON, Ronald
    Nocturne on the Rhine
      (In Black Fire)
    Notes from a Savage God
      (In Black Fire)
The Dreaded Batter Pudding Hurler (of Bexhill-on-Sea) (see Milligan,
    Spike)
A Dream (see Zimmerman, Armand L.)
The Dream Doctor (see Lenormand, Henri R.)
Dream Girl (see Rice, Elmer L.)
A Dream in Winter (see Thomas, Dylan)
A Dream of a Türk (see Turkish Theatre. Meddah)
A Dream of Love (see Williams, William Carlos)
The Dream of Scipio (see Metastasio, Pietro A.)
The Dream of Vasavadatta (see Bhasa)
Dream on Monkey Mountain (see Walcott, Derek)
The Dream Physician (see Martyrn, Edward)
A Dream Play (see Strindberg, August)
The Dream Weaver (see Buero Vallejo, Antonio)
The Dreaming Dust (see Johnston, Denis)
The Dreaming of the Bones (see Yeats, William Butler)
The Dreamlost (see Johnson, Robert E.) ·
The Dreamy Kid (see O'Neill, Eugene)

DREISER, Theodore, 1871-1945
  **An American Tragedy; scenario (see Eisenstein, Sergei M.)
LA DREVETIERE, Delisle de, Louis François, sieur de l'Isle,
    1682-1756
  Arlequin Sauvage
    (In Theatre de XVIII Siècle, Vol. 1)
DREXLER, Rosalyn, 1926-
  The Bed Was Full
    (In The Line of Least Existence and Other Plays)
  Home Movies
    (In The Line of Least Existence and Other Plays)
    (In The Off Off Broadway Book)
  Hot Buttered Roll
    (In her The Investigation and Hot Buttered Roll)
    (In The Line of Least Existence and Other Plays)
  The Investigation
    (In her The Investigation and Hot Buttered Roll)
    (In The Line of Least Existence and Other Plays)
  The Line of Least Existence
    (In The Line of Least Existence and Other Plays)
  Skywriting
    (In Collision Course)
  Softly, and Consider the Nearness
    (In The Line of Least Existence and Other Plays)
Dreyfus, Alfred, 1859-1935
  *Dreyfus (see Grumberg, Jean-Claude)
DRIEULA ROCHELLE, Pierre, 1893-1945
  **Le Feu Follet; filmscript (see Malle, Louis)
The Drinking Gourd (see Hansberry, Lorraine)
DRINKWATER, John, 1882-1937
  Abraham Lincoln
    (In his Collected Plays, Vol. 2)
  Cophetua
    (In his Collected Plays, Vol. 1)
  An English Medley
    (In his Collected Plays, Vol. 1)
  The God of Quiet
    (In his Collected Plays, Vol. 1)
  **The King's People; film sequence (see Shaw, George Bernard)
  Little Johnny
    (In his Collected Plays, Vol. 2)
  Mary Stuart
    (In his Collected Plays, Vol. 1)
  Oliver Cromwell
    (In his Collected Plays, Vol. 2)
  The Only Legend, a Masque of the Scarlet Pierrot
    (In his Collected Plays, Vol. 1)
  The Pied Piper, a Tale of Hamelin City
    (In his Collected Plays, Vol. 1)
  Rebellion
    (In his Collected Plays, Vol. 1)
  Robert E. Lee
    (In his Collected Plays, Vol. 2)

Robin Hood and the Pedlar
(In his Collected Plays, Vol. 1)
The Storm
(In his Collected Plays, Vol. 1)
X=0: A Night of the Trojan War
(In his Collected Plays, Vol. 1)
DRISCOLL, Louise
The Poor House
(In More One-Act Plays by Modern Authors)
DRIVER, Donald
Your Own Thing, a rock musical comedy by Donald Driver, Hal
Lester and Danny Apolinar, suggested by Shakespeare's
"Twelfth Night"
(In All the World's a Stage)
Le Droit aux Etrennes (see Moinaux, Georges)
Dronning Margareta (see Oehlenachläger, Adam G.)
Drug Store Sketch; radio script (see Fields, W. C.)
Drum Head; radio script (see Stevens, Thomas Wood)
DRUMMOND, Alexander Magnus, 1884-
Traffic Signals
(In One-Act Plays for Stage and Study, 6th Series)
The Drums Are Out (see Coulter, John)
Drums in the Night (see Brecht, Bertolt)
The Drums of Oude (see Strong, Austin)
The Drums of Snow (see Pinner, David)
The Drunkard (see Sedley, William H.)
The Drunkard; or, The Fallen Saved (see Smith, W. H.)
Drunken Angel; filmscript; text in Japanese and English (see Kuro-
sawa, Akira)
The Drunken Sisters (see Wilder, Thornton)
The Dry August (see Sebree, Charles)
DRYDEN, John, 1631-1700
Albion and Albanius
(In his Dramatic Works, Vol. 5)
All for Love; or, The World Well Lost, written in imitation of
Shakespeare's stile, "Antony and Cleopatra"
(In his Dramatic Works, Vol. 4)
(In Five Restoration Tragedies)
(In The London Stage, Vol. 3)
(In Plays of the Restoration and 18th Century)
Amboyna; or, The Cruelties of the Dutch
(In his Dramatic Works, Vol. 3)
Amphitryon; or, The Two Socias, with music by Henry Purcell,
based on the works of Plautus and Molière
(In his Dramatic Works, Vol. 6)
The Assignation; or, Love in a Nunnery
(In his Dramatic Works, Vol. 3)
Aureng-Zebe, based on François Bernier's "Histoire de la
Derniere Revolution des Etats du Grand Mogo!"
(In his Dramatic Works, Vol. 4)
(In Five Heroic Plays)
Cleomenes, The Spartan Heroe, by John Dryden, as completed
by Thomas Southerne, founded on Plutarch

(In his Dramatic Works, Vol. 6)
The Conquest of Granada by the Spaniards, pts. 1 & 2
    (In his Dramatic Works, Vol. 3)
**Cymon (see Garrick, David)
Don Sebastian, King of Portugal
    (In his Dramatic Works, Vol. 6)
The Duke of Guise, by John Dryden and Nathaniel Lee
    (In his Dramatic Works, Vol. 5)
    (In Lee's Works, Vol. 2)
An Evening's Love; or, The Mock Astrologer, based on Pedro
    Calderon's "El Astrologo Fingido"
    (In his Dramatic Works, Vol. 3)
The Indian Emperour; or, The Conquest of Mexico by the
    Spaniards, being the sequel to "The Indian Queen"
    (In his Dramatic Works, Vol. 1)
The Indian Queen, by John Dryden and Sir Robert Howard
    (In his Dramatic Works, Vol. 1)
    (In Plays of the Restoration and 18th Century)
The Kind Keeper; or, Mr. Limberham
    (In Restoration Comedy, Vol. 2)
King Arthur; or, The British Worthy, based on "Historiae
    Regum Britanniae," of Geoffrey Monmouth; with music by
    Henry Purcell
    (In his Dramatic Works, Vol. 6)
Limberham; or, The Kind Keeper
    (In his Dramatic Works, Vol. 4)
Love Triumphant; or, Nature Will Prevail
    (In his Dramatic Works, Vol. 6)
Marriage-a-la-mode
    (In his Dramatic Works, Vol. 3)
The Mistaken Husband
    (In his Dramatic Works, Vol. 4)
Oedipus, by John Dryden and Nathaniel Lee, based on the works
    of Sophocles, Seneca, and Corneille
    (In his Dramatic Works, Vol. 4)
    (In Lee's Works, Vol. 1)
The Rival Ladies
    (In his Dramatic Works, Vol. 1)
Secret Love; or, The Maiden Queen
    (In his Dramatic Works, Vol. 2)
The Secular Masque
    (In his Dramatic Works, Vol. 6)
Sir Martin Mar-all; or, The Feign'd Innocence, adapted from
    Molière's "L'Etourde" and "L'Amant Indiscret"
    (In his Dramatic Works, Vol. 2)
    (In Plays from Molière)
    (In Restoration Comedy, Vol. 1)
The Spanish Fryar; or, The Double Discovery
    (In British Plays from the Restoration to 1820)
    (In his Dramatic Works, Vol. 5)
The State of Innocence and Fall of Man
    (In his Dramatic Works, Vol. 3)
The Tempest; or, The Enchanted Island, adapted from Shake-
    speare by John Dryden and William D'Avenant

(In D'Avenant, Dramatic Works, Vol. 5)
(In his Dramatic Works, Vol. 2)
(In Five Restoration Adaptations of Shakespeare)
(In Shakespeare Adaptations)
Troilus and Cressida; or, Truth Found Too Late, based on the
work of Shakespeare
(In his Dramatic Works, Vol. 5)
The True Widow (see Shadwell, Thomas)
Tyrannick Love; or, The Royal Martyr
(In his Dramatic Works, Vol. 2)
The Wild Gallant
(In his Dramatic Works, Vol. 1)
DUARTE CLARK, Rodrigo
Brujerías
(In El Teatro de la Esperanza)
Du Barry, Jeanne Becu, comtesse, 1743-1793
*Du Barry (see Belasco, David)
DUBE, Marcel, 1930-
L'Aiguillage
(In his De L'Autre Côte du Mur Suivi de Cinq Courtes
Pièces)
Au Retour des Oies Blanches
(In Collection Théâtre Canadien, no. 10)
Avant de T'En Aller
(In Collection Théâtre Canadien, no. 10)
Les Beaux Dimanches
(In Collection Théâtre Canadien, no. 3, 1968)
Bilan
(In Collection Théâtre Canadien, no. 4, 1968)
La Cellule
(In Le Monde de Marcel Dubé, 2)
Le Coup de l'Etrier
(In Collection Théâtre Canadien, no. 17, 1970)
De L'Autre Côte du Mur
(In his De L'Autre Côte du Mur Suivi de Cinq Courtes
Pièces)
Entre Midi et Soir
(In Le Monde de Marcel Dubé, 1)
Florence
(In Collection Théâtre Canadien, no. 16, 1970)
Les Freres Ennemis
(In his De L'Autre Côte du Mur Suivi de Cinq Courtes
Pièces)
Manuel
(In Collection Les Beau Texts, Editions Lemeac, 1973)
Un Matin Comme les Autres
(In Collection Théâtre Canadien, no. 14, 1971)
Médée
(In Collection Théâtre Canadien, no. 27)
Le Naufrage
(In Collection Théâtre Canadien, no. 22, 1971)
Pauvre Amour
(In Collection Théâtre Canadien, no. 6, 1969)

Le Pere Ideal
   (In his De L'Autre Côte du Mur Suivi de Cinq Courtes
     Pièces)
Rendez-vous du Lendemain
   (In his De L'Autre Côte du Mur Suivi de Cinq Courtes
     Pièces)
Le Temps de Lilas
   (In Collection Théâtre Canadien, no. 7, 1969)
Le Visiteur
   (In his De L'Autre Côte du Mur Suivi de Cinq Courtes
     Pièces)
The White Geese
   (In New Drama 5 Series, 1972)
Zone
   (In Collection Théâtre Canadien, no. 1, 1968)
DUBERMAN, Martin, 1930-
   The Colonial Dudes
     (In The Best Short Plays 1973)
   Metaphors
     (In Collision Course)
DUBILLARD, Roland, 1923-
   The House of Bones
     (In Calder & Boyars Playscripts Series, no. 41)
   La Maison d'Os
     (In Le Théâtre d'Aujourd'hui)
   Naives Hirondelles
     (In Le Théâtre d'Aujourd'hui)
   The Swallows, translated by Barbara Wright
     (In Calder & Boyars Playscript Series no. 16)
DU BOIS, Theodore
   Exorcism for Now: A Ritual
     (In Break Out!)
DUBOURG, Augustus William, 1830-1910
   New Men and Old Acres (see Taylor, Tom)
The Duce Is in Him (see Colman, George, The Elder)
The Duchess of Malfi (see Brecht, Bertolt)
The Duchess of Padua (see Wilde, Oscar)
La Duchesse de Langeais (see Tremblay, Michel)
La Duchesse des Folies-Bergère (see Feydeau, Georges)
The Duck Variations (see Mamet, David)
Dudley, Robert, 1st Earl of Leicester, 1532?-1588
  *Amy Robsart (see Hugo, Victor)
  *Mary Stuart (see Schiller, Johann C.)
DUDLEY, Sir Henry Bate, bart. , 1745-1824
   The Rival Candidates
     (In A Collection of the Most Esteemed Farces ..., Vol. 4)
   The Woodman
     (In The London Stage, Vol. 4)
Le Due Frecce (see Volodin, Aleksandr)
Los Duendes (see Hernández, Luisa J.)
The Duenna (see Sheridan, Richard Brinsley)
DUER, Edward Rush
   John-a-Dreams

(In One-Act Plays for Stage and Study, 8th Series)
The Duke of Milan (see Massinger, Philip)
The Dumb Waiter (see Pinter, Harold)
DÜRRENMATT, Friedrich, 1921-
    Amleto Principe de Danimarca, di autore vari (see Brecht, Bertolt)
    Incident at Twilight
      (In Postwar German Theatre)
      (In Themes of Drama)
    The Meteor
      (In Cape Plays Series, 1973)
    Play Strindberg; the Dance of Death, choreographed by Dürrenmatt
      (In Evergreen Playscripts Series, 1973)
Duetto (see Burgess, Katherine S.)
DUFFET, Thomas, fl. 1678
    The Empress of Morocco, a Farce
      (In The Empress of Morocco & Its Critics)
      (In his Three Burlesque Plays)
    The Mock-Tempest
      (In his Three Burlesque Plays)
      (In Shakespeare Adaptations)
    Psyche Debauch'd
      (In his Three Burlesque Plays)
DUFFY, Maureen, 1933-
    Rites
      (In New Short Plays, Vol. 2)
      (In Plays By and About Women)
DUFRESNE, Guy, 1915-
    The Call of the Whippoorwill
      (In New Drama 6 Series, 1972)
DUFRESNY, Charles Riviere, 1648-1724
    La Coquette de Village ou Le Lot Suppose
      (In Théâtre du XVIII Siècle, Vol. 1)
DU HALDE, Jean Baptiste, 1674-1743
**The Orphan of China (see Murphy, Arthur)
DUHAMEL, Marcel, 1900-
    Des Souris et des Hommes; adaptation Marcel Duhamel
      (In L'Avant-Scène Théâtre, no. 589, June 15, 1976)
The Duke of Gandia (see Swinburne, Algernon Charles)
The Duke of Guise (see Dryden, John)
The Duke of Milan (see Massinger, Philip)
Duke or No Duke; or, Trapolin's Vagaries (see Tate, Nahum)
DUKES, Ashley, 1885-1959
    From Morn to Midnight; English version (see Kaiser, Georg)
    In Theatre Street (see Lenormand, Henri R.)
    The Machine-Wreckers; English version (see Toller, Ernst)
The Duke's Miracle; a play for radio (see Curnow, Allen)
The Duke's Mistress (see Shirley, James)
Dulcy (see Kaufman, George S.)
Dullin, Charles, 1885-1949
    *Baptism (see Tembeck, Robert)
DUMAS, Alexandre, Pere, 1802-1870
    The Corsican Brothers (see Bowen, John)

*Dumas le Magnifique (see Decaux, Alain)
DUMAS, Alexandre, Fils, 1824-1895
    L'Ami des Femmes
        (In his Théâtre Complet IV)
    Le Bijou de la Reine
        (In his Théâtre Complet I)
    Camille
        (In Camille and Other Plays)
    La Dame aux Camilias
        (In his Théâtre Complet I)
    The Demi-Monde
        (In World Drama, Vol. 2)
    Le Demi-monde; text in French
        (In his Théâtre Complet II)
    Denise
        (In his Théâtre Complet VII)
    Diane de Lys
        (In his Théâtre Complet I)
    L'Etranger
        (In his Théâtre Complet VI)
    La Femme de Claude
        (In his Théâtre Complet V)
    Le Fils Naturel
        (In his Théâtre Complet III)
    Francillon
        (In his Théâtre Complet VII)
    Les Ides de Madame Aubray
        (In his Théâtre Complet IV)
**Kean (see Sartre, Jean-Paul)
    The Lady of the Camellias
        (In Victorian Melodramas)
    Monsieur Alphonse
        (In his Théâtre Complet VI)
    La Pere Prodigue
        (In his Théâtre Complet III)
    La Princesse de Bagdad
        (In his Théâtre Complet VII)
    Le Princesse Georges
        (In his Théâtre Complet V)
    La Question d'Argent
        (In his Théâtre Complet II)
    Une Visite de Noces
        (In his Théâtre Complet V)
Dumas le Magnifique (see Decaux, Alain)
DUNBAR-NELSON, Alice, 1875-1935
    Mine Eyes Have Seen
        (In Black Theater U.S.A., 1847-1974)
DUNCAN, Ronald Frederick Henry, 1914-
    The Gift
        (In Best Short Plays of the World Theatre, 1968-1973)
        (In Gambit, Vol. 3, no. 11)
DUNCAN, Thelma Myrtle
    Sacrifice

DURHAM, Frank
    A Little More Than Kin
        (In One-Act Plays for Stage and Study, 10th Series)
DURSI, Massimo, 1902-
    Il Tumulto dei Ciompi
        (In Sipario, no. 318, Nov. 1972)
DU RYER, Pierre, c. 1600-1658
    Esther
        (In More Plays by Rivals of Corneille and Racine)
    Saul
        (In The Chief Rivals of Corneille and Racine)
    Scevole (Scaevola)
        (In The Chief Rivals of Corneille and Racine)
Dust in Your Eyes (see Labiche, Eugene)
The Dust of Suns (see Rousel, Raymond)
The Dutch Courtezan (see Marston, John)
The Dutch Lover (see Behn, Mrs. Aphra)
The Dutchesse of Malfy (see Webster, John)
The Dutchman (see Jones, LeRoi)
DUVERNOIS, Henri, 1875-1937
    The Bronze Lady and the Crystal Gentleman
        (In Modern One-Act Plays from the French)
DVORAK, Anton, 1841-1904
    Dvořàk's Song of the New World (see Schneideman, Rose)
The Dwarfs (see Pinter, Harold)
The Dweller in the Darkness (see Berkeley, Reginald)
DYAR, R. E.
    Horseshoe Luck
        (In Prize Plays of 1927-28, Vol. 2)
The Dybbuk (Between Two Worlds) (see Rappoport, Schloyme Z.)
DYER, Charles
    Staircase
        (In Evergreen Playscript Series, 1966)
The Dying Wife (see Taylor, Laurette)
Dynamo (see O'Neill, Eugene)

Each in His Own Way (see Pinero, Sir Arthur Wing)
The Eagle and the Serpent (see Fuentes, Ernesto)
The Ear of Malchus (see De Prins, Peter)
The Earl of Essex (see Jones, Henry)
The Earl of Warwick (see Francklin, Thomas)
Early Morning (see Bond, Edward)
Early Spring; filmscript (excerpt) (see Ozu, Yasujiro)
Earp, Wyatt, 1848-1929
    *Doc; screenplay (see Hamill, Pete)
    *Frontier Fighters, a historical adventure (see Berlin, Nathan)
E'Arrivato Pietro Gori (see Castri, Massimo)
Earth (see Dovzhenko, Oleksandr P.)
Earth Spirit (see Wedekind, Frank)
Earthquake (see Fox, George)
The Easiest Way (see Walter, Eugene)
East (see Berkoff, Steven)

East of Eden (see Morley, Christopher)
East of Eden; screenplay (see Kazan, Elia. A l'Est d'Eden; text in French)
East of Suez (see Maugham, William Somerset)
East Side/West Side television script Who Do You Kill? (see Perl, Arnold)
East-West: A Dialogue in Suzdal (see Amalrik, Andrei)
Easter (see Strindberg, August)
The Easter Egg (see Reaney, James C.)
EASTMAN, Charles
    The All-American Boy; screenplay for the film written and directed by Charles Eastman
        (A Noonday Original Screenplay, 1973)
EASTMAN, Fred, 1886-
    Bread
        (In The Play Book)
EASTON, William Edgar
    Dessalines; a dramatic tale, a single chapter from Haiti's history
        (In Early Black American Prose)
Eastward Ho (see Chapman, George)
Easy Money (see Ostrovskii, Alexandr N.)
Easy Virtue (see Coward, Noël)
Eat Cake! (see Van Itallie, Jean-Claude)
EATON, Walter Prichard, 1878-1957
    Grandma--Old Style
        (In One-Act Plays for Stage and Study, 7th Series)
    Period House
        (In One-Act Plays for Stage and Study, 10th Series)
    The Purple Door Knob
        (In One-Act Plays for Stage and Study, 8th Series)
Les Eaux de Merlin (see Lesage, Alian-Rene)
EBB, Fred, 1932-
    Cabaret (see Kander, John)
Eboli, Princesa de (Ana de Mendoza), Mistress of King Philip II of Spain, 1540-1592
    *Don Carlos: A Dramatic History (see Schiller, Johann C.)
ECARE, Desire
    Conserto pour un Exil
        (In L'Avant-Scène du Cinéma, no. 134, Mar. 1973)
The Eccentricities of a Nightingale (see Williams, Tennessee)
The Ecclesiazusae; or, Women in Council (see Aristophanes)
L'Echange (see Claudel, Paul)
ECHEVERRIA LORIA, Arturo, 1909-1966
    La Espera
        (In Obras Breves del Teatro Costarricense, Vol. 1)
Die Echten Sedemunds (see Barlach, Ernst)
ECKART, Dietrich, 1868-1923
    Der Erbgraf
        (In his Eight Plays)
    Familienväter
        (In his Eight Plays)
    Froschkönig

(In his Eight Plays)
Heinrich der Hohenstaufe
    (In his Eight Plays)
Ein Kerl, der Spekuliert
    (In his Eight Plays)
Der Kleine Zacharias
    (In his Eight Plays)
Lorenzaccio
    (In his Eight Plays)
Peer Gynt (see Ibsen, Henrik)
L'Eclisse; filmscript (see Antonioni, Michelangelo)
Eco-man (see San Francisco Mime Troup)
L'Ecole des Amants (see Lesage, Alain-Rene)
L'Ecole des Manages (see Balzac, Honoré de)
L'Ecole des Meres (see Marivaux, Pierre C.)
L'Ecole des Peres (see Anouilh, Jean)
The Ecstasy of Rita Joe (see Ryga, George)
The Eddie Doll Case; radio script (see Lord, Phillips H.)
The Eddying Ford (see Richards, Ivor A.)
Eden End (see Priestley, John B.)
EDGAR, David
    Destiny
        (In Methuen's New Theatrescripts, no. 3, 1976)
    Wreckers; with music by the 7:84 Company Band
        (In Methuen's New Theatrescripts, no. 6, 1977)
Edgar and Emmeline (see Hawkesworth, John)
The Edgar Bergen Show; CBS radio comedy (see Rose, Si)
Edgard et sa Bonne (see Labiche, Eugene)
Edipo (see Peman, José M.)
The Editor (see Bjørnson, Bjørnstjerne)
EDMONDS, Randolph, 1900-
    Bad Man
        (In Black Theater U.S.A., 1847-1974)
        (In The Negro Caravan)
        (In his Six Plays for a Negro Theatre)
    Bleeding Hearts
        (In his Six Plays for a Negro Theatre)
    Breeders
        (In his Six Plays for a Negro Theatre)
    Nat Turner
        (In The New Negro Renaissance)
        (In his Six Plays for a Negro Theatre)
    The New Window
        (In his Six Plays for a Negro Theatre)
    Old Man Pete
        (In his Six Plays for a Negro Theatre)
Edouard et Agrippine (see Obaldia, Rene de)
EDSON, Russell
    The Children
        (In Falling Sickness: A Book of Plays)
    The Crawlers
        (In Falling Sickness: A Book of Plays)
        (In New Directions in Prose and Poetry, Vol. 26, 1973)

The Falling Sickness
   (In Falling Sickness: A Book of Plays)
Ketchup
   (In New Directions in Prose and Poetry, Vol. 23, 1971)
Education de Prince (see Donnay, Maurice C.)
The Education of Skinny Spew (see Brenton, Howard)
EDWARD, H. F. V. , 1898-1973
   Job Hunters
      (In Black Theater U. S. A. , 1847-1974)
Edward, called the Confessor, King of England, 1002-1066
   *Harold (see Tennyson, Alfred Lord)
Edward the Black Prince, 1330-1376
   *Edward the Black Prince; or, The Battle of Poictiers
      (In The London Stage, Vol. 4)
Edward I, King of England, 1239-1307
   *The Chronicle of King Edward I (see Peele, George)
Edward II, King of England, 1284-1327
   *Edward the Second (see Marlowe, Christopher)
   *The Life of Edward II of England (see Brecht, Bertolt)
Edward III, King of England, 1327-1377
   *King Edward the Third (Anon.)
      (In Disputed Plays of William Shakespeare)
Edward IV, King of England, 1442-1483
   *King Edward the Fourth; the first and second parts (see Heywook,
      Thomas)
Edward V, King of England, 1470-1483
   *George A. Green, the Pinner of Wakefield (see Greene, Robert)
Edward VIII, King of Great Britain & Ireland, Duke of Windsor,
      1894-1972
   *Crown Matrimonial (see Ryton, Royse)
Edward and Agrippina (see Obaldia, Rene de)
EDWARDS, Sherman
   1776; music and lyrics by Sherman Edwards, book by Peter
      Stone, based on a conception of Sherman Edwards
      (In Best American Plays, 7th Series, 1967-1973)
      (In Ten Great Musicals of the American Theatre)
The Effect of Gamma Rays on Man-in-the-Moon Marigolds (see Zin-
   del, Paul)
EGAN, Michael
   The Dominant Sex
      (In Famous Plays of 1934-35)
   To Love and to Cherish
      (In Famous Plays of 1938-39)
Egelykke (see Munk, Jaj)
EGERTON, Lady Alix
   The Masque of the Two Strangers
      (In One-Act Plays by Modern Authors)
Egloga de la Natividad (see López de Yanguas, Hernán)
Egmont, Lamoral, Comte d', Prince of Gaure, 1522-1568
   *Egmont (see Goethe, Johann Wolfgang von)
Egotist and Pseudo-Critic (see Kotzebue, August F.)
Eh? (see Livings, Henry)
Ehe der Hahn Kraht (see Bukovcan, Ivan)

Ehrengericht (see Ignatow, Rangel)
EHRLICHT, Mrs. Ida Lublenski, 1886-
    Changing Places
        (In One-Act Plays for Stage and Study, 3rd Series)
    Cured
        (In One-Act Plays for Stage and Study, 4th Series)
EICHELBAUM, Samuel, 1894-
    Dos Brasas
        (In Teatro Argentino Contemporaneo)
EIDAM, Klaus
    Reise mit Joujou; musikalische komödie (see Hanell, Robert)
8 e $\frac{1}{2}$ (see Fellini, Federico)
The Eight Mrs. Blue-Beards (see Daudet, Alphonse)
1810 (see Rodriguez, Yamandu)
1837: The Farmer's Revolt (see Salutin, Rick)
Ein Bauspiel (see Brust, Alfred)
Ein Dorf Ohne Männer (see Horvath, Odön von)
Ein Mann Wird Jünger (see Svevo, Italo)
Der Einsame Weg (see Schnitzler, Arthur)
Einstein, Albert, 1879-1955
    *Einstein (see Michel, Karl)
Eirete (see Ortiz Guerrero, Manuel)
EISENSTEIN, Sergei Mikailovitch, 1898-1948
    Alexander Nevsky
        (In Lorrimer Screenplay Series, 1974)
        (In his Three Films)
    An American Tragedy; scenario for the uncompleted film, based
      upon the novel by Theodore Dreiser
        (In With Eisenstein in Hollywood)
    Battleship Potemkin
        (In Lorrimer Screenplay Series, 1974)
        (In his Three Films)
    October (The Ten Days That Shook the World)
        (In Lorrimer Screenplay Series, 1974)
        (In his Three Films)
    Sutter's Gold; scenario for the uncompleted film, based upon the
      novel "L'Or," by Blaise Cendrars
        (In With Eisenstein in Hollywood)
EISLER, Hanns, 1898-1962
    Johann Faustus
        (In Theater Heute, no. 5, May 1974)
Eiszeit (see Dorst, Tankred)
Eix! (see Donnay, Maurice C.)
El Ejemplo Mayor de la Desdicha (see Mira de Amescua, Antonio)
Elder, Kate
    *Doc; screenplay (see Hamill, Pete)
ELDER, Lonne III
    Ceremonies in Dark Old Men
        (In Best American Plays, 7th Series, 1967-1973)
        (In Black Theater)
    Charades on East Fourth Street
        (In Black Drama Anthology)
The Elder Brother (see Beaumont, Francis)

Eleanor of Aquitaine, Consort of Henry II, 1122?-1170
  *Left-handed Liberty; a play about Magna Carta (see Arden, John)
Eleanor of Castille, Queen of England, d. 1290
  *The Chronicle of King Edward I (see Peele, George)
Electra (see Giraudoux, Jean)
Electra, a tragedy in one act freely rendered after Sophocles (see
  Hofmannsthal, Hugo von H.)
Electre; text in French (see Chénier, Marie-Joseph B.)
Electre; text in French (see Crebillon, Prosper)
Electre; text in French (see Giraudoux, Jean)
Elektra; text in German (see Hofmannsthal, Hugo von H.)
The Elephant Calf (see Brecht, Bertolt)
The Elephant's Child (see Kipling, Rudyard)
The Elevator (see Howells, William Dean)
Elevator (see Thiessen, Cherie S.)
The Elf of Discontent (see Benton, Rita)
The Eligible Mr. Bangs (see Housum, Robert)
ELINSON, Jack
  The Visitor; television script for an episode in "Good Times, "
    by Jack Elinson and Norman Paul
    (In Samuel French's Tandem Library Series)
ELIOT, Thomas Stearns, 1888-1965
  Cocktail Party; text in Spanish
    (In Teatro Ingles Contemporaneo)
  The Family Reunion
    (In Four Modern Verse Plays)
Elisha and the Long Knives; television script (see Wasserman, Dale)
Elizabeth Bam (see Kharms, Daniil I.)
Elizabeth I, Queen of England, 1533-1603
  *Amy Robsart (see Hugo, Victor)
  *Le Comte d'Essex (The Earl of Essex) (see Corneille, Thomas)
  *The Dark Lady of the Sonnets (see Shaw, George Bernard)
  *Elizabeth I (see Foster, Paul)
  *The Heart of Kings (see Biro, Lajos)
  *Henry VIII (see Chénier, Marie-Joseph B.)
  *If You Know Not Me, You Know No Bodie; or, The Troubles of
    Queen Elizabeth (see Heywood, Thomas)
  *Mary Stuart (see Schiller, Johann C.)
  *Mary Stuart (see Swinburne, Algernon Charles)
  *Queen Mary (see Tennyson, Alfred Lord)
  *Vivat! Vivat Regina! (see Bolt, Robert)
Elizabeth of Valois, Queen of Spain, 1545-1568
  *Don Carlos: a Dramatic History (see Schiller, Johann C.)
  *Philippe II (see Chénier, Marie-Joseph B.)
ELLIOTT, Sumner Locke
  Rusty Bugles
    (In Three Australian Plays)
ELLISON, Harlan
  City on the Edge of Forever; television script for an episode in
    "Star Trek"
    (In Six Science Fiction Plays)
Eloisa Está Debajo de un Almendro (see Jardiel Poncela, Enrique)

ELWARD, James
    Paper Foxhole; television script from the "Kraft Television
    Theatre," Apr. 4, 1956
       (In Prize Plays of Television and Radio, 1956)
Embrassons-nous (see Labiche, Eugene)
L'Embroc (see Montherlant, Henry de)
An Emergency Case (see Flavin, Martin)
EMERSON, John, 1874-1956
    The Love Expert, scenario by John Emerson and Anita Loos
      (In their How To Write Photoplays)
    The Whole Town's Talking, by John Emerson and Anita Loos
      (In Longman's Players Prompt Book Play Series, 1925)
L'Emigre de Brisbane (see Schehade, Georges)
Emma Instigated Me (see Owens, Rochelle)
Emma's Time (see Mercer, David)
EMORY, William Closson
    Love in the West: A Scenario
      (In Transition, no. 13, Summer 1928)
Emperor and Galilean (see Ibsen, Henrik)
The Emperor Jones (see O'Neill, Eugene)
The Emperor of the East (see Massinger, Philip)
The Emperor of the Moon (see Behn, Mrs. Aphra)
The Emperor of the West End (see Shatzky, Joel)
The Emperor's Doll (see Van der Veer, Ethel)
The Empire Builders (see Vian, Boris)
The Employee (see Quiles, Eduardo)
The Empress of Morocco (see Duffet, Thomas)
An Empty Room (see Key-Aaberg, Sandro)
En Attendant Godot (see Beckett, Samuel)
En el Escorial, Carino Mio (see Paso, Alfonso)
En Gggarrrde! (see Daumal, Rene)
En la Ardiente Oscuridad (see Buero Vallejo, Antonio)
En la Diestra de Dois Padre (see Buenaventura, Enrique)
En la Red (see Sastre, Alfonso)
En Pieces Detachees (see Tremblay, Michel)
En Qué Piensas? (see Villaurrutia, Xavier)
Enchanted Night (see Mrozek, Slawomir)
The Enchanter; or, Love and Magic (see Garrick, David)
Encontro no Anhangabau (see Laura, Ida)
Encore (see Korr, David)
The End of Me Old Cigar (see Osborne, John)
End of Story; television script (see Lehman, Leo)
The End of Summer; filmscript (excerpt) (see Ozu, Yasujiro)
The End of the Beginning (see O'Casey, Sean)
Endicott, John, 1588?-1665
    *John Endicott (see Longfellow, Henry Wadsworth)
ENDLER, Adolf
    Das Bucklige Pferdchen; Märchenspiel in Versen von Adolf Endler
    und Elke Erb nach dem Poem von P. Jerschow
      (In Theater der Zeit, no. 3, March 1973)
L'Endormie (see Claudel, Paul)
Enemies (see Gor'kii, Maskim)
Enemy! (see Maugham, Robin)

An Enemy of the People (see Ibsen, Henrik)
The Enemy Within (see Friel, Brian)
L'Enfant de la Balle (see Fortuno, Claude)
L'Enfant Prodigue (see Becque, Henri)
L'Enfant Savage; filmscript (see Truffaut, Francois.   The Wild
    Child)
L'Enfer Sur Terre (see Hugo, Victor)
Engaged (see Gilbert, William S.)
Los Engañados (see Rueda, Lope de)
Engels, Friedrich, 1820-1895
    *Salut an Alle, Marx (see Kaltofen, Günter)
L'Enigme (see Hervieu, Paul Ernest)
Engineer Sergeyev (see Rokk, Vsevolod)
Der Englische Sender (see Kaiser, Georg)
The English Friar; or, The Town Sparks (see Crowne, John)
An English Medley (see Drinkwater, John)
The English Moor; or, The Mock-marriage (see Brome, Richard)
The English Traveller As It Hath Beene (see Heywood, Thomas)
The Englishman in Paris (see Foote, Samuel)
The Englishman Return'd from Paris (see Foote, Samuel)
L'Enigme de Kaspar Hauser (see Herzog, Werner)
ENRICO, Robert
    On Owl Creek; a film adaptation of "An Occurrence at Owl
        Creek Bridge "
        (In Contact with Drama)
Enrico IV (see Pirandello, Luigi)
Ensalada de Nochebuena (see Solana, Rafael)
Ensayando a Molière (see Magana, Sergio)
Enter a Free Man (see Stoppard, Tom)
Enter Solly Gold (see Kops, Bernard)
Entertaining Mr. Sloane (see Orton, Joe)
Entertainment at Rutland House (see D'Avenant, Sir William)
Entertainment of King James (see Middleton, Thomas)
Entra in Casa una Montagna (see Fiume, Salvatore)
Entre Cuatro Paredes (see Galich, Manuel)
Entre Medina y Olmedo (see Arauz, Alvaro)
Entre Midi et Soir (see Dubé, Marcel)
Entretiens avec le Professeur Y (see Celine, Louis-Ferdinand)
The Envoi Messages (see Phillips, Louis)
L'Envres d'une Sainte (see Curel, François)
L'Epee (see Hugo, Victor)
The Ephesian Matron (see Bickerstaff, Isaac)
Epicoene; or, The Silent Woman (see Jonson, Ben)
An Episode at the Dentist; filmscript (see Fields, W. C.)
Episode on the Life of an Author (see Anouilh, Jean)
L'Epouvantail (see Schatzberg, Jerry)
L'Epreuve (see Marivaux, Pierre C.)
Epsom-Wells (see Shadwell, Thomas)
EPSTEIN, Julius J., 1909-
    Casablanca; screenplay (see Curtiz, Michael)
EPSTEIN, Philip G., 1910-1952
    Casablanca; screenplay (see Curtiz, Michael)
L'Equarrissage pour Tous (see Vian, Boris)

Equus (see Schaffer, Peter)
Era Notte a Roma; filmscript (see Rossellini, Roberto)
ERASMUS, Desiderius, d. 1536
  **Pleasant Dialogues and Dramas (see Heywood, Thomas)
Der Erbgraf (see Eckart, Dietrich)
ERDMAN, Nikolai, 1902-1970
    The Mandate
      (In his Two Plays)
    The Suicide
      (In Russian Literature Triquarterly, no. 7, Fall 1973)
      (In his Two Plays)
Erechtheus (see Swinburne, Algernon Charles)
Der Erfinder (see Schneider, Hansjörg)
Erik og Abel (see Oehlenschläger, Adam G.)
Erika (see Krechel, Ursula)
The Ermine (see Anouilh, Jean)
Eros at Breakfast (see Davies, William R.)
The Erpingham Camp (see Orton, Joe)
ERSKINE, John, 1879-1951
    Hearts Enduring
      (In More One-Act Plays by Modern Authors)
ERVINE, St. John Greer, 1883-1971
    John Ferguson
      (In 20th Century Plays)
Es 1st Krieg! (see Ronchi, Teresa)
Es Urgente el Amor (see Rebello, Luiz F.)
Esa Luna Que Empieza (see Gibson Parra, Percy)
Escape (see Galsworthy, John)
The Escape (see Power, Victor)
The Escape; or, A Leap for Freedom (see Brown, William W.)
Escape by Balloon (see La Farge, W. E. R.)
ESCHNER, Eugen
    König Jörg
      (In Theater der Zeit, no. 7, 1974)
El Esclavo del Demonio (see Mira de Amescua, Antonio)
ESCOBAR, Luis
    El Amor es un Potro Descobado, Luis Escobar y Luis Saslawski
      (In Teatro Español, 1958-59)
Escuela de Pillos (see Salmon, Raul)
Escuradra Hacia la Muerte (see Sastre, Alfonso)
Escurial (see Ghelderode, Michel de)
Esker Mike & His Wife, Agiluk (see Hardin, Herschel)
Esmeralda (see Hugo, Victor)
Les Espagnols en Danemarck (see Mérimée, Prosper)
El Espectro Acrobata (see Marsicovetere y Duran, Miguel)
Espejo de Avarica (see Aub, Max)
La Espera (see Echeverria Loria, Arturo)
Esperando a Godot (En Attendant Godot) (see Beckett, Samuel)
La Esperanza de la Patria (see Tamayo y Baus, Manuel)
Espetáculo (see Kühner, Maria H.)
Un Espiritu Burlon (see Coward, Noël)
Essex, Robert Devereaux, Earl of, 1566-1603
    *Le Comte d'Essex (The Earl of Essex) (see Corneille, Thomas)

Est Dans Les Oeufs (see Ionesco, Eugene)
Esta Noche, Tampoco (see Lopez Rubio, José)
Esta Noche es la Vispera (see Ruiz Iriarte, Victor)
Estado de Secreto (see Usigli, Rudolfo)
El Estano Ero Limachi (see Salmon, Raul)
Esther (see Du Ryer, Pierre)
Esther (see Hochwälder, Fritz)
Esther (see Masefield, John)
Esther (see Racine, Jean Baptiste)
ESTORINO, Abelardo, 1925-
    El Robo del Cochino
        (In El Teatro Hispanoamericano Contemporaneo, Vol. 2)
O Estranho (see Rocha Miranda, Edgard da)
Estudio en Blanco y Negro (see Pinera, Virgilio)
... Et a la Fin Etait le Bang (see Obaldia, Rene de)
... Et Ils Passerent des Menottes aux Fleurs (see Arrabal, Fer-
    nando)
L'Eté (see Weingarten, Romain)
The Eternal Song (see Arnstein, Marc)
Ethan Frome (see Davis, Owen)
ETHEREGE, Sir George, 1635?-1691
    The Man of Mode; or, Sir Fopling Flutter
        (In Plays of the Restoration and 18th Century)
        (In Restoration Comedy, Vol. 1)
        (In British Plays from the Restoration to 1820)
    She Would If She Could
        (In Restoration Comedy, Vol. 1)
Ethiopia at the Bar of Justice (see McCoo, Edward J.)
Etoiles Rouges (see Bourgeade, Pierre)
L'Etouffe-Chrétien (see Marceau, Felicien)
L'Etranger (see Dumas, Alexandre, Fils)
Eugenie (see Beaumarchais, Pierre A.)
Eumenides (see Aeschylus)
Les Eumenides (see Aeschylus)
The Eunuch (see Terence)
Eupalinos; ou, L'Architecte (see Valèry, Paul)
EURIPIDES, 480 or 484-406 B.C.
    Alcestis
        (In his Three Plays, 1968)
        (In his Three Plays, 1974)
        (In World Drama, Vol. 1)
    **Alkestis des Euripides (see Hofmannsthal, Hugo von H.)
    The Bacchae
        (In Themes of Drama)
        (In his Three Plays, 1974)
    *The Bacchae of Euripides (see Soyinka, Wole)
    Hippolytus
        (In his Three Plays, 1968)
    **Iphigenia at Aulus; a dance play (see Rexroth, Kenneth)
    **Jason and Media (see Baring, Maurice)
    Iphigenia in Tauris
        (In his Three Plays, 1968)
    Medea

            (In his Three Plays, 1974)
  **Medea (see Jahnn, Hans H.)
  **Medea, freely adapted from the "Medea" of Euripides (see
      Jeffers, Robinson)
  **Medea; filmscript (see Pasolini, Pier P.)
  **Médée; text in French (see Anouilh, Jean)
  **Médée; text in French (see Corneille, Pierre)
  **Médée; text in French (see Lamartine, Alphonse M.)
  **Oreste; text in Italian (see Alfieri, Vittorio)
    The Trojan Women; radio script adapted by Harry MacFayden,
      Oct. 16, 1938
            (In Best Broadcasts of 1938-39)
Europa (see Kaiser, Georg)
Eurydice (see Fielding, Henry)
Eurydice (Legend of Lovers) (see Anouilh, Jean)
Eurydise Hiss'd; or, A Word to the Wise (see Fielding, Henry)
Eva Maria (see Järner, V. V.)
Eva Peron (see Copi)
"O Evangelho Segundo Zebedeu" (see Vieira, Cesar)
Une Evasion de Latude (see Moinaux, Georges)
The Eve of the Execution; or, Genesis Was Tomorrow (see Diaz,
    Jorge)
EVELING, Harry Stanley, 1925-
    The Balachites
            (In Calder & Boyars Playscript Series, no. 20)
    Come and Be Killed
            (In Calder & Boyars Scottish Library Series)
    The Lunatic, the Secret Sportsman and the Woman Next Door
            (In Calder & Boyars Playscript Series, no. 30)
    The Strange Case of Martin Richter
            (In Calder & Boyars Playscript Series, no. 20)
    Vibrations
            (In Calder & Boyars Playscript Series, no. 30)
Even a Wise Man Stumbles (see Ostrovskii, Alexandr N.)
Even the Blind (see Hartwig, Edward A.)
Evening Dress (see Howells, William Dean)
An Evening for Merlin Finch (see Dizenzo, Charles)
An Evening in Sorrento (see Turgenev, Ivan S.)
An Evening's Love; or, The Mock Astrologer (see Dryden, John)
L'Eventail (see Goldoni, Carlo)
Events, 1968-1969 (see Baker, Fred)
Events While Guarding the Bofors Gun (see McGrath, John)
Ever Since Paradise (see Priestley, John B.)
Ever Young (see Gerstenberg, Alice)
The Everest Hotel (see Wilson, Snoo)
Every Man in His Humour (see Jonson, Ben)
Every Man in His Humour (Italian Edition) (see Jonson, Ben)
Every Man Out of His Humour (see Jonson, Ben)
Everybody's a Jew (see Figueroa, John)
Everyman (Anon.)
            (In A Book of Short Plays, XV-XX Centuries)
            (In On the High Road)
            (In The Drama, Vol. 4)

(In Themes of Drama)
(In World Drama, Vol. 1)
EVREINOV, Nikolai Nikolaevich, 1879-1953
    Les Coulisses de l'Ame
        (In L'Avant-Scène Théâtre, no. 544, July 1, 1974)
    A Merry Death; a harlequinade in one act with brief, although
       extremely amusing, prologue and a few concluding words on
       behalf of the author, N. Evreinov
        (In Life as Theater)
        (In Theatre Wagon Plays)
    The Ship of the Righteous; a dramatic Epopee in three acts
        (In Life as Theater)
    Styopik and Manya
        (In Theatre Wagon Plays)
    The Theater of the Soul; a one-act mono-drama with prologue
        (In Life as Theater)
    Le Triangle Immortel; adaptation de Genia Cannac
        (In L'Avant-Scene Théâtre, no. 566, June 15, 1975)
    The Unmasked Ball (The Theater of Eternal War); a play in
       three acts and four scenes
        (In Life as Theater)
Der Ewige Mensch (see Brust, Alfred)
El Examen de Maridos (see Ruiz de Alarcón y Mendoza, Juan)
The Examination (see Pinter, Harold)
The Example (see Shirley, James)
Exaustacao (see Calvet, Aldo)
The Exception and the Rule (see Brecht, Bertolt)
L'Exil (see Montherlant, Henry de)
Exit Muttering (see Jack, Donald)
Exit the King (see Ionesco, Eugene)
Exorcism for Now: Ritual (see DuBous, Theodore)
Expert Opinion; radio script (see Boardman, True)
The Explorer (see Jupp, Kenneth)
Explosion; an Overpopulation Farce for Two Actors and Percussion
    (see Gerould, Dan)
La Exposicion (see Usigli, Rudolfo)
Expressing Willie (see Crothers, Rachel)
Exterior (see Rice, Elmer L.)
The Exterminating Angel; screenplay (see Buñuel, Luis)
L'Extra-Lucide (see Moinaux, Georges)
Un Extrano en la Niebla (see Roman A., Sergio)
Extreme Unction (see Aldis, Mrs. Mary Reynolds)
EYEN, Thomas Lee, 1941-
    Aretha in the Ice Palace
        (In his Sarah B. Divine & Other Plays)
    The Death of Off-Broadway, a street play
        (In his Sarah B. Divine & Other Plays)
    Grand Tenement
        (In his Sarah B. Divine & Other Plays)
    The Kama Sutra, an Organic Happening
        (In his Sarah B. Divine & Other Plays)
    My Next Husband Will Be a Beauty!
        (In his Sarah B. Divine & Other Plays)

November 22
    (In his Sarah B. Divine & Other Plays)
Pouquoi le Robe d'Anna Ne Veut Pas Redescendre; adaptation
    française de Bernard Da Costa
    (In L'Avant-Scène Théâtre, no. 549, Oct. 1, 1974)
Sarah B. Divine!
    (In his Sarah B. Divine & Other Plays)
The Three Sisters from Springfield, Illinois
    (In his Sarah B. Divine & Other Plays)
The White Whore and the Bit Player
    (In his Sarah B. Divine & Other Plays)
Why Hanna's Skirt Won't Stay Down
    (In The Off Off Broadway Book)
Eyes and No Eyes (see Gilbert, William S.)

Fa Men Ssu (Buddha's Temple)
    (In Famous Chinese Plays)
FABBRI, Diego
    Inquisicion
        (In Teatro Italian Contemporaneo)
FABIO, Sarah Webster
    Saga of the Black Man
        (In Ohio Review, Vol. 6, no. 2, Spring 1975)
Fabius Cunctator, d. 203 B.C.
    *Before Cannae (see Munk, Kaj H.)
A Fable (see Van Itallie, Jean-Claude)
Fables Here and Then (see Feldshuh, David)
El Fabricante de Deudas (see Salazar Bondy, Sebastian)
Fabrik im Walde (see Schutz, Stefan)
Fabula de las Cinco Caminantes (see Garcia, Ivan)
The Fabulous Miss Marie (see Bullins, Edward A.)
Façades (see Shearer, Marjorie)
The Face; screenplay (see Bergman, Ingmar. The Magician)
Face of God (see Kennedy, Charles Rann)
Face to Face; screenplay (see Bergman, Ingmar)
Facing Westward (see Guaedinger, Arthur)
The Factory Lad (see Walker, John)
Fagan, Alison Mary
    *Alison Mary Fagan (see Selbourne, David)
FAGAN, Barthelemi-Christophe, 1702-1755
    **The Guardian (see Garrick, David)
    **The Old Maid (see Murphy, Arthur)
    La Pupille
        (In Théâtre de XVIII Siècle, Vol. 1)
Der Fahrend Schuler im Paradeis (see Sachs, Hans)
The Fair Favourite (see D'Avenant, Sir William)
Fair Ladies at a Game of Poem-Cards (see Chikamatsu, Monzae-
    mon)
The Fair Maid of the Inn (see Fletcher, John)
The Fair Maid of the West; or, A Girle Worth Gold, pts. 1 & 2
    (see Heywood, Thomas)
The Fair Penitent (see Rowe, Nicholas)

A Fair Quarrel (see Middleton, Thomas)
Faire sans Dire (see Musset, Alfred de)
The Fairies (see Garrick, David)
Fairy Tales of New York (see Donleavy, James Patrick)
Le Faiseur (see Balzac, Honoré de)
Le Faiseur; adaptation (see Franck, Pierre)
Fait Divers (see Sabatier, Pierre)
The Faith Hawker; television script (see Rodman, Howard)
The Faith Healer (see Moody, William Vaughn)
The Faithful (see Masefield, John)
Faithful! A Sentimental Fragment (see Wolff, Pierre)
The Faithful Friend (see Scala, Flamminio)
The Faithful Shepherdess (see Beaumont, Francis)
The Faithless (see Hayden, John)
The Falcon (see Tennyson, Alfred Lord)
Faliero, Marino, Doge of Venice, 1278?-1355
    *Marino Faliero (see Swinburne, Algernon Charles)
Der Fall des Schülers Vehgesack (see Kaiser, Georg)
The Fall of British Tyranny; or, American Liberty (see Leacock,
    John)
The Fall of the House of Usher (see Berkoff, Steven)
Fallen Angels (see Coward, Noël)
The Falling of an Apple (see Kennedy, Charles O'Brien)
The Falling Sickness (see Edson, Russell)
The False Count; or, A New Way to Play an Old Game (see Behn,
    Mrs. Aphra)
False Delicacy (see Kelly, Hugh)
The False Friend (see Vanbrugh, Sir John)
False Impressions (see Cumberland, Richard)
The False One (see Beaumont, Francis)
I Falsi Galantuomini (see Federici)
Falso Drama (see Usigli, Rudolfo)
Las Faltas Justificadas (see Martinez Queirolo, José)
La Familia Cena en Case (see Usigli, Rudolfo)
Familienvater (see Eckart, Dietrich)
La Familla Swedenhielm (see Bergman, Hjalmar)
La Famille de Carvajal (see Mérimée, Prosper)
La Famille Extravagante (see Legrand, Gabriel-Marie-Jean-Baptiste)
Family Affairs (see Jennings, Gertrude E.)
A Family and a Fortune (see Mitchell, Julian)
The Family Charge (see Turgenev, Ivan S.)
Family Life; screenplay (see Mercer, David)
The Family of Love (see Middleton, Thomas)
Family Portrait (see Coffee, Lenore)
The Family Reunion (see Eliot, T. S.)
The Famous Mrs. Fair (see Forbes, James)
The Fan (see Goldoni, Carlo)
Le Fanatisme; ou, Mahomet le Prophète (see Voltaire)
Fando and Lis (see Arrabal, Fernando)
Fando et Lis; text in French (see Arrabal, Fernando)
Fanny's First Play (see Shaw, George Bernard)
Fanshen (see Hare, David)
Fantasio (see Musset, Alfred de)

Fantasio; text in French (see Musset, Alfred de)
O Fantasma (see Pongetti, Henrique)
Fantastic Suite (see Bellido, José M.)
The Fantastics (see Jones, Tom)
Los Fantoches (see Solórzano, Carlos)
Le Fantôme de la Liberté; screenplay (see Buñuel, Luis)
Far Taiga (see Afinogenov, Alexander N.)
The Far-off Hills (see Robinson, Lennox)
FARAGOH, Francis Edwards
    Frankenstein; screenplay (see Whale, James)
The Farce of the Worthy Master Pierre Patelin (Anon.)
    (In World Drama, Vol. 1)
The Farewell Case (see Cohan, George M.)
Farewell to Greatness! (see Carroll, Paul Vincent)
Farfetched Fables (see Shaw, George Bernard)
The Farm (see Storey, David)
FARMER, Gene
    This Land Is Whose Land? Television script for an episode in
    "Sanford and Son"
    (In Samuel French's Tandem Library Series)
Farmer's Almanac (see Owens, Rochelle)
The Farmers Hotel (see O'Hara, John)
The Farmer's Wife (see Dibdin, Charles, The Younger)
Farmyard (see Kroetz, Franz X.)
FARNUM, Dorothy
    Jew Süss; screenplay (see Rawlinson, Arthur)
FARQUHAR, George, 1677?-1707
    The Adventures of Covent-Garden
        (In his Complete Works, Vol. 2)
    The Beaux' Stratagem
        (In British Plays from the Restoration to 1820)
        (In his Complete Works, Vol. 2)
        (In The Drama, Vol. 22)
        (In World Drama, Vol. 1)
        (In Plays of the Restoration and 18th Century)
        (In Restoration Comedy, Vol. 4)
    The Constant Couple; or, A Trip to the Jubilee
        (In his Complete Works, Vol. 1)
        (In Restoration Comedy, Vol. 4)
    The Inconstant; or, The Way to Win Him
        (In his Complete Works, Vol. 1)
    Love and a Bottle
        (In his Complete Works, Vol. 1)
    The Recruiting Officer
        (In his Complete Works, Vol. 2)
        (In Restoration Comedy, Vol. 4)
    Sir Henry Wildair; being a sequel to "A Trip to the Jubilee"
        (In his Complete Works, Vol. 1)
    The Stage Coach
        (In his Complete Works, Vol. 2)
  **Trumpets and Drums (see Brecht, Bertolt)
    The Twin-Rivals
        (In his Complete Works, Vol. 1)

FARRAR, John, 1896-
  Here Are Sailors!
    (In One-Act Plays for Stage and Study, 7th Series)
  The Wedding Rehearsal
    (In One-Act Plays for Stage and Study, 5th Series)
Farsa de la Concordia (see López de Yanguas, Hernán)
Farsa del Mundo y Moral (see López de Yanguas, Hernán)
Farsa Infantil de la Cabeza del Dragon (see Valle-Inclan, Ramon
  del)
Farsa Italiana de la Enamorada del Rey (see Valle-Inclan, Ramon
  del)
Farsa Sacramental (see López de Yanguas, Hernán)
Farsa y Licencia de la Reina Castiza (see Valle-Inclan, Ramon del)
Farvorfen Vinkel (see Hirschbein, Peretz)
FARWELL, George
  The House That Jack Built
    (In Australian Theatre Workshop no. 4, 1970)
The Fascinating Foundling (see Shaw, George Bernard)
Fashion; or, Life in New York (see Mowatt, Anna Cora)
Fashionable Follies (see Hutton, Joseph)
The Fashionable Lover (see Cumberland, Richard)
Fashions for Men (see Molnar, Ferenc)
FASSBINDER, Rainer Werner
  Pre-Paradise Story Now
    (In Gambit, Vol. 6, no. 21)
Fastes d'Enfer (see Ghelderode, Michel de)
Fatal Curiosity (see Lillo, George)
The Fatal Dowry (see Massinger, Philip)
The Fatal Error (see McClarchie, Thomas R.)
The Fatal Glass of Beer; filmscript (see Fields, W. C.)
Fate of a Cockroach (see Al Hakim, Tewfik)
FATH'ALI, Akhund-Zãdah, 1812-1878
  The Alchemist, by Mirza Fath-Ali and Mirza Ja'afar
    (In The Drama, Vol. 3)
The Father (see Strindberg, August)
A Father and a Son (see Taylor, Peter H.)
Father Hubbard's Tales (see Middleton, Thomas)
Father Unknown (see Shkvarkin, Vassily V.)
The Fathers; or, The Good-Natured Man (see Fielding, Henry)
FAULKNER, George H.
  The Thinking Heart, NBC Kraft Television Theatre script, Feb.
    11, 1954
    (In Top TV Shows of the Year, 1954-55)
FAULKNER, William, 1897-1962
  Tomorrow (see Foote, Horton)
Les Fausses Confidences (see Marivaux, Pierre C.)
La False Suivante; ou, Le Fourbe Puni (see Marivaux, Pierre C.)
Faust; filmscript; text in French (see Rohmer, Eric)
Faust; text in German (see Kaiser, Georg)
Faust: The Tragedy, Part One (see Goethe, Johann Wolfgang von)
Faustine (see Musset, Alfred de)
Faustine; text in French (see Musset, Alfred de)
Faustus Kelly (see O'Nolan, Brian)

Favola del Figlio Cambiato (see Pirandello, Luigi)
La Favola d'Orfeo (see Binazzi, Massimo)
The Fayre Mayde of the Exchange (see Heywood, Thomas)
Fear (see Afinogenyev, Alexander)
Fear (see Lind, Jakov)
The Fearless Vampire Killers; screenplay (see Polanski, Roman.
     Le Bal des Vampires)
The Feast at Solhoug (see Ibsen, Henrik)
The Feast of Barking Women (see Van der Veer, Ethel)
The Feast of Ortolans (see Anderson, Maxwell)
FECHTER, Charles Albert, 1824-1879
     Monte Cristo; James O'Neill's version, based on the novel by
     Alexandre Dumas
FEDERICI
     I Falsi Galantuomini
          (In Teatro Comico Moderno)
FEDERSPIEL, Jürg, 1931-
     The Dogs of Salonika.   Both German and English texts are given
          (In Dimension, Vol. 2, no. 1, 1969)
Ein Feierabend (see Kaiser, Georg)
FEIFFER, Jules, 1929-
     Carnal Knowledge; screenplay of film produced and directed by
     Mike Nichols
          (A Noonday Original Screenplay, 1971)
     Cohn of Arc
          (In Partisan Review, Vol. 40, no. 2, 1973)
     Dick and Jane
          (In Evergreen Black Cat Playscript Series, 1970)
          (In Ramparts Magazine, Vol. 8, Aug. 1969)
     Little Murders
          (In Best American Plays, 7th Series, 1967-1973)
          (A Random House Play, 1968)
     The Unexpurgated Memoirs of Bernard Mergendeiler
          (In Collision Course)
     The White House Murder Case
          (In Evergreen Black Cat Playscript Series, 1970)
The Feign'd Curtezans; or, A Night's Intrigue (see Behn, Mrs.
     Aphra)
Feinde; text in German (see Gor'kii, Maksim)
FELDHAUS-WEBER, Mary
     The Virgin, the Lizard, and the Lamb
          (In New Directions in Prose and Poetry, Vol. 20, 1968)
FELDSHUH, David
     Fables Here and Then, by David Feldshuh and the Guthrie
     Theater Company
          (In Minnesota Showcase: Four Plays, Minnesota Drama Edi-
          tions, no. 9)
Der Feldzug nach Sizilien (see Heym, Georg)
Felicidad; a Play for Dolls, Dummies, Mannequins, Masks, Puppets
     and People (see Chalfi, Raquel)
Felicie (see Marivaux, Pierre C.)
FELIPE, Carlos, 1914-
     El Travieso Jimmy

(In <u>Teatro Cubano Contemporaneo</u>)
Th' Feller from Omaha (see Conkle, Ellsworth P.)
FELLINI, Federico, 1920-
   Amarcord
      (In <u>Dal Soggetto al Film</u> Series, no. 48, 1974)
   Il Bidone
      (In <u>Dal Soggetto al Film</u> Series Retrospettiva, no. 1, 1963)
   Boccaccio '70
      (In <u>Dal Soggetto al Film</u>, no. 22, 1962)
   I Clowns; la sceneggiatura de Federico Fellini e Bernardino
    Zapponi
      (In <u>I Clowns, a Cura di Renzo Renzi</u>)
   La Dolce Vita
      (In <u>Dal Soggetto al Film</u> Series, no. 13, 1960)
   8 e $\frac{1}{2}$
      (In <u>Dal Soggetto al Film</u> Series, no. 27, 1963)
   Fellini Satyricon
      (In <u>Dal Soggetto al Film</u> Series, no. 38, 1969)
   Fellini TV
      (In <u>Dal Soggetto al Film</u> Series, no. 46, 1972)
   Giulietta Degli Spiriti
      (In <u>Dal Soggetto al Film</u> Series, no. 33, 1965)
   Le Notti di Cabiria; screenplay
      (In <u>Dal Soggetto al Film</u>,. no. 5, 1965)
   Open City (Roma Città Aperta); screenplay (see Rossellini,
    Roberto)
   Roma, Città Aperta (Rome, Open City); screenplay (see Rossel-
    lini, Roberto)
   Lo Sceicco Bianco
      (In <u>Dal Soggetto al Film</u> Series Retrospettiva, no. 1, 1963)
   La Strada
      (In <u>Dal Soggetto al Film</u> Series Retrospettiva, no. 1, 1963)
   Le Tentazioni del Dottor Antonio
      (In <u>Dal Soggetto al Film</u>, no. 22, 1962)
   Toby Dammit, screenplay based on Edgar Allan Poe's story
    "Non Scommettete la Testa Col Diavolo." Directed by
    Federico Fellini
      (In <u>Dal Soggetto al Film</u> Series, no. 37, 1968)
   I Vitelloni
      (In <u>Dal Soggetto al Film</u> Series Retrospettiva, no. 1, 1963)
Fellini Satyricon; screenplay (see Fellini, Federico)
Fellini TV (see Fellini, Federico)
FELTON, Norman
   Sam 'n' Ella
      (In <u>One-Act Plays for Stage and Study</u>, 10th Series)
FELTZMAN, Oscar
   The Young Guard (see Aleksin, Anatoly)
Female Transport; parts 1 & 2 (see Gooch, Steve)
La Femme de Claude (see Dumas, Alexandre, Fils)
La Femme de Paille (see Arley, Catherine)
La Femme en Fleur (see Amiel, Denys)
Une Femme est un Diable (see Mérimée, Prosper)
Une Femme est une Femme; filmscript (see Godard, Jean-Luc. A
   Woman Is a Woman)

La Femme et Son Ombre (see Claudel, Paul)
La Femme Fidele (see Marivaux, Pierre C.)
Une Femme Libre (see Salacrou, Armand)
La Femme Qui a Raison (see Voltaire)
Les Femmes du Boeuf (see Audiberti, Jacques)
Fen Ho Wan (At the Bend of Fen River)
    (In Famous Chinese Plays)
Fénélon, François de Salignac de la Mothe, 1698-1762
    *Fénélon (see Chénier, Marie-Joseph B.)
La Fénix de Salamanca (see Mira de Amescua, Antonio)
FENN, Frederick
    'Ope-o'-Me-Thumb, by Frederick Fenn and Richard Pryce
        (In One-Act Plays for Stage and Study, 1st Series)
FERBER, Edna, 1887-1968
    Dinner at Eight (see Kaufman, George S.)
Ferdinand, called the Catholic, King of Spain, 1452-1516
    *The Conquest of Granada by the Spaniards, pts. 1 & 2 (see
    Dryden, John)
FERDINAND, Val, 1947-
    Blk Love Song #1
        (In Black Theater U.S.A., 1847-1974)
FERET, René
    La Communion Solennelle
        (In L'Avant-Scène Cinéma, no. 185, Apr. 1, 1977)
FERLINGHETTI, Lawrence
    Servants of the People
        (In New Directions, Vol. 18, 1964)
FERNANDEZ ARDAVIN, Luis, 1891-
    La Sombra Pasa
        (In Teatro Español, 1950-51)
FERNANDEZ DE LIZARDI, José Joaquin, 1776-1827
    Todos Contra el Payo y el Payo Contra Todos o La Visita del
    Payo en el Hospital de Locos
        (In Teatro Méxicano del Siglo XIX, Vol. 1)
Festival (see Williams, Albert N.)
The Festival of Bacchus (see Schnitzler, Arthur)
The Festival of Our Lord of the Ship (see Pirandello, Luigi)
La Fête Noire (see Audiberti, Jacques)
Le Feu Follet; filmscript (see Malle, Louis)
Feu la Mere de Madame (see Feydeau, Georges)
FEUCHTWANGER, Lion, 1884-1958
    **Jew Süss; screenplay (see Rawlinson, Arthur)
    The Visions of Simon Marchard (see Brecht, Bertolt)
FEYDEAU, Georges, León Jules Marie, 1862-1921
    L'Affaire Edouard
        (In his Théâtre Complet I)
    L'Age d'Or
        (In his Théâtre Complet IX)
    Amour et Piano
        (In his Théâtre Complet I)
    Un Bain de Ménage
        (In his Théâtre Complet VII)
    Le Bourgeon

(In his <u>Théâtre Complet IX</u>)
Cent Millions Qui Tombent
    (In his <u>Théâtre Complet VI</u>)
C'est une Femme du Monde
    (In his <u>Théâtre Complet IV</u>)
Champignol Malgre Lui
    (In his <u>Théâtre Complet VI</u>)
Chat en Poche
    (In his <u>Théâtre Complet II</u>)
Le Circuit
    (In his <u>Théâtre Complet V</u>)
La Dame de Chez Maxim
    (In his <u>Théâtre Complet VII</u>)
Le Dindon
    (In his <u>Théâtre Complet II</u>)
Don't Walk Around Stark Naked
    (In <u>Yale/Theatre</u>, Vol. 5, no. 1, Fall 1973)
Dormez, Je le Veux!
    (In his <u>Théâtre Complet III</u>)
La Duchesse des Folies-Bergeres
    (In his <u>Théâtre Complet VIII</u>)
Feu la Mere de Madame
    (In his <u>Théâtre Complet VII</u>)
Les Fiances de Loche
    (In his <u>Théâtre Complet VII</u>)
Fiances en Herbe
    (In his <u>Théâtre Complet I</u>)
Un Fil a la Patte
    (In his <u>Théâtre Complet VI</u>)
Get Out of My Hair!
    (In <u>Three French Farces</u>)
Gibier de Potence
    (In his <u>Théâtre Complet VI</u>)
Going to Pot
    (In his <u>Four Farces</u>)
Hortense a Dit "Je M'En Fous!"
    (In his <u>Théâtre Complet I</u>)
L'Hotel du Libre Echange
    (In his <u>Théâtre Complet IV</u>)
The Lady from Maxim's, translated by John Morrimer
    (A <u>National Theatre Play</u>, 1977)
Le ne Trompe Pas Mon Mari!
    (In his <u>Théâtre Complet III</u>)
Leonie est en Avance
    (In his <u>Théâtre Complet IV</u>)
**Look After Lulu! (see Coward, Noël)
La Lycéenne
    (In his <u>Théâtre Complet VIII</u>)
La Main Passe
    (In his <u>Théâtre Complet III</u>)
Mais n'te Promene Donc pas Toute Nue
    (In his <u>Théâtre Complet VIII</u>)
Le Mariage de Barillon

          (In his Works, Vol. 2)
    Don Quixote in England
          (In his Works, Vol. 3)
    Eurydice
          (In his Works, Vol. 3)
    Eurydice Hiss'd; or, A Word to the Wise
          (In his Works, Vol. 3)
    The Fathers; or, The Good-Natured Man
          (In his Works, Vol. 4)
    The Grub-Street Opera
          (In his Works, Vol. 2)
    The Historical Register for the Year 1736
          (In 18th Century Drama: Afterpieces)
          (In his Works, Vol. 3)
    The Intriguing Chambermaid
          (In A Collection of the Most Esteemed Farces ..., Vol. 3)
          (In his Works, Vol. 3)
    The Letter Writers; or, A New Way to Keep a Wife at Home
          (In his Works, Vol. 2)
    The Lottery
          (In A Collection of the Most Esteemed Farces ..., Vol. 2)
          (In his Works, Vol. 2)
    The Miser, adapted from Molière's "L'Avare"
          (In Plays from Molière)
          (In his Works, Vol. 2)
    Miss Lucy in Town; a sequel to The Virgin Unmask'd
          (In his Works, Vol. 3)
    The Mock Doctor; or, The Dumb Lady Cured, done from Molière's
    "Medecin Malgré Lui"
          (In A Collection of the Most Esteemed Farces ..., Vol. 1)
          (In his Works, Vol. 2)
    The Modern Husband
          (In his Works, Vol. 2)
    The Old Man Taught Wisdom; or, The Virgin Unmask'd
          (In A Collection of the Most Esteemed Farces ..., Vol. 2)
          (In his Works, Vol. 3)
    Pasquin: A Dramatic Satire of the Times
          (In his Works, Vol. 3)
    Tumble-Down Dick; or, Phaeton in the Suds
          (In his Works, Vol. 3)
    The Universal Gallant; or, The Different Husbands
          (In his Works, Vol. 3)
  **The Upholsterer; or, What News? (see Murphy, Arthur)
    The Virgin Unmasked
          (In The London Stage, Vol. 3)
    The Wedding-Day
          (In his Works, Vol. 3)
FIELDS, Joseph, 1895-1966
    Wonderful Town (see Bernstein, Leonard)
FIELDS, W. C. (William Claude Dunkinfield), 1879-1946
    The Baby Austin; vaudeville script
          (In W. C. Fields by Himself)
    The Bank Dick; screenplay by Mahatma Kane Jeeves (W. C.
    Fields); film directed by Edward Cline

(In <u>Classic Filmscripts Series</u>, 1973)
(In <u>Lorrimer Screenplay Series</u>, 1973)
The Barber Shop, directed by Arthur Ripley
  (In <u>"Godfrey Daniels!"</u>)
The Caledonian Express; filmscript
  · (In <u>W. C. Fields by Himself</u>)
Charlie McCarthy Scripts; excerpts from three scripts featuring
W. C. Fields
  (In <u>W. C. Fields by Himself</u>)
Crudd Boys; radio script
  (In <u>W. C. Fields by Himself</u>)
The Day I Drank the Glass of Water; radio script
  (In <u>W. C. Fields by Himself</u>)
The Dentist, a Mack Sennett comedy, directed by Leslie Pearce
  (In <u>"Godfrey Daniels!"</u>)
Doctor W. C. Fields; radio script
  (In <u>W. C. Fields by Himself</u>)
Drug Store Sketch; radio script
  (In <u>W. C. Fields by Himself</u>)
An Episode at the Dentist; filmscript
  (In <u>W. C. Fields by Himself</u>)
The Fatal Glass of Beer; directed by Clyde Bruckman
  (In <u>"Godfrey Daniels!"</u>)
Honky-Tonk, or Husband in Name Only; filmscript
  (In <u>W. C. Fields by Himself</u>)
Mr. Whipsande Looks for Work--for His Nephew; being the first
of a radio series of slices of life in a great American depart-
ment store
  (In <u>W. C. Fields by Himself</u>)
Motel; a story for the stage, motion picture, or radio or printed
matter
  (In <u>W. C. Fields by Himself</u>)
Mumbling Radio Talk--Catalina; radio script
  (In <u>W. C. Fields by Himself</u>)
Notes of Rocket; vaudeville script
  (In <u>W. C. Fields by Himself</u>)
Off to the Country; vaudeville script
  (In <u>W. C. Fields by Himself</u>)
The Pharmacist; directed by Arthur Ripley
  (In <u>"Godfrey Daniels!"</u>)
Playing the Sticks; filmscript, earlier version of The Old
Fashioned Way
  (In <u>W. C. Fields by Himself</u>)
The Pullman Sleeper; vaudeville script
  (In <u>W. C. Fields by Himself</u>)
The Sport Model; vaudeville script
  (In <u>W. C. Fields by Himself</u>)
Ten Thousand People Killed; a musical review and vaudeville
sketch
  (In <u>W. C. Fields by Himself</u>)
What a Night! Vaudeville script
  (In <u>W. C. Fields by Himself</u>)
What W. C. Fields Thinks He Heard on the Quiz Kids Hour;
radio script

(In W. C. Fields by Himself)
   You Can't Cheat an Honest Man; scenario
      (In W. C. Fields by Himself)
Fiesco; or, The Genoese Conspiracy (see Schiller, Johann C.)
Fiesta (see Hanel, Robert)
Fifteen Miles of Broken Glass (see Hendry, Tom)
15-Minute Red Revue, an Agit-Prop Play (see Bonn, John E.)
Figaro, Lässt sich Scheiden (see Horvath, Odön von)
Fight for Shelton Bar (see Cheeseman, Peter)
The Fighting Cock (see Anouilh, Jean)
Fighting on the Plain (see China. Peking Opera Troupe)
FIGUEROA, John, 1936-
   Everybody's a Jew
      (In The Disinherited: Plays)
La Figurante (see Curel, François)
Un Fil a la Patte (see Feydeau, Georges)
Il Filantropo (see Hampton, Christopher)
Filippo (see Alfieri, Vittorio)
FILIPPO, Eduardo de, 1900-
   Filumena Marturano
      (In Masterpieces of the Modern Italian Theatre)
      (In his Three Plays)
   Grand Magic
      (In his Three Plays)
   The Local Authority
      (In his Three Plays)
   Mi Familia
      (In Teatro Italiano Contemporaneo)
La Fille Bien Gardée (see Labiche, Eugene)
La Fille Sauvage (see Curel, François)
Fils de Personne; ou, Plus Que le Sang (see Montherlant, Henry de)
Le Fils Naturel (see Dumas, Alexandre, Fils)
Filumena Marturano (see Filippo, Eduardo de)
Fin de Partie (see Beckett, Samuel)
Fin de Siegfried (see Giraudoux, Jean)
The Final Hour; The Shadow radio script (see McGill, Jerry)
The Final War of Olly Winter; television script (see Ribman, Ronald)
The Final Word (see Albright, Hardie)
FINCH, Robert Voris, 1900-
   The Day They All Came Back
      (In his Plays of the American West)
   The Desert Shall Rejoice
      (In his Plays of the American West)
   The Desert Shall Rejoice, by Robert Finch and Betty Smith;
      radio version
      (In On the Air: 15 Plays for Broadcast)
   From Paradise to Butte
      (In his Plays of the American West)
   Ghost Town, by Robert Finch and Betty Smith
      (In his Plays of the American West)
   Gone Today
      (In his Plays of the American West)
   Goodbye to the Lazy K

(In his Plays of the American West)
Johnny, by Robert Finch and Betty Smith
(In his Plays of the American West)
Miracle at Dublin Gulch
(In his Plays of the American West)
Murder in the Snow, by Robert Finch and Betty Smith
(In his Plays of the American West)
Near Closing Time, by Robert Finch and Betty Smith
(In his Plays of the American West)
The Old Grad
(In his Plays of the American West)
The Return
(In his Plays of the American West)
Rodeo
(In his Plays of the American West)
Summer Comes to the Diamond O, by Robert Finch and Betty
Smith
(In his Plays of the American West)
Western Night (see Smith, Betty)
Find Me (see Mercer, David)
Find the Girl (see Bohanon, Mary)
Find Your Way Home (see Hopkins, John R.)
Der Findling (see Barlach, Ernst)
A Fine Companion (see Marmion, Shakerly)
FINEBERG, Larry
Death
(In Performing Arts in Canada, Vol. 10, no. 2, Summer
1973)
The Finger Meal (see Pringle, Ronald J.)
Fings Ain't Wot They Used T'Be (see Bart, Lionel)
FINNEGAN, Edward
A Fool of a Man
(In Types of Modern Dramatic Composition)
FINSTERWALD, Maxine
The Ladder Under the Maple Tree
(In 100 Non-Royalty Radio Plays)
May Moon
(In One-Act Plays for Stage and Study, 9th Series)
Fiorello! (see Bock, Jerry)
Fire in the Opera House (see Kaiser, Georg)
The Fire Raisers (see Frisch, Max)
FIREHOUSE THEATRE CO.
Escape by Balloon (see La Farge, W. E. R.)
The Fires of St. John (see Sudermann, Hermann)
THE FIRESIGN THEATRE
Don't Crush That Dwarf, Hand Me the Pliers
(In The Firesign Theatre's Big Book of Plays)
How Can You Be in Two Places at Once When You're Not Any-
where at All
(In The Firesign Theatre's Big Book of Plays)
I Think We're All Bozos on This Bus
(In The Firesign Theatre's Big Book of Plays)
Waiting for the Electrician or Somebody Like Him

     (In <u>The Firesign Theatre's Big Book of Plays</u>)
First Communion (see Arrabal, Fernando)
First Corinthians (see Rubinstein, Harold F.)
First Cousins (see Kasznar, Kurt)
The First Distiller (see Tolstoi, Lev N.)
The First Dress-Suit (see Medcraft, Russell)
The First Floor (see Cobb, James)
First Love (see Cumberland, Richard)
The First Man (see O'Neill, Eugene)
The First Night of Lent (see Bradbury, Ray)
The First Part of Ieronimo (see Kyd, Thomas)
The First Part of Sir John Oldcastle (Anon.)
     (In <u>Disputed Plays of William Shakespeare</u>)
The First President (see Williams, William Carlos)
FISCHER, Jürgen
    Richards Korkbein; text in German (see Simpson, Alan)
Fish in the Sea (see McGrath, John)
FISHER, Terence, 1904-
    Le Cauchemar de Dracula; titre original anglais "Dracula, "
    "Horror of Dracula, " scenario Jimmy Sangster, d'après le
    roman de Bram Stoker
     (In <u>L'Avant-Scène Cinéma</u>, no. 160-161, July/Sept. 1975)
Fishing (see Weller, Michael)
FISKE, Minnie Maddern, 1865-1932
    A Light from St. Agnes
     (In <u>One-Act Plays for Stage and Study</u>, 9th Series)
FITCH, Clyde, 1865-1909
    Barbara Fritchie
     (In his <u>Plays</u>, Vol. 2)
    Beau Brummell
     (In his <u>Plays</u>, Vol. 1)
    Captain Jinks of the Horse Marines
     (In his <u>Plays</u>, Vol. 2)
    The City
     (In <u>Dramas from the American Theatre</u>, 1762-1909)
     (In his <u>Plays</u>, Vol. 4)
     (In <u>Representative American Dramas</u>)
    The Climbers
     (In his <u>Plays</u>, Vol. 2)
    The Girl with the Green Eyes
     (In his <u>Plays</u>, Vol. 3)
     (In <u>Representative American Plays</u>, 1792-1949)
    Her Own Way
     (In his <u>Plays</u>, Vol. 3)
    Lover's Lane
     (In his <u>Plays</u>, Vol. 1)
    The Moth and the Flame
     (In <u>Representative Plays by American Dramatists</u>, Vol. 3)
    Nathan Hale
     (In his <u>Plays</u>, Vol. 1)
    The Stubbornness of Geraldine
     (In his <u>Plays</u>, Vol. 3)
    The Truth

(In his Plays, Vol. 4)
The Woman in the Case
(In his Plays, Vol. 4)
FITZGERALD, Edward, 1809-1883
**Omar and Oh My! A burlesque dramatization of the celebrated
    poem "Rubâiyât," by Omar Khayyam, translated by Edward
    Fitzgerald. (Author of burlesque anonymous)
    (In The Drama, Vol. 21)
FITZGERALD, Francis Scott Key, 1896-1940
    The Debutante
        (In The Apprentice Fiction of F. Scott Fitzgerald)
    **Le Dernier Nabab (see Pinter, Harold)
    Shadow Laurels
        (In The Apprentice Fiction of F. Scott Fitzgerald)
FIUME, Salvatore
    Entra in Casa una Montagna
        (In Sipario, Vol. 31, nos. 361-362, June-July, 1976)
Five Evenings (see Volodin, Aleksandr M.)
Five Finger Exercise (see Shaffer, Peter)
Five O'Clock Tea (see Howells, William Dean)
Five Revue Sketches (see Pinter, Harold)
Fixin's; The Tragedy of a Tenant Farm Woman (see Green, Paul)
The Flame (see Clarke, Austin)
Flaming Ministers (see Kennedy, Charles Rann)
FLANAGAN, Hallie
    Arena, a documentary of the Federal Theatre, adapted for radio
    by Amita Fairgrieve
        (In 100 Non-Royalty Radio Plays)
FLAVIN, Martin, 1883-
    The Blind Man; a pantomime
        (In his Brains and Other One-Act Plays)
    Brains
        (In his Brains and Other One-Act Plays)
    Caleb Stone's Death Watch
        (In his Brains and Other One-Act Plays)
    Casualties
        (In his Brains and Other One-Act Plays)
    An Emergency Case
        (In his Brains and Other One-Act Plays)
    A Question of Principle
        (In his Brains and Other One-Act Plays)
        (In One-Act Plays for Stage and Study, 2nd Series)
FLEISSER, Marieluise
    Der Starke Stamm
        (In Theater Heute, no. 4, April 1974)
FLETCHER, John, 1579-1625
    Beggars Bush, by Beaumont and Fletcher
        (In their Works, Vol. 1)
    The Bloody Brother; or, Rollo, by Beaumont and Fletcher
        (In their Works, Vol. 4)
    Bonduca, by Beaumont and Fletcher
        (In their Works, Vol. 6)
    The Captain (see Beaumont, Francis)

Valentinian, by Beaumont and Fletcher
     (In their Works, Vol. 4)
The Widow (see Middleton, Thomas)
A Wife for a Month (see Beaumont, Francis)
The Wild-Goose Chase, by Beaumont and Fletcher
     (In their Works, Vol. 4)
Wit at Several Weapons (see Beaumont, Francis)
Wit Without Money, by Beaumont and Fletcher
     (In their Works, Vol. 2)
The Woman-Hater (see Beaumont, Francis)
The Woman's Prize; or, The Tamer Tam'd (see Beaumont,
     Francis)
Women Pleas'd (see Beaumont, Francis)
FLETCHER, Lucille
     My Client, Curley (see Corwin, Norman)
La Fleur des Pois (see Bourdet, Edouard)
The Flies (see Sartre, Jean-Paul)
Flight; a Play in Eight Dreams and Four Acts (see Bulgakov, Mik-
     hail A.)
Flight into Danger (see Hailey, Arthur)
Flight into Geography; a scenario (see Jolas, Eugene)
The Flight of the Natives (see Richardson, Willis)
Flint (see Mercer, David)
Floating Weeds; filmscript (excerpt) (see Ozu, Yasujiro)
The Flood (see Barlach, Ernst)
Flora; or, Hob in the Well (see Cibber, Colley)
Florence (see Dubé, Marcel)
FLORENTINO, Alberto S. , 1931-
     Oli Impan
          (In 3 Filipino Playwrights)
     Wedding Dance
          (In 3 Filipino Playwrights)
Las Flores (see Alvarez Quintero, Serafin)
Flores de Papel (see Wolff, Egon)
Florizel and Perdita (see Garrick, David)
Das Floss der Medusa (see Kaiser, Georg)
A Flower of Yeddo (see Mapes, Victor)
Flowers for the Trashman (see Jackmon, Marvin E.)
Flowers of the Forest (see Van Druten, John)
Die Flucht Nach Venedig (see Kaiser, Georg)
La Flûte Enchantée (see Mozart, Wolfgang Amadeus)
Fly Blackbird (see Jackson, C. Bernard)
The Flying Doctor (La Médecin Volant) (see Molière, Jean Baptiste)
Flying Scud (see Boucicault, Dion)
FO, Dario
     Bezahlt Wird Nicht!
          (In Theater Heute, no. 8, August 1977)
Foch, Marshall Ferdinand, 1851-1929
     *The War Indemnities (see Shaw, George Bernard)
FOELLBACH, Lena
     Jahresringe
          (In Theater der Zeit, no. 11, 1974)
Fog (see O'Neill, Eugene)

La Foi, l'Espérance et la Charité (see Horvath, Odön von)
Foiled by President Fred; The Goon Show Script (see Milligan,
    Spike)
La Foire d'Empoigne (see Anouilh, Jean)
La Folle de Chaillot (see Giraudoux, Jean)
Folle Enterprise (see Donnay, Maurice C.)
La Folle Journée; ou, Le Mariage de Figaro (see Beaumarchais,
    Pierre A.)
Folleville! (see Labiche, Eugene)
The Follies of Marianne (see Musset, Alfred de)
Follow the Yellow Brick Road; television script (see Potter, Dennis)
FOLPRECHT, William
    The Christmas Story
        (In 100 Non-Royalty Radio Plays)
A Fond Husband; or, The Plotting Sisters (see D'Urfey, Thomas)
FONVIZIN, Denis Ivanovich, 1745-1792
    The Brigadier
        (In The Literature of 18th Century Russia, Vol. 2)
    The Minor
        (In Nineteenth-Century Russian Plays)
    The Young Hopeful
        (In Masterpieces of the Russian Drama, Vol. 1)
FOO-HSI, Hsiung
    The Genius
        (In One-Act Plays for Stage and Study, 9th Series)
The Fool from the Hills (see Kennedy, Charles Rann)
A Fool of a Man (see Finnegan, Edward)
Fool's Errand (see Wood, Margaret)
The Fool's Revenge (see Hugo, Victor)
The Foot of the Wall (see Ionesco, Eugene)
Football (see Bellido, José-Maria)
FOOTE, Horton
    The Chase; play based on the author's novel
        (A Dramatists Play Service Play, 1952)
        (In Signet Film Book Series, 1966)
    The Midnight Caller
        (A Dramatists Play Service Play, 1959)
    Only the Heart
        (A Dramatists Play Service Play, 1944)
    Roots in a Parched Ground; originally produced on television's
    DuPont Show of the Month, under the title "Night of the Storm"
        (A Dramatists Play Service Play, 1962)
    Tomorrow; a play adapted from a story by William Faulkner;
    originally presented on television's "Playhouse 90"
        (A Dramatists Play Service Play, 1963)
    The Traveling Lady; the original play from which the author
    wrote his screenplay "Baby, the Rain Must Fall"
        (A Dramatists Play Service Play, 1955)
    Trip to Bountiful
        (A Dramatists Play Service Play, 1954)
FOOTE, Samuel, 1720-1777
    The Author
        (In A Collection of the Most Esteemed Farces ..., Vol. 3)

(In his Dramatic Works, Vol. 1)
The Bankrupt
(In his Dramatic Works, Vol. 2)
The Capuchin
(In his Dramatic Works, Vol. 2)
The Commissary
(In A Collection of the Most Esteemed Farces ..., Vol. 4)
(In his Dramatic Works, Vol. 2)
(In 18th Century Drama: Afterpieces)
The Cozeners
(In his Dramatic Works, Vol. 2)
The Devil upon Two Sticks
(In his Dramatic Works, Vol. 2)
The Englishman in Paris
(In A Collection of the Most Esteemed Farces ..., Vol. 3)
(In his Dramatic Works, Vol. 1)
The Englishman Return'd from Paris
(In A Collection of the Most Esteemed Farces ..., Vol. 3)
(In his Dramatic Works, Vol. 1)
The Knights
(In A Collection of the Most Esteemed Farces ..., Vol. 1)
(In his Dramatic Works, Vol. 1)
The Lame Lover
(In A Collection of the Most Esteemed Farces ..., Vol. 6)
(In his Dramatic Works, Vol. 2)
The Lyar
(In A Collection of the Most Esteemed Farces ..., Vol. 2)
(In his Dramatic Works, Vol. 1)
The Maid of Bath
(In his Dramatic Works, Vol. 2)
The Mayor of Garrat
(In A Collection of the Most Esteemed Farces ..., Vol. 1)
(In his Dramatic Works, Vol. 1)
The Minor
(In A Collection of the Most Esteemed Farces ..., Vol. 5)
(In his Dramatic Works, Vol. 1)
The Nabob
(In his Dramatic Works, Vol. 2)
The Orators
(In A Collection of the Most Esteemed Farces ..., Vol. 4)
(In his Dramatic Works, Vol. 1)
The Patron
(In A Collection of the Most Esteemed Farces ..., Vol. 4)
(In his Dramatic Works, Vol. 1)
Taste
(In A Collection of the Most Esteemed Farces ..., Vol. 1)
(In his Dramatic Works, Vol. 1)
A Trip to Calais
(In his Dramatic Works, Vol. 2)
Footfalls (see Beckett, Samuel)
For Better, for Worse (see Watkyn, Arthur)
For Our Sake (see Vega Carpio, Lope F.)
For Richer--For Richer; a radio script (see Boardman, True)

For Services Rendered (see Maugham, William Somerset)
For Tea on Sunday (see Mercer, David)
For Unborn Children (see Livingston, Myrtle S.)
FORBES, James, 1871-1938
    The Famous Mrs. Fair
        (In Representative American Dramas)
Forbes, Kathryn
    I Remember Mama (see Van Druton, John)
La Force du Sang (see Hardy, Alexandre)
Force Majeure (see John, Errol)
The Forc'd Marriage; or, The Jealous Bridegroom (see Behn, Mrs.
    Aphra)
The Forced Marriage (Le Mariage Forcé) (see Molière, Jean Bap-
    tiste)
The Forced Physician (Le Médecin Malgré Lui) (see Molière, Jean
    Baptiste)
FORD, Harriet
    Are Men Superior?
        (In One-Act Plays for Stage and Study, 7th Series)
    The Dickey Bird (see O'Higgins, Harvey)
    In-Laws
        (In One-Act Plays for Stage and Study, 4th Series)
    Youth Must Be Served
        (In One-Act Plays for Stage and Study, 3rd Series)
FORD, John, 1586?- ca. 1640
    C'Est Pitié Qu'elle Soit une Putain; adaptation Française de
        Christiane Barry
        (In L'Avant-Scène Théâtre, no. 565, June 1, 1975)
FORD, John, 1895-1973
    Stagecoach; screenplay by Dudley Nichols, from an original
        story by Ernest Haycox, directed by John Ford. Pictures
        and complete dialogue edited by Richard J. Anobile
        (In The Film Classics Library, 1975)
A Foregone Conclusion (see Howells, William Dean)
FOREMAN, Carl
    Young Winston; screenplay, based on Winston Churchil's book
        "My Early Life," film directed by Richard Attenborough
        (A Ballantine Books Screenplay, 1972)
FOREMAN, Richard, 1937-
    Angelface
        (In his Plays and Manifestos)
    Classical Therapy or A Week Under the Influence ...
        (In his Plays and Manifestos)
    HċOhTiEħLà (or) Hotel China
        (In his Plays and Manifestos)
    Hotel for Criminals; libretto by Richard Foreman, music by
        Stanley Silverman
        (In Yale/Theatre, Vol. 7, no. 1, Fall 1975)
    Ontological-Hysteric Manifesto I
        (In his Plays and Manifestos)
    Ontological-Hysteric Manifesto II
        (In his Plays and Manifestos)
    Ontological-Hysteric Manifesto III

Fortunato (see Alvarez Quintero, Serafin)
Fortune and Men's Eyes (see Peabody, Josephine P.)
Fortune by Land and Sea (see Heywood, Thomas)
Fortune, My Foe (see Davies, William R.)
FORTUNO, Claude
    Apprenez à Conduire par Correspondance
       (In L'Avant-Scène Théâtre, no. 579, Jan. 15, 1976)
    L'Enfant de la Balle
       (In L'Avant-Scène Théâtre, no. 608, Apr. 15, 1977)
The 'Forty-Niners, a Drama of the Gold Mines (see Hanshew,
    Thomas W.)
FORZANO, Giovacchino
    A Gust of Wind
       (In Gambit, no. 7)
    To Live in Peace
       (In Gambit, no. 7)
The Fossil (see Sternheim, Carl)
Les Fossiles; text in French (see Curel, François)
The Fossils (see Curel, François)
FOSTER, Paul, 1931-
    "Balls"
       (In his "Balls" and Other Plays)
       (In Calder & Boyars Playscripts no. 2)
    Elizabeth I
       (In his Elizabeth I and Other Plays)
    Heimskringla! or, The Stoned Angels
       (In Calder & Boyars Playscript Series no. 39, 1970)
    The Hessian Corporal
       (In his "Balls" and Other Plays)
       (In Calder & Boyars Playscripts no. 2)
    Hurrah for the Bridge
       (In his "Balls" and Other Plays)
       (In Calder & Boyars Playscripts no. 2)
    The Madonna in the Orchard
       (In his Elizabeth I and Other Plays)
    Marcus Brutus
       (In his Marcus Brutus and The Silver Queen)
    The Recluse
       (In his "Balls" and Other Plays)
       (In Calder & Boyars Playscripts no. 2)
    Satyricon
       (In his Elizabeth I and Other Plays)
       (In The Off Off Broadway Book)
    The Silver Queen
       (In his Marcus Brutus and The Silver Queen)
    Tom Paine
       (In Best American Plays, 7th Series, 1967-1973)
       (In Calder & Boyars Playscript Series no. 1)
The Foundling (see Moore, Edward)
The Foundling; The Waltons television script (see McGreevey, John)
The Fountain (see Calderon, George)
The Fountain (see O'Neill, Eugene)
FOUNTAIN, John, fl. 1661
  **The Royal Shepherdess (see Shadwell, Thomas)

The Four Freedoms (see Rivera, Vicente, Jr.)
4-H Club (see Shepard, Sam)
The 400 Blows; filmscript (see Truffaut, François)
The Four Little Girls (see Picasso, Pablo)
Four Plays; or, Moral Representations in One (see Beaumont,
     Francis)
Four Plays from "The Little Theatre of the Green Goose" (see
     Galcynski, Konstanty)
The Four Prentises of London (see Heywood, Thomas)
Four Saints in Three Acts (see Stein, Gertrude)
The Four Twins (see Copi)
LA FOURCHARDIERE, Georges de, 1874-1943
     **La Chienne (see Renoir, Jean)
La Fourmi dans le Corps (see Audiberti, Jacques)
The Fourposter (see Hartog, Jan de)
Fourteen (see Gerstenberg, Alice)
Fourteen Hundred Thousand (see Shepard, Sam)
The Fourteen Lovers of Ugly Mary-Ann (see Amalrik, Andrei)
A Fourth for Bridge (see Johnston, Denis)
The Fourth Mrs. Phillips (see Glick, Carl)
The Fourth Monkey (see Nicol, Eric)
The Fourth Room (see Reid, Ben)
FOWLER, Gene, 1891-1960
     The Mighty Barnum, screenplay by Gene Fowler and Bess
        Meredyth, film directed by Walter Lang
           (In Garland Classics of Film Literature Series)
FOX, George
     Earthquake; filmscript by George Fox and Mario Puzo, for the
        film directed by Mark Robson
           (In Signet Film Series, 1974)
Fox, Hound, & Huntress (see Lee, Lance)
FOY, Helen
     Newgate's the Fashion
           (In Best One-Act Plays of 1938, London)
     What is Hys Lyflode?
           (In Best One-Act Plays of 1941, London)
Fra un Allo e L'Altro (see Lopez, Sabatino)
Fragment of a Greek Tragedy (see Housman, A. E.)
Fragmente und Varianten (see Horvath, Odön von)
Fragments de Romet et Juiette (see Vigny, Alfred V.)
Les Fraises Musclées (extracts) (see Ribes, Jean-Michel)
Francesca da Rimini, d. 1285?
     *Francesca da Rimini (see Boker, George Henry)
Francesco d'Assisi, St., 1182-1226
     *Francesco e Galileo (see Cavani, Liliana)
Francillon (see Dumas, Alexandre, Fils)
Francis I, King of France, 1494-1547
     *The Tragedy of Chabct Admiral of France (see Chapman,
        George)
FRANCK, Pierre
     Les Deux Augures (see l'Isle-Adam, Villiers de)
     Le Faiseur. Pièce d'Honoré de Balzac, adaptation nouvelle et
        mise en scène de Pierre Franck

(In L'Avant-Scène du Théâtre, no. 524, Sept. 1973)
Monsieur Teste (see Valery, Paul)
FRANCKLIN, Thomas, 1721-1784
    The Earl of Warwick
        (In The London Stage, Vol. 3)
Françoise's Luck (see Porto-Riche, Georges de)
FRANCOVICH, Guillermo, 1901-
    Un Punal en la Noche
        (In El Teatro Actual Latinoamericano)
FRANJU, Georges
    Les Yeux sans Visage, d'après le roman de Jean Redon
        (In L'Avant-Scène Cinéma, no. 188, June 1, 1977)
FRANK, Bruno
    Moon Watch, adapted for radio by Edward Goldberger
        (In 100 Non-Royalty Radio Plays)
FRANK, Christopher
    **L'Important c'Est d'Aimer (see Zulawski, Adrzej)
Frankenstein; screenplay (see Whale, James)
Frankenstein, the True Story; teleplay (see Isherwood, Christopher)
Franklin, Benjamin, 1706-1790
    *1776 (see Edwards, Sherman)
FRANKLIN, Pearl
    Young America (see Ballard, Fred)
FRATTI, Mario, 1927-
    The Academy
        (In Masterpieces of the Modern Italian Theatre)
    Dolls No More
        (In Drama and Theatre, Vol. 11, no. 2, Winter 1972-73)
    The Return
        (In Masterpieces of the Modern Italian Theatre)
Die Frau im Fenster (see Hofmannsthal, Hugo von H.)
Die Frau mit dem Dolche (see Schnitzler, Arthur)
Die Frau Ohne Schatten (see Hofmannsthal, Hugo von H.)
Frau Warheit Will Niemand Herbergen (see Sachs, Hans)
Das Frauenopfer (see Kaiser, Georg)
FRAYN, Michael, 1933-
    Chinamen
        (In The Best Short Plays 1973)
Freaks; screenplay; text in French (see Browning, Tod)
The Fred Allen Show radio script (see Allen, Fred)
FREDERIC, Phyllis
    What Time Is It?
        (In 100 Non-Royalty Radio Plays)
Free Treat (see Bernard, Tristan)
Freedom for Clemens (see Dorst, Tankred)
FREEMAN, Carol, 1941-
    The Suicide
        (In Black Fire)
FREEMAN, David, 1941-
    Battering Ram
        (In Talonplays Series, 1972)
    You're Gonna Be Alright, Jamie Boy
        (In Talonplays Series, 1974)

Frei Caneca (see Telles, Carlos de Queiroz)
Freibrief (see Salvatore, Gaston)
Freiwild (see Schnitzler, Arthur)
FRENCH, Helen
    Charlie Who?
        (In Performing Arts in Canada, Vol. 8, no. 2, Summer 1971)
The French Revolution, Year One (see Lemasson, Sophie)
Les Frénétiques (see Salacrou, Armand)
Frenzy for Two (see Ionesco, Eugene)
Le Frere Aine (see Daudet, Alphonse)
Les Freres Ennemis (see Dubé, Marcel)
Fric-Frac (see Bourdet, Edouard)
Friday's Hiding (see Arden, John)
FRIDELL, Folke, 1904-
    One Man's Bread
        (In Modern Nordic Plays: Sweden)
FRIED, Emanuel
    The Dodo Bird
        (In Drama and Theatre, Vol. 11, no. 2, Winter 1972-73)
FRIEDMAN, Bruce Jay, 1930-
    Scuba Duba
        (In Best American Plays, 7th Series, 1967-1973)
Friedrich und Anna (see Kaiser, Georg)
FRIEL, Brian
    Crystal and Fox
        (In his Crystal and Fox and Mundy Scheme)
    The Enemy Within
        (In The Journal of Irish Literature, Vol. 4, no. 2, May 1975)
    Losers
        (In his Lovers)
    The Loves of Cass McGuire
        (In Noonday Plays Series, 1966)
    The Mundy Scheme
        (In his Crystal and Fox and Mundy Scheme)
    Philadelphia, Here I Come!
        (In Best Plays of the Sixties)
        (In Noonday Plays Series, 1966)
    Winners
        (In his Lovers)
Friends (see Abe, Kobo)
Friends and Relations (see Hood, Hugh)
FRINGS, Ketti
    Look Homeward, Angel; based on the novel by Thomas Wolfe
        (In 50 Best Plays of the American Theatre, Vol. 4)
FRISCH, Max, 1911-
    Als der Krieg zu Ende War
        (In his Stücke, Band 1)
    Andorra
        (In Hill & Wang Spotlight Drama Series, 1962)
        (In his Stücke, Band 2)
        (In his Three Plays, 1962)
    Biedermann et les Incendiaires; adaptation Française Philippe
    Pilliod. Titre original: "Biedermann und die Brandstifter"

        (In L'Avant-Scène Théâtre, no. 587, May 15, 1976)
Biedermann und die Brandstifter
        (In his Stücke, Band 2)
Die Chinesische Mauer
        (In his Stücke, Band 1)
Count Oederland
        (In his Three Plays, 1962)
Don Juan oder Die Lieber zur Geometrie
        (In his Stücke, Band 2)
Don Juan; or, The Love of Geometry; Acts IV and V
        (In The Theatre of Don Juan)
The Fire Raisers
        (In his Three Plays, 1962)
Graf Oederland
        (In his Stücke, Band 1)
La Grande Muraille
        (In L'Avant-Scène du Théâtre, no. 512, Feb. 15, 1973)
The Great Fury of Philip Holtz
        (In Postwar German Theatre)
Die Grosse Wut des Philipp Holtz
        (In his Stücke, Band 2)
Now They Sing Again
        (In Contemporary German Theater)
Nun Singen Sie Wieder
        (In his Stücke, Band 1)
Phillip Holtz's Fury
        (In Gambit, no. 4)
Santa Cruz
        (In his Stücke, Band 1)
Frisette (see Labiche, Eugene)
FRITZ, Walter Helmut
    Now He's There, Now He's Not; a radio play; both German and
        English texts are given
        (In Dimension, Vol. 3, no. 2, 1970)
The Frogs (see Aristophanes)
Frolic Wind (see Pryce, Richard)
From Core to Rind (see Sartoris, Ramón)
From Morn to Midnight (see Kaiser, Georg)
From Paradise to Butte (see Finch, Robert V.)
Fromont Jeune et Risler Aine (see Daudet, Alphonse)
The Front (see Korneichuk, Alexander E.)
The Front Page (see Hecht, Ben)
Frontier Fighters, A Historical Adventure (see Berlin, Nathan)
Froschkönig (see Eckart, Dietrich)
FROST, Rex
    Small Hotel
        (In Plays of the Year, Vol. 13, 1955)
FROST, Robert, 1875-1963
    A Way Out
        (In More One-Act Plays by Modern Authors)
Frühlingespiel (see Brust, Alfred)
FRUET, William
    Wedding in White

Funny Business (see Hughes, Glenn)
Funny Girl (see Styne, Jule)
The Funny Old Man (see Rozewicz, Tadeusz)
Funny Peculiar (see Stott, Mike)
Funnyhouse of a Negro (see Kennedy, Adrienne)
FURTH, George, 1932-
    Company (see Sondheim, Stephen)
The Fussy Man (Den Studeslöse) (see Holberg, Ludvig von)
FUST, Johann, 1400?-1466
    *Fust and His Friends (see Browning, Robert)
The Future Is in Eggs; or, It Takes All Sorts to Make a World (see
    Ionesco, Eugene)
Futz (see Owens, Rochelle)
FYLEMAN, Rose
    Cabbages and Kings
    (In Types of Modern Dramatic Composition)

Gabriel (see Mason, Clifford)
The Gadfly; or, The Son of the General (see Shaw, George Bernard)
Der Gärtner von Toulouse (see Kaiser, Georg)
Gage, Lyman Judson, U. S. Sect'y of the Treasury, 1836-1927
    *Two Administrations (see Bierce, Ambrose)
GAINES, Frederick
    A Christmas Carol, adapted from the work of Charles Dickens
    (In Five Plays from the Children's Theatre Company of
    Minneapolis)
    The Legend of the Sleepy Hollow, adapted from the work of
    Washington Irving
    (In Five Plays from the Children's Theatre Company of
    Minneapolis)
    The New Chautauqua Plays Without Playwright
    (In Break Out!)
GAINES, J. E.
    What If It Had Turned Up Heads
    (In The New Lafayette Theatre Presents)
GAINES-SHELTON, Ruth, 1873-
    The Church Fight
    (In Black Theater U. S. A., 1847-1974)
Les Gaites de l'Escardron (see Moinaux, Georges)
GALA, Antonio
    Anillos Para una Dama
    (In Teatro Español, 1973-74)
    Los Buenos Días Perdidos
    (In Teatro Español, 1972-73)
    Los Verdes Campos del Eden
    (In Teatro Español, 1963-64
Les Galanteries du Duc d'Ossonne, Vice-Roi de Naples (see Mairet,
    Jean de)
Galba, Servius Sulpicius, Roman Emperor, 5 B. C. ?-69 A. D.
    *Othon (Otho) (see Corneille, Pierre)
GAŁCYNSKI, Konstanty Ildefons
    The Little Theatre of "The Green Goose"; four plays

(In <u>Twentieth-Century Polish Avant-Garde Drama</u>)
The Little Theatre of "The Green Goose"; twenty-two short
  plays
    (In <u>Twentieth-Century Polish Avant-Garde Drama</u>)
GALE, Zona (Breese), 1874-1938
    Uncle Jimmy
      (In <u>Types of Modern Dramatic Composition</u>)
GALEEN, Henrik, 18??-19??
    The Golem; film scenario (see Wegener, Paul)
    Nosferatu; film scenario (see Murnau, Friedrich W.)
Los Galeotes (see Alvarez Quintero, Serafin)
La Galerie du Palais (see Corneille, Pierre)
La Galette des Rois (see Marais, Jean-Bernard)
GALEY, Matthieu, 1934-
    Butley; adaptation Française (see Gray, Simon)
GALICH, Manuel, 1913-
    Entre Cuatro Paredes
      (In <u>Teatro Guatemalteco Contemporaneo</u>)
Galilei, Galileo, 1564-1642
    *Francesco e Galileo (see Cavani, Liliana)
    *Galileo (see Brecht, Bertolt)
    *Life of Galileo (see Brecht, Bertolt)
Galizien (see Krleza, Miroslav)
GALLACHER, Tom
    Mr. Joyce Is Leaving Paris
      (In <u>Calder & Boyars Scottish Library Series</u>)
GALLEGOS, Daniel, 1930-
    La Colina
      (In <u>El Teatro Actual Latinoamericano</u>)
      (In <u>El Teatro de Hoy en Costa Rica</u>)
Gallows Humor (see Richardson, Jack)
GALLU, Samuel
    "Give 'em Hell Harry, " play presented on stage and screen,
      about Harry S Truman
        (An <u>Avon Books Playscript,</u> 1976)
GALSWORTHY, John, 1867-1933
    Escape
      (In his <u>Ten Famous Plays</u>)
    Joy
      (In his <u>Ten Famous Plays</u>)
    Justice
      (In his <u>Ten Famous Plays</u>)
    The Little Man
      (In <u>One-Act Plays by Modern Authors</u>)
    Loyalties
      (In <u>Masterpieces of the Modern English Theatre</u>)
      (In <u>his Ten Famous Plays</u>)
    Old English
      (In his <u>Ten Famous Plays</u>)
    The Roof
      (In his <u>Ten Famous Plays</u>)
    The Silver Box
      (In <u>Representative British Dramas</u>)

(In his Ten Famous Plays)
The Skin Game
(In his Ten Famous Plays)
Strife
(In his Ten Famous Plays)
Windows
(In his Ten Famous Plays)
GAMBETTI, Giacomo, 1932-
Il Vangelo Secundo Matteo, un film di Pier Paolo Pasolini
(In Garzanti Filmscripts, 1964)
The Gamblers (see Gogol, Nikolai)
GAMBOA, Federico, 1864-1939
La Venganza de la Gleba
(In Teatro Méxicano del Siglo XX, Vol. 1)
GAMBOA, José Joaquin, 1878-1931
Via Crucis
(In Teatro Méxicano del Siglo XX, Vol. 1)
A Game of Chess (see Middleton, Thomas)
Game of Hearts (see Molnar, Ferenc)
The Game of Love (Liebelei) (see Schnitzler, Arthur)
The Game of Love and Chance (see Marivaux, Pierre C.)
Games (see Bass, George H.)
The Gamester (see Moore, Edward)
The Gamester (see Shirley, James)
The Gamesters (see Garrick, David)
Ganar Amigos (see Ruiz de Alarcón y Mendoza, Juan)
Gang Busters radio script
The Eddie Doll Case (see Lord, Phillips H.)
GANLY, Andrew
Documents: The Dear Queen
(In The Journal of Irish Literature, Vol. 5, no. 2, May 1976)
GANZL, Serge
Candide; une pièce de Serge Ganzl d'après Voltaire
(In L'Avant-Scène Théâtre, no. 617, Nov. 1, 1977)
The Gaol Gate (see Gregory, Isabella A.)
Garbo, Greta, 1905-
*Greta Garbo, Quem Diria, Acabou No Irajo (see Melo, Fernando)
*What Does Greta Garbo Mean to You? (see Parlakian, Nishan)
GARCIA GUERRA, Ivan, 1938-
Don Quijote de Todo el Mundo
(In Teatro Contemporaneo Hispanoamericano, Vol. 2)
Fabula de las Cinco Caminantes
(In Teatro Breve Hispanoamericano Contemporaneo)
GARCIA LORCA, Federico, 1899-1936
Amor de Don Perlimplin con Belisa en su Jardin
(In his Obras Completas)
Asi Que Pasen Cinco Años
(In his Obras Completas)
(In Teatro Inquieto Español)
The Billy-Club Puppets
(In All the World's a Stage)
Blood Wedding
(In New Directions, Vol. 4, 1939)

Bodas de Sangre
  (In his Obras Completas)
Buster Keaton Rides Again: a Sequel; translated by Jack Spicer
  (In The Collected Books of Jack Spicer)
Buster Keaton's Ride, translated by Jack Spicer
  (In The Collected Books of Jack Spicer)
La Casa de Bernarda Alba
  (In his Obras Completas)
Dialogue of Amargo
  (In New Directions, Vol. 8, 1944)
Doña Rosita la Soltera, o El Lenguaje de las Flores
  (In his Obras Completas)
La Doncella, el Marinero y el Estudiante
  (In his Obras Completas)
The House of Bernarda Alba
  (In Contemporary Drama: 13 Plays)
  (In Enclosure)
In the Frame of Don Cristobal; a puppet farce
  (In New Directions, Vol. 8, 1944)
The Love of Don Perlimplin and Belisa in the Garden
  (In Masterpieces of the Modern Spanish Theatre)
El Maleficio de la Mariposa
  (In his Obras Completas)
Mariana Pineda
  (In his Obras Completas)
El Paseo de Buster Keaton
  (In his Obras Completas)
El Publico
  (In his Obras Completas)
Quimera
  (In his Obras Completas)
Retablillo de Don Cristobal
  (In his Obras Completas)
The Shoemaker's Prodigious Wife
  (In Modern Spanish Theatre)
Los Titeres de Cachiporra
  (In his Obras Completas)
Yerma; text in Spanish
  (In his Obras Completas)
La Zapatera Prodigiosa
  (In his Obras Completas)
GARCIA PONCE, Juan, 1932-
  Doce y Una, Trece
    (In Teatro Méxicano del Siglo XX, Vol. 4)
Un Garçon de Chez Véry (see Labiche, Eugene)
Le Garçon et l'Aveugle; text in English (Anon.)
    (In Medieval French Plays)
The Garden God (see Powell, Anthony)
Garden of Delights (see Arrabal, Fernando)
The Garden of the Hesperides (see Shaw, George Bernard)
Gardenias: Ten Cents (see Julian, Joseph)
GARDNER, Herb, 1934-
  The Goodbye People

(Noonday Original Plays Series, 1974)
GARNER, Hugh
  The Magnet
    (In A Collection of Canadian Plays, Vol. 2)
  Some Are So Lucky
    (In A Collection of Canadian Plays, Vol. 2)
  A Trip for Mrs. Taylor
    (In A Collection of Canadian Plays, Vol. 2)
Garnett, Constance (Black), 1862-1946
  *The Idiots Karamazov (see Durang, Christopher)
GARRETT, Jimmy, 1944-
  We Won the Night
    (In Black Fire)
GARRICK, David, 1717-1779
  Arthur and Emmeline
    (In his Dramatic Works, Vol. 3)
  Bon Ton; or, High Life Above Stairs
    (In A Collection of the Most Esteemed Farces ..., Vol. 4)
    (In his Dramatic Works, Vol. 3)
    (In The London Stage, Vol. 3)
  Bucks, Have at Ye All
    (In A Collection of the Most Esteemed Farces ..., Vol. 4)
  Catharine and Petruchio, adapted from Shakespeare's "Taming
    of the Shrew"
    (In A Collection of the Most Esteemed Farces ..., Vol. 3)
    (In his Dramatic Works, Vol. 1)
  The Clandestine Marriage (see Colman, George, The Elder)
  Cymbeline, adapted from the work of Shakespeare
    (In his Dramatic Works, Vol. 2)
  Cymon, altered from Dryden's "Cymon and Iphigenia"
    (In A Collection of the Most Esteemed Farces ..., Vol. 3)
    (In The London Stage, Vol. 3)
  The Enchanter; or, Love and Magic
    (In his Dramatic Works, Vol. 2)
  Every Man in His Humor (see Jonson, Ben)
  The Fairies, adapted from Shakespeare's "A Midsummer Night's
    Dream"
    (In his Dramatic Works, Vol. 1)
  Florizel and Perdita, adapted from Shakespeare's "Winter's
    Tale"
    (In A Collection of the Most Esteemed Farces ..., Vol. 1)
    (In his Dramatic Works, Vol. 1)
  The Gamesters
    (In his Dramatic Works, Vol. 2)
  The Guardian, founded on "La Pupille," by Barthelemi-Christophe
    Fagan
    (In A Collection of the Most Esteemed Farces ..., Vol. 1)
    (In his Dramatic Works, Vol. 2)
    (In The London Stage, Vol. 3)
  Harlequin's Invasion
    (In his Three Plays)
  High Life Below Stairs (see Townley, James)
  The Irish Widow; based on Molière's "Le Marriage Force"

(In A Collection of the Most Esteemed Farces ..., Vol. 5)
(In his Dramatic Works, Vol. 3)
(In The London Stage, Vol. 3)
Isabella; or, The Fatal Marriage
(In his Dramatic Works, Vol. 2)
The Jubilee
(In his Three Plays)
Lethe; or, Aesop in the Shades, based on James Miller's "An
Hospital for Fools"
(In A Collection of the Most Esteemed Farces ..., Vol. 1)
(In his Dramatic Works, Vol. 1)
Lilliput, based on parts of Swift's "Gulliver's Travels"
(In A Collection of the Most Esteemed Farces ..., Vol. 6)
(In his Dramatic Works, Vol. 2)
The Lying Valet; based on the second act, entitled "All Without
Money," of the play "Novelty; or, Every Act a Play," by
Peter Antony Motteux
(In A Collection of the Most Esteemed Farces ..., Vol. 2)
(In his Dramatic Works, Vol. 1)
May-Day; or, The Little Gypsy
(In A Collection of the Most Esteemed Farces ..., Vol. 6)
(In his Dramatic Works, Vol. 3)
The Meeting of the Company; or, Baye's Art of Acting; based
on Buckingham's "The Rehearsal"
(In his Three Plays)
Miss in Her Teens; or, The Medley of Lovers, founded on "La
Parisienne," by Florent Carton sieus Dancourt
(In A Collection of the Most Esteemed Farces ..., Vol. 1)
(In his Dramatic Works, Vol. 1)
(In 18th Century Drama: Afterpieces)
Neck of Nothing; The Narrow Escape, by David Garrick and
James Lacy, based on the work of Alain Rene Le Sage
(In A Collection of the Most Esteemed Farces ..., Vol. 2)
A Peep Behind the Curtain; or, The New Rehearsal
(In his Dramatic Works, Vol. 3)
Romeo and Juliet, adapted from the work of Shakespeare
(In his Dramatic Works, Vol. 1)
GARRO, Elena, 1920 or 1922-
Los Perros
(In 12 Ombras en un Acto)
La Señora en Su Balcón
(In Teatro Breve Hispanoamericano Contemporaneo)
(In Teatro Méxicano del Siglo XX, Vol. 5)
The Garroters (see Howells, William Dean)
GARZA, Roberto J., 1934-
No Nos Venceremos
(In Contemporary Chicano Theatre)
Gas (see Kaiser, Georg)
The Gas Heart (see Rosenstock, Sami)
GASKILL, William
The Speakers, by William Gaskill and Max Stafford-Clark,
freely adapted from the book by Heathcote Williams
(In Gambit, Vol. 7, no. 25, 1974)

I Gaspiri (The Upholsterers) (see Lardner, Ring)
Gastone, the Animal Tamer (see Morselli, Ercole L.)
The Gates of Summer (see Whiting, John)
Gats (see Kaiser, Georg)
GATTI, Armand, 1924-
    The Imaginary Life of the Street Cleaner Auguste G.
      (In Contemporary French Theater)
    Passion du Général Franco
      (In L'Avant-Scène Théâtre, no. 586, May 1, 1976)
Il Gattopardo; screenplay (see Visconti, Luchino)
Le Gaucher (see Penn, Arthur)
The Gauntlet (see Bjørnson, Bjørnstjerne)
GAY, John, 1685-1732
    Achilles
      (In his Poetical Works)
    Acis and Galatea; founded on Ovid's "Metamorphoses"
      (In his Poetical Works)
    The Beggar's Opera
      (In British Plays from the Restoration to 1820)
      (In Plays of the Restoration and 18th Century)
      (In his Poetical Works)
    The Captives
      (In his Poetical Works)
    Dione
      (In his Poetical Works)
    The Distress'd Wife (fragment)
      (In his Poetical Works)
    The Mohocks
      (In his Poetical Works)
  **L'Opéra de Quat'sous (Die Dreigroschenoper) (see Pabst, Georg
    W.)
    Polly
      (In his Poetical Works)
    The Rehearsal at Gotham (fragment)
      (In his Poetical Works)
    Three Hours After Marriage, by John Gay, Alexander Pope and
    John Arbuthnot
      (In his Poetical Works)
  **The Threepenny Opera; screenplay (see Lania, Leo)
    The What D'Ye Call It
      (In A Collection of the Most Esteemed Farces ..., Vol. 5)
      (In his Poetical Works)
    The Wife of Bath
      (In his Poetical Works)
The Gay Lord Quex (see Pinero, Arthur Wing)
The Gay White Way (see Rice, Elmer L.)
O "Gazeteiro" (see Pongetti, Henrique)
Gazul, Clara, pseud. (see Mérimée, Prosper)
Die Gefährtin (see Schnitzler, Arthur)
Der Gehörnte Siegfried (see Hebbel, Friedrich)
GEIGER, Milton
      In the Fog; a radio script
      (In Best Broadcasts of 1939-40)

The Twilight Shore; a radio script, Mar. 17, 1938
      (In Best Broadcasts of 1938-39)
GEIST, Peter von
      A Piscatorial Eclogue: Vel Isaacus Walton in Novamm Scalam
      Redivivus
      (In The Knickerbocker, Vol. 23, no. 5, May 1844)
Der Geist der Antike (see Kaiser, Georg)
Das Gelbe Fenster, der Gelbe Stein (see Hammel, Claus)
GELBER, Jack, 1932-
      Sleep
      (In Hill & Wang Spotlight Drama Series, 1972)
GELMAN, Alexander
      Protokoll einer Sitzung; original title: "Protokol Odnogo
      Zasedanija, " aus dem Russischen Günter Jäniche
      (In Theater der Zeig, no. 4, 1976)
      Rückkopplung; original title: "Obratnaja Svjaz, " aus dem
      Russischen von Regine Kühn
      (In Theater der Zeit, no. 11, 1977)
Le Gendarme est sans Pitié (see Moinaux, Georges)
The General (see Keaton, Buster)
General Confession (see Davis, Robertson)
El General del Diablo (see Zuckmayer, Carl)
GENET, Jean, 1910-
      Le Balcon
      (In Le Théâtre d'Aujourd'hui)
      Les Bonnes
      (In Le Théâtre d'Aujourd'hui)
      Les Paravents
      (In Le Théâtre d'Aujourd'hui)
Geneva: Another Political Extravaganza (see Shaw, George Bernard)
Genghis Khan, 1162-1227
      *The Orphan of China (see Voltaire)
The Genie of Sutton Place; a television play (see Heuer, Kenneth)
The Genius (see Foo-Hsi, Hsiung)
Genousie (see Obaldia, Rene de)
The Gentle Gunman (see MacDougall, Roger)
The Gentle Invasion (see Curteis, Ian)
Gentle Jack (see Bolt, Robert)
The Gentleman Caller (see Bullins, Edward A.)
The Gentleman Dancing-Master (see Wycherley, William)
A Gentleman from Cambridge (pseud.) (see Rich, John)
Gentleman Jim; screenplay, text in French (see Walsh, Raoul)
The Gentleman of Venice (see Shirley, James)
The Gentleman Usher (see Chapman, George)
The Genuine Sedemunds (see Barlach, Ernst)
GEOFFREY OF MONMOUTH, c. 1110-1154
      **King Arthur; or, The British Worthy (see Dryden, John)
Geographie und Liebe (see Bjørnson, Bjørnstjerne)
Geography of a Horse Dreamer (see Shepard, Sam)
George, Ernest (pseud.) (see Wise, Ernest George)
George A Green, the Pinner of Wakefield (see Greene, Robert)
The George Burns and Gracie Allen Show; television script, "Carna-
      tions" (see Burns, George)

George Dandin; or, The Wanton Wife (see Molière, Jean Baptiste)
The George Gobel Show television script (see Kanter, Hal)
George Reborn (see Cregan, David)
George III, King of Great Britain & Ireland, 1760-1820
*A Dialogue and Ode (see Hopkinson, Francis)
Georgette Lemeunier (see Donnay, Maurice C.)
GERALDY, Paul, 1885-
    Just Boys
        (In Modern One-Act Plays from the French)
Der Gerettete Alkibiades (see Kaiser, Georg)
Das Gerettete Venedig (see Hofmannsthal, Hugo von H.)
Germania Anno Zero; filmscript (see Rossellini, Roberto)
Germania Tod in Berlin (see Müller, Heiner)
Germany--Year Zero; filmscript (see Rossellini, Roberto)
GERMI, Pietro
    Sedotta e Abbandonata
        (In Dal Soggetto al Film, no. 31; 1964)
    L'Uomo di Paglia
        (In Dal Soggetto al Film, no. 9, 1958)
Germinal (see Orozco Castro, Jorge)
GEROULD, Daniel
    Explosion; an Overpopulation Farce for Two Actors and Percussion
        (In Break Out!)
    Triptych; Three Short Plays for Dummies
        (In Drama and Theatre, Vol. 11, no. 2, Winter 1972-73)
GERROLD, David
    Trouble with Tribbles; television script for an episode in
    "Star Trek"
        (In On the Air)
GERSHWIN, George, 1898-1937
    Of Thee I Sing; book by George S. Kaufman and Morrie Ryskind;
    music by George Gershwin; lyrics by Ira Gershwin
        (In Ten Great Musicals of the American Theatre)
    Porgy and Bess; music by George Gershwin; libretto by DuBose
    Heyward; lyrics by DuBose Heyward and Ira Gershwin; based
    on the play "Porgy," by Dorothy and DuBose Heyward
        (In Ten Great Musicals of the American Theatre)
GERSHWIN, Ira, 1896-
    Lady in the Dark (see Weill, Kurt)
    Of Thee I Sing (see Gershwin, George)
    Porgy and Bess (see Gershwin, George)
GERSTENBERG, Alice
    Attuned
        (In Ten One-Act Plays)
    Beyond
        (In Ten One-Act Plays)
    The Buffer
        (In Ten One-Act Plays)
    Ever Young
        (In her Four Plays for Four Women)
    Fourteen
        (In Ten One-Act Plays)

He Said and She Said-
  (In Ten One-Act Plays)
Hearts
  (In Ten One-Act Plays)
The Illuminati in Drama Libre
  (In Ten One-Act Plays)
Mah-jongg
  (In her Four Plays for Four Women)
Overtones
  (In Plays by and About Women)
  (In Ten One-Act Plays)
The Pot Boiler
  (In Ten One-Act Plays)
Seaweed
  (In her Four Plays for Four Women)
Their Husband
  (In her Four Plays for Four Women)
The Unseed
  (In Ten One-Act Plays)
GERSTL, Elfriede
  Legitimate Questions: A Radio Play
    (In The Malahat Review, Vol. 37, Jan. 1976)
Gertrude; or, Would She Be Pleased to Receive It? (see Leach,
  Wilford)
Geschichten aus dem Wiener Wald (see Horvath, Odön von)
Das Gespräch Alexandri Magni mit dem Philosopho Diogeni (see
  Sachs, Hans)
El Gesticulador (see Usigli, Rudolfo)
Der Gestohlene Gott (see Jahnn, Hans H.)
Get Out of My Hair! (see Feydeau, Georges)
Geta, Publius Septimius, Joint Emperor of Rome, 189-212
  *Geta (see Pechantre)
GETO, Alfred D.
  Pack Up Your Troubles
    (In The Army Play by Play)
Getting Married (see Shaw, George Bernard)
Gettysburg (see MacKaye, Percy)
GHELDERODE, Michel de, 1898-1962
  Barabbas
    (In his Seven Plays, Vol. 1)
  The Blind Men
    (In his Seven Plays, Vol. 1)
  Christopher Columbus; a dramatic fairy tale in three scenes
    (In Masterpieces of the Modern French Theatre)
    (In his Seven Plays, Vol. 2)
  Chronicles of Hell
    (In his Seven Plays, Vol. 1)
  The Death of Doctor Faust
    (In his Seven Plays, Vol. 2)
  Escurial
    (In Le Théâtre d'Aujourd'hui)
  Fastes d'Enfer
    (In Le Théâtre d'Aujourd'hui)

Halewyn
  (In Teatro Belga Contemporaneo)
Hop, Signor!
  (In his Seven Plays, Vol. 2)
Lord Halewyn
  (In his Seven Plays, Vol. 1)
Mademoiselle Jaïre
  (In Le Théâtre d'Aujourd'hui)
Miss Jairus
  (In his Seven Plays, Vol. 2)
A Night of Pity
  (In his Seven Plays, Vol. 2)
Pantagleize
  (In his Seven Plays, Vol. 1)
Piet Bouteille
  (In his Seven Plays, Vol. 2)
Red Magic
  (In his Seven Plays, Vol. 2)
The Strange Rider
  (In Chicago Review, Vol. 9, no. 4, Winter 1956)
  (In The Chicago Review Anthology)
Three Actors and Their Drama
  (In his Seven Plays, Vol. 1)
The Women at the Tomb
  (In his Seven Plays, Vol. 1)
The Ghost Dance (see Hart, Joseph)
The Ghost of Jerry Bundler (see Jacobs, William W.)
The Ghost of Molière (L'Ombre de Molière) (see Molière, Jean
  Baptiste)
The Ghost Sonata (see Strindberg, August)
Ghost Town (see Finch, Robert V.)
Ghost Trio; a television play (see Beckett, Samuel)
Ghosts (see Ibsen, Henrik)
The Ghosts of Windsor Park (see Brighouse, Harold)
GIACOSA, Giuseppe, 1847-1906
  Diritti dell'Anima
  (In Modern Italian One-Act Plays)
  Like Falling Leaves
  (In Representative Continental Dramas)
  Tosca; opera (see Puccini, Giacomo)
The Giants in the Earth (see Bernard, Kenneth)
La Giara (see Pirandello, Luigi)
GIBBS, Arthur Hamilton
  Meredew's Right Hand
  (In Types of Modern Dramatic Composition)
Gibier de Potence (see Feydeau, Georges)
GIBSON, William, 1914-
  Two for the Seesaw
  (In 50 Best Plays of the American Theatre, Vol. 4)
GIBSON PARRA, Percy, 1908-
  Esa Luna Que Empieza
  (In Teatro Peruano Contemporaneo)
The Gift (see Duncan, Ronald F.)

The Gift of Friendship; a play for television (see Osborne, John)
I Gigante della Montagna (see Pirandello, Luigi)
O Gigante Egoista (see Luna, Nelson)
GILBERT, Charles
    La Preuve du Contraire
        (In L'Avant-Scène Théâtre, no. 612, June 15, 1977)
GILBERT, Michael
    A Clean Kill
        (In Plays of the Year, Vol. 21, 1959/60)
GILBERT, William Schwenck, 1836-1911
    Ages Ago, with music by Frederic Clay
        (In Gilbert Before Sullivan)
    Engaged
        (In English Plays of the 19th Century, Vol. III: Comedies)
    Eyes and No Eyes, with music by Frederic Clay
        (In Gilbert Before Sullivan)
    The Gondoliers; or, The King of Barataria, by Gilbert and Sullivan
        (In Complete Plays of Gilbert and Sullivan)
    The Grand Duke; or, The Statutory Duel, by Gilbert and Sullivan
        (In Complete Plays of Gilbert and Sullivan)
    H. M. S. Pinafore; or, The Lass That Loved a Sailor, by Gilbert and Sullivan
        (In Complete Plays of Gilbert and Sullivan)
        (In Representative British Dramas)
    Happy Arcadia, with music by Frederic Clay
        (In Gilbert Before Sullivan)
    Iolanthe; or, The Peer and the Peri, by Gilbert and Sullivan
        (In Complete Plays of Gilbert and Sullivan)
    The Mikado; or, The Town of Titipu, by Gilbert and Sullivan
        (In Complete Plays of Gilbert and Sullivan)
    No Cards, with music by Frederic Clay
        (In Gilbert Before Sullivan)
    Our Island Home, with music by Frederic Clay
        (In Gilbert Before Sullivan)
    Patience; or, Bunthorne's Bride, by Gilbert and Sullivan
        (In Complete Plays of Gilbert and Sullivan)
    The Pirates of Penzance; or, The Slave of Duty, by Gilbert and Sullivan
        (In Complete Plays of Gilbert and Sullivan)
        (In The Play Book)
    Princess Ida; or, Castle Adamant, by Gilbert and Sullivan
        (In Complete Plays of Gilbert and Sullivan)
    Ruddigore; or, The Witch's Curse, by Gilbert and Sullivan
        (In Complete Plays of Gilbert and Sullivan)
    A Sensational Novel, with music by Frederic Clay
        (In Gilbert Before Sullivan)
    The Sorcerer, by Gilbert and Sullivan
        (In Complete Plays of Gilbert and Sullivan)
    Sweethearts
        (In The Drama, Vol. 16)
    Thespis; or, The Gods Grown Old, by Gilbert and Sullivan

Tom Cobb; or, Fortune's Toy
  (In English Plays of the 19th Century, Vol IV: Farces)
Trial by Jury, by Gilbert and Sullivan
  (In Complete Plays of Gilbert and Sullivan)
Utopia, Limited; or, The Flowers of Progress, by Gilbert and
  Sullivan
  (In Complete Plays of Gilbert and Sullivan)
The Yeomen of the Guard; or, The Merryman and His Maid, by
  Gilbert and Sullivan
  (In Complete Plays of Gilbert and Sullivan)
GILBERT-LECOMTE, Roger, 1907-1943
  The Odyssey of Ulysses the Palmiped
  (In Modern French Theatre)
Giles Corey of the Salem Farms (see Longfellow, Henry Wadsworth)
GILL, Peter
  Small Change
  (In Plays and Players, Vol. 23, no. 11 & 12, Aug. & Sept.
  1976)
GILLE, Andre
  Les Vilains; d'après Ruzzante
  (In L'Avant-Scène du Théâtre, no. 514, Mar. 15, 1973)
GILLES, Ange
  Un Lache; d'après Guy de Maupassant
  (In L'Avant-Scène du Théatre, no. 545, July 15, 1974)
  Noces d'Argent
  (In L'Avant-Scène du Théatre, no. 525, Sept. 1973)
Gilles und Jeanne (see Kaiser, Georg)
GILLETTE, William Hooker, 1855-1937
  The Red Owl
  (In One-Act Plays for Stage and Study, 1st Series)
  Secret Service; a drama of the Southern Confederacy
  (In Representative American Plays, 1792-1949)
  Sherlock Holmes, based on stories by Sir Arthur Conan Doyle
  (In Plays of the Year, Vol. 44, 1975)
GILROY, Frank D., 1925-
  Les Jeux de la Nuit; adaptation de Marcel Mithois
  (In L'Avant-Scène Théâtre, no. 554, Dec. 15, 1974)
  Present Tense
  (In Best Short Plays, 1974)
GIMENEZ-ARNAU, José Antonio
  Murio Hace Quince Años
  (In Teatro Español, 1952-53)
Gimme Shelter (see Keeffe, Barrie)
The Ginger Man (see Donleavy, James Patrick)
GINSBURY, Norman
  The Safety Match
  (In Best Short Plays of the World Theatre, 1968-1973)
  Viceroy Sarah
  (In Famous Plays of 1934-35)
GINZBURG, Natalia
  The Advertisement
  (In New Theatre of Europe, Vol. 4)
  (In Plays by and About Women)

Giochi di Mano (see Bordon, Furio)
Il Gioco delle Parti (see Pirandello, Luigi)
GIORLOFF, Ruth
    Maizie
        (In One-Act Plays for Stage and Study, 5th Series)
    The Way Out
        (In One-Act Plays for Stage and Study, 7th Series)
Giovanni in London; or, The Libertine Reclaimed (see Moncrieff,
    William T.)
GIOVANNINETTI, Silvio
    Lidia o el Infinito
        (In Teatro Italian Contemporaneo)
Uma Girafinha das Arabias (see Monteiro, José M.)
GIRAUD, Giovanni, conte, 1776-1834
    Il Prognosticante Fanatico
        (In Teatro Comico Moderno)
GIRAUDOUX, Jean, 1882-1944
    Amphitryon 38; text in French
        (In his Théâtre I)
    L'Apollon de Bellac
        (In his Théâtre IV)
    Cantique des Cantiques
        (In his Théâtre III)
    Electra; a play in two acts
        (In Masterpieces of the Modern French Theatre)
    Electre; text in French
        (In his Théâtre III)
    Fin de Siegfried
        (In his Théâtre I)
    La Folle de Chaillot
        (In his Théâtre IV)
    La Guerre de Troie n'Aura Pas Lieu
        (In The French Theater Since 1930)
        (In his Théâtre II)
    L'Impromptu de Paris
        (In his Théâtre III)
    Intermezzo; text in French
        (In his Théâtre II)
    Judith; text in French
        (In his Théâtre I)
    Ondine
        (In Contemporary Drama: 13 Plays)
    Ondine; text in French
        (In his Théâtre III)
    Pour Lucréce
        (In his Théâtre IV)
    Siegfried; text in French
        (In his Théâtre I)
    Sodome et Gomorrhe
        (In his Théâtre IV)
    Supplément; ou, Voyage de Cook
        (In his Théâtre III)
    Tessa; text in French

(In his Théâtre II)
GIRETTE, Marcel, 1849-
The Weaver of Dreams
(In Modern One-Act Plays from the French)
The Girl (see People, Edward)
The Girl from Kavalla, an historical romance (see Wang, William
H.)
The Girl in the Tube (see Allom, Mikhail)
The Girl of the Golden West (see Belasco, David)
The Girl Who Did Not Want to Go to Kuala Lumpur (see Mavor,
Osborne Henry)
The Girl with the Cut-Off Hands (see Quillard, Pierre)
The Girl with the Golden Voice (see Shaw, George Bernard)
The Girl with the Green Eyes (see Fitch, Clyde)
Gishiki; screenplay (see Oshima, Nagisa. La Ceremonie; text in
French)
GIUDICELLI, Christian, 1942-
La Reine de la Nuit
(In L'Avant-Scène Théâtre, no. 611, June 1, 1977)
Giulietta Degli Spiriti; filmscript (see Fellini, Federico)
Giulietta e Romeo; filmscript (see Castellani, Renato)
"Give 'em Hell Harry" (see Gallu, Samuel)
Give Me Wings, Brother (see Delston, Vernon)
The Gladiator (see Bird, Robert Montgomery)
Gladly, My Cross-eyed Bear (see Hopkins, John R.)
Gladly Otherwise (see Simpson, Norman F.)
Glamour (see Bernard, Jean J.)
GLASGOW, Alex
Close the Coalhouse Door (see Plater, Alan)
GLASPELL, Susan, 1882-1948
Alison's House
(In Six Plays: Famous Plays Series, 1930)
Suppressed Desires
(In 10 Short Plays)
Trifles
(In By Women)
(In Types of Modern Dramatic Composition)
The Glass Menagerie (see Williams, Tennessee)
The Glass of Water (see Scribe, Eugene)
The Glass Slipper (see Molnar, Ferenc)
Glastonbury Skit (see Shaw, George Bernard)
Glaube Liebe Hoffnung (see Horvath, Odön von)
GLAZE, Harriet
The Old Oaken Bucket
(In 100 Non-Royalty Plays)
GLEASON, Jackie, 1916-
The Honeymooners television script, "A Letter to the Boss"
(see Marx, Marvin)
The Honeymooners television script, "The $99,000 Answer"
(see Stern, Leonard)
GLEBOV, Anatole, 1899-
Inga
(In Six Soviet Plays)

GLICK, Carl
    The Fourth Mrs. Phillips
        (In One-Act Plays for Stage and Study, 4th Series)
The Glimpse of Reality (see Shaw, George Bernard)
GLINES, John
    In the Desert of My Soul
        (In Best Short Plays, 1976)
Glissements Progressifs du Plaisir (see Robbe-Grillet, Alain)
Gloria (see Marinković, Ranko)
Gloria and Esperanza (see Bovasso, Julie)
Le Glorieux (see Destoughes, Philippe N.)
The Glorious First of June (see Sheridan, Richard Brinsley)
Glorious Morning (see Macowan, Norman)
The Glory of Columbia: Her Yeomanry! (see Dunlap, William)
Gnaeus Pompeius Magnus, "Pompey the Great," 106-48 B.C.
    *La Morte de Pompee (The Death of Pompey)(see Corneille,
      Pierre)
    *Pompee (see Corneille, Pierre)
    *Sertorius (see Corneille, Pierre)
    *The Tragedy of Caesar and Pompey (see Chapman, George)
Go West (see Keaton, Buster)
Goa (see Currimbhoy, Asif)
The Goat (see Keaton, Buster)
Goatsong for Glutt (see Schrock, Gladden)
Gobierno de Alcoba (see Rovinski, Samuel)
God Have Mercy on the June-Bug (see Phillips, Louis)
The God of Quiet (see Drinkwater, John)
God of Vengeance (see Asch, Sholem)
GODARD, Jean-Luc, 1930-
    Les Carabiniers; screenplay
        (In L'Avant-Scène Cinéma, nos. 171-172, July-Sept. 1976)
    A Married Woman (Une Femme Mariée); filmscript
        (In Lorrimer Screenplay Series, 1975)
        (In his Three Films)
    Masculine Feminine; screenplay based on two stories by Guy de
      Maupassant
        (In Grove Press Film Script Series, 1969)
    Pierrot le Fou; d'après "Obsession," un roman de Lionel White
        (In L'Avant-Scène Cinema, nos. 171-172, July-Sept. 1976)
    Two or Three Things I Know About Her
        (In Lorrimer Screenplay Series, 1975)
        (In his Three Films)
    A Woman Is a Woman
        (In Lorrimer Screenplay Series, 1975)
        (In his Three Films)
Godefroy (see Moinaux, Georges)
GODEFROY, Philip
    Intermezzo
        (In Best One-Act Plays of 1941, London)
GODEFROY, Vincent
    Full Circle
        (In Best One-Act Plays of 1939, London)
GODFREY, Thomas, 1736-1763
    The Prince of Parthia

(In <u>Representative American Plays</u>, 1792-1949)
(In <u>Representative Plays by American Dramatists</u>, Vol. 1)
GODLOVITCH, Charles Z., 1921-
  Timewatch
    (In <u>Contemporary Canadian Drama</u>)
The Gods Are Not to Blame (see Rotimi, Ola)
The Gods of the Mountain (see Dunsany, Edward John)
The Godsend (see Hooke, Nina W.)
Godunov, Boris Fedorovich, Czar of Russia, 1552-1605
  *Boris Godunov (see Pushkin, Aleksandr)
  *Demetrius (see Hebbel, Friedrich)
  *Tsar Fyodor Ivanovich (see Tolstoi, Aleksei K.)
Goebbels, Joseph Paul, 1897-1945
  *Germania Tod in Berlin (see Müller, Heiner)
GOERING, Reinhard, 1887-1936
  Naval Encounter
    (In <u>Vision and Aftermath: Four Expressionist War Plays</u>)
GÖRLING, Lars, 1931-1966
  The Sandwiching
    (In <u>Modern Nordic Plays: Sweden</u>)
GOETHE, Johann Wolfgang von, 1749-1832
  **The Death of Doctor Faust (see Ghelderode, Michel de)
  **Doctor Faustus (see Marlowe, Christopher)
  Egmont
    (In <u>World Drama</u>, Vol. 2)
  **Faust; filmscript; text in French (see Rohmer, Eric)
  **Faust; text in German (see Kaiser, Georg)
  Faust: The Tragedy, Part One, translated by John Prudhoe
    (In <u>Classics of Drama in English Translation</u> Series, 1973)
  Iphigenia in Tauris
    (In <u>Classics of Drama in English Translation</u> Series, 1966)
    (In <u>The Drama</u>, Vol. 11)
  **Johann Faustus (see Eisler, Hanns)
  **Luste; or, The Crystal Girl (see Valery, Paul)
  **The Only One; or, The Curses of the Cosmos (see Valery, Paul)
  Stella
    (In <u>The Drama</u>, Vol. 12)
GOGGAN, John Patrick, 1907-
  La Case de Té de la Luna de Agosto, por John Patrick, pseud.
    (In <u>Teatro Norteamericano Contemporaneo</u>)
  The Story of Mary Surratt, by John Patrick, pseud.
    (A <u>Dramatists Play Service</u> Play, 1947)
  The Teahouse of the August Moon, by John Patrick, pseud.
    (In <u>50 Best Plays of the American Theatre</u>, Vol. 4)
GOGOL, Nikolai Vasil'evich, 1809-1852
  The Gamblers
    (In his <u>Collected Tales and Plays</u>)
  The Government Inspector
    (In <u>The Storm and Other Russian Plays</u>)
  The Government Inspector, adapted by Peter Raby
    (In <u>Minnesota Drama Editions</u>, no. 7)
  The Inspector

GOLDMAN, James
 Robin and Marian; screenplay of the film directed by Richard
 Lester
 (A Bantam Books Screenplay, 1976)
GOLDMAN, William
 The Great Waldo Pepper; screenplay by William Goldman, based
 on a story by George Roy Hill, directed by George Roy Hill
 (A Dell Books Screenplay, 1975)
GOLDMANN, Friedrich
 R. Hot; musik Friedrich Goldmann; text-buch Thomas Körner
 (In Theater der Zeit, no. 8, 1976)
GOLDONI, Carlo, 1707-1793
 **L'Amant Militaire (see San Francisco Mime Troup)
 Il Campiello
 (In L'Avant-Scène Théâtre, no. 596, Oct. 15, 1976)
 Un Curioso Accidente
 (In Teatro Comico Moderno)
 L'Eventail
 (In L'Avant-Scène Théâtre, no. 570, 1975)
 The Fan
 (In World Drama, Vol. 2)
 Mirandolina, translated and adapted by Lady Gregory
 (In Complete Plays of Lady Gregory, Vol. 4)
 The Post-Inn
 (In The Drama, Vol. 5)
GOLDSMITH, Clifford
 The Aldrich Family; radio script, Oct. 31, 1939: A Halloween
 Story
 (In Best Broadcasts of 1939-40)
GOLDSMITH, Oliver, 1728-1774
 The Good Natur'd Man
 (In his Collected Works, Vol. 5)
 She Stoops to Conquer; or, The Mistakes of a Night
 (In British Plays from the Restoration to 1820, Vol. 2)
 (In his Collected Works, Vol. 5)
 (In Plays of the Restoration and 18th Century)
 (In World Drama, Vol. 1)
GOLEA, Antoine
 La Prison
 (In L'Avant-Scène Théâtre, no. 580, July 1, 1976)
 The Golem (see Leivick, Halper)
 The Golem; film scenario (see Wegener, Paul)
GOLL, Ivan, 1891-1950
 Methusalem
 (In Seven Expressionist Plays)
GOMBROWICZ, Witold
 The Marriage
 (In Calder & Boyars Playscripts Series, no. 34)
 Operetta
 (In Calder & Boyars Playscript Series, no. 48)
 Princess Ivona
 (In Calder & Boyars Playscript Series, no. 13)
GOMEZ DE LA SERNA, Ramón, 1888-1963
 Los Medios Seres

(In Teatro Inquieto Español)
GONDINET, Edmond
   The Happiest of the Three (see Labiche, Eugene)
The Gondoliers; or, The King of Barataria (see Gilbert, William S.)
Gone (see Abse, Dannie)
Gone for a Soldier (see Biel, Nicholas)
Gone Out (see Rosewicz, Tadeusz)
Gone Today (see Finch, Robert V.)
GONZALEZ, Gloria
   Curtains
      (In Best Short Plays, 1976)
GONZALEZ BOCANEGRA, Francisco, 1824-1861
   Vasco Nuñez de Balboa
      (In Teatro Méxicano del Siglo XIX, Vol. 1)
GONZALEZ CABALLERO, Antonio, 1931-
   El Medio Pelo
      (In Teatro Méxicano, 1964)
   Señoritas a Disgusto
      (In Teatro Méxicano del Siglo XX, Vol. 5)
GOOCH, Steve
   Female Transport; parts 1 & 2
      (In Plays and Players, Vol. 21, nos. 4 & 5, Jan. and Feb.
      1974)
The Good and Faithful Servant (see Orton, Joe)
The Good and Obedient Young Man (see Barr, Betty)
Good Day (see Peluso, Emanuel)
The Good Fairy (see Molnar, Ferenc)
Good Friday; a dramatic poem (see Masefield, John)
Good Morning; filmscript (excerpt) (see Ozu, Yasujiro)
The Good Natur'd Man (see Goldsmith, Oliver)
Good Theatre (see Morley, Christopher)
Good Times television scripts
   Getting Up the Rent (see Monte, Eric)
   Junior the Senior (see Derman, Lou)
   Michael Gets Suspended (see Monte, Eric)
   Springtime in the Ghetto (see Paul, Norman)
   The Visitor (see Elinson, Jack)
Good Vintage (see Totheroh, Dan)
The Good Woman of Sitzuan (see Brecht, Bertolt)
Good-bye, Gray Flannel; television script (see Howells, J. Harvey)
Goodbye, My Gentle (see Nolledo, Wilfredo D.)
The Goodbye People (see Gardner, Herb)
Goodbye to the Lazy K (see Finch, Robert V.)
Goodbye to the Summer (see Carroll, Paul Vincent)
GOODCHILD, Roland
   The Grand Duchess
      (In Canada on Stage)
GOODMAN, Kenneth Sawyer, 1883-1918
   The Wonder Hat
      (In The Play Book)
GOODMAN, Paul, 1911-
   Saul
      (In New Directions, Vol. 8, 1944)

The Tower of Babel; a puppet show
(In New Directions, Vol. 5, 1940)
GOODRICH, Frances
The Diary of Anne Frank, by Frances Goodrich and Albert
Hackett
(In 50 Best Plays of the American Theatre, Vol. 4)
GOODRICH, John F.
The Last Command, screenplay by John F. Goodrich, film
directed by Josef von Sternberg
(In Motion Picture Continuities)
Goon Show television scripts (see Milligan, Spike)
Gopaleen, Myles na (see O'Nolan, Brian)
GORAGUER, Alain
La Planete Sauvage (see Laloux, Rene)
Garboduc; or, Ferrex and Porrex (see Norton, Thomas)
GORDON, Robert
The Tunes of Chicken Little
(In Playwrights for Tomorrow, Vol. 13, 1975)
GORDONE, Charles F. (Oyamo), 1925-
The Breakout, by Oyamo, pseud.
(In Black Drama Anthology)
Gordone Is a Muthah
(In The Best Short Plays, 1973)
His First Step, by Oyamo, pseud.
(In The New Lafayette Theatre Presents)
No Place to Be Somebody
(In Black Theater)
(In Contemporary Black Drama)
Gordone Is a Muthah (see Gordone, Charles F.)
GORELIK, Mordecai
The Big Day
(In Best Short Plays, 1977)
The Gorge; television script (see Nichols, Peter)
Gorilla Queen (see Tavel, Ronald)
GOR'KII, Maksim, 1868-1936
Barbarians
(In his Seven Plays)
Les Derniers; adaptation de Lily Denis
(In L'Avant-Scène Théâtre, no. 618, Nov. 15, 1977)
Dostigaeff and the Others
(In The Last Plays of Maxim Gorki)
Down and Out
(In Masterpieces of the Russian Drama, Vol. 2)
Enemies
(In his Seven Plays)
Feinde; text in German
(In Theater Heute, Vol. 14, no. 3, March 1973)
In the Depths
(In The Drama, Vol. 18)
The Lower Depths
(In Masterpieces of the Modern Russian Theatre)
(In The Moscow Art Theatre Series of Russian Plays)
(In his Seven Plays)

(In The Storm and Other Russian Plays)
(In 20th Century Russian Plays)
Night's Lodging
    (In Dramas of Modernism)
Queer People
    (In his Seven Plays)
Vassa Zheleznova (Mother)
    (In his Seven Plays)
Yegor Bulichoff
    (In The Last Plays of Maxim Gorki)
Yegor Bulychov and the Others
    (In his Seven Plays)
Gorky, Maxim (see Gor'kii, Maksim)
GOROSTIZA, Carlos, 1920-
    El Pan de la Locura
        (In El Teatro Actual Latinoamericano)
GOROSTIZA, Celestino, 1904-
    El Color de Nuestra Piel
        (In Teatro Méxicano del Siglo XX, Vol. 2)
        (In Teatro Méxicano Contemporaneo)
    La Malinche
        (In Teatro Méxicano, 1958)
        (In Teatro Méxicano del Siglo XX, Vol. 4)
GOROSTIZA, Manuel Eduardo de, 1798-1851
    Contigo Pan y Cebolla
        (In Teatro Méxicano del Siglo XIX, Vol. 1)
The Gospel According to St. Matthew; screenplay (see Pasolini, Pier
    Paolo. Il Vangelo Secondo Matteo)
GOSS, Clay
    Andrew
        (In his Homecookin': Five Plays)
    Homecookin'
        (In his Homecookin': Five Plays)
    Mars: Monument to the Last Black Eunuch
        (In his Homecookin': Five Plays)
    On Being Hit
        (In his Homecookin': Five Plays)
        (In The New Lafayette Theatre Presents)
    OurSides
        (In his Homecookin': Five Plays)
GOTTLIEB, Alex
    September Song
        (In Best Short Plays, 1976)
GOUNOD, Charles François, 1818-1893
    Le Mythe de Faust 1: Faust
        (In L'Avant-Scène Opéra, no. 2, Mar./Apr. 1976)
Le Gouter des Generaux (see Vian, Boris)
The Government Inspector (see Gogol, Nikolai)
The Governor's Lady (see Mercer, David)
GOW, Ronald, 1897-
    Ann Veronica, adapted by Ronald Gow from the novel by H. G.
    Wells
        (In Plays of the Year, Vol. 2, 1949)

GOZZI, Carlo, conte, 1722-1806
  Turandot, Prizessin von China; ein Tragikomisches Mährchen
  nach Gozzi von Schiller
    (In Schiller's Works, Vol. 4)
GRABBE, Christian Dietrich, 1801-1836
  Don Juan and Faust
    (In The Theatre of Don Juan)
Gracchus, Caius Sempronius, c. 159-121 B. C.
  *Caius Gracchus (see Chénier, Marie-Joseph B.)
  Les Gracques (see Lamarche, Gustave)
Graf Orderland (see Frisch, Max)
Der Graf von Ratzenburg (see Barlach, Ernst)
La Grammaire (see Labiche, Eugene)
Gramps; radio script (see Rogers, Merrill)
El Gran Minue (see Ruiz Iriarte, Victor)
GRANBERRY, Edwin, 1897-
  A Trip to Czardis
    (In The Mentor Book of Short Plays)
  **A Trip to Czardis; radio script (see Hart, Elizabeth)
Le Grand Autobus (see Rigoir, Vincent)
The Grand Ceremonial (see Arrabal, Fernando)
The Grand Duchess (see Goodchild, Roland)
The Grand Duke; or, The Statutory Duel (see Gilbert, William S.)
Grand Illusion; filmscript (see Renoir, Jean)
Grand Magic (see Filippo, Eduardo de)
Grand Tenement (see Eyen, Tom)
La Grande Casa (see Behan, Brendan)
La Grande Guerra; screenplay (see Monicelli, Mario)
Le Grande Muraille (see Frisch, Max)
La Grande Oreille (see Breal, Pierre-Aristide)
La Grande Revue du XXe Siecle; ou, "Marie Satanas c'est pas
  Degueulasse" (see Arrabal, Fernando)
La Grande y la Pequeña Maniobra (see Adamov, Arthur)
Grandma Faust (see Bond, Edward)
Grandma--Old Style (see Eaton, Walter P.)
Grandma Pulls the String (see Delano, Edith B.)
La Grand'mere (see Hugo, Victor)
Grania (see Gregory, Isabella A.)
Granville, George (see Lansdowne, George Granville, baron)
GRANVILLE-BARKER, Harley Granville, 1877-1946
  Fortunato (see Alvarez Quintero, Serafin)
  A Hundred Years Old (see Alvarez Quintero, Serafin)
  The Lady from Alfaqueque (see Alvarez Quintero, Serafin)
  The Madras House
    (In Edwardian Plays)
    (In Representative British Dramas)
  **The Madras House (see Shaw, George Bernard)
  The Women Have Their Way (see Alvarez Quintero, Serafin)
GRASS, Günther, 1927-
  Amleto Principe di Danimarca (see Brecht, Bertolt)
  Rocking Back and Forth
    (In Postwar German Theatre)
  Uptight (Scenes 1, 3, 5, 6) Both German and English texts are
  given

(In Dimension, Vol. 3, Special issue, 1970)
Grass and Wild Strawberries (see Ryga, George)
The Grateful Servant (see Shirley, James)
GRAU, Jacinto, 1877-1962
    El Señor de Pigmalion
        (In Teatro Inquieto Español)
Graven Images (see Miller, May)
GRAVES, Warren C., 1933-
    The Proper Perspective
        (In Contemporary Canadian Drama)
GRAY, Simon James Holliday
    Butley
        (In Methuen's Modern Plays Series, 1971)
    Butley, de Simon Gray, adaptation Française de Matthieu Galley
        (In L'Avant-Scène Théâtre, no. 547, Sept. 1, 1974)
    Dog Days
        (In Methuen's Modern Plays Series, 1976)
        (In The New Review, Vol. 2, no. 20, Nov. 1975)
    Otherwise Engaged
        (In his Otherwise Engaged and Other Plays)
    Plaintiffs and Defendants; a television play
        (In The New Review, Vol. 1, no. 11, Feb. 1975)
        (In his Otherwise Engaged and Other Plays)
    Sleeping Dog; a play for television
        (In Faber & Faber Plays Series, 1968)
    Spoiled
        (In Methuen Modern Plays Series, 1971)
    Two Sundays, a BBC television play
        (In The New Review, Vol. 1, no. 8, Nov. 1974)
        (In his Otherwise Engaged and Other Plays)
GRAY, Stanley
    If You Give a Dance, You Gotta Pay the Band
        (In Great Television Plays, Vol. 2)
GREANIAS, George
    Wilson
        (In Playwrights for Tomorrow, Vol. 12)
Grease (see Casey, Warren)
The Great American Desert (see Oppenheimer, Joel)
The Great Caper; a visionary drama (see Campbell, Ken)
Great Catherine (Whom Glory Still Adores) (see Shaw, George Bernard)
The Great Collision of Monday Last (see Bradbury, Ray)
The Great Dark (see Totheroh, Dan)
The Great Diamond Robbery (see Alfriend, Edward M.)
The Great Divide (see Moody, William Vaughn)
The Great Duke of Florence (see Massinger, Philip)
The Great Elixir (see Baker, George M.)
The Great Fury of Philip Holz (see Frisch, Max)
The Great God Brown (see O'Neill, Eugene)
Great Goodness of Life; a Coon Show (see Jones, LeRoi)
The Great Highway (see Strindberg, August)
The Great MacDaddy (see Carter-Harrison, Paul)
The Great Speckled Band; a radio script (see Hardwick, Michael)

The Great Stage of the World (see Calderon de la Barca)
The Great String Robberies (see Milligan, Spike)
The Great Waldo Pepper; screenplay (see Goldman, William)
The Great White Hope (see Sackler, Howard)
GREAVES, Donald, 1943-
    The Marriage
       (In Black Drama Anthology)
The Grecian Daughter (see Murphy, Arthur)
GREDY, Jean-Pierre, 1920-
    Peau de Vache (see Barillet, Pierre)
    Une Rose au Petit Dejeuner (see Barillet, Pierre)
Greed, screenplay (see Von Stroheim, Erich)
Greek to You (see Hughes, Babette)
GREEN, Adolph, 1915-
    Applause (see Strouse, Charles)
    Wonderful Town (see Bernstein, Leonard)
GREEN, Cara Mae
    Jumpin' the Broom
       (In One-Act Plays for Stage and Study, 5th Series)
GREEN, Cliff
    Marion; parts 1-4
       (In Australian Theatre Workshop, no. 12, 1974)
GREEN, Erma, 1897-
    Fixin's; the Tragedy of a Tenant Farm Woman (see Green, Paul)
GREEN, Janet
    Murder Mistaken
       (In Plays of the Year, Vol. 8, 1952/53)
GREEN, Julien
    South
       (In Plays of the Year, Vol. 12, 1954/55)
GREEN, Paul, 1894-1947
    Alma Mater
       (In One-Act Plays for Stage and Study, 9th Series)
    Blue Thunder
       (In One-Act Plays for Stage and Study, 4th Series)
    Fixin's; the Tragedy of a Tenant Farm Woman, by Paul and
    Erma Green
       (In The Disinherited: Plays)
    The Last of the Lowries
       (In More One-Act Plays by Modern Authors)
    The Man Who Died at Twelve O'Clock
       (In One-Act Plays for Stage and Study, 2nd Series)
    Native Son (see Wright, Richard)
    Quare Medicine
       (In 10 Short Plays)
    The Southern Cross
       (In Best One-Act Plays of 1938, London)
    Supper for the Dead
       (In The American Caravan, 1927)
    Unto Such Glory
       (In One-Act Plays for Stage and Study, 3rd Series)
Green Fields (see Hirshbein, Peretz)
The Green Helmet (see Yeats, William Butler)

The Green Pastures (see Connelly, Marcus C.)
GREENE, Graham, 1904-
    El Curato en Que Se Vive
      (In Teatro Ingles Contemporaneo)
    The Third Man (see Reed, Sir Carol)
GREENE, Robert, 1558-1592
    The Comicall Historie of Alphonsus, King of Aragon
      (In his Plays & Poems, Vol. 1)
    George A Green, the Pinner of Wakefield
      (In his Plays & Poems, Vol. 2)
    The Historie of Orlando Furioso; one of the twelve pieres of
      France; founded on a portion of Ariosto's poem
      (In his Plays and Poems, Vol. 1)
    The Honorable Historie of Frier Bacon and Frier Bongay
      (In his Plays and Poems, Vol. 2)
    A Looking Glasse for London and England by Robert Greene and
      Thomas Lodge
      (In his Plays & Poems, Vol. 1)
    The Scottish Hystorie of James the Fourth, slaine at Flodden
      (In his Plays & Poems, Vol. 2)
GREENE, Robert S.
    Decision for Freedom; NBC radio documentary script, Oct. 9,
      1955
      (In Prize Plays of Television and Radio, 1956)
GREENLAND, Bill
    We Three, You and I
      (In The Factory Lab Anthology)
GREGORY, Isabella Augusta (Persse) Lady, 1859-1932
    A la Salida de la Luna
      (In Teatro Irlandes Contemporaneo)
    Aristotle's Bellows
      (In The Collected Plays of Lady Gregory, Vol. 3)
    The Bogie Men
      (In The Collected Plays of Lady Gregory, Vol. 1)
    The Canavans
      (In The Collected Plays of Lady Gregory, Vol. 3)
    Coats
      (In The Collected Plays of Lady Gregory, Vol. 1)
    Colman & Guaire
      (In The Collected Plays of Lady Gregory, Vol. 3)
      (In One-Act Plays for Stage and Study, 6th Series)
    Damer's Gold
      (In The Collected Plays of Lady Gregory, Vol. 1)
    Dave
      (In The Collected Plays of Lady Gregory, Vol. 3)
      (In One-Act Plays for Stage and Study, 3rd Series)
    The Deliverer
      (In The Collected Plays of Lady Gregory, Vol. 2)
    Dervorgilla
      (In The Collected Plays of Lady Gregory, Vol. 2)
    The Dispensary
      (In The Collected Plays of Lady Gregory, Vol. 1)
    The Doctor in Spite of Himself (see Molière, Jean Baptiste)

The Dragon
   (In The Collected Plays of Lady Gregory, Vol. 3)
The Full Moon
   (In The Collected Plays of Lady Gregory, Vol. 3)
The Gaol Gate
   (In The Collected Plays of Lady Gregory, Vol. 2)
The Golden Apple
   (In The Collected Plays of Lady Gregory, Vol. 3)
Grania
   (In The Collected Plays of Lady Gregory, Vol. 2)
Hanrahan's Oath
   (In The Collected Plays of Lady Gregory, Vol. 1)
Heads or Harps (see Yeats, William Butler)
Hyacinth Halvey
   (In The Collected Plays of Lady Gregory, Vol. 1)
The Image
   In The Collected Plays of Lady Gregory, Vol. 2)
The Jackdaw
   (In The Collected Plays of Lady Gregory, Vol. 1)
The Jester
   (In The Collected Plays of Lady Gregory, Vol. 3)
Kinora
   (In The Collected Plays of Lady Gregory, Vol. 2)
The Lighted Window
   (In The Collected Plays of Lady Gregory, Vol. 1)
A Losing Game
   (In The Collected Plays of Lady Gregory, Vol. 1)
McDonough's Wife
   (In The Collected Plays of Lady Gregory, Vol. 2)
The Meadow Gate
   (In The Collected Plays of Lady Gregory, Vol. 1)
Michelin
   (In The Collected Plays of Lady Gregory, Vol. 1)
Mirandolina (see Goldoni, Carlo)
The Miser (see Molière, Jean Baptiste)
The Old Woman Remembers
   (In The Collected Plays of Lady Gregory, Vol. 2)
On the Racecourse
   (In The Collected Plays of Lady Gregory, Vol. 1)
   (In One-Act Plays for Stage and Study, 2nd Series)
The Poorhouse (see Hyde, Douglas)
The Rising of the Moon
   (In The Collected Plays of Lady Gregory, Vol. 1)
   (In The Mentor Book of Short Plays)
The Rogueries of Scapin (see Molière, Jean Baptiste)
Sancho's Master (see Cervantes, Miguel de)
Shanwalla
   (In The Collected Plays of Lady Gregory, Vol. 3)
The Shoelace
   (In The Collected Plays of Lady Gregory, Vol. 1)
Spreading the News
   (In The Collected Plays of Lady Gregory, Vol. 1)
   (In One-Act Plays by Modern Authors)

(In One-Act Plays for Stage and Study, 1st Series)
(In The Play Book)
The Story Brought by Brigit
    (In The Collected Plays of Lady Gregory, Vol. 3)
Teja (see Sudermann, Hermann)
The Travelling Man
    (In The Collected Plays of Lady Gregory, Vol. 3)
Twenty Five
    (In The Collected Plays of Lady Gregory, Vol. 1)
The Unicorn from the Stars (see Yeats, William Butler)
The White Cockade
    (In The Collected Plays of Lady Gregory, Vol. 2)
The Worked-Out Ward
    (In The Collected Plays of Lady Gregory, Vol. 1)
The Workhouse Ward
    (In The Collected Plays of Lady Gregory, Vol. 1)
    (In Representative British Dramas)
The Would-Be Gentleman (see Molière, Jean Baptiste)
The Wrens
    (In The Collected Plays of Lady Gregory, Vol. 1)
GREINER, Peter
    Kiez
        (In Theater Heute, no. 7, July 1977)
GRESSET, Jean-Baptiste-Louis, 1709-1777
    Le Méchant
        (In Théâtre de XVIII Siècle, Vol. 1)
Greta Garbo, Quem Diria, Acabou No Iraja (see Melo, Fernando)
GREY, Bernice G.
    Widows Shouldn't Weep
        (In 100 Non-Royalty Radio Plays)
Grey, Jane, Lady, 1537-1554
    *Lady Jane Grey (see Rowe, Nicholas)
GRIBOEDOV, Aleksandr Sergeevich, 1795-1829
    The Misfortune of Being Clever (selection)
        (In A Treasury of Classic Russian Literature)
    The Trouble with Reason
        (In Nineteenth-Century Russian Plays)
    Wit Works Woe
        (In Masterpieces of the Russian Drama, Vol. 1)
Griboyedov, Alexander Sergeyevich (see Griboedov, Aleksandr Ser-
    geevich)
Il Grido; filmscript (see Antonioni, Michelangelo)
GRIEG, Nordahl, 1902-1943
    The Defeat: a Play About the Paris Commune
        (In Masterpieces of the Modern Scandinavian Theatre)
        (In Scandinavian Plays of the 20th Century, Series 2)
    La Derrota
        (In Teatro Noruego Contemporaneo)
    Our Power and Our Glory
        (In Five Modern Scandinavian Plays)
GRIFFIN, G. W. H.
    Camille; a Minstrel Show
        (In Dramas from the American Theatre, 1762-1909)

GRIFFITHS, Howard
    Of All the Crowd That Assembled There; an episode from the
    Rush television series
      (In Australina Theatre Workshop, no. 13)
GRIFFITHS, Trevor
    Apricots
      (In Gambit, Vol. 8, no. 29, 1976)
    Such Impossibilities
      (In his Two Plays for Television)
    Through the Night
      (In his Two Plays for Television)
Grifone (see Heym, Georg)
GRILLO, John
    Hello Goodbye Sebastian
      (In Gambit, Vol. 4, no. 16)
    Number Three
      (In New Short Plays: 3)
GRIMKE, Angelina Weld, 1880-1958
    Rachel
      (In Black Theater U.S.A., 1847-1974)
GRIMM, Jakob Ludwig Karl, 1785-1863
    Clever Gretel; from Grimm's Fairy Tales. Written by Jakob
    and Wilhelm Grimm
      (In Readers Theatre Handbook)
  **The Miniature Darzis (see Smith, Moyne Rice)
GRIMM, Wilhelm Karl, 1786-1859
    Clever Gretel (see Grimm, Jakob)
  **The Miniature Darzis (see Smith, Moyne Rice)
GRIPARI, Pierre
    Le No de Saint-Denis
      (In L'Avant-Scène du Théâtre, no. 535, Feb. 1974)
GRISMER, Frank A., 1899-
    Ladee-ee-s and Gentlemen!
      (In One-Act Plays for Stage and Study, 9th Series)
GRISOLLI, Paulo Affonso
    Avatar
      (In Revista de Teatro, no. 408, Nov./Dec. 1975)
GRONOWICZ, Antoni
    The League of Animals
      (In 100 Non-Royalty Radio Plays)
Gros Chagrins (see Moinaux, Georges)
Un Gros Mot (see Labiche, Eugene)
Die Grosse Wut des Philipp Holtz (see Frisch, Max)
GROSSMAN, Budd
    Maude's Reunion; television script for an episode in "Maude,"
    by Budd Grossman, Alan J. Levitt and Leo Rifkin
      (In Samuel French's Tandem Library Series)
La Grotte (see Anouilh, Jean)
The Group (see Warren, Mrs. Mercy)
GRUAULT, Jean
    The Wild Child; screenplay (see Truffaut, François)
The Grub-Street Opera (see Fielding, Henry)
GRUBB, Davis
    Speak o' the Devil, a modern miracle play

(In 100 Non-Royalty Radio Plays)
Der Grüne Kakadu (see Schnitzler, Arthur)
La Grulla Crepuscular (see Kinoshita, Funji)
GRUMBERG, Jean-Claude, 1939-
    Dreyfus
        (In L'Avant-Scène du Théâtre, no. 543, June 15, 1974)
    Michu
        (In L'Avant-Scène du Théâtre, no. 543, June 15, 1974)
    Tomorrow from Any Window
        (In New Theatre of Europe, Vol. 4)
Gruppo di Fameglia in un Interno; screenplay (see Visconti, Lucino)
GRUZA, Jerzy, 1932-
    Aquarium 2, by Jerzy Gruza and Krysztof T. Toeplitz
        (In Modern International Drama, Vol. 7, no. 1, Fall 1973)
GUAEDINGER, Arthur
    Facing Westward, by Arthur Guaedinger and Henry Nash Smith
        (In 100 Non-Royalty Radio Plays)
The Guardian (see Garrick, David)
The Guardian (see Massinger, Philip)
The Guardian of the Tomb (see Kafka, Franz)
The Guardsman (see Molnar, Ferenc)
GUARE, John Edward, 1938-
    Cop-Out
        (In his Cop Out, Muzeeka, Home Fires)
        (In The Great American Life Show)
        (In Off-Broadway Plays, Vol. 1)
    Home Fires
        (In his Cop Out, Muzeeka, Home Fires)
    The House of Blue Leaves
        (In Best American Plays, 7th Series, 1967-1973)
    The Loveliest Afternoon of the Year
        (In The Off Off Broadway Book)
    Muzeeka
        (In his Cop Out, Muzeeka, Home Fires)
        (In Off-Broadway Plays, Vol. 1)
    Un Pape a New-York, adaptation Française de Jacques Sigurd
        (In L'Avant-Scène du Théâtre, no. 509, Jan. 1, 1973)
    Something I'll Tell You Tuesday
        (In The Off Off Broadway Book)
Guatemotzin, or Cuauhtèmoc, Last Aztec Emperor of México, 1495?-
    1525
    *Corona de Fuego; tragedia antihistórica Americana (see Usigli,
        Rudolfo)
    *Cuauhtèmoc (see Novo, Salvador)
GUERDON, David
    Laundry
        (In New Theatre in Europe, Vol. 3)
Guernica (see Arrabal, Fernando)
La Guerra (see Lopez, Sabatino)
La Guerra de las Gordas (see Novo, Salvador)
Guerra e Pace; screenplay (see Vidor, King)
Le Guerra Empieza en Cuba (see Ruiz Iriarte, Victor)
Guerre au Troisième Etage (see Kohout, Pavel)

La Guerre Civile (see Montherlant, Henry de)
La Guerre de Troie n'Aura Pas Lieu (see Giraudoux, Jean)
GUEULLETTE, Thomas Simon, 1683-1766
    La Chaste Isabelle
        (In Théâtre de XVIII Siècle, Vol. 1)
    Isabelle Grosse par Vertu
        (In Théâtre de XVIII Siècle, Vol. 1)
    Leandre Fiacre
        (In Théâtre de XVIII Siècle, Vol. 1)
Les Gueux (see Hugo, Victor)
Le Guichet (see Tardieu, Jean)
GUILLE, Frances V.
    **L'Histoire d'Adele H. (see Truffaut, François)
GUILLERMIN, John
    King Kong; screenplay (see Simple, Lorenzo, Jr.)
Guillermo Tell Tiene los Ojos Tristes (see Sastre, Alfonso)
GUILLOUX, Louis, 1899-
    Cripure
        (In L'Avant-Scène Théâtre, no. 619, Nov. 15, 1977)
GUINAN, John
    Black Oliver
        (In One-Act Plays for Stage and Study, 5th Series)
GUINN, Dorothy C.
    Out of the Dark
        (In Plays and Pageants from the Life of the Negro)
GUINON, Albert, 1863-1923
    The Yoke, by M. Albert Guinon and Mme. J. Marni, pseud.
        (In The Drama, Vol. 21)
Guise, Henry, 3rd Duke, "La Belafre," 1550-1588
    *Charles IX; ou, La Saint-Barthelemi (see Chènier, Marie-
        Joseph B.)
    *The Duke of Guise (see Dryden, John)
    *The Massacre of Paris (see Marlowe, Christopher)
GUITRY, Sacha, 1885-1957
    Beaumarchais
        (In his Theatre: Works, Vol. 12)
    Don't Listen Ladies! Adapted by Stephen Powys and Guy Bolton
        (In Plays of the Year, Vol. 1, 1948-49)
    Monsieur Prudhomme a-t-il Vecu?
        (In his Theatre: Works, Vol. 12)
    Talleyrand
        (In his Theatre: Works, Vol. 12)
    Villa for Sale
        (In Modern One-Act Plays from the French)
GULLETTE, William Hooker, 1855-1937
    Among Thieves
        (In One-Act Plays for Stage and Study, 2nd Series)
Gum and Goo (see Brenton, Howard)
A Gun Play (see Udoff, Yale M.)
GUNNER, Frances
    The Light of the Women
        (In Plays and Pageants from the Life of the Negro)
GURIK, Robert, 1932-
    API 2967

(In Talonplays Series, 1974)
The Hanged Man
    (In New Drama 4 Series, 1972)
Le Pendu
    (In Collection Théâtre Canadien, no. 12, 1970)
The Trial of Jean-Baptiste M.
    (In Talonplays Series, 1972)
GURNEY, Albert R., Jr., 1930-
    Children, suggested by a story by John Cheever
        (In Plays and Players, Vol. 21, no. 8-9, May-June, 1974)
    The Golden Fleece
        (In The Off Off Broadway Book)
GURNEY, Claude
    Mary Read (see Mavor, Osborne Henry)
A Gust of Wind (see Forzano, Giovacchino)
Gustavus Vasa (see Brooke, Henry)
Die Gute Zeit (see Barlach, Ernst)
GUTHRIE, Arthur, d. 1914
    The Probationer, by Anthony Rowley, pseud.
        (In Scottish Repertory Plays Series, no. 6, 1911)
    Weaver's Shuttle, by Anthony Rowley, pseud.
        (In Scottish Repertory Plays Series, no. 5, 1910)
GUTHRIE, Thomas Anssey, 1856-1934
  **One Touch of Venus (see Weill, Kurt)
GUTHRIE, Sir Tyrone, 1900-
    Fables Here and Then (see Feldshuh, David)
    Top of the Ladder
        (In Plays of the Year, Vol. 3, 1949-50)
    Uncle Vanya (see Chekhov, Anton)
GUTIERREZ, Antonio Garcia, 1813-1884
    El Trovador
        (In Tres Dramas Romanticos)
Guy, or Guido of Lusignan, king of Jerusalem, 1140-1194
    *Zaire (see Voltaire)
Guy Domville (see James, Henry)
Gwyn, Eleanor, known as Nell, 1650-1687
    *"In Good King Charles's Golden Days": A True History That
        Never Happened (see Shaw, George Bernard)
Gyges and His Ring (see Hebbel, Friedrich)
Gyges und Sein Ring (see Hebbel, Friedrich)
Gypsy (see Styne, Jule)
Gyubal Wahazar; or, Along the Cliffs of the Absurd (see Witkiewicz,
    Stanislaw)

H. M. S. Pinafore; or, The Lass That Loved a Sailor (see Gilbert,
    William S.)
Ha Vagas Para Mocas de Fino Trato (see Araujo, Alcine)
Ha Vuelto Ulises (see Novo, Salvador)
Haakon VI Magnusson, King of Norway, 1340-1380
    *Queen Margaret of Norway (see Kiel'and, Trygve)
HAAVIKKO, Paavo, 1931-
    The Superintendent

(In <u>Modern Nordic Plays</u>:   Finland)
Superintendent, translated by Philip Binham
(In <u>Literary Review</u>, Vol. 14, Fall 1970)
Habeas Corpus (see Bennett, Alan)
L'Habit Vert (see Musset, Alfred de)
Los Habitantes de la Casa Deshabitada (see Jardiel Poncela, Enrique)
Hacia la Meta (see Parada Leon, Ricardo)
Hacket Gets Ahead (see Hannan, Bill)
HACKETT, Albert, 1900-
    The Diary of Anne Frank (see Goodrich, Frances)
HACKETT, Walter, 1876-1944
    It Pays to Advertise (see Megrue, Roi Cooper)
HACKS, Peter
    Amleto Principe di Danimarca (see Brecht, Bertolt)
    Omphale; both German and English texts are given
        (In <u>Dimension</u>, Vol. 6, no. 3, 1973)
    Prexaspes
        (In <u>Theater der Zeit</u>, no. 2, 1975)
        (In <u>Theater Heute</u>, no. 5, May 1976)
Hadad (see Hillhouse, James A.)
Hadrian VII (see Luke, Peter)
HADRICH, Rolf, 1931-
    Murder in Frankfurt; both German and English texts are given
        (In <u>Dimension</u>, Vol. 3, no. 1, 1970)
Hagbarth og Signe (see Oehlenschläger, Adam G.)
Hail Scrawdyke! Little Malcolm and His Struggle Against the Eunuchs
    (see Halliwell, David)
HAILEY, Arthur, 1920-
    Flight into Danger
        (In <u>Ten Canadian Short Plays</u>)
HAILEY, Oliver, 1932-
    Animal
        (In <u>Collision Course</u>)
    Picture
        (In <u>New Theatre in America</u>, Vol. 2)
HAIM, Victor, 1935-
    Abraham et Samuel
        (In <u>L'Avant-Scène Théâtre</u>, no. 548, Sept. 15, 1974)
    Comment Harponner le Requin
        (In <u>L'Avant-Scène Théâtre</u>, no. 548, Sept. 15, 1974)
    Isaac et la Sage-Femme
        (In <u>L'Avant-Scène Théâtre</u>, no. 600, Dec. 15, 1976)
    La Visite
        (In <u>L'Avant-Scène Théâtre</u>, no. 562, April 15, 1975)
HAINES, William Wister, 1908-
    Command Decision
        (In <u>Representative American Plays</u>, 1792-1949)
The Hairy Ape (see O'Neill, Eugene)
HAITOV, Nicolai
    The Boat in the Forest
        (In <u>Gambit</u>, Vol. 3, no. 12)
HAITOW, Einakter von Nikolai
    Wege

(In Theater der Zeit, no. 5, May 1973)
Hakon Karl Hiin Rige (see Oehlenschläger, Adam G.)
HALE, Lucretia Peabody, 1820-1900
  **The Lady Who Put Salt in Her Coffee (see Smith, Moyne Rice)
Halewyn (see Ghelderode, Michel de)
Half a Basket of Peanuts, a Shaohsing Opera. A collective work of
  a group of writers and actors in Chekiang
        (In Chinese Literature, no. 5, 1973)
Half an Hour (see Barrie, James M.)
Half-Life (see Mitchell, Julian)
HALL, Willis, 1929-
    Qui Est Qui? (see Waterhouse, Keith)
    Who's Who? (see Waterhouse, Keith)
Hall of Healing (see O'Casey, Sean)
HALLDORSSON, Erlingur E.   1930-
    Mink
        (In Modern Nordic Plays: Iceland)
HALLE, Adam de la, c.1235-1287
    Le Jeu de la Feuillée; text in English
        (In Medieval French Plays)
    Le Jeu de Robin et de Marion; text in English
        (In Medieval French Plays)
    The Play of Robin and Marion (Le Jeu de Robin et Marion)
        (In Five Comedies of Medieval France)
Hallelujah (see Lebović, Djorde)
HALLIDAY, Andrew, 1830-1877
    The Area Belle (see Brough, William)
HALLIWELL, David
    Hail Scrawdyke! Little Malcolm and His Struggle Against the
    Eunuchs
        (In Evergreen Playscripts Series, 1967)
Hallo und Adieu (see Fugard, Athol)
Hallowed Ground (see Brighouse, Harold)
HALMAN, Doris F.
    The Closet
        (In Types of Modern Dramatic Composition)
    Johnny Pickup
        (In Best Television Plays, 1954)
    Lenna Looks Down
        (In One-Act Plays for Stage and Study, 4th Series)
    The Voice of the Snake
        (In One-Act Plays for Stage and Study, 3rd Series)
HALPER, Leivick, 1888-1962
    The Golem
        (In The Great Jewish Plays)
HALPERN, Joseph
    Mother and Son
        (In One-Act Plays from the Yiddish)
Hamal the Porter (see Turkish Theatre. Meddah)
Haman's Downfall (see Sloves, Chaim)
HAMBLIN, Louisa (Medina), d. 1838
    Nick of the Woods
        (In Victorian Melodramas)

"Hambre" (see Rozsa, Jorge)
HAMER, Maimie
    A Living Thing, by Maimie Hamer and Helen Lustig
      (In Women Write for the Theatre Series, Vol. 1)
HAMER, Robert, 1911-
    Kind Hearts and Coronets; directed and screenplay by Robert
    Hamer
      (In Masterworks of the British Cinema)
HAMILL, Pete, 1935-
    Doc; screenplay of the film directed by Frank Perry
      (A Paperback Library Original Screenplay, 1971)
HAMILTON, Patrick, 1904-1962
    Angel Street
      (In Best Mystery and Suspense Plays of the Modern Theatre)
Hamlet; d'après la moralité legendaire (see Huster, Francis)
Un Hamlet de Moins; screenplay (see Bene, Carmelo)
Hamlet em Brasília (see Laura, Ida)
Die Hamletmaschine (see Müller, Heiner)
HAMMEL, Claus
    Das Gelbe Fenster, der Gelbe Stein
      (In Theater der Zeit, no. 3, 1977)
    Rom Oder die Zweite Erschaffung der Welt
      (In Theater der Zeit, no. 3, 1975)
HAMMERSTEIN, Oscar, 1895-1960
    Allegro (see Rodgers, Richard)
    Carousel (see Rodgers, Richard)
    The King and I (see Rodgers, Richard)
    Me and Juliet (see Rodgers, Richard)
    Oklahoma! (see Rodgers, Richard)
    South Pacific (see Rodgers, Richard)
HAMMETT, Dashiell, 1894-1961
  **The Maltese Falcon; screenplay (see Huston, John)
HAMON, Franck, 1949-
    La Chasse au Dahut
      (In L'Avant-Scène du Théâtre, no. 540, May 1974)
HAMPDEN, John, 1898-
    Mrs. Adis (see Kaye-Smith, Sheila)
HAMPTON, Christopher, 1946-
    Il Filantropo
      (In Sipario, no. 313, June 1972)
    Uncle Vanya (see Chekhov, Anton)
    Die Wilden
      (In Theater Heute, no. 2, Feb. 1974)
Hancock, John, 1737-1793
    *1776 (see Edwards, Sherman)
HANDELSMAN, J. B.
    Kephas and Elohenu
      (In Playboy, Vol. 19, no. 4, April 1972)
HANDKE, Peter, 1942-
    Amleto Principe di Danimarca (see Brecht, Bertolt)
    Calling for Help
      (In his The Ride Across Lake Constance and Other Plays)
    Kaspar

(In Methuen's Modern Plays Series; 1972)
My Foot My Tutor
    (In his The Ride Across Lake Constance and Other Plays)
Offending the Audience
    (In Methuen's Modern Plays Series, 1971)
Prophecy
    (In his The Ride Across Lake Constance and Other Plays)
Quodlibet
    (In The Malahat Review, Vol. 37, Jan. 1976)
    (In his The Ride Across Lake Constance and Other Plays)
The Ride Across Lake Constance
    (In Contemporary German Theater)
    (In Methuen's Modern Plays Series; 1973)
    (In his The Ride Across Lake Constance and Other Plays)
Self-Accusation
    (In Methuen's Modern Plays Series, 1971)
    (In New Theatre of Europe, Vol. 4)
They Are Dying Out
    (In his The Ride Across Lake Constance and Other Plays)
Die Unvernünftigen Sterben Aus
    (In Theater Heute, no. 7, July 1974)
Handsome Is- (see Hanford, Helen)
HANELL, Robert, 1925-
    Fiesta; Al Fresco für Musiktheater frei nach einem Roman von
    Prudencio de Pereda
        (In Theater der Zeit, no. 5, 1974)
    Reise mit Joujou; musikalische komödie nach Maupassant, von
    Robert Hanell, Klaus Eidam
        (In Theater der Zeit, no. 6, 1976)
HANFORD, Helen
    Handsome Is-
        (In 100 Non-Royalty Radio Plays)
The Hanged Man (see Gurik, Robert)
Hanging and Wiving (see Manners, John Hartley)
HANJURO, Tsuuchi
    Saint Narukami and the God Fudō, by Tsuuchi Hanjurō, Yasuda
    Abun, and Nakada Mansuke
        (In Kabuki: Five Classic Plays)
HANKIN, St. John Emile Clavering, 1869-1909
    The Burglar Who Failed
        (In his Plays, Vol. 2)
    The Cassilis Engagement
        (In his Plays, Vol. 2)
        (In Representative British Dramas)
    The Charity That Began at Home
        (In his Plays, Vol. 1)
    The Constant Lover
        In his Plays, Vol. 2)
    The Last of the De Mullins
        (In his Plays, Vol. 2)
        (In 20th Century Plays)
    Return of the Prodigal
        (In Edwardian Plays)

(In his <u>Plays</u>, Vol. 1)
Thompson
(In his <u>Plays</u>, Vol. 2)
The Two Mr. Wetherbys
(In his <u>Plays</u>, Vol. 1)
Hank's Night   A Sea-Blue Comedy
HANLEY, James
The Inner Journey
(In his <u>Plays One</u>)
A Stone Flower
(In his <u>Plays One</u>)
HANLEY, William
Mrs. Dally Has a Lover
(In <u>New Theatre in America</u>, Vol. 1)
No Answer
(In <u>Collision Course</u>)
HANLON, Daniel E., 1877-
The Wolf at the Door
(In <u>One-Act Plays for Stage and Study</u>, 6th Series)
HANNAN, Bill
Hacket Gets Ahead, by Bill & Lorna Hannan and John Romeril
(In <u>Australian Theatre Workshop</u>, Vol. 11)
Hannele (see Hauptmann, Gerhart)
Hannibal, "The Grace of Baal," 247-182 B. C.
*Before Cannae (see Munk, Kaj H.)
*Sophonisba; or, Hannibal's Overthrow (see Lee, Nathaniel)
Hanrahan's Oath (see Gregory, Isabella A.)
Hans Heinrich (see Jahnn, Hans H.)
HANSBERRY, Lorraine, 1931-1965
The Drinking Gourd
(In <u>Black Theater U. S. A.</u>, 1847-1974)
A Raisin in the Sun
(In <u>Black Insights</u>)
(In <u>Black Theater</u>)
(In <u>By Women</u>)
(In <u>Contemporary Black Drama</u>)
(In <u>Eight American Ethnic Plays</u>)
What Use Are Flowers?
(In <u>The Best Short Plays</u> 1973)
HANSHEW, Thomas W., 1857-1914
The 'Forty-Niners, a Drama of the Gold Mines
(In <u>The Drama</u>, Vol. 20)
HANSON, Meyer
The Comeback
(In <u>100 Non-Royalty Radio Plays</u>)
The Happening in the Bungalow (see Joo For, Lee)
The Happiest Days of Your Life (see Dighton, John)
The Happiest of the Three (see Labiche, Eugene)
Happiness (see Veber, Pierre)
Happy Arcadia (see Gilbert, William S.)
Happy as Larry (see MacDonagy, Donagh)
Happy Birthday Bernadette (see Goldberg, Jeff)
Happy Birthday, Wanda June (see Vonnegut, Kurt, Jr.)

A Happy Day (see Kock, Charles P.)
Happy Ending (see Ward, Douglas Turner)
The Happy Housewife (see Rosten, Hedda)
The Happy Journey (see Wilder, Thornton)
The Happy Journey to Trenton and Camden (see Wilder, Thornton)
The Happy Man (see Williams, Hugh)
The Happy Prince (see Benton, Rita)
HARBOU, Thea von, 1888-1954
    **M; film scenario and dialogue (see Lang, Fritz)
    **Metropolis; screenplay (see Lang, Fritz)
The Hard Boiled Egg (see Ionesco, Eugene)
A Hard Day's Night; filmscript (see Owen, Alun)
HARDIN, Herschel
    Esker Mike & His Wife, Agiluk: Scenes from Life in the
        Mackenzie River Delta
        (In Talonplays Series; 1973)
HARDING, John
    The Golden Pathway Annual, by John Harding and John Burrows
        (In Plays and Players, Vol. 21, no. 11-12, August-Sept. 1974)
HARDWICK, Michael
    The Great Speckled Band. A radio script by Michael and Mollie
        Hardwick, based on the story "The Adventure of the Great
        Speckled Band, " by Sir Arthur Conan Doyle
        (In On the Air)
HARDY, Alexandre, 1575-1632
    La Force du Sang
        (In Théâtre du XVIIe Siècle, Vol. 1)
    Lucrece; ou, l'Adultère Puni
        (In Théâtre du XVIIe Siècle, Vol. 1)
    Mariamne
        (In More Plays by Rivals of Corneille and Racine)
    Scédase; ou, l'Hospitalité Violée
        (In Théâtre du XVIIe Siècle, Vol. 1)
HARDY, Thomas, 1840-1928
    **The Day After the Fair (see Harvey, Frank)
    A Sequelula to "The Dynasts"
        (In Parodies)
HARE, David
    Fanshen
        (In Plays and Players, Vol. 22, no. 12, and Vol. 23, no. 1,
            Sept., Oct. 1975)
HARLAN, Walter, 1867-1931
    The Nüremberg Egg
        (In Eight European Plays)
Harlequin's Invasion (see Garrick, David)
HARNICK, Sheldon, 1924-
    Fiddler on the Roof (see Bock, Jerry)
    Fiorello! (see Bock, Jerry)
Harold II, Earl of Wessex, afterward King of England, 1022?-1066
    *Harold (see Tennyson, Alfred Lord)
HARRIGAN, Edward, 1845-1911
    The Mulligan Guard Ball
        (In Dramas from the American Theatre, 1762-1909)

HARRIS, Andrew B.
  Tausk
    (In Drama & Theatre, Vol. 12, no. 2, Spring 1975)
HARRIS, Aurand
  Androcles and the Lion, based on Italian version of the legend
    in style of Italian Commedia dell'arte
    (In his Six Plays for Children)
  Peck's Bad Boy
    (In his Six Plays for Children)
  Punch and Judy
    (In his Six Plays for Children)
  Rags to Riches
    (In his Six Plays for Children)
  Steal Away Home
    (In his Six Plays for Children)
  Yankee Doodle
    (In his Six Plays for Children)
HARRIS, Clarence
  The Trip
    (In Black Voices from Prison)
HARRIS, Susan
  Like Mother, Like Daughter; television script for an episode in
    "Maude"
    (In Samuel French's Tandem Library Series)
HARRISON, Carey, 1944-
  Lovers
    (In New Short Plays, Vol. 2)
  Twenty-six Efforts at Pornography
    (In New Short Plays, Vol. 1)
Harrison, Paul Carter (see Carter-Harrison, Paul)
Harrison, William Henry, Pres. U. S., 1777-1852
  *Daniel Webster (see Chevigny, Hector)
Harry and the Angel; a vaudeville for two players (see Dietz, Nor-
  man D.)
HARSHA or HARSHAVARDHANA, King of Northern India, 590?-647
  Nagananda
    (In Six Sanskrit Plays)
    (In Sri Harsa's Plays)
  Pridyadarshika
    (In Sri Harsa's Plays)
  Ratnavali; or, The Necklace
    (In Great Sanskrit Plays)
    (In Sri Harsa's Plays)
HART, Elizabeth
  A Trip to Czardis, radio script by Elizabeth and James Hart,
    adapted from the story by Edwin Granberry
    (In Best Broadcasts of 1938-39)
HART, Joseph
  The Dark Moon and the Full; a chamber play
    (In Best Short Plays, 1977)
  The Ghost Dance
    (In Drama and Theatre, Vol. 11, no. 2, Winter 1972-73)
  Sonata for Mott Street

(In Drama and Theatre, Vol. 11, no. 1, Fall 1972)
HART, Moss, 1904-1961
    Lady in the Dark (see Weill, Kurt)
    The Man Who Came to Dinner (see Kaufman, George S.)
    You Can't Take It With You, by Moss Hart and George S. Kaufman
        (In 50 Best Plays of the American Theatre, Vol. 2)
HARTOG, Jan de, 1914-
    Capitan Después de Dios
        (In Teatro Neerlandes Contemporaneo)
    The Fourposter
        (In 50 Best Plays of the American Theatre, Vol. 4)
HARTWIG, Edward Anthony
    Even the Blind
        (In 100 Non-Royalty Radio Plays)
Harvest in the North (see Hodson, James L.)
Harvey (see Chase, Mary)
HARVEY, Frank
    The Day After the Fair, based on a story by Thomas Hardy
        (In Plays of the Year, Vol. 43, 1972-73)
HARWOOD, Harold Marsh, 1874-
    Old Folks at Home
        (In Famous Plays of 1934)
HARWOOD, Ronald
    One Day in the Life of Ivan Denisovich, screenplay based on the
    novel by Aleksandr Solzenitsyn
        (In Making of "One Day in the Life of Ivan Denisovich")
HASENCLEVER, Walter, 1890-1940
    Antigone
        (In Vision and Aftermath: Four Expressionist War Plays)
    Christopher Columbus (see Tucholsky, Kurt)
Hasta Luego (see John, Errol)
HASTINGS, Charlotte
    Bonaventure
        (In Plays of the Year, Vol. 3, 1949-50)
    Uncertain Joy
        (In Plays of the Year, Vol. 12, 1954-55)
HASTINGS, Hugh
    Seagulls over Sorrento
        (In Plays of the Year, Vol. 4, 1950)
The Hastings Flyer; The Goon Show Scripts no. 141 (see Milligan,
    Spike)
HATCH, James V., 1928-
    Fly Blackbird (see Jackson, C. Bernard)
The Haunted Coal Mine (see Pride, Leo B.)
The Haunted Host (see Patrick, Robert)
HAUPTMAN, Ira
    Cinema of the Year Zero
        (In Yale/Theatre, Vol. 5, no. 1, Fall 1973)
HAUPTMAN, William
    Comanche Cafe
        (In his Comanche Cafe/Domino Courts)
    Domino Courts

(In Best Short Plays, 1977)
(In his Comanche Cafe/Domino Courts)
Heat
    (In Yale/Theatre, Vol. 6, no. 3, Spring 1975)
Shearwater
    (In Performance, Vol. 1, no. 5, Mar. /Apr.
1973)
HAUPTMANN, Carl Ferdinand Maximilian, 1858-1921
    War A Te Deum
    (In Vision and Aftermath: Four Expressionist War Plays)
HAUPTMANN, Gerhart Johann Robert, 1862-1946
    Hannele
    (In The Drama, Vol. 12)
    The Sunken Bell
    (In Representative Continental Dramas)
    The Weavers
    (In Masterpieces of the Modern German Theatre)
Das Haus Erinnerung (see Kästner, Erich)
Hauser, Kaspar, 1812?-1833
    *L'Enigme de Kaspar Hauser (see Herzog, Werner)
Havana Jo Jo (see Argelander, Ron)
Havana Moon (see Hughes, Glenn)
HAVARD, Lezley
    Victims
    (In Women Write for the Theatre Series, Vol. 4)
HAVEL, Václav
    Audienz
    (In Theater Heute, no. 1, Jan. 1977)
    Udienza
    (In Sipario, no. 369, Feb. 1977)
    Vernissage
    (In Sipario, no. 372, May 1977)
HAVREVOLD, Finn 1905-
    The Injustice
    (In Modern Nordic Plays: Norway)
HAWEMANN, Horst, 1940-
    Tschapai... Tschapai... Tschapajew
    (In Theater der Zeit, no. 10, 1977)
The Hawk (see Mednick, Murray)
HAWKES, John, 1925-
    The Innocent Party
    (In his The Innocent Party: Four Short Plays)
    The Question
    (In his The Innocent Party: Four Short Plays)
    The Undertaker
    (In his The Innocent Party: Four Short Plays)
    The Wax Museum
    (In his The Innocent Party: Four Short Plays)
HAWKESWORTH, John, 1715?-1773
    Edgar and Emmeline
    (In A Collection of the Most Esteemed Farces ..., Vol. 4)
HAWKS, Howard Winchester, 1896-1977
    Scarface; filmscript; text in French (see Hecht, Ben)
HAWORTH, Don
    There's No Point in Arguing the Toss

Heaven Is Deep (see Day, Frederic L.)
Heavenly and Earthly Love (see Molnar, Ferenc)
HEBBEL, Friedrich, 1813-1863
    Der Gehörnte Siegfried
        (In his Werke: Dramen und Prosa, Vol. 2)
    Gyges and His Ring
        (In his Three Plays)
    Gyges und Sein Ring
        (In his Werke: Dramen und Prosa, Vol. 1)
    Herod and Mariamne
        (In his Three Plays)
    Herodes und Mariamne
        (In his Werke: Dramen und Prosa, Vol. 1)
    Judith
        (In his Three Plays)
    Judith; text in German
        (In his Werke: Dramen und Prosa, Vol. 1)
    Kriemhilds Rache
        (In his Werke: Dramen und Prosa, Vol. 2)
    Maria Magdalena
        (In Masterpieces of the Modern German Theatre)
    Maria Magdalena; text in German
        (In his Werke: Dramen und Prosa, Vol. 1)
HEBEL, Johann Peter, 1760-1826
    Das Bergwerk zu Falun (The Mine at Falun) (see Hofmannsthal,
    Hugo von H.)
HECHT, Ben, 1893-1964
    The Front Page, by Ben Hecht and Charles MacArthur
        (In 50 Best Plays of the American Theatre, Vol. 1)
        (In The Stage Works of Charles MacArthur)
    Ladies and Gentlemen, by Ben Hecht and Charles MacArthur,
        derived from a play by Ladislaus Bus-Fekete
        (In The Stage Works of Charles MacArthur)
    Scarface; screenplay; text in French. A film by Howard Hawks
        (In L'Avant-Scène du Cinéma, no. 132, Jan. 1973)
    Swan Song, by Ben Hecht and Charles MacArthur based on a
        story by Ramón Romero and Harriet Hinsdale
        (In The Stage Works of Charles MacArthur)
    Twentieth Century, by Ben Hecht and Charles MacArthur,
        based on a play by Charles Bruce Milholland
        (In The Stage Works of Charles MacArthur)
Hector (see Montchretien, Antoine de)
Hedda Gabler (see Ibsen, Henrik)
HEERMAN, Victor
    Animal Crackers; screenplay (see Ryskind, Morris)
HEGGEN, Thomas Orlo, 1919-1949
    Mister Roberts, by Thomas O. Heggen and Joshua Logan, based
        on the novel by Thomas O. Heggen
        (In 50 Best Plays of the American Theatre, Vol. 3)
HEIDE, Robert, 1939-
    Moon
        (In The Off Off Broadway Book)
Das Heilige Experiment (see Hochwälder, Fritz)

Heiligung (see Brust, Alfred)
Heimskringla! or, The Stoned Angels (see Foster, Paul)
Heinrich der Hohenstaufe (see Eckart, Dietrich)
Heinrich Schlaghands Höllenfahrt (see Kirsch, Rainer)
Heinrich von Kleist (see Jahnn, Hans H.)
Heir of the Ages; screenplay (see Lathrop, William A.)
HEIREMANS, Luis Alberto
    El Abanderado
        (In Teatro Contemporaneo Chileño)
The Heiress (see Burgoyne, John)
Das Heiss Eisen (see Sachs, Hans)
Held Wilder Willen; ein film (see Kaiser, Georg)
HELLER, Joseph
    Clevinger's Trial
        (In Best Short Plays, 1976)
HELLMAN, Lillian, 1905-
    Another Part of the Forest
        (In her Collected Plays)
    The Autumn Garden
        (In her Collected Plays)
    Candide, a comic operetta based upon Voltaire's satire; lyrics
     by Richard Wilbur, score by Leonard Bernstein, with two addi-
     tional lyrics by John Latouche
        (In her Collected Plays)
    The Children's Hour
        (In her Collected Plays)
        (In 50 Best Plays of the American Theatre, Vol. 2)
        (In Plays by and About Women)
        (In Plays of the Year, Vol. 5, 1950/51)
    Days to Come
        (In her Collected Plays)
    The Lark (see Anouilh, Jean)
    The Little Foxes
        (In her Collected Plays)
    Montserrat, adapted from the French play by Emmanuel Roblès
        (In her Collected Plays)
    My Mother, My Father, and Me, based upon the novel "How
     Much?" by Burt Blechman
        (In her Collected Plays)
    Scene from an Unfinished Play
        (In New Republic, Vol. 171, Nov. 30, 1974)
    The Searching Wind
        (In her Collected Plays)
    Toys in the Attic
        (In her Collected Plays)
    Watch on the Rhine
        (In her Collected Plays)
Hello and Goodbye (see Fugard, Athol)
Hello from Bertha (see Williams, Tennessee)
Hello Goodbye Sebastian (see Grillo, John)
Hellseherei (see Kaiser, Georg)
Help, I Am; a monologue (see Patrick, Robert)
The Helper (see Bullins, Edward A.)

HELTAI, Eugene, 1871-
    Death Sends for the Doctor
      (In One-Act Plays for Stage and Study, 9th Series)
HENDRY, Tom
    Fifteen Miles of Broken Glass
      (In Talonplays Series, 1975)
    That Boy, Call Him Back
      (In Performing Arts in Canada, Vol. 9, no. 4, Winter 1972)
HENKEL, Heinrich
    Die Betriebsschliebung
      (In Theater Heute, no. 4, April 1975)
    Olaf und Albert
      (In Theater Heute, no. 9, Sept. 1973)
Der Henno (see Sachs, Hans)
HENRY, Ann
    Lulu Street
      (In Talonplays Series, 1975)
Henry II, King of England, 1133-1189
    *Becket (see Tennyson, Alfred Lord)
    *Becket; ou, l'Honneur de Dieu (see Anouilh, Jean)
    *Rosamund (see Swinburne, Algernon Charles)
    *Rosamund, Queen of the Lombards (see Swinburne, Algernon
      Charles)
Henry II, King of Navarre, 1503-1555
    *The Queen-Mother (see Swinburne, Algernon Charles)
Henry II de Bourbon (Prince de Conde), 1588-1646
    *La Maréchale d'Ancre (see Vigny, Alfred Victor)
Henri III, King of France, 1551-1589
    *Bussy d'Ambois (see Chapman, George)
    *The Revenge of Bussy d'Ambois (see Chapman, George)
Henry IV, German Holy Roman Emperor, 1050-1106
    *Henry IV (see Pirandello, Luigi)
Henri IV "Henri de Navarre", King of France, 1553-1610
    *The Conspiracy of Charles, Duke of Byron (see Chapman,
      George)
    *The Tragedy of Charles, Duke of Byron (see Chapman, George)
Henry V, King of Great Britain, 1387-1422
    *The First Part of Sir John Oldcastle (Anon.)
      (In Disputed Plays of William Shakespeare)
Henry VIII, King of England, 1491-1547
    *Anne Boleyn (see Albery, Peter)
    *Anne Boleyn (see Boker, George H.)
    *Cant; a play of Henry VIII and Anne Boleyn (see Munk, Kaj H.)
    *Catherine Parr; or, Alexander's Horse (see Baring, Maurice)
    *Henri VIII (see Chénier, Marie-Joseph B.)
    *A Man for All Seasons (see Bolt, Robert)
    *The Private Life of Henry VIII, screenplay (see Biro, Lajos)
Henry and Ribsy (see Cleary, Beverly)
Henry Hudson, a historical drama; radio script (see Monroe, Robert)
HENSEN, Herwig, 1917-
    Agamemnon (see Aeschylus)
HENSON, Bertram
    Plans for the Coronation

(In Best One-Act Plays of 1938, London)
Her Master's Voice (see Kummer, Mrs. Clare)
Her Opinion of His Story (see Howells, William Dean)
Her Own Way (see Fitch, Clyde)
Heraclius, Emperor of the Eastern Roman Empire, 575?-641
    *Heraclius (see Corneille, Pierre)
Die Herberge (see Hochwälder, Fritz)
HERBERT, Alan Patrick, 1890-
    Two Gentlemen of Soho
        (In Atlantic Harvest)
HERBERT, John
    Some Angry Summer Songs
        (In Talonplays Series, 1975)
Herbert III (see Shine, Ted)
Here Are Sailors! (see Farrar, John)
Here Come the Clowns (see Barry, Philip)
Here Comes the Chopper (see Ionesco, Eugene)
La Herencia (see Calvo Sotelo, Joaquin)
Here's a Howdy-do (see Stone, Weldon)
La Herida Luminosa (see Sagarra, José M.)
L'Heritier de Village (see Marivaux, Pierre C.)
Les Heritiers Rabourdin (see Zola, Emile)
HERNANDEZ, Luisa Josefina, 1928-
    Los Duendes
        (In Teatro Méxicano, 1963)
    Los Frutos Caidos
        (In Teatro Méxicano Contemporaneo)
        (In Teatro Méxicano del Siglo XX, Vol. 3)
    Los Huespedes Reales
        (In Teatro Méxicano del Siglo XX, Vol. 4)
Hernani (see Hugo, Victor)
HERNE, James A. (James Ahern), 1839-1901
    Margaret Fleming
        (In Representative American Plays, 1792-1949)
    Shore Acres
        (In Dramas from the American Theatre, 1762-1909)
The Herne's Egg (see Yeats, William Butler)
The Hero (see Martinez Ballesteros, Antonio)
Hero and Leander (see Marlowe, Christopher)
Hero and Leander: a Comic Burletta (see Jackman, Isaac)
Herod Antipas, ruler of Galilee, d. after 40 A.D.
    *The Divine Tragedy (see Longfellow, Henry Wadsworth)
    *Herod and Mariamne (see Hebbel, Friedrich)
    *Herod the King (see Munk, Kaj H.)
    *Herodes (see Herzberg, Abel J.)
    *Herodes und Mariamne (see Hebbel, Friedrich)
    *Mariamne (see Hardy, Alexandre)
    *Mariamne (see Voltaire)
    *The Play of Herod (Anon.)
        (In Medieval Church Music-Dramas)
    *The Slaughter of the Innocents (Anon.)
        (In Medieval Church Music-Dramas)
El Heroe (see Canas, Alberto)

Heroes of Labour; a play for television (see Barker, Howard)
HERRERA, Ernesto, 1886-1917
    El Leon Ciego
        (In Teatro Uruguayo Contemporaneo)
HERRY, Ginette, 1933-
    La Comédie sans Titre; ou, La Régénération (see Svevo, Italo)
HERVIEU, Paul Ernest, 1857-1915
    Connais-Toi
        (In his Oeuvres: Théâtre IV)
    La Course du Flambeau
        (In his Oeuvres: Théâtre II)
    Le Dedale
        (In his Oeuvres: Théâtre III)
    L'Enigme
        (In his Oeuvres: Théâtre II)
    La Loi de l'Homme
        (In his Oeuvres: Théâtre I)
    Modestie
        (In his Oeuvres: Théâtre IV)
    Les Paroles Restent
        (In his Oeuvres: Théâtre I)
    Le Reveil
        (In his Oeuvres: Théâtre IV)
    Les Tenailles
        (In his Oeuvres: Théâtre I)
    Theroigne de Mericourt
        (In his Oeuvres: Théâtre III)
HERZBERG, Abel J.
    Herodes
        (In Teatro Neerlandes Contemporaneo)
HERZOG, Werner, 1942-
    L'Enigme de Kaspar Hauser; titre original: "Jeder für Sich
    und Gott Gegen Alle"
        (In L'Avant-Scène Cinéma, no. 176, Nov. 15, 1976)
He's Much to Blame (see Holcroft, Thomas)
The Hessian Corporal (see Foster, Paul)
HESTER, Hal
    Your Own Thing; a rock musical comedy (see Driver, Donald)
HEUER, Kenneth
    The Genie of Sutton Place, a television play by Kenneth Heuer
    and George Selden
        (In All the World's a Stage)
L'Heure du Berger (see Bourdet, Edouard)
L'Heureux Stratagème (see Marivaux, Pierre C.)
HEURTE, Yves
    La Nuit, les Clowns
        (In L'Avant-Scène Théâtre, no. 604, Feb. 15, 1977)
Hey for Honesty (see Randolph, Thomas)
Hey, There--Hello! (see Mamlin, Gennadi)
HEYM, Georg, 1887-1912
    Antonius in Athen
        (In his Dichtungen und Schriften: 2, Prosa und Dramen)
    Arnold von Brescia

(In his Dichtungen und Schriften: 2, Prosa und Dramen)
Cenci
    (In his Dichtungen und Schriften: 2, Prosa und Dramen)
Der Feldzug nach Sizilien
    (In his Dichtungen und Schriften: 2, Prosa und Dramen)
Grifone
    (In his Dichtungen und Schriften: 2, Prosa und Dramen)
Die Hochzeit des Bartolomeo Ruggieri
    (In his Dichtungen und Schriften: 2, Prosa und Dramen)
Iugurtha
    (In his Dichtungen und Schriften: 2, Prosa und Dramen)
Lucius Sergius Catilina
    (In his Dichtungen und Schriften: 2, Prosa und Dramen)
Die Revolution
    (In his Dichtungen und Schriften: 2, Prosa und Dramen)
Spartacus
    (In his Dichtungen und Schriften: 2, Prosa und Dramen)
Der Sturm auf die Bastille
    (In his Dichtungen und Schriften: 2, Prosa und Dramen)
Der Tod des Helden
    (In his Dichtungen und Schriften: 2, Prosa und Dramen)
Heyns, Roger
    *"Heyns" (see Radical Arts Troups of Berkeley)
HEYWARD, Dorothy Hertzell (Kuhns), 1890-1961
    Porgy (see Heyward, Dubose)
    Porgy and Bess (see Gershwin, George)
HEYWARD, Dubose, 1885-1940
    Porgy, by Dorothy and Dubose Heyward, from the novel by Du-
    bose Heyward
        (In 50 Best Plays of the American Theatre, Vol. 1)
    Porgy and Bess (see Gershwin, George)
HEYWOOD, John, 1497?-1580
    Maandazi; a play "Johan Johan" by John Heywood translated
    into Swahili by E. A. Ibrek from a modern English version by
    Doreen Newlyn.   Text in Swahili
        (In Zuka, no. 1, Sept. 1967)
    The Play of the Wether
        (In A Book of Short Plays, XV-XX Centuries)
HEYWOOD, Thomas, d. 1641
    The Brazen Age
        (In his Dramatic Works, Vol. 3)
    A Challenge for Beautie
        (In his Dramatic Works, Vol. 5)
    The English Traveller As It Hath Beene
        (In his Dramatic Works, Vol. 4)
    The Fair Maid of the West; or, A Girlie Worth Gold, pts. 1 & 2
        (In his Dramatic Works, Vol. 2)
    The Fayre Mayde of the Exchange
        (In his Dramatic Works, Vol. 2)
    Fortune by Land and Sea, by Thomas Heywood and William
    Rowley
        (In Heywood's Dramatic Works, Vol. 6)
    The Four Prentises of London

(In his <u>Dramatic Works</u>, Vol. 2)
The Golden Age
    (In his <u>Dramatic Works</u>, Vol. 3)
If You Know Not Me, You Know No Bodie; or, The Troubles of
    Queen Elizabeth
        (In his <u>Dramatic Works</u>, Vol. 1)
The Iron Age
    (In his <u>Dramatic Works</u>, Vol. 3)
King Edward the Fourth; the first and second parts
    (In his <u>Dramatic Works</u>, Vol. 1)
A Mayden-Head Well Lost
    (In his <u>Dramatic Works</u>, Vol. 4)
Pleasant Dialogues and Drammas; selected out of Lucian, Eras-
    mus, Textor, Ovid, etc.
        (In his <u>Dramatic Works</u>, Vol. 6)
The Rape of Lucrece
    (In his <u>Dramatic Works</u>, Vol. 5)
The Royall King, and the Loyall Subject
    (In his <u>Dramatic Works</u>, Vol. 6)
The Silver Age
    (In his <u>Dramatic Works</u>, Vol. 3)
The Wise-Woman of Hogsdon
    (In his <u>Dramatic Works</u>, Vol. 5)
The Witches of Lancashire
    (In his <u>Dramatic Works</u>, Vol. 4)
A Woman Kilde with Kindnesse
    (In his <u>Dramatic Works</u>, Vol. 2)
    (In <u>World Drama</u>, Vol. 1)
HICKEY, E. and D. E.
    Victory at Trafalgar
        (In <u>Best One-Act Plays of 1939</u>, London)
Hickok, James Butler, known as Wild Bill Hickok, 1837-1876
    *Frontier Fighters, a historical adventure (see Berlin, Nathan)
    *Indians (see Kopit, Arthur L.)
The High-Backed Chair (see Holland, Norman)
The High Bid (see James, Henry)
·High in Vietnam, Hot Damn (see Pomerance, Bernard)
High Life Below Stairs (see Townley, James)
High Summer (see Rattigan, Sir Terence)
High Tor (see Anderson, Maxwell)
High Water; radio script (see Levenstein, Aaron)
HIGLEY, Philo
    The "America's" Cup, a historical drama
        (In <u>100 Non-Royalty Radio Plays</u>)
La Hija de Rappaccini (see Paz, Octavio)
Hija y Madre (see Tamayo y Baus, Manuel)
Los Hijos del Alcohol (see Salmon, Raul)
HILDESHEIMER, Wolfgang, 1916-
    Nightpiece
        (In <u>Postwar German Theatre</u>)
    Pastorale; a grotesque in one act. Both German and English
    texts are given
        (In <u>Dimension</u>, Vol. 3, no. 3, 1970)

HILL, Aaron, 1685-1750
   Zara
      (In The London Stage, Vol. 4)
HILL, Abram, 1911-
   Walk Hard
      (In Black Theater U. S. A., 1847-1974)
HILL, Errol
   Strictly Matrimony
      (In Black Drama Anthology)
HILL, George Roy
   **The Great Waldo Pepper; screenplay (see Goldman, William)
   A Night to Remember; television script adapted by George Roy
   Hill and John Whedon from the book by Walter Lord, Kraft
   Television Theatre, Mar. 28, 1956
      (In Prize Plays of Television and Radio, 1956)
HILL, Kay, 1917-
   Cobbler, Stick to Thy Last
      (In Ten Canadian Short Plays)
HILLHOUSE, James Abraham, 1789-1841
   Demetria
      (In his Dramas, Discourses, & Other Pieces, Vol. 1)
   Hadad
      (In his Dramas, Discourses, & Other Pieces, Vol. 1)
   Percy's Masque
      (In his Dramas, Discourses, & Other Pieces, Vol. 1)
Der Himbeerpflücker (see Hochwälder, Fritz)
Himmel und Erde (see Reinshagen, Gerlind)
HIMMELSTRUP, Kaj
   "Welcome to Dallas, Mr. Kennedy"
      (In Calder & Boyars Playscript Series no. 29)
Himmelwärts (see Horvath, Odön von)
Hin und Her (see Horvath, Odön von)
Hinkemann (see Toller, Ernst)
Die Hinterhältigkeit der Windmaschinen (see Jonke, G. F.)
Hinze und Kunze (see Braun, Volker)
Hippolytus (see Euripides)
Hiroshima Mon Amour; screenplay (see Duras, Marguerite)
Hirsh Lekert (see Leivich, Halper)
HIRSHBEIN, Peretz, 1880-1948
   Farvorfen Vinkel
      (In Epic and Folk Plays of the Yiddish Theatre)
   Green Fields
      (In The Great Jewish Plays)
   The Snowstorm
      (In One-Act Plays from the Yiddish)
   The Stranger
      (In One-Act Plays from the Yiddish)
   When the Dew Falleth
      (In One-Act Plays from the Yiddish)
His Excellency (see Christie, Dorothy)
His First Step (see Gordon, Charles F.)
His Helpmate (see Schnitzler, Arthur)
His House in Order (see Pinero, Arthur Wing)

His Name Shall Be: Remember (see Reines, Bernard)
L'Histoire d'Adele H.; screenplay (see Truffaut, François)
Histoire de Rire (see Salacrou, Armand)
L'Histoire de Todie et de Sara (see Claudel, Paul)
Histoire de Vasco (see Schehade, Georges)
L'Histoire du Soldat (see Ramuz, Charles F.)
Histoires de l'Oncle Jakob (see Kraemer, Jacques)
Histoires Extraordinaires; filmscript (episode) (see Vadim, Roger. Metzengerstein)
Historia de Hizen (see Tanaka, Chikao)
La Historia de los Tarantos (see Manas Navascues, Alfredo)
Historia de un Numero (see Pla, Josefina)
Historia de un Resentido (see Calvo Sotelo, Joaquin)
Historia de una Escalera (see Buero Vallejo, Antonio)
Historia de Vasco (Histoire de Vasco) (see Schehade, Georges)
Historia del Hombre Que Se Convirtio en Perro (see Dragun, Oswaldo)
A Historia do Juiz (see Pallottini, Renata)
The Historical Register for the Year 1736 (see Fielding, Henry)
The Historie of Orlando Furiosol one of the twelve pieres of France (see Greene, Robert)
History Doesn't Pay the Rent (see Ward, Edmund)
The History of Charles the Eighth of France; or, The Invasion of Naples by the French (see Crowne, John)
The History of King Lear (see Tate, Nahum)
The History of King Richard III (see Cibber, Colley)
The History of Timon of Athens, the Man-Hater (see Shadwell, Thomas)
Histrio-Mastix; or, The Player (see Marston, John)
HITCHCOCK, Alfred, 1899-
    Psycho; screenplay; directed by Alfred Hitchcock. Pictures and complete dialogue edited by Richard J. Anobile
        (In The Film Classics Library, 1974)
HITE, Barbara Allan
    Birdwatchers
        (In Theatre Wagon Plays)
    Sandcastle
        (In Theatre Wagon Plays)
Hitler, Adolph, 1889-1945
    *Germania Tod in Berlin (see Müller, Heiner)
Hitting Town (see Poliakoff, Stephen)
HIVNOR, Robert
    Love Reconciled to War
        (In Break Out!)
    The Ticklish Acrobat
        (In Playbook: Five Plays for a New Theatre)
Hoboken Blues (see Gold, Michael)
HOCHHUTH, Rolf, 1931-
    Amleto Principe di Danimarca (see Brecht, Bertolt)
HOCHWALDER, Fritz, 1911-
    Der Befehl
        (In his Dramen, Vol. 2)
    Donadieu

(In his <u>Dramen,</u> VoL 2)
Esther
   (In his <u>Dramen,</u> VoL 1)
Das Heilige Experiment
   (In his <u>Dramen,</u> VoL 1)
Die Herberge
   (In his <u>Dramen,</u> VoL 2)
Der Himbeerpflüker
   (In his <u>Dramen,</u> VoL 2)
The Holy Experiment
   (In <u>Themes of Drama</u>)
Hotel du Commerce
   (In his <u>Dramen,</u> VoL 1)
Meier Helmbrecht
   (In his <u>Dramen,</u> VoL 1)
Der Offentliche Ankläger
   (In his <u>Dramen,</u> VoL 1)
The Raspberry Picker
   (In <u>New Theatre of Europe</u>, VoL 4)
The Strong Are Lonely, translated by Eva Le Gallienne
   (In <u>Plays of the Year</u>, VoL 14, 1955/56)
Der Unschuldige
   (In his <u>Dramen,</u> VoL 2)
Die Hochzeit der Sobeide (see Hofmannsthal, Hugo von H.)
Die Hochzeit der Sobeide (The Marriage of Zobeide); both German
   and English texts (see Hofmannsthal, Hugo von H.)
Die Hochzeit des Bartolomeo Ruggieri (see Heym, Georg)
Die Hochzeit des Papstes (see Bond, Edward)
HODSON, James Lansdale, 1891-
   Harvest in the North
     (In <u>Famous Plays of 1938-39</u>)
   Red Light
     (In <u>Famous Plays of 1935-36</u>)
HOECK, Josef van, 1921-
   Sentencia Provisional
     (In <u>Teatro Flamenco Contemporaneo</u>)
HÖLJER, Björn-Erik, 1907-
   Isak Juntti Had Many Sons
     (In <u>Modern Nordic Plays: Sweden</u>)
Hölderlin; text in French (see Weiss, Peter)
Hölle Weg Erde (see Kaiser, Georg)
Höllenspiel (see Brust, Alfred)
HOFFENSTEIN, Samuel
   Dr. Jekyll and Mr. Hyde; screenplay (see Mamoulian, Rouben)
HOFFMAN, Ernst Theodor Amadeus, 1776-1822
   Das Bergwerk zu Falun (The Mine at Falun) (see Hofmannsthal,
   Hugo von H.)
   The Tales of Hoffman; filmscript (see Powell, Michael)
HOFFMAN, William Moses, 1939-
   A Quick Nut Bread to Make Your Mouth Water
     (In <u>Spontaneous Combustion</u>; The Winter Repertory, VoL 6)
   Saturday Night at the Movies
     (In <u>The Off Off Broadway Book</u>)

HOFMAN, Gert
On Vacation
(In Best Short Plays, 1974)
HOFMANNSTHAL, Hugo von Hoffman, Elder von, 1874-1929
Der Abenteurer und die Sängerin
(In his Dramen I)
Die Agyptische Helena
(In his Dramen IV)
Alekestis des Euripides)
(In his Dramen I)
Arabella
(In his Selected Plays and Liberetti)
Das Bergwerk zu Falun (The Mine at Falun); act one, based on
the work of E. T. A. Hoffman and an anecdote by J. P. Hebel;
both German and English texts are given
(In his Poems and Verse Plays)
The Cavalier of the Rose
(In his Selected Plays and Liberetti)
The Difficult Man
(In his Selected Plays and Liberetti)
Electra, a tragedy in one act freely rendered after Sophocles
(In Masterpieces of the Modern Central European Theatre)
(In his Selected Plays and Liberetti)
Elektra
(In his Dramen I)
Die Frau im Fenster
(In his Dramen I)
Die Frau ohne Schatten
(In his Dramen III)
Fuchs
(In his Dramen I)
Das Gerettete Venedig
(In his Dramen II)
Die Hochzeit der Sobeide
(In his Dramen I)
Die Hochzeit der Sobeide (The Marriage of Zobeide); both Ger-
man and English texts are included
(In his Poems and Verse Plays)
Jedermann
(In his Dramen III)
Der Kaiser und die Hexe (The Emperor and the Witch); both
German and English texts are included
(In his Poems and Verse Plays)
Das Kleine Welttheater (The Little Theatre of the World); both
German and English texts are included
(In his Poems and Verse Plays)
König Ödipus
(In his Dramen II)
Das Leben ein Traum
(In his Dramen III)
Ödipus und die Sphinx
(In his Dramen II)
Die Ruinen von Athen

(In his Dramen IV)
The Salzburg Great Theatre of the World
   (In his Selected Plays and Libretti)
Das Salzburger Grosse Welttheater
   (In his Dramen III)
Der Schüler
   (In his Dramen I)
Der Tor und der Tod (Death and the Fool); both German and
   English texts are included
   (In his Poems and Verse Plays)
The Tower
   (In his Selected Plays and Libretti)
Der Triumph der Zeit
   (In his Dramen I)
Der Turm
   (In his Dramen III)
Vorspiel für ein Puppentheater
   (In his Dramen II)
Vorspiel zur Antigone des Sophokles
   (In his Dramen I)
Vorspiel zur "Antigone" des Sophokles (Prologue to the "Antigone"
   of Sophocles); both German and English texts are included
   (In his Poems and Verse Plays)
Hogan's Goat (see Alfred, William)
HOLBERG, Ludvig von, baron, 1684-1754
The Arabian Powder
   (In his Seven One-Act Plays)
   (In his Three Comedies)
The Changed Bridegroom
   (In his Seven One-Act Plays)
The Christmas Party
   (In his Seven One-Act Plays)
Diderich the Terrible
   (In his Seven One-Act Plays)
The Fussy Man (Den Stundeslöse)
   (In his Four Plays)
The Healing Spring
   (In his Three Comedies)
Jeppe of the Hill
   (In World Drama, Vol. 2)
The Loquacious Barber
   (In The Drama, Vol. 17)
The Masked Ladies (De Usynlige)
   (In his Four Plays)
Masquerades (Maskarade)
   (In his Four Plays)
Master Gert Westphaler; or, The Talkative Barber
   (In his Seven One-Act Plays)
The Peasant in Pawn
   (In his Seven One-Act Plays)
Sganarel's Journey to the Land of the Philosophers
   (In his Seven One-Act Plays)
The Transformed Peasant

(In his Three Comedies)
The Weathercock (Den Vaegelsindede)
(In his Four Plays)
HOLCROFT, Thomas, 1745-1809
The Deserted Daughter
(In The London Stage, Vol. 3)
He's Much to Blame
(In The London Stage, Vol. 4)
The School for Arrogance
(In The London Stage, Vol. 4)
Seduction
(In The London Stage, Vol. 4)
Hold On, Hortense (see Moinaux, Georges)
Holding a Husband (see Hopkins, Arthur M.)
The Hole (see Simpson, Norman F.)
Holiday (see Barry, Philip)
HOLLAND, Norman
The High-Backed Chair
(In Best One-Act Plays of 1938, London)
Telltale Heart; adapted from the short story by Edgar Allan Poe
(In The Best One-Act Plays of 1958-59, London)
Holland's Leaguer (see Marmion, Shakerly)
Holliday, John Henry, (Doc), 1852?-1887
*Doc; screenplay (see Hamill, Pete)
HOLLINGSWORTH, Michael
Strawberry Fields
(In The Factory Lab Anthology)
The Holly and the Ivy (see Browne, Wynyard)
HOLMAN, Joseph George, 1764-1817
Abroad and at Home
(In The London Stage, Vol. 4)
The Votary of Wealth
(In The London Stage, Vol. 4)
The Holy Experiment (see Hochwälder, Fritz)
The Holy Ghostly (see Shepard, Sam)
Holy Ghosts (see Linney, Romulus)
Holy Isle (see Mavor, Osborne Henry)
The Homage of the Arts (see Schiller, Johann C.)
Un Hombre Como los Demas (see Salacrou, Armand)
Un Hombre Puro (see Calvo Sotelo, Joaquin)
El Hombre sin Cuerpo (see Teirlinck, Herman)
El Hombre y Su Máscara (see Ureta, Margarita)
El Hombre y Sus Sueños (see Marques, Rene)
Los Hombres de Bien (see Tamayo y Baus, Manuel)
Hombres de los Mundos (see Cid Perez, José)
HOME, John, 1722-1808
Douglas
(In British Plays from the Restoration to 1820)
(In The Drama, Vol. 14)
(In 18th Century Tragedy)
(In Plays of the Restoration and 18th Century)
HOME, William Douglas, 1912-
Lloyd George Knew My Father

(In Plays of the Year, Vol. 42, 1972)
    The Thistle and the Rose
        (In Plays of the Year, Vol. 4, 1950)
Home (see Maeterlinck, Maurice)
Home Ain't So Sweet (see Corrie, Joe)
Home and Beauty (see Maugham, William Somerset)
Home Chat (see Coward, Noël)
Home Fires (see Guare, John Edward)
The Home for Heroes (see Bowering, George)
Home Front (see Walser, Martin)
Home Is Tomorrow (see Priestley, John B.)
Home Movies (see Drexler, Rosalyn)
Homecoming (see O'Neill, Eugene)
The Homecoming of Beorhtnoth, Beorhthelm's Son (see Tolkien, J.
    R. R.)
Homecookin' (see Goss, Clay)
HOMER, 8th Century B.C.
    **La Teyedora de Sueños (see Buero Vallejo, Antonio)
Un Homme Comme les Autres (see Salacrou, Armand)
L'Homme en Question (see Marceau, Felicien)
L'Homme Enchaine (see Bourdet, Edouard)
L'Homme et Son Désir (see Claudel, Paul)
The Homosexual; or, The Difficulty of Expressing Oneself (see Copi)
The Honest Man's Fortune (see Beaumont, Francis)
The Honest Thieves (see Knight, Thomas)
The Honeymoon (see Tobin, John)
The Honeymooners television scripts
    A Letter to the Boss (see Marx, Marvin)
    The $99,000 Answer (see Stern, Leonard)
HONIG, Edwin
    Orpheus Below; a verse play
        (In New Directions in Prose and Poetry, Vol. 24, 1972)
Honky-Tonk, or Husband in Name Only; filmscript (see Fields,
    W. C.)
Les Honnêtes Femmes (see Becque, Henri)
Honni Soit Qui Mal y Pense; text in French (see Barnes, Peter)
The Honor and the Glory (see Chipp, Elinor)
The Honorable Histoire of Frier Bacon and Grier Bongay (see
    Greene, Robert)
Honoria and Mammon (see Shirley, James)
HOOD, Hugh
    Friends and Relations
        (In The Play's the Thing)
HOOKE, Nina Warner
    The Godsend
        (In The Best One-Act Plays of 1958-59, London)
HOORINK, Eduardo
    El Agua
        (In Teatro Neerlandes Contemporaneo)
Hop, Signor! (see Ghelderode, Michel de)
HOPE, Bob (Leslie Townes), 1904-
    The Bob Hope Show; radio script, Mar. 12, 1940
        (In Best Broadcasts of 1939-40)

HOPGOOD, Alan
   And the Big Men Fly
      (In Australian Theatre Workshop no. 2, 1969)
HOPKINS, Arthur Melancthon, 1878-1950
   Holding a Husband
      (In One-Act Plays for Stage and Study, 9th Series)
   Moonshine
      (In Five Plays from the Other Side)
      (In One-Act Plays for Stage and Study, 1st Series)
HOPKINS, John Richard, 1931-
   Any Time You're Ready, I'll Sparkle
      (In his Talking to a Stranger)
   Find Your Way Home
      (In Penguin Plays Series, 1971)
   Gladly, My Cross-eyed Bear
      (In his Talking to a Stranger)
   The Innocent Must Suffer
      (In his Talking to a Stranger)
   No Skill or Special Knowledge Is Required
      (In his Talking to a Stranger)
   This Story of Yours
      (In Penguin Modern Playwrights Series, no. 9, 1969)
HOPKINSON, Francis, 1737-1791
   A Dialogue and Ode; on the accession of his present gracious
   Majesty George III
      (In Dramas from the American Theatre, 1762-1909)
HOPKINSON, Simon
   The Crazy World of Advertising
      (In Australian Theatre Workshop no. 13, 1975)
Horace, Quintus Horatius Flaccus, 65-8 B.C.
   *Another "Lay of Ancient Rome," not by Macauley
      (In The Knickerbocker, Vol. 21, no. 5, May 1843)
   *Horace, text in French (see Corneille, Pierre)
   *Horace (The Horatii); text in English (see Corneille, Pierre)
L'Horloger de Saint-Paul (see Tavernier, Bertrand)
HORNE, Kenneth
   Trial and Error
      (In Plays of the Year, Vol. 9, 1953)
Las Hornigas (see Yglesias, Antonio)
HOROVITZ, Israel, 1939-
   Acrobates
      (In L'Avant-Scène du Théâtre, no. 529, Nov. 15, 1973)
   The Indian Wants the Bronx
      (In Off-Broadway Plays, Vol. 1)
   It's Called the Sugar Plum
      (In Off-Broadway Plays, Vol. 1)
   Line
      (In The Off Off Broadway Book)
   Live
      (In Best Short Plays of the World Theatre, 1968-1973)
   Morning
      (In Best American Plays, 7th Series, 1967-1973)
   Le Premier (Le 1er) Piece d'Israel Horovitz; adaptation de

Claude Roy
    (In L'Avant-Scène du Théâtre, no. 529, Nov. 15, 1973)
Rats
    (In Collision Course)
Spared
    (In Best Short Plays of 1975)
Stage Directions
    (In Best Short Plays, 1977)
Horror of Dracula; screenplay (see Fisher, Terence. Le Cauchemar
    de Dracula)
El Horroroso Crimen de Penaranda del Campo (see Baroja y Nessi,
    Pio)
Hors Service (see Berreby, Georges)
The Horse Latitudes (see Black, Stephen)
Horseshoe Luck (see Dyar, R. E.)
Horse-shoe Robinson (see Tayleure, Clifton W.)
Hortense a Dit: "Je M'En Fous!" (see Feydeau, Georges)
Hortense, Couche-Toi! (see Moinaux, Georges)
HORVATH, Odön von, 1901-1938
    Don Juan Kommt aus dem Krieg
        (In his Gesammelte Werke 2: Schauspiele)
    Ein Dorf ohne Männer
        (In his Gesammelte Werke 4: Komödien II)
    Ein Epilog
        (In his Gesammelte Werke 2: Schauspiele)
    Figaro Lässt sich Scheiden
        (In his Gesammelte Werke 4: Komödien II)
    La Foi, l'Espérance et la Charité; adaptation Française de
        Renée Saurel
        (In L'Avant-Scène Théâtre, no. 580, July 1, 1976)
    Fragmente und Varianten
        (In his Gesammelte Werke 7: Szenisches)
    Geschichten aus dem Wiener Wald
        (In his Gesammelte Werke 1: Volksstücke)
    Glaube Liebe Hoffnung
        (In his Gesammelte Werke 1: Volksstücke)
    Himmelwärts
        (In his Gesammelte Werke 3: Komödien I)
    Hin und Her
        (In his Gesammelte Werke 3: Komödien I)
    Italienische Nacht
        (In his Gesammelte Werke 1: Volksstücke)
    Der Juan Jungste Tag
        (In his Gesammelte Werke 2: Schauspiele)
    Kasimir und Karoline
        (In his Gesammelte Werke 1: Volksstücke)
    Mit dem Kopf Durch die Wand
        (In his Gesammelte Werke 4: Komödien II)
    Mord in der Mohrengasse
        (In his Gesammelte Werke 2: Schauspiele)
    Notte Italiana
        (In Sipario, no. 327-328, Aug. /Sept. 1973)
    Pompeji

(In his <u>Gesammelte Werke 4:   Komödien II</u>)
Revolte auf Côte 3018
(In his <u>Gesammelte Werke 1:   Volksstücke</u>)
Rund um den Kongress
(In his <u>Gesammelte Werke 3:   Komödien I</u>)
Ein Sklavenball
(In his <u>Gesammelte Werke 4:   Komödien II</u>)
Sladek oder Die Schwarze Armee
(In his <u>Gesammelte Werke 2:   Schauspiele</u>)
Die Unbekannte aus der Sein
(In his <u>Gesammelte Werke 3:   Komödien I</u>)
Zur Schönen Aussicht
(In his <u>Gesammelte Werke 3:   Komödien I</u>)
HORWITZ, Simi
   The Opening Up
      (In <u>South of the Navel</u>)
Hosanna (see Tremblay, Michel)
Hospital (see Pomerance, Bernard)
The Host (see Molnar, Ferenc)
Hostile Witness (see Roffey, Jack)
Hot Buttered Roll (see Dexler, Rosalyn)
Hot Ice (see Ludlam, Charles)
Hot Lemonade (see Ryerson, Florence)
Hot Stuff (see Pokalsky, Peter)
Hotel du Commerce (see Hochwälder, Fritz)
L'Hotel du Libre Echange (see Feydeau, Georges)
Hotel for Criminals (see Foreman, Richard)
The Hotel in Amsterdam (see Osborne, John)
Hotel Universe (see Barry, Philip)
HOUDAR DE LA MOTTE, Antoine, 1672-1731
   Ines de Castro
      (In <u>Théâtre de XVIII Siècle</u>, Vol. 1)
HOUGHTON, Stanley, 1881-1913
   The Dear Departed
      (In More One-Act Plays by Modern Authors)
   Phipps
      (In One-Act Plays for Stage and Study, 1st Series)
The Hour-Glass (see Yeats, William Butler)
The Hour of Recognition (see Schnitzler, Arthur)
The Hour of the Dog (see Dorall, Edward)
The House (see Borgen, Johan)
The House by the Lake (see Mills, Hugh)
The House of Atreus (see Aeschylus)
The House of Bernarda Alba (see Garcia Lorca, Federico)
The House of Blue Leaves (see Guare, John)
The House of Bones (see Dubillard, Roland)
House of Cowards (see Abse, Dannie)
The House of Sham (see Richardson, Willis)
The House of Teeth; The Goon Show Scripts no. 145 (see Milligan, Spike)
The House on Chestnut Street (see Nichol, James W.)
The House That Jack Built (see Farwell, George)
Household Bread (see Renard, Jules)

The Household Peace (see Maupassant, Guy de)
The Houses by the Green (see Cregan, David)
HOUSMAN, Alfred Edward, 1859-1936
    Fragment of a Greek Tragedy
        (In Parodies)
HOUSMAN, Laurencem 1865-1959
    Bethlehem
        (In Types of Modern Dramatic Composition)
    Royal Favour
        (In A Book of Short Plays, XV-XX Centuries)
HOUSUM, Robert, 1886-
    The Corsican Lieutenant
        (In One-Act Plays for Stage and Study, 2nd Series)
    The Despot
        (In One-Act Plays for Stage and Study, 9th Series)
    The Eligible Mr. Bangs
        (In One-Act Plays for Stage and Study, 3rd Series)
HOUWENINGE, Chiem van, 1940-
    Le Dernier Train; adaptation Française de Maryse et Michel
    Caillol
        (In L'Avant-Scène Théâtre, no. 589, June 15, 1976)
How Are They at Home? (see Priestley, John B.)
How Are You? A Day in Five Movie Details (see Maiakovskii,
    Vladimir V.)
How Bitter the Bread (see Ridler, Anne B.)
How Can You Be in Two Places at Once When You're Not Anywhere
    at All (see The Firesign Theatre)
How Could You? (see Donahue, John C.)
How Do You Do (see Bullins, Edward A.)
How He Lied to Her Husband (see Shaw, George Bernard)
How I Met My Husband (see Munro, Alice)
How Mr. Mockinpott Was Cured of His Sufferings (see Weiss, Peter)
How to Settle Accounts with Your Laundress (see Coyne, Joseph S.)
How to Train a Dog; a radio monologue (see Clark, Sylvia)
HOWARD, Bronson Crocker, 1842-1908
    The Banker's Daughter
        (In Favorite American Plays of the 19th Century)
    Shenandoah
        (In Dramas from the American Theatre, 1762-1909)
        (In Representative Plays by American Dramatists, Vol. 3)
HOWARD, Sir Robert, 1626-1698
    The Indian Queen (see Dryden, John)
HOWARD, Roger, 1938-
    The Carrying of X from A to Z
        (In New Short Plays, Vol. 1)
    Dis
        (In New Short Plays, Vol. 1)
    The Love Suicides at Havering
        (In New Short Plays, Vol. 1)
    Seven Stations on the Road to Exile
        (In New Short Plays, Vol. 1)
HOWARD, Sidney Coe, 1891-1939
    Lucky Sam McCarver

Olympia (see Molnar, Ferenc)
Salvation by Sidney Howard and Charles MacArthur
   (In The Stage Works of Charles MacArthur)
The Silver Cord
   (In Dramas of Modernism)
   (In Representative American Plays, 1792-1949)
HOWARD, William K. , 1899-1954
Back Door to Heaven; screenplay (see Bright, John)
HOWARTH, Donald
Three Months Gone
   (In Plays of the Year, Vol. 39, 1969/70)
HOWELLS, J. Harvey
Good-by, Gray Flannel; television script from the "Schick Tele-
vision Theatre, " Oct. 22, 1956
   (In Prize Plays of Television and Radio)
HOWELLS, William Dean, 1837-1920
The Albany Depot
   (In his Complete Plays)
Bride Roses
   (In his Complete Plays)
Colonel Sellers as a Scientist, by W. D. Howells and Samuel L.
Clemens
   (In his Complete Plays)
A Counterfeit Presentment
   (In his Complete Plays)
The Elevator
   (In his Complete Plays)
Evening Dress
   (In his Complete Plays)
Five O'Clock Tea
   (In his Complete Plays)
A Foregone Conclusion
   (In his Complete Plays)
The Garroters
   (In his Complete Plays)
A Hazard of New Fortunes
   (In his Complete Plays)
Her Opinion of His Story
   (In his Complete Plays)
The Impossible: a Mystery Play
   (In his Complete Plays)
An Indian Giver
   (In his Complete Plays)
A Letter of Introduction
   (In his Complete Plays)
   (In Dramas from the American Theatre, 1762-1909)
A Likely Story
   (In his Complete Plays)
A Masterpiece of Diplomacy
   (In his Complete Plays)
The Mother and the Father
   (In his Complete Plays)
The Mouse Trap

(In his Complete Plays)
The Night Before Christmas
   (In his Complete Plays)
Out of the Question
   (In his Complete Plays)
The Parlor Car
   (In his Complete Plays)
Parting Friends
   (In his Complete Plays)
A Previous Engagement
   (In his Complete Plays)
Priscilla: a Comedy
   (In his Complete Plays)
The Register
   (In his Complete Plays)
The Rise of Silas Lapham
   (In his Complete Plays)
Room Forty-Five
   (In his Complete Plays)
Samson
   (In his Complete Plays)
Saved: an Emotional Drama
   (In his Complete Plays)
A Sea Change; or, Love's Stowaway
   (In his Complete Plays)
Self-Sacrifice: a Farce Tragedy
   (In his Complete Plays)
The Sleeping Car
   (In his Complete Plays)
The Smoking Car
   (In his Complete Plays)
A True Hero: Melodrama
   (In his Complete Plays)
The Unexpected Guests
   (In his Complete Plays)
Yorick's Love
   (In his Complete Plays)
Hoy Es Fiesta (see Buero Vallejo, Antonio)
Hoy Invita la Güera (see Inclan, Federico Schroeder)
HOYT, Charles Hale, 1860-1900
   A Temperance Town
     (In Dramas from the American Theatre, 1762-1909)
   A Texas Steer; or, "Money Makes the Mare Go"
     (In Representative American Dramas)
   A Trip to Chinatown
     (In Favorite American Plays of the 19th Century)
Hsueh Pei Yuan (Affinity of the Snow Cup)
   (In Famous Chinese Plays)
Hu Tieh Meng (The Butterfly's Dream)
   (In Famous Chinese Plays)
Huang Ho Lou (The Yellow Crane Tower)
   (In Famous Chinese Plays)
HUBAY, Miklos
   Il Carnevale

(In <u>Sipario</u>, no. 373-374, June/July 1977)
HUBBARD, Philip
   The Crumbs That Fall
      (In <u>Types of Modern Dramatic Composition</u>)
Hudson, Henry,   -1611?
   *Henry Hudson, a historical drama (see Monroe, Robert)
HUDSON, Holland, 1889-
   The Kite
      (In <u>One-Act Plays for Stage and Study</u>, 3rd Series)
Huelguistas (see Valdez, Luis)
Los Huespedes Reales (see Hernandez, Luisa Josefina)
HUFHAM, B. Gary
   Peace on Earth, a Christmas play of today
      (In <u>100 Non-Royalty Radio Plays</u>)
HUGHES, Mrs. Babbette (Plechner), 1906-
   Angelica
      (In <u>One-Act Plays for Stage and Study</u>, 8th Series)
   Bilora, the Second Rustic Play (see Beolco, Angelo)
   Greek to You
      (In <u>One-Act Plays for Stage and Study</u>, 9th Series)
   The March Heir
      (In <u>One-Act Plays for Stage and Study</u>, 7th Series)
   Murder! Murder! Murder!
      (In <u>One-Act Plays for Stage and Study</u>, 6th Series)
   No More Americans
      (In <u>One-Act Plays for Stage and Study</u>, 5th Series)
   One Egg; a play edited for radio
      (In <u>On the Air: 15 Plays for Broadcast</u>)
   Sisters Under the Skin
      (In <u>One-Act Plays for Stage and Study</u>, 10th Series)
   Three Players, a Fop and a Duchess
      (In <u>One-Act Plays for Stage and Study</u>, 4th Series)
   The Wise Virgins and the Foolish Virgins (Anon.), translated
   by Babbette and Glenn Hughes
      (In <u>World Drama</u>, Vol. 1)
HUGHES, Glenn, 1894-
   Art and Mrs. Palmer
      (In <u>One-Act Plays for Stage and Study</u>, 5th Series)
   Babbitt's Boy
      (In <u>One-Act Plays for Stage and Study</u>, 6th Series)
   Bilora, the Second Rustic Play (see Beolco, Angelo)
   Blue Sea and Red Rose
      (In <u>One-Act Plays for Stage and Study</u>, 8th Series)
   Dinner for Two
      (In <u>One-Act Plays for Stage and Study</u>, 9th Series)
   Funny Business
      (In <u>One-Act Plays for Stage and Study</u>, 7th Series)
   Havana Moon
      (In <u>One-Act Plays for Stage and Study</u>, 10th Series)
   Red Carnations
      (In <u>One-Act Plays for Stage and Study</u>, 2nd Series)
   Red Carnations; a play edited for radio
      (In <u>On the Air: 15 Plays for Broadcast</u>)

The Wise Virgins and the Foolish Virgins (Anon.), translated by
   Babbette and Glenn Hughes
   (In World Drama, VoL 1)
HUGHES, John
   The Ship of Dreams
   (In Canada on Stage)
HUGHES, John, 1677-1720
   The Siege of Damascus
   (In The London Stage, VoL 3)
HUGHES, Langston, 1902-1967
   Don't You Want to Be Free?
     (In Black Theater U. S. A. , 1847-1974
     (In The New Negro Renaissance)
   Limitations of Life
     (In Black Theater U. S. A. , 1847-1974)
   Little Ham
     (In Black Theater U. S. A. , 1847-1974)
   Mother and Child
     (In Black Drama Anthology)
   Simply Heavenly
     (In Black Theater)
   Soul Gone Home
     (In All the World's a Stage)
     (In Blackamerican Literature 1760-Present)
     (In The Disinherited: Plays)
Hugo, Adele, 1830-1915
   *L'Histoire d'Adele H. ; filmscript; text in French (see Truffaut,
   François)
   *The Story of Adele H. ; filmscript (see Truffaut, François)
HUGO, Victor Marie, comte, 1802-1885
   A Quelque Chose Hasard Est Bon
     (In his Théâtre Complet I)
   Amy Robsart
     (In his Dramas, VoL 1)
   Amy Robsart; text in French
     (In his Théâtre Complet I)
   Angelo
     (In his Dramas, VoL 1)
   Angelo, Tyran de Padoue; text in French
     (In his Théâtre Complet II)
   Athelie; ou, Les Scandinaves
     (In his Théâtre Complet II)
   The Burgraves
     (In his Dramas, VoL 3)
   Les Burgraves; text in French
     (In his Théâtre Complet II)
   Le Chateau du Diable
     (In his Théâtre Complet II)
   Corneille
     (In his Théâtre Complet II)
   Cromwell
     (In his Dramas, VoL 3)
   Cromwell; text in French

(In his <u>Théâtre Complet</u> I)
Don Cesar de Bazan
(In his <u>Théâtre Complet</u> II)
L'Enfer sur Terre
(In his <u>Théâtre Complet</u> II)
L'Epée
(In his <u>Théâtre Complet</u> II)
Esmeralda
(In his <u>Dramas</u>, Vol. 2)
La Esmeralda; text in French
(In his <u>Théâtre Complet</u> II)
The Fool's Revenge
(In his <u>Dramas</u>, Vol. 4)
La Forêt Mouilée
(In his <u>Théâtre Complet</u> II)
La Grand'mere
(In his <u>Théâtre Complet</u> II)
Les Gueux
(In his <u>Théâtre Complet</u> II)
Hernani
(In his <u>Dramas</u>, Vol. 1)
(In <u>World Drama</u>, Vol. 2)
Hernani; text in French
(In his <u>Théâtre Complet</u> I)
*L'Histoire d'Adele H.; filmscript; text in French (see Truffaut, François)
Inez de Castro; text in French
(In his <u>Théâtre Complet</u> I)
L'Intervention
(In his <u>Théâtre Complet</u> II)
Irtamene; text in French
(In his <u>Théâtre Complet</u> I)
Les Jumeaux
(In his <u>Théâtre Complet</u> II)
Lucrece Borgia; text in French
(In <u>L'Avant-Scène Théâtre</u>, no. 574, Nov. 1, 1975)
(In his <u>Théâtre Complet</u> II)
Lucretia Borgia
(In his <u>Dramas</u>, Vol. 4)
Maglia
(In his <u>Théâtre Complet</u> II)
Mangeront-ils?
(In his <u>Théâtre Complet</u> II)
Marie Tudor; text in French
(In his <u>Théâtre Complet</u> II)
Marion de Lorme
(In his <u>Dramas</u>, Vol. 4)
Marion de Lorme; text in French
(In his <u>Théâtre Complet</u> I)
Mary Tudor
(In his <u>Dramas</u>, Vol. 2)
Mille Francs de Recompense
(In his <u>Théâtre Complet</u> II)

HUSTON, John, 1906-
   The Maltese Falcon; screenplay and direction by John Huston,
   based upon the novel by Dashiell Hammett.   Pictures and
   complete dialogue edited by Richard J. Anobile
      (In The Film Classics Library, 1974)
HUTCHINS, Maude Phelps
   The Case of Astrolabe
      (In New Directions, Vol. 8, 1944)
   A Short Play About Joseph Smith, Jr.
      (In New Directions, Vol. 9, 1946)
   The Wandering Jew
      (In New Directions, Vol. 13, 1951)
HUTTON, Joseph, 1787-1828
   Fashionable Follies
      (In Representative Plays by American Dramatists, Vol. 2)
Hyacinth Halvey (see Gregory, Isabella A.)
HYDE, Douglas, Pres. Irish Free State, 1860-1949
   The Bursting of the Bubble (Pleusgadh na Bulgoide)
      (In Poets and Dreamers)
   King James
      (In Poets and Dreamers)
   The Lost Saint
      (In Poets and Dreamers)
   The Marriage
      (In Poets and Dreamers)
   The Matchmaking
      (In Poets and Dreamers)
   The Nativity
      (In Poets and Dreamers)
   The Poorhouse, by Douglas Hyde and Lady Gregory
      (In Complete Plays of Lady Gregory, Vol. 4)
   The Schoolmaster
      (In Poets and Dreamers)
   The Tinker and the Sheeog
      (In Poets and Dreamers)
   The Twisting of the Rope
      (In Poets and Dreamers)
Hyde Park (see Shirley, James)
Hyetad (see Kedjian, Yetvart)
Hyginus, Gaius Julius, 1st Century B. C.
   *Merope (see Voltaire)
Hymen (see Torres Naharro, Bartolome de)
Hymenée (see Bourdet, Edouard)
Die Hypochonder (see Strauss, Botho)
The Hypochondriac (Le Malade Imaginaire) (see Molière, Jean
   Baptiste)
The Hypocrite (see Bickerstaff, Isaac)
The Hypocrite (see McLellan, Robert)
Hypocrite(s) (see Jones, LeRoi)
The Hypothesis (see Pinget, Robert)

I Came to New York to Write (see Patrick, Robert)

"I Can't Sleep" (see Odets, Clifford)
I Didn't Always Live Here (see Conn, Stewart)
I Have Been Here Before (see Priestley, John B.)
I Heard the Owl Call My Name; television script (see Di Pego, Gerald)
I Love You Sylvia Plath (see Langford, Gary)
I P'eng Hsueh (A Double Handful of Snow)
   (In Famous Chinese Plays)
I Remember Mama (see Van Druten, John)
I Spy (see Mortimer, John Clifford)
I Think We're All Bozos on This Bus (see The Firesign Theatre)
I Vecchi (see Wesker, Arnold)
I Was Born, But ...; filmscript (excerpt) (see Ozu, Yasujiro)
IBARGUENGOITIA, Jorge, 1928-
   Clotilde en Su Casa
      (In Teatro Méxicano del Siglo XX, Vol. 3)
   Susana y lod Jóvenes
      (In Teatro Méxicano Contemporaneo)
IBBITSON, John
   The Ritual
      (In Performing Arts in Canada, Vol. 11, no. 3, Fall 1974)
IBREK, Emil A.
   Maandazi (see Heywood, John)
IBSEN, Henrik Johan, 1828-1906
   Archer; The Feast at Solhough
      (In his Works, Vol. 1)
   Brand
      (In The Oxford Ibsen, Vol. 3)
      (In his Works, Vol. 3)
   The Burial Mound; 1st and 2nd versions
      (In The Oxford Ibsen, Vol. 1)
   Catiline, 1st and 2nd versions
      (In The Oxford Ibsen, Vol. 1)
   La Dame de la Mer; version Française de Gilbert Sigaux
      (In L'Avant-Scène Théâtre, no. 610, May 15, 1977)
   A Doll's House
      (In his Eleven Plays)
      (In The Oxford Ibsen, Vol. 5)
      (In his Works, Vol. 7)
   A Doll's House, translated by William Archer
      (In World Drama, Vol. 2)
   Emperor and Galilean
      (In The Oxford Ibsen, Vol. 4)
      (In his Works, Vol. 5)
   An Enemy of the People
      (In his Eleven Plays)
      (In The Oxford Ibsen, Vol. 6)
      (In his Works, Vol. 8)
   An Enemy of the People, adapted by Stan Darstow
      (In Calder & Boyars Playscript Series, 1977)
   The Feast at Solhoug
      (In The Oxford Ibsen, Vol. 1)
   Ghosts

(In his Eleven Plays)
(In The Oxford Ibsen, Vol. 5)
(In his Works, Vol. 7)
Ghosts, translated by William Archer
(In The Drama, Vol. 17)
Hedda Gabler
(In Contact with Drama)
(In his Eleven Plays)
(In Masterpieces of the Modern Scandinavian Theatre)
(In The Oxford Ibsen, Vol. 7)
(In his Works, Vol. 10)
John Gabriel Borkman
(In his Eleven Plays)
(In his Works, Vol. 11)
The Lady from the Sea
(In The Oxford Ibsen, Vol. 7)
(In his Works, Vol. 9)
Lady Inger; 1st and 2nd versions
(In The Oxford Ibsen, Vol. 1)
Lady Inger of Ostrat
(In his Works, Vol. 1)
.The League of Youth
(In his Eleven Plays)
(In The Oxford Ibsen, Vol. 4)
(In his Works, Vol. 6)
Little Eyolf
(In his Works, Vol. 11)
Love's Comedy
(In The Oxford Ibsen, Vol. 2)
(In his Works, Vol. 1)
The Master Builder
(In his Eleven Plays)
(In The Oxford Ibsen, Vol. 6)
(In his Works, Vol. 10)
Norma; or, A Politician's Love
(In The Oxford Ibsen, Vol. 1)
Olaf Liljekrans
(In The Oxford Ibsen, Vol. 1)
Peer Gynt
(In his Eleven Plays)
(In The Oxford Ibsen, Vol. 3)
(In his Works, Vol. 4)
Peer Gynt, adapted by Dietrich Eckart
(In Eckart's Eight Plays)
Pillars of Society
(In his Eleven Plays)
(In The Oxford Ibsen, Vol. 5)
(In his Works, Vol. 6)
The Pretenders
(In The Oxford Ibsen, Vol. 2)
(In his Works, Vol. 2)
Quand Nous Nous Réveillerons d'Entre les Morts
(In L'Avant-Scène Théâtre, no. 599, Dec. 1, 1976)

Ikiru; screenplay (see Kurosawa, Akira)
IKO, Momoko, 1940-
 The Gold Watch
  (In Aiiieeeee!)
Il Faut Passer par les Nuages (see Billetdoux, François P.)
Il Faut Que le Sycomore (see Ribes, Jean-Michel)
Il Faut Qu'une Porte Soit Ouverte ou Fermée (see Musset, Alfred de)
Ile (see O'Neill, Eugene)
L'Ile de la Raison; ou, Les Petits Hommes (see Marivaux, Pierre C.)
L'Ile des Esclaves (see Marivaux, Pierre C.)
ILF, Ilya
 The Power of Love, by Ilya Ilf and Evgeny Petrov
  (In Modern International Drama, Vol. 8, no. 1, 1974)
"I'll Leave It to You" (see Coward, Noël)
The Illuminati in Drama Libre (see Gerstenberg, Alice)
L'Illusion (see Corneille, Pierre)
ILYENKOV, Vassily Pavlovich, 1897-
 The Square of Flowers
  (In Soviet Scene)
I'm a Star (see Inge, William M.)
I'm Dreaming, But Am I? (see Pirandello, Luigi)
I'm Somebody, I'm Nobody; a stereo radio play; German and English
 texts given (see Weyraunch, Wolfgang)
I'm Talking About Jerusalem (see Wesker, Arnold)
The Image (see Gregory, Isabella A.)
The Image of St. Nicholas (Anon.)
  (In Medieval Church Music-Dramas)
Imaginame Infinita (see Potts, Renee)
The Imaginary Cuckold (Le Cocu Imaginaire) (see Molière, Jean
 Baptiste)
The Imaginary Life of the Street Cleaner Auguste G. (see Gatti,
 Armand)
The Imbecile (see Pirandello, Luigi)
L'Imbecille; text in French (see Pirandello, Luigi)
The Immortal Husband (see Merrill, James L.)
The Immortal One (see Robbe-Grillet, Alain)
L'Immortelle; text in French (see Robbe-Grillet, Alain)
The Impertinents (Les Facheux) (see Molière, Jean Baptiste)
The Importance of Being a Woman (see Crothers, Rachel)
The Importance of Being Clothed (see Crothers, Rachel)
The Importance of Being Earnest (see Wilde, Oscar)
The Importance of Being Married (see Crothers, Rachel)
The Importance of Being Nice (see Crothers, Rachel)
L'Important c'Est d'Aimer; screenplay (see Zulawski, Andrzej)
The Impossible: a Mystery Play (see Howells, William Dean)
The Imposture (see Shirley, James)
L'Impromptu de l'Alma (see Ionesco, Eugene)
L'Impromptu de Paris (see Giraudoux, Jean)
The Impromptu of Versailles (see Molière, Jean Baptiste)
Improvisation; or, The Shepherd's Chameleon (see Ionesco, Eugene)
The Impure Tragedians and the Leprous Playwrights (see Chekhov,
 Anton)
In a Balcony (see Browning, Robert)

In a Cold Hotel (see Maddow, Ben)
In Camera (see Sartre, Jean-Paul)
"In Good King Charles's Golden Days" (see Shaw, George Bernard)
In-Laws (see Ford, Harriet)
In Mizzoura (see Thomas, Augustus)
In Portineria (see Verga, Giovanni)
In Search of Justice (see Brecht, Bertolt)
In Splendid Error (see Branch, William)
In the Cage (see Abse, Dannie)
In the Darkness (see Totheroh, Dan)
In the Depths (see Gor'kii, Maksim)
In the Desert of My Soul (see Glines, John)
In the Fog; radio script (see Geiger, Milton)
In the Frame of Don Cristobal; a puppet farce (see Garcia Lorca,
    Federico)
In the Jungle of Cities (see Brecht, Bertolt)
In the Lyons Den. A dramatic sequel to Bulwer-Lytton's The Lady
    of Lyons, by "Mr. Punch"
        (In The Drama, Vol. 22)
In the Net (see Sastre, Alfonso)
In the Swamp (see Brecht, Bertolt)
In the Wine Time (see Bullins, Edward A.)
In the Zone (see O'Neill, Eugene)
In This Hung-up Age (see Corso, Gregory)
In Two Minds (see Mercer, David)
Inadmissable Evidence (see Osborne, John)
The Inauguration Speech: an Interlude (see Shaw, George Bernard)
The Inca of Perusalem: An Almost Historical Comedietta (see Shaw,
    George Bernard)
INCE, Thomas H. , 1913-
    Stan McAllister's Heir; film scenario (see Sullivan, C. Garner)
Les Incendiaires (see Clavel, Maurice)
INCHBALD, Mrs. Elizabeth (Simpson), 1755-1831
    Animal Magnetism
        (In The London Stage, Vol. 4)
    Appearance Is Against Them
        (In The London Stage, Vol. 4)
    The Midnight Hour
        (In The London Stage, Vol. 1)
    The Mogul Tale
        (In The London Stage, Vol. 4)
    Wives As They Were, and Maids As They Are
        (In The London Stage, Vol. 2)
Incident at Eureka Bumps (see Conkle, Ellsworth P.)
Incident at Twilight (see Dürrenmatt, Friedrich)
El Inciso Hache (see Andreu Iglesias, César)
INCLAN, Federico Schroeder, 1910-
    Cordelia!
        (In Teatro Méxicano, 1958)
    Detrás de Esa Puerta
        (In Teatro Méxicano, 1959)
    Hoy Invita la Güera
        (In Teatro Méxicano del Siglo XX, Vol. 3)

L'Avenir
  (In his Théâtre II)
The Bald Primadonna
  (In his Plays, Vol. 1)
La Cantatrice Chauve
  (In his Théâtre I)
  (In Le Théâtre d'Aujourd'hui)
Ce Formidable Bordel!
  (In L'Avant-Scène du Théâtre, no. 542, June 1, 1974)
The Chairs
  (In his Plays, Vol. 1)
Les Chaises
  (In his Théâtre I)
La Colère
  (In his Théâtre III)
Delire a Deux
  (In his Théâtre III)
Est dans les Oeufs
  (In his Théâtre II)
Exit the King
  (In his Plays, Vol. 5)
The Foot of the Wall
  (In his Plays, Vol. 8)
Frenzy for Two
  (In his Plays, Vol. 6)
The Future Is in Eggs; or, It Takes All Sorts to Make a World
  (In his Plays, Vol. 4)
The Hard Boiled Egg
  (In his Plays, Vol. 10)
Here Comes the Chopper
  (In his Plays, Vol. 8)
Hunger and Thirst
  (In his Plays, Vol. 7)
L'Impromptu de l'Alma
  (In his Théâtre II)
Improvisation; or, The Shepherd's Chameleon
  (In Masterpieces of the Modern French Theatre)
  (In his Plays, Vol. 3)
Jacques; ou, La Soumission
  (In his Théâtre I)
Jacques; or, Obedience
  (In his Plays, Vol. 1)
La Jeune Fille
  (In his Théâtre II)
The Killer
  (In his Plays, Vol. 3)
The Leader
  (In his Plays, Vol. 4)
Learning to Walk
  (In his Plays, Vol. 9)
La Leçon
  (In his Théâtre I)
The Lesson

(In his Plays, Vol. 1)
Macbett
  (In Evergreen Plays Series, 1973)
  (In his Plays, Vol. 9)
Maid to Marry
  (In his Plays, Vol. 3)
La Maître
  (In his Théâtre II)
A Marier
  (In his Théâtre II)
The Mine
  (In his Plays, Vol. 9)
The Motor Show
  (In his Plays, Vol. 5)
The New Tenant
  (In his Plays, Vol. 2)
Le Nouveau Locataire
  (In his Théâtre II)
Oh What a Bloody Circus
  (In his Plays, Vol. 10)
Ou Comment
  (In his Théâtre I)
The Oversight
  (In his Plays, Vol. 8)
The Painting
  (In Modern French Theatre)
The Picture
  (In his Plays, Vol. 7)
Le Pieton de l'Air
  (In his Théâtre III)
Rhinoceros
  (In his Plays, Vol. 4)
Rhinoceros; text in French
  (In his Théâtre III)
Le Roi se Meurt
  (In Le Théâtre d'Aujourd'hui)
Salutations
  (In his Plays, Vol. 7)
Les Salutations
  (In his Théâtre III)
Scène a Quatre
  (In his Théâtre III)
S'en Debarrasser
  (In his Théâtre I)
Las Sillas (Les Chaises)
  (In Teatro Frances de Vanguardia)
A Stroll in the Air
  (In his Plays, Vol. 6)
Le Tableau
  (In his Théâtre III)
Tueur sans Gages
  (In L'Avant-Scène du Théatre, no. 510, Jan. 15, 1973)
  (In his Théâtre II)

Victimes du Devoir
   (In his Théâtre I)
Victims of Duty
   (In his Plays, VoL 2)
Iphigenia (see Racine, Jean Baptiste)
Iphigenia at Aulis; a dance play (see Rexroth, Kenneth)
Iphigenia in Tauris (see Euripides)
Iphigenia in Tauris (see Goethe, Johann Wolfgang von)
IREDYNSKI, Ireneusz
   Women; a Radio Play
      (In Mundus Artium, VoL 8, no. 1, 1975)
IRELAND, William Henry, 1717-1835
   Vortigern
      (In The Drama, VoL 22)
   *William Ireland's Confession (see Miller, Arthur)
Irene (see Johnson, Samuel)
Irene; o, El Tesoro (see Buero Vallejo, Antonio)
Iris (see Pinero, Arthur Wing)
The Irish Widow (see Garrick, David)
The Iron Age (see Heywood, Thomas)
The Iron Chest (see Colman, George, The Younger)
The Iron Harp (see O'Conor, Joseph)
The Iron Manufacturer (see Ohnet, Georges)
Der Irre (see Bond, Edward)
The Irrepressible Conflict ... (see Carpenter, S. D.)
Irtamene; text in French (see Hugo, Victor)
IRVING, Washington, 1783-1859
   Charles the Second (see Payne, John H.)
   **The Legend of the Sleepy Hollow (see Gaines, Frederick)
   **Rip Van Winkle (see Burke, Charles St. Thomas)
Is Uncle Jack a Conformist? (see Amalrik, Andrei)
Isaac et la Sage-Femme (see Haim, Victor)
Isabella; or, The Fatal Marriage (see Garrick, David)
Isabella, Queen of Castile, 1451-1504
   *Christopher Columbus (see Ghelderode, Michel de)
   *The Conquest of Granada by the Spaniards, pts. 1 & 2 (see
      Dryden, John)
   *Don Sancho of Aragon (Don Sanche d'Aragon) (see Corneille,
      Pierre)
   *La Vivre de Christoph Colomb (see Claudel, Paul)
Isabella II, Queen of Spain, 1830-1904
   *Donde Vas, Alfonso XII? (see Luca de Tena, Juan Ignacio)
   *Donde Vas, Triste de Ti? (see Luca de Tena, Juan Ignacio)
Isabelle Grosse par Vertu (see Gueullette, Thomas S.)
Isak Juntti Had Many Sons (see Höijer, Björn-Erik)
ISHERWOOD, Christopher, 1904-
   The Ascent of F6 (see Auden, W. H.)
   **Cabaret (see Kander, John)
   The Dog Beneath the Skin (see Auden, W. H.)
   Frankenstein, the True Story; teleplay by Christopher Isherwood
      and Don Bachardy, from a classic novel by Mary W. Shelley
      (An Avon Books Original Teleplay, 1973)
ISKANDAR, Y. A. M., Raja Ismail
   **Lela Mayang (see Das, K.)

La Isla Desierta (see Defresne, Augusto)
The Island (see Fugard, Athol)
The Island of the Mighty (see Arden, John)
The Island Princess (see Fletcher, John)
L'ISLE-ADAM, Villiers de
     Les Deux Augures, par Villiers de l'Isle-Adam, adaptation
       Pierre Franck
Isles of the Blest (see Kennedy, Charles R.)
Isma; ou, Ce Qui s'Appelle Rien (see Sarrante, Nathalie)
It Bees Dat Way (see Bullins, Edward A.)
It Has No Choice (see Bullins, Edward A.)
It Pays to Advertise (see Megrue, Roi C.)
It Runs in the Family (see Parke, J. H.)
It Should Happen to a Dog (see Mankowitz, Wolf)
Itaca! Itaca! (see Chiara, Ghigo de)
The Italian Straw Hat (see Labiche, Eugene)
The Italian Straw Hat; film scenario (see Clair, Rene)
Italienische Nacht (see Horvath, Odön von)
Itie et Bernice (see Corneille, Pierre)
It's Been Ages! (see Panova, Vera F.)
It's a Family Affair; We'll Settle It Ourselves (see Ostrovskii,
     Aleksandr, N.)
It's an Ill Wind (see Baumer, Marie)
It's Called the Sugar Plum (see Horovitz, Israel)
It's Really Quite Simple; television script (see Anderson, Harold L.)
Iugurtha (see Heym, Georg)
Ivan IV, called "The Terrible," 1st Czar of Russia, 1530-1584
    *The Death of Ivan the Terrible (see Tolstoy, Alexey K.)
Ivan the Fool (see Benton, Rita)
Ivan Vasilievich (see Bulgakov, Mikhail A.)
Ivanov (see Chekhov, Anton)
IVERNEL, Philippe
    Hölderlin; traduction Française (see Weiss, Peter)
IVORY, James
    Savages; filmscript (see Trow, George S.)
    Shakespeare Wallah; filmscript (see Jhabvala, R. Prawer)

J. Wilkes Booth; or, The National Tragedy (see Luby, William A.)
La Jacassiere (see Leautier, Gilbert)
Jack (see Daudet, Alphonse)
JACK, Donald
    Exit Muttering
      (In A Collection of Canadian Plays, Vol. 1)
The Jack Benny Show radio script (see Benny, Jack)
Jack Cade, the Captain of the Commons (see Conrad, Robert T.)
Jack in the Box (see Cregan, David)
Jack Straw (see Maugham, William Somerset)
The Jackass (see Ruibal, José)
Jacke Drum's Entertainment; or, The Comedie of Pasquill and
    Katherine (see Marston, John)
JACKER, Corinne
    Bits and Pieces

(In Best Short Plays, 1977)
JACKMAN, Isaac, fl. 1795
    All the World's a Stage
       (In A Collection of the Most Esteemed Farces ..., Vol. 4)
       (In The London Stage, Vol. 1)
    Hero and Leander: a Comic Burletta
       (In The London Stage, Vol. 3)
JACKMON, Marvin E.
    Flowers for the Trashman
       (In Black Fire)
JACKSON, Sir Barry
    Doctor's Delight (see Molière, Jean Baptiste)
JACKSON, C. Bernard, 1927-
    Fly Blackbird; written by C. Bernard Jackson and James V. Hatch
       (In Black Theater U.S.A., 1847-1974)
JACKSON, Elaine
    Toe Jam
       (In Black Drama Anthology)
Jacob Comes Home (see Kozlenko, William)
Jacob y el Angel (see Regio, José)
JACOBS, Jim
    Grease (see Casey, Warren)
JACOBS, Lewis
    Prague Is Quiet
       (In 100 Non-Royalty Radio Plays)
JACOBS, William Wymark, 1863-1943
    The Ghost of Jerry Bundler
       (In One-Act Plays for Stage and Study, 1st Series)
Jacob's Wake (see Cook, Michael)
JACOBSON, Egon
  **M; film scenario and dialogue (see Lang, Fritz)
JACQUEMARD, Yves
    Angelo; di Yves Jacquemard e Jean Michel Senecal
       (In Sipario, no. 348, May 1975)
Jacques; or, Obedience (see Ionesco, Eugene)
Jacques; ou, La Soumission (see Ionesco, Eugene)
JÄRNER, Väinö Vilhelm, 1910-
    Eva Maria
       (In Modern Nordic Plays: Finland)
JAGENDORF, Moritz Adolf, 1888-
    Buffalmacco's Jest
       (In One-Act Plays for Stage and Study, 8th Series)
    The Pie and the Tart
       (In One-Act Plays for Stage and Study, 6th Series)
JAHNN, Hans Henry, 1894-1959
    Armut, Reichtum, Mensch und Tier
       (In his Dramen II)
    Der Arzt, Sein Weib, Sein Sohn
       (In his Dramen I)
    Des Buches Erstes und Letztes Blatt
       (In his Dramen I)
    Der Gestohlene Gott
       (In his Dramen I)

Hans Heinrich
   (In his Dramen I)
Heinrich von Kleist
   (In his Dramen I)
Medea
   (In his Dramen I)
Neuer Lübecker Totentanz
   (In his Dramen II)
Pastor Ephraim Magnus
   (In his Dramen I)
Die Schüler
   (In his Dramen I)
Spur des Dunklen Engels
   (In his Dramen II)
Strassenecke
   (In his Dramen II)
Thomas Chatterton
   (In his Dramen II)
Der Tod
   (In his Dramen I)
Die Trümmer des Gewissens
   (In his Dramen II)
Jahresringe (see Foellbach, Lena)
JAKES, John
   Stranger with Roses, adapted from a short story by John Jakes
   (In Six Science Fiction Plays)
JAKOBS, Karl-Heinz, 1929-
   Rauhweiler
   (In Theater der Zeit, no. 10, 1976)
JAKOBSSON, Jökull, 1933-
   The Seaway to Baghdad
   (In Modern Nordic Plays: Iceland)
JAMES, Grace
   **The Good and Obedient Young Man (see Barr, Betty)
JAMES, Henry, 1843-1916
   The Album
   (In his Complete Plays)
   (In his Theatricals, Vol. 2)
   The American
   (In his Complete Plays)
   **The Aspern Papers (see Redgrave, Sir Michael)
   A Change of Heart
   (In his Complete Plays)
   The Chaperon
   (In his Complete Plays)
   Daisy Miller
   (In his Complete Plays)
   Disengaged
   (In his Complete Plays)
   (In his Theatricals, Vol. 1)
   Guy Domville
   (In his Complete Plays)
   The High Bid
   (In his Complete Plays)

**The Innocents (see Archibald, William)
The Other House
   (In his Complete Plays)
· The Outcry
   (In his Complete Plays)
Pyramus and Thisbe
   (In his Complete Plays)
The Reprobate
   (In his Complete Plays)
   (In his Theatricals, Vol. 2)
The Saloon
   (In his Complete Plays)
Still Waters
   (In his Complete Plays)
Summersoft
   (In his Complete Plays)
Tenants
   (In his Complete Plays)
   (In his Theatricals, Vol. 1)
James I, King of Great Britain, 1566-1625
  *The Burning (see Conn, Stewart)
  *Entertainment to King James (see Middleton, Thomas)
James IV, King of Scotland, 1473-1513
  *The Burning (see Conn, Stewart)
  *George A Green, the Pinner of Wakefield (see Greene, Robert)
  *The Scottish Hystorie of James the Fourth, Slaine at Flodden
    (see Greene, Robert)
JAMIAQUE, Yves
  Acapulco Madame
    (In L'Avant-Scène Cinéma, no. 598, Nov. 15, 1976)
  Monsieur Amilcar
    (In L'Avant-Scène Théatre, no. 560, Mar. 15, 1975)
Jamie the Saxt (see McClellan, Robert)
JANCSO, Miklos, 1921-
  La Pacifista
    (In Dal Soggetto al Film Series, no. 43, 1971)
Jane, Jean and John (see Kreymborg, Alfred)
Jane Shore (see Rowe, Nicholas)
Jano es una Muchacha (see Usigli, Rudolfo)
La Jaquerie (see Mérimée, Prosper)
The Jar (see Pirandello, Luigi)
JARDIEL PONCELA, Enrique, 1901-1952
  Angelina o El Honor de un Brigadier
    (In Teatro Selecto Enrique Jardiel Poncela)
  Eloisa Está Debajo de un Almendro
    (In Teatro Selecto Enrique Jardiel Poncela)
  Los Habitantes de la Casa Deshabitada
    (In Teatro Selecto Enrique Jardiel Poncela)
  Los Ladrones Somos Gente Honorada
    (In Teatro Selecto Enrique Jardiel Poncela)
  Madre (El Drama Padre)
    (In Teatro Selecto Enrique Jardiel Poncela)
Le Jardin des Délices (see Arrabal, Fernando)

JARRY, Alfred, 1873-1907
  L'Amour en Visites
    (In his Oeuvres Complètes, Vol. 1)
  César, Antechrist
    (In his Oeuvres Complètes, Vol. 4)
  King Ubu
    (In Modern French Theatre)
    (In Themes of Drama)
  Les Minutes de Sable Mémorial
    (In his Oeuvres Complètes, Vol. 4)
  Les Paralipomènes d'Ubu
    (In his Oeuvres Complètes, Vol. 4)
  Ubu Cocu (Ubu Cuckolded); a version by Cyril Connolly
    (In his Selected Works)
  Ubu, Colonialist; a version by Cyril Connolly
    (In his Selected Works)
  Ubu Cuckolded (Ubu Cocu)
    (In Evergreen Plays Series, 1969)
    (In Methuen Theatre Classic Plays, 1968)
    (In The Ubu Plays)
  Ubu Enchainé
    (In his Oeuvres Complètes, Vol. 4)
  Ubu Enchained
    (In Evergreen Plays Series, 1969)
    (In Methuen Theatre Classic Plays, 1968)
    (In The Ubu Plays)
  Ubu Rex (Ubu Roi)
    (In Evergreen Plays Series, 1969)
    (In Methuen Theatre Classic Plays, 1968)
    (In The Ubu Plays)
  Ubu Roi; text in English
    (In Four Modern French Comedies)
  Ubu Roi; text in French
    (In his Oeuvres Complètes, Vol. 4)
Der Jasager; a school opera (see Brecht, Bertolt)
Jason and Medea (see Baring, Maurice)
Der Jaun Jungste Tag (see Horvath, Odön von)
Jazz Band; comedia musical (see Men Desleal, Alvaro)
The Jeallusest ob Her Sect; a Minstrel Show (Anon.)
        (In Dramas from the American Theatre, 1762-1909)
The Jealous Husband (La Jalousie de Barbouille) (see Molière, Jean
    Baptiste)
The Jealous Lovers (see Randolph, Thomas)
Jean (see Colquhon, Donald)
Jean Calas, ou, L'Ecole des Juges (see Chénier, Marie-Joseph B.)
Jean de la Lune (see Achard, Marcel)
Jean Marais Artisan du Rêve (see Devillers, Gerard)
Jeanne d'Arc (see Peguy, Charles P.)
Jeanne d'Arc au Bucher (see Claudel, Paul)
JEANS, Ronald, 1887-
  Count Your Blessings
    (In Plays of the Year, Vol. 5, 1950/51)
  Young Wives' Tale

(In Plays of the Year, VoL 3, 1949-50)
Jeb (see Ardrey, Robert)
Jedermann (see Hofmannsthal, Hugo von H.)
Jedgement Day (see Pawley, Thomas D.)
El Jefe (see Calvo Sotelo, Joaquin)
JEFFERS, Robinson, 1887-1962
  Medea, freely adapted from the "Medea" of Euripides
    (In 50 Best Plays of the American Theatre, VoL 3)
JEFFERSON, Joseph, 1829-1905
  Rip Van Winkle, based on the work by Washington Irving
    (In Representative American Plays, 1792-1949)
Jefferson, Thomas, Pres. U. S. , 1743-1826
  *1776 (see Edwards, Sherman)
JELLICOE, Ann
  Shelley; or, The Idealist
    (In Evergreen Playscripts Series, 1966)
The Jellyfish's Banquet (see Obaldia, Rene de)
JENNINGS, Gertrude E.
  Family Affairs
    (In Famous Plays of 1934)
Jens (see Mowat, David)
Jenusia (see Obaldia, Rene de)
JEPHERSON, Robert, 1736-1803
  Braganza
    (In The London Stage, VoL 4)
  The Count of Narbonne
    (In The London Stage, VoL 3)
  The Law of Lombardy
    (In The London Stage, VoL 4)
  Two Strings to Your Bow
    (In The London Stage, VoL 3)
Jephté ou le Voeu (see Buchanan, George)
Jeppe of the Hill (see Holberg, Ludwig von)
Jerome; a radio play (see Bieler, Manfred)
JERROLD, Douglas William, 1803-1857
  Black-Eyed Susan; or, All in the Downs
    (In English Plays of the 19th Century, VoL I: Dramas 1800-
    1850)
    (In Representative British Dramas)
  Mr. Paul Pry; or, I Hope I Don't Intrude
    (In English Plays of the 19th Century, VoL IV: Farces)
The Jester (see Gregory, Isabella A.)
Jesus Christ
  *The Crucifixion (see Solórzano, Carlos)
  *The Divine Tragedy (see Longfellow, Henry Wadsworth)
  *Jesus As Seen by His Friends (see Kenan, Amos)
  *Jésus II (see Liger, Christian)
  *The Lament of Mary (Anon.)
    (In Medieval Church Music-Dramas)
  *Passion Play (see Shaw, George Bernard)
  *The Pilgrim (Anon.)
    (In Medieval Church Music-Dramas)
  *The Raising of Lazarus (Anon.)

(In Medieval Church Music-Dramas)
*The Shepherds (Anon.)
    (In Medieval Church Music-Dramas)
*Il Vangelo Secondo Matteo ("The Gospel According to St.
    Matthew") (see Pasolini, Pier)
*The Visit to the Sepulcher (Anon.)
    (In Medieval Church Music-Dramas)
Le Jet de Pierre (see Claudel, Paul)
Jet of Blood (see Artaud, Antonin)
Jete Donat (see Kaiser, Georg)
Le Jeu d'Adam; text in English (Anon.)
    (In Medieval French Plays)
Le Jeu de l'Amour et du Hasard (see Marivaux, Pierre C.)
Le Jeu de la Feuillée (see Halle, Adam de la)
Le Jeu de Robin et de Marion; text in English (see Halle, Adam de
    la)
Le Jeu de Saint Nicholas; text in English (see Bodel, Jean)
La Jeune Fille (see Ionesco, Eugene)
La Jeune Fille Violaine (see Claudel, Paul)
Un Jeune Homme Pressé (see Labiche, Eugene)
La Jeunesse Illustrée (see Arrabal, Fernando)
Les Jeux de la Nuit (see Gilroy, Frank D.)
Jew! (see Perr, Harvey)
The Jew of Malta (see Marlowe, Christopher)
The Jew of Venice (see Lansdowne, George G.)
Jew Süss; screenplay (see Rawlinson, Arthur)
The Jewish Wife (see Brecht, Bertolt)
Jezabel (see Anouilh, Jean)
Jezebel, Queen of Samaria, fl. 9th cent. B. C.
    *A King's Daughter (see Masefield, John)
JHABVALA, R. Prawer
    Shakespeare Wallah, a film by James Ivory from a screenplay
      by R. Prawer Jhabvala and James Ivory
      (In Savages & Shakespeare Wallah)
JIHEI, Tsuuchi II
    Sukeroku: Flower of Edo, by Tsuuchi Jihei II and Tsuuchi Hane-
    mon
      (In Kabuki: Five Classic Plays)
Jill and Jack; a play for television (see Osborne, John)
JIMENEZ RUEDA, Julio, 1898-
    La Silueta de Humo
      (In Teatro Méxicano del Siglo XX, Vol. 1)
The Jingo Ring (see Canale, Raymond)
Joan of Arc, St., c. 1412-1431
    *L'Alouette (see Anouilh, Jean)
    *Jeanne d'Arc (see Péguy, Charles P.)
    *Jeanne d'Arc au Bûcher (see Claudel, Paul)
    *The Lark (see Anouilh, Jean)
    *Maid of France (see Brighouse, Harold)
    *The Maid of Orleans (see Schiller, Johann C.)
    *Le Mystère de la Charité de Jeanne d'Arc (see Péguy, Charles
      P.)
    *Saint Joan: a Chronical Play in Six Scenes and an Epilogue
      (see Shaw, George Bernard)

*The Trial of Joan of Arc at Rouen, 1431 (see Brecht, Bertolt)
*The Visions of Simone Marchard (see Brecht, Bertolt)
JOAQUIN, Nick, 1917-
    A Portrait of the Artist as Filipino
        (In New Writing from the Philippines)
The Job (see Caldwell, Ben)
Job (see Kokoschka, Oscar)
Job Hunters (see Edward, H. F. V.)
Job Security (see Charles, Martie)
Job's Comforting (see Richards, Ivor A.)
JODELLE, Etienne, 1532-1573
    Didon Se Sacrifiant
        (In Four Renaissance Tragedies)
Joe; screenplay (see Wexler, Norman)
O Jogo da Verdade (see Rocha, Aurimar)
Johann Faustus (see Eisler, Hanns)
JOHN, Errol
    The Dispossessed
        (In his Force Majeure, The Dispossessed, and Hasta Luego)
    Force Majeure
        (In his Force Majeure, The Dispossessed, and Hasta Luego)
    Hasta Luego
        (In his Force Majeure, The Dispossessed, and Hasta Luego)
John, King of England, 1167-1216
    *Left-handed Liberty; a play about Magna Carta (see Arden, John)
John V, Calo-John Paleologus, ruler of the Byzantine Empire, 1332-1391
    *Andronic (Andronicus) (see Campistron, Jean-Galbert de)
John-a-Dreams (see Duer, Edward R.)
John Bull; or, The Englishman's Fireside (see Colman, George, The Younger)
John Bull's Other Island (see Shaw, George Bernard)
John Endicott (see Longfellow, Henry Wadsworth)
John Ferguson (see Ervine, St. John G.)
John Ford's Cuban Missile Crisis (see Bradford Art College Theatre Group)
John Gabriel Borkman (see Ibsen, Henrik)
John Thomas (see Wood, Charles)
John Whiffle Concentrates (see Sak, Norman)
Johnny (see Finch, Robert Voris)
Johnny Comes Marching Home (see Bread and Puppet Theater)
Johnny Guitar; screenplay; text in French (see Ray, Nicholas)
Johnny on a Spot (see MacArthur, Charles)
Johnny Pickup (see Halman, Doris)
Johnny So Long (see Welburn, Vivienne C.)
JOHNSON, Douglas
    Nancy Clare
        (In 100 Non-Royalty Radio Plays)
JOHNSON, Georgia Douglas, 1886-1966
    Plumes: a Folk Tragedy
        (In The New Negro Renaissance)
    A Sunday Morning in the South
        (In Black Theater U.S.A., 1847-1974)

JOHNSON, Greer
  The Rights of Man, 1: The Exile; 2: Racial Freedom; 3: Cul-
    tural Freedom; 4: The Right to Organize
    (In 100 Non-Royalty Radio Plays)
Johnson, Jack, 1878-1946
  *The Great White Hope (see Sackler, Howard)
Johnson, Nunnally, 1897-
  Stag at Bay, by Nunnally Johnson and Charles MacArthur
    (In The Stage Works of Charles MacArthur)
JOHNSON, Page
  Sweet of You to Say So
    (In Southwest Review, Vol. 59, Winter 1974)
JOHNSON, Philip, 1900-
  Hullaballoo
    (In Best One-Act Plays of 1941, London)
  Lovers' Leep
    (In Famous Plays of 1934-35)
JOHNSON, Robert E.
  The Dreamlost
    (In One-Act Plays for Stage and Study, 10th Series)
JOHNSON, Samuel, 1709-1784
  Irene
    (In 18th Century Tragedy)
JOHNSON, Wallace
  Don't Leave Me Alone
    (In Drama and Theatre, Vol. 11, no. 2, Winter 1972-73)
Johnson Over Jordan (see Priestley, John B.)
JOHNSTON, Denis, 1901-
  A Bride for the Unicorn
    (In his Storm Song and A Bride for the Unicorn)
  The Dreaming Dust
    (In The Old Lady Says "No!")
  A Fourth for Bridge
    (In The Old Lady Says "No!")
  La Luna en el Rio Amarillo
    (In Teatro Irlandes Contemporaneo)
  The Moon in the Yellow River
    (In The Old Lady Says "No!")
    (In Three Irish Plays)
  The Old Lady Says "No!"
    (In The Old Lady Says "No!" and Other Plays)
  The Scythe and the Sunset
    (In The Old Lady Says "No!")
  Storm Song
    (In his Storm Song and A Bride for the Unicorn)
  Strange Occurrence on Ireland's Eye
    (In The Old Lady Says "No!")
La Joie Imprevue (see Marivaux, Pierre C.)
JOLAS, Eugene, 1894-
  Flight into Geography; a scenario
    (In Transition, Vol. 1, no. 10, Jan. 1928)
JONA, Emilio
  Il 29 Luglio del 1900 (see Liberovici, Sergio)

Jonah and the Whale (see Mavor, Osborne Henry)
Jonah 3 (see Mavor, Osborne Henry)
JONES, Helena
  Lorna
    (In The Best One-Act Plays of 1958-59, London)
JONES, Henry, 1721-1770
  The Earl of Essex
    (In The London Stage, Vol. 3)
JONES, Henry Arthur, 1851-1929
  Chatterton
    (In One-Act Plays for Stage and Study, 7th Series)
  Dolly Reforming Herself
    (In 20th Century Plays)
  Dolly's Little Bills
    (In One-Act Plays for Stage and Study, 1st Series)
  The Knife
    (In One-Act Plays for Stage and Study, 2nd Series)
  The Masqueraders
    (In Representative British Dramas)
  Mrs. Dane's Defence
    (In English Plays of the 19th Century, Vol. II: Dramas
      1850-1900)
JONES, Joseph Stevens, 1809-1877
  The People's Lawyer (Solon Shingle)
    (In Representative Plays by American Dramatists, Vol. 2)
  Solon Shingle
    (In The Drama, Vol. 20)
JONES, Le Roi, 1934-
  Ba-Ra-Ka
    (In Spontaneous Combustion: The Winter Repertory, Vol. 6)
  Bloodrites
    (In Black Drama Anthology)
  Blues for Mister Charlie
    (In Contemporary Black Drama)
  Dutchman
    (In Black Theater)
    (In New Theatre in America, Vol. 1)
  Great Goodness of Life: a Coon Show
    (In A Black Quartet)
    (In The Disinherited: Plays)
    (In Kuntu Drama)
  Hypocrite(s)
    (In The Moderns)
  Junkies Are Full of (SHHH...)
    (In Black Drama Anthology)
  Madheart
    (In Black Fire)
  The Slave
    (In Black Theater U.S.A., 1847-1974)
  Slaveship
    (In The Great American Life Show)
    (In The Off Off Broadway Book)
  Thieves
    (In The Moderns)

JONES, Paul
    Birthday Honours
        (In Plays of the Year, Vol. 9, 1953)
JONES, Tom
    Celebration, by Tom Jones and Harvey Schmidt
        (In their 2 Musicals)
    The Fantastics, by Tom Jones and Harvey Schmidt
        (In their 2 Musicals)
JONKE, G. F.
    Die Hinterhältigkeit der Windmaschinen
        (In Theater Heute, Vol. 14, no. 7, July 1973)
JONSON, Ben, 1573?-1637
    The Alchemist
        (In his Plays, Vol. 2)
    Bartholomew Fair
        (In his Plays, Vol. 2)
  *Bingo: Scenes of Money and Death (see Bond, Edward)
    The Case Is Altered
        (In his Plays, Vol. 2)
    Catiline His Conspiracy
        (In his Plays, Vol. 2)
    Cynthia's Revels; or, The Fountain of Self-Love
        (In his Plays, Vol. 1)
    The Devil Is an Ass
        (In his Plays, Vol. 2)
    Eastward Ho (see Chapman, George)
    Epicoene; or, The Silent Woman
        (In his Plays, Vol. 1)
    Every Man in His Humour
        (In The Drama, Vol. 14)
        (In The London Stage, Vol. 3)
        (In World Drama, Vol. 1)
    Everyman in His Humour, adapted from the work of Ben Jonson
    by David Garrick
        (In Garrick's Dramatic Works, Vol. 1)
    Every Man in His Humour (Anglicized Edition)
        (In his Plays, Vol. 1)
    Every Man in His Humour (Italian Edition)
        (In his Plays, Vol. 1)
    Every Man Out of His Humour
        (In his Plays, Vol. 1)
    The Magnetic Lady; or, Humours Reconciled
        (In his Plays, Vol. 2)
    The New Inn; or, The Light Heart
        (In his Plays, Vol. 2)
    The Poetaster; or, His Arraignment
        (In his Plays, Vol. 1)
    The Sad Shepherd; or, A Tale of Robin Hood
        (In his Plays, Vol. 2)
    Sejanus: His Fall
        (In his Plays, Vol. 1)
    The Staple of News
        (In his Plays, Vol. 2)

A Tale of a Tub
   (In his Plays, Vol. 2)
The Tobacconist
   (In The London Stage, Vol. 2)
Volpone; or, The Fox
   (In his Plays, Vol. 1)
The Widow (see Middleton, Thomas)
JOO FOR, Lee, 1929-
The Happening in the Bungalow
   (In New Drama One: Oxford in Asia Modern Authors)
When the Sun Sits on the Branches of That Jambu Tree)
   (In New Drama Two: Oxford in Asia Modern Authors)
JOSELOVITZ, Ernest A.
The Inheritance
   (In Playwrights for Tomorrow, Vol. 13, 1975)
Sammi
   (In Best Short Plays, 1976)
JOSEPH, Allen
Anniversary on Weedy Hill
   (In Playwrights for Tomorrow, Vol. 8)
Josephine (see Crocker, Bosworth)
Josephine (nee Marie Josephine Rose Tascher de la Pagerie), 1763-
  1814
  *Bonaparte (see Unruh, Fritz von)
JOSEPHSON, Ragnar, 1891-
Perhaps a Poet
   (In Scandinavian Plays of the 20th Century)
Quiza un Poeta
   (In Teatro Sueco Contemporaneo)
Josua Lässt Grüssen (see Wander, Fred)
Le Jour se Leve; filmscript (see Carne, Marcel)
Des Journees Entieres dans les Arbres (see Duras, Marguerite)
The Journey of the Fifth Horse (see Ribman, Ronald B.)
A Journey to London (see Vanbrugh, Sir John)
Journey's End (see Sherriff, Robert C.)
Jovanka e le Altre (see Ritt, Martin)
Joven, Rica 7 Plebeya (see Salmon, Raul)
A Joviall Crew; or, The Merry Beggars (see Brome, Richard)
Joy (see Galsworthy, John)
Joy in Earnest (see The Bim-Bom Troupe and the Afanasjeff Family
  Circus)
JOYCE, James, 1882-1941
  *Travesties (see Stoppard, Tom)
  Verbannte; text in German
   (In Theater Heute, Vol. 14, no. 8, August 1973)
Joyce Dynel, an American Zarzuela (see Patrick, Robert)
Juan Palmieri Tupamaro (see Larreta, Antonio)
Juana (see Kaiser, Georg)
Juana de Arco (see Tamayo y Baus, Manuel)
Juana Sanchez (see Salmon, Raul)
The Jubilee (see Garrick, David)
Judas Maccabaeus (see Longfellow, Henry Wadsworth)
The Judge (see Mortimer, John C.)

Judge Lynch (see Rogers, John W.)
Judgement Day (see Rice, Elmer L.)
Judgment of Paris (see Marcus, Joseph)
Judith; text in French (see Giraudoux, Jean)
Judith (see Hebbel, Friedrich)
Judith et Allori (see Musset, Alfred de)
Die Jüdische Witwe (see Kaiser, Georg)
Juego de Niños (see Ruiz Iriarte, Victor)
Juego Limpio (see Castro, H. Alfredo)
El Juego Sagrado (see Canton, Wilberto)
Juegos de Medianoche (see Moncada, Santiago)
Juegos de Sociedad (see Alonso Millan, Juan J.)
Jueves (see Alban Gomez, Ernesto)
El Juez (see Branner, H. C.)
JUGAND, Jean-Phillippe
    Il Suffit d'un Bâton
        (In L'Avant-Scène Théâtre, no. 605, Mar. 1, 1977)
Le Juge et l'Assassin; film scenario and dialogue (see Tavernier,
    Bertrand)
El Jugo de la Tierra (see Prieto, Carlos)
El Juicio (see Leñero, Vicente)
Juicio Contra un Sinverguenza (see Paso, Alfonso)
Juicio Final (see Martinez, José de Jesus)
Le Juif de Malte (see Marlowe, Christopher)
JULIAN, Joseph
    Gardenias: Ten Cents
        (In 100 Non-Royalty Radio Plays)
Juliana; or, The Princess of Poland (see Crowne, John)
JULIEN, Martin
    Rooster Cogburn; written by Martin Julien, suggested by the
        character "Rooster Cogburn" from the novel "True Grit, " by
        Charles Portis, directed by Stuart Millar
        (In Signet Film Series, 1975)
Juliet of the Spirits; screenplay (see Fellini, Federico. Giulietta
    Degli Spiriti)
Julius Caesar (see Shakespeare, William)
JULLIEN, Jean, 1854-1919
    The Serenade
        (In Four Plays of the Free Theater)
Les Jumeaux (see Hugo, Victor)
Jumpers (see Stoppard, Tom)
Jumpin' the Broom (see Green, Cara Mae)
June/Moon (see Larson, Jack)
Junebug Graduates Tonight (see Shepp, Archie)
Der Junge Medardus (see Schnitzler, Arthur)
Junkies Are Full of (SHHH...) (see Jones, LeRoi)
Juno and the Paycock (see O'Casey, Sean)
Juno y el Pavo Real (see O'Casey, Sean)
JUPP, Kenneth
    The Explorer
        (In his A Chelsea Trilogy)
    The Photographer
        (In his A Chelsea Trilogy)

The Tycoon
    (In his A Chelsea Trilogy)
The Just (see Camus, Albert)
Just Boys (see Geraldy, Paul)
The Just Italian (see D'Avenant, Sir William)
Justice (see Galsworthy, John)
The Justice Box (see David, Michael R.)

Ka Mountain and Guardenia Terrace (see Trilling, Ossia)
Kabnis (see Toomer, Jean)
Das Kälterbrüten (see Sachs, Hans)
KÄSTNER, Erich, 1899-
    Chauvelin, oder Lang Lebe der König!
        (In his Gesammelte Schriften 4: Theater)
    Das Haus Erinnerung
        (In his Gesammelte Schriften 4: Theater)
    Leben in Dieser Zeit
        (In his Gesammelte Schriften 4: Theater)
    Münchhausen
        (In his Gesammelte Schriften 4: Theater)
    Peter Pan; oder das Märchen vom Junger der Nicht Gross Wer-
    den Wollte ein stück in Fünf von J. M. Barrie
        (In his Gesammelte Schriften 4: Theater)
    Die Schule der Diktatoren
        (In his Gesammelte Schriften 4: Theater)
    Zu Treuen Händen
        (In his Gesammelte Schriften 4: Theater)
KAFKA, Franz, 1883-1924
    The Guardian of the Tomb
        (In Seven Expressionist Plays)
    Metamorfosis (see Reyes, Carlos J.)
KAISER, Georg, 1878-1945
    Achtung des Kriegers
        (In his Stücke Erzählungen Aufsätze Gedichte)
        (In his Werke 3)
    Adrienne Ambrossat
        (In his Werke 3)
    Agnete
        (In his Werke 3)
    Alain und Elise
        (In his Werke 3)
    Ballade vom Schönen Mädchen
        (In his Werke 1)
    Bellerophon
        (In his Werke 6)
    Der Brand im Opernhaus
        (In his Werke 1)
    Die Bürger von Calais
        (In his Stücke Erzählungen Aufsätze Gedichte)
        (In his Werke 1)
    The Burghers of Calais
        (In his Five Plays)

Claudius
  (In his Werke 5)
The Coral
  (In his Five Plays)
David & Goliath
  (In his A Day in October & Other Plays)
David und Goliath
  (In his Werke 1)
A Day in October
  (In his A Day in October & Other Plays)
De la Mañana a la Medianoche
  (In his Teatro)
Un Día de Octobre
  (In his Teatro)
Die Dornfelds
  (In his Werke 5)
Der Englische Sender
  (In his Werke 6)
Europa
  (In his Werke 1)
Der Fall des Schülers Vehgesack
  (In his Werke 1)
Faust; text in German
  (In his Werke 5)
Ein Feierabend
  (In his Werke 5)
Fire in the Opera House
  (In Eight European Plays)
Das Floss der Medusa
  (In his Werke 3)
Die Flucht Nach Venedig
  (In his Werke 2)
Das Frauenopfer
  (In his Werke 5)
Friedrich und Anna
  (In his Werke 5)
From Morn to Midnight; English version by Ashley Dukes
  (In Dramas of Modernism)
From Morning to Midnight
  (In his Five Plays)
Der Gärtner von Toulouse
  (In his Werke 3)
Gas; text in German
  (In his Stücke Erzählungen Aufsätze Gedichte)
  (In his Werke 2)
Gas; text in Spanish
  (In his Teatro)
Gas I, Gas II; text in English
  (In his Five Plays)
Gas. Zweiter Teil; text in German
  (In his Stücke Erzählungen Aufsätze Gedichte)
  (In his Werke 2)
Gats; text in German

(In his Werke 2)
Der Geist der Antike
    (In his Werke 5)
Der Gerettete Alkibiades
    (In his Werke 1)
Gilles und Jeanne
    (In his Werke 5)
Held Wilder Willen; ein film
    (In his Werke 4)
Hellseherei
    (In his Werke 3)
Hete Donat
    (In his Werke 5)
Hölle Weg Erde
    (In his Werke 2)
Infanticide
    (In his A Day in October & Other Plays)
Juana
    (In his Werke 5)
Die Jüdische Witwe
    (In his Werke 1)
Kanzlist Krehler
    (In his Werke 2)
Kidnapper; ein film
    (In his Werke 4)
Klawitter
    (In his Werke 6)
König Hahnrei
    (In his Werke 1)
König Heinrich
    (In his Werke 5)
Kolportage
    (In his Stücke Erzählungen Aufsätze Gedichte)
    (In his Werke 2)
Die Koralle
    (In his Werke 1)
Die Lederköpfe
    (In his Stücke Erzählungen Aufsätze Gedichte)
    (In his Werke 3)
Die Letzte Geliebte; ein film
    (In his Werke 4)
Das Los des Ossian Balvesen
    (In his Werke 6)
Der Mann Wir; filme
    (In his Stücke Erzählungen Aufsätze Gedichte)
    (In his Werke 4)
Margarine; text in German
    (In his Werke 1)
Die Melkende Kuh
    (In his Werke 5)
Mississippi; text in German
    (In his Werke 2)
Mörder ohne Mord; ein film

(In his Stücke Erzählungen Aufsätze Gedichte)
(In his Werke 4)
The Musical Box
(In his A Day in October & Other Plays)
Der Mutige Seefahrer
(In his Werke 5)
Nachwort
(In his Werke 5)
Napoleon in New Orleans; text in German
(In his Stücke Erzählungen Aufsätze Gedichte)
(In his Werke 3)
Nebeneinander
(In his Stücke Erzählungen Aufsätze Gedichte)
(In his Werke 2)
Noli Me Tangere
(In his Werke 2)
Oktobertag
(In his Werke 2)
Papiermühle
(In his Werke 2)
Die Pfarrerwahl
(In his Werke 5)
Pferdewechsel
(In his Werke 6)
Der Präsident
(In his Werke 5)
The President
(In his A Day in October & Other Plays)
The Protagonist
(In Seven Expressionist Plays)
Der Protagonist
(In his Werke 5)
Pygmalion
(In his Werke 6)
The Raft of the Medusa
(In Postwar German Theatre)
Rektor Kleist
(In his Werke 5)
Rosamunde Floris
(In his Werke 3)
Schellenkönig, Eine Blutige Groteske
(In his Stücke Erzählungen Aufsätze Gedichte)
(In his Werke 1)
Der Schuss in die Offentlichkeit
(In his Werke 3)
Der Silbersee
(In his Werke 3)
Singspiel zum Weihnachtsball
(In his Werke 5)
Der Soldat Tanaka
(In his Werke 3)
Die Sorina
(In his Werke 5)

Die Spieldose
    (In his Stücke Erzählungen Aufsätze Gedichte)
    (In his Werke 3)
Symphonie; ein film
    (In his Werke 4)
Die Versuchung
    (In his Werke 1)
Vincent Verkauft ein Bild
    (In his Werke 6)
Vollkommenheit Sind Zwei; Filmexposé
    (In his Stücke Erzählungen Aufsätze Gedichte)
    (In his Werke 4)
Von Morgens Bis Mitternachts
    (In his Stücke Erzählungen Aufsätze Gedichte)
    (In his Werke 1)
Xenia; ein film
    (In his Stücke Erzählungen Aufsätze Gedichte)
    (In his Werke 4)
Der Zar Lässt Sich Photographieren
    (In his Werke 2)
Zwei Krawatten
    (In his Werke 3)
Zweimal Amphitryon
    (In his Werke 6)
Zweimal Oliver
    (In his Werke 2)
Der Kaiser und die Hexe (The Emperor and the Witch); both German
    and English texts are given (see Hofmannsthal, Hugo von H.)
KALCHEIM, Lee
    Match Play
        (In New Theatre in America, Vol. 1)
KALIDASA, 5th Century
    Malavika and Agnimitra
        (In his Shakuntala and Other Writings)
    Shakuntala; or, The Recovered Ring
        (In Great Sanskrit Plays)
        (In his Shakuntala and Other Writings)
        (In Six Sanskrit Plays)
    Sákoontalá
        (In World Drama, Vol. 1)
    Urvashi
        (In his Shakuntala and Other Writings)
    Vikramorvacie; or, The Hero and the Nymph
        (In Six Sanskrit Plays)
KALTOFEN, Günter
    Salut an Alle, Marx; ein stück nach briefen von Karl und Jenny
        Marx und Friedrich Engels, von Günther Kalofen und Hans
        Pfeiffer
        (In Theater der Zeit, no. 7, 1976)
The Kama Sutra, an Organic Happening (see Eyen, Tom)
KAMINKA, Didier
    Viens Chez Moi J'Habite Chez une Copine (see Rego, Luis)

KANDER, John, 1927-
    Cabaret. Book by Joe Masteroff, based on the play "I Am a
    Camera," by John van Druten and stories by Christopher
    Isherwood; lyrics by Fred Ebb; music by John Kander
        (A Random House Play, 1966)
        (In Ten Great Musicals of the American Theatre, Vol. 2)
KANIGHER, Robert
    The Odyssey of Homer, by Robert Kanigher and Robert Black
        (In 100 Non-Royalty Radio Plays)
    Visitation, a fantasy by Robert Kanigher and Robert Black
        (In 100 Non-Royalty Radio Plays)
KANIKU, John Willis, 1948-
    Cry of the Cassowary
        (In Australian Theatre Workshop No. 3, 1970)
KANIN, Garson, 1912-
    Born Yesterday
        (In 50 Best Plays of the American Theatre, Vol. 3)
KANTER, Hal
    The George Gobel Show; television script by Hal Kanter, Howard
    Leeds, Harry Winkler, Everett Greenbaum, NBC, Nov. 12, 1955
        (In Prize Plays of Television and Radio, 1956)
KANTOUKAS, Haralimbus Medea, 1947-
    Invocations of a Haunted Mind
        (In The Off Off Broadway Book)
Kanzlist Krehler (see Kaiser, Georg)
KAO HUNG
    Storm Warning
        (In Chinese Literature, no. 8, 1973)
KAPLAN, Jack A.
    Alligator Man
        (In Best Short Plays, 1976)
KARDISH, Larry
    Brussels Sprouts
        (In The Factory Lab Anthology)
KARIARA, Jonathan
    Tonight We Shall Pray to My Gods
        (In Zuka, no. 4, Dec. 1969)
Karl Damerow 1st Tot (see Schuster, Uew)
The Karl Marx Play (see Owens, Rochelle)
Karla, Valeu a Pena? (see Bloch, Pedro)
KARNAD, Girish
    Tuglakh (excerpts)
        (In Indian Writing Today, Vol. 4, 1970)
Kasimir und Karoline (see Horvath, Odön von)
Kaspar (see Handke, Peter)
KASZNAR, Kurt
    First Cousins
        (In The Army Play by Play)
KATAIEV, Valentin Petrovich, 1097-
    La Cuadratura del Circulo
        (In Teatro Comico Sovietico)
    Squaring the Circle
        (In Six Soviet Plays)

Kataki (see Wincelberg, Shimon)
The Kate Smith Hour radio script (see Smith, Kate)
Katie Roche (see Deevey, Teresa)
KATTAN, Naim
    Le Trajet
        (In L'Avant-Scène Théâtre, no. 577, Feb. 1, 1975)
KATZ, Leon, 1919-
    Dracula: Sabbat
        (In The Off Off Broadway Book)
Katzenspiel; original title: "Macskajatek" (see Örkeny, Istvan)
KAUFFMANN, Stanley, 1916-
    Mr. Flemington Sits Down
        (In One-Act Plays for Stage and Study, 9th Series)
KAUFMAN, George Simon, 1889-1961
    Animal Crackers; screenplay (see Ryskind, Morrie)
    Dinner at Eight, by George S. Kaufman and Edna Ferber
        (In Six Plays)
    Dulcy, by George S. Kaufman and Marc Connelly
        (In Representative American Dramas)
    Of Thee I Sing (see Gershwin, George)
        (In 50 Best Plays of the American Theatre, Vol. 2)
    The Still Alarm
        (In One-Act Plays for Stage and Study, 6th Series)
    You Can't Take It with You (see Hart, Moss)
KAWATAKE MOKUAMI, 1816-1893
    The Thieves
        (In Modern Japanese Literature)
KAYE-SMITH, Sheila, 1887-1956
    Mrs. Adis, by Sheila Kay-Smith and John Hampden
        (In One-Act Plays for Stage and Study, 5th Series)
KAZAN, Elia, 1909-
    Le Dernier Nabab; scenario, "The Last Tycoon" (see Pinter,
        Harold)
    A l'Est d'Eden; titre original: "East of Eden"; realization,
        Elia Kazan; scenario, Paul Osborn, d'après le roman de John
        Steinbeck
        (In L'Avant-Scène Cinéma, no. 163, Nov. 1975)
    Viva Zapata; screenplay (see Steinbeck, John)
Kean (see Sartre, Jean-Paul)
KEANE, John Brendan, 1928-
    Many Young Men of Twenty
        (In 7 Irish Plays)
    Sharon's Grave
        (In 7 Irish Plays)
KEARNEY, Gene
    Silent Snow, Secret Snow, screenplay adapted and directed by
        Gene Kearney from the story by Conrad Aiken
        (In Dickenson Literature and Film Series: From Fiction to
        Film: Conrad Aiken's "Silent Snow, Secret Snow")
KEATON, Buster (Joseph Francis Keaton), 1895-1966
    *Buster Keaton Rides Again (see Garcia Lorca, Federico)
    *Buster Keaton's Ride (see Garcia Lorca, Federico)
    The General; written and directed by Buster Keaton and Clyde
        Bruckman

(In The Film Classics Library, 1975)
Go West
   (In The Best of Buster)
The Goat
   (In The Best of Buster)
Le Mecano de la "General"; d'après un sujet de Buster Keaton
   et Clyde Bruckman, inspiré par "The Great Locomotive
   Chase," récit de William Pittenger
   (In L'Avant-Scène Cinéma, no. 155, Feb. 1975)
The Navigator
   (In The Best of Buster)
  *El Paseo de Buster Keaton (see Garcia Lorca, Federico)
Sherlock Jr.
   (In The Best of Buster)
KEDJIAN, Yetvart
   Hyetard
      (In Canadian Fiction Magazine, Vol. 20, Spring 1976)
KEEFEE, Barrie
   Abide with Me
      (In Methuen's New Theatrescripts, no. 7, 1977)
   Gimme Shelter
      (In Methuen's Theatrescripts, no. 7, 1977)
   A Mad World, My Masters; adaptation of the Jacobean original
      by Thomas Middleton for present times
      (In Methuen's New Theatrescripts, no. 9, 1977)
KELLER, Evelyn L.
   The Quality of Mercy
      (In 100 Non-Royalty Radio Plays)
KELLERMAN, Don
   No Man Is an Island; television script (see Benjamin, James)
Kellers Abend (see Kuschg, Adolf)
KELLY, George Edward, 1887-1975
   Craig's Wife
      (In Dramas of Modernism)
   One of Those Things
      (In One-Act Plays for Stage and Study, 3rd Series)
   The Show-off
      (In Representative American Dramas)
KELLY, Hugh, 1739-1777
   Clementina
      (In his Works)
   False Delicacy
      (In Plays of the Restoration and 18th Century)
      (In his Works)
   The Romance of an Hour
      (In A Collection of the Most Esteemed Farces ..., Vol. 5)
      (In his Works)
   The School for Wives
      (In The London Stage, Vol. 4)
      (In his Works)
   A Word to the Wise
      (In his Works)
KELLY, Robert
   The Well Wherein a Deer's Head Bleeds

    (In A Play and Two Poems)
KELLY, Thomas
    The University Today, 3:   The Freshman
      (In 100 Non-Royalty Radio Plays)
The Kelly Kid (see Norris, Kathleen)
Kelly's Eye (see Livings, Henry)
KENAN, Amos
    Jesus As Seen by His Friends
      (In Drama and Theatre, Vol. 11, no. 3, Spring 1973)
KENNEDY, Adrienne, 1931-
    Cities in Bézique: The Owl Answers and A Beast Story
      (In Kuntu Drama)
    Funnyhouse of a Negro
      (In Anthology of the American Negro in the Theatre)
      (In Contemporary Black Drama)
    The Lennon Play: In His Own Write, by Adrienne Kennedy,
    John Lennon, and Victor Spinetti
      (In Best Short Plays of the World Theatre, 1968-1973)
    A Lesson in Dead Language
      (In Collision Course)
    The Owl Answers
      (In Black Theater U. S. A., 1847-1974
    A Rat's Mass
      (In The Off Off Broadway Book)
    Sun
      (In Spontaneous Combustion; The Winter Repertory Vol. 6)
KENNEDY, Charles O'Brien
    And There Was Light
      (In One-Act Plays for Stage and Study, 2nd Series)
    The Falling of an Apple
      (In One-Act Plays for Stage and Study, 8th Series)
    Men, Women and Goats
      (In One-Act Plays for Stage and Study, 6th Series)
    Some Words in Edgewise
      (In One-Act Plays for Stage and Study, 7th Series)
KENNEDY, Charles Rann, 1871-1950
    The Admiral
      (In his A Repertory of Plays for a Company of Three Players,
      Vol. 1)
    The Army with Banners
      (In his A Repertory of Plays for a Company of Seven Players)
    Beggar's Gift
      (In his A Repertory of Plays for a Company of Three Players)
    The Chastening
      (In his A Repertory of Plays for a Company of Three Players,
      Vol. 1)
    Crumbs
      (In his A Repertory of Plays for a Company of Three Players,
      Vol. 2)
    Face of God
      (In his A Repertory of Plays for a Company of Three Players,
      Vol. 3)

Flaming Ministers
  (In his A Repertory of Plays for a Company of Three Players,
  Vol 2)
The Fool from the Hills
  (In his A Repertory of Plays for a Company of Seven Players)
The Idol-Breaker
  (In his A Repertory of Plays for a Company of Seven Players)
Isles of the Blest
  (In his A Repertory of Plays for a Company of Three Players,
  Vol 3)
The Necessary Evil
  (In his A Repertory of Plays for a Company of Seven Players)
Old Nobody
  (In his A Repertory of Plays for a Company of Three Players,
  Vol 2)
The Rib of the Man
  (In his A Repertory of Plays for a Company of Seven Players)
The Salutation
  (In his A Repertory of Plays for a Company of Three Players,
  Vol 1)
The Servant in the House
  (In his A Repertory of Plays for a Company of Seven Players)
The Winterfeast
  (In his A Repertory of Plays for a Company of Seven Players)
Kennedy, John Fitzgerald, Pres. U.S., 1917-1963
  *"Welcome to Dallas, Mr. Kennedy" (see Himmelstrup, Kaj)
Kennedy's Children (see Patrick, Robert)
KENNEY, James, 1780-1849
  Raising the Wind
    (In English Plays of the 19th Century, Vol IV: Farces)
KENNY, Maurice
  Forked Tongues
    (In Drama & Theatre, Vol 12, no. 2, Spring 1975)
Kephas and Elohenu (see Handelsman, J. B.)
The Kept Mistress; or, The Mock Orators (Anon.)
    (In 18th Century Drama: Afterpieces)
Ein Kerl, der Spekuliert (see Eckart, Dietrich)
KERNDL, Rainer, 1928-
  Nacht mit Kompromissen
    (In Theater der Zeit, no. 11, 1973)
  Der Vierzehnte Sommer
    (In Theater der Zeit, no. 5, 1977)
  Die Wilde Rotte
    (In Theater der Zeit, no. 11, 1975)
KERR, Jean (Collins)
  The Ten Worst Things About a Man
    (In Readers Theatre Handbook)
KESSELRING, Joseph, 1902-1967
  Arsenic and Old Lace
    (In Best Mystery and Suspense Plays of the Modern Theatre)
    (In 50 Best Plays of the American Theatre, Vol 3)
KESSLER, Jascha
  Perfect Days

(In <u>Modern Occasions</u>)
Ketchup (see Edson, Russell)
Der Ketzermeister mit den Viel Kessel Suppen (see Sachs, Hans)
The Key, a drama for women (see Boylston, Helen D.)
KEY, Ted
 The Clinic; radio script, June 8, 1940
  (In <u>Best Broadcasts of 1939-40</u>)
KEY-AABERG, Sandro, 1922-
 An Empty Room
  (In <u>Calder & Boyars Playscript Series,</u> no. 28)
 O
  (In <u>Calder & Boyars Playscript Series,</u> no. 28)
The Keys of Heaven (see Strindberg, August)
KHAMINWA, Charles
 Dead
  (In <u>Zuka,</u> no. 5, Oct. 1970)
KHARMS, (born Yuvachev) Daniil Ivanovich, 1905-1942
 Elizabeth Bam
  (In <u>Russia's Lost Literature of the Absurd</u>)
KHAYTOV, Nikolay
 Paths, translated by A.D. Maser
  (In <u>Literary Review,</u> Vol. 16, Winter 1973)
KHLEBNIKOV, Velimir, 1885-1922
 Death's Mistake: The Thirteenth Guest
  (In <u>Russian Literature Triquarterly,</u> no. 7)
Khosrau II, called Khosrau Parvez, king of Persia, d. 628
 *Cosroes (Chosroes) (see Rotrou, Jean)
KIELLAND, Axel
 The Lord and His Servants
  (In <u>Modern Nordic Plays: Norway</u>)
KIELLAND, Trygve
 Queen Margaret of Norway
  (In <u>Modern Scandinavian Plays</u>)
Kiez (see Greiner, Peter)
KIHM, Jean-Jacques, 1923-
 Oedipe ou le Silence des Dieux
  (In <u>L'Avant-Scène Théâtre,</u> no. 567, July 1, 1975)
KIKUCHI, Kwan 1888-1948
 The Madman on the Roof
  (In <u>Modern Japanese Literature</u>)
 The Savior of the Moment
  (In <u>The Passion</u>)
The Killdeer (see Reaney, James C.)
The Killer (see Cowles, Albert)
The Killer (see Ionesco, Eugene)
KILLIGREW, Thomas 1612-1683
 Bellamira Her Dream; or, The Love of Shadows; pts. 1 & 2
  (In his <u>Comedies & Tragedies</u>)
 Cicilia & Clorinda; or, Love in Arms
  (In his <u>Comedies & Tragedies</u>)
 Claricilla
  (In his <u>Comedies & Tragedies</u>)
 The Parson's Wedding
  (In his <u>Comedies & Tragedies</u>)

(In Restoration Comedy, Vol. 1)
(In Six Caroline Plays)
The Pilgrim
    (In his Comedies & Tragedies)
The Princesse; or, Love at First Sight
    (In his Comedies & Tragedies)
The Prisoners
    (In his Comedies & Tragedies)
The Rover; or, The Banish'd Cavaliers, pts. 1 & 2 (see Behn,
    Mrs. Aphra)
Thomaso; or, The Wanderer, pts. 1 & 2
    (In his Comedies & Tragedies)
The Killing of Sister George (see Marcus, Frank)
KIMMINS, Anthony
    The Amorous Prawn
        (In Plays of the Year, Vol. 21, 1959-60)
Kind Hearts and Coronets (see Hamer, Robert)
The Kind Keeper; or, Mr. Limberham (see Dryden, John)
Kind Lady (see Chodorov, Edward)
Kindly Observe the People (see Berg, Barry)
The King (see Bjørnson, Bjørnstjerne)
King, Martin Luther, Jr., 1929-1968
    *We Can't All Be Martin Luther King (see Nkosi, Lewis)
KING, Norman 1921-
    The Shadow of Doubt
        (In Plays of the Year, Vol. 12, 1954-55)
KING, Philip
    Sailor, Beware! by Philip King and Falkland Cary
        (In Plays of the Year, Vol. 12, 1954-55)
The King and I (see Rodgers, Richard)
A King, and No King (see Beaumont, Francis)
King Arthur; or, The British Worthy (see Dryden, John)
King Belshazzar's Feast (see Calderon de la Barca, Pedro)
King David and His Wives (see Pinski, David)
King Edward the Fourth; the first and second parts (see Heywood,
    Thomas)
King Edward the Third (Anon.)
        (In Disputed Plays of William Shakespeare)
King James (see Hyde, Douglas)
King Kong; screenplay (see Simple, Lorenzo, Jr.)
The King of Friday's Men (see Molloy, Michael J.)
The King of Gee-Whiz (see Baum, Lyman Frank)
The King of Nowhere (see Mavor, Osborne Henry)
The King of Soul; or, The Devil and Otis Redding (see Caldwell, Ben)
The King of the Great Clock Tower (see Yeats, William Butler)
King Phoenix (see Davies, Robertson)
The King, the Greatest Alcalde (see Vega Carpio, Lope F.)
King Ubu (see Jarry, Alfred)
King Victor and King Charles (see Browning, Robert)
Kingdom of Earth (see Williams, Tennessee)
A King's Daughter (see Masefield, John)
The King's Dilemma (see Richardson, Willis)
The King's People (see Shaw, George Bernard)

KISHON, Ephraim
    The Blaumilch Canal
        (In Gambit, Vol. 3, no. 12)
The Kiss (see Clarke, Austin)
A Kiss for Cinderella (see Barrie, James M.)
A Kiss for Cinderella; filmscript (see Goldbeck, Willis)
Kiss Me, Kate (see Porter, Cole)
The Kitchen (see Wesker, Arnold)
The Kitchen Comedy (see Mavor, Osborne Henry)
The Kite (see Hudson, Holland)
Kites (see The American Playground)
Klara und der Gänserich (see Stopler, Armin)
Klawitter (see Kaiser, Georg)
KLEBAN, Monte
    The Golden Age; a play edited for radio
        (In On the Air: 15 Plays for Broadcast)
Das Kleine Welttheater (The Little Theatre of the World); both Ger-
    man and English texts are included (see Hofmannsthal, Hugo von H.)
Der Kleine Zacharias (see Eckart, Dietrich)
KLEINEIDAM, Horst
    Polterabend
        (In Theater der Zeit, no. 12, Dec. 1973)
KLEIST, Heinrich von, 1777-1811
    Amphitryon, a Comedy after Molière, translated by Charles E.
    Passage
        (In Amphitryon: Three Plays in New Verse Translations)
    The Broken Jug, translated by Roger Jones
        (In Classics of Drama in English Translation Series, 1977)
KLIEWER, Warren
    A Lean and Hungry Priest
        (In Playwrights for Tomorrow, Vol. 12)
The Knacker's ABC; a Para-military Vaudeville in One Long Act
    (see Vian, Boris)
KNAUTH, Joachim
    Der Prinz von Portugal
        (In Theater der Zeit, no. 1, 1973)
KNIAZHIN, Iakov Borisovich, 1742-1791
    Misfortune from a Coach; a comic opera, with music by V.A.
    Paskevich
        (In The Literature of 18th Century Russia, Vol. 2)
The Knife (see Jones, Henry A.)
Knife in the Water; filmscript (see Polanski, Roman)
KNIGHT, Thomas, d. 1820
    The Honest Thieves
        (In The London Stage, Vol. 1)
    The Turnpike Gate
        (In The London Stage, Vol. 4)
The Knight of Malta (see Beaumont, Francis)
The Knight of the Burning Pestle (see Beaumont, Francis)
Knight of the Twelfth Saucer (see Zagoren, Marc Alan)
The Knights (see Foote, Samuel)
Knives from Syria (see Riggs, Lynn)

Knock (see Romains, Jules)
Knock Three Times (see Davis, Donald)
KNOTT, Frederick
 Dial "M" for Murder
  (In Best Mystery and Suspense Plays of the Modern Theatre)
The Knotty (see Cheeseman, Peter)
Know Your Own Mind (see Murphy, Arthur)
KNOWLES, James Sheridan, 1784-1862
 Virginius
  (In English Plays of the 19th Century, Vol. 1: Dramas 1800-
  1850)
  (In Representative British Dramas)
KNOWLES, Leo
 The Last Victim
  (In Best Short Plays, 1974)
KOBRIN, Leon, 1872-1948
 Yankel Boyla
  (In Epic and Folk Plays of the Yiddish Theatre)
KOCH, Howard, 1902-
 Casablanca; screenplay (see Curtiz, Michael)
KOCH, Jurij
 Landvermesser
  (In Theater der Zeit, no. 12, 1977)
KOCK, Charles Paul de, 1794-1871
 A Happy Day
  (In The Drama, Vol. 9)
Der Konig (see Bjørnson, Bjørnstjerne)
König Hahnrei (see Kaiser, Georg)
König Heinrich (see Kaiser, Georg)
König Jorg (see Eschner, Eugen)
König Öedipus (see Hofmannsthal, Hugo von H.)
KÖRNER, Thomas
 **R. Hot (see Goldmann, Friedrich)
KOHOUT, Pavel
 Guerre au Troisième Etage
  (In L'Avant-Scène Théâtre, no. 604, Feb. 15, 1977)
KOKOSCHKA, Oscar, 1886-
 Assassino Speranza delle Donne
  (In Sipario, no. 326, July 1973)
 Job
  (In German Drama Between the Wars)
 Murderer Hope of Womankind
  (In Seven Expressionist Plays)
KOLB, Kenneth
 She Walks in Beauty; television script from the "Medic" program,
 NBC
  (In Prize Plays of Television and Radio, 1956)
Kolportage (see Kaiser, Georg)
Komtesse Mizzi, oder, Der Familienstag (see Schnitzler, Arthur)
Kontraption (see Owens, Rochelle)
KOOPMAN, Romance C.
 The Bottle Imp, adapted for radio from the story by Robert Louis
 Stevenson
  (In 100 Non-Royalty Radio Plays)

KOPIT, Arthur L., 1937-
  **Buffalo Bill and the Indians; or, Sitting Bull's History Lesson
    (see Rudolph, Alan)
  Indians
    (In Best American Plays, 7th Series, 1967-1973)
  Oh Dad, Poor Dad, Mamma's Hung You in the Closet and I'm
    Feelin' So Sad
    (In 50 Best Plays of the American Theatre, Vol. 4)
    (In Off-Broadway Plays, Vol. 1)
KOPS, Bernard, 1926-
  Enter Solly Gold
    (In Masterpieces of the Modern English Theatre)
Die Koralle (see Kaiser, Georg)
KORDA, Alexander, 1893-1956
  The Private Life of Henry VIII; screenplay (see Biro, Lajos)
KORN, ILSE & VILMOS
  **Meister Röckle; oper (see Werzlau, Joachim)
KORN, Reneke, 1938-
  Die Reise des Eugin Ozkartal von Nevsehir nach Herne und Zur-
    ück
    (In Theater Heute, no. 8, 1975)
KORNEICHUK, Alexander Evdokimovich, 1905-
  The Front
    (In Seven Soviet Plays)
KORR, David
  Encore
    (In Playwrights for Tomorrow, Vol. 9)
KOTZEBUE, August Frederich Ferdinand von, 1761-1819
  Egotist and Pseudo-Critic
    (In The Drama, Vol. 11)
  Lovers' Vows; or, The Natural Son
    (In The Drama, Vol. 21)
    (In The London Stage, Vol. 3)
  **Pizarro (see Sheridan, Richard Brinsley)
  The Stranger
    (In The London Stage, Vol. 3)
    (In Plays of the Restoration and 18th Century)
KOVAK, Primož, 1929-
  An Affair
    (In Five Modern Yugoslav Plays)
KOZLENKO, William
  Jacob Comes Home
    (In New Fields for the Writer)
  The Rebel Saint
    (In 100 Non-Royalty Radio Plays)
KRAEMER, Jacques, 1938-
  Les Ciseaux d'Anastasie
    (In L'Avant-Scène Théâtre, no. 601, Jan. 1, 1977)
  Histoires de l'Oncle Jakob
    (In L'Avant-Scène Théâtre, no. 601, Jan. 1, 1977)
Der Krämerkorb (see Sachs, Hans)
The Kramer (see Medoff, Mark)

KRAUS, Karl, 1874-1936
  The Last Days of Mankind; excerpt
    (In German Drama Between the Wars)
  Literatur oder Man Wird Dach da Sehn
    (In his Dramen)
  Marginalien
    (In his Dramen)
  Perichole
    (In his Dramen)
  Traumstück
    (In his Dramen)
  Traumtheater
    (In his Dramen)
  Die Unüberwindlichen
    (In his Dramen)
  Wolkenkuckucksheim
    (In his Dramen)
KRAUSS, Ruth Ida, 1901-
  A Beautiful Day
    (In The Off Off Broadway Book)
  Poem-Plays
    (In All the World's a Stage)
KRECHEL, Ursula
  Erika
    (In Theater Heute, no. 8, Aug. 1974)
Krechinsky's Wedding (see Sukhovo-Kobylin, Aleksandr V.)
KREYMBORG, Alfred, 1883-1966
  Ballad of Youth
    (In One-Act Plays for Stage and Study, 9th Series)
  Brother Bill
    (In One-Act Plays for Stage and Study, 4th Series)
  The Dead Are Free
    (In The New Caravan)
  Jane, Jean, and John
    (In One-Act Plays for Stage and Study, 3rd Series)
  Limping Along
    (In One-Act Plays for Stage and Study, 5th Series)
Der Krieg Bricht Nach der Pause Aus (see Daněk, Oldřich)
Kriemhilds Rache (see Hebbel, Friedrich)
KRLEZA, Miroslav
  Galizien
    (In Theater Heute, no. 4, April 1973)
KROETZ, Franz Xaver, 1946-
  Agnes Bernauer
    (In Theater Heute, no. 10, Oct. 1976)
  Alta Austria
    (In Sipario, no. 336, May 1974)
  Amleto Principe di Danimarca (see Brecht, Bertolt)
  La Corte delle Stalle (Stallerhof)
    (In Sipario, no. 319, Dec. 1972)
  Farmyard
    (In his Farmyard & Four Plays)

A Man, a Dictionary
   (In his Farmyard & Four Plays)
Maria Magdalena
   (In Theater Heute, no. 6, June 1973)
Men's Business
   (In his Farmyard & Four Plays)
Michi's Blood
   (In his Farmyard & Four Plays)
Das Nest
   (In Theater der Zeit, no. 1, 1975)
   (In Theater Heute, no. 5, May 1975)
Oberösterreich
   (In Theater Heute, no. 2, Feb. 1973)
Request Concert
   (In his Farmyard & Four Plays)
   (In Yale/Theatre, Vol. 6, no. 3, Spring 1975)
Stallerhof
   (In Theater: Chronik und Bilanz des Buhenjahres, 1971)
Verfaussungsfeinde
   (In Theater der Zeit, no. 12, 1976)
KROG, Helge, 1889-
   La Ruptura
      (In Teatro Noruego Contemporaneo)
   The Sounding Shell
      (In Scandinavian Plays of the 20th Century, Series 2)
KUAN HAN-CH'ING, 1241?-1322?
   The Injustice Done to Tou Ngo
      (In Six Yüan Plays)
KUHNER, Maria Helena
   Espetáculo
      (In her Teatro Popular: Uma Experiência)
Kulubob (see Wabei, Turuk)
KUMMER, Mrs. Clare (Beecher)
   Bridges
      (In her Selected Plays)
   Her Master's Voice
      (In her Selected Plays)
   Open Storage
      (In One-Act Plays for Stage and Study, 9th Series)
   Papers
      (In One-Act Plays for Stage and Study, 3rd Series)
   The Rescuing Angel
      (In her Selected Plays)
   The Robbery
      (In One-Act Plays for Stage and Study, 1st Series)
   So's Your Old Antique!
      (In One-Act Plays for Stage and Study, 4th Series)
   A Successful Calamity
      (In her Selected Plays)
KUNAD, Rainer, 1936-
   Litauische Claviere; musik von Rainer Kunad und Gerhard Wolf,
   libretto
      (In Theater der Zeit, no. 9, 1975)

KUNERT, Günter
    Affair of Honor; a radio play.   Both German and English texts
    are given
    (In Dimension, Vol. 5, no. 3, 1972)
KUPER, Hilda
    A Witch in My Heart; a play about the Swazi people
    (In Oxford Three Crowns Series, 1970)
KUROSAWA, Akira, 1910-
    The Bad Sleep Well; screenplay; text in Japanese and English
    (In his Complete Works, Vol. 9)
    Dodesukaden; filmscript; text in Japanese and English
    (In his Complete Works, Vol. 1)
    Drunken Angel; filmscript; text in Japanese and English
    (In his Complete Works, Vol. 3)
    The Idiot; screenplay, based on the novel by Dostoevsky; text in
    English
    (In his Complete Works, Vol. 6)
    Ikiru; screenplay; text in Japanese and English
    (In his Complete Works, Vol. 6)
    (In Lorrimer Screenplay Series, 1968)
    No Regrets for Our Youth; filmscript; text in Japanese and Eng-
    lish
    (In his Complete Works, Vol. 2)
    One Wonderful Sunday; filmscript; text in Japanese and English
    (In his Complete Works, Vol. 3)
    Quiet Duel; screenplay; text in Japanese and English
    (In his Complete Works, Vol. 4)
    Sanshiro Sugata; filmscript; text in Japanese and English
    (In his Complete Works, Vol. 2)
    Stray Dog; screenplay; text in Japanese and English
    (In his Complete Works, Vol. 4)
    Three Bad Men in a Hidden Fortress; screenplay; text in Japan-
    ese and English
    (In his Complete Works, Vol. 9)
KUTUZOV, Mikhail Illarionovich, 1745-1813
    *Field Marshall Kutuzov (see Solovyov, Vladimir A.)
KUZMIN, Mikhail Alexeevich, 1875-1936
    The Venetian Madcaps
    (In Russian Literature Triquarterly, no. 7, Fall 1973)
KYD, Thomas, 1558-1594
    Cornelia
    (In his Works)
    The First Part of Ieronimo; with The Warres of Portugall and
    The Life and Death of Don Andraea
    (In his Works)
    The Spanish Tragedy; or, Hieronimo Is Mad Againe
    (In his Works)
    The Spanish Tragedy; edited by T.W. Craik
    (In Minor Elizabethan Tragedies)
    Tragedia, von dem Griegischen Keyser zu Constantinopel und
    Seiner Tochter Pelimperia mit dem Ghengten Horatio; adapta-
    tion of "The Spanish Tragedy" by Jacob Ayrer of Nürnberg
    (In his Works)

The Tragedye of Solyman and Perseda; wherein is laide open,
loves, constancy, fortunes inconstancy, and deaths triumphs
(In his <u>Works)</u>

L. S. B., Le Salamandre's Business (see Pommeret, Xavier-Agnan)
El Laberinto (see Rovinski, Samuel)
LABICHE, Eugene Marin, 1815-1888
   L'Affaire de la Rue de Lourcine
      (In his <u>Théâtre Complet,</u> Vol. 1)
   L'Ai Compromis Ma Femme
      (In his <u>Théâtre Complet,</u> Vol. 10)
   L'Avare en Gants Jaunes
      (In his <u>Théâtre Complet,</u> Vol. 6)
   Le Baron de Fourchevif
      (In his <u>Théâtre Complet,</u> Vol. 3)
   Le Cachemire X. B. T.
      (In his <u>Théâtre Complet,</u> Vol. 6)
   La Cagnotte
      (In his <u>Théâtre Complet,</u> Vol. 5)
   Celimare le Bien-aimé
      (In his <u>Théâtre Complet,</u> Vol. 3)
   Un Chapeau de Paille d'Italie
      (In his <u>Théâtre Complet,</u> Vol. 1)
   La Chasse aux Corbeaux
      (In his <u>Théâtre Complet,</u> Vol. 8)
   Le Choix d'un Gendre
      (In his <u>Théâtre Complet,</u> Vol. 5)
   La Cigale Chez Fourmis
      (In his <u>Théâtre Complet,</u> Vol. 10)
   Le Clou aux Maris
      (In his <u>Théâtre Complet,</u> Vol. 8)
   Le Club Champenois
      (In his <u>Théâtre Complet,</u> Vol. 3)
   La Commode de Victorine
      (In his <u>Théâtre Complet,</u> Vol. 6)
   Deux Merles Blancs
      (In his <u>Théâtre Complet,</u> Vol. 8)
   Deux Papas Très Bien
      (In his <u>Théâtre Complet,</u> Vol. 1)
   Les Deux Timides
      (In his <u>Théâtre Complet,</u> Vol. 4)
   Doit-on le Dire?
      (In his <u>Théâtre Complet,</u> Vol. 9)
   Dust in Your Eyes
      (In his <u>Two Plays)</u>
   Edgard et sa Bonne
      (In his <u>Théâtre Complet,</u> Vol. 1)
   Embrassons-nous
      (In his <u>Théâtre Complet,</u> Vol. 4)
   La Fille Bien Gardée
      (In his <u>Théâtre Complet,</u> Vol. 1)

Folleville!
(In his <u>Théâtre Complet,</u> Vol. 4)
Frisette
(In his <u>Théâtre Complet,</u> Vol. 3)
Un Garçon de Chez Véry
(In his <u>Théâtre Complet,</u> Vol. 4)
La Grammaire
(In his <u>Théâtre Complet,</u> Vol. 2)
Un Gros Mot
(In his <u>Théâtre Complet,</u> Vol. 5)
The Happiest of the Three, by Eugene Labiche and Edmond Gondinet
(In <u>Three French Farces</u>)
L'Invite le Colonel
(In his <u>Théâtre Complet,</u> Vol. 3)
The Italian Straw Hat
(In his <u>The Italian Straw Hat and The Spelling Mistakes</u>)
The Italian Straw Hat; screenplay (see Calir, Rene)
Un Jeune Homme Pressé
(In his <u>Théâtre Complet,</u> Vol. 1)
La Main Loste
(In his <u>Théâtre Complet,</u> Vol. 7)
Le Major Cravachon
(In his <u>Théâtre Complet,</u> Vol. 7)
Maman Sabouleux
(In his <u>Théâtre Complet,</u> Vol. 4)
Un Mari Qui Lance Sa Femme
(In his <u>Théâtre Complet,</u> Vol. 10)
Les Marquises de la Fourchette
(In his <u>Théâtre Complet,</u> Vol. 4)
Le Misanthrope et l'Auvergnat
(In his <u>Théâtre Complet,</u> Vol. 1)
Moi
(In his <u>Théâtre Complet,</u> Vol. 4)
Mon Isménie
(In his <u>Théâtre Complet,</u> Vol. 3)
Un Monsieur Qui a Brulé une Dame
(In his <u>Théâtre Complet,</u> Vol. 8)
Un Monsieur Qui Prend la Mouche
(In his <u>Théâtre Complet,</u> Vol. 3)
90° in the Shade
(In his <u>Two Plays</u>)
Les Noces de Bouchencoeur
(In his <u>Théâtre Complet,</u> Vol. 9)
La Perle de la Canebière
(In his <u>Théâtre Complet,</u> Vol. 5)
Le Petit Voyage
(In his <u>Théâtre Complet,</u> Vol. 7)
Les Petites Oiseaux
(In his <u>Théâtre Complet,</u> Vol. 2)
Les Petites Mains
(In his <u>Théâtre Complet,</u> Vol. 8)

Un Pied dans le Crime
   (In his Théâtre Complet, Vol. 7)
Le Plus Heureux des Trois
   (In his Théâtre Complet, Vol. 6)
Le Point de Mire
   (In his Théâtre Complet, Vol. 9)
Pots of Money
   (In Three Popular French Comedies)
La Poudre aux Yeux
   (In his Théâtre Complet, Vol. 2)
Le Premier Pas
   (In his Théâtre Complet, Vol. 5)
Le Prix Martin
   (In his Théâtre Complet, Vol. 10)
La Sensitive
   (In his Théâtre Complet, Vol. 6)
Si Jamais Je Te Pince!
   (In his Théâtre Complet, Vol. 10)
The Spelling Mistakes
   (In his The Italian Straw Hat and The Spelling Mistakes)
La Station Champbaudet
   (In his Théâtre Complet, Vol. 9)
Les Suites d'un Premier Lit
   (In his Théâtre Complet, Vol. 4)
Les Trente Millions de Gladiator
   (In his Théâtre Complet, Vol. 7)
Les 37 Sous de M. Montaudoin
   (In his Théâtre Complet, Vol. 5)
29 Degrés a l'Ombre
   (In his Théâtre Complet, Vol. 7)
Les Vivacites du Capitaine Tic
   (In his Théâtre Complet, Vol. 2)
Voyage Autour de Ma Marmite
   (In L'Avant-Scène Théâtre, no. 562, April 15, 1975)
Le Voyage de Monsieur Perrichon
   (In his Théâtre Complet, Vol. 2)
Laboremus (see Bjørnson, Bjørnstjerne)
LABRELY, Flamen de
   The Song of Songs of Solomon (see Roinard, Paul N.)
LA BRUYERE, Jean de, 1645-1696
  **The Absent Man (see Bickerstaff, Isaac)
Laburnum Grove (see Priestley, John B.)
The Labyrinth (see Arrabal, Fernando)
Le Labyrinth le Tricycle (see Arrabal, Fernando)
LA CALPRENDE, Gautier de Costes de, 1614-1663
  **The Young King; or, The Mistake (see Behn, Mrs. Aphra)
Lace on Her Petticoat (see Stuart, Aimee)
LACEY, Jackson
   The Prince, the Wolf and the Firebird
      (In Gambit, Vol. 4, no. 14)
Un Lache (see Gilles, Ange)
Die Lachtaube (see Baieri, Helmut)

LACLOS, Pierre Ambroise Françoise Choderlos de, 1741-1803
  Les Liaisons Dangereuses; screenplay (see Vailland, Roger)
Lacombe Lucien; screenplay (see Malle, Louis)
The Ladder Under the Maple Tree (see Finsterwald, Maxine)
Ladee-ee-s and Gentlemen! (see Grismer, Frank A.)
Ladies and Gentlemen (see Hecht, Ben)
Ladies' Day (see Aristophanes)
Ladies in Retirement (see Smith, Edward P.)
Ladies in Waiting (see DeAnda, Peter)
The Ladies Should Be in Bed (see Zindel, Paul)
Los Ladrones Somos Gente Honorada (see Jardiel Poncela, Enrique)
The Lady-Errant (see Cartweight, William)
Lady Frederick (see Maugham, William Somerset)
The Lady from Alfaqueque (see Alvarez Quintero, Serafin)
The Lady from Maxim's (see Feydeau, Georges)
The Lady from the Sea (see Ibsen, Henrik)
Lady in the Dark (see Weill, Kurt)
Lady Inger (see Ibsen, Henrik)
Lady Inger of Ostrat (see Ibsen, Henrik)
Lady Jane Grey (see Rowe, Nicholas)
Lady Johanna Gray (see Wieland, Christoph M.)
Lady Julie (see Strindberg, August)
The Lady of Pleasure (see Shirley, James)
The Lady of the Camellias (see Dumas, Alexandre)
The Lady or the Tiger? a radio script (see Olfson, Lewy)
Lady Strass (see Manet, Eduardo)
The Lady Who Put Salt in Her Coffee (see Smith, Moyne Rice)
Lady Windemere's Fan (see Wilde, Oscar)
The Lady's Last Stake; or, The Wife's Resentment (see Cibber, Colley)
LA FARGE, W.E.R.
  Escape by Balloon; in collaboration with the Firehouse Theatre
    (In Playwrights for Tomorrow, Vol. 10)
Lafayette, Marie Joseph Paul Yves Roch Gilbert Motier, Marquis de, 1757-1834
  *Mount Vernon Interlude (see Meyer, Lewis)
LAFORGUE, Jules, 1860-1887
  **Hamlet; d'après la moralité legendaire "Hamlet ou Les Suites de la Piété Filiale" (see Huster, Francis)
LA FOSSE, Antoine de, c. 1653-1708
  Manlius Capitolinus
    (In The Chief Rivals of Corneille and Racine)
LAGERKVIST, Pär Fabian, 1891-
  The Difficult Hour
    (In Masterpieces of the Modern Scandinavian Theatre)
  Let Man Live
    (In Scandinavian Plays of the 20th Century, Series 3)
  The Man Who Lived His Life Over
    (In Five Modern Scandinavian Plays)
  The Man Without a Soul
    (In Scandinavian Plays of the 20th Century, Series 1)
  El Rey
    (In Teatro Sueco Contemporaneo)

LAGRANGE-CHANCEL, Joseph de, 1677-1758
    Ino et Melicerte (Ino and Melicertes)
        (In More Plays by Rivals of Corneille and Racine)
LaGuardia, Fiorello Henry, 1882-1947
    *Fiorello! (see Bock, Jerry)
Le Lai de Barabbas (see Arrabal, Fernando)
Laid Off (see Pinsky, David)
LAIGLESIA, Alvaro de
    Amor Sin Pasaporte
        (In Teatro Español, 1952-53)
LAIGLESIA, Juan Antonio de, 1917-
    La Rueda
        (In Teatro Español, 1954-55)
LALOUX, Rene
    La Planète Sauvage; scenario et dialogues par Rene Laloux et
    Roland Topor, d'après un roman de Stefan Wul; musique par
    Alain Goraguer
        (In L'Avant-Scène du Cinéma, no. 149/50, July/Sept. 1974)
LAMARCHE, Gustave, 1895-
    Abraham, l'Ami de Dieu
        (In his Oeuvres Théâtrales, Vol. 1)
    L'Areopage
        (In his Oeuvres Théâtrales, Vol. 1)
    Les Gracques
        (In his Oeuvres Théâtrales, Vol. 1)
    La Loi de Feu
        (In his Oeuvres Théâtrales, Vol. 1)
    Le Petit Juif Laid
        (In his Oeuvres Théâtrales, Vol. 1)
    Prélude pour la Nuit de Noël
        (In his Oeuvres Théâtrales, Vol. 1)
LAMARTINE, Alphonse Marie Louis de, 1790-1869
    Chant du la Veille des Armes
        (In his Oeuvres Poétiques Complétes)
    Confidences
        (In his Oeuvres Poétiques Complètes)
    Médée
        (In his Oeuvres Poétiques Complètes)
    Saul; text in French
        (In his Oeuvres Poétiques Complètes)
    Toussaint Louverture
        (In his Oeuvres Poétiques Complètes)
    Zoraide
        (In his Oeuvres Poétiques Complètes)
Lamb, Charles, 1775-1834
    *The Night of "Mr. H." (see Brighouse, Harold)
LAMB, Myrna, 1931-
    Scyklon Z, But What Have You Done for Me Lately? or, Pure
    Polemic
        (In The Disinherited: Plays)
The Lame Lover (see Foote, Samuel)
Lament for Harmonica (Maya) (see Ringwood, Gwen P.)

The Lament of Mary (Anon.)
     (In <u>Medieval Church Music-Dramas</u>)
Lament the Days That Are Gone By; television script (see Borg, So-
     nia
The Lancashire Witches and Teque O. Divelly (see Shadwell, Thomas)
Lancelot, (see Mavor, Osborne Henry)
Lances de Honor (see Tamayo y Baus, Manuel)
LANCHBERY, John
     Tales of Beatrix Potter; an EMI Film Production with music by
          John Lanchbery, choreography by Frederick Ashton, directed
          by Reginald Mills
     (In <u>The Tale of the Tales</u>)
The Land (see Colum, Padraic)
The Land of Heart's Desire (see Yeats, William Butler)
The Land of Laughingstock (see Weinberg, Dan)
The Land of Milk and Funny; or, Portrait of a Scientist as a Dumb
     Broad; a film scenario (see Yankowitz, Susan)
The Land of Promise (see Maugham, William Somerset)
The Land of the Palms (see Cregan, David)
Landet Fundet og Forsvundet (see Oehlenschläger, Adam G.)
El Lando de Seis Caballos (see Ruiz Iriarte, Victor)
LANDON, Joseph
     Blessing
     (In <u>Playwrights for Tomorrow,</u> Vol. 13, 1975)
LANDON, Margaret Dorothea (Mortenson), 1903-
   **The King and I (see Rodgers, Richard)
Landscape (see Pinter, Harold)
Landscape with Figures (see Rice, Elmer L.)
Landslide (see Betti, Ugo)
Landvermesser (see Koch, Juij)
LANG, Fritz, 1890-1976
     M; scenario and dialogue of the film by Thea von Harbou, after
          an article by Egon Jacobson, film directed by Fritz Lang
     (In <u>Lorrimer Screenplay Series,</u> 1968)
     (In <u>Masterworks of the German Cinema</u>)
     Metropolis; screenplay based on the novel by Thea von Harbou,
          film directed by Fritz Lang
     (In <u>Classic Filmscripts Series,</u> 1973)
     (In <u>Lorrimer Screenplay Series,</u> 1973)
LANG, Walter, 1896-
     The Mighty Barnum; screenplay (see Fowler, Gene)
LANGFORD, Gary, 1947-
     I Love You Sylvia Plath
     (In <u>Landfall,</u> Vol. 29, no. 4, Dec. 1975)
LANGLEY, <u>Rod</u>
     Bethune
     (In <u>Talonplays Series,</u> 1975)
LANGNER, Lawrence, 1890-
     Accidents Will Happen
     (In <u>One-Act Plays for Stage and Study</u>, 7th Series)
LANGUIRAND, Jacques
     The Departures
     (In <u>Gambit,</u> no. 5)

LANIA, Leo
    The Threepenny Opera; screenplay by Leo Lania, Ladislas Vaj-
    da and Bela Balasz, based on John Gay's "Beggar's Opera,"
    adapted from the play by Bertolt Brecht, music by Kurt Weill,
    directed by G.W. Pabst
      (In Masterworks of the German Cinema)
LANKESH, P.
    Teregalu; excerpts
      (In Indian Writing Today, Vol. 4, no. 4, 1970)
LANOUX, Victor, 1936-
    Le Peril Bleu; ou, Mefiez-vous des Autobus
      (In L'Avant-Scène Théâtre, no. 556, Jan. 15, 1975)
LANSDOWNE, George Granville, baron, 1667-1735
    The Jew of Venice, by George Granville, based on the work of
    Shakespeare
      (In Five Restoration Adaptations of Shakespeare)
The Lansky Soliloquies (see Weitz, Elissa-Raquel)
Lanuza (see Rivas, Angel P.)
The Laocoon Group (see Rosewicz, Tadeusz)
Laodice (see Corneille, Thomas)
Les Larbins (see Menthon, Henri de)
LARDNER, Ring Wilmer, 1885-1933
    Clemo Uti--"The Water Lilies"
      (In Parodies)
    Dinner Bridge
      (In Parodies)
    I Gaspiri (The Upholsterers)
      (In Parodies)
The Lark (see Anouilh, Jean)
Les Larmes d'une Mère (see Mace, Jean)
LARRETA, Antonio, 1928-
    Juan Palmieri Tupamaro
      (In Sipario, no. 322, Mar. 1973)
LARRIMORE, Lida
    The Third Floor Front
      (In Prize Plays of 1927-28, Vol. 2)
    Yesterday's Roses
      (In Prize Plays of 1927-28, Vol. 1)
Larry Parks' Day in Court (see Bentley, Eric Russell)
LARSON, Jack
    Chuck
      (In Collision Course)
    June/Moon
      (In New Theatre in America, Vol. 2)
LASAYGUES, Maurice
    Les Deux Vierges (see Bricaire, Jean-Jacques)
LASCELLES, Kendrew, 1935-
    Tigers
      (In The Best Short Plays 1973)
LAS COVERAS, Francisco de
  **The Dutch Lover (see Behn, Mrs. Aphra)

LASKER-SCHULER, Else
    Die Wupper
        (In Theater Heute, no. 8, August 1976)
Lassie television script, "The Visitor, " (see Robinson, Thelma)
The Last Clock (see Thurber, James)
The Last Command; screenplay (see Goodrich, John F.)
The Last Days of Mankind; excerpt (see Kraus, Karl)
The Last Enemy (see Curteis, Ian)
The Last Feast of the Fianna (see Milligan, Alice)
The Last Joke (see Bagnold, Enid)
The Last Laugh; filmscript (see Mayer, Carl. Le Dernier des Hommes)
The Last Man In (see Maxwell, William B.)
The Last Night of Don Juan (see Rostand, Edmond)
The Last of the Cheesecake (see Mankowitz, Wolf)
The Last of the De Mullins (see Hankin, St. John)
The Last of the Lowries (see Green, Paul)
The Last Refuge (see Derbes, Claude)
The Last Romantic (see Brabbe, Kerry Lee)
The Last Straw (see Dizenzo, Charles)
Last Tango in Paris; screenplay (see Bertolucci, Bernardo)
The Last Trump (see Mavor, Osborne Henry)
The Last Tycoon; screenplay (see Pinter, Harold. Le Dernier Nabab)
The Last Victim (see Knowles, Leo)
The Last Word (see Patricelli, Anthony)
The Last Words of Dutch Schultz; filmscript (see Burroughs, William
    S.)
Last Year at Marienbad; screenplay (see Robbe-Grillet. L'Annee
    Dernière à Marienbad)
LASZLO, Carl
    The Chinese Icebox
        (In Postwar German Theatre)
    Let's Eat Hair!
        (In Postwar German Theatre)
Late Autumn; filmscript (excerpt) (see Ozu, Yasujiro)
The Late Captain Crow (see Armstrong, Louise Van V.)
The Late Edwina Black (see Dinner, William)
The Late Witches of Lancashire (see Heywood, Thomas, The Witches
    of Lancashire)
The Later Story of Rama (see Bhavabhuti)
LATHAM, John
    One in Twelve, by John Latham and Betty Lord
        (In Best Television Plays, 1954)
LATHROP, William Addison
    Heir of the Ages; screenplay of the 1917 film, directed by E.J.
    LeSaint
        (In Little Stories from the Screen)
LATTUADA, Alberto, 1914-
    La Steppa
        (In Dal Soggetto al Film, no. 25, 1962)
    La Tempesta; filmscript, based on the work of Pushkin
        (In Dal Soggetto al Film, no. 10, 1958)

LATZKO, Andreas
    Royal March, adapted for radio by Charles O'Neill
       (In 100 Non-Royalty Radio Plays)
LAUBE, Horst
    Der Dauerklavierspieler
       (In Theater Heute, no. 11, Nov. 1974)
Laughing Anne (see Conrad, Joseph)
LAUNDER, Frank
    Meet a Body, by Frank Launder and Sidney Gilliat
       (In Plays of the Year, Vol. 10, 1953/54)
Laundry (see Guerdon, David)
LAURA, Ida
    Encontro no Anhangabau
       (In Hamlet em Brasilia e Outras Pecas)
    Hamlet em Brasilia
       (In Hamlet em Brasilia e Outras Pecas)
    Lobisomem
       (In Hamlet em Brasilia e Outras Pecas)
Laure Persecutée (see Rotrou, Jean)
LAURENDEAU, Andre
    Deux Femmes Terribles
       (In his Théâtre)
    Marie-Emma
       (In his Théâtre)
    La Vertu des Chattes
       (In his Théâtre)
LAURENTS, Arthur, 1918-
    West Side Story (see Bernstein, Leonard)
LAVEDAN, Henri, 1859-1940
    The King's Pet
       (In Modern One-Act Plays from the French)
Lavender Gloves (see Conkle, Ellsworth P.)
LAVILLE, Pierre
    La Celestine, d'après "le Livre de Calixte et Melibee et da la
      Vielle Putain Celestine," de Fernando de Royas
       (In L'Avant-Scène Théâtre, no. 556, June 15, 1975)
Il Lavora (see Visconti, Luchino)
The Law Against Lovers (see D'Avenant, Sir William)
The Law of Lombardy (see Jepherson, Robert)
LAWRENCE, David Herbert, 1885-1933
    **D. H. Lawrence's The Rocking-Horse Winner (see Fuller, Clark)
    **The Rocking-Horse Winner; screenplay (see Pelissier, Anthony)
LAWRENCE, Jerome, 1915-
    The Incomparable Max Beerbohm, by Jerome Lawrence and Rob-
      ert E. Lee
       (In Hill & Wang Spotlight Dramabook Series, 1972)
    The Night Thoreau Spent in Jail, by Jerome Lawrence and Rob-
      ert E. Lee
       (In Hill & Wang Spotlight Dramabook Series, 1971)
Lawrence, Thomas Edward (Lawrence of Arabia) 1888-1935
    *Ross, a Dramatic Portrait (see Rattigan, Terence)
LAWRENCE, Vincent
    Gentleman Jim; scenario (see Walsh, Raoul)

The Laws of Candy (see Beaumont, Francis)
The Lawyer (see Molnar, Ferenc)
LAXNESS, Halldór
    The Pigeon Banquet
        (In Modern Nordic Plays: Iceland)
Lay the Bosses Off--Not the Workers (see San Francisco Red Theatre)
Lazare (see Zola, Emile)
Lazarus Laughed (see O'Neill, Eugene)
LAZO, Agustin, 1898-
    El Caso de Don Juan Manuel
        (In Teatro Méxicano del Siglo XX, Vol. 3)
Lazzaro (see Pirandello, Luigi)
LE GALLIENNE, Eva, 1899-
    The Strong Are Lonely (see Hochwalder, Fritz)
Le ne Trompe Pas Mon Mari! (see Feydeau, Georges)
LEACH, Wilford, 1929-
    Gertrude; or, Would She Be Pleased to Receive It?
        (In The Off Off Broadway Book)
LEACOCK, John
    The Fall of British Tyranny; or, American Liberty
        (In Representative Plays by American Dramatists, Vol. 1)
LEACOCK, Stephen Butler, 1869-1944
    The Raft: An Interlude
        (In Ten Canadian Short Plays)
The Leader (see Ionesco, Eugene)
The Leader (see White, Joseph)
Leäna (see Brust, Alfred)
The League of Animals (see Gronowicz, Antoni)
The League of Youth (see Ibsen, Henrik)
A Leak in the Universe (see Richards, Ivor A.)
LEAN, David, 1908-
    Brief Encounter; directed by David Lean, produced and screenplay by Nöel Coward
        (In Masterworks of the British Cinema)
    Doctor Zhivago; screenplay (see Bolt, Robert)
A Lean and Hungry Priest (see Kliewer, Warren)
The Lean Years (see Reely, Mary K.)
Leandre Fiacre (see Gueullette, Thomas S.)
Lear (see Bond, Edward)
The Learned Ladies (see Molière, Jean Baptiste)
Learning to Walk (see Ionesco, Eugene)
LEAUTIER, Gilbert
    La Jacassiere
        (In L'Avant-Scène Théâtre, no. 584, April 1, 1976)
Leave It to Me! (see Porter, Cole)
LEAVITT, A.J.
    The Thumping Process; a minstrel show
        (In Dramas from the American Theatre, 1762-1909)
Das Leben ein Traum (see Hofmannsthal, Hugo von H.)
Leben in Dieser Zeit (see Kästner, Erich)
Lebendige Stunden (see Schnitzler, Arthur)

LEBOVIC, Djorde, 1928-
  Hallelujah
    (In Five Modern Yugoslav Plays)
LECHLITNER, Ruth
  We Are the Rising Wing; a play in verse for radio
    (In New Directions, Vol. 3, 1938)
La Leçon (see Ionesco, Eugene)
La Leçon de Geographie (see Mace, Jean)
Lecture to a Fire Company; a minstrel show (Anon.)
    (In Dramas from the American Theatre, 1762-1909)
Die Lederköpfe (see Kaiser, Georg)
LEE, Charlotte I.
  Hunk Is a Punk; a comedy of college life
    (In 100 Non-Royalty Radio Plays)
Lee, Gypsy Rose, 1914-1970
  *Gypsy (see Styne, Jule)
LEE, Jeannie
  On the Corner of Cherry and Elsewhere
    (In Theatre Wagon Plays)
LEE, Lance
  Fox, Hound, & Huntress
    (In Playwrights for Tomorrow, Vol. 10)
LEE, Nathaniel, 1653-1692
  Caesar Borgia, Son of Pope Alexander the Sixth
    (In his Works, Vol. 2)
  Constantine the Great
    (In his Works, Vol. 2)
  The Duke of Guise (see Dryden, John)
  Lucius Junius Brutus, Father of His Country
    (In his Works, Vol. 2)
  The Massacre of Paris
    (In his Works, Vol. 2)
  Mithridates, King of Pontus
    (In his Works, Vol. 1)
  Oedipus (see Dryden, John)
  The Princess of Cleve
    (In his Works, Vol. 2)
  The Rival Queens, or The Death of Alexander the Great
    (In Plays of the Restoration and 18th Century)
    (In his Works, Vol. 1)
  Sophonisba; or, Hannibal's Overthrow
    (In Five Heroic Plays)
    (In his Works, Vol. 1)
  Theodosius; or, The Force of Love
    (In his Works, Vol. 2)
  The Tragedy of Nero, Emperour of Rome
    (In his Works, Vol. 1)
Lee, Robert Edward, 1807-1870
  *Lee at Gettysburg (see Sapinsley, Alvin)
  *Robert E. Lee (see Drinkwater, John)
LEE, Robert Edwin, 1918-
  The Incomparable Max Beerbohm (see Lawrence, Jerome)
  The Night Thoreau Spent in Jail (see Lawrence, Jerome)

Lenna Looks Down
LENNART, Isobel
    Funny Girl (see Styne, Jule)
LENNON, John
    The Lennon Play: In His Own Write (see Kennedy, Adrienne)
Lenny (see Barry, Julian)
LENORMAND, Henri Rene, 1882-1952
    The Coward
        (In his Three Plays)
        (In 20th Century Plays)
    La Dent Rouge
        (In his Théâtre Complet, Vol. 3)
    The Dream Doctor
        (In Dramas of Modernism)
        (In his Three Plays)
    Man and His Phantoms
        (In his Three Plays)
    La Mangeur de Rêves
        (In his Théâtre Complet, Vol. 2)
    Les Rates
        (In his Théâtre Complet, Vol. 1)
    Le Simoun
        (In his Théâtre Complet, Vol. 2)
    Le Temps Est un Songe
        (In his Théâtre Complet, Vol. 1)
    In Theatre Street, adapted by Ashley Dukes
        (In Famous Plays of 1937)
    Une Vie Secrète
        (In his Théâtre Complet, Vol. 3)
LENZ, Jakob Michael Reinhold
    The Courtesan
        (In Yale/Theatre, Vol. 5, no. 1, Fall 1973)
    **The Tutor (see Brecht, Bertolt)
Leocadia (see Anouilh, Jean)
El Leon Ciego (see Herrera, Ernesto)
Leon Toral, Jose de, 1901-1929
    *El Juicio: El Jurado de Leon Toral y la Madre Conchita (see
        Leñero, Vicente)
LEONARD, Hugh
    DA
        (In Plays and Players, Vol. 21, no. 3, Dec. 1973)
        (In Plays of the Year, Vol. 44, 1975)
Leonarda (see Bjørnson, Bjørnstjerne)
Leonie est en Avance (see Feydeau, Georges)
Leonor De Guzman (see Boker, George Henry)
LEONOV, Leonid Maximovich, 1899-
    The Orchards of Polovchansk
        (In Seven Soviet Plays)
The Leopard; screenplay (see Visconti, Luchino. 11 Gattopardo)
LERMONTOV, Mikhail IU'evich, 1814-1841
    Masquerade
        (In Russian Literature Triquarterly, no. 7, Fall 1973)

LERNER, Alan Jay, 1918-
    Brigadoon (see Loewe, Frederick)
    Camelot (see Loewe, Frederick)
LESAGE, Alain-Rene, 1668-1747
    Arlequin Roi de Serendib
      (In Théâtre du XVIII Siècle, Vol. 1)
    Crispin Rival de Son Maître
      (In Théâtre du XVIII Siècle, Vol. 1)
    Les Eaux de Merlin
      (In Théâtre du XVIII Siècle, Vol. 1)
    L'Ecole des Amants
      (In Théâtre du XVIII Siècle, Vol. 1)
    Turcaret
      (In Théâtre du XVIII Siècle, Vol. 1)
LeSAINT, E. J.
    Heir of the Ages; screenplay (see Lathrop, William Addison)
LESSING, Doris, 1921-
    Play with a Tiger
      (In Plays by and About Women)
LESSING, Gotthold Ephraim, 1729-1781
    Minna von Barnhelm; or, The Soldier's Fortune
      (In The Drama, Vol. 10)
    Miss Sara Sampson
      (In World Drama, Vol. 2)
The Lesson (see Ionesco, Eugene)
A Lesson in Dead Language (see Kennedy, Adrienne)
LESTER, Richard, 1932-
    A Hard Day's Night; filmscript (see Owen, Alun)
    Robin and Marian; screenplay (see Goldman, James)
Let Man Live (see Lagerkvist, Pär F.)
Let Me Hear You Whisper (see Zindel, Paul)
Let the People Speak (see Canoy, Reuben, R.)
Lethe; or, Aesop in the Shades (see Garrick, David)
Let's Eat Hair! (see Laszlo, Carl)
Let's Get a Divorce! (see Sardou, Victorien)
Let's Murder Vivaldi (see Mercer, David)
Let's Pretend radio script
    The Nuremberg Stove (see Mack, Nila)
The Letter (see Aldis, Mrs. Mary)
The Letter (see Maugham, William Somerset)
A Letter of Introduction (see Howells, William Dean)
The Letter Writers; or, A New Way to Keep a Wife at Home (see
    Fielding, Henry)
LETTON, Jeanette (Dowling)
    The Young Elizabeth, by Jeanette Dowling and Francis Letton
      (In Plays of the Year, Vol. 7, 1951/52)
Une Lettre (see Mace, Jean)
Une Lettre Chargée (see Moinaux, Georges)
Lettre Morte (see Pinget, Robert)
Letty (see Pinero, Arthur Wing)
Die Letzte Geliebte; ein film (see Kaiser, Georg)
Die Letzten Masken (see Schnitzler, Arthur)

LEVENSTEIN, Aaron
    Going Home
      (In 100 Non-Royalty Radio Plays)
    High Water
      (In 100 Non-Royalty Radio Plays)
LEVI, Clovis
    "A Criminosa, Grotesca, Sofrida e Sempre Gloriosa Caminhada
    de Alqui Caba la Silva em Busca da Grande Luz" de Clovis Le-
    ve e Tania Pacheco
      (In Revista de Teatro, no. 398, Mar./Apr. 1974)
LEVI, Paolo
    The Pinedus Affair
      (In Gambit, no. 2)
    Unpublished Story
      (In Gambit, Vol. 3, no. 11)
LEVINSON, Richard
    My Sweet Charlie; television script by Richard Levinson and
    William Link, from the novel and stage play by David Westhei-
    mer. NBC, Jan. 20, 1970
      (In Electronic Drama)
LEVITT, Alan J.
    Florida's Affair; television script for an episode in "Maude"
      (In Samuel French's Tandem Library Series)
LEVITT, Paul M.
    Act the Second: The Norwich Incident
      (In The Ohio Review, Vol. 7, no. 1, Fall 1975)
LEWERTH, Margaret
    Sandhogs; radio script from "Americans at Work"
      (In Best Broadcasts of 1938-39)
LEWIN, Albert E.
    The Will; television script for an episode in "Maude"
      (In Samuel French's Tandem Library Series)
LEWIN, John
    The House of Atreus (see Aeschylus)
LEWIS, Herbert
  **Surprise for the Boys; a radio script (see Smith, Victor)
LEWIS, Matthew Gregory, 1775-1818
    The Castle Spectre
      (In The London Stage, Vol. 1)
LEWIS, Saunders
    Siwan, translated by Emyr Humphreys
      (In Plays of the Year, Vol. 21, 1959/60)
La Leyenda de Juan de Alzante (see Baroja y Nessi, Pio)
LI HAO-KU, early 13th Cent.
    Chang Boils the Sea
      (In Six Yüan Plays)
Les Liaisons Dangereuses; screenplay, text in English (see Vailland,
    Roger)
LIBEROVICI, Sergio
    Il 29 Luglio del 1900, di Sergio Liberovici ed Emilio Jona; vita
    e morte di Gaetano Bresci
      (In Sipario, no. 321, Feb. 1973)

The Libertine (see Shadwell, Thomas)
The Liberty Bell (see Benton, Rita)
The License (see Pirandello, Luigi)
Lichter der Boheme (see Valle-Inclan, Ramón M.)
Lickrish; a radio tale (see Schallüch, Paul)
Lidia o el Infinito (see Giovanninetti, Silvio)
Lidoire (see Moinaux, Georges)
The Lie (see Sarraute, Nathalie)
Liebelei (see Schnitzler, Arthur)
Liebestraum (see Cregan, David)
The Life and Death of Thomas, Lord Cromwell (Anon.)
        (In Disputed Plays of William Shakespeare)
The Life and Times of J. Walter Smintheus (see White, Edgar)
The Life of Edward II of England (see Brecht, Bertolt)
Life of Galileo (see Brecht, Bertolt)
Life of Hercules: Page One (see Cruden, Thomas)
The Life of Man (see Andreev, Leonid N.)
Life with Father (see Lindsay, Howard)
LIGER, Christian, 1935-
    Jésus II, une pièce tirée du roman de Joseph Delteil, adapte par
        Christian Liger
        (In L'Avant-Scène Théâtre, no. 605, Mar. 1, 1977)
A Light from St. Agnes (see Fiske, Minnie Maddern)
The Light of Heart (see Williams, Emlyn)
The Light of the Women (see Gunner, Frances)
The Light Shines in Darkness (see Tolstoi, Lev N.)
The Lighted Window (see Gregory, Isabella A.)
The Lighthouse Keepers; radio script (see Cloquemin, Paul)
Lights/Camera/Action (see Patrick, Robert)
'Lijah (see Smith, Edgar V.)
Like Falling Leaves (see Giacosa, Giuseppe)
Like Father, Like Fun (see Nicol, Eric)
A Likely Story (see Howells, William Dean)
LILAR, Suzanne, 1901-
    The Burlador
        (In Two Great Belgian Plays About Love)
    El Burlador o el Angel del Demonio
        (In Teatro Belga Contemporaneo)
Liliom (see Molnar, Ferenc)
Lilliput (see Garrick, David)
LILLO, George, 1693-1739
    Arden of Feversham
        (In The London Stage, Vol. 2)
    Fatal Curiosity
        (In The London Stage, Vol. 3)
    The London Merchant
        (In 18th Century Tragedy)
        (In Plays of the Restoration and 18th Century)
Liluli (see Rolland, Romain)
Limberham; or, The Kind Keeper (see Dryden, John)
Limitations of Life (see Hughes, Langston)
Limping Along (see Kreymborg, Alfred)

Lincoln, Abraham, Pres. U.S., 1809-1865
 *Abe Lincoln in Illinois (see Sherwood, Robert E.)
 *Abraham Lincoln (see Drinkwater, John)
 *The Irrepressible Conflict; or, The Rise, Progress and Decline
   of "One Idea," including the principal acts in the life of Abra-
   ham the First (see Carpenter, S.D.)
 *J. Wilkes Booth; or, The National Tragedy (see Luby, William
   A.)
 *Madame Surrat (see Rogers, James Webb)
 *The Story of Mrs. Surratt (see Goggan, John Patrick)
 *Unfinished Symphony (see Morgan, Albert)
LIND, Jakov
   Anna Laub
     (In The Silver Foxes Are Dead)
   Fear
     (In The Silver Foxes Are Dead)
   Hunger
     (In The Silver Foxes Are Dead)
   The Silver Foxes Are Dead
     (In The Silver Foxes Are Dead)
The Linden Tree (see Priestley, John B.)
LINDSAY, Howard, 1889-1968
   Life with Father, by Howard Lindsay and Russel Crouse
     (In 50 Best Plays of the American Theatre, Vol. 2)
   State of the Union, by Howard Lindsay and Russel Crouse
     (In 50 Best Plays of the American Theatre, Vol. 3)
Line (see Horovitz, Israel A.)
The Line of Least Existence (see Drexler, Rosalyn)
LINK, William
   My Sweet Charlie (see Levinson, Richard)
LINLEY, Thomas 1732-1795
   The Duenna (see Sheridan, Richard Brinsley)
LINNEY, Romulus
   Holy Ghosts
     (In his The Sorrows of Frederick/Holy Ghosts)
   The Sorrows of Frederick
     (In his The Sorrows of Frederick/Holy Ghosts)
Liola (see Pirandello, Luigi)
The Lion and the Jewel; excerpt (see Soyinka, Wole)
The Lion in Love (see Delaney, Shelagh)
The Lion Roars (see Swanson, Bud)
Lion with Corset (see Soya, Carl Erik)
Lionel and Clarissa (see Bickerstaff, Isaac)
LIRA, Miguel N., 1905-
   Vuelta a la Tierra
     (In Teatro Méxicano del Siglo XX, Vol. 2)
Lise Tavernier (see Daudet, Alphonse)
LISLE, William de
   Tragic Christening
     (In One-Act Plays for Stage and Study, 9th Series)
LISS, Joseph
   Story in Dogtown Common, a poetic play
     (In 100 Non-Royalty Radio Plays)

Listen to the Wind (see Reaney, James)
Litauische Claviere (see Kunad, Rainer)
Literatur; text in German (see Schnitzler, Arthur)
Literatur oder Man Wird Dach da Sehn (see Kraus, Karl)
Literature (see Schnitzler, Arthur)
The Litigants (see Racine, Jean Baptiste)
Little, Malcolm, 1925-1965
    *One Day, When I Was Lost; a scenario (see Baldwin, James)
The Little Blue Light (see Wilson, Edmund)
Little Boxes: The Coffee Lace and Trevor (see Bowen, John)
The Little Clay Cart (see Sudraka, Rajah of Magadha)
A Little Dancing (see Smith, Robert K.)
Little Eyolf (see Ibsen, Henrik)
The Little Father of the Wilderness (see Strong, Austin)
Little Fears (see Peluso, Emanuel)
The Little Foxes (see Hellman, Lillian)
The Little France Lawyer (see Beaumont, Francis)
Little Ham (see Hughes, Langston)
Little Johnny (see Drinkwater, John)
A Little Journey (see Crothers, Rachel)
The Little Man (see Galsworthy, John)
A Little More Than Kin (see Durham, Frank)
Little Murders (see Feiffer, Jules)
A Little Night Music; screenplay (see Sondheim, Stephen)
The Little Poor Man (Le Petit Pauvre) (see Copeau, Jacques)
Little Red Riding Hood (see Schwartz, Eugene)
The Little Saint (see Bracco, Robert)
The Little Stranger (see Craven, Frank)
A Little Teatable Chitchat ... (see Smith, John)
The Little Theatre of "The Green Goose" (see Gałcyński, Konstanty
    I.)
Live (see Horovitz, Israel)
The Live Corpse (see Tolstoi, Lev N.)
To Live in Peace (see Forzano, Giovacchino)
Living Koheiji (see Suzuki, Sensaburo)
LIVING NEWSPAPER. EDITORIAL STAFF
    Triple-A Plowed Under
       (In The Anxious Years)
       (In Federal Theatre Plays)
THE LIVING THEATRE
    Six Public Acts
       (In The Drama Review, Vol. 19, no. 3, Sept. 1975)
    Turning the Earth
       (In The Drama Review, Vol. 19, no. 3, Sept. 1975)
LIVING THEATRE COLLECTIVE
    The Money Tower; scenario
       (In The Drama Review, Vol. 18, no. 2, June 1974)
A Living Thing (see Hamer, Maimie)
LIVINGS, Henry, 1929-
    Big Soft Nellie
       (In Kelly's Eye and Other Plays)
    Eh?
       (In Hill & Wang Spotlight Drama Series, 1967)

The ffinest ffamily in the Land
   (In Methuen Playscript Series, 1973)
Kelly's Eye
   (In Kelly's Eye and Other Plays)
There's No Room for You Here for a Start
   (In Kelly's Eye and Other Plays)
This Jockey Drives Late Nights; a play from "The Power of
   Darkness" by Leo Tolstoy
   (In Methuen Playscripts Series, 1972)
LIVINGSTON, Myrtle Smith, 1901-
   For Unborn Children
   (In Black Theater U.S.A., 1847-1974)
Le Livre de Christophe Colomb (see Claudel, Paul)
LIZZANI, Carlo, 1922-
   L'Oro di Roma
   (In Dal Soggetto al Film Series, no. 20, 1961)
   Il Processo di Verona
   (In Dal Soggetto al Film Series, no. 28, 1963)
LLANDERAS, Nicolas de las, 1938-
   Asi Es la Vida, de Nicolas de las Llanderas y Arnaldo M. Mal-
   ffatti
   (In Teatro Argention Contemporaneo)
Llegada de Noche (see Rothe, Hans)
Llovet, Enrique
   Socrates
   (In Teatro Español, 1972-73)
Lloyd George, David, 1st Earl of Dwyfor, British Prime Minister,
   1863-1945
   *The War Indemnities (see Shaw, George Bernard)
   *Wilson (see Greanias, George)
Lloyd George Knew My Father (see Home, William Douglas)
Llywelyn ab Gruffydd, Prince of Wales, d. 1282
   *The Chronicle of King Edward I (see Peele, George)
Lo Positivo (see Tamayo y Baus, Manuel)
Lo Que Dejo la Tempestad (see Rengifo, Cesar)
Lo Que No Se Dice (see Williams, Tennessee)
LOACH, Kenneth, 1936-
   Family Life; scenario; text in French (see Mercer, David)
Loaves and Fishes (see Maugham, William Somerset)
Lobisomen (see Laura, Ida)
The Local Authority (see Filippo, Eduardo de)
The Local Stigmatic (see Williams, Heathcote)
LOCKE, Matthew, 1630?-1677
   Psyche (see Shadwell, Thomas)
The Locked Chest (see Masefield, John)
El Loco y la Muerte (see Brandão, Raúl)
Locrine (Anon.)
   (In Disputed Plays of William Shakespeare)
Locrine (see Swinburne, Algernon Charles)
La Locura de Amor (see Tamayo y Baus, Manuel)
Lodge, Henry Cabot, 1850-1924
   *Wilson (see Greanias, George)

LODGE, Thomas, 1558?-1625
   A Looking Glasse for London and England (see Greene, Robert)
LOEPELMANN, Götz
   Darwins Reise
      (In Theater Heute, Vol. 16, no. 1, Jan. 1975)
LOEWE, Frederick, 1901-
   Brigadoon; book and lyrics by Alan Jay Lerner; music by Fred-
      erick Loewe
      (In Ten Great Musicals of the American Theatre)
   Camelot. Book and lyrics by Alan Jay Lerner; based on "The
      Once and Future King, " by T.H. White; music by Frederick
      Loewe
      (A Random House Play, 1961)
      (In Ten Great Musicals of the American Theatre, Vol. 2)
LOGAN, Joshua, 1908-
   Mister Roberts (see Heggen, Thomas O.)
   South Pacific (see Rodgers, Richard)
La Logeuse (see Audiberti, Jacques)
La Loi de l'Homme (see Hervieu, Paul E.)
La Loi du Feu (see Lamarche, Gustave)
LOISELEUX, Jacques, 1937-
   La Parcelle
      (In L'Avant-Scène Cinéma, no. 199, Feb. 1976)
Lolita; screenplay (see Nabokov, Vladimir)
London Assurance (see Boucicault, Dion)
London by Night (Anon.)
      (In Victorian Melodramas)
The London Cuckolds (see Ravenscroft, Edward)
The London Merchant (see Lillo, George)
London Prodigal (Anon.)
      (In Disputed Plays of William Shakespeare)
The Londonderry Air (see Field, Rachel)
The Londoner (see Thomas, Dylan)
The Lone Ranger radio script
   No. 1, 000 (see Striker, Fran)
The Lonely Way (see Schnitzler, Arthur)
Lonesome-Like (see Brighouse, Harold)
Long, John Davis, U.S. Sect'y of the Navy, 1838-1915
   *Two Administrations (see Bierce, Ambrose)
LONG, John Luther, 1861-1927
   Adrea (see Belasco, David)
   The Darling of the Gods (see Belasco, David)
  **Madam Butterfly; a tragedy of Japan (see Belasco, David)
Long and Short Division (see Smith, Moyne Rice)
The Long Hour, a fantasy for St. Patrick's Day; radio script (see
      O'Connell, Thomas E.)
The Long Sunset (see Sherriff, Robert C.)
The Long Voyage Home (see O'Neill, Eugene)
Longbaugh, Harry
   Butch Cassidy and the Sundance Kid (see Goldman, William)
LONGFELLOW, Henry Wadsworth, 1807-1882
   The Divine Tragedy
      (In his Poetical Works, Vol. 5)

Giles Corey of the Salem Farms
   (In his Poetical Works, Vol. 5)
The Golden Legend
   (In his Poetical Works, Vol. 5)
John Endicott
   (In his Poetical Works, Vol. 5)
Judas Maccabaeus
   (In his Poetical Works, Vol. 6)
The Masque of Pandora
   (In his Poetical Works, Vol. 3)
Michael Angelo; a fragment with additional scenes omitted for
  the first form
   (In his Poetical Works, Vol. 6)
The Spanish Student
   (In The Drama, Vol. 19)
   (In his Poetical Works, Vol. 1)
LONGNECKER, Edna B.
  References
   (In Prize Plays of 1927-28, Vol. 2)
Look After Lulu! (see Coward, Nöel)
Look and Long (see Stein, Gertrude)
Look Homeward, Angel (see Frings, Ketti)
Look Up and Live television scripts
  The Faith Hawker (see Rodman, Howard)
  No Man Is an Island (see Benjamin, James)
  Plenty of Rein (see Roskam, Clair)
  The Puzzle (see Roskam, Clair)
  A Thing of Beauty (see Rodman, Howard)
  The Will to Win (see Rodman, Howard)
A Looking Glasse for London and England (see Greene, Robert)
LOOS, Anita, 1894-
  The Love Expert; scenario (see Emerson, John)
  The Whole Town's Talking (see Emerson, John)
Loot (see Orton, Joe)
Lope de Vega, Felix (see Vega Carpio, Lope Felix de)
LOPEZ, Sabatino, 1867-1951
  Daceapo
   (In his Il Teatro)
  Fra un Allo e l'Altro
   (In his Il Teatro)
  La Guerra
   (In his Il Teatro)
  Il Punto d'Appoggio
   (In his Il Teatro)
  Il Segreto
   (In his Il Teatro)
  The Sparrow
   (In Plays of the Italian Theatre)
LOPEZ ARANDA, Ricardo
  Cerca de las Estrellas
   (In Teatro Español, 1960-61)
López de Yanguas, Fernán (see López de Yanguas, Hernán)

LOPEZ DE YANGUAS, Hernán, b. 1486 or 1487
  Egloga de la Natividad
    (In Clásicos Castellanos, Vol. 162)
  Farsa de la Concordia
    (In Clásicos Castellanos, Vol. 162)
  Farsa del Mundo y Moral
    (In Clásicos Castellanos, Vol. 162)
  Farsa Sacramental
    (In Clásicos Castellanos, Vol. 162)
LOPEZ MOZO, Jerónimo
  The Testament
    (In New Generation Spanish Drama)
LOPEZ RUBIO, José, 1903-
  The Blindfold
    (In The Modern Spanish Stage: Four Plays)
  Celos del Aire
    (In Teatro Español, 1949-50)
    (In his Teatro Selecto)
  Diana Está Comunicando
    (In Teatro Español, 1959-60)
  Esta Noche, Tampoco
    (In Teatro Español, 1961-62)
  Una Madeja de Lana Azul Celeste
    (In Teatro Español, 1951-52)
  Las Manos Son Inocentes
    (In Teatro Español, 1958-59)
    (In his Teatro Selecto)
  Nunca Es Tarde
    (In Teatro Español, 1964-65)
    (In Teatro Selecto)
  La Otra Orilla
    (In Teatro Español, 1954-55)
    (In his Teatro Selecto)
  Veinte y Cuarenta
    (In Teatro Español)
  La Venda en los Ojos
    (In Teatro Español, 1953-54)
    (In his Teatro Selecto)
The Loquacious Barber (see Holberg, Ludvig von)
The Loquacious Barber (see also Holberg, Ludvig von. Master Gert
  Westphaler; or, The Talkative Barber)
LORD, Phillips H.
  The Eddie Doll Case; radio script from "Gang Busters" Jan. 18,
  1939
    (In Best Broadcasts of 1938-39)
LORD, Walter
  **A Night to Remember (see Hill, George R.)
The Lord and His Servants (see Kielland, Axel)
Lord Byron's Love Letter (see Williams, Tennessee)
Lord Eldred's Other Daughter (see Downing, Henry F.)
Lord Halewyn (see Ghelderode, Michel de)
LORDE, Andre de
  At the Telephone
    (In One-Act Plays for Stage and Study, 2nd Series)

The System of Doctor Gourdon and Professor Plume
  (In The Drama Review, Vol. 18, no. 1, March 1974)
Lorenzaccio (see Eckhart, Dietrich)
Lorenzaccio (see Musset, Alfred de)
Loretta Strong (see Copi)
LORING, Emilie
  Where's Peter?
    (In Prize Plays of 1927-28, Vol. 2)
Lorna (see Jones, Helena)
Los del Cuarto (see Diaz, Gregor)
Das Los des Ossian Balvesen (see Kaiser, Georg)
Losers (see Friel, Brian)
LOSEY, Joseph, 1909-
  Mr. Klein
    (In L'Avant-Scène Cinéma, no. 175, Nov. 1, 1976)
A Losing Game (see Gregory, Isabella A.)
Lost in the Stars (see Weill, Kurt)
The Lost Princess (see Totheroh, Dan)
The Lost Saint (see Hyde, Douglas)
The Lottery (see Fielding Henry)
Lottie Dundass (see Bagnold, Enid)
Lou Gehrig Did Not Die of Cancer (see Miller, Jason)
Louis VII, called the Young, King of France, 1137-1180
  *Becket (see Tennyson, Alfred Lord)
Louis XIII, King of France, 1601-1643
  *Marion de Lorme (see Hugo, Victor)
  *Richelieu; or, The Conspiracy (see Lytton, Edward George)
Louis XV, King of France, 1710-1774
  *Une Comedie sous le Regne de Louis XV (see Musset, Alfred de)
  *Du Barry (see Belasco, David)
Louis Ferdinand, Prince of Prussia, 1772-1806
  Louis Ferdinand Prinz von Preussen (see Unruh, Fritz von)
Louison (see Musset, Alfred de)
LOUKI, Pierre
  La Petite Cuiller
    (In L'Avant-Scène Théâtre, no. 576, Dec. 1, 1975)
LOURENCO, Pasqual
  A Chuva de Sorrisos
    (In Revista de Teatro, no. 397, Jan./Feb. 1974)
LOURSON, Laurent
  Narcissus
    (In Gambit, no. 2)
La Louve (see Thomas, Robert)
Love A-la-Mode (see Macklin, Charles)
Love and a Bottle (see Farquhar, George)
Love and Anarchy (see Wertmüller, Lina)
Love and Geography (see Bjørnson, Bjørnstjerne)
Love and Honour (see D'Avenant, Sir William)
Love and Intrigue (see Schiller, Johann C.)
Love and Learning (see Weil, Rene)
Love at Twenty; screenplay (see Truffaut, François)
Love Crowns the End (see Tatham, John)
Love Cure; or, The Martial Maid (see Beaumont, Francis)
The Love Expert; scenario (see Emerson, John)

Love for Love (see Congreve, William)
The Love-Girl and the Innocent (see Solzhenitsyn, Aleksandr I.)
Love in a French Kitchen (see Clements, Colin C.)
Love in a Village (see Bickerstaffe, Isaac)
Love in a Wood (see Wycherley, William)
Love in '76 (see Bunce, Oliver Bell)
Love in the City (see Bickerstaff, Isaac. The Romp)
Love in the West (see Emory, William C.)
Love Is a Daisy (see Collins, Margaret)
Love Is a Fallacy (see Shulman, Max)
Love Is Enough; or, The Freeing of Pharamond (see Morris, William)
The Love Letter (see Woolf, Douglas)
Love Letter from the Licensed Quarter (see Bunshō, Kuruwa)
Love Makes the Man (see Cibber, Colley)
Love Mouse (see Rosen, Sheldon)
The Love of Don Perlimplin and Belisa in the Garden (see Garcia
     Lorca, Federico)
The Love of Four Colonels (see Ustinov, Peter)
The Love of King David and Fair Bethsaba (see Peele, George)
Love Reconciled to War (see Hivnor, Robert)
A Love Song (see Brownjohn, Alan)
The Love Suicides at Havering (see Howard, Roger)
Love the Best Physician (L'Amour Medecin) (see Molière, Jean Bap-
     tiste)
Love Tricks; or, The School of Complement (see Shirley, James)
Love Triumphant; or, Nature Will Prevail (see Dryden, John)
Love Will Finde Out the Way (see Shirley, James, The Constant
     Maid)
Loveless, George
     *Six Men of Dorset (see Malleson, Miles)
The Loveliest Afternoon of the Year (see Guare, John E.)
Lovely Rita (see Brasch, Thomas)
The Lover (see Pinter, Harold)
The Lovers (see Bernard, Kenneth)
Lovers (see Donnay, Maurice C.)
Lovers (see Harrison, Carey)
Lover's Lane (see Fitch, Clyde)
Lovers' Leap (see Johnson, Philip)
Lover's Pilgrimage (see Beaumont, Francis)
The Lover's Progress (see Beaumont, Francis)
Lovers' Quarrels (see Vanbrugh, Sir John)
Lovers' Vows; or, The Natural Son (see Kotzebue, Augustus F.)
Love's Comedy (see Ibsen, Henrik)
Love's Cruelty (see Shirley, James)
Love's Last Shift: or, The Fool in Fashion (see Cibber, Colley)
The Loves of Cass McGuire (see Friel, Brian)
The Lovesick Count; or, The Ambitious Politique (see Brome, Rich-
     ard)
LOW, Samuel, b. 1765
     The Politician Out-Witted
          (In Representative Plays by American Dramatists, Vol. 1)

LOWE, Allen D.
   The Window
      (In <u>Modern International Drama</u>, Vol. 7, no. 1B, Spring 1976)
LOWE, Stephen
   Touched
      (In <u>Plays and Players</u>, Vol. 24, nos. 11-12, Aug. /Sept.1977)
LOWELL, Robert, 1917-
   Benito Cereno
      (In <u>Revolution: a Collection of Plays</u>)
The Lower Depths (see Gor'kii, Maksim)
The Lower Depths (see also Gor'kii, Maksim, Night's Lodging)
The Loyal Subject (see Fletcher, John)
Loyalties (see Galsworthy, John)
LOZANO GARCIA, Carlos, 1902-
   Al Fin Mujer (see Lozano Garcia, Lazaro)
LOZANO GARCIA, Lazaro, 1899-
   Al Fin Mujer, por Lazaro y Carlos Lozano Garcia
      (In <u>Teatro Méxicano del Siglo XX</u>, Vol. 1)
Lu Hsün (pseud.) (see Chou, Shu-jen)
LUBIEZ-MILOSZ, Oscar Vladislas de, 1877-1939
   Rubezahl
      (In <u>L'Avant-Scène du Théâtre</u>, no. 534, Feb. 1974)
LUBITSCH, Ernst, 1892-1947
   Ninotchka; screenplay by Charles Brackett, Billy Wilder and Wal-
   ter Reisch, based on the original story by Melchior Lengyel,
   directed by Ernst Lubitsch. Pictures and complete dialogue
   edited by Richard J. Anobile
      (In <u>The Film Classics Library</u>, 1975)
LUBY, William A.
   J. Wilkes Booth; or, The National Tragedy
      (In <u>Magazine of History</u>, Vol. 8, Extra no. 29, 1914)
LUCA DE TENA, Juan Ignacio, 1897-
   El Condor s in Alas
      (In <u>Teatro Español</u>, 1951-1952)
   Donde Vas, Alfonso XII?
      (In <u>Teatro Español</u>, 1956-57)
   Donde Vas, Triste de Ti?
      (In <u>Teatro Español</u>, 1959-60)
   Hay una Luz Sobre la Cama
      (In <u>Teatro Español</u>, 1969-70)
   Dos Mujeres a las Nueve
      (In <u>Teatro Español</u>, 1949-50)
LUCAS, George
   American Graffiti, scenario by George Lucas, Gloria Katz and
   Willard Huyck; directed by George Lucas
      (In <u>Evergreen Filmscript Series</u>, 1973)
LUCE, Clare (Boothe) 1903-
   The Women
      (In <u>Famous Plays of 1937</u>)
      (In <u>Plays by and About Women</u>)
Luces de Bohemia (see Valle-Inclán, Ramón)
LUCIAN (Lucianus Samosatiensis), c. 117-180 A.D.
  **Pleasant Dialogues and Drammas (see Heywood, Thomas)

Lucienne et le Boucher (see Aymé, Marcel)
Lucius Junius Brutus, Father of His Country (see Lee, Nathaniel)
Lucius Sergius Catilina (see Heym, Georg)
Luck; radio adaptation (see Steele, Wilbur D.)
The Lucky Chance; or, An Alderman's Bargain (see Behn, Mrs.
    Aphra)
Lucky Per's Journey (see Strindberg, August)
Lucky Sam McCarver (see Howard, Sidney Coe)
Lucrece; ou, l'Adultère Puni (see Hardy, Alexandre)
Lucrece Borgia (see Hugo, Victor)
Lucretia Borgia (see Hugo, Victor)
Lucullus, Lucius Licinius, c. 110-57 B.C.
    *The Trial of Lucullus (see Brecht, Bertolt)
LUDLAM, Charles, 1943-
    Bluebeard
        (In The Off Off Broadway Book)
    Hot Ice
        (In The Drama Review, Vol. 18, no. 2, June 1974)
Ludwig II, King of Bavaria, 1845-1886
    *Ludwig (see Visconti, Luchino)
Lui (see Pillement, Georges)
Luira (see Browning, Robert)
LUKE, Peter, 1919-
    Hadrian VII, based on "Hadrian the Seventh" and other works by
        Frederick Rolfe, "Baron Corvo"
        (In Best Plays of the Sixties)
Lulu Belle (see Sheldon, Edward)
Lulu Street (see Henry, Ann)
Lumie di Sicilia (see Pirandello, Luigi)
LUNA, Nelson, 1938-
    O Gigante Egoista
        (In Revista de Teatro, no. 396, Nov./Dec. 1973)
Luna de Miel (Santander, Felipe)
La Luna en el Rio Amarillo (see Johnston, Denis)
The Lunatic, the Secret Sportsman and the Woman Next Door (Eve-
    ling, Stanley)
Lunch Hour (see Mortimer, John C.)
Lunchtime (see Wymark, Olwen)
Lunchtime Concert (see Wymark, Olwen)
La Lune a la Recherche d'Elle-meme (see Claudel, Paul)
La Lupa (see Verga, Giovanni)
Lusignan (see Guy, or Guido of Lusignan)
Lust, La Demoiselle de Cristal ("Mon Faust") (see Valery, Paul)
Luste; or, The Crystal Girl (see Valery, Paul)
LUSTIG, Helen
    A Living Thing, by Maimie Hamer and Helen Lustig
        (In Women Write for the Theatre Series, Vol. 1)
Luther, Martin, 1483-1546
    *Thomas Muntzer (see Pfeiffer, Hans)
La Lutte pour la Vie (see Daudet, Alphonse)
Lux in Tenebris (see Brecht, Bertolt)
The Lyar (see Foote, Samuel)
La Lycéenne (see Feydeau, Georges)

The Lying Lover; or, The Ladies Friendship (see Steele, Richard)
The Lying Valet (see Garrick, David)
LYNCH, Hal
    3 Miles to Poley
        (In Playwrights for Tomorrow, Vol. 10)
Lysistrata (see Aristophanes)
Lysistrata (see Donnay, Maurice C.)
LYTTON, Edward George Earle Lytton Bulwer-Lytton, 1st Baron,
    1803-1873
    **In the Lyons Den. A dramatic sequel to Bulwer-Lytton's The
        Lady of Lyons, by "Mr. Punch."
        (In The Drama, Vol. 22)
    Money
        (In The Drama, Vol. 16)
        (In English Plays of the 19th Century, Vol. III: Comedies)
    Richelieu; or, The Conspiracy
        (In English Plays of the 19th Century, Vol. 1: Dramas,
        1800-1850)
        (In Representative British Dramas)
Lyubov Yarovaya (see Trenyov, Konstantin)

M; screenplay (see Lang, Fritz)
MA CHIH-YUAN, 1250?-1320?
    Autumn in Han Palace
        (In Six Yüan Plays)
Ma Liberte (see Amiel, Denys)
Ma Non e una Cosa Seria (see Pirandello, Luigi)
Maada and Ulka (see Dunn, Theo M.)
Maandazi (see Heywood, John)
Le Macano de la "General" (see Keaton, Buster)
MacARTHUR, Charles 1895-1956
    The Front Page (see Hecht, Ben)
    Johnny on a Spot, based on a script by Parke Levy and Alan
        Lipscott
        (In The Stage Works of Charles MacArthur)
    Ladies and Gentlemen (see Hecht, Ben)
    Lulu Belle (see Sheldon, Edward)
    Salvation (see Howard, Sidney C.)
    Stag at Bay (see Johnson, Nunnally)
    Swan Song (see Hecht, Ben)
    Twentieth Century (see Hecht, Ben)
MACAYA LAHMANN, Enrique
    Preludio a la Noche
        (In Obras Breves del Teatro Costarricense, Vol. 2)
Macbeth; adaptation (see D'Avenant, Sir William)
Macbeth; text in German (see Shakespeare, William)
Macbeth Skit (see Shaw, George Bernard)
Macbett (see Ionesco, Eugene)
McCLARCHIE, Thomas Russell Hillier, d. 1886
    The Fatal Error, from the Japanese of Kaga-Sodo
        (In The Drama, Vol. 21)

McCLELLAN, Robert
   The Hypocrite
     (In <u>Calder & Boyars Scottish Library</u> Series, no. 19)
   Jamie the Saxt
     (In <u>Calder & Boyars Scottish Library</u> Series)
McCLOSKEY, James J., 1825-1913
   Across the Continent; or, Scenes from New York Life and the
   Pacific Railroad
     (In <u>Dramas from the American Theatre</u>, 1762-1909)
McCLURE, Michael
   The Masked Choir; Masque in the Shape of an Enquiry
     (In <u>Performing Arts Journal</u>, Vol. 1, no. 2, Fall 1976)
McCOO, Edward J.
   Ethiopia at the Bar of Justice
     (In <u>Plays and Pageants from the Life of the Negro</u>)
McCULLERS, Carson (Smith), 1917-1967
   The Member of the Wedding
     (In <u>50 Best Plays of the American Theatre</u>, Vol. 3)
MacDonagy, Donagh, 1912-
   Happy as Larry
     (In <u>Four Modern Verse Plays</u>)
   Step-in-the-Hollow
     (In <u>Three Irish Plays</u>)
MacDONALD, John D.
   **The Trap of Solid Gold (see Violett, Ellen M.)
MacDONALD, Robert David
   Chinchilla ... Figures in a Classical Landscape with Ruins ...
     (In <u>Plays and Players</u>, Vol. 24, nos 9-10, June-July, 1977)
McDonough's Wife (see Gregory, Isabella A.)
MacDOUGALL, Roger
   The Gentle Gunman
     (In <u>Plays of the Year</u>, Vol. 5, 1950/51)
   To Dorothy, a Son
     (In <u>Plays of the Year</u>, Vol. 4, 1950)
MACE, Jean 1815-1894
   L'Annee Nouvelle
     (In <u>Théâtre du Petit Chateau</u>)
   A Brebis Tondue Dieu Mesure Le Vent
     (In <u>Théâtre du Petit Chateau</u>)
   La Composition d'Histoire
     (In <u>Théâtre du Petit Chateau</u>)
   Les Larmes d'une Mere
     (In <u>Théâtre du Petit Chateau</u>)
   La Leçon de Geographie
     (In <u>Théâtre du Petit Chateau</u>)
   Une Lettre
     (In <u>Théâtre du Petit Chateau</u>)
   Le Palais du Temps
     (In <u>Théâtre du Petit Chateau</u>)
   Le Revolte des Fleurs
     (In <u>Théâtre du Petit Chateau</u>)
   Les Ricochets
     (In <u>Théâtre du Petit Chateau</u>)

Souvenirs de Pension
   (In Théâtre du Petit Chateau)
L'Utilite de la Douleur
   (In Théâtre du Petit Chateau)
MacFARLANE, Donald
   Blood of the Martyrs, radio script based on the story by Stephen
   Vincent Benét and the play by Percival Wilde, Dec. 7, 1938
      (In Best Broadcasts of 1938-39)
MacFAYDEN, Harry
   The Trojan Women; radio script (see Euripides)
McGILL, Jerry
   The Final Hour; The Shadow radio script
      (In On the Air)
McGRATH, John, 1935-
   Events While Guarding the Bofors Gun
      (In Methuen Playscripts Series, 1966)
   Fish in the Sea
      (In Plays and Players, Vol. 22, nos. 7 & 8, April & May
      1975)
McGREEVY, John
   The Foundling; The Waltons television script
      (In On the Air)
McGUANE, Thomas
   The Missouri Breaks; screenplay, directed by Arthur Penn
      (A Ballantine Books Screenplay, 1976)
MACHADO, Maria Clara
   Pluft, el Fantasmita
      (In Teatro Contemporaneo Hispanoamericano, Vol. 2)
La Machine Infernale (see Cocteau, Jean)
The Machine-Wreckers (see Toller, Ernst)
Les Machins de l'Existence (see Dion, Jean-François)
Die Macht der Gewohnheit (see Bernhard, Thomas)
MacINTYRE, John, 1869-
   The Charge-House, by John Brandane, pseudonym
      (In More One-Act Plays by Modern Authors)
MACK, Nila
   The Nuremberg Stove; a radio script, for "Let's Pretend"
      (In Best Broadcasts of 1938-39)
MacKAY, Isabel E.
   Two Too Many
      (In Prize Plays of 1927-28, Vol. 1)
MacKAYE, Percy, 1875-1956
   Gettysburg
      (In One-Act Plays by Modern Authors)
   Napoleon Crossing the Rockies
      (In One-Act Plays for Stage and Study, 3rd Series)
   The Scarecrow; a tragedy of the ludicrous
      (In Representative American Dramas)
      (In Representative American Plays, 1792-1949)
MacKAYE, Steele, 1842-1894
   Hazel Kirke
      (In Representative American Plays, 1792-1949)

Paul Kavar; or, Anarchy
(In Representative Plays by American Dramatists, Vol. 3)
McKENNEY, Ruth, 1911-
**Wonderful Town (see Bernstein, Leonard)
MacKENZIE, Kent
"Saturday Morning"; a transcript of the film
(An Avon Books Filmscript, 1971)
MacKENZIE, Ronald
The Maitlands
(In Famous Plays of 1934)
MACKEY, William Wellington
Requiem for Brother X
(In Black Drama Anthology)
MACKIE, Philip
The Whole Truth
(In Plays of the Year, Vol. 13, 1955)
McKinley, William, Pres. U.S., 1843-1901
*Two Administrations (see Bierce, Ambrose)
McKINNEL, Norman, 1870-1932
The Bishop's Candlesticks
(In The Play Book)
McKINNEY, Jack, d. 1966
The Well
(In Three Australian Plays)
MACKINTOSH, Elizabeth, 1896-1952
Queen of Scots, by Gordon Daviot, pseud.
(In Famous Plays of 1934)
MACKLIN, Charles, 1697?-1797
Love A-la-Mode
(In his Four Comedies)
(In The London Stage, Vol. 3)
The Man of the World
(In his Four Comedies)
The School for Husbands
(In his Four Comedies)
The True-Born Irishman
(In his Four Comedies)
A Will and No Will
(In 18th Century Drama: Afterpieces)
McLEAN, Kathryn (Anderson) 1909-
*I Remember Mama (see Van Druten, John)
MacLEISH, Archibald, 1892-
Air Raid; radio script
(In Best Broadcasts of 1938-39)
MacMAHON, Bryan, 1909-
Song of the Anvil
(In 7 Irish Plays)
MacMANUS, Seumas, 1869-1960
The Townland of Tamney
(In Irish Drama Series, Vol. 7)
McMENAMIN, Elizabeth
The University Today, 2: The Library; 4: The University Social
Life
(In 100 Non-Royalty Radio Plays)

McMORROW, Will
    Peter Stuyvesant; a radio script, from "The Cavalcade of Ameri-
        ca" Series
        (In Best Broadcasts of 1938-39)
McNALLY, Terrence, 1939-
    "... And Things That Go Bump in the Night"
        (In The Off Off Broadway Book)
        (In his The Ritz and Other Plays)
    Bad Habits
        (In his The Ritz and Other Plays)
    Botticelli
        (In New Theatre in America, Vol. 2)
        (In Off-Broadway Plays, Vol. 2)
    Bring It All Back Home
        (In his The Ritz and Other Plays)
    Noon
        (In Best American Plays, 7th Series, 1967-1973)
    Ravenswood
        (In Best Short Plays of 1975)
    The Ritz
        (In his The Ritz and Other Plays)
    Sweet Eros
        (In Off-Broadway Plays, Vol. 2)
    Tour
        (In Collision Course)
    Where Has Tommy Flowers Gone?
        (In his The Ritz and Other Plays)
    Whiskey
        (In his The Ritz and Other Plays)
MACOWAN, Norman, 1877-
    Glorious Mornings
        (In Famous Plays of 1938-39)
MacRAE, Arthur
    Both Ends Meet
        (In Plays of the Year, Vol. 10, 1953/54)
Macrune's Guevara (see Spurling, John)
McVEIGH, Christopher
    Sunday News
        (In Landfall, Vol. 29, no. 4, Dec. 1975)
The Mad Bomber (see Rapid Transit Guerrilla Communications, Chi-
    cago)
A Mad Couple Will Matched (see Brome, Richard)
Mad Dog Blues (see Shepard, Sam)
The Mad Lover (see Beaumont, Francis)
A Mad World, My Masters; adaptation (see Keeffe, Barrie)
A Mad World, My Masters (see Middleton, Thomas)
Madam Butterfly; a tragedy of Japan (see Belasco, David)
Madam Fickle; or, The Witty False One (see D'Urfey, Thomas)
Madam Legros (see Mann, Heinrich)
Madam Popov (see Schrock, Gladden)
Madame Marguerite (see Athayde, Roberto)
Madame Surratt (see Rogers, James Webb)

The Madcap (see Forssell, Lars)
Madd Couple Well Matcht (see Brome, Richard)
MADDEN, Richard
    Portrait of an Old Lady
       (In One-Act Plays for Stage and Study, 8th Series)
MADDOW, Ben
    In a Cold Hotel
       (In New Theatre in America, Vol. 1)
Una Madeja de Lana Azul Celeste (see Lopez Rubio, José)
Madeleine (see Zola, Emile)
Mademoiselle Jaire (see Ghelderode, Michel de)
Mademoiselle Löwenzorn (see Becher, Ulrich)
Madheart (see Jones, LeRoi)
Madly in Love: A Sky-Blue Comedy (see Ableman, Paul)
The Madman and the Nun (see Witkiewicz, Stanislaw I.)
The Madman on the Roof (see Kikuchi Kan)
Madman's Diary (see Gogol, Nikolai V.)
Madmen and Specialists (see Soyinka, Wole)
The Madness of Lady Bright (see Wilson, Lanford)
Mado (see Sautet, Claude)
The Madonna in the Orchard (see Foster, Paul)
The Madras House (see Granville-Barker, Harley)
The Madras House (see Shaw, George Bernard)
Las Madres (see Usigli, Rudolfo)
Madretta (see Young, Stark)
La Madriguera (see Rodriguez Buded, Ricardo)
Madro (El Drama Padre) (see Jardiel Poncela, Enrique)
Madrugada (see Buero Vallejo, Antonio)
MAETERLINCK, Maurice, 1862-1949
    Aglavaine et Selysette; text in French
       (In his Théâtre, Vol. 3)
    Alladine and Palomides
       (In his Plays, Vol. 2)
    Alladine et Palomides: text in French
       (In his Théâtre, Vol. 2)
    Ariane et Barbe-Bleue
       (In his Théâtre, Vol. 3)
    Les Aveugles
       (In his Théâtre, Vol. 1)
    The Blind
       (In his Plays, Vol. 1)
    The Death of Tintagiles
       (In The Drama, Vol. 21)
       (In his Plays, Vol. 2)
    Home
       (In his Plays, Vol. 2)
    Interieur
       (In his Théâtre, Vol. 2)
    The Intruder
       (In On the High Road)
       (In One-Act Plays by Modern Authors)
       (In his Plays, Vol. 1)

The Magnet (see Garner, Hugh)
The Magnetic Lady; or, Humours Reconciled (see Jonson, Ben)
The Magnificent Cuckold (see Crommelyneck, Fernand)
The Magnificent Lovers (Les Amans Magnifiques) (see Molière, Jean
    Baptiste)
The Magnolia Tree (see Manson, H. W. D.)
MAGRE, Maurice, 1877-
    The Tin Soldier and the Paper Dancer
        (In Modern One-Act Plays from the French)
Mah-Jongg (see Gerstenberg, Alice)
Mahabharatha (see Rangacharya, Adya)
Mahomet (see Voltaire)
MAIA, Luiz
    A Cigarra e a Formiga (see Almeida, Lyad de)
MAIAKOVSKII, Vladimir Vladimirovich, 1893-1930
    The Bedbug
        (In Masterpieces of the Modern Russian Theatre)
        (In 20th Century Russian Plays)
    Championship of the Universal Class Struggle
        (In Drama Review, Vol. 17, March 1973)
    La Chinche
        (In Teatro Comico Sovietico)
    How Are You? A Day in Five Movie Details
        (In Russian Literature Triquarterly, no. 7, Fall 1973)
    Moscow Is Burning
        (In Drama Review, Vol. 17, March 1973)
    Mystery-Bouffe
        (In Masterpieces of the Russian Drama, Vol. 2)
The Maid in the Mill (see Fletcher, John)
The Maid of Athens (see Baum, Lyman Frank)
The Maid of Bath (see Foote, Samuel)
Maid of France (see Brighouse, Harold)
The Maid of Honour (see Massinger, Philip)
The Maid of Orleans (see Schiller, Johann C.)
The Maid of the Mill (see Bickerstaffe, Isaac)
The Maid of the Oakes (see Burgoyne, John)
Maid to Marry (see Ionesco, Eugene)
The Maid's Revenge (see Shirley, James)
The Maid's Tragedy (see Beaumont, Francis)
Mail Call (see Nelson, Ralph)
Main Basse sur la Ville (see Rosi, Francesco)
La Main Loste (see Labiche, Eugene)
La Main Passe (see Feydeau, Georges)
The Main Thing (see Evreinov, Nikolai N.)
MAINARDI, Renato, 1931-
    Antonio von Elba
        (In Sipario, nos. 349-350, June-July, 1975)
Les Mains Sales (see Sartre, Jean-Paul)
MAIRET, Jean de, 1604-1686
    Les Galanteries du Duc d'Ossonne, Vice-Roi de Naples
        (In Théâtre du XVIIᵉ Siècle, Vol. 1)
    La Silvanire; ou, La Morte Vive
        (In Théâtre du XVIIᵉ Siècle, Vol. 1)

La Sophonisbe; text in French
(In Théâtre du XVIIe Siècle, Vol. 1)
Sophonisbe (Sophonisba)
(In The Chief Rivals of Corneille and Racine)
La Sylvie
(In Théâtre du XVIIe Siècle, Vol. 1)
Mais n'te Promene Donc pas Toute Nue (see Feydeau, Georges)
Mai Qu'est-ce Qui Fait Courir les Femmes, la Nuit a Madrid? (see
  Ceccaldi, Daniel)
La Maison d'Os (see Dubillard, Roland)
The Maitlands (see Mackenzie, Ronald)
Le Maître (see Ionesco, Eugene)
La Maître de Santiago (see Montherlant, Henry de)
Maizie (see Giorloff, Ruth)
Major Barbara (see Shaw, George Bernard)
La Major Cravachon (see Labiche, Eugene)
The Maker of Dreams (see Down, Oliphant)
La Mal Court (see Audiberti, Jacques)
Malandragens de Escapino (see Molière, Jean Baptiste)
Malatesta (see Montherlant, Henry de)
Malavika and Agnimitra (see Kalidasa)
Marlborough s'en Va-t-en Guerre (see Achard, Marcel)
Malcochon; or, The Six in the Rain (see Walcott, Derek)
MALCOLM, Ian
  A Moment of Existence
    (In Canada on Stage)
Malcolm X (see Little, Malcolm)
The Malcontent (see Marston, John)
Malditos (see Cantón, Wilberto)
Male of the Species (see Owen, Alun)
El Maleficio de la Mariposa (see Garcia Lorca, Federico)
Les Malefilatre (see Porto-Riche, Georges de)
Le Malentendu (see Camus, Albert)
MALERBA, Luigi, 1927-
  Ossido di Carbonio
    (In Sipario, no. 351-352, Oct./Nov. 1975)
MALFATTI, Arnaldo M., 1922-
  Asi Es la Vida (see Llanderas, Nicolas de las)
MALINA, Judith
  Mysteries and Smaller Pieces, by Judith Malina and Julian Beck
    (In The Great American Life Show)
La Malinche (see Gorostiza, Celestino)
MALLE, Louis, 1932-
  Le Feu Follet; filmscript based on the novel by Pierre La Ro-
  chelle
    (In Deux Films Français)
  Lacombe Lucien
    (In Lorrimer Screenplay Series, 1975)
    (A Viking/Compass Book Screenplay, 1975)
  William Wilson, screenplay based on the story by Edgar Allan
  Poe, directed by Louis Malle
    (In Dal Soggetto al Film Series, no. 37, 1968)

MALLESON, Miles, 1888-
    Maurice's Own Idea
        (In Types of Modern Dramatic Composition)
    The Miser (see Molière, Jean Baptiste)
    The School for Wives (see Molière, Jean Baptiste)
    Six Men of Dorset, by Miles Malleson and H. Brooks
        (In Famous Plays of 1938-39)
    Tartuffee (see Molière, Jean Baptiste)
The Maltese (see Schiller, Johann C.)
The Maltese Falcon; screenplay (see Huston, John)
MALTZ, Albert, 1908-
    Red Head Baker
        (In 100 Non-Royalty Radio Plays)
Maman Sabouleux (see Labiche, Eugene)
MAMET, David
    The Duck Variations
        (In Best Short Plays, 1977)
MAMLIN, Gennadi
    Hey, There--Hello! (Hey, Ty-Z-drastvuy!)
        (In Russian Plays for Young Audiences)
Mammon and the Whittler (see Stone, Weldon)
MAMOULIAN, Rouben, 1897-
    Dr. Jekyll and Mr. Hyde; screenplay by Samuel Hoffenstein and
        Percy Heath, based on the novel by Robert Louis Stevenson;
        directed by Rouben Mamoulian. Pictures and complete dialogue
        edited by Richard J. Anobile
        (In The Film Classics Library, 1975)
A Man, A Dictionary (see Kroetz, Franz X.)
Man and His Phantoms (see Lenormand, Henri R.)
Man and Superman: a Comedy and a Philosophy (see Shaw, George
    Bernard)
The Man and the Fly (see Ruibal, José)
A Man for All Seasons (see Bolt, Robert)
Man from Inner Space (see Nicol, Eric)
The Man-Hater (Le Misanthrope) (see Molière, Jean Baptiste)
The Man in the Bowler Hat (see Milne, Alan A.)
The Man in the Green Muffler (see Conn, Stewart)
The Man of Destiny (see Shaw, George Bernard)
A Man of God (see Marcel, Gabriel)
Man of La Mancha (see Leigh, Mitch)
The Man of Mode; or, Sir Fopling Flutter (see Etherege, Sir George)
The Man of the World (see Macklin, Charles)
The Man Upstairs (see Augustus, Thomas)
The Man Who Broke Bingo (see Golden, David T.)
The Man Who Came to Dinner (see Kaufman, George S.)
The Man Who Could Work Miracles; scenario from the film (see
    Wells, H.G.)
The Man Who Died at Twelve O'Clock (see Green, Paul)
The Man Who Dug Fish (see Bullins, Edward A.)
The Man Who Lived His Life Over (see Lagerkvist, Pär)
The Man with the Bundle (see Williams, Frayne)
The Man with the Demijohn (see Baker, George M.)
The Man with the Flower in His Mouth (see Pirandello, Luigi)

The Man with the Heart in the Highlands (see Saroyan, William)
The Man with the Mandoline (see Tanizaki, Junichiro)
The Man Without a Soul (see Lagerkvist, Pär)
MANAS NAVASCUES, Alfredo
  La Historia de los Tarantos
    (In Teatro Español, 1961-62)
The Mandarin Coat (see Riley, Mrs. Alice C.)
The Mandate (see Erdman, Nikolai)
MANDEL, Loring
  Do Not Go Gentle into That Good Night; television script, CBS,
    Oct. 17, 1967
    (In Electronic Drama)
    (In Great Television Plays, Vol. 2)
MANET, Eduardo, 1927-
  Lady Strass
    (In L'Avant-Scène Théâtre, no. 613, July 1, 1977)
Mangeront-ils? (see Hugo, Victor)
La Mangeur de Reves (see Lenormand, Henri R.)
MANHATTAN PROJECT (THEATRE COMPANY)
  Alice in Wonderland, based on Lewis Carroll's "Alice in Won-
    derland & Through the Looking Glass"
    (In Manhattan Project: The Forming of a Company, the Mak-
    ing of a Play)
MANKIEWICZ, Joseph Leo, 1909-
  All About Eve; screenplay, based on a short story by Mary Orr.
    (In More About All About Eve)
  Applause (see Strouse, Charles)
  Notre Pain Quotidien (see Vidor, King)
MANKOWITZ, Wolf, 1924-
  The Baby; based on a story by Chekhov
    (In his Five One-Act Plays)
  The Bespoke Overcoat
    (In his Five One-Act Plays)
  It Should Happen to a Dog, a Serio-Comic Strip; based on the
    story of Jonah and the Whale
    (In his Five One-Act Plays)
  The Last of the Cheesecake; based on a story by Chekhov
    (In his Five One-Act Plays)
  The Mighty Hunter
    (In his Five One-Act Plays)
Manlius Capitolinus (see La Fosse, Antoine de)
MANN, Heinrich, 1871-1950
  Madam Legros
    (In Eight European Plays)
MANN, Philip Grenville
  Eight Days a Week
    (In Australian Theatre Workshop, Vol. 9, 1972)
Der Mann Wir; filme (see Kaiser, Georg)
MANNER, Eeva-Liisa, 1921-
  Snow in May
    (In Modern Nordic Plays: Finland)
MANNERS, John Hartley, 1870-1927
  Hanging and Wiving
    (In One-Act Plays for Stage and Study, 1st Series)

MANNING, Hilda
    A Young Man's Fancy; a play edited for radio
        (In On the Air: 15 Plays for Broadcast)
MANOFF, Arnold
    All You Need Is One Good Break; adapted for radio by Edward
        Goldberg
        (In 100 Non-Royalty Radio Plays)
    Telegram from Heaven
        (In 100 Non-Royalty Radio Plays)
Las Manos de Dios (see Solórzano, Carlos)
Las Manos Son Inocentes (see López Rubio, José)
A Man's a Man (see Brecht, Bertolt)
The Man's Bewitch'd; or, The Devil to Do About Her (see Centlivre,
    Mrs. Susanna)
The Man's the Master (see D'Avenant, Sir William)
MANSFIELD, Richard, 1854-1907
    As You Find It
        (In One-Act Plays for Stage and Study, 8th Series)
MANSON, H. W. D.
    The Magnolia Tree; based on a Japanese tale by Ryunosuke Aku-
        tagawa
        (In Gambit, no. 8)
Os Mansos da Terra (see Alberto, Raimundo)
Mansur, Al-, "Abdullah Al-Mansur," Second Abbasside Caliph, 712?-
    775
*Revenge for Honour (see Chapman, George)
Manuel (see Dubé, Marcel)
Many Loves (see Williams, William Carlos)
Many Loves (see also Williams, William Carlos, Trail Horse no. 1)
Many Young Men of Twenty (see Keane, John Brendan)
MAPES, Victor
    A Flower of Yeddo
        (In One-Act Plays for Stage and Study, 1st Series)
MARAINI, Dacia
    Don Juan
        (In Sipario, no. 358, Mar. 1976)
MARAIS, Jean-Bernard
    La Galette des Rois
        (In L'Avant-Scène Théâtre, no. 547, Sept. 1, 1974)
MARASCO, Robert
    Child's Play
        (In Best Mystery and Suspense Plays of the Modern Theatre)
La Maratre (see Balzac, Honore de)
MARCEAU, Felicien (pseud.), 1913-
    L'Etouffé-Chrétien
        (In Le Théâtre d'Aujourd'hui)
    L'Homme en Question
        (In L'Avant-Scène du Théâtre, no. 546, August 1974)
    L'Oeuf
        (In Le Théâtre d'Aujourd'hui)
    Le Preuve par Quatre
        (In Le Théâtre d'Aujourd'hui)

Les Secrets de la Comédie Humaine
    (In L'Avant-Scène Théâtre, no. 563, May 1, 1975)
MARCEL, Gabriel, 1889-
    Anastasia; adapted by Guy Bolton
       (In Plays of the Year, Vol. 9, 1953)
    Ariadne
       (In his Three Plays)
    Colombyre; ou, Le Brasier de la Paix
       (In his Théâtre Comique)
    Le Divertissement Posthume
       (In his Théâtre Comique)
    La Double Expertise
       (In his Théâtre Comique)
    The Funeral Pyre
       (In his Three Plays)
    A Man of God
       (In his Three Plays)
March (see Adellach, Alberto)
March, William (pseud.) (see Campbell, William March)
The March Heir (see Hughes, Babette)
The March on Chumley Hollow (see Page, Myra)
Le Marchand d'Estampes (see Porto-Riche, Georges de)
Marching Song (see Whiting, John)
Marco Millions (see O'Neill, Eugene)
MARCUS, Frank, 1928-
    Blank Pages
       (In Best Short Plays, 1974)
    The Killing of Sister George
       (In Best Plays of the Sixties)
    Notes on a Love Affair
       (In Plays of the Year, Vol. 42, 1972)
MARCUS, Joseph
    Judgment of Paris
       (In The Journal of Irish Literature, Vol. 5, no. 2, May 1976)
MARCUS, Ysidro R.
    The Ultimate Pendejada
       (In Contemporary Chicano Theatre)
Marcus Brutus (see Foster, Paul)
Il Mare (see Bond, Edward)
La Maréchale d'Ancre (see Vigny, Alfred V.)
Margaret, Queen of Norway, 1353-1412
    *Queen Margaret of Norway (see Kielland, Trygve)
Margaret Fleming (see Herne, James A.)
Margaret of Parma, 1522-1586
    *Egmont (see Goethe, Johann Wolfgang von)
Margaret's Bed (see Inge, William M.)
Margarine (see Kaiser, Georg)
Marginalien (see Kraus, Karl)
Margot (see Bourdet, Edouard)
Marguerite (see Salacrou, Armand)
Le Mari, la Femme, et la Mort (see Roussin, Andre)
Un Mari Qui Lancé Sa Femme (see Labiche, Eugene)

Maria da Fe (see Domingos, Anselmo)
Maria Magdalena (see Hebbel, Friedrich)
Maria Magdalena (see Kroetz, Franz X.)
Maria Stuarda (see Alfieri, Vittorio)
Le Mariage de Barillon (see Feydeau, Georges)
Mariamne (see Hardy, Alexandre)
Mariamne (see Voltaire)
Mariana o El Alba (see Marques, René)
Mariana Pineda (see Garcia Lorca, Federico)
La Mariane (Mariamne) (see Tristan L'Hermite, François)
Maribel y la Extrana Familia (see Mihura, Miguel)
Marie (see Babel, Isaac)
Marie Couche-toi La (see Pillement, Georges)
Marie-Emma (see Laurendeau, Andre)
Marie Tudor; text in French (see Hugo, Victor)
A Marier (see Ionesco, Eugene)
Les Mariés de la Tour Eiffel (see Cocteau, Jean)
MARINETTI, Filippo Tommaso, 1876-1944
    Marinetti's Short Plays (Nine Scripts)
        (In The Drama Review, Vol. 17, no. 4, 1973)
MARINKOVIC, Ranko, 1913-
    Gloria
        (In Five Modern Yugoslav Plays)
Marino Faliero (see Swinburne, Algernon Charles)
Marion; parts 1-4 (see Green, Cliff)
MARION, Frances, 1890-
    The Scarlet Letter, script by Frances Marion based on the novel
        by Nathaniel Hawthorne, directed by Victor Sjostrom
        (In Motion Picture Continuities)
Marion de Lorme (see Hugo, Victor)
MARIVAUX, Pierre Carlet de Chamblain de, 1688-1793
    Les Acteurs de Bonne Foi
        (In his Théâtre Complet, 1964)
    L'Amour et la Vérité
        (In his Théâtre Complet, 1964)
    Annibal; text in French
        (In his Théâtre Complet, 1964)
    Arlequin Poli par l'Amour
        (In his Théâtre Complet, 1964)
    Le Chemin de la Fortune; ou, Le Saut du Fosse
        (In his Théâtre Complet, 1964)
    La Colonie
        (In his Théâtre Complet, 1964)
    Le Dénoûement Imprévu
        (In his Théâtre Complet, 1964)
    La Dispute
        (In his Théâtre Complet, 1964)
    La Double Inconstance
        (In his Théâtre Complet, 1964)
    Double Infidelity
        (In his Seven Comedies)
    L'Ecole des Mères
        (In his Théâtre Complet, 1964)

L'Epreuve
    (In his Théâtre Complet, 1964)
La Fausse Suivante; ou, Le Fourbe Puni
    (In his Théâtre Complet, 1964)
Les Fausses Confidences
    (In his Théâtre Complet, 1964)
Felicie
    (In his Théâtre Complet, 1964)
La Femme Fidèle
    (In his Théâtre Complet, 1964)
The Fame of Love and Chance
    (In his Seven Comedies)
L'Héritier de Village
    (In his Théâtre Complet, 1964)
L'Heureux Stratagème
    (In his Théâtre Complet, 1964)
L'Ile de la Raison; ou, Les Petits Hommes
    (In his Théâtre Complet, 1964)
L'Ile des Esclaves
    (In his Théâtre Complet, 1964)
Le Jeu de l'Amour et du Hasard
    (In his Théâtre Complet, 1964)
Le Joie Imprévue
    (In his Théâtre Complet, 1964)
Le Legs
    (In his Théâtre Complet, 1964)
La Méprise
    (In his Théâtre Complet, 1964)
La Mère Confidente
    (In his Théâtre Complet, 1964)
Money Makes the World Go Round
    (In his Seven Comedies)
Le Père Prudent et Equitable; ou, Crispin l'Heureux Fourbe
    (In his Théâtre Complet, 1964)
Le Petit-Maître Corrigé
    (In his Théâtre Complet, 1964)
Le Préjugé Vaincu
    (In his Théâtre Complet, 1964)
Le Prince Travesti; ou, L'Illustre Aventurier
    (In his Théâtre Complet, 1964)
La Provinciale
    (In his Théâtre Complet, 1964)
La Réunion des Amours
    (In his Théâtre Complet, 1964)
Robin, Bachelor of Love
    (In his Seven Comedies)
La Seconde Surprise de l'Amour
    (In his Théâtre Complet, 1964)
Les Serments Indiscrets
    (In his Théâtre Complet, 1964)
Les Sincères
    (In his Théâtre Complet, 1964)

La Surprise de l'Amour
    (In his Théâtre Complet, 1964)
Sylvia Hears a Secret
    (In his Seven Comedies)
The Test
    (In his Seven Comedies)
Le Triomphe de l'Amour
    (In his Théâtre Complet, 1964)
Le Triomphe de Plutus
    (In his Théâtre Complet, 1964)
The Wiles of Love
    (In his Seven Comedies)
MARKS, Jeannette Augustus, 1875-1964
Welsh Honeymoon
    (In One-Act Plays by Modern Authors)
Markurells of Wadköping (see Bergman, Hjalmar F.)
Marlborough, Sarah (Jennings) Churchill, Duchess of, 1660-1744
    *Viceroy Sarah (see Ginsbury, Norman)
MARLOWE, Christopher, 1564-1593
    **Abdelazer; or, The Moore's Revenge (see Behn, Mrs. Aphra)
    Dido, Queen of Carthage
    (In his Complete Plays)
    Doctor Faustus
    (In his Complete Plays)
    Edward the Second
    (In his Complete Plays)
    Hero and Leander; a poem left unfinished and completed by
    George Chapman
    (In The London Stage, Vol. 3)
    The Jew of Malta
    (In his Complete Plays)
    Le Juif de Malte; texte Français de Max Denes et François Rey
    (In L'Avant Scéne Théâtre, no. 588, June 1, 1976)
    The Massacre of Paris
    (In his Complete Plays)
    Tamburlaine the Great, pts. 1 & 2
    (In his Complete Plays)
    The Tragical History of Dr. Faustus
    (In World Drama, Vol. 1)
MARMION, Shakerly, 1603-1639
    The Antiquary
    (In his Dramatic Works)
    A Fine Companion
    (In his Dramatic Works)
    Holland's Leaguer
    (In his Dramatic Works)
MARMONTEL, Jean François, 1723-1799
    **The Sultan; or, A Peep into the Seraglio (see Bickerstaff, Isaac)
Marni, J. (pseud.) (see Marnière, Jeanne Marie Françoise)
MARNIERE, Jeanne Marie Françoise, 1854-1910
    The Yoke (see Guinon, Albert)
MAROWITZ, Charles
    Measure for Measure (see Shakespeare, William)

MARQUES, René
El Apartamiento
    (In his Teatro, Vol. 3)
La Casa Sin Reloj
    (In his Teatro, Vol. 3)
El Hombre y Sus Sueños
    (In his Teatro, Vol. 2)
Mariana o El Alba
    (In Teatro Puertorriqueño: Octavo Festival)
La Muerte No Entrara en Palacio
    (In El Teatro Hispanoamericano Contemporaneo, Vol. 1)
The Oxcart
    (In Eight American Ethnic Plays)
El Sol y los Macdonald
    (In his Teatro, Vol. 2)
The Marquis of Keith (see Wedekind, Frank)
The Marquise (see Coward, Nöel)
La Marquise d'O; screenplay (see Rohmer, Eric)
Les Marquises de la Fourchette (see Labiche, Eugene)
The Marriage (see Gombrowicz, Witold)
The Marriage (see Greaves, Donald)
The Marriage (see Hyde, Douglas)
Marriage A-la-Mode (see Dryden, John)
Marriage, a Quite Incredible Incident (see Gogol, Nikolai V.)
Marriage, an Absolutely Incredible Incident in Two Acts (see Gogol,
    Nikolai V.)
Marriage Is No Joke (see Mavor, Osborne Henry)
The Marriage of Bette and Boo (see Durang, Christopher)
The Marriage of Drama and Censorship (see Campos Garcia, Jesus)
A Marriage Proposal (see Chekhov, Anton P.)
The Married Beau; or, The Curious Impertinent (see Crowne, John)
A Married Woman (Une Femme Mariée); filmscript (see Godard,
    Jean-Luc)
Mars: Monument to the Last Black Eunuch (see Goss, Clay)
Marsh Hay (see Denison, Merrill)
MARSHAK, Samuel Yakovlevich, 1887–
    Twelve Months
        (In Soviet Scene)
Marshal (see Molnar, Ferenc)
MARSHALL, George, 1891-1975
    The Blue Dahlia; screenplay (see Chandler, Raymond)
MARSICOVETERE Y DURAN, Miguel, 1912–
    El Espectro Acrobata
        (In Teatro Guatemalteco Contemporaneo)
MARSTON, John, 1575?-1634
    Antonio and Mellida
        (In his Plays, Vol. 1)
    Antonio's Revenge; the second part of the Historie of Antonio and
        Mellida
        (In his Plays, Vol. 1)
    The Dutch Courtezan
        (In his Plays, Vol. 2)

Eastward Ho (see Chapman, George)
Histrio-Mastix; or, The Player
    (In his Plays, Vol. 3)
The Insatiate Countesse
    (In his Plays, Vol. 3)
Jacke Drum's Entertainment; or, The Comedie of Pasquill and
Katherine
    (In his Plays, Vol. 3)
The Malcontent
    (In his Plays, Vol. 3)
Parasitaster; or, The Fawne
    (In his Plays, Vol. 2)
What You Will
    (In his Plays, Vol. 2)
The Wonder of Women; or, The Tragedie of Sophonisba
    (In his Plays, Vol. 2)
MARTIN, John
There's a Change from the Old to the New; an episode from the
Rush television series
    (In Australian Theatre Workshop, no. 13)
MARTIN, Townsend
A Kiss for Cinderella; filmscript (see Goldbeck, Willis)
MARTIN RECUERDA, José
Las Salvajes en Puente San Gil
    (In Teatro Español, 1962-63)
Martine (see Bernard, Jean Jacques)
MARTINEZ, Jose de Jesus, 1929-
Juicio Final
    (In El Teatro Hispanoamericano Contemporaneo, Vol. 2)
Segundo Asalto
    (In Teatro Breve Hispanoamericano Contemporaneo)
MARTINEZ BALLESTEROS, Antonio, 1929-
The Best of All Possible Worlds
    (In The New Wave Spanish Drama)
    (In Themes of Drama)
The Hero
    (In The New Wave Spanish Drama)
MARTINEZ CUITINO, Vicente
Servidumbre
    (In Teatro Uruguayo Contemporaneo)
MARTINEZ DE LA ROSA, Francisco, 1787-1862
Aben Humeya
    (In Clásicos Castellanos, Vol. 107)
La Conjuración de Venecia
    (In Clásicos Castellanos, Vol. 107)
La Viuda de Padilla
    (In Clásicos Castellanos, Vol. 107)
MARTINEZ QUEIROLO, José, 1931-
Las Faltas Justificadas
    (In Teatro Ecuatoriano Contemporaneo, Vol. 2)
Los Unos Vrs. los Otros
    (In Teatro Contemporaneo Hispanoamericano, Vol. 1)

MARTINEZ RUIZ, (Azorin) José, 1873-
    Angelita
       (In Teatro Inquieto Español)
MARTINEZ-SIERRA, Gregorio, 1881-1947
    The Cradle Song
       (In Masterpieces of the Modern Spanish Theatre)
Os Martírios de Jorge e de Rosa (see Santos, Vital)
MARTYN, Edward, 1859-1923
    The Dream Physician
       (In Irish Drama Series, Vol. 7)
    The Heather Field
       (In Irish Drama Series, Vol. 1)
    Maeve
       (In Irish Drama Series, Vol. 2)
The Martyrdom of Ali; a Persian drama (Anon.)
       (In The Drama, Vol. 3)
The Martyrdom of Peter Chey (see Mrozek, Slawomir)
Le Martyre de Hourh-Ibn-Iazid (see Al Khonsari, Aboul-Kassim-
    Mohamed)
Marx, Karl, 1818-1883
    *Salut an Alle, Marx (see Kaltofen, Günter)
    *The Karl Marx Play (see Owens, Rochelle)
MARX, Marvin, & Others
    The Honeymooners; "A Letter to the Boss," The Jackie Gleason
    Show, Mar. 6, 1954
       (In Top TV Shows of the Year, 1954-55)
MARX BROTHERS
    Animal Crackers (see Ryskind, Morris)
    *The Marx Brothers Meet Karl (see Schecter, Joel)
Mary, Queen Consort of George V, 1867-1953
    *Crown Matrimonial (see Ryton, Royse)
    *Queen Mary (see Tennyson, Alfred Lord)
Mary, Queen of Scots, 1542-1587
    *Bothwell (see Swinburne, Algernon Charles)
    *Chaslelard (see Swinburne, Algernon Charles)
    *Maria Stuarda; text in Italian (see Alfieri, Vittorio)
    *Mary Stuart (see Drinkwater, John)
    *Mary Stuart (see Schiller, Johann C.)
    *Mary Stuart (see Swinburne, Algernon Charles)
    *Mary Tudor (see Hugo, Victor)
    *Queen of Scots, (see Mackintosh, Elizabeth)
    *Vivat! Vivat Regina! (see Bolt, Robert)
Mary Jane (see Bernard, Kenneth)
Mary Jones (see Mitchell, Ronald E.)
Mary Means What She Says (see Rogers, John William)
Mary Read (see Mavor, Osborne Henry)
Mary Rose (see Barrie, James M.)
Mary Stuart (see Drinkwater, John)
Mary Stuart (see Schiller, Johann C.)
Mary Stuart (see Swinburne, Algernon Charles)
Mary the Third (see Crothers, Rachel)
Mary Tudor (see Hugo, Victor)

Mas Vale Mana Que Fuera (see Tamayo y Baus, Manuel)
Masaniello (see Porta, Elvio)
Masculine Feminine (see Godard, Jean-Luc)
MASEFIELD, John, 1878-1967
    Bernice; adapted from the work of Racine
        (In his Verse Plays)
    The Campden Wonder
        (In his Prose Plays)
    Esther; adapted from the work of Racine
        (In his Verse Plays)
    The Faithful
        (In his Prose Plays)
    Good Friday; a dramatic poem
        (In his Verse Plays)
    A King's Daughter
        (In his Verse Plays)
    The Locked Chest
        (In his Prose Plays)
    Melloney Holtspur; or, The Pangs of Love
        (In his Prose Plays)
    Mrs. Harrison
        (In his Prose Plays)
    Philip the King
        (In his Verse Plays)
    The Sweeps of Ninety-Eight
        (In his Prose Plays)
    The Tragedy of Nan
        (In his Prose Plays)
    The Tragedy of Pompey the Great
        (In his Prose Plays)
        (In Representative British Dramas)
The Masked Choir (see McClure, Michael)
The Masked Ladies (De Usynlige) (see Holberg, Ludvig von)
MASON, Clifford
    Gabriel
        (In Black Drama Anthology)
MASON, Timothy
    Kidnapped in London, inspired by John Bennett's "Master Skylark"
        (In Five Plays from the Children's Theatre Company of Minne-
            apolis)
    Robin Hood: A Story of the Forest
        (In Five Plays from the Children's Theatre Company of Minne-
            apolis)
A Masque (see Cokayne, Sir Aston)
The Masque of Kings (see Anderson, Maxwell)
The Masque of Pandora (see Longfellow, Henry Wadsworth)
The Masque of the Gentlemen of Grays-Inne and the Inner-Temple
    (see Beaumont, Francis)
The Masque of the Middle Temple and Lincoln's Inn (see Chapman,
    George)
The Masque of Two Strangers (see Egerton, Lady Alix)
The Masquerade (see Clark, John P.)

Masquerade (see Lermontov, Mikhail I.)
The Masqueraders (see Jones, Henry Arthur)
Masquerades (Maskarade) (see Holberg, Ludvig von)
MASS TRANSIT STREET THEATER
    Ursula Underdog vs. The Money Grabbers; or, Tenants Go Round
      (In Guerilla Street Theater)
Massachusetts Trust (see Terry, Megan)
The Massacre of Paris (see Lee, Nathaniel)
The Massacre of Paris (see Marlowe, Christopher)
MASSINGER, Philip, 1583-1640
    The Bashful Lover
      (In his Plays, Vol. 4)
    The Bondman
      (In his Plays, Vol. 2)
  **The City Heiress; or, Sir Timothy Treat-All (see Behn, Mrs.
    Aphra)
    The City Madam
      (In his Plays, Vol. 4)
    The Duke of Milan
      (In The London Stage, Vol. 2)
      (In his Plays, Vol. 1)
    The Emperor of the East
      (In his Plays, Vol. 3)
    The Fatal Dowry
      (In his Plays, Vol. 3)
    The Great Duke of Florence
      (In his Plays, Vol. 2)
    The Guardian
      (In his Plays, Vol. 4)
    Love Cure; or, The Martial Maid (see Beaumont, Francis)
    The Maid of Honour
      (In his Plays, Vol. 3)
    A New Way to Pay Old Debts
      (In The Drama, Vol. 13)
      (In his Plays, Vol. 3)
    The Old Law, by Philip Massinger, Thomas Middleton, and Wil-
    liam Rowley
      (In his Plays, Vol. 4)
      (In Middleton's Works, Vol. 2)
    The Parliament of Love
      (In his Plays, Vol. 2)
    The Picture
      (In his Plays, Vol. 3)
    The Renegado
      (In his Plays, Vol. 2)
    The Roman Actor
      (In his Plays, Vol. 2)
    The Unnatural Combat
      (In his Plays, Vol. 1)
    A Very Woman; or, The Prince of Tarent
      (In his Plays, Vol. 4)
    The Virgin-Martyr
      (In his Plays, Vol. 1)

The Master Builder (see Ibsen, Henrik)
Master Gert Westphaler; or, The Talkative Barber (see Holberg, Ludvig von)
MASTEROFF, Joe, 1919-
    Cabaret (see Kander, John)
A Masterpiece of Diplomacy (see Howells, William Dean)
Match a la Une (see Novak, Ana)
Match Play (see Kalcheim, Lee)
The Matchmaker (see Wilder, Thornton)
The Matchmaking (see Hyde, Douglas)
MATHEUS, John, 1887-
    'Cruiter
        (In Black Theater U.S.A., 1847-1974)
        (In Blackamerican Literature 1760-Present)
    Ti Yette
        (In Plays and Pageants from the Life of the Negro)
MATHEW, Ray, 1920-
    We Find the Bunyip
        (In Three Australian Plays)
MATHEWS, Charles James, 1803-1878
    Patter Versus Clatter
        (In English Plays of the 19th Century, Vol. IV: Farces)
MATILLA, Luis
    Post Mortem
        (In Modern International Drama, Vol. 7, no. 2, Spring 1974)
        (In New Generation Spanish Drama)
Un Matin Comme les Autres (see Dubé, Marcel)
La Matinée de Don Juan (see Musset, Alfred de)
A Matter of Life and Death (see Atlas, Leopold)
Maude television scripts
    The Convention (see Schiller, Bob)
    Florida's Affair (see Levitt, Alan J.)
    Like Mother, Like Daughter (see Harris, Susan)
    Maude's Reunion (see Levitt, Alan E.)
    The Will (see Lewin, Albert E.)
MAUGHAM, Robin, 1916-
    Enemy!
        (In Plays of the Year, Vol. 39, 1969/70)
MAUGHAM, William Somerset, 1874-1965
  **Before the Party (see Ackland, Rodney)
    The Bread-Winner
        (In Collected Plays, Vol. 2)
        (In Six Comedies)
        (In 20th Century Plays)
    Caesar's Wife
        (In Collected Plays, Vol. 3)
    The Circle
        (In Collected Plays, Vol. 2)
        (In Dramas of Modernism)
        (In Six Comedies)
    The Constant Wife
        (In Collected Plays, Vol. 2)

(In The Maugham Reader)
(In Six Comedies)
East of Suez
    (In Collected Plays, Vol. 3)
For Services Rendered
    (In Collected Plays, Vol. 3)
Home and Beauty
    (In Collected Plays, Vol. 2)
    (In Six Comedies)
Jack Straw
    (In Collected Plays, Vol. 1)
Lady Frederick
    (In Collected Plays, Vol. 1)
The Land of Promise
    (In Collected Plays, Vol. 1)
The Letter
    (In Best Mystery and Suspense Plays of the Modern Theatre)
Loaves and Fishes
    (In Edwardian Plays)
Mrs. Dot
    (In Collected Plays, Vol. 1)
Our Betters
    (In Collected Plays, Vol. 2)
    (In The Maugham Reader)
    (In Six Comedies)
Penelope
    (In Collected Plays, Vol. 1)
**Rain (see Colton, John)
The Sacred Flame
    (In Collected Plays, Vol. 3)
Sheppey
    (In Collected Plays, Vol. 3)
    (In Six Plays)
Smith
    (In Collected Plays, Vol. 1)
The Unattainable
    (In Collected Plays, Vol. 2)
    (In Six Comedies)
The Unknown
    (In Collected Plays, Vol. 3)
MAUPASSANT, Henri René Guy de, 1850-1893
  **Un Lâche (see Gilles, Ange)
    The Household Peace
        (In The Drama, Vol. 9)
  **Masculine Feminine; screenplay (see Godard, Jean-Luc)
    La Paix du Ménage; or, A Comedy of Marriage
        (In his Life Work, Vol. 14)
  **Reise mit Joujou (see Hanell, Robert)
MAURIAC, François, 1805-
  Asmodee
      (In Port-Royal)
Maurice (see Bolt, Carol)

Maurice's Own Idea (see Malleson, Miles)
MAVOR, Osborne Henry, 1888-1951
    The Amazed Evangelist
      (In his <u>A Sleeping Clergyman and Other Plays</u>)
    The Anatomist
      (In his <u>A Sleeping Clergyman and Other Plays</u>)
    Babes in the Wood
      (In his <u>The King of Nowhere and Other Plays</u>)
    The Black Eye
      (In his <u>Moral Plays</u>)
    Colonel Wotherspoon
      (In his <u>Colonel Wotherspoon and Other Plays</u>)
    The Dancing Bear
      (In his <u>Colonel Wotherspoon and Other Plays</u>)
    The Dragon and the Dove; or, How the Hermit Abraham Fought
    the Devil for His Niece, by James Bridie, pseud.
      (In his <u>Plays for Plain People</u>)
    The Girl Who Did Not Want to Go to Kuala Lumpur
      (In his <u>Colonel Wotherspoon and Other Plays</u>)
    The Golden Legend of Shults
      (In his <u>Susannah and the Elders and Other Plays</u>)
    Holy Isle, by James Bridie, pseud.
      (In his <u>Plays for Plain People</u>)
    Jonah and the Whale
      (In <u>A Sleeping Clergyman and Other Plays</u>)
    Jonah 3; a new version of Jonah and the Whale, by James Bridie,
    pseud.
      (In his <u>Plays for Plain People</u>)
    The King of Nowhere
      (In his <u>The King of Nowhere and Other Plays</u>)
    The Kitchen Comedy
      (In his <u>Susannah and the Elders and Other Plays</u>)
    Lancelot, by James Bridie, pseud.
      (In his <u>Plays for Plain People</u>)
    The Last Trump
      (In his <u>The King of Nowhere and Other Plays</u>)
    Marriage Is No Joke
      (In his <u>Moral Plays</u>)
    Mary Read, by James Bridie, pseud., and Claude Gurney
      (In his <u>Moral Plays</u>)
    Mr. Bolfry, by James Bridie, pseud.
      (In his <u>Plays for Plain People</u>)
    The Sign of the Prophet Jonah; a play for broadcasting, by James
    Bridie, pseud.
      (In his <u>Plays for Plain People</u>)
    A Sleeping Clergyman
      (In his <u>A Sleeping Clergyman and Other Plays</u>)
    Susannah and the Elders
      (In his <u>Susannah and the Elders and Other Plays</u>)
    Tobias and the Angel
      (In his <u>A Sleeping Clergyman and Other Plays</u>)
    What It Is to Be Young
      (In his <u>Colonel Wotherspoon and Other Plays</u>)

What Say They?
(In his Susannah and the Elders and Other Plays)
Maximian, Marcus Aurelius Valerius Maximianus I, Roman emperor, d. 310
*Maximian (see Corneille, Thomas)
*Saint Genest (Saint Genesius) (see Rotrou, Jean)
Maximilian (Ferdinand Maximilian Joseph), Emperor of México, 1832-1867
    Corona de Sombra: pieza antihistórica (see Usigli, Rudolfo)
MAXWELL, William Babington, 1866-1938
    The Last Man In
        (In Scottish Repertory Plays Series, no. 1, 1910)
MAY, Elaine, 1932-
    The Real You; a compass scenario
        (In Yale/Theatre, Vol. 5, no. 2, Spring 1974)
MAY, Karl Friedrich, 1842-1912
    **Winnetou; filmscript (see Rialto-Film Preben Phillipsen & Jardran-Film)
May Moon (see Finsterwald, Maxine)
Mayakovsky, Vladimir (see Maiakovskii, Vladimir Vladimir-ovich)
A Mayden-Head Well Lost (see Heywood, Thomas)
MAYER, Carl, 1894-1944
    Le Cabinet du Docteur Caligari; scenario (see Weine, Robert)
    Le Dernier des Hommes, titre original: "Der Letzte Mann, " aux U.S.A.: "The Last Laugh, " film directed by Friedrich-Wilhelm Murnau
        (In L'Avant-Scène Cinéma, no. 190-191, July/Sept. 1977)
    Tartuffe; filmscript, titre original "Herr Tartüff, " d'apres la pièce de Molière; film directed by Friedrich-Wilhelm Murnau
        (In L'Avant-Scène Cinéma, no. 190-191, July/Sept. 1977)
The Mayor and the Manicure (see Ade, George)
The Mayor of Garrat (see Foote, Samuel)
The Mayor of Queensborough (see Middleton, Thomas)
Mayores con Reparos (see Alfonso Millan, José)
MAYSLES, Albert
    Salesman, a film by Albert and David Maysles and Charlotte Zwerin
        (A Signet Film Series Book, 1969)
Mazeppa (see Milner, Henry M.)
Me and Juliet (see Rodgers, Richard)
The Meadow Gate (see Gregory, Isabella A.)
Measure for Measure (see Shakespeare, William)
The Measures Taken (see Brecht, Bertolt)
The Mechanical Bride (see Leiber, Fritz)
Le Mechant (see Gresset, Jean-Baptiste-Louis)
A Medal for Willie (see Branch, William)
MEDCRAFT, Russell Graham, 1900-
    The First Dress-Suit
        (In One-Act Plays for Stage and Study, 5th Series)

Poetry and Plaster
    (In <u>One-Act Plays for Stage and Study</u>, 6th Series)
Medea (see Anouilh, Jean)
Medea (see Euripides)
Medea (see Jahnn, Hans H.)
Medea (see Jeffers, Robinson)
Medea (see Seneca)
Medea; screenplay (see Pasolini, Pier P.)
Médée; text in French (see Anouilh, Jean)
Médée; text in French (see Corneille, Pierre)
Médée; text in French (see Dubé, Marcel)
Médée; text in French (see Lamartine, Alphonse)
Media Hora Antes (see Delgado Benavente, Luis)
A Media Luz los Tres (see Mihura, Miguel)
Medic television script, "She Walks in Beauty" (see Kolb, Kenneth)
Medici, Alessandro de, 1510-1537
    *Lorenzaccio (see Musset, Alfred de)
El Médico de Su Honra (see Calderon de la Barca, Pedro)
El Medio Pelo (see Gonzáles Caballero, Antonio)
Medio Tono (see Usigli, Rudolfo)
Los Medios Seres (see Gomez de la Serna, Ramón)
MEDNICK, Murray, 1939-
    The Hawk, by Murray Mednick and Anthony Barsha
        (In <u>The Off Off Broadway Book</u>)
MEDOFF, Mark
    Doing A Good One for the Red Man
        (In <u>Best Short Plays of 1975</u>)
    The Kramer
        (In <u>Playwrights for Tomorrow</u>, Vol. 13, 1975)
    Wann Kommst'n Wieder Roter Reiter?
        (In <u>Theater Heute</u>, no. 3, Mar. 1976)
Médor (see Vitrac, Roger)
Medora (see Rueda, Lope de)
Meet a Body (see Launder, Frank)
Meet Noah Smith (see Bennett, Gordon C.)
Meet the Missus (see Nicholson, Kenyon)
The Meeting of the Company; or, Baye's Art of Acting (see Garrick, David)
MEGRUE, Roi Cooper, 1883-1927
    It Pays to Advertise, by Roi Cooper Megrue and Walter Hackett
        (In <u>Representative American Dramas</u>)
    The Same Old Thing
        (In <u>One-Act Plays for Stage and Study</u>, 2nd Series)
Mehemet Ali, Viceroy of Egypt, 1769-1849
    *The Girl from Kavella, an historical romance (see Wang, William H.)
Meier Halmbrecht (see Hochwälder, Fritz)
La Meilleure Façon de Marcher (see Miller, Claude)
Meister Röckle; oper (see Werzlau, Joachim)
Mel Says to Give You His Best (see Rosenberg, James L.)
Melanide (see La Chausee, Pierre-Claude N.)
MELFI, Leonard Anthony, 1935-
    Birdbath
        (In <u>New Short Plays</u>, Vol. 1)

(In The Off Off Broadway Book)
Cinque
        (In Spontaneous Combustion; The Winter Repertory Vol. 6)
Niagara Falls
        (In New Theatre in America, Vol. 2)
Night
        (In Best American Plays, 7th Series, 1967-1973)
Stars and Stripes
        (In Collision Course)
Melgarejo, Mariano, Pres. Bolivia, 1820-1870
    *Juana Sanchez (see Salmon, Raul)
Melicerta, an Heroick Pastoral (see Molière, Jean Baptiste)
Melite (see Corneille, Pierre)
Die Melkende Kuh (see Kaiser, Georg)
Melloney Holtspur; or, The Pangs of Love (see Masefield, John)
MELO, Fernando, 1945-
        Greta Garbo, Quem Diria, Acabou No Iraja
        (In Revista de Teatro, no. 400, July/Aug. 1974)
Melocoton en Almibar (see Mihura, Miguel)
Melodrama Play (see Shepard, Sam)
Melville, Alan, pseud. (see Caverhill, William Melville)
MELWOOD, Mary
        The Tingalary Bird
        (In All the World's a Stage)
The Member of the Wedding (see McCullers, Carson)
A Memory of Two Mondays (see Miller, Arthur)
Men and No (see Pedrolo, Manuel de)
Men in White (see Kingsley, Sidney)
Men, Women and Goats (see Kennedy, Charles O'Brien)
Menagerie; or, The Elephant's Escapades (see Witkiewicz, Stanislaw
        I.)
MENCKEN, Henry Louis, 1880-1956
    **Bring on the Angels; radio script (see Sloane, Allan)
MENDES, Lothar, 1894-
        Jew Süss; screenplay (see Rawlinson, Arthur)
        The Man Who Could Work Miracles; scenario from the film (see
        Wells, H.G.)
MENDEZ, Moses, d. 1758
        The Chaplet, a musical entertainment with music composed by
        Dr. Boyce
        (In A Collection of the Most Esteemed Farces ..., Vol. 1)
MENDEZ BALLESTER, Manuel
        Tiempo Muerto
        (In Teatro Puertorriqueño: Quinto Festival)
MENDOZA, Hector, 1932
        Las Cosas Simples
        (In Teatro Méxicano del Siglo XX, Vol. 3)
MENEN DESLEAL, Alvaro, 1913-
        El Circo
        (In Teatro Breve Hispanoamericano Contemporaneo)
        Jazz-Band; comedia musical
        (In Teatro Breve Hispanoamericano Contemporaneo)

Retablo
    (In <u>Teatro Breve Hispanoamericano Contemporaneo</u>)
Ternura
    (In <u>Teatro Breve Hispanoamericano Contemporaneo</u>)
MENESTREL, Marie
    On Tue Toujours Celle Qu'on Aime
        (In <u>L'Avant-Scène du Théâtre</u>, no. 546, August 1974)
Las Meninas (see Buero Vallejo, Antonio)
MENOTTI, Gian-Carlo, 1911-
    Amahl and the Night Visitors
        (In <u>All the World's a Stage</u>)
Men's Business (see Kroetz, Franz X.)
Le Mensonge (see Sarraute, Nathalie)
Le Menteur (see Corneille, Pierre)
La Menteuse (see Daudet, Alphonse)
MENTHON, Henri de
    Les Larbins
        (In <u>L'Avant-Scène Théâtre</u>, no. 567, July 1, 1975)
El Menu (see Buenaventura, Enrique)
MENZEL, Jiri, 1938-
    Closely Observed Trains; screenplay, by Jiri Menzel and Bohumil
        Hrabal, film directed by Jiri Menzel
        (In <u>Lorrimer Screenplay Series</u>, 1971)
La Méprise (see Marivaux, Pierre C.)
Mercadet (see Balzac, Honore de)
The Mercenary (see Spunde, Walter G.)
MERCER, David, 1928-
    An Afternoon at the Festival
        (In his <u>The Bankrupt and Other Plays</u>)
    And Did Those Feet
        (In his <u>Three TV Comedies</u>)
    The Bankrupt
        (In his <u>The Bankrupt and Other Plays</u>)
    Belcher's Luck
        (In <u>Hill & Wang Spotlight Drama</u> Series, 1967)
    The Birth of a Private Man
        (In his <u>Generations: A Trilogy of Plays</u>)
    The Cellar and the Almond Tree
        (In his <u>On the Eve of Publication and Other Plays</u>)
    A Climate of Fear
        (In his <u>Generations: A Trilogy of Plays</u>)
    Dopo Haggerty
        (In <u>Sipario</u>, no. 330, Nov. 1973)
    Emma's Time
        (In his <u>On the Eve of Publication and Other Plays</u>)
Family Life; scenario de David Mercer d'après sa pièce "In Two
    Minds"; realization Kenneth Loach
        (In <u>L'Avant-Scène du Cinéma</u>, no. 133, Feb. 1973)
Find me
    (In his <u>The Bankrupt and Other Plays</u>)
Flint
    (In <u>Methuen Modern Plays Series</u>, 1970)

For Tea on Sunday
    (In his Three TV Comedies)
The Governor's Lady
    (A Methuen Playscript, 1968)
In Two Minds
    (In his The Parachute with Two More TV Plays)
Let's Murder Vivaldi
    (In Best Short Plays, 1974)
    (In his The Parachute with Two More TV Plays)
On the Eve of Publication
    (In his On the Eve of Publication and Other Plays)
The Parachute
    (In his The Parachute with Two More TV Plays)
Providence: scenario: text in French (see Resnais, Alain)
Ride a Cock Horse
    (In Hill & Wang Spotlight Drama Series, 1966)
A Suitable Case for Treatment
    (In his Three TV Comedies)
Where the Difference Begins
    (In his Generations: A Trilogy of Plays)
You and Me and Him
    (In his The Bankrupt and Other Plays)
Mercier and Camier (see Beckett, Samuel)
MERCURE, Jean
    La Création du Monde et Autre Bisness (see Miller, Arthur)
La Mère Confidente (see Marivaux, Pierre C.)
La Mère Coupable (see Beaumarchais, Pierre A.)
Meredew's Right Hand (see Gibbs, Arthur H.)
MEREDYTH, Bess
    The Mighty Barnum; screenplay (see Fowler, Gene)
MERI, Veijo, 1928-
    Private Jokinen's Marriage Leave
    (In Modern Nordic Plays: Finland)
MERIMEE, Prosper, 1803-1870
    L'Amour Africain
    (In his Théâtre de Clara Gazul)
    Le Carrosse du Saint-Sacrement
    (In his Théâtre de Clara Gazul)
    Le Ciel et l'Enfer
    (In his Théâtre de Clara Gazul)
    Les Espagnols en Danemarck
    (In his Théâtre de Clara Gazul)
    La Famille de Carvajal
    (In his Théâtre de Clara Gazul)
    Une Femme est un Diable
    (In his Théâtre de Clara Gazul)
    Ines Mendo; or, The Triumph of Prejudice, by Clara Gazul, pseud.
    (In The Drama, Vol. 21)
    Inès Mendo; ou, Le Préjugé Vaincu
    (In his Théâtre de Clara Gazul)
    Inès Mendo; ou, Le Triomphe du Préjugé
    (In his Théâtre de Clara Gazul)

La Jacquerie
    (In his <u>Théâtre de Clara Gazul</u>)
L'Occasion
    (In his <u>Théâtre de Clara Gazul</u>)
Mérope (see Alfieri, Vittorio)
Mérope (see Voltaire)
MERRILL, Bob
    Funny Girl (see Styne, Jule)
    New Girl in Town, based on the play "Anna Christie," by Eugene
        O'Neill. Book by George Abbott; music and lyrics by Bob Mer-
        rill
        (A <u>Random House Play</u>, 1958)
MERRILL, James Lee, 1930-
    The Immortal Husband
        (In <u>Playbook</u>; Five Plays for a New Theatre)
A Merry Death (see Evreinov, Nikolai N.)
The Merry Devil of Edmonton (Anon.)
    (In <u>Disputed Plays of William Shakespeare</u>)
The Merry Jests of Hershel Ostropolier; television script (see Kinoy,
    Ernest)
La Mesonera del Cielo (see Mira de Amescua, Antonio)
La Metafísica di un Vitello a Due Testa (see Witkiewicz, Stanislaw
    I.)
Metamora; or, The Last of the Wampanoags (see Stone, John A.)
Metamorfosis (see Reyes, Carlos J.)
Metaphors (see Duberman, Martin)
Metaphysics of a Two-Headed Calf (see Witkiewicz, Stanislaw I.)
METASTASIO, Pietro Antonio Domenico Buonaventura, 1698-1782
    **The Desert Island (see Murphy, Arthur)
    The Dream of Scipio
        (In <u>The Drama</u>, Vol. 5)
The Meteor (see Dürrenmatt, Friedrich)
Meter Maid (see The San Francisco Mime Troupe)
Methusalem (see Goll, Ivan)
La Métromanie ou le Poète (see Piron, Alexis)
Metropolis; screenplay (see Lang, Fritz)
Metzengerstein; screenplay (see Vadim, Roger)
MEYER, Ernst Hermann
    Reiter der Nacht, oper nach dem gleichnamigen Roman von Peter
        Abraham; libretto von Gunther Deicke; music von Ernst Hermann
        Meyer
        (In <u>Theater der Zeit,</u> no. 6, June 1973)
MEYER, Lewis
    Mount Vernon Interlude
        (In <u>100 Non-Royalty Radio Plays</u>)
Meyer's Room (see Rosen, Sheldon)
MEYRINK, Gustav
    **The Golem; film scenario (see Wegener, Paul)
Mi Adorado Juan (see Mihura, Miguel)
Mi Compadre, el Ministro (see Salmon, Raul)
Mi Familia (see Filippo, Eduardo de)
Micaela (see Calvo-Sotelo, Joaquin)

MICALLEF, Lexie
    Tripe
        (In Gambit, Vol. 7, no. 25, 1974)
Michael Angelo (see Longfellow, Henry Wadsworth)
Michael Auclair (see Vildrac, Charles)
Michael Pauper (see Becque, Henri)
Michaelma's Term (see Middleton, Thomas)
MICHEL, Georges, 1926-
    Aggression
        (In Contemporary French Theater)
    The Sunday Walk
        (In Methuen Playscript Series, 1967)
Michelangelo Buonarroti, 1475-1564
    *Michael Angelo: A Fragment (see Longfellow, Henry Wadsworth)
Michelin (see Gregory, Isabella A.)
MICHENER, James Albert, 1907-
    **South Pacific (see Rodgers, Richard)
Michi's Blood (see Kroetz, Franz X.)
Michu (see Grumberg, Jean-Claude)
MICINSKI, Tadeusz,   -1918
    The Ballad of the Seven Sleeping Brothers of China
        (In Yale/Theatre, Vol. 7, no. 1, Fall 1975)
MICKEL, Karl
    Einstein
        (In Theater der Zeit, no. 4, March 1974)
Micro-cynicon (see Middleton, Thomas)
Microdramas: Ramses, The Three Musketeers, William Tell, Cali-
    gula, Columbus, Romeo and Juliet (see Bauer, Wolfgang)
Mid Channel (see Pinero, Arthur Wing)
Midas (see O'Hara, Kane)
Middleman (see Workers Theater, 1930s)
MIDDLETON, Thomas, 1570?-1627
    Anything for a Quiet Life, by Thomas Middleton and John Web-
      ster
        (In his Works, Vol. 5)
        (In Webster's Works, Vol. 4)
    The Black Book
        (In his Works, Vol. 8)
    Blurt, Master-Constable
        (In his Works, Vol. 1)
    The Changeling, by Thomas Middleton and William Rowley
        (In his Works, Vol. 6)
    A Chaste Maid in Cheapside
        (In his Works, Vol. 5)
  **The City Heiress; or, Sir Timothy Treat-All (see Behn, Mrs.
    Aphra)
    Entertainment to King James
        (In his Works, Vol. 7)
    A Fair Quarrel, by Thomas Middleton and William Rowley
        (In his Works, Vol. 4)
    The Family of Love
        (In his Works, Vol. 3)

Father Hubbard's Tales
  (In his Works, Vol. 8)
A Game of Chess
  (In his Works, Vol. 7)
The Inner-Temple Masque
  (In his Works, Vol. 7)
A Mad World, My Masters
  (In his Works, Vol. 3)
**A Mad World, My Masters; adaptation   (see Keeffe, Barrie)
The Mayor of Queensborough
  (In his Works, Vol. 2)
Michaelma's Term
  (In his Works, Vol. 1)
Micro-cynicon
  (In his Works, Vol. 8)
More Dissemblers Besides Women
  (In his Works, Vol. 6)
No Wit (Help) Like a Woman's
  (In his Works, Vol. 4)
The Old Law (see Massinger, Philip)
Una Partita a Scacchi
  (In Sipario, no. 334, Mar. 1974)
The Phoenix
  (In his Works, Vol. 1)
The Roaring Girl, by Thomas Middleton and Thomas Dekker
  (In his Works, Vol. 4)
The Spanish Gipsy, by Thomas Middleton and William Rowley
  (In his Works, Vol. 6)
A Trick to Catch the Old One
  (In his Works, Vol. 2)
The Widow, by Thomas Middleton, Ben Jonson, and John Fletcher
  (In his Works, Vol. 5)
The Wisdom of Solomon Paraphrased
  (In his Works, Vol. 8)
The Witch
  (In his Works, Vol. 5)
Woman Beware Women
  (In his Works, Vol. 6)
The World Lost at Tennis, by Thomas Middleton and William
  Rowley
  (In his Works, Vol. 7)
Your Five Gallants
  (In his Works, Vol. 3)
The Midnight Caller (see Foote, Horton)
The Midnight Hour (see Inchbald, Mrs. Elizabeth)
Midsummer Night (see Biro, Lajos)
A Midwinter Story (see Schildt, Runar)
Miedo de si Mismo (see Bompiano, Valentino)
Mientras Amemos (see Usigli, Rudolfo)
The Mighty Barnum; screenplay (see Fowler, Gene)
The Mighty Dollar (see Woolf, Benjamin)
The Mighty Hunter (see Mankowitz, Wolf)

The Mighty Wurlitzer; The Goon Show Script no. 140 (see Milligan,
  Spike)
MIHURA, Miguel
  La Bella Dorotea
    (In Teatro Español, 1963-64)
  Carlota
    (In Teatro Español, 1956-57)
  La Decente
    (In Teatro Español, 1967-68)
  Maribel y la Extrana Familia
    (In Teatro Español, 1959-60)
    (In Teatro Selecto de Miguel Mihura)
  A Media Luz los Tres
    (In Teatro Español, 1953-54)
    (In Teatro Selecto de Miguel Mihura)
  Melocoton en Almibar
    (In Teatro Selecto de Miguel Mihura)
  Mi Adorado Juan
    (In Teatro Español, 1955-56)
  Ninette (Modas de Paris)
    (In Teatro Español, 1966-67)
  Ninette y un Señor de Murcia
    (In Teatro Español, 1964-65)
    (In Teatro Selecto de Miguel Mihura)
  Sublime Decision!
    (In Teatro Español, 1954-55)
    (In Teatro Selecto de Miguel Mihura)
  Three Top Hats
    (In Modern Spanish Theatre)
  Tres Sombreros de Copa
    (In Teatro Español, 1952-53)
    (In Tcatro Selecto de Miguel Mihura)
The Mikado; or, The Town of Titipu (see Gilbert, William S.)
Milagro en la Plaza del Progreso (see Calvo Sotelo, Joaquin)
Milarepa (see Cavani, Liliana)
MILGATE, Rodney, 1934-
  A Refined Look at Existence
    (In Methuen Playscript Series, 1968)
MILHOLLAND, Charles Bruce
  **Twentieth Century (see Hecht, Ben)
The Militants (see Valdez, Luis)
The Milk Train Doesn't Stop Here Anymore (see Williams, Tennessee)
MILLAN, Juan José Alonso
  Se Vuelve a Llevar la Guerra Larga
    (In Teatro Español, 1973-74)
MILLAR, Ronald
  Abelard and Heloise
    (In Plays of the Year, Vol. 39, 1969/70)
  Waiting for Gillian
    (In Plays of the Year, Vol. 10, 1953/54)
MILLAUD, Fernand
  Díner au Champagne
    (In L'Avant-Scène Théâtre, no. 613, July 1, 1977)

MILLAY, Edna St. Vincent, 1862-1950
  Heavenly and Earthly Love (see Molnar, Ferenc)
Mille Francs de Recompense (see Hugo, Victor)
MILLER, Arthur, 1915-
  After the Fall
    (A Bantam Books Play, 1965)
    (A Penguin Play, 1968)
  After the Fall (selection)
    (In This Is My Best in the Third Quarter Century)
  All My Sons
    (In his Collected Plays)
  La Creation du Monde et Autre Bisness; adaptation Française:
  Jean Mercure
    (In L'Avant-Scène Théâtre, no. 552, Nov. 15, 1974)
  The Crucible
    (In his Collected Plays)
    (In 50 Best Plays of the American Theatre, Vol. 4)
  Death of a Salesman
    (In his Collected Plays)
    (In Contact with Drama)
    (In 50 Best Plays of the American Theatre, Vol. 3)
  A Memory of Two Mondays
    (In his Collected Plays)
  The Misfits
    (In Film Scripts Three)
    (A Penguin Books Script, 1961)
  La Muerte de un Viajante
    (In Teatro Norteamericano Contemporaneo)
  The Poosidin's Resignation
    (In Boston University Journal, Vol. 24, no. 2, 1976)
  The Price
    (In Best American Plays, 7th Series, 1967-1973)
  The Pussycat and the Expert Plumber Who Was a Man
    (In 100 Non-Royalty Radio Plays)
  A View from the Bridge
    (In his Collected Plays)
    (In Contemporary Drama: 13 Plays)
  William Ireland's Confession
    (In 100 Non-Royalty Radio Plays)
MILLER, Claude, 1942-
  La Meilleure Façon de Marcher
    (In L'Avant-Scène Cinéma, no. 168, April 1976)
MILLER, James, 1706-1744
  **Lethe; or, Aesop in the Shades (see Garrick, David)
  Mohomet, the Impostor
    (In The London Stage, Vol. 4)
MILLER, Jason, 1939-
  Circus Lady
    (In The Best Short Plays 1973)
  Lou Gehrig Did Not Die of Cancer
    (In Best Short Plays of the World Theatre, 1968-1973)
MILLER, Joaquin, 1841-1913
  The Danites in the Sierras
    (In The Disinherited: Plays)

MILLER, May
    Graven Images
        (In Black Theater U.S.A., 1847-1974)
        (In Plays and Pageants from the Life of the Negro)
    Riding the Goat
        (In Plays and Pageants from the Life of the Negro)
MILLER, Sigmund
    One Bright Day
        (In Plays of the Year, Vol. 14, 1955/56)
The Miller and His Men (see Pocock, Isaac)
The Miller of Mansfield (see Dodsley, Robert)
MILLIGAN, Alice
    The Last Feast of the Fianna
        (In Irish Drama Series, Vol. 2)
MILLIGAN, Spike
    The Affair of the Lone Banana; the Goon Show Script no. 104
        (5th Series, no. 5)
        (In The Goon Show Scripts)
    The Canal; The Goon Show Script no. 105 (5th Series, no. 6)
        (In The Goon Show Scripts)
    The Dreaded Batter Pudding Hurler (of Bexhill-on-Sea). Goon
        Show Script no. 102 (5th Series no. 3)
        (In The Goon Show Scripts)
    Foiled by President Fred; The Goon Show Scripts no. 132 (6th
        Series, no. 7)
        (In The Goon Show Scripts)
    The Great String Robberies
        (In The Book of the Goons)
    The Hastings Flyer; The Goon Show Scripts no. 141 (6th Series,
        no. 16)
        (In The Goon Show Scripts)
    The House of Teeth; The Goon Show Scripts no. 145 (6th Series,
        no. 20)
        (In The Goon Show Scripts)
    The Mighty Wurlitzer; The Goon Show Scripts no. 140 (6th Se-
        ries, no. 15)
        (In The Goon Show Scripts)
    Napoleon's Piano; The Goon Show Scripts no. 129 (6th Series,
        no. 4)
        (In The Goon Show Scripts)
    The Phantom Head-Shaver (of Brighton); The Goon Show Scripts
        no. 103 (5th Series, no. 4)
        (In The Goon Show Scripts)
    Robin's Post
        (In The Book of the Goons)
    The Spon Plague
        (In The Book of the Goons)
    The Terrible Revenge of Fred Fumanchu
        (In The Book of the Goons)
The Millionairess (see Shaw, George Bernard)
MILLS, Hugh
    The House by the Lake
        (In Plays of the Year, Vol. 14, 1955/56)

MILNE, Alan Alexander, 1882-1956
   The Artist
      (In More One-Act Plays by Modern Authors)
   The Man in the Bowler Hat
      (In One-Act Plays for Stage and Study, 1st Series)
   The Truth About Blayds
      (In Dramas of Modernism)
   Wurzel-Flummery
      (In One-Act Plays by Modern Authors)
MILNER, Henry M., fl. 1820-1840
   Mazeppa
      (In Victorian Melodramas)
MILNER, Ronald Scott, 1938-
   The Warning--a Theme for Linda
      (In Black Quartet)
   Who's Got His Own
      (In Black Drama Anthology)
MILTON, John, 1608-1674
   Comus
      (In The London Stage, Vol. 2)
   Comus, altered by George Colman
      (In A Collection of the Most Esteemed Farces ..., Vol. 4)
   Milton's Paradise Lost: Screenplay for Cinema of the Mind
      (see Collier, John)
   *The Story of John Milton; radio script (see Walpole, Helen)
Mima (see Molnar, Ferenc)
Mimosa Pudica (see Dempster, Curt)
Mimsy (see Bourder, Edouard)
The Mine (see Ionesco, Eugene)
Mine Eyes Have Seen (see Dunbar-Nelson, Alice)
Minetti (see Bernhard, Thomas)
The Miniature Darzis (see Smith, Moyne Rice)
Miniatures (see Cregan, David)
The Minister's Seal (see Visakha-Datta, Prince)
Mink (see Halldórsson, Erlingur E.)
Minna Von Barnhelm; or, The Soldier's Fortune (see Lessing, Gotthold E.)
Minnie and Moskowitz; screenplay (see Cassavetes, John)
The Minor (see Fonvizin, Denis I.)
The Minor (see Foote, Samuel)
A Minor Scene (see Bullins, Edward A.)
Minstrel Boy (see Dean, Phillip Hayes)
A Minuet (see Parker, Louis)
Les Minutes de Sable Mémorial (see Jarry, Alfred)
MIRA DE AMESCUA, Antonio, fl. 1600
   Auto Sacramental
      (In Clásicos Castellanos, Vol. 171)
   De la Jura del Principe
      (In Clásicos Castellanos, Vol. 171)
   El Ejemplo Mayor del la Desdicha
      (In Clásicos Castellanos, Vol. 82)
   El Esclavo del Demonio
      (In Clásicos Castellanos, Vol. 70)

La Fénix de Salamanca
   (In Clásicos Castellanos, Vol. 82)
La Mesonera del Cielo
   (In Clásicos Castellanos, Vol. 171)
Pedro Telonario (Auto Sacramental)
   (In Clásicos Castellanos, Vol. 70)
Miracle at Dublin Gulch (see Finch, Robert Voris)
The Miracle at Verdun (see Chlumberg, Hans)
Le Miracle de Théophile; text in English (see Rutebeuf)
The Miracle-Merchant (see Munro, Hector H.)
The Miracle of Saint Martin (see Dondo, Mathurin)
MIRACLES DE NOSTRA DAME PAR PERSONNAGES
   La Nonne Qui Laissa Son Abbaie
     (In Two Miracles)
   Saint Valentin
     (In Two Miracles)
Mirandolina (see Goldoni, Carlo)
Miriam; television script (see Capote, Truman)
Mirra (see Alfieri, Vittorio)
The Mirror (see Carballido, Emilio)
The Mirror-Wardrobe One Fine Evening (see Aragon, Louis)
Mirthful Marionettes (see Totheroh, Dan)
Misalliance (see Shaw, George Bernard)
The Misanthrope (see Schiller, Johann C.)
Le Misanthrope et l'Auvergnat (see Labiche, Eugene)
The Miser (see Fielding, Henry)
The Miser (see Molière, Jean Baptiste)
The Miser (see Shadwell, Thomas)
A Miserable Day; or Honesty Is the Best Soviet Policy (see Schweid, Mark)
The Misfits; filmscript (see Miller, Arthur)
Misfortune from a Coach; opera (see Kniazhin, Iakov B.)
The Misfortune of Being Clever (selection) (see Griboedov, Aleksandr S.)
Miss ChiJini (see Salmon, Raul)
Miss in Her Teens; or, The Medley of Lovers (see Garrick, David)
Miss Jairus (see Ghelderode, Michel de)
Miss Julie (see Strindberg, August)
Miss Lucy in Town: a Sequel to The Virgin Unmask'd (see Fielding, Henry)
Miss Myrtle Says "Yes" (see O'Dea, Mark L.)
Miss Sara Sampson (see Lessing, Gotthold E.)
The Missing Links (see Antrobus, John)
Missing Person (see Taylor, Peter H.)
Mississippi (see Bread and Puppet Theater)
Mississippi; text in German (see Kaiser, Georg)
The Missouri Breaks; screenplay (see McGuane, Thomas)
The Mistake (see Vanbrugh, Sir John)
The Mistaken Husband (see Dryden, John)
Mr. Bolfry (see Mavor, Osborne Henry)
Mr. Curator's Proposal (see Trainer, David)
Mr. F. (see Wilde, Percival)

Mr. Flemington Sits Down (see Kauffmann, Stanley)
Mr. Joyce Is Leaving Paris (see Gallacher, Tom)
Mr. Klein; screenplay (see Losey, Joseph)
Mr. Klevs and Rosalie (see Obaldia, Rene de)
Mr. Leonida Face to Face with the Reaction (see Caragiale, Ion L.)
Mr. Paul Pry; or, I Hope I Don't Intrude (Jerrold, Douglas W.)
Mr. Price; or: Tropical Madness (see Witkiewicz, Stanislaw I.)
Mister Roberts (see Heggen, Thomas O.)
Mr. Siggie Morrison with His Comb and Paper (see Reed, Bill)
Mr. Sleeman Is Coming (see Bergman, Hjalmar F.)
Mr. Sydney Smith Coming Upstairs (see Oulton, Brian)
Mr. Whipsnade Looks for Work--for His Nephew; radio script (see
    Fields, W. C.)
I Misteri de Roma (Rocca San Casciano); screenplay (see Bolzoni)
O Misterioso Caso do Queijo Desaparecido (see Braga, J. Alberto)
Mrs. Adis (see Kaye-Smith, Sheila)
Mrs. Bumpstead-Leigh (see Smith, Harry J.)
Mrs. Dally Has a Lover (see Hanley, William)
Mrs. Dane's Defense (see Jones, Henry Arthur)
Mrs. Dot (see Maugham, William Somerset)
Mrs. Harrison (see Masefield, John)
Mrs. Pat and the Law (see Aldis, Mrs. Mary)
Mrs. Warren's Profession (see Shaw, George Bernard)
Mit dem Kopf Durch die Wand (see Horvath, Odön von)
MITCHELL, Julian
    A Family and a Fortune; from the novel by Ivy Compton-Burnett
        (In Plays of the Year, Vol. 45, 1976)
    Half-Life
        (A National Theatre Play, 1977)
MITCHELL, Ken
    This Train
        (In Performing Arts in Canada, Vol. 10, no. 1, Spring 1973)
MITCHELL, Langdon Elwyn, 1862-1935
    The New York Idea
        (In Dramas from the American Theatre, 1762-1909)
        (In Representative American Plays, 1792-1949)
        (In Representative Plays by American Dramatists, Vol. 3)
MITCHELL, Loften, 1919-
    Star of the Morning
        (In Black Drama Anthology)
        (In Black Theater U.S.A., 1847-1974)
MITCHELL, Ronald Elwy
    Mary Jones
        (In One-Act Plays for Stage and Study, 9th Series)
    The Road to Ruin
        (In The Best One-Act Plays of 1958-59, London)
MITCHELL, W. O.
    The Devil's Instrument
        (In A Collection of Canadian Plays, Vol. 2)
MITCHISON, Naomi, 1897-
    Nix-Nought-Nothing
        (In A Book of Short Plays, XV-XX Centuries)

MITHOIS, Marcel, 1922-
    L'Arc de Triomphe; comédie de Marcel Mithois d'apres Franca
    Valeri. Mise-en-scène de Jacques Charon
       (In L'Avant-Scène du Théâtre, no. 535, Feb. 1974)
    Les Jeux de la Nuit (see Gilroy, Frank D.)
Mithridates IV, Philopator Philadelphus, King of Pontus, 170?-150
    B.C.
    *Mithridates (see Racine, Jean Baptiste)
    *Mithridates, King of Pontus (see Lee, Nathaniel)
MIZOGUCHI, Kenji
    Les Contes de la Lune Vague après le Pluie; titre original:
    "Ugetsu Monogatari"
       (In L'Avant-Scène Cinéma, no. 179, Jan. 1, 1977)
Moa a Mo'i, Chicken into King (see Charlot, Jean)
MOBERG, Vilhelm, 1898-
    La Mujer del Hombre
       (In Teatro Sueco Contemporaneo)
As Mocas: O Beijo Final (see Camara, Isabel)
The Mock Doctor; or, The Dumb Lady Cured (see Fielding, Henry)
The Mock-Tempest (see Duffet, Thomas)
The Modern Husband (see Fielding, Henry)
Modestie (see Hervieu, Paul Ernest)
MOELLER, Philip, 1880-1958
    The Glass Slipper (see Molnar, Ferenc)
    The Guardsman (see Molnar, Ferenc)
Mörder ohne Mord; ein film (see Kaiser, Georg)
MOGIN, Jean, 1921-
    A Cada Cual Segun Su Apetito
       (In Teatro Belga Contemporaneo)
The Mogul Tale (see Inchbald, Mrs. Elizabeth)
Mohammed (see Muhammad, the Prophet)
Mohammed Ali (see Mehemet Ali, Viceroy of Egypt)
The Mohocks (see Gay, John)
Mohomet, the Impostor (see Miller, James)
Moi (see Labiche, Eugene)
Moi, Pierre Rivière, Ayant Egorgé Ma Mère, Ma Soeur et Mon
    Frère ...; screenplay (see Allio, Rene)
MOINAUX, Georges, 1861-1929
    Article 330, by Georges Courteline, pseud.
       (In his Plays, Vol. 1)
    L'Article 330; text in French; by Georges Courteline, pseud.
       (In his Théâtre Complet)
    Badin the Bold, by Georges Courteline, pseud.
       (In his Plays, Vol. 1)
    Les Balances, by Georges Courteline, pseud.
       (In his Théâtre Complet)
    Boubouroche, by Georges Courteline, pseud.
       (In his Plays, Vol. 1)
    Boubouroche; text in French; by Georges Courteline, pseud.
       (In his Théâtre Complet)
    Les Boulingrin, by Georges Courteline, pseud.
       (In his Théâtre Complet)
    La Cinquantaine, by Georges Courteline, pseud.

(In his <u>Théâtre Complet</u>)
Un Client Serieux, by Georges Courteline, pseud.
(In his <u>Théâtre Complet</u>)
Le Commissaire est Bon Enfant, by Georges Courteline, pseud.
(In his <u>Théâtre Complet</u>)
The Commissioner
(In <u>Four Modern French Comedies</u>)
The Commissioner Has a Big Heart, by Georges Courteline,
pseud.
(In <u>Three Popular French Comedies</u>)
La Conversion d'Alceste, by Georges Courteline, pseud.
(In his <u>Théâtre Complet</u>)
La Cruche, by Georges Courteline, pseud.
(In his <u>Théâtre Complet</u>)
Le Droit aux Etrennes, by Georges Courteline, pseud.
(In his <u>Théâtre Complet</u>)
Une Evasion de Latude, by Georges Courteline, pseud.
(In his <u>Théâtre Complet</u>)
L'Extra-Lucide, by Georges Courteline, pseud.
(In his <u>Théâtre Complet</u>)
Les Gaites de l'Escadron; par Georges Courteline, pseud.
(In his <u>Théâtre Complet</u>)
Le Gendarme est sans Pitie, by Georges Courteline, pseud.
(In his <u>Théâtre Complet</u>)
Godefroy, by Georges Courteline, pseud.
(In his <u>Théâtre Complet</u>)
Gros Chagrins, by Georges Courteline, pseud.
(In his <u>Théâtre Complet</u>)
Hold On, Hortense, by Georges Courteline, pseud.
(In his <u>Plays</u>, Vol. 1)
Hortense, Couche-Toi, by Georges Courteline, pseud.
(In his <u>Théâtre Complet</u>)
Une Lettre Chargée, by Georges Courteline, pseud.
(In his <u>Théâtre Complet</u>)
Lidoire, by Georges Courteline, pseud.; text in French
(In his <u>Théâtre Complet</u>)
Monsieur Badin, by Georges Courteline, pseud.
(In his <u>Théâtre Complet</u>)
La Paix Chez Soi, by Georges Courteline, pseud.
(In his <u>Théâtre Complet</u>)
Pantheon-Courcelles, by Georges Courteline, pseud.
(In his <u>Théâtre Complet</u>)
Peace at Home, by Georges Courteline, pseud.
(In <u>Modern One-Act Plays from the French</u>)
Petin, Mauillarbourg et Consorts, by Georges Courteline, pseud.
(In his <u>Théâtre Complet</u>)
La Peur des Coups, par Georges Courteline, pseud.
(In his <u>Théâtre Complet</u>)
Sigismond, by Georges Courteline, pseud.
(In his <u>Théâtre Complet</u>)
Theodore Cherche des Allumettes, by Georges Courteline, pseud.
(In his <u>Théâtre Complet</u>)
La Voiture Versee, by Georges Courteline, pseud.

(In his <u>Théâtre Complet</u>)
Moise et Aaron; filmscript (see Straub, Jean-Marie)
MOISSEY, Alexander Guillaume Mouslier de, 1712-1777
    *The Way to Keep Him (see Murphy, Arthur)
Mojo (see Childress, Alice)
The Moke-eater (see Bernard, Kenneth)
MOLETTE, Barbara J., 1940-
    Rosalee Pritchett (see Molette, Carlton W.)
MOLETTE, Carlton W., II, 1939-
    Rosalee Pritchett, by Carlton W. Molette II and Barbara J. Molette
        (In <u>Black Writers of America</u>)
MOLIERE, Jean Baptiste Poquelin, 1622-1673
    The Affected Ladies (Les Précieuses Ridicules)
        (In his <u>Works,</u> Vol. 1)
    Alcestes (see Usigli, Rudolfo)
    **All in the Wrong (see Murphy, Arthur)
    The Amorous Quarrel (Depit Amoureux)
        (In his <u>Works,</u> Vol. 1)
    Amphitryon; translated by Charles E. Passage
        (In <u>Amphitryon: Three Plays in New Verse Translations</u>)
    Amphitryon; or, The Two Sosias
        (In his <u>Works,</u> Vol. 3)
    **Amphitryon; or, The Two Sosias; adaptation with music (see
        Dryden, John)
    **Barnaby Brittle; or, A Wife at Her Wits' End (see Betterton,
        Thomas)
    The Cheats of Scapin (Les Fourberies de Scapin)
        (In his <u>Works,</u> Vol. 5)
    The Cit Turned Gentleman
        (In <u>World Drama</u>, Vol. 2)
    The Countess of Escarbagnas
        (In his <u>Works,</u> Vol. 6)
    The Doctor in Spite of Himself, translated and adapted by Lady
        Gregory
        (In <u>Complete Plays of Lady Gregory,</u> Vol. 4)
    **Dr. Last in His Chariot (see Bickerstaff, Isaac)
    Doctor's Delight, adapted by Sir Barry Jackson
        (In <u>Plays of the Year</u>, Vol. 5, 1950/51)
    Don Garcia of Navarre; or, The Jealous Prince
        (In his <u>Works,</u> Vol. 5)
    **Don Juan (see Brecht, Bertolt)
    Don John; or, The Libertine
        (In <u>The Theatre of Don Juan</u>)
        (In his <u>Works,</u> Vol. 6)
    Ensayando a Molière (see Magana, Sergio)
    **The False Count; or, A New Way to Play an Old Game (see
        Behn, Mrs. Aphra)
    The Flying Doctor (Le Médecin Volant)
        (In <u>One-Act Comedies of Molière</u>)
    The Forced Marriage (Le Mariage Forcé)
        (In <u>One-Act Comedies of Molière</u>)

**Psyche; adaptation from Molière and Corneille (see Shadwell,
    Thomas)
  The Rehearsal at Versailles (L'Impromptu de Versailles)
      (In One-Act Comedies of Molière)
  The Rogueries of Scapin, after Molière by Lady Gregory
      (In Complete Plays of Lady Gregory, Vol. 4)
**The School for Guardians (see Murphy, Arthur)
  The School for Husbands (L'Ecole des Maris)
      (In The Drama, Vol. 7)
      (In his Works, Vol. 2)
  The School for Wives, adapted by Miles Malleson
      (In Plays of the Year, Vol. 10, 1953/54)
  A School for Women (L'Ecole des Femmes)
      (In his Works, Vol. 2)
  The School for Women Criticised (La Critique de l'Ecole des
    Femmes)
      (In his Works, Vol. 2)
  The Seductive Countess (La Comtesse d'Escarbagnas)
      (In One-Act Comedies of Molière)
  Sganarelle; or, The Imaginary Cuckold (Sganarelle; ou, Le Cocu
    Imaginaire)
      (In One-Act Comedies of Molière)
  The Sicilian; or, Love Makes a Painter (Le Sicilien; ou, L'Amour
    Peintre)
      (In his Works, Vol. 3)
  Sir Martin-Mar-all (L'Estourdi)
      (In his Works, Vol. 1)
**Sir Martin Mar-all; or, The Feign'd Innocence (see Dryden, John)
**Sir Patient Fancy (see Behn, Mrs. Aphra)
  Tartuffe; adapted by Miles Malleson
      (In Plays of the Year, Vol. 3, 1949-50)
  Tartuffe; or, The Hypocrite (Tartuffe; ou, L'Imposteur)
      (In his Works, Vol. 4)
  Two Precious Maidens Ridiculed (Les Précieuses Ridicules)
      (In One-Act Comedies of Molière)
  The Would-Be Gentleman
      (In Themes of Drama)
  The Would-Be Gentleman, translated and adapted by Lady Gregory
      (In Complete Plays of Lady Gregory, Vol. 4)
Molina, Tirso de, pseud. (see Tellez, Gabriel)
MOLLOY, Michael Joseph, 1917-
  The King of Friday's Men
      (In Plays of the Year, Vol. 2, 1949)
  The Visiting House
      (In 7 Irish Plays)
Molly's Dream (see Fornes, Maria I.)
MOLNAR, Ferenc, 1878-1952
  Actor from Vienna
      (In his Romantic Comedies)
  Anniversary Dinner
      (In his Romantic Comedies)
  Arthur
      (In his Romantic Comedies)

Blue Danube
   (In his <u>Romantic Comedies</u>)
Carnival
   (In his <u>Plays</u>)
**Carousel (see Rodgers, Richard)
The Devil
   (In his <u>Plays</u>)
Fashions for Men
   (In his <u>Plays</u>)
Game of Hearts
   (In his <u>Romantic Comedies</u>)
The Glass Slipper; acting version by Philip Moeller
   (In his <u>Plays</u>)
The Good Fairy
   (In his <u>Romantic Comedies</u>)
The Guardsman; acting version by Philip Moeller
   (In his <u>Plays</u>)
Heavenly and Earthly Love; adapted by Edna St. Vincent Millay
   (In his <u>Plays</u>)
The Host
   (In <u>One-Act Plays for Stage and Study</u>, 2nd Series)
The Lawyer
   (In his <u>Plays</u>)
Liliom
   (In <u>Dramas of Modernism</u>)
   (In his <u>Plays</u>)
Marshal
   (In his <u>Plays</u>)
Mima; adapted from "The Red Mill, " by David Belasco
   (In his <u>Plays</u>)
Olympia; adapted by Sidney Howard
   (In his <u>Plays</u>)
The Play's the Thing
   (In <u>Masterpieces of the Modern Central European Theatre</u>)
The Play's the Thing; adapted by P. G. Wodehouse
   (In his <u>Plays</u>)
President
   (In his <u>Romantic Comedies</u>)
A Prologue to "King Lear"
   (In his <u>Plays</u>)
Riviera
   (In his <u>Plays</u>)
Still Life
   (In his <u>Plays</u>)
The Swan
   (In his <u>Plays</u>)
   (In <u>20th Century Plays</u>)
The Tale of the Wolf
   (In his <u>Plays</u>)
The Violet
   (In his <u>Plays</u>)
Waxworks
   (In his <u>Romantic Comedies</u>)

The White Cloud
    (In his <u>Plays</u>)
The Witch
    (In his <u>Plays</u>)
The Moment Next to Nothing (see Clarke, Austin)
A Moment of Existence (see Malcolm, Ian)
The Moment of Truth (see Ustinov, Peter)
El Momento de Tu Vida (see Saroyan, William)
Les Momes (see Hugo, Victor)
Momma As She Became-But Not As She Was (see Rechy, John)
Mon Isménie (see Labiche, Eugene)
MONCADA, Santiago
    Juegos de Medianoche
        (In <u>Teatro Español</u>, 1970-71)
MONCRIEFF, William Thomas, 1794-1857
    The Bashful Man
        (In <u>The London Stage,</u> Vol. 4)
    Giovanni in London; or, The Libertine Reclaimed
        (In <u>The London Stage,</u> Vol. 4)
        (In <u>The Theatre of Don Juan</u>)
    Monsieur Tonson
        (In <u>The London Stage</u>, Vol. 3)
Las Monedas de Heliogabalo (see Suarez, Marcial)
Money (see Lytton, Edward G.)
Money Makes the World Go Round (see Marivaux, Pierre C.)
The Money Tower; scenario (see Living Theatre Collective)
MONICELLI, Mario, 1915-
    I Compagni ("The Organizer")
        (In <u>Dal Soggetto al Film</u> Series, no. 30, 1963)
    La Grande Guerra
        (In <u>Dal Soggetto al Film</u> Series, no. 12, 1959)
    Renzo e Luciana
        (In <u>Dal Soggetto al Film</u> Series, no. 22, 1962)
The Monkeys in the Organ Grinder (see Bernard, Kenneth)
MONKHOUSE, Allan Noble, 1858-1936
    The Wily One
        (In <u>One-Act Plays for Stage and Study</u>, 4th Series)
Monna Vanna (see Maeterlinck, Maurice)
Monologues from Division Street (see Terkel, Louis "Studs,")
MONROE, Robert Allan
    And The Gods Play
        (In <u>100 Non-Royalty Radio Plays</u>)
    Henry Hudson, a historical drama
        (In <u>100 Non-Royalty Radio Plays</u>)
Monsieur Alphonse (see Dumas, Alexandre, Fils)
Monsieur Amilcar (see Jamiaque, Yves)
Monsieur Badin (see Moinaux, Georges)
Monsieur Barnett (see Anouilh, Jean)
Monsieur Chasse (see Feydeau, Georges)
Monsieur de Pourceaugnac; or, Squire Trelooby (see Molière, Jean
    Baptiste)
Monsieur D'Olive (see Chapman, George)
Monsieur le Modere (see Adamov, Arthur)

Monsieur Prudhomme a-t-il Vecu? (see Guitry, Sacha)
Un Monsieur Qui a Brulé une Dame (see Labiche, Eugene)
Un Monsieur Qui Prend la Mouche (see Labiche, Eugene)
Monsieur Teste (see Valery, Paul)
Monsieur Thomas (see Beaumont, Francis)
Monsieur Tonson (see Moncrieff, William T.)
Monsieur Vernet (see Renard, Jules)
MONSON, William N.
  The Nihilist
    (In Playwrights for Tomorrow, Vol. 8)
La Monstruese Parade; screenplay (see Browning, Tod. Freaks)
MONTCHRETIEN, Antoine de, c. 1575-1621
  Hector; text in French
    (In Théâtre du XVIIe Siècle, Vol. 1)
MONTE, Eric
  Getting Up the Rent; television script for an episode in "Good
    Times"
    (In Samuel French's Tandem Library Series)
  Michael Gets Suspended; television script for an episode in "Good
    Times"
    (In Samuel French's Tandem Library Series)
Monte Cristo (see Fechter, Charles A.)
MONTEIRO, José Maria
  Uma Girafinha das Arabias
    (In Revista de Teatro, no. 393, May/June 1973)
MONTERDE, Francisco, 1894-
  Proteo
    (In Teatro Méxicano del Siglo XX, Vol. 2)
Montespan, Françoise Athenais (de Rockechouart) de Pardaillan de
  Gondrin, Marquise de, 1641-1707
  *The Montespan (see Rolland, Romain)
MONTEVERDI, Claudio, 1567-1643
  L'Orfeo; musica di Claudio Monteverdi, libretto d'Allesandro
    Stiggio
    (In L'Avant-Scène Opéra, no. 5, Sept./Oct. 1976)
Montezuma II, Emperor of México, 1466-1520
  The Indian Emperour; or, The Conquest of Mexico by the Span-
    iards (see Dryden, John)
MONTGOMERY, Robert, 1946-
  Subject to Fits
    (In Best American Plays, 7th Series, 1967-1973)
A Month in the Country (see Turgenev, Ivan S.)
MONTHERLANT, Henry de, 1896-1972
  Brocèliande; text in French
    (In his Théâtre)
  Le Cardinal d'Espagne
    (In his Théâtre)
  Celles Qu'on Prend dans ses Bras; ou, Les Chevaux de Bois
    (In his Théâtre)
  Demain il Fera Jour
    (In his Théâtre)
  Don Juan; Act II
    (In The Theatre of Don Juan)

L'Embroc
  (In his Théâtre)
L'Exil
  (In his Théâtre)
Fils de Personne; ou, Plus Que le Sang
  (In his Théâtre)
La Guerre Civile
  (In his Théâtre)
Un Incompris
  (In his Théâtre)
Le Maître de Santiago
  (In his Théâtre)
Malatesta; text in French
  (In his Théâtre)
Le Mort Qui Fait le Trottoir
  (In his Théâtre)
Pasipháe; text in French
  (In his Théâtre)
Port-Royal; text in French
  (In Port-Royal)
  (In his Théâtre)
Queen After Death
  (In Masterpieces of the Modern French Theatre)
La Reine Morte
  (In The French Theater Since 1930)
  (In his Théâtre)
La Ville Dont le Prince est un Enfant
  (In his Théâtre)
Montserrat (see Hellman, Lillian)
Mood Indigo (see Vian, Boris)
MOODY, William Vaughan, 1869-1910
    The Faith Healer
      (In Representative American Plays, 1792-1949)
    The Great Divide
      (In Dramas from the American Theatre, 1762-1909)
Moon (see Heide, Robert)
The Moon in the Yellow River (see Johnston, Denis)
The Moon of the Caribees (see O'Neill, Eugene)
Moon Watch; radio script (see Frank, Bruno)
Moonshine (see Hopkins, Arthur M.)
MOORE, Edward, 1712-1757
    The Foundling
      (In The London Stage, Vol. 3)
    The Gamester
      (In 18th Century Tragedy)
      (In The London Stage, Vol. 1)
MOORE, Elvie A., 1942-
    Angela Is Happening
      (In The Disinherited: Plays)
MOORE, Eugene W.
    Back to 1960!
      (In 100 Non-Royalty Radio Plays)

Unidentified
    (In <u>100 Non-Royalty Radio Plays</u>)
MOORE, George, 1852-1933
    The Bending of the Bough
    (In <u>Irish Drama Series</u>, Vol. 3)
MOORE, Mavor
    The Argument
    (In <u>Performing Arts in Canada</u>, Vol. 10, no. 4, Winter 1973)
    Inside Out
    (In <u>A Collection of Canadian Plays</u>, Vol. 2)
    The Pile
    (In <u>A Collection of Canadian Plays</u>, Vol. 2)
    The Roncarelli Affair, based on a story by F. R. Scott
    (In <u>The Play's the Thing</u>)
    The Store
    (In <u>A Collection of Canadian Plays</u>, Vol. 2)
MORATIN, Leandro Fernandes de, 1760-1828
    La Comedia Nueva
    (In <u>Clásicos Castellanos</u>, Vol. 58)
    El Si de las Niñas
    (In <u>Clásicos Castellanos</u>, Vol. 58)
Mord in der Mohrengasse (see Horvath, Odön von)
La Mordaza (see Sastre, Alfonso)
More, Sir Thomas, 1478-1535
    *The Life and Death of Thomas, Lord Cromwell (Anon.)
    (In <u>Disputed Plays of William Shakespeare</u>)
    *A Man for All Seasons (see Bolt, Robert)
Le More de Venise (see Vigny, Alfred V.)
More Dissemblers Besides Women (see Middleton, Thomas)
MORENO, Luis
    Los Sueños Encendidos
    (In <u>Teatro Méxicano</u>, 1958)
MORGAN, Albert E.
    This Obscene Pomp
    (In <u>100 Non-Royalty Radio Plays</u>)
    Unfinished Symphony
    (In <u>100 Non-Royalty Radio Plays</u>)
MORLEY, Christopher Darlington, 1890-1957
    Bedroom Suite
    (In his <u>One Act Plays</u>)
    East of Eden
    (In his <u>One Act Plays</u>)
    Good Theatre
    (In <u>More One-Act Plays by Modern Authors</u>)
    On the Shelf
    (In his <u>One Act Plays</u>)
    Rehearsal
    (In his <u>One Act Plays</u>)
    Thursday Evening
    (In his <u>One Act Plays</u>)
    Walt
    (In his <u>One Act Plays</u>)
Morning (see Horovitz, Israel)

A Morning with Don Juan (see Musset, Alfred de)
MORRIS, Andres, 1928-
    Oficio de Hombres
        (In Teatro Contemporaneo Hispanoamericano, Vol. 1)
MORRIS, Thomas Badden
    Cats of Egypt
        (In Best One-Act Plays of 1938, London)
    Progress to Fotheringay
        (In Best One-Act Plays of 1941, London)
    Wild for to Hold
        (In Best One-Act Plays of 1939, London)
MORRIS, William, 1834-1896
    Love Is Enough; or, The Freeing of Pharamond
        (In his Collected Works, Vol. 9)
MORRISON, Anne
    Their First Anniversary
        (In One-Act Plays for Stage and Study, 8th Series)
MORRISON, Bill, 1940-
    Sam Slade Is Missing
        (In The Best Short Plays 1973)
La Morsa (see Pirandello, Luigi)
MORSELLI, Ercole Luigi, 1882-1921
    Gastone, the Animal Tamer
        (In Plays of the Italian Theatre)
    Water upon Fire
        (In Plays of the Italian Theatre)
La Mort de Sénèque (The Death of Seneca) (see Tristan L'Hermite,
    François)
La Mort Qui Fait le Trottoit (see Montherlant, Henry de)
La Morte de Pompée (The Death of Pompey) (see Corneille, Pierre)
La Morte de Tintagiles (see Maeterlinck, Maurice)
A Morte do Imortal (see Muniz, Lauro C.)
Mortgaged (see Richardson, Willis)
MORTIMER, John Clifford, 1923-
    Bermondsey
        (In Best Short Plays of the World Theatre, 1968-1973)
    Call Me a Liar; a play for television
        (In Lunch Hour and Other Plays)
    Collect Your Hand Baggage
        (In his Five Plays)
        (In Lunch Hour and Other Plays)
    David and Broccoli; a play for television
        (In Lunch Hour and Other Plays)
    The Dock Brief
        (In his Five Plays)
        (In Plays of the Year, Vol. 17, 1957/58)
        (In his Three Plays, 1962)
    I Spy
        (In his Five Plays)
        (In his Three Plays)
    The Judge
        (In Methuen's Modern Plays Series, 1967)

Lunch Hour
    (In The Best One-Act Plays of 1958-59, London)
    (In his Five Plays)
    (In Lunch Hour and Other Plays)
Two Stars for Comfort
    (In Methuen's Modern Plays Series, 1962)
What Shall We Tell Caroline?
    (In his Five Plays)
    (In Plays of the Year, Vol. 17, 1957/58)
    (In his Three Plays, 1962)
MORTON, John Maddison, 1811-1891
  Box and Cox
    (In English Plays of the 19th Century, Vol. IV: Farces)
MORUM, William
  The Late Edwina Black (see Dinner, William)
Moscow Is Burning (see Maiakovskii, Vladimir V.)
MOSEL, Tad
  That's Where the Town's Going! television script, CBS, Apr. 14,
  1962
    (In Electronic Drama)
MOSELEY, Katharine Prescott
  Daggers and Diamonds
    (In Types of Modern Dramatic Composition)
Moses, 14th-15th Century B.C.
  *The Procession of the Prophets
    (In Medieval Church Music-Dramas)
Moses Was an Oyster Man (see Ruthenburg, Grace D.)
MOSS, Howard
  No Strings Attached
    (In New Directions, Vol. 8, 1944)
MOSS, Winston
  A House Is Not a Poolroom; television script for an episode in
  "Sanford and Son"
    (In Samuel French's Tandem Library Series)
Un Mot pour un Autre (see Tardieu, Jean)
Motel; radio script (see Fields, W.C.)
Motel: A Masque for Three Dolls (see Van Itallie, Jean-Claude)
Motel from American Hurrah (see Van Itallie, Jean-Claude)
The Moth and the Flame (see Fitch, Clyde)
The Mother (see Brecht, Bertolt)
The Mother (see Chayefsky, Paddy)
Mother; screenplay (see Pudovkin, Vsevolod I.)
The Mother (see Witkiewicz, Stanislaw I.)
Mother and Child (see Hughes, Langston)
Mother and Son (see Halpern, Joseph)
The Mother and the Father (see Howells, William Dean)
Mother Courage (see Brecht, Bertolt)
Mother Courage and Her Children (see Brecht, Bertolt)
The Motor Show (see Ionesco, Eugene)
MOTTEUX, Peter Anthony, 1663-1718
  **The Lying Valet (see Garrick, David)
Mount Vernon Interlude (see Meyer, Lewis)
Mourning Becomes Electra (see O'Neill, Eugene)

The Mourning Bride (see Congreve, William)
The Mouse Trap (see Howells, William Dean)
Move! (see Nicholls, Bronwen)
The Movie Man (see O'Neill, Eugene)
The Moving; a minstrel show (Anon.)
    (In Dramas from the American Theatre, 1762-1909)
MOWAT, David, 1944-
    Anna-Luse
      (In Calder & Boyars Playscript Series, no. 27)
    Jens
      (In Calder & Boyars Playscript Series, no. 27)
    Purity
      (In Calder & Boyars Playscript Series, no. 27)
MOWATT, Anna Cora (Ritchie), 1819-1870
    Fashion; or, Life in New York
      (In Dramas from the American Theatre, 1762-1909)
      (In Representative American Plays, 1792-1949)
      (In Representative Plays by American Dramatists, Vol. 2)
MOZART, Johan Chrysostom Wolfgang Amadeus, 1756-1791
    La Flute Enchantée
      (In L'Avant-Scène Opéra, no. 1, Jan./Feb. 1976)
   *Mozart and Salieri (see Pushkin, Aleksandr S.)
Mozartement Votre (see Westphal, Eric)
MROZEK, Slawomir, 1930-
    Un Caso Fortunato
      (In Sipario, no. 315-316, Aug./Sept. 1972)
    Charlie
      (In his Six Plays)
    Enchanted Night
      (In his Six Plays)
    The Martyrdom of Peter Chey
      (In his Six Plays)
    Out at Sea
      (In his Three Plays)
    The Party
      (In his Six Plays)
    The Police
      (In his Six Plays)
    The Professor
      (In Twentieth-Century Polish Avant-Garde Drama)
    The Prophets
      (In his Three Plays, 1973)
    Repeat Performance
      (In his Three Plays, 1973)
    Striptease
      (In his Three Plays, 1973)
    Tango
      (In Evergreen Playscript Series, 1968)
    Vatzlav; a play in 77 scenes
      (In Evergreen Playscript Series, 1970)
Mu Yang Chuan (The Shepherd's Pen)
    (In Famous Chinese Plays)

Mucedorus 380

Mucedorus (Anon.)
(In <u>Disputed Plays of William Shakespeare</u>)
La Muchacha del Sombrerito Rosa (see Ruiz Iriarte, Victor)
Una Muchachita de Valladolid (see Calvo Sotelo, Joaquin)
MÜHL, Karl Otto
Rheinpromenade
.. (In <u>Theater: Chronik und Bilanz des Bühenjahres,</u> 1973)
MÜLLER, Armin
Der Goldene Vogel
(In <u>Theater der Zeit,</u> no. 6, 1975)
Sieben Wünsche
.. (In <u>Theater der Zeit,</u> no. 3, Feb. 1974)
MÜLLER, Heiner
Amleto Principe di Danimarca (see Brecht, Bertolt)
Germania Tod in Berlin
(In <u>Theater: Chronik und Bilanz des Bühenjahres,</u> 1977)
Die Hamletmaschine
(In <u>Theater Heute,</u> no. 12, Dec. 1977)
Die Schlacht
(In <u>Theater: Chronik und Bilanz des Bühenjahres,</u> 1975)
Traktor
(In <u>Theater der Zeit,</u> no. 8, 1975)
Zement
(In <u>Theater der Zeit,</u> no. 6, 1974)
(In <u>Theater Heute,</u> no. 10, Oct. 1975)
Münchhausen (see Kästner, Erich)
MUNTZER, Thomas, 1489?-1525
*Thomas Müntzer (see Pfeiffer, Hans)
La Muerte de Atahualpa (see Roca Tey, Bernardo)
La Muerte de un Viajante (see Miller, Arthur)
La Muerte No Entrara en Palacio (see Marques, Rene)
Muhammad, the Prophet, 570-632 A.D.
*The Death of Mohammed (see Hakim, Tawfiq Al)
*Le Fanatisme ou Mahomet le Prophete (see Voltaire)
La Mujer del Hombre (see Moberg, Vilhelm)
La Mujer del Tambor (see Tanaka, M. Magdalena)
La Mujer No Hace Milagros (see Usigli, Rudolfo)
The Mulberry Garden (see Sedley, Sir Thomas)
The Mulligan Guard Ball (see Harrigan, Edward)
Mumbling Radio Talk--Catalina; radio script (see Fields, W.C.)
The Mummer's Play (see White, Edgar)
Un Mundo Para Mi (see Sada, Concepcion)
The Mundy Scheme (see Friel, Brian)
MUNFORD, Colonel Robert, c. 1730-1784
The Candidates; or, The Humours of a Virginia Election
(In <u>Dramas from the American Theatre,</u> 1762-1909)
MUNIZ, Lauro Cesar, 1938-
A Morte do Imortal
(In <u>Revista de Teatro,</u> no. 391, Jan. /Feb. 1973)
MUNK, Kaj Harald Leininger, 1898-1944
Before Cannae
(In <u>Anthology of Danish Literature</u>)

(In his Five Plays)
Cant: A Play of Henry VIII and Anne Boleyn
    (In his Five Plays)
Egelykke
    (In Modern Scandinavian Plays)
He Sits at the Melting Pot
    (In his Five Plays)
Herod the King
    (In his Five Plays)
Niels Ebbesen
    (In Scandinavian Plays of the 20th Century, Series 2)
La Palabra
    (In Teatro Danes Contemporaneo)
The Word
    (In his Five Plays)
Muñoz, Visitador de México (see Rodriguez Galvan, Ignacio)
MUNRO, Alice
    How I Met My Husband
        (In The Play's the Thing)
MUNRO, Hector Hugh, 1870-1916
    The Miracle Merchant, by "Saki," pseud.
        (In One-Act Plays for Stage and Study, 8th Series)
La Muralla (see Calvo Sotelo, Joaquin)
Murder Among the Psychologists (see Cantor, Eli)
Murder in Baghdad (Ma'sat al-Hallaj) (see 'Abd Al-Sabur, Salah)
Murder in Frankfurt; German and English texts (see Hädrich, Rolf)
Murder in the Snow (see Finch, Robert V.)
Murder Mistaken (see Green, Janet)
Murder! Murder! Murder! (see Hughes, Mrs. Babbette)
Murdered; a minstrel show (Anon.)
        (In Dramas from the American Theatre, 1762-1909)
Murderer Hope of Womankind (see Kokoschka, Oscar)
MURDOCH, Frank, 1843-1872
    Davy Crockett; or, Be Sure You're Right, Then Go Ahead
        (In Favorite American Plays of the 19th Century)
Murieta, Joaquin (see Murrieta, Joaquin)
Murio Hace Quince Años (see Gimenez-Arnau, José)
MURNAU, Friedrich Wilhelm, 1889-1931
    L'Aurore; titre original "Sunrise," le script; Fox film, 1927,
        d'après le roman "Le Voyage a Tilsitt," d'Hermann Sudermann
        (In L'Avant-Scène du Cinéma, no. 148, June 1974)
    Le Dernier des Hommes; filmscript (see Mayer, Carl)
    Faust; filmscript (see Rohmer, Eric)
    Tartuffe; filmscript (see Mayer, Carl)
    Nosferatu; a symphony of horror based on the novel "Dracula"
        by Bram Stoker and freely adapted by Henrik Galeen; directed
        by F.W. Murnau
        (In Masterworks of the German Cinema)
        (In Murnau)
Muro de Arrimo (see Telles, Carlos Q.)
MURPHY, Arthur, 1727-1805
    All in the Wrong, based on Molière's "Sganarelle; ou, Le Cocu
    Imaginaire"

(In his Works, Vol. 3)
Alyuma
    (In his Works, Vol. 1)
The Apprentice
    (In A Collection of the Most Esteemed Farces ..., Vol. 1)
    (In The London Stage, Vol. 4)
    (In his Works, Vol. 2)
The Citizen
    (In A Collection of the Most Esteemed Farces ..., Vol. 3)
    (In The London Stage, Vol. 1)
    (In his Works, Vol. 2)
The Desert Island; founded on the Isola Disabitata of the cele-
brated Abbe Metastasio
    (In A Collection of the Most Esteemed Farces ..., Vol. 5)
    (In his Works, Vol. 3)
The Grecian Daughter
    (In The London Stage, Vol. 3)
    (In his Works, Vol. 1)
Know Your Own Mind, founded on the "Irresolu" of Destouches
    (In his Works, Vol. 4)
News from Parnassus
    (In his Works, Vol. 4)
No One's Enemy but His Own, based on Voltaire's "L'Indiscret"
    (In his Works, Vol. 2)
The Old Maid; adapted from Fagan's "L'Etourderie"
    (In A Collection of the Most Esteemed Farces ..., Vol. 2)
    (In his Works, Vol. 2)
The Orphan of China, based on the Chinese tragedy in Du Halde's
Zenobia, from Crebillon's "Rhadamisthe et Zenobie" and Vol-
taire's "Orphelin de la Chine"
    (In The London Stage, Vol. 2)
    (In his Works, Vol. 1)
The School for Guardians, based on Molière's "L'Ecole des Femmes"
later turned into an opera "Love Finds the Way"
    (In his Works, Vol. 4)
Three Weeks After Marriage; or, What We Must All Come To
    (In A Collection of the Most Esteemed Farces ..., Vol. 4)
    (In The London Stage, Vol. 1)
    (In his Works, Vol. 2)
The Upholsterer; or, What News? Avowedly taken from the
"Tatler" nos. 155 & 160 by Addison & Steele, but owing more
to Fielding's "Coffee-House Politician"
    (In A Collection of the Most Esteemed Farces ..., Vol. 1)
    (In 18th Century Drama: Afterpieces)
    (In his Works, Vol. 2)
The Way to Keep Him, based in part on De Moissey's "Nouvelle
Ecole des Femmes"
    (In 18th Century Drama: Afterpieces)
    (In The London Stage, Vol. 1)
    (In his Works, Vol. 3)
MURPHY, J. B.
If I May So Speak; a burlesque stump oration, a minstrel show
    (In Dramas from the American Theatre, 1762-1909)

MURRAY, Anne
    Zee-Zee
        (In Prize Plays of 1927-28, Vol. 1)
MURRAY, Thomas Cornelius, 1873-1959
    The Pipe in the Fields
        (In One-Act Plays for Stage and Study, 4th Series)
MURRAY, William Henry, 1790-1852
    Diamond Cut Diamond
        (In English Plays of the 19th Century, Vol. IV: Farces)
Murrieta, Joaquin, 1828/9-1853
    *Radiance and Death of Joaquin Murieta (see Neruda, Pablo)
MUSCHG, Adolf
    Kellers Abend
        (In Theater Heute, no. 6, June 1975)
The Muses' Looking-Glass (see Randolph, Thomas)
MUSHAKOJI, Saneatsu, 1885-
    The Passion
        (In The Passion)
Music Night (see Priestley, John B.)
The Music-Cure: A Piece of Utter Nonsense (see Shaw, George
    Bernard)
La Musica (see Duras, Marguerite)
The Musical Box (see Kaiser, Georg)
The Musical Lady (see Colman, George)
MUSSET, Alfred de, 1810-1857
    Andre del Sarto
        (In his Complete Writings, Vol. 3)
    Andre del Sarto; text in French
        (In his Théâtre Complet)
    L'Ane et le Ruisseau
        (In his Théâtre Complet)
    Barberine
        (In his Complete Writings, Vol. 3)
    Barberine; text in French
        (In his Théâtre Complet)
    Bettine
        (In his Complete Writings, Vol. 5)
    Bettine; text in French
        (In his Théâtre Complet)
    A Caprice
        (In his Complete Writings, Vol. 5)
    Un Caprice; text in French
        (In his Théâtre Complet)
    Les Caprices de Marianne
        (In his Théâtre Complet)
    Carmosine
        (In his Complete Writings, Vol. 5)
    Carmosine; text in French
        (In his Théâtre Complet)
    The Chandelier
        (In The Drama, Vol. 9)
    Le Chandelier; text in French
        (In his Théâtre Complet)

The Chandler
   (In his <u>Complete Writings</u>, Vol. 4)
Chestnuts from the Fire
   (In his <u>Complete Writings</u>, Vol. 1)
Une Comédie sous le Règne de Louis XV
   (In his <u>Théâtre Complet</u>)
The Cup and the Lip
   (In his <u>Complete Writings,</u> Vol. 1)
Les Deux Magnétismes
   (In his <u>Théâtre Complet</u>)
The Donkey and the Stream
   (In his <u>Complete Writings</u>, Vol. 10)
A Door Must Be Either Open or Shut
   (In his <u>Complete Writings</u>, Vol. 5)
Faire sans Dire
   (In his <u>Théâtre Complet</u>)
Fantasio
   (In his <u>Complete Writings</u>, Vol. 3)
Fantasio; text in French
   (In his <u>Théâtre Complet</u>)
Faustine
   (In his <u>Complete Writings</u>, Vol. 10)
Faustine; text in French
   (In his <u>Théâtre Complet</u>)
Il Faut Qu'une Porte Soit Ouverte ou Fermée
   (In his <u>Théâtre Complet</u>)
The Follies of Marianne
   (In his <u>Complete Writings</u>, Vol. 3)
L'Habit Vert
   (In his <u>Théâtre Complet</u>)
Il Ne Faut Jurer de Rien
   (In his <u>Théâtre Complet</u>)
Judith et Allori
   (In his <u>Théâtre Complet</u>)
Lorenzaccio
   (In his <u>Complete Writings</u>, Vol. 4)
Lorenzaccio; étude de Robert Abirached, spectacle de Guy Rétoré,
   musique Andre Chamoux
   (In <u>L'Avant-Scène Théâtre</u>, no. 603, Feb. 1, 1977)
Lorenzaccio; text in French
   (In his <u>Théâtre Complet</u>)
Louison
   (In his <u>Complete Writings</u>, Vol. 5)
Louison; text in French
   (In his <u>Théâtre Complet</u>)
La Matinée de Don Juan
   (In his <u>Théâtre Complet</u>)
A Morning with Don Juan
   (In his <u>Complete Writings</u>, Vol. 10)
No Trifling with Love
   (In his <u>Complete Writings</u>, Vol. 3)
La Nuit Vénitienne; ou, Les Noces de Laurette
   (In his <u>Théâtre Complet</u>)

The Nabob (see Foote, Samuel)
NABOKOV, Vladimir Vladimirovich, 1899-
    Lolita: a screenplay; based on the author's novel, but not the
    screenplay produced as the motion picture
        (A McGraw-Hill Screenplay, 1974)
    The Waltz Invention (Izobretenie Val'sa)
        (A Phaedra Playscript, 1966)
Nacht mit Kompromissen (see Kerndl, Rainer)
Die Nacht Nach der Abschlussfeier (see Tendrjakow, Wladimir F.)
Nachwort (see Kaiser, Georg)
Nagananda (see Harsha)
Naives Hirondelles (see Dubillard, Roland)
NAJAC, Emile de, 1828-1889
    Let's Get a Divorce! (see Sardou, Victorien)
Nakamitsu (see Seami Motokiyo)
The Naked King (see Shvarts, Evgenii L.)
NALE ROXLO, Conrado, 1898-
    La Cola de la Sirena
        (In Teatro Argentino Contemporaneo)
NAMBOKU, Tsuruya IV
    The Scarlet Princess of Edo, by Tsuruya Namboku IV, Sajurada
    Jisuke II, and Tsuuchi Genshichi
        (In Kabuki: Five Classic Plays)
Nancy Clare (see Johnson, Douglas)
Nanine; ou, Le Préjugé Vaincu (see Voltaire)
NANUS, Susan
    The Autumn Ladies and Their Lovers' Lovers
        (In The Yale Literary Magazine, Vol. 142 no. 5, Oct. 1973)
Napoleon I (Napoleon Bonaparte). Emperor of the French, 1769-1821
    *Bonaparte (see Unruh, Fritz von)
    *La Foire d'Empoigne (see Anouilh, Jean)
    *St. Helena (see Sherriff, Robert C.)
Napoleon III (Charles Louis Napoleon Bonaparte), 1808-1873
    *Corona de Sombra; pieza antihistórica (see Usigli, Rudolfo)
    *Napoleon in New Orleans; text in German (see Kaiser, Georg)
    *Napoléon III a la Barre de l'Histoire (see Castelot, Andre)
Napoleon Crossing the Rockies (see MacKaye, Percy)
Napoleon's Piano; Goon Show Script no. 129 (see Milligan, Spike)
NARANJO, Carmen
    La Voz
        (In Obras Breves del Teatro Costarricense, Vol. 2)
Narcissus (see Lourson, Laurent)
The Narcissus Cantata (see Valéry, Paul)
Das Narrenschneiden (see Sachs, Hans)
Narrow Road to the Deep North (see Bond, Edward)
NASH, N. Richard, 1913-
    The Rainmaker; play and screenplay by N. Richard Nash; film
    directed by Joseph Anthony; film edition of the play
        (A Bantam Books Play, 1957)
NASH, Ogden, 1902-
    One Touch of Venus (see Weill, Kurt)
Nashville; screenplay (see Tewkesbury, Joan)
Nat Turner (see Edmonds, Randolph)

Nathan and Tabileth (see Bermange, Barry)
Nathan Hale (see Fitch, Clyde)
Nathan Le Sage (see Chénier, Marie-Joseph B.)
The National Health (see Nichols, Peter)
Native Dancer; television script (see Shaw, David)
Native Son (see Wright, Richard)
The Nativity (see Hyde, Douglas)
Natural Man (see Browne, Theodore)
Les Naturels du Bordelais (see Audiberti, Jacques)
Le Naufrage (see Dubé, Marcel)
Le Naufrage au Port-a-l'Anglais ou les Nouvelles Dabaraquées (see
    Arteau, Jacques)
Naval Encounter (see Goering, Reinhard)
La Navette (see Becque, Henri)
The Navigator (see Keaton, Buster)
Nazarin; screenplay (see Buñuel, Luis)
Il Ne Faut Jurer de Rien (see Musset, Alfred de)
Near Closing Time (see Finch, Robert V.)
Nebeinander (see Kaiser, Georg)
The Necessary Evil (see Kennedy, Charles R.)
Neck of Nothing: The Narrow Escape (see Garrick, David)
The Necklace; a Hindoo drama (Anon.)
        (In The Drama, Vol. 3)
The Necromancer (Il Negromante) (see Ariosto, Lodovico)
The Need for Polygamy (see Sampaio, Silveira)
The Need to Be (see Yeoh, Patrick)
Los Negocios Registrados (see Vulgarin M., Agustin)
Der Neidhart mit dem Feiel (see Sachs, Hans)
Neighbours (see Saunders, James)
NEIMAN, Irving Gaynor
    Button Your Lip
        (In The Army Play by Play)
Nekrassov (see Sartre, Jean-Paul)
Nel Nome del Padre (see Bellocchio, Marco)
NELSON, Ralph
    Mail Call
        (In The Army Play by Play)
Nepal (see Widmer, Urs)
Nero Claudius Caesar Drusus Germanicus, 37-68 A.D.
    *La Mort de Seneque (The Death of Seneca) (see Tristan L'Her-
        mite, François)
    *Satyricon (see Foster, Paul)
    *The Tragedy of Nero, Emperour of Rome (see Lee, Nathaniel)
NERON, Claude
    **Vincent, François, Paul et les Autres ... (see Sautet, Claude)
Neron-Paso (see Paso, Alfonso)
NERUDA, Pablo
    Radiance and Death of Joaquin Murieta
        (In Modern International Drama, Vol. 10, no. 1, 1976)
The Nerve of It! (see Kirkpatrick, John)
Nesbit, Edith (see Bland, Mrs. Edith Nesbit)
Das Nest (see Kroetz, Franz X.)
Neue Götter-Gespräche (see Wieland, Christoph M.)

Neuer Lübecker Totentanz (see Jahnn, Hans H.)
Die Neuvermahlten (see Bjørnson, Bjørnstjerne)
NEVEUX, Georges, 1900-
    Plainte Contre Inconnu
        (In Le Théâtre d'Aujourd'hui)
    Robert Macaire; d'après la pièce de Saint-Amand, Antier et
    Frederic Lemaître
        (In L'Avant-Scène Théâtre, no. 578, Jan. 1, 1976)
    Zamore
        (In Le Théâtre d'Aujourd'hui)
NEVILLE, Edgar, 1899-
    Alta Fidelidad
        (In Teatro Español, 1957-58)
        (In Teatro Selecto Edgar Neville)
    El Baile
        (In Teatro Español, 1952-53)
        (In Teatro Selecto Edgar Neville)
    Prohibido en Otoño
        (In Teatro Selecto Edgar Neville)
    Rapto
        (In Teatro Selecto Edgar Neville)
    Veinte Anitos
        (In Teatro Selecto Edgar Neville)
    La Vida en un Hilo
        (In Teatro Español, 1958-59)
        (In Teatro Selecto Edgar Neville)
The New Academy; or, The New Exchange (see Brome, Richard)
The New Chautauqua Plays Without Playwright (see Gaines, Frederick)
The New Deliverance (see Witkiewicz, Stanislaw I.)
New-Found Land (see Stoppard, Tom)
New Girl in Town (see Merrill, Bob)
New Horizons; radio script (see Adamson, Hans Christian)
The New Inn; or, The Light Heart (see Jonson, Ben)
New Men and Old Acres (see Taylor, Tom)
The New System (see Bjørnson, Bjørnstjerne)
The New Tenant (see Ionesco, Eugene)
A New Way to Pay Old Debts (see Massinger, Phillip)
The New Window (see Edmonds, Randolph)
The New Wing at Elsinore; a dramatic sequel to Hamlet by "Mr.
    Punch. "
        (In The Drama, Vol. 22)
The New World (see Barrie, James M.)
The New York Idea (see Mitchell, Langdon E.)
Newgate's the Fashion (see Foy, Helen)
The Newly-Married Couple (see Bjørnson, Bjørnstjerne)
NEWMAN, Ellis
    Cask of Amontillado, adapted for radio from the story by Edgar
    Allan Poe
        (In 100 Non-Royalty Radio Plays)
News from Parnassus (see Murphy, Arthur)
News from Plymouth (see D'Avenant, Sir William)
The News Item (see Olmo, Lauro)

Newton, Sir Isaac, 1642-1727
  *"In Good King Charles's Golden Days": a True History That Nev-
    er Happened (see Shaw, George Bernard)
Next Year in Jerusalem (see Osborn, Murray S.)
NGUNJIRI, Julius
  The Return
    (In Zuka, no. 4, Dec. 1969)
Ni Ku Ssu Fan (A Nun Craves Wordly Vanities)
    (In Famous Chinese Plays)
Niagara Falls (see Melfi, Leonard)
NICCODEMI, Dario
  Dawn, Day, Night
    (In Gambit, no. 6)
Nice People (see Crothers, Rachel)
The Nice Valour; or, The Passionate Mad-Man (see Beaumont, Fran-
    cis)
NICHOL, James W.
  The House on Chestnut Street
    (In Performing Arts in Canada, Vol. 10, no. 3, Fall 1973)
NICHOLL, Don
  Archie in the Hospital; television script for an episode in "All
    in the Family"
    (In Samuel French's Tandem Library Series)
NICHOLLS, Bronwen
  Move!
    (In Australian Theatre Workshop, Vol. 8)
NICHOLS, Dudley, 1895-
  Stagecoach; screenplay (see Ford, John)
NICHOLS, Mike, 1931-
  Carnal Knowledge; screenplay (see Feiffer, Jules)
NICHOLS, Peter, 1927-
  The Gorge
    (In The Television Dramatist)
  The National Health
    (In Evergreen Playscript Series, 1975)
NICHOLS, Robert Malise Bowyer, 1893-
  Wings over Europe, by Robert Nichols and Maurice Browne
    (In Dramas of Modernism)
NICHOLSON, Kenyon, 1894-
  Meet the Missus
    (In One-Act Plays for Stage and Study, 2nd Series)
  The Snake Eater
    (In One-Act Plays for Stage and Study, 4th Series)
  Wanderlust
    (In Types of Modern Dramatic Composition)
  Words and Music
    (In One-Act Plays for Stage and Study, 5th Series)
Nick of the Woods (see Hamblin, Louisa Medina)
Nicodemus (see Corrie, Joe)
NICOL, Eric
  The Citizens of Calais
    (In Canadian Theatre Review, Vol. 5, Winter 1975)

NICOL, Eric Patrick, 1919-
   The Fourth Monkey
     (In his Three Plays)
   Like Father, Life Fun
     (In his Three Plays)
   Man from Inner Space
     (In The Play's the Thing)
   Pillar of Sand
     (In his Three Plays)
NICOLAEFF, Ariadne
   Five Evenings (see Volodin, Aleksandr)
   A Month in the Country (see Turgenev, Ivan S.)
Nicomedes II (Epiphanes) King of Bithynia, fl. 142-91 B.C.
   *Nicomede (Nicomedes) (see Corneille, Pierre)
Niels Ebbesen (see Munk, Kaj H.)
Niemandsland (see Pinter, Harold)
NIETZSCHE, Friedrich Wilhelm, 1844-1900
   Thus Spake Zarathustra, adapted by Jean-Louis Barrault
     (In Calder & Boyars Playscript Series, 1977)
NIGGLI, Josephina
   Sunday Costs Five Pesos
     (In Best One-Act Plays of 1938, London)
Night (see Melfi, Leonard)
Night (see Pinter, Harold)
The Night; screenplay (see Antonioni, Michelangelo, La Notte)
Night and War in the Prado Museum (see Alberto, Rafael)
A Night at the Inn (see Dunsany, Edward J.)
The Night Before Christmas (see Howells, William Dean)
The Night Before the Trial (see Chekhov, Anton)
Night Club (Bubi's Hide-Away) (see Bernard, Kenneth)
Night Freight (see Yates, J. Michael)
Night Must Fall (see Williams, Emlyn)
The Night of "Mr. H." (see Brighouse, Harold)
A Night of Pity (see Ghelderode, Michel de)
Night of the Beast (see Bullins, Edward A.)
Night of the Iguana (see Williams, Tennessee)
Night of the Storm; television script (see Foote, Horton. Roots in
   a Parched Ground)
A Night Out (see Pinter, Harold)
Night School (see Pinter, Harold)
The Night Thoreau Spent in Jail (see Lawrence, Jerome)
A Night to Remember; television script (see Hill, George Roy)
The Night-Walker; or, The Little Thief (see Beaumont, Francis)
The Nightingale of the Cemetery (see Daudet, Alphonse)
Nightmare Abbey (see Sharp, Anthony)
Nightpiece (see Hildesheimer, Wolfgang)
Night's Lodging (see Gor'kii, Maksim)
Nightwalk (see Open Theater)
The Nihilist (see Monson, William N.)
Nin, Anaïs, 1903-1977
   *The Idiots Karamazov (see Durnag, Christopher)
Nina + Georg: When the Music's Over (see Bergmann, Alfred)
Nine O'Clock Mail (see Sackler, Howard)

1913 (see Sternheim, Carl)
Ninette (Moda de Paris) (see Mihura, Miguel)
Ninette y un Señor de Murcia (see Mihura, Miguel)
The Ninety and Nine: A Scenario (see Paul, Elliot)
90° in the Shade (see Labiche, Eugene)
El Niño y la Niebla (see Usigli, Rudolfo)
Ninotchka; screenplay (see Lubitsch, Ernst)
NIRDLINGER, Charles Frederic
    The World and His Wife
        (In Representative Continental Dramas)
NISS, Stanley
    The Penny; CBS radio script presented on the 21st Pre-
    cinct Program, Jan. 20, 1956
        (In Prize Plays of Television and Radio, 1956)
Nivelle de la Chaussée (see La Chaussée, Pierre-Claude Nivelle de)
Nix-Nought-Nothing (see Mitchison, Naomi)
NKOSI, Lewis, 1936-
    The Rhythm of Violence
        (In Themes of Drama)
    We Can't All Be Martin Luther King
        (In The Benin Review, Vol. 1, June 1974)
No Answer (see Hanley, William)
No Cards (see Gilbert, William S.)
No Cure, No Pay (see Baker, George M.)
Le No de Saint-Denis (see Gripari, Pierre)
No Exit (see Sartre, Jean-Paul)
No Hay Cosa Como Callar (see Calderon de la Barca, Pedro)
No Hay Isla Feliz (see Salazar Bondy, Sebastian)
No Hay Mal que por Bien No Venga (see Tamayo y Baus, Manuel)
No Help Wanted; radio script (see Robson, William N.)
No Man Is an Island; television script (see Benjamin, James)
No Man's Land (see Pinter, Harold)
No More Americans (see Hughes, Babette)
No More Peace! (see Toller, Ernst)
No Nos Venceremos (see Garza, Roberto J.)
No One's Enemy but His Own (see Murphy, Arthur)
No Place to Be Somebody (see Gordone, Charles)
No Regrets for Our Youth; filmscript (see Kurosawa, Akira)
No Saco Nada de la Escuela (see Valdez, Luis)
No Se Culpe a Nadie (see Solana, Rafael)
No Sign of the Dove (see Ustinov, Peter)
No Skill or Special Knowledge Is Required (see Hopkins, John R.)
No Strings Attached (see Moss, Howard)
No Thank You, Mr. Smart (see Shearer, Marjorie)
No Trams to Lime Street; television script (see Owen, Alun)
No Trifling with Love (see Musset, Alfred de)
No Why (see Whiting, John)
No Wit (Help) Like a Woman's (see Middleton, Thomas)
Noah (Noe) (see Obey, Andre)
NOAH, Mordecai Manuel, 1785-1851
    She Would Be a Soldier; or, The Plains of Chippewa
        (In Dramas from the American Theatre, 1762-1909)
        (In Representative Plays by American Dramatists, Vol. 1)

The Noble Gentleman (see Beaumont, Francis)
Noces d'Argent (see Gilles, Ange)
Les Noces de Bouchencoeur (see Labiche, Eugene)
Noche de Estio (see Usigli, Rudolfo)
La Noche de la Iguana (see Williams, Tennessee)
Una Noche en la Posada (see Dunsany, Edward J.)
Nocturne (see Arlette, Vera I.)
Nocturne on the Rhine (see Drayton, Ronald)
El "Nocturno" del Hermano Beltran (see Baroja y Nessi, Pio)
Noli Me Tangere (see Kaiser, Georg)
NOLLEDO, Wilfredo D.
    Goodbye, My Gentle
        (In 3 Filipino Playwrights)
    Legend of the Filipino Guitar
        (In 3 Filipino Playwrights)
NOLTE, Charles M.
    Do Not Pass Go
        (In Minnesota Showcase: Four Plays, Minnesota Drama Editions, no. 9)
Noman and the Nomads (see Whiting, John)
The Non-Juror (see Cibber, Colley)
Non si sa Come (see Pirandello, Luigi)
La Nonne Qui Laissa Son Abbaie (see Miracles de Nostra Dame par Personnages)
Noon (see McNally, Terrence)
Noon Wine; television script (see Peckinpah, Sam)
NOONAN, John Ford
    Older People; revised version
        (In Yale/Theatre, Vol. 6, no. 3, Spring 1975)
    Rainbows for Sale
        (In The Off Off Broadway Book)
NORIEGA HOPE, Carlos, 1896-1934
    La Señorita Voluntad
        (In Teatro Méxicano del Siglo XX, Vol. 1)
Norma; or, A Politician's Love (see Ibsen, Henrik)
NORMAN, Frank
    Fings Ain't Wot They Used T'Be (see Bart, Lionel)
NORRIS, Frank, 1870-1902
    **Greed (see Von Stroheim, Erich)
NORRIS, June
    The Soldiers of Fortune
        (In 100 Non-Royalty Radio Plays)
NORRIS, Kathleen (Thompson), 1880-1966
    The Kelly Kid, by Kathleen Norris and Dan Totheroh
        (In Types of Modern Dramatic Composition)
The Northern Lasse (see Brome, Richard)
NORTON, Bill L.
    Cisco Pike; screenplay, written and directed by Bill L. Norton
        (A Bantam Books Screenplay, 1971)
NORTON, Thomas, 1532-1584
    Gorboduc; or, Ferrex and Porrex, by Thomas Norton and Thomas Sackville
        (In Minor Elizabethan Tragedies)

Norwegian Wood; a radio play (see Wohmann, Gabriele)
Nose! Nose? No-se! (see Amalrik, Andrei)
Nosferatu (see Murnau, Friedrich W.)
Not a Thing Out of Place (see Al Hakim, Tewfik)
Not by Bed Alone (see Feydeau, Georges)
Not I (see Beckett, Samuel)
Not in the Book (see Watkyn, Arthur)
Not in the Lessons (see O'Dea, Mark L.)
NOTA, Alberto, 1775-1847
    Il Progittista
        (In Teatro Comico Moderno)
Notes from a Savage God (see Drayton, Ronald)
Notes of Rocket; vaudeville script (see Fields, W. C.)
Notes on a Love Affair (see Marcus, Frank)
Nothing Personal (see Pomerantz, Edward)
The Notorious Mrs. Ebbsmith (see Pinero, Arthur Wing)
Nôtre Futur (see Feydeau, Georges)
Nôtre Pain Quotidien (see Vidor, King)
La Notte; filmscript (see Antonioni, Michelangelo)
Notte Italiana (see Horvath, Odön von)
Le Notti Bianche (see Visconti, Luchino)
Le Notti di Cabiria (see Fellini, Federico)
Nous Ne Viellirons Pas Ensemble; screenplay (see Pialat, Maurice)
La Nouva Isola (see Balducci, Alfredo)
Le Nouveau Locataire (see Ionesco, Eugene)
La Nouvelle Idole (see Curel, François)
NOVAK, Ana
    Match à la Une
        (In L'Avant-Scène Théâtre, no. 568, July 15, 1975)
The Novella (see Brome, Richard)
November 22 (see Eyen, Tom)
Una Novia en la Mañana (see Claus, Hugo)
NOVO, Salvador, 1004-
    Cuauhtémoc
        (In Teatro Méxicano del Siglo XX, Vol. 4)
    La Culta Dama
        (In Teatro Méxicano del Siglo XX, Vol. 3)
    La Guerra de las Gordas
        (In Teatro Méxicano, 1963)
    Ha Vuelto Ulises
        (In 12 Obras en un Acto)
Now He's There, Now He's Not; a radio play (see Fritz, Walter H.)
Now There's Just the Three of Us (see Weller, Michael)
Now They Sing Again (see Frisch, Max)
NOWAK, Tadeusz
    Und Wenn Du König, und Wenn Du Henker Bist
        (In Theater der Zeit, no. 10, 1975)
Noziere, Fernand, pseud. (see Weyl, Fernand)
Nude with Violin (see Coward, Noël)
The Nüremberg Egg (see Harlan, Walter)
Nuestra Natacha (see Rodrigues Alvarez, Alejandro)
Nuestro Pueblo (see Wilder, Thornton)
La Nuit de Noël 1914 (see Claudel, Paul)

La Nuit, Les Clowns (see Heurte, Yves)
La Nuit Vénitienne; ou, Les Noces de Laurette (see Musset, Alfred
    de)
Les Nuits de la Colère (see Salacrou, Armand)
Numa Roumestan (see Daudet, Alphonse)
Number 9 (see Vilalta, Maruxa)
Number Three (see Grillo, John)
Nun Singen Sie Wieder (see Frisch, Max)
Nunca Es Tarde (see López Rubio, José)
La Nuova Colonia (see Pirandello, Luigi)
La Nuova Isola (see Balducci, Alfredo)
... Nur Noch Gewölk ... (see Beckett, Samuel)
The Nuremberg Stove; a radio script (see Mack, Nila)
NUTTALL, Jeff
    The People Show
        (In Gambit, Vol. 4, no. 16)

O (see Key-Aaberg, Sandro)
O. K. Certaldo (see Owens, Rochelle)
O Lucky Man! screenplay (see Anderson, Lindsay)
O Be Living, O Be Dying (see Dietz, Norman D.)
Oak Leaves and Lavender (see O'Casey, Sean)
Oakley, Annie (Phoebe Anne Oakley Mozee) 1860-1926
    *Buffalo Bill and the Indians; or, Sitting Bull's History Lesson
        (see Rudolph, Alan)
    *Indians (see Kopit, Arthur L.)
OBALDIA, René de
    And Suddenly There Came the Bang!
        (In his Plays, Vol. 4)
    The Babysitter
        (In his Plays, Vol. 3)
    Du Vent dans les Branches de Sassafras
        (In Le Théâtre d'Aujourd'hui)
    Edouard et Agrippine
        (In Le Théâtre d'Aujourd'hui)
    Edward and Agrippina
        (In Gambit, no. 2)
    ... Et à la Fin Etait le Bang
        (In L'Avant-Scène Théâtre, no. 551, no. 1, 1974)
    Genousie
        (In Le Théâtre d'Aujourd'hui)
    The Jellyfish's Banquet
        (In his Plays, Vol. 3)
    Jenusia
        (In his Plays, Vol. 1)
    Mr. Klebs and Rosalie
        (In his Plays, Vol. 4)
    Satyr of La Villette
        (In his Plays, Vol. 2)
    Seven Impromptus for Leisure
        (In his Plays, Vol. 1)
    Two Women for One Ghost
        (In his Plays, Vol. 3)

The Unknown General
  (In his Plays, Vol. 2)
Wide Open Spaces
  (In his Plays, Vol. 2)
Wind in the Branches of the Sassafras
  (In Calder & Boyars Playscript Series, no. 14)
Oberösterreich (see Kroetz, Franz X.)
OBEY, Andre, 1892-
  Noah (Noe)
    (In Three Plays)
  One for the Wind (Une Fille pour du Vent)
    (In Three Plays)
  The Phoenix (L'Homme de Cendres)
    (In Three Plays)
OBOLER, Arch, 1907-
  This Lonely Heart; radio script, Jan. 14, 1940
    (In Best Broadcasts of 1939-40)
  The Steel Worker; radio script
    (In Best Broadcasts of 1938-39)
OBRENOVIC, Aleksandar, 1928-
  The Bird
    (In Five Modern Yugoslav Plays)
O'Brien, Flann (see O'Nolan, Brian)
O'BRIEN, Seumas, 1880-
  The Black Bottle
    (In One-Act Plays for Stage and Study, 2nd Series)
  Christmas Eve
    (In One-Act Plays for Stage and Study, 4th Series)
  The Cobbler's Den
    (In One-Act Plays for Stage and Study, 3rd Series)
O'BRIEN, William, d. 1815
  Cross Purposes
    (In A Collection of the Most Esteemed Farces..., Vol. 6)
Les Observateurs (see Danaud, Jean-Claude)
L'Obstacle (see Daudet, Alphonse)
Obstinacy (see Benedix, Roderich)
The Obstinate Lady (see Cokayne, Sir Aston)
OCAMPO, Maria Luisa, 1907-
  Al Otro Día
    (In Teatro Méxicano del Siglo XX, Vol. 1)
O'CASEY, Sean, 1880-1964
  Bedtime Story
    (In his Collected Plays, Vol. 4)
  Cock-a-Doodle Dandy
    (In his Collected Plays, Vol. 4)
    (In Masterpieces of the Modern Irish Theatre)
  The End of the Beginning
    (In All the World's a Stage)
    (In his Collected Plays, Vol. 1)
  Hall of Healing
    (In his Collected Plays, Vol. 3)
  Juno and the Paycock
    (In his Collected Plays, Vol. 1)

    (In <u>Contemporary Drama: 13 Plays</u>)
Juno y el Pavo Real
    (In <u>Teatro Irlandes Contemporaneo</u>)
Oak Leaves and Lavender
    (In his <u>Collected Plays</u>, Vol. 4)
The Plow and the Stars
    (In his <u>Collected Plays</u>, Vol. 1)
    (In <u>Revolution: A Collection of Plays</u>)
A Pound on Demand
    (In his <u>Collected Plays</u>, Vol. 1)
Purple Dust
    (In his <u>Collected Plays</u>, Vol. 3)
Red Roses for Me
    (In his <u>Collected Plays</u>, Vol. 3)
The Shadow of a Gunman
    (In his <u>Collected Plays</u>, Vol. 1)
The Silver Tassie
    (In his <u>Collected Plays</u>, Vol. 2)
    (In <u>Masterpieces of the Modern Irish Theatre</u>)
The Star Turns Red
    (In his <u>Collected Plays</u>, Vol. 2)
Time to Go
    (In his <u>Collected Plays</u>, Vol. 4)
Within the Gates
    (In his <u>Collected Plays</u>, Vol. 2)
L'Occasion (see Mérimée, Prosper)
Occupe-toi d'Amelie (see Feydeau, Georges)
An Occurrence at Owl Creek Bridge; screenplay (see Vidor, Charles)
O'CONNELL, Thomas E.
    The Long Hour, a fantasy for St. Patrick's Day
    (In <u>100 Non-Royalty Radio Plays</u>)
O'Connor (see Brown, Alan)
O'CONNOR, Frank
    The Statue's Daughter
    (In <u>The Journal of Irish Literature</u>, Vol. 4, no. 1, Jan. 1975)
O'CONOR, Joseph
    The Iron Harp
    (In <u>Three Irish Plays</u>)
October; filmscript (see Eisenstein, Sergei M.)
The Octoroon; or, Life in Louisiana (see Boucicault, Dion)
The Odd Couple (see Simon, Neil)
O'DEA, John B.
    Where E'er We Go
    (In <u>The Army Play by Play</u>)
O'DEA, Mark Leland Hill
    Miss Myrtle Says "Yes"
    (In his <u>Red Bud Women</u>)
    Not in the Lessons
    (In his <u>Red Bud Women</u>)
    Shivaree
    (In his <u>Red Bud Women</u>)
    The Song of Solomon
    (In his <u>Red Bud Women</u>)

Odessea Nuda (see Rossi, Jean-Baptiste)
ODETS, Clifford, 1906-1963
    Awake and Sing!
        (In <u>Enclosure</u>)
        (In <u>Famous Plays of 1935-36</u>)
        (In <u>50 Best Plays of the American Theatre</u>, Vol. 2)
        (In <u>Literature of American Jews</u>)
        (In <u>Representative American Dramas</u>)
        (In his <u>Six Plays</u>)
    The Country Girl
        (In <u>Contemporary Drama: 13 Plays</u>)
    Golden Boy
        (In <u>Famous Plays of 1938-39</u>)
        (In <u>50 Best Plays of the American Theatre</u>, Vol. 2)
        (In his <u>Six Plays</u>)
    "I Can't Sleep"
        (In <u>The Anxious Years</u>)
    Paradise Lost
        (In his <u>Six Plays</u>)
    Rocket to the Moon
        (In his <u>Six Plays</u>)
        (In <u>This Is My Best</u>)
    Till the Day I Die
        (In his <u>Six Plays</u>)
    Waiting for Lefty
        (In his <u>Six Plays</u>)
Odipus und die Sphinx (see Hofmannsthal, Hugo von H.)
Ododo (see Walker, Joseph A.)
O'DONOVAN, John, 1921-
    Copperfaced Jack
        (In <u>7 Irish Plays</u>)
The Odyssey of Homer; radio script (see Kanigher, Robert)
The Odyssey of Ulysses the Palmiped (see Gilbert-Lecomte, Roger)
Oedipe (see Corneille, Pierre)
Oedipe (see Voltaire)
Oedipe a Colone (see Chénier, Marie-Joseph B.)
Oedipe ou le Silence des Dieux (see Kihm, Jean-Jacques)
Oedipe-Roi (see Chénier, Marie-Joseph B.)
Oedipus (see Dryden, John)
Oedipus (see Voltaire)
Oedipus Nix: A Mythical Tragedy (see Brustein, Robert)
Oedipus Rex; screenplay (see Pasolini, Pier P.)
Oedipus the King (see Sophocles)
Der Öffentliche Ankläger (see Hochwälder, Fritz)
Die Öffentliche Meinung (see Baranga, Aurel)
OEHLENSCHLAGER, Adam Gottlob, 1779-1850
    Axel og Valborg
        (In his <u>Tragoedier</u>, Vol. 2)
    Baldur hiin Gode
        (In his <u>Tragoedier</u>, Vol. 1)
    Correggio
        (In his <u>Tragoedier</u>, Vol. 2)

Den Lille Hyrdedreng
    (In his <u>Tragoedier</u>, Vol. 3)
Dina
    (In his <u>Tragoedier</u>, Vol. 4)
Dronning Margareta
    (In his <u>Tragoedier</u>, Vol. 4)
Erik og Abel
    (In his <u>Tragoedier</u>, Vol. 3)
Hagbarth og Signe
    (In his <u>Tragoedier</u>, Vol. 3)
Hakon Jarl Hiin Rige
    (In his <u>Tragoedier</u>, Vol. 1)
Landet Fundet og Forsvundet
    (In his <u>Tragoedier</u>, Vol. 4)
Palnatoke
    (In his <u>Tragoedier</u>, Vol. 1)
Starkodder
    (In his <u>Tragoedier</u>, Vol. 2)
Tordenskiold
    (In his <u>Tragoedier</u>, Vol. 4)
Vaeingerne i Miklagard
    (In his <u>Tragoedier</u>, Vol. 3)
L'Oeillet Blanc (see Daudet, Alphonse)
ÖRKENY, Istvan
    Katzenspiel; originaltitel: "Macskajatek"
    (In <u>Theater der Zeit</u>, no. 10, 1974)
L'Oeuf (see Marceau, Felicien)
Les Oeufs à la Moutarde (see Roudy, Pierre)
Of All the Crowd That Assembled There; television script (see Griffiths, Howard)
Of Thee I Sing (see Gershwin George)
Of These Thousand Pleasures; screenplay (see Visconti, Luchino. Vaghe Stelle dell'Orsa)
Of What Young Maidens Dream (see Musset, Alfred de)
Off to the Country; vaudeville script (see Fields, W. C.)
OFFENBACH, Jacques, 1819-1880
    **The Tales of Hoffman (see Powell, Michael)
Offending the Audience (see Handke, Peter)
Offiziere (see Unruh, Fritz von)
Oficio de Hombres (see Morris, Andres)
Oficio de Tinieblas (see Sastre, Alfonso)
O'Flaherty, V. C.: a Recruiting Pamphlet (see Shaw, George Bernard)
Oh (see Simpson, Norman F.)
Oh Dad, Poor Dad, Mamma's Hung You in the Closet and I'm Feelin' So Sad (see Kopit, Arthur L.)
Oh David, Are You There? (see Ritchie, Paul)
Oh What a Bloody Circus (see Ionesco, Eugene)
Oh What a Lovely War (see Theatre Workshop, London)
Ohad's Woman (see Rubinstein, Harold F.)
O'HARA, John, 1905-
    The Champagne Pool
    (In his <u>Five Plays</u>)

The Farmers Hotel
(In his <u>Five Plays</u>)
The Searching Sun
(In his <u>Five Plays</u>)
Veronique
(In his <u>Five Plays</u>)
The Way It Was
(In his <u>Five Plays</u>)
O'HARA, Kane, 1714?-1782
The Golden Pippin
(In <u>A Collection of the Most Esteemed Farces ...</u>, Vol. 3)
Midas
(In <u>A Collection of the Most Esteemed Farces ...</u>, Vol. 2)
The Two Misers
(In <u>The London Stage,</u> Vol. 3)
O'HIGGINS, Harvey
The Dickey Bird, by Harvey O'Higgins and Harriet Ford
(In <u>One-Act Plays for Stage and Study</u>, 2nd Series)
OHNET, Georges, 1848-1918
The Iron Manufacturer
(In <u>The Drama,</u> Vol. 9)
El Okapi (see Diosdada, Ana)
OKE, Richard
**Frolic Wind (see Pryce, Richard)
O'KEEFE, John
Chamber Piece
(In <u>Playwrights for Tomorrow,</u> Vol. 11)
O'KELLY, Seumas, 1881-1918
The Shuiler's Child
(In <u>Irish Drama Series,</u> Vol. 5)
Oklahoma! (see Rodgers, Richard)
Oktobertag (see Kaiser, Georg)
Olaf Liljekrans (see Ibsen, Henrik)
Olaf und Albert (see Henkel, Heinrich)
The Old Batchelour (see Congreve, William)
Old English (see Galsworthy, John)
Old Folks at Home (see Harwood, Harold M.)
An Old Friend (see See, Edmond)
Old Friends (see Barrie, James M.)
Old Gentleman Gay (see Benton, Rita)
The Old Grads (see Finch, Robert V.)
Old Kieg of Malfi (see Donahue, John C.)
The Old Ladies (see Ackland, Rodney)
The Old Lady Says "No!" (see Johnston, Denis)
The Old Lady Shows Her Medals (see Barrie, James M.)
"Old Lady 31" (see Crothers, Rachel)
The Old Law (see Massinger, Philip)
The Old Maid (see Murphy, Arthur)
Old Man Pete (see Edmonds, Randolph)
The Old Man Taught Wisdom; or, The Virgin Unmask'd (see Fielding, Henry)
Old Movies (see Bryden, Bill)
Old Nobody (see Kennedy, Charles R.)

The Old Oaken Bucket (see Glaze, Harriet)
Old Pipes (see Smith, Moyne Rice)
Old Times (see Pinter, Harold)
The Old Tune (see Pinget, Robert)
Old Verily (see Corrie, Joe)
The Old Wives Tale (see Peele, George)
The Old Woman Remembers (see Gregory, Isabella A.)
Old Ymir's Clay Pot (see Dietz, Norman D.)
Oldcastle, Sir John, 1377?-1417
    *The First Part of Sir John Oldcastle (Anon.)
        (In Disputed Plays of William Shakespeare)
OLDENBURG, Claes
    Injun: A Happening
        (In The Great American Life Show)
Older People (see Noonan, John F.)
OLFSON, Lewy
    The Lady or the Tiger? a radio script based on the story by
      Frank R. Stockton
        (In On the Air)
Oli Impan (see Florention, Alberto S.)
Olimpica (see Azar, Hector)
Olivada los Tambores (see Diosdada, Ana)
Oliveira, Vlademar de
    Terra Adorada
        (In Revista de Teatro, no. 416, Mar./Apr. 1977)
Oliver Cromwell (see Drinkwater, John)
OLMO, Lauro
    La Camisa
        (In Teatro Español, 1961-62)
    El Cuerpo
        (In Teatro Español, 1965-66)
    The News Item
        (In Modern Spanish Theatre)
OLSEN, Ernst Bruun
    The Bookseller Cannot Sleep
        (In Modern Nordic Plays: Denmark)
Los Olvidados; screenplay (see Buñuel, Luis)
Olympe's Marriage (see Augier, Emile)
Olympia (see Molnar, Ferenc)
Olympia (see Voltaire)
O'MALLEY, Mary
    Once a Catholic
        (In Plays and Players, Vol. 25, nos. 1 & 2, Oct. & Nov.
          1977)
OMAR KHAYYAM, d. 1123?
    **Omar and Oh My! a burlesque dramatization of the celebrated
      poem "Rubâiyât," by Omar Khayyam translated by Edward Fitz-
      gerald
        (In The Drama, Vol. 21)
L'Ombra di Banquo ossia La Lezione di Potere di Potere (see Cagli,
  Bruno)
L'Omosessuale o la Difficolta de Esprimersi (see Copi)
Omphale (see Hacks, Peter)
Omphalos Hotel (see Ribes, Jean-Michel)

On Baile's Strand (see Yeats, William Butler)
On Being Hit (see Goss, Clay)
On Borrowed Time (see Osborn, Paul)
On la Faire la Cocotte (see Feydeau, Georges)
On Loge la Nuit--Cafe a l'Eau (see Ribes, Jean-Michel)
On Ne Badine pas avec l'Amour (see Musset, Alfred de)
On Ne Saurait Penser à Tout (see Musset, Alfred de)
On Owl Creek; a film adaptation (see Enrico, Robert)
On Purge Bébé (see Feydeau, Georges)
On the Corner of Cherry and Elsewhere (see Lee, Jeannie)
On the Eve (see Afinogenov, Alexander N.)
On the Eve of Publication (see Mercer, David)
On the High Road (see Chekhov, Anton)
On the Marry-Go-Wrong (see Feydeau, Georges)
On the Plain of Dura (see Bennett, Gordon C.)
On the Portsmouth Road (see Rubinstein, Harold F.)
On the Racecourse (see Gregory, Isabella A.)
On the Rocks: a Political Comedy (see Shaw, George Bernard)
On the Shelf (see Morley, Christopher D.)
On Trial (see Rice, Elmer L.)
On Tue Toujours Celle Qu'on Aime (see Menestrel, Marie)
On Vacation (see Hofmann, Gert)
On with the New (see Wiener, Frantz)
Once a Catholic (see O'Malley, Mary)
Once a Giant (see Bush, Stephen)
Once Below a Time (see Quackenbush, Jan)
Oncilda e Zé Buscapé (see Amado, João J.)
Ondine (see Giraudoux, Jean)
The One (see Pitcher, Oliver)
One Big Family (see Wang, Fa)
One Blast and Have Done (see Simpson, Norman F.)
One Bright Day (see Miller, Sigmund)
One Can Not Think of Everything (see Musset, Alfred de)
One Crowded Hour (see Fielden, Charlotte)
One Day at Nixon High School (see San Francisco Red Theatre)
One Day in the Life of Ivan Denisovich; screenplay (see Harwood,
    Ronald)
One Day More (see Conrad, Joseph)
One Day, When I Was Lost; scenario (see Baldwin, James)
One Egg; radio play (see Hughes, Babette)
One for the Wind (Une Fille pour du Vent) (see Obey, Andre)
$100, 000 for a Wife; radio script (see Saks, Sol)
One in Twelve; television play (see Latham, John)
One Man's Bread (see Fridell, Folke)
One of These Days (see Usigli, Rudolfo)
One of Those Letters (see Brighouse, Harold)
One of Those Things (see Kelly, George E.)
One Person (see Patrick, Robert)
One Touch of Venus (see Weill, Kurt)
One Way for Another (see Tardieu, Jean)
One Way Pendulum (see Simpson, Norman F.)
One Wonderful Sunday; filmscript (see Kurosawa, Akira)

O'NEILL, Eugene Gladstone, 1888-1953
  Abortion
    (In his Ten "Lost" Plays)
  Ah, Wilderness!
    (In his Plays, Vol. 2)
  All God's Chillun Got Wings
    (In The Disinherited: Plays)
    (In his Plays, Vol. 2)
  "Anna Christie"
    (In his Plays, Vol. 3)
  Before Breakfast
    (In his Plays, Vol. 1)
  Beyond the Horizon
    (In his Plays, Vol. 3)
    (In Representative American Plays, 1792-1949)
  Bound East for Cardiff
    (In his Plays, Vol. 1)
  Days Without End
    (In his Plays, Vol. 3)
  Desire Under the Elms
    (In Dramas of Modernism)
    (In 50 Best Plays of the American Theatre, Vol. 1)
    (In his Plays, Vol. 1)
    (In 20th Century American Writing)
  Diff'rent
    (In his Plays, Vol. 2)
  The Dreamy Kid
    (In his Plays, Vol. 1)
  Dynamo
    (In his Plays, Vol. 3)
  The Emperor Jones
    (In Contact with Drama)
    (In The Nobel Prize Library)
    (In his Plays, Vol. 3)
    (In Representative American Dramas)
  The First Man
    (In his Plays, Vol. 2)
  Fog
    (In his Ten "Lost" Plays)
  The Fountain
    (In his Plays, Vol. 1)
  Gold
    (In his Plays, Vol. 2)
  The Great God Brown
    (In his Plays, Vol. 3)
  The Great God Brown (selection)
    (In This Is My Best)
  "The Hairy Ape"
    (In 50 Best Plays of the American Theatre, Vol. 1)
    (In his Plays, Vol. 3)
  Homecoming
    (In The Nobel Prize Library)

The Iceman Cometh
    (In his Plays, Vol. 3)
Ile
    (In his Plays, Vol. 1)
In the Zone
    (In his Plays, Vol. 1)
Lazarus Laughed
    (In The American Caravan, 1927)
    (In his Plays, Vol. 1)
The Long Voyage Home
    (In his Plays, Vol. 1)
Marco Millions
    (In his Plays, Vol. 2)
    (In 20th Century Plays)
The Moon of the Caribbees
    (In his Plays, Vol. 1)
Mourning Becomes Electra
    (In his Plays, Vol. 2)
The Movie Man
    (In his Ten "Lost" Plays)
**New Girl in Town   (see Merrill, Bob)
  Recklessness
    (In his Ten "Lost" Plays)
The Rope
    (In his Plays, Vol. 1)
Servitude
    (In his Ten "Lost" Plays)
The Sniper
    (In his Ten "Lost" Plays)
Strange Interlude
    (In his Plays, Vol. 1)
The Straw
    (In his Plays, Vol. 3)
Thirst
    (In his Ten "Lost" Plays)
Warnings
    (In his Ten "Lost" Plays)
The Web
    (In his Ten "Lost" Plays)
Welded
    (In his Plays, Vol. 2)
Where the Cross Is Made
    (In More One-Act Plays by Modern Authors)
    (In On the High Road)
    (In The Play Book)
    (In his Plays, Vol. 1)
  The Wife for a Life
    (In his Ten "Lost" Plays)
The Only Jealousy of Emer (see Yeats, William Butler)
The Only Legend, a Masque of the Scarlet Pierrot (see Drinkwater, John)
The Only One; or, The Curses of the Cosmos (see Valéry, Paul)

L'Orfeo (see Monteverdi, Claudio)
The Organizer; screenplay (see Monicelli, Mario. I Compagni)
The Orgy (see Buenaventura, Enrique)
An Original Idea (see Baker, George M.)
Orison (see Arrabal, Fernando)
Orlando, Vittorio Emanuele, Italian Prime Minister, 1860-1952
  *Wilson (see Greanias, George)
L'Oro di Roma (see Lizzani, Carlo)
Oroonoko (see Southerne, Thomas)
Oropaste (Oropastes) (see Boyer, L'Abbe Claude)
OROZCO CASTRO, Jorge, 1891-
  Germinal
    (In Obras Breves del Teatro Costarricense, Vol. 1)
The Orphan (see Otway, Thomas)
The Orphan of Chao (see Chi Chun-hsiang)
The Orphan of China (see Murphy, Arthur)
The Orphan of China (see Voltaire)
Orpheus Below (see Honig, Edwin)
Orpheus Descending (see Williams, Tennessee)
ORR, Mary
  **All About Eve; screenplay (see Mankiewicz, Joseph L.)
ORTEGA, Julio, 1942-
  La Campana
    (In Teatro Breve Hispanoamericano Contemporaneo)
ORTIZ DE MONTELLANO, Bernardo
  Salome's Head
    (In New Directions, Vol. 8, 1944)
ORTIZ GUERRERO, Manuel, 1897-1933
  La Conquista; drama de la Conquista Español en Tierra y Alma
  Guarani
    (In his Obras Completas)
  El Crimen de Tintalila
    (In his Obras Completas)
  Eirete
    (In his Obras Completas)
ORTON, Joe, 1933-1967
  Entertaining Mr. Sloane
    (In his Complete Plays)
    (Evergreen Playscript Series, 1965)
  The Erpingham Camp
    (In his Complete Plays)
    (In his Crimes of Passion)
  Funeral Games
    (In his Complete Plays)
    (In his Funeral Games and The Good and Faithful Servant)
  The Good and Faithful Servant
    (In his Complete Plays)
    (In his Funeral Games and The Good and Faithful Servant)
  Loot
    (In his Complete Plays)
  The Ruffian on the Stair
    (In his Complete Plays)
    (In his Crimes of Passion)

What the Butler Saw
    (In his Complete Plays)
    (Evergreen Playscript Series, 1970)
OSBORN, Murray S.
    Next Year in Jerusalem
        (In Modern International Drama, Vol. 7, no. 1B, Spring 1976)
OSBORN, Paul, 1901-
    A l'Est d'Eden; scenario (see Kazan, Elia)
    On Borrowed Time
        (In 50 Best Plays of the American Theatre, Vol. 2)
OSBORNE, John, 1929-
    The Blood of the Bambergs
        (In Plays for England)
    The End of Me Old Cigar
        (In The End of Me Old Cigar and Jill and Jack)
    The Gift of Friendship; a play for television
        (In Faber & Faber Plays Series, 1972)
    The Hotel in Amsterdam
        (In his Four Plays, 1973)
    Inadmissable Evidence
        (In New Theatre in Europe, Vol. 3)
    Jill and Jack; a play for television
        (In The End of Me Old Cigar and Jill and Jack)
        (In Faber & Faber Plays, 1975)
    A Patriot for Me
        (In Faber & Faber Plays, 1966)
        (In his Four Plays, 1973)
    The Picture of Dorian Gray, adapted from the novel by Oscar
    Wilde
        (In Faber & Faber Plays, 1975)
    A Place Calling Itself Rome; based on Shakespeare's play
    "Coriolanus"
        (In Faber & Faber Plays Series, 1973)
    The Right Prospectus; a play for television
        (In Faber & Faber Plays, 1970)
    A Sense of Detachment
        (In Faber & Faber Plays Series, 1973)
    Time Present
        (In his Four Plays, 1973)
    Under Plain Cover
        (In Plays for England)
    Very Like a Whale
        (Faber & Faber Plays, 1971)
    Watch It Come Down
        (Faber & Faber Plays, 1975)
    West of Suez
        (In his Four Plays, 1973)
    The World of Paul Slickey
        (In Plays for England)
OSBOURNE, Lloyd, 1868-1947
    The Little Father of the Wilderness (see Strong, Austin)
OSGOOD, Lawrence
    Rook
        (In New Theatre in America, Vol. 1)

OSHIMA, Nagisa
    La Ceremonie. Scenario original Tsutomu Tamura, Mamoru
    Sasaki, Nagisa Oshima. Titre original: "Gishiki"
        (In L'Avant-Scène du Cinéma no. 136, May 1973)
Osman (see Tristan L'Hermite, François)
Osman, Sultan, Ottoman Empire (see Othman)
Ossessione; screenplay (see Visconti, Luchino)
Ossido di Carbonio (see Malerba, Luigi)
Ostrom (see Brust, Alfred)
OSTROVSKII, Alexandr Nikolaevich, 1823-1886
    Artistes and Admirers
        (In Classics of Drama in English Translation Series, 1970)
    A Domestic Picture; a Scene from Moscow Life
        (In A Treasury of Classic Russian Literature)
    Easy Money
        (In Easy Money and Two Other Plays)
    Even a Wise Man Stumbles
        (In Easy Money and Two Other Plays)
    The Forest
        (In his Five Plays)
    It's a Family Affair; We'll Settle It Ourselves
        (In his Five Plays)
    The Poor Bride
        (In his Five Plays)
        (In Masterpieces of the Russian Drama, Vol. 1)
    The Scoundrel
        (In his Five Plays)
    The Storm
        (In his Five Plays)
        (In Nineteenth-Century Russian Plays)
        (In The Storm and Other Russian Plays)
    The Thunderstorm
        (In World Drama, Vol. 2)
    Wolves and Sheep
        (In Easy Money and Two Other Plays)
O'SULLIVAN, Maurice
    **Twenty Years a-Growing Up (see Thomas, Dylan)
L'Otage (see Claudel, Paul)
Otello; text in French (see Verdi, Giuseppe)
Othello (see Shakespeare, William)
The Other House (see James, Henry)
The Other Side of the Swamp (see Ryton, Royce)
The Other Son (see Pirandello, Luigi)
Otherwise Engaged (see Gray, Simon)
Othman, or Osman I, Sultan, Ottoman Empire, 1259-1326
    *Osman (see Tristan L'Hermite, François)
    *Zoraide (see Lamartine, Alphonse M.)
Otho, Marcus Salvius, Roman Emperor, 32-69 A.D.
    *Othon (Otho) (see Corneille, Pierre)
OTHON, Manuel José, 1858-1906
    El Ultimo Capitulo
        (In Teatro Méxicano del Siglo XX, Vol. 1)

La Otra Orilla (see López Rubio, José)
Otra Primavera (see Usigli, Rudolfo)
Ottavia (see Alfieri, Vittorio)
OTWAY, Thomas, 1652-1685
   The Cheats of Scapin
     (In The London Stage, Vol. 4)
   The Orphan
     (In The London Stage, Vol. 3)
   Venice Preserv'd; or, A Plot Discovered
     (In British Plays from the Restoration to 1820, Vol. 1)
     (In Five Restoration Tragedies)
     (In Plays of the Restoration and 18th Century)
Ou Comment (see Ionesco, Eugene)
Le Ouallou (see Audiberti, Jacques)
OULD, Hermon
   Claude
     (In One-Act Plays for Stage and Study, 2nd Series)
OULMONT, Charles
   Trois Couverts
     (In L'Avant-Scène du Théâtre, no. 528, Nov. 1, 1973)
OULTON, Brian, 1908-
   Mr. Sydney Smith Coming Upstairs
     (In Plays of the Year, Vol. 42, 1972)
Our Betters (see Maugham, William Somerset)
Our Daily Bread; screenplay (see Vidor, King. Notre Pain Quati-
   dien)
Our Island Home (see Gilbert, William S.)
Our Love: A Radio Romance (see Thompson, Palmer)
Our Power and Our Glory (see Grieg, Nordahl)
Our Town (see Wilder, Thornton)
L'Ouragan (see Zola, Emile)
L'Ours et la Lune (see Claudel, Paul)
OurSides (see Goss, Clay)
Out at Sea (see Mrozek, Slawomir)
Out of Synch (see Lees, Richard)
Out of the Dark (see Guinn, Dorothy C.)
Out of the Question (see Howells, William Dean)
The Outcry (see James, Henry)
The Outcry; filmscript (see Antonioni, Michelangelo, Il Grido)
Outport (see Braid, Angus)
The Outsider (see Borchert, Wolfgang)
Un Ouvrage de Dames (see Danaud, Jean-Claude)
Over the Wire (see Cocteau, Jean)
Overlaid (see Davies, Robertson)
Overruled (see Shaw, George Bernard)
The Overseas Expert (see Curnow, Allen)
The Oversight (see Ionesco, Eugene)
Overtones (see Gerstenberg, Alice)
OVID, (Publius Ovidius Naso), 43 B.C.-17? A.D.
  **Acis and Galatea (see Gay, John)
  **The Contention of Ajax and Ulysses for the Armour of Achilles
    (see Shirley, James)

**Pleasant Dialogues and Drammas (see Heywood, Thomas)
  *The Tragedy of Ovid (see Cokayne, Sir Aston)
OWEN, Alun Davies, 1926-
    After the Funeral
        (In Three TV Plays)
    A Hard Day's Night; filmscript by Alun Owen, directed by Rich-
    ard Lester
        (In Film Scripts Four)
    Lena, Oh My Lena
        (In Three TV Plays)
    Male of the Species
        (In Best Short Plays of the World Theatre, 1968-1973)
    No Trams to Lime Street
        (In Three TV Plays)
OWENS, Rochelle, 1936-
    Coconut Folk-Singer
        (In The Karl Marx Play and Others)
    Emma Instigated Me
        (In Performing Arts Journal, Vol. 1, no. 1, Spring 1976)
    Farmer's Almanac
        (In The Karl Marx Play and Others)
    Futz
        (In New Short Plays, Vol. 2)
        (In The Off Off Broadway Book)
    He Wants Shih!
        (In The Karl Marx Play and Others)
        (In Spontaneous Combustion; The Winter Repertory Vol. 6)
    The Karl Marx Play
        (In The Karl Marx Play and Others)
    Kontraption
        (In The Karl Marx Play and Others)
    O.K. Certaldo
        (In The Karl Marx Play and Others)
    The Widow and the Colonel
        (In Best Short Plays, 1977)
The Owl Answers (see Kennedy, Adrienne)
The Owl Killer (see Dean, Phillip H.)
Owners (see Churchill, Caryl)
The Oxcart (see Marques, Rene)
Oyamo, pseud. (see Gordon, Charles F.)
OYONO-MBIA, Guillaume, 1939-
    Three Suitors: One Husband
        (In Three Suitors: One Husband & Until Further Notice)
    Until Further Notice
        (In Three Suitors: One Husband & Until Further Notice)
Ozidi (see Clark, John P.)
OZU, Yasujiro, 1903-1963
    An Autumn Afternoon; excerpt from the script of the film
        (In Ozu)
    Early Spring; excerpt from the script of the film
        (In Ozu)
    The End of Summer; excerpt of the working script of the film
        (In Ozu)

Floating Weeds; excerpt from the script of the film
    (In Ozu)
Good Morning; excerpt from the script of the film
    (In Ozu)
I Was Born, But ...; excerpt of the working script of the film
    (In Ozu)
Late Autumn; excerpt from the script of the film
    (In Ozu)
There Was a Father; excerpt from the working script of the film
    (In Ozu)
Tokayo Story; excerpt from the script of the film
    (In Ozu)

PABST, Georg Wilhelm, 1887-1967
    L'Opéra de Quat'sous (Die Dreigroschenoper); d'après la pièce
    homonyme de Bertolt Brecht inspirée de "The Beggar's Opera, "
    pièce de John Gay; musique Kurt Weill
        (In L'Avant-Scène Cinéma, no. 177, Dec. 1, 1976)
    The Threepenny Opera; screenplay (see Lania, Leo)
PACHECO, Tania
    "A Criminosa, Grotesca, Sofrida e Sempre Gloriosa Caminhada
    de Alqui Cava la Silva em Busca da Grande Luz" (see Levi,
    Clovis)
Pacific 1860 (see Coward, Noël)
La Pacifista (see Jancso, Miklos)
PACK, Richard
    Frontier Fighters, a Historical Adventure (see Berlin, Nathan)
    What's in a Word? (see Berlin, Nathan)
Pack Up Your Troubles (see Geto, Alfred D.)
Paddle Your Own Canoe (see Reginer, Max)
The Padlock (see Bickerstaffe, Isaac)
Padre Mercader (see Diaz Dufoo, Carlos)
PAGANO, José Leon, 1875-
    El Secreto
        (In Teatro Argentino Contemporaneo)
PAGE, Myra
    The March on Chumley Hollow
        (In 100 Non-Royalty Radio Plays)
A Pageant of Plays and Players; sequence (see Shaw, George Ber-
    nard)
Le Pain de Menage (see Renard, Jules)
Le Pain Dur (see Claudel, Paul)
Paine, Thomas, 1737-1809
    *Tom Paine (see Foster, Paul)
Pain(T) (see Foreman, Richard)
The Painting (see Ionesco, Eugene)
A Pair of Drawers (see Sternheim, Carl)
Un Pais Feliz (see Vilalta, Maruxa)
Paisa; filmscript (see Rossellini, Roberto)
Paisan; filmscript (see Rossellini, Roberto)
La Paix Chez Soi (see Moinaux, Georges)

La Paix du Menage; or, A Comedy of Marriage (see Maupassant,
    Guy de)
La Palabra (see Munk, Kaj)
Le Palais du Temps (see Mace, Jean)
Palissy, Bernard, c. 1510-1589
    *Bernardo de Palissy (see Tapia y Rivera, Alejandro)
PALLOTTINI, Renata, 1931-
    O Crime de Cabra
        (In Revista de Teatro, no. 394, July/August 1973)
    A Historia do Juiz
        (In Revista de Teatro, no. 407, Sept. /Oct. 1975)
Palmieri, Juan
    *Juan Palmieri Tupamaro (see Larreta, Antonia)
Pamela Giraud (see Balzac, Honore de)
El Pan de la Locura (see Gorostiza, Carlos)
Pandora (see Voltaire)
Pandora's Box (see Wedekind, Frank)
Panfila la Curandera (see El Teatro de la Esperanza)
Panic in Salem; radio script (see Pettitt, Wilfrid H.)
PANIZZA, Oscar, 1853-1921
    Il Concilio d'Amore
        (In Sipario, no. 310, Mar. 1972)
PANOVA, Vera Fyodorovna, 1905-
    It's Been Ages!
        (In Contemporary Russian Drama)
Pantagleize (see Ghelderode, Michel de)
Pantaloon (see Barrie, James M.)
Pantheon-Courcelles (see Moinaux, Georges)
Panuco 137 (see Magdaleno, Mauricio)
Pao Lien Teng (Precious Lotus-Lantern)
        (In Famous Chinese Plays)
Los Papeleros (see Aguirre, Isadora)
Paolo Paoli (see Adamov, Arthur)
Papa Haydn (see Pemberton, Madge)
Un Pape a New-York (see Guare, John)
Paper Foxhole; television script (see Elward, James)
Papers (see Kummer, Clare)
Papiermuhle (see Kaiser, Georg)
La Paquebot Tenacity (see Vildrac, Charles)
Par dela les Marronniers (see Ribes, Jean-Michel)
Par le Fenetre (see Feydeau, Georges)
La Parabole du Festin (see Claudel, Paul)
Paracelsus (see Browning, Robert)
Paracelsus (see Schnitzler, Arthur)
The Parachute (see Mercer, David)
PARADA LEON, Ricardo, 1902-
    Hacia la Meta
        (In Teatro Méxicano del Siglo XX, Vol. 1)
Paradise Lost (see Odets, Clifford)
Paradise Lost; screenplay (see Collier, John. Milton's Paradise
    Lost: Screenplay for Cinema of the Mind)
Le Paradoxe sur le Comédien (see Baillon, Jacques)
The Paragon (see Pertwee, Roland)

Un Paraguas Bajo la Lluvia (see Ruiz Iriarte, Victor)
Paralelo al Sueño (see Cordero C., Gustavo)
Les Paralipomènes d'Ubu (see Jarry, Alfred)
Parasitaster; or, The Fawne (see Marston, John)
Les Paravents (see Genet, Jean)
La Parcelle (see Loiseleux, Jacques)
Parece Mentira (see Villaurrutia, Xavier)
Las Paredes Oyen (see Ruiz de Alarcón y Mendoza, Juan)
Parents Are People (see Weiss, Morton J.)
Les Parents Terribles (see Cocteau, Jean)
Paris and Helen (see Schwartz, Delmore)
Paris Bound (see Barry, Philip)
The Parisian Woman (see Becque, Henri)
La Parisienne (see Becque, Henri)
The Park (see Ursell, Geoffrey)
PARKE, J.H.
    It Runs in the Family
        (In Prize Plays of 1927-28, Vol. 2)
PARKER, Kenneth T.
    Cry on My Shoulders
        (In his Parker's Television Plays)
    A Cup of Tea
        (In his Parker's Television Plays)
    Double Identity
        (In his Parker's Television Plays)
    Shall We Dance?
        (In his Parker's Television Plays)
    Stand Up to Death
        (In his Parker's Television Plays)
    Star Minded
        (In his Parker's Television Plays)
    Voice of the Machines
        (In his Parker's Television Plays)
    Within the Family
        (In his Parker's Television Plays)
PARKER, Louis N.
    A Minuet
        (In One-Act Plays for Stage and Study, 1st Series)
Parker, Robert, 1866-?
    *Butch Cassidy and the Sundance Kid (see Goldman, William)
PARKER, Stewart
    Spokesong; or, The Common Wheel
        (In Plays and Players, Vol. 24, nos. 3 & 4, Dec. 1976 &
        Jan. 1977)
PARLAKIAN, Nishan
    What Does Greta Garbo Mean to You?
        (In Drama and Theatre, Vol. 11, no. 3, Spring 1973)
The Parliament of Love (see Massinger, Philip)
The Parlor Car (see Howells, William Dean)
La Parodia (see Adamov, Arthur)
Les Paroles Restent (see Hervieu, Paul E.)
Parr, Catherine, 6th wife of Henry VIII, 1512-1548
    *Catherine Parr; or, Alexander's Horse (see Baring, Maurice)

The Parson's Wedding (see Killigrew, Thomas)
Partage de Midi (see Claudel, Paul)
El Partido de la Contrapartida (see Salmon, Raul)
Parting Friends (see Howells, William Dean)
Una Partita a Scacchi (see Middleton, Thomas)
The Party (see Mrozek, Slawomir)
Party for Six (see Bauer, Wolfgang)
El Paseo de Buster Keaton (see Garcia Lorca, Federico)
PASHKEVICH, Vasilii Alekseevich, c. 1742-c. 1800
    Misfortune from a Coach (see Kniazhin, Iakov B.)
Pasiphae (see Montherlant, Henry de)
Paskevich, Vasilii (see Pashkevich, Vasilii Alekseevich)
PASO, Alfonso
    La Corbata
        (In Teatro Español, 1962-63)
    Cosas de Papa y Mama
        (In Teatro Español, 1959-60)
    Desde Isabel, con Amor
        (In Teatro Español, 1966-67)
    En el Escorial, Carino Mio
        (In Teatro Selecto de Alfonso Paso)
    Juicio Contra un Sinverguenza
        (In Teatro Selecto de Alfonso Paso)
    Neron-Paso
        (In Teatro Selecto de Alfonso Paso)
    Los Pobrecitos
        (In Teatro Español, 1956-57)
        (In Teatro Selecto de Alfonso Paso)
    Rebelde
        (In Teatro Español, 1961-62)
    Usted Puede Ser un Asesino
        (In Teatro Español, 1957-58)
        (In Teatro Selecto de Alfonso Paso)
    Veneno Para Mi Marido
        (In Teatro Español, 1953-54)
PASOLINI, Pier Paolo, 1923-1975
    Medea; screenplay from "Medea, " by Euripides
        (In Garzanti Filmscripts, 1964)
    Oedipus Rex; screenplay from "Oedipus Rex, " by Sophocles
        (In Lorrimer Screenplays Series, 1971)
        (In Modern Filmscripts, 1971)
    Il Vangelo Secundo Matteo; filmscript (see Gambetti, Giacomo)
Pasquin: A Dramatic Satire of the Times (see Fielding, Henry)
Le Passe (see Porto-Riche, Georges de)
Passe-Porc ou le Confessional (see Pech, Claude-Henri)
The Passenger; filmscript (see Antonioni, Michelangelo)
The Passing of Chow-Chow (see Rice, Elmer L.)
The Passion (see Mushakoji, Saneatsu)
La Passion d'Anna Karénini (see Arout, Gabriel)
Passion du Général Franco (see Gatti, Armand)
Passion Play (see Shaw, George Bernard)
Passion, Poison, and Petrifaction; or, The Fatal Gazogene (see Shaw, George Bernard)

The Past Is Past (see Wasley, Richard)
The Past Is Present (see Golden, David T.)
El Pastel (see Romashov, Boris S.)
PASTERNAK, Boris Leonidovich, 1890-1960
  **Doctor Zhivago; screenplay (see Bolt, Robert)
Pastor Ephraim Magnus (see Jahnn, Hans Henny)
Pastorale; A Grotesque in One Act (see Hildesheimer, Wolfgang)
Patchouli (see Salacrou, Armand)
La Patente (see Pirandello, Luigi)
Paths (see Khaytov, Nikolay)
Patience; or, Bunthorne's Bride (see Gilbert, William S.)
Les Patients (see Audiberti, Jacques)
Patiomkin, Prince (see Potëmkin, Grigori Aleksandrovich)
PATON, Alan, 1903-
  **Lost in the Stars (see Weill, Kurt)
La Patria Chica (see Alvarez Quintero, Serafin)
PATRICELLI, Anthony
    The Last Word
      (In 100 Non-Royalty Radio Plays)
Patrick, John (pseud.) (see Goggan, John Patrick)
PATRICK, Robert, 1937-
    The Arnold Bliss Show
      (In Cheep Theatricks)
    Un Bel Di
      (In Performance, Vol. 1, no. 5, Mar./Apr. 1973)
    Camera Obscura
      (In Collision Course)
    Cornered
      (In Cheep Theatricks)
    The Haunted Host
      (In Cheep Theatricks)
    Help, I Am; a monologue
      (In Cheep Theatricks)
    I Came to New York to Write
      (In Cheep Theatricks)
    Joyce Dynel, an American Zarzuela
      (In Cheep Theatricks)
    Kennedy's Children
      (In Plays and Players, Vol. 22, nos. 5 & 6, Feb. & Mar. 1975)
    Lights/Camera/Action
      (In Cheep Theatricks)
    One Person; a monologue
      (In Cheep Theatricks)
    Preggin and Liss
      (In Cheep Theatricks)
    The Richest Girl in the World Finds Happiness; an occasional
    play for all occasions
      (In Cheep Theatricks)
      (In The Off Off Broadway Book)
    Still-Love
      (In Cheep Theatricks)
A Patriot for Me (see Osborne, John)
The Patron (see Foote, Samuel)

Patter Versus Clatter (see Mathews, Charles J.)
PATTERSON, Charles, 1941-
    Black-Ice
      (In Black Fire)
    Legacy
      (In 19 Necromancers from Now)
PAUL, Elliot
    The Ninety and Nine; a scenario
      (In Transition, Vol. 1, no. 11, Feb. 1928)
PAUL, Norman
    Springtime in the Ghetto; television script for an episode in
    "Good Times," by Norman Paul and Jack Elinson
      (In Samuel French's Tandem Library Series)
Paul and Virginia (see Cobb, James)
Paul Kauvar; or, Anarchy (see MacKaye, Steele)
Paul Lange und Tora Parsberg (see Bjørnson, Bjørnstjerne)
Paul Schippel Esq. (see Sternheim, Carl)
La Paura (see Binazzi, Massimo)
Pauvre Amour (see Dubé, Marcel)
Pauvre Bitos; ou, Le Diner de Têtes (see Anouilh, Jean)
Les Paves de l'Ours (see Feydeau, Georges)
PAWLEY, Thomas D., Jr., 1917-
    Jedgement Day
      (In The Negro Caravan)
    The Tumult and the Shouting
      (In Black Theater U.S.A., 1847-1974)
PAYNE, John Howard, 1791-1852
    Brutus; or, The Fall of Tarquin
      (In Representative Plays by American Dramatists, Vol. 2)
    Charles the Second, by John Howard Payne and Washington Irv-
    ing
      (In Representative American Plays, 1792-1949)
    Therese, the Orphan of Geneva
      (In The Drama, Vol. 19)
PAZ, Octavio, 1914-
    La Hija de Rappaccini
      (In Teatro Méxicano del Siglo XX, Vol. 5)
Pazukhin's Death (see Saltykov-Shchedrin, Mikhail)
PEABODY, Josephine Preston (Mrs. Lionel S. Marks), 1874-1922
    Fortune and Men's Eyes
      (In One-Act Plays by Modern Authors)
    The Piper
      (In Representative American Dramas)
Peace at Home (see Moinaux, Georges)
"Peace in Our Time" (see Coward, Noël)
Peace Manoeuvers (see Davis, Richard H.)
Peace on Earth, a Christmas Play of Today (see Hufham, B. Gary)
The Peach (see Romains, Jules)
PEACOCK, Thomas Love, 1785-1866
  **Nightmare Abbey (see Sharp, Anthony)
PEARCE, Leslie
    The Dentist, a Mack Sennett Comedy (see Fields, W.C.)
Pearls (see Totheroh, Dan)

The Peasant in Pawn (see Holberg, Ludvig von)
Peau de Vache (see Barillet, Pierre)
PECH, Claude-Henri
  Passe-Porc ou le Confessional
    (In L'Avant-Scène Théâtre, no. 564, May 15, 1975)
PECHANTRE, 1638-1709
  Geta
    (In More Plays by Rivals of Corneille and Racine)
Los Pechos Privilegiados (see Ruiz de Alarcón y Mendoza, Juan)
PECK, George Wilbur, 1840-1916
  **Peck's Bad Boy (see Harris, Aurand)
PECKINPAH, Sam, 1926-
  Noon Wine; television script, based on the short novel by Katherine Ann Porter. ABC, Nov. 23, 1966
    (In Electronic Drama)
A Peculiar Position (see Scribe, Eugene)
The Pedagogue (see Saunders, James)
Pedro Telonario (Auto Sacramental) (see Mira de Amescua, Antonio)
PEDROLO, Manuel de
  Cruma
    (In Modern International Drama, Vol. 6, no. 2, Spring 1973)
    (In 3 Catalan Dramatists)
  Full Circle
    (In 3 Catalan Dramatists)
  Men and No
    (In Modern International Drama, Vol. 10, no. 1, 1976)
  The Room
    (In 3 Catalan Dramatists)
PEELE, George, 1558?-1597?
  The Battle of Alcazar
    (In his Life and Works, Vol. 2)
  The Chronicle of King Edward I
    (In his Life and Works, Vol. 2)
  The Love of King David and Fair Bethsaba
    (In his Life and Works, Vol. 3)
  The Old Wives Tale
    (In his Life and Works, Vol. 3)
A Peep Behind the Curtain; or, The New Rehearsal (see Garrick, David)
Peer Gynt (see Ibsen, Henrik)
Peggy (see Crothers, Rachel)
PEGUY, Charles Pierre, 1873-1914
  Jeanne d'Arc
    (In his Oeuvres Poetiques)
  Le Mystère de la Charité de Jeanne d'Arc
    (In his Oeuvres Poetiques)
PEIPER, Tadeusz
  Wenn Er Nicht Da Ist
    (In Theater der Zeit, no. 4, 1975)
Los Pelados (see Castro, Felipe)
Le Pelerin (see Vildrac, Charles)
The Pelican (see Strindberg, August)

The Pelicans (see Radiguet, Raymond)
PELISSIER, Anthony, 1912-
    The Rocking-Horse Winner, screenplay and direction of the film
    by Anthony Pelissier, from the story by D.H. Lawrence
    (In Dickenson Literature and Film Series: From Fiction to
    Film)
Pelleas and Melisande (see Maeterlinck, Maurice)
Pelleas et melisande (Opera) (see Debussy, Claude)
PELUSO, Emanuel
    Good Day
    (In Off-Broadway Plays, Vol. 2)
    Little Fears
    (In Off-Broadway Plays, Vol. 2)
PEMAN, José Maria, 1897-
    Callados Como Muertos
    (In Teatro Español, 1951-52)
    La Casa
    (In Teatro Selecto de José Maria Peman)
    El Divino Impaciente
    (In Teatro Selecto de José Maria Peman)
    Edipo
    (In Teatro Selecto de José Maria Peman)
    La Herida Luminosa (see Sagarra, José M.)
    Los Tres Etceteras de Don Simon
    (In Teatro Español, 1957-58)
    (In Teatro Selecto de José Maria Peman)
    Tres Testigos
    (In Teatro Español, 1969-70)
    Tyestes; inspirado en la tragedia de Seneca
    (In Teatro Español, 1955-56)
    El Viejo y las Niñas
    (In Teatro Selecto de José Maria Peman)
PEMBERTON, Madge
    Papa Haydn
    (In Best One-Act Plays of 1939, London)
PENDLETON, James D.
    The Brief and Violent Reign of Absalom
    (In Religious Theatre, no. 7, Spring 1969)
Le Pendu (see Gurik, Robert)
Penelope (see Maugham, William Somerset)
PENMAN, Margaret
    Wheelchair
    (In Women Write for the Theatre Series, Vol. 1)
PENN, Arthur, 1922-
    Le Gaucher; titre original "The Left-Handed Gun" d'après une
    pièce écrite pour la télévision de Gore Vidal. Titre de la
    pièce "La Mort de Billy the Kid"
    (In L'Avant-Scène du Cinéma, no. 141, Nov. 1973)
    The Missouri Breaks; screenplay (see McGuane, Thomas)
The Penny; radio script (see Niss, Stanley)
A Penny for a Song (see Whiting, John)
A Penny Saved; radio script (see Reed, Dena)
Pensaci, Giacomino! (see Pirandello, Luigi)

People at Sea (see Priestley, John B.)
The People Show (see Nuttall, Jeff)
The People's Lawyer (Solon Shingle) (see Jones, Joseph S.)
The People's Park in Berkeley (see Burning City Theater, New York)
PEOPLE'S STREET THEATER, N. Y.
    Play for People's Tribunal to Try the War Criminals
        (In Guerilla Street Theater)
    Song of the Mighty B-52
        (In Guerilla Street Theater)
    To Be Radical Is to Get to the Root of Things
        (In Guerilla Street Theater)
PEPLE, Edward, 1867-1924
    The Girl
        (In Five Plays from the Other Side)
        (In One-Act Plays for Stage and Study, 1st Series)
PEPLOE, Mark
    The Passenger; filmscript (see Antonioni, Michelangelo)
Pepper, Waldo, 1895-1931
    The Great Waldo Pepper; screenplay (see Goldman, William)
Pepper Young's Family radio script
    Back in the Old House (see Carrington, Elaine S.)
El Pequeño Caso de Jorge Livido (see Magaña, Sergio)
El Pequeño Juicio (see Sanchez Mayans, Fernando)
Per Uso di Memoria (see Castri, Massimo)
PERALTA, Jesus T.
    Scent of Fear
        (In 3 Filipino Playwrights)
    The Sign of the Sea Gulls
        (In 3 Filipino Playwrights)
Percy, Edward (pseud.) (see Smith, Edward Percy)
Percy's Masque (see Hillhouse, James A.)
Perdican (see Musset, Alfred de)
Père (see Bourdet, Edouard)
Le Père Humilie (see Claudel, Paul)
Le Père Ideal (see Dubé, Marcel)
Le Père Prodigue (see Dumas, Alexandre)
Le Père Prudent et Equitable; ou, Crispin l'Heureux Fourbe (see
    Marivaux, Pierre C.)
PEREDA, Pridencio de
    Fiesta; text in German (see Hanel, Robert)
PERELMAN, Sidney Joseph, 1904-
    One Touch of Venus (see Weill, Kurt)
    Waiting for Sanity
        (In The Anxious Years)
PEREZ, Isaac Loeb, 1851-1915
    Champagne
        (In One-Act Plays from the Yiddish)
PEREZ REY, Lupe
    Astucia Femenina
        (In Obras Breves del Teatro Costarricense, Vol. 1)
Perfect Days (see Kessler, Jascha)
Perhaps a Poet (see Josephson, Ragnar)
Perichole (see Kraus, Karl)

Le Peril Bleu; ou, Mefiez-vous des Autobus (see Lanoux, Victor)
Period House (see Eaton, Walter P.)
Period of Adjustment (see Williams, Tennessee)
Periodo de Ajuste (see Williams, Tennessee)
PERL, Arnold
    Who Do You Kill? television script from "East Side/West Side,"
        CBS, Nov. 4, 1963
        (In Electronic Drama)
La Perle de la Canebière (see Labiche, Eugene)
Perón, Eva Duarte de, 2nd wife of Argentina Pres., Juan Perón,
    1919 or 1922-1952
    *Eva Perón (see Copi)
PERR, Harvey
    Afternoon Tea
        (In Guthrie New Theater, Vol. 1)
    Jew!
        (In Collision Course)
    Upstairs Sleeping
        (In New Theatre in America, Vol. 1)
Los Perros (see Garro, Elena)
PERRY, Eleanor
    Among the Paths to Eden; television script (see Capote, Truman)
    A Christmas Memory; television script (see Capote, Truman)
    Miriam; television script (see Capote, Truman)
PERRY, Frank
    Doc; screenplay (see Hamill, Pete)
Persona; screenplay (see Bergman, Ingmar)
Le Personnage Combattant (see Vauthier, Jean)
Pertharite (see Corneille, Pierre)
PERTWEE, Roland, 1885-
    Counsel's Opinion
        (In One-Act Plays for Stage and Study, 7th Series)
    The Paragon, by Roland and Michael Pertwee
        (In Plays of the Year, Vol. 1, 1948-49)
    Speaking Terms
        (In One-Act Plays for Stage and Study, 6th Series)
Peter Pan; oder das Märchen vom Jungen der Nicht Gross Werden
    Wollte (see Kästner, Erich)
Peter Pan; or, The Boy Who Would Not Grow Up (see Barrie, James
    M.)
Peter Quill's Shenanigans (La Farce de Maître Pierre Pathelin)
    (Anon.)
        (In Five Comedies of Medieval France)
Peter Stuyvesant; radio script (see McMorrow, Will)
PETERKIN, Julia (Mood), 1880-1961
    Boy-Children
        (In One-Act Plays for Stage and Study, 7th Series)
Peter's Banquet; or, The Criminal Son (see Commedia dell'Arte)
PETERSEN, Eric Jens
    Who Called You Here? adapted for radio by Edward Goldberger
        (In 100 Non-Royalty Radio Plays)
PETERSON, Louis, 1922-
    Take a Giant Step

        (In <u>Black Insights</u>)
        (In <u>Black Theater</u>)
        (In <u>Black Theater U.S.A.</u>, 1847-1974)
Petin, Mauillarbourg et Consorts (see Moinaux, Georges)
Un Petit Drame (see Shaw, George Bernard)
Le Petit Juif Laid (see Lamarche, Gustave)
Le Petit-Maître Corrige (see Marivaux, Pierre C.)
Le Petit Voyage (see Labiche, Eugene)
La Petite Bête (see Roncoroni, Jean-Louis)
La Petite Cuiller (see Louki, Pierre)
La Petite Paroisse (see Daudet, Alphonse)
Les Petites Mains (see Labiche, Eugene)
Les Petites Oiseaux (see Labiche, Eugene)
A Petrarchan Sonnet (see Pogodin, Nikolai F.)
PETRESCO, Julia
        La Cité du Soleil
            (In <u>L'Avant-Scène du Théâtre</u>, no. 510, Jan. 15, 1973)
The Petrified Forest (see Sherwood, Robert E.)
PETRONIUS ARBITER, fl. 1st Cent. A.D., d. 66 A.D.
    **Satyricon (see Foster, Paul)
PETROV, Evgeny
        The Power of Love (see Ilf, Ilya)
PETTITT, Wilfrid H.
        Panic in Salem
            (In <u>100 Non-Royalty Radio Plays</u>)
        The Silver Coronet
            (In <u>100 Non-Royalty Radio Plays</u>)
La Peur des Coups (see Moinaux, Georges)
PEZZULO, Ted
        The Wooing of Lady Sunday
            (In <u>Best Short Plays</u>, 1974)
Der Pfarrer mit Sein Ehbrecher-Bauern (see Sachs, Hans)
Die Pfarrerwahl (see Kaiser, Georg)
PFEIFFER, Hans
        Salut an Alle, Marx (see Kaltofen Günter)
        Thomas Müntzer
            (In <u>Theater der Zeit</u>, no. 7, 1975)
Pferdewechsel (see Kaiser, Georg)
Phaea (see Unruh, Fritz von)
Phaedra (see Racine, Jean Baptiste)
Phaedra (see Rexroth, Kenneth)
The Phantom Head-Shaver (of Brighton); The Goon Show Script no.
    103 (see Milligan, Spike)
The Pharmacist; filmscript (see Fields, W.C.)
Philadelphia, Here I Come! (see Friel, Brian)
The Philadelphia Story (see Barry, Philip)
The Philanderer (see Shaw, George Bernard)
Philaster; or, Love Lies Bleeding (see Beaumont, Francis)
Philip II, King of France, 1165-1223
    *Left-Handed Liberty; a Play About Magna Carta (see Arden, John)
Philip II, King of Spain, 1527-1598
    *Don Carlos: A Dramatic History (see Schiller, Johann)
        Philip the King (see Masefield, John)

*Philippe II (see Chénier, Marie-Joseph B.)
*Queen Mary (see Tennyson, Alfred Lord)
*The Resources of Quinola (see Balzac, Honore de)
PHILIPS, Ambrose, 1674-1747
    The Distrest Mother
        (In The London Stage, Vol. 4)
Phillip Holtz's Fury (see Frisch, Max)
PHILLIPS, Louis, 1942-
    The Envoi Messages
        (In Modern International Drama, Vol. 7, no. 1B, Spring 1976)
    God Have Mercy on the June-Bug
        (In Modern International Drama, Vol. 7, no. 1A, Oct. 1973)
The Philosopher Duped by Love (see Corneille, Pierre)
Phipps (see Houghton, Stanley)
PHIRI, Desmond Dudwa, 1931-
    The Chief's Bride
        (In All the World's a Stage)
Phocas, Emperor of the Eastern Roman Empire, d. 610 A.D.
    *Heraclius (see Corneille, Pierre)
The Phoenix (see Middleton, Thomas)
The Phoenix (L'Homme de Cendres) (see Obey, Andre)
Phoenix Too Frequent (see Fry, Christopher)
Phormio (see Terence)
The Photographer (see Jupp, Kenneth)
Pi Yu Tsan (The Green Jade Hairpin)
        (In Famous Chinese Plays)
Il Piacere dell'Onesta (see Pirandello, Luigi)
PIALAT, Maurice, 1925-
    Nous ne Viellirons pas Ensemble
        (In L'Avant-Scène du Cinéma, no. 134, Mar. 1973).
PICASSO, Pablo, 1881-1973
    Desire Caught by the Tail
        (In Calder & Boyars Playscript Series, no. 25)
    The Four Little Girls
        (In Calder & Boyars Playscript Series, no. 32)
Piccolo, Brian, 1943-1970
    *Brian's Song
        (see Blinn, William)
Piccolomini, Octavio, 1599-1656
    *The Piccolomini (see Schiller, Johann)
Picnic (see Inge, William M.)
Picnic on the Battlefield (see Arrabal, Fernando)
A Picnic to Ialova (see Turkish Theatre, Karagöz)
PICO, Pedro E., 1882-
    Agua en las Manos
        (In Teatro Argentino Contemporaneo)
Picture (see Hailey, Oliver)
The Picture (see Ionesco, Eugene)
The Picture (see Massinger, Philip)
The Picture of Dorian Gray (see Osborne, John)
The Pie and the Tart (see Jagendorf, Moritz A.)
En Pièces Détachées (see Tremblay, Michel)
Un Pied dans le Crime (see Labiche, Eugene)

The Pied Piper, a Tale of Hamelin City (see Drinkwater, John)
Pierrot Before the Seven Doors (see Cantillon, Arthur)
Pierrot le Fou; screenplay (see Godard, Jean-Luc)
The Pierrot of the Minute (see Dowson, Ernest C.)
The Pierrot of the Present (see Dowson, Ernest C.)
Piet Bouteille (see Ghelderode, Michel de)
Le Pieton de l'Air (see Ionesco, Eugene)
The Pig Pen (see Bullins, Edward A.)
The Pigeon Banquet (see Laxness, Halldor)
Pilate, Pontius, 5th Roman Procurator of Judaea and Samaria, 1st
    half of 1st Cent. A.D.
    *The Divine Tragedy (see Longfellow, Henry Wadsworth)
    Good Friday; a dramatic poem (see Masefield, John)
The Pile (see Moore, Mavor)
The Pilgrim (Anon.)
        (In Medieval Church Music-Dramas)
The Pilgrim (see Beaumont, Francis)
The Pilgrim (see Killigrew, Thomas)
Pillar of Sand (see Nicol, Eric)
Pillars of Society (see Ibsen, Henrik)
PILLEMENT, Georges, 1898-
    L'Autobus
        (In Le Théâtre d'Aujourd'hui)
    Lui
        (In Le Théâtre d'Aujourd'hui)
    Marie Couche-toi La
        (In Le Théâtre d'Aujourd'hui)
PILLOT, Joseph Eugene
    The Sundial
        (In One-Act Plays for Stage and Study, 3rd Series)
PILON, Frederick, 1750-1788
    The Deaf Lover
        (In The London Stage, Vol. 3)
    He Would Be a Soldier
        (In The London Stage, Vol. 3)
The Pilots (see Schevill, James)
PINCHON, Edgcumb, 1883-
    Viva Zapata; screenplay (see Steinbeck, John)
The Pinedus Affair (see Levi, Paolo)
PINERA, Virgilio, 1912-
    Estudio en Blanco y Negro
        (In Teatro Breve Hispanoamericano Contemporaneo)
PINERO, Sir Arthur Wing, 1855-1934
    Each in His Own Way
        (In 20th Century Plays)
    The Gay Lord Quex
        (In Representative British Dramas)
        (In his Social Plays, Vol. 2)
    His House in Order
        (In his Social Plays, Vol. 3)
    Iris
        (In his Social Plays, Vol. 2)

Letty
    (In his <u>Social Plays</u>, Vol. 3)
The Magistrate
    (In <u>English Plays of the 19th Century,</u> Vol. IV: Farces)
MidChannel
    (In <u>Edwardian Plays</u>)
    (In his <u>Social Plays</u>, Vol. 4)
The Notorious Mrs. Ebbsmith
    (In his <u>Social Plays</u>, Vol. 1)
The Second Mrs. Tanqueray
    (In <u>English Plays of the 19th Century,</u> Vol. 11: Dramas
    (In his <u>Social Plays,</u> Vol. 1)
The Thunderbolt
    (In his <u>Social Plays</u>, Vol. 4)
The Widow of Wasdale Head
    (In <u>One-Act Plays for Stage and Study</u>, 1st Series)
Ping Pong (see Adamov, Arthur)
PINGET, Robert
  About Mortin
    (In his <u>Plays</u>, Vol. 2)
  Architruc
    (In <u>Modern French Theatre</u>)
    (In his <u>Plays</u>, Vol. 2)
  Clope
    (In his <u>Plays</u>, Vol. 1)
  Dead Letter
    (In his <u>Plays</u>, Vol. 1)
  The Hypothesis
    (In his <u>Plays</u>, Vol. 2)
  Ici ou Ailleurs
    (In <u>Le Théâtre d'Aujourd'hui</u>)
  Lettre Morte
    (In <u>Le Théâtre d'Aujourd'hui</u>)
  The Old Tune, adapted by Samuel Beckett
    (In his <u>Plays,</u> Vol. 1)
PINNER, David, 1940-
  The Drums of Snow
    (In <u>Plays of the Year</u>, Vol. 42, 1972)
PINSKI, David, 1872-1959
  King David and His Wives
    (In <u>The Great Jewish Plays</u>)
  Laid Off
    (In <u>One-Act Plays for Stage and Study</u>, 7th Series)
PINTER, Harold, 1930-
  Altri Tempi
    (In <u>Sipario</u>, no. 311, Apr. 1972)
  The Birthday Party
    (In his <u>Complete Works: One</u>)
  Black and White
    (In his <u>Complete Works</u>, Vol. 1)
  The Caretaker
    (In his <u>Complete Works: Two</u>)
  The Collection
    (In his <u>Complete Works: Two</u>)

L'Altro Figlio
    (In his <u>Teatro (Maschere Nude)</u>, Vol. 8)
L'Amica delle Mogli
    (In his <u>Teatro (Maschere Nude)</u>, Vol. 6)
At the Exit
    (In his <u>One-Act Plays</u>)
Bellavita
    (In his <u>One-Act Plays</u>)
Bellavita; text in Italian
    (In his <u>Teatro (Maschere Nude)</u>, Vol. 8)
Il Berretto a Sonagli
    (In his <u>Teatro (Maschere Nude)</u>, Vol. 7)
Cece
    (In his <u>Teatro (Maschere Nude)</u>, Vol. 7)
Chee-Chee
    (In his <u>One-Act Plays</u>)
Ciascuno a Suo Modo
    (In his <u>Teatro (Maschere Nude)</u>, Vol. 1)
Come Prima, Meglio di Prima
    (In his <u>Teatro (Maschere Nude)</u>, Vol. 4)
Come Tu Mi Vuoi
    (In his <u>Teatro (Maschere Nude)</u>, Vol. 4)
Cosi e (se Vi Pare)
    (In his <u>Teatro (Maschere Nude)</u>, Vol. 5)
O di Uno o di Nessuno
    (In his <u>Teatro (Maschere Nude)</u>, Vol. 8)
Diana e la Tuda
    (In his <u>Teatro (Maschere Nude)</u>, Vol. 2)
The Doctor's Duty
    (In his <u>One-Act Plays</u>)
Il Dovere del Medico
    (In his <u>Teatro (Maschere Nude)</u>, Vol. 7)
Enrico IV
    (In his <u>Teatro (Maschere Nude)</u>, Vol. 2)
Favola del Figlio Cambiato
    (In his <u>Teatro (Maschere Nude)</u>, Vol. 10)
The Festival of Our Lord of the Ship
    (In his <u>One-Act Plays</u>)
La Giara
    (In his <u>Teatro (Maschere Nude)</u>, Vol. 7)
I Giganti delle Montagna
    (In his <u>Teatro (Maschere Nude)</u>, Vol. 10)
Il Gioco delle Parti
    (In his <u>Teatro (Maschere Nude)</u>, Vol. 3)
Henry IV
    (In <u>Themes of Drama</u>)
I'm Dreaming, but Am I?
    (In his <u>One-Act Plays</u>)
The Imbecile
    (In his <u>One-Act Plays</u>)
L'Imbecille
    (In his <u>Teatro (Maschere Nude)</u>, Vol. 3)

L'Innesto
  (In his Teatro (Maschere Nude), Vol. 6)
The Jar
  (In All the World's a Stage)
  (In his One-Act Plays)
Lazzaro
  (In his Teatro (Maschere Nude), Vol. 10)
The License
  (In his One-Act Plays)
Liola
  (In his Teatro (Maschere Nude), Vol. 8)
Lumie di Sicilia
  (In his Teatro (Maschere Nude), Vol. 7)
Ma Non e una Cosa Seria
  (In his Teatro (Maschere Nude), Vol. 8)
The Man with the Flower in His Mouth
  (In his One-Act Plays)
La Morsa
  (In his Teatro (Maschere Nude), Vol. 6)
Non si sa Come
  (In his Teatro (Maschere Nude), Vol. 9)
La Nuova Colonia
  (In his Teatro (Maschere Nude), Vol. 10)
The Other Son
  (In his One-Act Plays)
La Patente
  (In his Teatro (Maschere Nude), Vol. 8)
Pensaci, Giacomino!
  (In his Teatro (Maschere Nude), Vol. 7)
Il Piacere dell'Onesta
  (In his Teatro (Maschere Nude), Vol. 3)
The Pleasure of Honesty
  (In Masterpieces of the Modern Italian Theatre)
Quando si e Qualcuno
  (In his Teatro (Maschere Nude), Vol. 9)
Questa Sera Si Recita a Soggetto
  (In his Teatro (Maschere Nude), Vol. 1)
La Ragione Degli i Altri
  (In his Teatro (Maschere Nude), Vol. 5)
Right You Are! (If You Think So)
  (In Dramas of Modernism)
Sagra del Signore della Nave
  (In his Teatro (Maschere Nude), Vol. 7)
Sei Personaggi in Cerca d'Autore
  (In his Teatro (Maschere Nude), Vol. 1)
Sicilian Limes
  (In his One-Act Plays)
  (In Plays of the Italian Theatre)
La Signora Morli, Una e Due
  (In his Teatro (Maschere Nude), Vol. 6)
Six Characters in Search of an Author
  (In Contact with Drama)
  (In Masterpieces of the Modern Italian Theatre)

Sogno (Ma Forse No)
    (In his Teatro (Maschere Nude), Vol. 6)
Trovarsi
    (In his Teatro (Maschere Nude), Vol. 9)
Tutto per Bene
    (In his Teatro (Maschere Nude), Vol. 5)
L'Uomo dal Fore in Bocca
    (In his Teatro (Maschere Nude), Vol. 3)
L'Uomo, la Bestia e la Virtu
    (In his Teatro (Maschere Nude), Vol. 3)
Vestire Gli Ignudi
    (In his Teatro (Maschere Nude), Vol. 4)
The Vise
    (In his One-Act Plays)
La Vita Che Ti Diedi
    (In his Teatro (Maschere Nude), Vol. 2)
The Pirates of Penzance; or, The Slave of Duty (see Gilbert, William
    S.)
PIRON, Alexis, 1689-1773
    Arlequin-Deucalion
        (In Théâtre de XVIII Siècle, Vol. 1)
    La Métromanie ou le Poète
        (In Théâtre de XVIII Siècle, Vol. 1)
A Piscatorial Eclogue: Vel Isaacus Walton in Novamm Scalam Redi-
    vivus (see Geist, Peter von)
PISEMSKII, Aleksei Feofilakovich, 1821-1881
    Baal
        (In Russian Literature Triquarterly, no. 9, Spring 1974)
    A Bitter Fate
        (In Masterpieces of the Russian Drama, Vol. 1)
Pisemsky, Alexey (see Pisemskii, Aleksei Feofilakovich)
Pistols for Two (see Shellan, David)
PITCHER, Oliver
    The One
        (In Black Drama Anthology)
Pizarro, Francisco Marques, 1470?-1541
    *Pizatto (see Sheridan, Richard Brinsley)
    *The Royal Hunt of the Sun (see Shaffer, Peter)
PLA, Josefina, 1909-
    Historia de un Numero
        (In Teatro Breve Hispanoamericano Contemporaneo)
        (In Teatro Contemporaneo Hispanoamericano, Vol. 1)
A Place Calling Itself Rome (see Osborne, John)
La Place de L'Etoile (see Desnos, Robert)
A Place in the World (see Sternheim, Carl)
La Place Royale (see Corneille, Pierre)
Les Plaideurs; or, The Suitors (see Racine, Jean)
The Plaindealer (see Wycherley, William)
Plainte Contre Inconnu (see Neveux, Georges)
Plaintiff in a Pretty Hat (see Williams, Hugh)
Plaintiffs and Defendants (see Gray, Simon)
Le Plaisir de Rompre (see Renard, Jules)

PLANCHE, James Robinson, 1796-1880
    Returned "Killed"
        (In The London Stage, Vol. 4)
    Plans for the Coronation (see Henson, Bertram)
La Planète Sauvage; film scenario (see Laloux, Rene)
Plaster (see Alson, Lawrence)
PLATER, Alan, 1935-
    Close the Coalhouse Door; based on stories by Sid Chaplin; songs
        by Alex Glasgow
        (In Methuen Playscript Series, 1971)
Plato, 427-347 B.C.
    *Socrates (see Llovet, Enrique)
Plato Paceno (see Salmon, Raul)
The Platonic Lovers (see D'Avenant, Sir William)
Platonov (see Chekhov, Anton)
PLAUTUS, Titus Maccius, 254?-184 B.C.
    Amphitruo, translated by James H. Mantinband
        (In Amphitryon: Three Plays in New Verse Translations)
    Amphitryon; or, Jupiter in Disguise
        (In The Drama, Vol. 21)
  **Amphitryon; or, The Two Socias (see Dryden, John)
    The Captives
        (In World Drama, Vol. 1)
Play for a Dark Room; a radio play (see Piontek, Heinz)
Play for People's Tribunal to Try the War Criminals (see People's
    Street Theater, N.Y.)
Play It Again, Sam; play and screenplay (see Allen, Woody)
The Play of Daniel (Anon.)
        (In Medieval Church Music-Dramas)
The Play of Herod (Anon.)
        (In Medieval Church Music-Dramas)
The Play of Robin and Marion (see Halle, Adam de la)
The Play of St. George (Anon.)
        (In World Drama, Vol. 1)
The Play of St. Nicholas (see Bodel, Jean)
The Play of the Annunciation (Anon.)
        (In Medieval Church Music-Dramas)
The Play of the Wether (see Heywood, John)
The Play of William Cooper and Edmund Dew-Nevett (see Selbourne,
    David)
Play Strindberg (see Dürrenmatt, Friedrich)
Play with a Tiger (see Lessing, Doris)
La Playa Vacia (see Salom, Jaime)
The Playboy of Seville; or, Supper with a Statue (see Tellez, Gabriel)
Playboy of the Western World (see Synge, John M.)
The Player Queen (see Yeats, William Butler)
The Playhouse to Be Let (see D'Avenant, Sir William)
Playing the Sticks; filmscript (see Fields, W.C.)
The Play's the Thing (see Molnar, Ferenc)
A Playwright's Dilemma (see Sturm, Richard F.)
Pleasant Dialogues and Drammas (see Heywood, Thomas)
The Pleasure of Honesty (see Pirandello, Luigi)
The Pleasure of Parting (see Renard, Jules)

The Pleasures of the Inchanted Island (see Molière, Jean Baptiste)
Plenty of Rein; television script (see Roskam, Clair)
The Plot Is Ready (see Clarke, Austin)
The Plot Succeeds (see Clarke, Austin)
The Plough and the Stars (see O'Casey, Sean)
Pluft, el Fantasmita (see Machado, Maria C.)
La Pluga (see Zamiatin, Evgeni I.)
Plumes: A Fold Tragedy (see Johnson, Georgia D.)
Le Plus Heureux des Trois (see Labiche, Eugene)
PLUTARCH (PLOUTARCHOS), c. 46-c. 120 A.D.
  **Cleomenes, The Spartan Heroe (see Dryden, John)
POBLACION, Pablo
    La Sesion
        (In Teatro Español, 1969-70)
El Pobrecito Embustero (see Ruiz Iriarte, Victor)
Los Pobrecitos (see Paso, Alfonso)
Pocahontas (American Indian Princess Matoaka), 1595?-1617
    *Po-ca-hon-tas; or, The Gentle Savage (see Brougham, John)
    *Pocahontas; or, The Settlers of Virginia (see Curtis, George W.)
POCOCK, Isaac, 1782-1835
    The Miller and His Men
        (In English Plays of the 19th Century, Vol. 1: Dramas 1800-
        1850)
El Poder (see Calvo Sotelo, Joaquin)
POE, Edgar Allan, 1809-1849
    **Cask of Amontillado; radio script (see Newman, Ellis)
    **The Fall of the House of Usher (see Berkoff, Steven)
    **Metzengerstein; screenplay (see Vadim, Roger)
    **The Purloined Letter; radio script (see Andrews, Charleton)
    **Telltale Heart (see Holland, Norman)
    **Toby Dammit; screenplay (see Fellini, Federico)
    **William Wilson; screenplay (see Malle, Louis)
Poem-Plays (see Krauss, Ruth)
Le Poème de l'Elève Mikovsky (see Thomas, Pascal)
The Poetaster; or, His Arraignment (see Jonson, Ben)
Poetry and Plaster (see Medcraft, Russell G.)
The Poet's Secret (see Bernard, Jean-Jacques)
The Poet's Well (see Riley, Mrs. Alice C.)
POGODIN, (born Stukalov) Nikolai Fydorovich, 1900-1962
    The Chimes of the Kremlin
        (In Soviet Scene)
    A Petrarchan Sonnet
        (In Contemporary Russian Drama)
    Tempo
        (In Six Soviet Plays)
Poil de Carotte (see Renard, Jules)
Le Point de Mire (see Labiche, Eugene)
Point of Departure (see Anouilh, Jean)
Point Valaine (see Coward, Noël)
POIRET, Jean
    La Cage aux Folles
        (In L'Avant-Scène du Théâtre, no. 518, May 15, 1973)
Les Poissons Rouges; ou, Mon Père ce Héros (see Anouilh, Jean)

POKALSKY, Peter
  Hot Stuff
      (In The Yale Literary Magazine, Vol. 146, nos. 4/5, 1977)
POLANSKI, Roman, 1933-
  Le Bal des Vampires; titre original "The Fearless Vampire
  Killers"
      (In L'Avant-Scène Cinéma, no. 154, Jan. 1975)
  Cul-de-Sac; screenplay by Roman Polanski and Gerard Brach,
  film directed by Roman Polanski
      (In Lorrimer Modern Film Scripts Series, 1975)
      (In his Polanski: 3 Filmscripts)
  Knife in the Water; screenplay by Roman Polanski, Jerzy Sko-
  limowski and Jakub Goldberg, film directed by Roman Polanski
      (In Lorrimer Modern Film Scripts Series, 1975)
      (In his Polanski: 3 Filmscripts)
  Repulsion; screenplay by Roman Polanski and Gerard Brach, film
  directed by Roman Polanski
      (In Lorrimer Modern Film Scripts Series, 1975)
      (In his Polanski: 3 Filmscripts)
  What?
      (In Lorrimer Modern Film Scripts Series, 1974)
POLIAKOFF, Stephen
  City Sugar
      (In Methuen's New Theatrescripts, no. 1, 1976)
      (In Plays and Players, Vol. 23, nos. 4 & 5, Jan. & Feb. 1976)
  Hitting Town
      (In Methuen's New Theatrescripts, no. 1, 1976)
  Strawberry Fields
      (In Methuen's New Theatrescripts, no. 8, 1977)
The Police (see Mrozek, Slawomir)
Polinice (see Alfieri, Vittorio)
The Politician (see Shirley, James)
The Politician Out-Witted (see Low, Samuel)
Politics of Passion (see Callaghan, Barry)
POLLOCK, Sharon
  Walsh
      (In Talonplays Series, 1973)
Pollution; text in French (see Tholy, Rene)
Polly (see Gay, John)
Polly Honeycombe (see Colman, George, The Younger)
Polterabend (see Kleineidam, Horst)
Polyeucte (see Corneille, Pierre)
POMERANCE, Bernard
  High in Vietnam, Hot Damn
      (In Gambit, Vol. 6, no. 22)
  Hospital
      (In Gambit, Vol. 6, no. 22)
  Thanksgiving in Detroit
      (In Gambit, Vol. 6, no. 22)
POMERANTZ, Edward
  Change of Pace
      (In Ms., Vol. 2, June 1974)
  Nothing Personal
      (In Ms., Vol. 2, June 1974)

Pomme, Pomme, Pomme (see Audiberti, Jacques)
POMMERET, Xavier-Agnan, 1932-
    L. S. B. , Le Salamandre's Business
        (In L'Avant-Scène Théâtre, no. 606, Mar. 15, 1977)
    Pour Agnès, ou L'Agnèserie
        (In L'Avant-Scène Théâtre, no. 606, Mar. 15, 1977)
Pompée (see Corneille, Pierre)
Pompeji (see Horvath, Odön von)
Pompey the Great (Gnaeus Pompeus Magnus), 106-48 B. C.
    *La Morte de Pompée (The Death of Pompey) (see Corneille,
        Pierre)
    *The Tragedy of Pompey the Great (see Masefield, John)
PONFERRADE, Juan Oscar, 1908-
    El Carnaval del Diablo
        (In Teatro Argentino Contemporaneo)
PONGETTI, Henrique
    A Arca de Noe Nao Parte Hoje
        (In Revista de Teatro, no. 392, Mar. /Apr. 1973)
    Com a Rainha e Assim
        (In Revista de Teatro, no. 392, Mar. /Apr. 1973)
    Dois Primos ... Do Outro Mundo
        (In Revista de Teatro, no. 392, Mar. /Apr. 1973)
    E da Sua Conta?
        (In Revista de Teatro, no. 392, Mar. /Apr. 1973)
    O Fantasma
        (In Revista de Teatro, no. 392, Mar. /Apr. 1973)
    O "Gazeteiro"
        (In Revista de Teatro, no. 392, Mar. /Apr. 1973)
    Precisa-se de um Sapato
        (In Revista de Teatro, no. 392, Mar. /Apr. 1973)
Le Pont de l'Europe (see Salacrou, Armand)
Ponteach; or, The Savages of America (see Rogers, Robert)
PONTES, Paulo
    Dr. Fausto Da Silva
        (In Revista de Teatro, no. 405, May-June 1975)
POOLE, John, 1786?-1872
    The Scape-Goat
        (In The London Stage, Vol. 4)
POOLE, John F.
    Dat's What's de Matter; a burlesque lecture, a minstrel show
        (In Dramas from the American Theatre, 1762-1909)
POOLER, James
    Boy Waiting, adapted for radio by Edward Goldberger
        (In 100 Non-Royalty Radio Plays)
The Poor Boy (see Witkiewicz, Stanislaw I.)
The Poor Bride (see Ostrovskii, Alexandr N.)
The Poor House (see Driscoll, Louise)
Poor Judas (see Bagnold, Enid)
Poor Tom (see Cregan, David)
The Poorhouse (see Hyde, Douglas)
The Poosidin's Resignation (see Miller, Arthur)
POPE, Alexander, 1688-1744
    Three Hours After Marriage (see Gay, John)

The Pope's Wedding (see Bond, Edward)
POPPLEWELL, Jack
    Dead on Nine
       (In Plays of the Year, Vol. 13, 1955)
Por los Caminos Van los Campesions (see Cuarda, Pablo A.)
Por un Plato de Arroz (see Salazar Tamariz, Hugo)
Porch (see Sweet, Jeffrey)
Porfirio (see Robles, Emmanuel)
Porgy (see Heyward, Dubose)
Porgy and Bess (see Gershwin, George)
Porsena, Lars, King of Clusium, 6th Cent. B.C.
    *Scevole (Scaevola) (see Du Ryer, Pierre)
Port-Royal (see Montherlant, Henry de)
PORTA, Elvio, 1945-
    Masaniello, di Elvio Porta e Armando Pugliese
       (In Sipario, no. 343, Dec. 1974)
PORTER, Cole, 1892-1964
    Kiss Me, Kate; book by Samuel and Bella Spewack; music and
    lyrics by Cole Porter; based on William Shakespeare's "The
    Taming of the Shrew"
       (In Ten Great Musicals of the American Theatre, Vol. 1)
    Leave It to Me! Book by Bella and Samuel Spewack; music and
    lyrics by Cole Porter
       (In Ten Great Musicals of the American Theatre, Vol. 2)
PORTER, Katherine Anne, 1890-
  **Noon Wine (see Peckinpah, Sam)
PORTILLO, Estela
    The Day of the Swallows
       (In Contemporary Chicano Theatre)
PORTO-RICHE, Georges de, 1849-1930
    Amoureuse
       (In his Théâtre d'Amour, Vol. 1)
    La Chance de François
       (In his Théâtre d'Amour, Vol. 1)
    Françoise' Luck
       (In Four Plays of the Free Theater)
    L'Infidèle
       (In his Théâtre d'Amour, Vol. 1)
    Les Malefilatre
       (In his Théâtre d'Amour, Vol. 2)
    Le Marchand d'Estampes
       (In his Théâtre d'Amour, Vol. 2)
    Le Passe
       (In his Théâtre d'Amour, Vol. 1)
    Le Vieil Homme
       (In his Théâtre d'Amour, Vol. 2)
    Zubiri
       (In his Théâtre d'Amour, Vol. 2)
The Portrait (see Scala, Flaminio)
Portrait by Proxy (see Barker, Albert)
Le Portrait de Dorian Gray (see Boutron, Pierre)
Portrait of an Old Lady (see Madden, Richard)
Portrait of Dora (see Cixous, Helene)

A Portrait of the Artist as Filipino (see Joaquin, Nick)
Portraits de Famille (see Chénier, Marie-Joseph B.)
Posada (see Richards, Ivor A.)
The Possessed (see Camus, Albert)
The Post-Inn (see Goldoni, Carlo)
Post-Mortem (see Coward, Noël)
The Post Office (see Tagore, Sir Rabindranath)
The Pot Boiler (see Gerstenberg, Alice)
The Pot of Broth (see Yeats, William Butler)
Potemkin; screenplay (see Eisenstein, Sergei M. Battleship Potemkin)
Potëmkin, Grigori Aleksandrovich, 1739-1791
    *Great Catherine (Whom Glory Still Adores) (see Shaw, George
    Bernard)
Pots of Money (see Labiche, Eugene)
POTTER, Beatrix, 1866-1943
    **Tales of Beatrix Potter; filmscript (see Lanchberry, John)
POTTER, Dennis, 1935-
    Follow the Yellow Brick Road
        (In The Television Dramatist)
POTTS, Renee, 1908-
    Imaginame Infinita
        (In Teatro Cubano Contemporaneo)
Poucette (see Vildrac, Charles)
La Poudre aux Yeux (see Labiche, Eugene)
A Pound on Demand (see O'Casey, Sean)
Pour Agnès, ou L'Agnèserie (see Pommeret, Xavier-Agnan)
Pour Lucrece (see Giraudoux, Jean)
Pourquoi le Robe d'Anna Ne Veut Pas Redescendre (see Eyen, Tho-
    mas L.)
POWELL, Anthony, 1905-
    The Garden God
        (In his Two Plays, 1972)
    The Rest I'll Whistle
        (In his Two Plays, 1972)
POWELL, Michael
    The Red Shoes; written, directed and produced by Michael Pow-
    ell and Emeric Pressburger, based on the work of Hans Chris-
    tian Andersen
        (In Garland Classics of Film Literature Series)
    The Tales of Hoffman; written, directed and produced by Mich-
    ael Powell and Emeric Pressburger, based on the opera by
    Jacques Offenbach
        (In Garland Classics of Film Literature Series)
Power; a Living Newspaper (see Arent, Arthur)
POWER, Victor
    The Escape
        (In Drama and Theatre, Vol. 10, no. 2, Winter 1971-72)
The Power of Darkness (see Tolstoi, Lev N.)
The Power of Love (see Ilf, Ilya)
Der Präsident (see Kaiser, Georg)
PRAGA, Andre
    Salle d'Attente
        (In L'Avant-Scène Théâtre, no. 581, Jan. 15, 1976)

The Pragmatists (see Witkiewicz, Stanislaw I.)
Prague Is Quiet (see Jacobs, Lewis)
The Prairie Doll (see Carpenter, Edward C.)
Prayer Meeting; or, The First Militant Minister (see Caldwell, Ben)
Pre-Paradise Story Now (see Fassbinder, Rainer W.)
Precious Moments from the Family Album to Provide You with Comfort in the Long Years to Come (see Yavin, Naftali)
Precisa-se de um Sapato (see Pongetti, Henrique)
Preggin and Liss (see Patrick, Robert)
Le Prejuge Vaincu (see Marivaux, Pierre C.)
PRELOVSKY, Anatoly
    Common Man, translated by J.C. Gulick
        (In Literary Review, Vol. 13, Spring 1970)
Prelude pour la Nuit de Noël (see Lamarche, Gustave)
Preludio a la Noche (see Macaya Lahmann, Enrique)
Le Premier (Le 1er) (see Horovitz, Israel)
Le Premier Combat (see Bonneau, Jean-Pierre)
Le Premier Pas (see Labiche, Eugene)
Preparing (see Simons, Beverly)
Present Laughter (see Coward, Noël)
Present Tense (see Gilroy, Frank D.)
The President (see Kaiser, George)
President (see Molnar, Ferenc)
El Presidenta y el Ideal (see Usigli, Rudolfo)
PRESS, Steve, 1934
    We Need Another Man
        (In Modern International Drama, Vol. 7, no. 1A, Oct. 1973)
Press Cuttings (see Shaw, George Bernard)
PRESSBURGER, Emeric
    The Red Shoes (see Powell, Michael)
    The Tales of Hoffman (see Powell, Michael)
Le Prestige Mâle (see Costine, Jacques)
PRESTON, Peter S.
    The Tricolor Suite
        (In The Best One-Act Plays of 1958-59, London)
PRESTON, Thomas, 1537-1598
    Cambises
        (In Minor Elizabethan Tragedies)
The Pretenders (I Suppositi) (see Ariosto, Lodovico)
The Pretenders (see Ibsen, Henrik)
La Preuve de Contraire (see Gilbert, Charles)
La Preuve par Quatre (see Marceau, Felicien)
PREVERT, Jacques, 1900-
    Le Jour se Levé; filmscript (see Carne, Marcel)
    Les Visiteurs du Soir: filmscript
        (In Deux Films Française)
A Previous Engagement (see Howells, William Dean)
Prexaspes (see Hacks, Peter)
The Price (see Miller, Arthur)
The Price of Coal (see Brighouse, Harold)
PRIDE, Leo B., 1896-
    The Haunted Coal Mine
        (In One-Act Plays for Stage and Study, 5th Series)

PRIDEAUX, James, 1927-
    An American Sunset
      (In Best Short Plays, 1974)
    Lemonade
      (In The Off Off Broadway Book)
PRIESTLEY, John Boynton, 1894-
    Bees on the Boat Deck
      (In his Plays, Vol. 2)
    Cornelius
      (In his Plays, Vol. 3)
    Dangerous Corner
      (In Best Mystery and Suspense Plays of the Modern Theatre)
      (In his Plays, Vol. 1)
      (In Six Plays)
    Eden End
      (In his Plays, Vol. 1)
    Ever Since Paradise
      (In his Plays, Vol. 2)
    The Golden Fleece
      (In his Plays, Vol. 2)
    Home Is Tomorrow
      (In his Plays, Vol. 3)
    How Are They at Home
      (In his Plays, Vol. 2)
    I Have Been Here Before
      (In his Plays, Vol. 1)
    An Inspector Calls
      (In his Plays, Vol. 3)
      (In 10 Classic Mystery and Suspense Plays of the Modern
        Theatre)
    Johnson over Jordan
      (In his Plays, Vol. 1)
    Laburnum Grove
      (In his Plays, Vol. 2)
    The Linden Tree
      (In his Plays, Vol. 1)
    Music at Night
      (In his Plays, Vol. 1)
    People at Sea
      (In his Plays, Vol. 3)
    Summer Day's Dream
      (In his Plays, Vol. 3)
    They Came to a City
      (In his Plays, Vol. 3)
    El Tiempo y los Conway
      (In Teatro Ingles Contemporaneo)
    Time and the Conways
      (In his Plays, Vol. 1)
    When We Are Married
      (In his Plays, Vol. 2)
  PRIETO, Carlos
    El Jugo de la Tierra
      (In Teatro Méxicano, 1959)

Le Primitif (see Rosselson, Leon)
The Prince d'Amour (see D'Avenant, Sir William)
LE PRINCE DE BEAUMONT, Marie, 1711-1780
   **Le Baron Fantôme (see Cocteau, Jean)
The Prince of Parthia (see Godfrey, Thomas)
The Prince, the Wolf and the Firebird (see Lacey, Jackson)
Le Prince Travesti; ou, L'Illustre Aventurier (see Marivaux, Pierre
   C.)
Princess Ida; or, Castle Adamant (see Gilbert, William S.)
Princess Ivona (see Gombrowicz, Witold)
Princess Magdalena; or, The Importunate Prince (see Witkiewicz,
   Stanislaw I.)
Princess Maleine (see Maeterlinck, Maurice)
The Princess of Clive (see Lee, Nathaniel)
The Princess of Elis, Being the Second Day of the Inchanted Island
   (see Molière, Jean Baptiste)
The Princesse; or, Love at First Sight (see Killigrew, Thomas)
La Princesse de Bagdad (see Dumas, Alexandre, Fils)
Le Princesse Georges (see Dumas, Alexandre, Fils)
El Principe Constante (see Calderon de la Barca, Pedro)
PRINGLE, Ronald John, 1942-
   The Finger Meal
      (In 19 Necromancers from Now)
Der Prinz von Portugal (see Knauth, Joachim)
Priscilla: A Comedy (see Howells, William Dean)
La Prison (see Goléa, Antoine)
The Prisoner (see Boland, Bridget)
Prisoner and Escort (see Wood, Charles)
The Prisoner of Second Avenue (see Simon, Neil)
The Prisoners (see Killigrew, Thomas)
La Prisonniere (see Bourdet, Edouard)
The Private Ear (see Shaffer, Peter)
Private Jokinen's Marriage Leave (see Meri, Veijo)
The Private Life of Henry VIII; screenplay (see Biro, Lajos)
Private Lives (see Coward, Noël)
Le Prix Martin (see Labiche, Eugene)
Priyadarshika of Harsa (see Harsavardhana)
The Probationer (see Guthrie, Arthur)
The Problem (see Cregan, David)
El Proceso del Arzobisop Carranza (see Calvo Sotelo, Joaquin)
The Procession of the Prophets (Anon.)
      (In Medieval Church Music-Dramas)
Il Processo di Verona (see Lizzani, Carlo)
PROCUNIER, Edwin R.
   Voices of Desire
      (In Canada on Stage)
The Prodigal (see Voltaire)
El Profesor Taranne (see Adamov, Arthur)
Professor Storitsyn (see Andreev, Leonid N.)
Professor Taranne (see Adamov, Arthur)
Il Progittista (see Nota, Alberto)
Il Prognosticante Fanatico (see Giraud, Giovanni)
Progress to Fotheringay (see Morris, Thomas B.)

Prohibido en Otoño (see Neville, Edgar)
Prohibido Suicidarse en Primavera (see Rodrigues Alvarez, Alejan-
    dro)
The Projectors (see Wilson, John)
A Prologue to "King Lear" (see Molnar, Ferenc)
Promenade (see Fornes, Maria I.)
La Promesa (see Santareno, Bernardo)
Prometheus Bound (see Aeschylus)
Prometheus in Granada, a verse play (see Rosten, Norman)
The Promise of May (see Tennyson, Alfred Lord)
The Proper Perspective (see Graves, Warren C.)
Prophecy (see Handke, Peter)
The Prophetess (see Beaumont, Francis)
The Prophets (see Mrozek, Slawomir)
The Proposal (see Chekhov, Anton)
The Protagonist (see Kaiser, Georg)
Protée (see Claudel, Paul)
Proteo (see Monterde, Francisco)
Protest (see William, Norman)
Protokoll einer Sitzung (see Gelman, Alexander)
PROUST, Marcel, 1871-1922
    **Remembrance of Things Past; screenplay (see Pinter, Harold)
Providence; scenario (see Resnais, Alain)
La Provinciale (see Marivaux, Pierre C.)
Provinzanekdoten (see Wampilow, Alexander)
The Provok'd Husband (see Vanbrugh, Sir John)
The Provok'd Wife (see Vanbrugh, Sir John)
Der Prozesc (see Weiss, Peter)
The Prude (see Voltaire)
Prudence Spurns a Wager (see Musset, Alfred de)
La Prueba de las Promesas (see Ruiz de Alarcón y Mendoza, Juan)
PRYCE, Richard, 1864-
    Frolic Wind, from the novel by Richard Oke
        (In Famous Plays of 1934-35)
    'Ope-o'-Me Thumb (see Fenn, Frederick)
Psalms of Two Davids (see Schwartz, Joel)
Psiche (see Molière, Jean Baptiste)
Psyche (see Corneille, Pierre)
Psyche (see Shadwell, Thomas)
Psyche Debauch'd (see Duffet, Thomas)
Psycho; screenplay (see Hitchcock, Alfred)
Ptolemy I, King of Egypt, d. 283 B.C.
    *Cleomenes, The Spartan Heroe (see Dryden, John)
Ptolemy XIII (or XII or XIV), King of Egypt, 61-48 B.C.
    *Caesar and Cleopatra: A History (see Shaw, George Bernard)
    *La Morte de Pompee (The Death of Pompey) (see Corneille,
        Pierre)
The Public Eye (see Shaffer, Peter)
El Publico (see García Lorca, Federico)
PUCCINI, Giacomo, 1858-1924
    Tosca; opéra en trois actes d'après le drame de Victorien Sar-
        dou, libretto di G. Giacosa e L. Illica
        (In L'Avant-Scène Opéra, no. 11, Sept./Oct. 1977)

La Puce a l'Oreille (see Feydeau, Georges)
Pucelle (see Audiberti, Jacques)
PUDOVKIN, Vsevolod Ilarionovich, 1893-1953
    Mother
        (In Lorrimer Screenplay Series, 1973)
        (In Two Russian Film Classics)
PUGLIESE, Armando, 1947-
    Masaniello (see Porta, Elvio)
I Pugni in Tasca (see Bellocchio, Marco)
Pulcheria (Aelia Pulcheria Augusta), Byzantine Empress, 399-453
    *Pulcheria (see Corneille, Pierre)
The Pullman Sleeper; vaudeville script (see Fields, W. C.)
PULMAN, Jack
    David Copperfield, screenplay by Jack Pulman and Frederick
        Brogger, based on the work of Charles Dickens
        (In Copperfield '70)
Un Punal en la Noche (see Francovich, Guillermo)
Punch and Judy (see Harris, Aurand)
The Punished Libertine; or, Don Giovanni (see Da Ponte, Lorenzo)
Il Punto d'Appoggio (see Lopez, Sabatino)
La Pupille (see Fagan, Christopher B.)
Der Puppenspieler (see Schnitzler, Arthur)
The Puppet Show (see Blok, Alexandr A.)
The Puppets (see Solórzano, Carlos)
PURCELL, Henry C. 1659-1695
    Amphitryon; or, The Two Socias (see Dryden, John)
    King Arthur; or, The British Worthy (see Dryden, John)
PURDY, James
    Q & A
        (In Esquire, Vol. 79, Mar 1973)
    True
        (In New Directions in Prose and Poetry, Vol. 34)
    Wedding Finger
        (In New Directions, Vol. 28, 1974)
Purgatory (see Yeats, William Butler)
The Purging (see Feydeau, Georges)
The Purification (Anon.)
        (In Medieval Church Music-Dramas)
The Puritan; or, The Widow of Watling Street (Anon.)
        (In Disputed Plays of William Shakespeare)
Purity (see Mowat, David)
Purlie Victorious (see Davis, Ossie)
The Purloined Letter; radio script (see Andrews, Charlton)
The Purple Door Knob (see Eaton, Walter P.)
Purple Dust (see O'Casey, Sean)
The Purple Flower (see Bonner, Marita)
The Purse (see Cross, James C.)
The Pursuit of Happiness; radio script (see Barnouw, Erik)
PUSHKIN, Aleksandr Sergeyevich, 1799-1837
    Boris Godunov
        (In Nineteenth-Century Russian Plays)
        (In his Poems, Prose & Plays)
    The Covetous Knight
        (In his Poems, Prose & Plays)

Mozart and Salieri
    (In his <u>Poems, Prose & Plays</u>)
**La Tempesta (see Lattuada, Alberto)
The Pussycat and the Expert Plumber Who Was a Man (see Miller,
    Arthur)
The Puzzle; television script (see Rosham, Clair)
Pygmalion (see Kaiser, Georg)
Pygmalion: A Romance in Five Acts (see Shaw, George Bernard)
Pyramus and Thisbe (see James, Henry)
Pyrrhus, King of Epirus, 318?-272 B.C.
    *Pyrrhus (see Crebillon, Prosper J.)

Q & A (see Purdy, James)
QUACKENBUSH, Jan
    Inside Out
        (In <u>Calder & Boyars Playscripts</u> no. 15)
    Once Below a Time; three plays for child actors: "Still Fires,"
        "Rolly's Grave," and "Come Tomorrow."
        (In <u>Calder & Boyars Playscripts</u>, no. 15)
    Still Fires
        (In <u>Gambit</u>, Vol. 3, no. 11)
    Talking of Michaelangelo
        (In <u>Calder & Boyars Playscripts</u>, no. 15)
Quadrille (see Coward, Noël)
The Quality of Mercy (see Keller, Evelyn L.)
Quality Street (see Barrie, James M.)
Quand Nous Nous Réveillerons d'Entre les Morts (se Ibsen, Henrik)
Quando si e Qualcuno (see Pirandello, Luigi)
Quare Medicine (see Green, Paul)
4 Chemins 4 (see Usigli, Rudolfo)
Les Quatre Cubes (see Arrabal, Fernando)
Queen After Death (see Montherlant, Henri de)
The Queen and Concubine (see Brome, Richard)
The Queen and the Rebels (see Betti, Ugo)
Queen Cross-Patch and the Scullery Wench (see Benton, Rita)
Queen Margaret of Norway (see Kielland, Trygve)
Queen Mary (see Tennyson, Alfred Lord)
The Queen-Mother (see Swinburne, Algernon Charles)
The Queen of Corinth (see Beaumont, Francis)
Queen of Scots (see Mackintosh, Elizabeth)
The Queen of Sheba (see Young, Stark)
The Queen Was in the Parlour (see Coward, Noël)
The Queen's Exchange (see Brome, Richard)
Queer People (see Gor'kii, Maksim)
QUEIROLO, José Martínez, 1931-
    R.I.P.
        (In <u>The Orgy</u>)
The Quest of the Bride (see Turkish Theatre. Meddah)
Questa Sera Si Recita a Soggetto (see Pirandello, Luigi)
The Question (see Hawks, John)
La Question d'Argent (see Dumas, Alexandre, Fils)

A Question of Principle (see Flavin, Martin)
Questioning the Irrevocable (see Schnitzler, Arthur)
Qui Est Qui? (see Waterhouse, Keith)
A Quick Nut Bread to Make Your Mouth Water (see Hoffman, William M.)
Quien Soy Yo? (see Soya, C.E.)
Quiet Duel; screenplay (see Kurosawa, Akira)
QUILES, Eduardo
    The Bridal Chamber
        (In Modern International Drama, Vol. 7, no. 1, Fall 1973)
    The Employee
        (In Modern International Drama, Vol. 9, no. 1, Fall 1975)
        (In New Generation Spanish Drama)
    The Refrigerator
        (In Modern International Drama, Vol. 7, no. 1, Fall 1973)
        (In New Generation Spanish Drama)
QUILLARD, Pierre
    The Girl with the Cut-Off Hands
        (In The Drama Review, Vol. 20, no. 3, Sept. 1976)
Quimera (see Garcia Lorca, Federico)
QUINAULT, Philippe, 1635-1688
    Astrate (Astrates)
        (In More Plays by Rivals of Corneille and Racine)
Quinta Temporada (see Valdez, Luis)
La Quittance du Diable (see Musset, Alfred de)
Quitte pour la Peur (see Vigny, Alfred V.)
Quiza un Poeta (see Josephson, Ragnar)
Quoat-Quoat (see Audiberti, Jacques)
Quodlibet (see Handke, Peter)

R. Hot (see Goldman, Friedrich)
R.I.P. (see Queirolo, José Martínez)
R.U.R. (see Capek, Karel)
RABAN, Jonathan
    The Water Baby
        (In The New Review, Vol. 1, no. 12, Mar. 1975)
RABE, David William, 1940-
    The Basic Training of Pavlo Hummel
        (In The Off Off Broadway Book)
    Sticks and Bones
        (In Best American Plays, 7th Series, 1967-1973)
RABELAIS, François, c. 1490-1553?
    **Rabelais: A Dramatic Game in Two Parts Taken from the Five
        Books of François Rabelais (see Barrault, Jean-Louis)
RABINOWITZ, Shalom, 1859-1916
    **Fiddler on the Roof (see Bock, Jerry)
RABY, Peter
    The Government Inspector (see Gogol, Nikolai)
RACAN, Honorat de Bueil, Marquis de, 1589-1670
    Les Bergeries
        (In Théâtre du XVIIe Siècle, Vol. 1)

Rachel (see Grimke, Angelina W.)
Rachel, (Elisa Felix) c. 1820-1858
   *A Supper at the House of Mademoiselle Rachel (see Musset, Al-
     fred de)
RACINE, Jean Baptiste, 1639-1699
   Alexander the Great
     (In his Complete Plays, Vol. 1)
   Andromache
     (In his Complete Plays, Vol. 1)
   Athaliah
     (In his Complete Plays, Vol. 2)
     (In Enclosure)
   Bajazet
     (In his Complete Plays, Vol. 2)
   Berenice
     (In his Complete Plays, Vol. 1)
     (In World Drama, Vol. 2)
   Bernice (see Masefield, John)
   Britannicus
     (In his Complete Plays, Vol. 1)
   The Distrest Mother
     (In The London Stage, Vol. 4)
   Esther
     (In his Complete Plays, Vol. 2)
   Esther (see Masefield, John)
   Iphigenia
     (In his Complete Plays, Vol. 2)
   The Litigants
     (In his Complete Plays, Vol. 1)
   Mithridates
     (In his Complete Plays, Vol. 2)
   Phaedra
     (In his Complete Plays, Vol. 2)
   Phädra; ein Trauerspiel von Racine von Schiller; fragment
     (In Schiller's Works, Vol. 4)
   Les Plaideurs; or, The Suitors
     (In The Drama, Vol. 7)
   The Theban Brothers
     (In his Complete Plays, Vol. 1)
RADDE, Ronald
   Apaga a Luz e Faz de Conta que Estamos Bebados
     (In Revista de Teatro, no. 397, Jan./Feb. 1974)
Radiance and Death of Joaquin Murieta (see Neruda, Pablo)
RADICAL ARTS TROUPE, CHICAGO
   A Tale of Two Cities
     (In Guerilla Street Theater)
RADICAL ARTS TROUPE OF BERKELEY
   "Heyns"
     (In Guerilla Street Theater)
   Reserve Liberal Training Corps
     (In Guerilla Street Theater)
RADICAL ARTS TROUPE, UNIVERSITY OF CALIFORNIA, DAVIS
   The Turn of the Screw
     (In Guerilla Street Theater)

RADICAL ARTS TROUPE, UNIVERSITY OF CONNECTICUT
  A Bosses' Christmas Carol
    (In Guerilla Street Theater)
  UConn GE Varsity Quiz
    (In Guerilla Street Theater)
RADIGUET, Raymond, 1903-1923
  The Pelicans
    (In Modern French Theatre)
RADIN, Ben
  A Seacoast in Bohemia
    (In Best Television Plays, 1954)
Radio (see Riley, Mrs. Alice C.)
Radio I & II (see Beckett, Samuel)
The Raft (see Clark, John P.)
The Raft: An Interlude (see Leacock, Stephen B.)
The Raft of the Medusa (see Kaiser, Georg)
La Ragione Degli Altri (see Pirandello, Luigi)
The Ragpickers (see Smythe, Norman)
Rags and Riches (see Harris, Aurand)
Raid on the White Tiger Regiment (see China. Shantung Provincial
    Peking Opera Troupe)
Rain (see Colton, John)
Rainbows for Sale (see Noonan, John F.)
The Rainmaker (see Nash, N. Richard)
A Raisin in the Sun (see Hansberry, Lorraine)
The Raising of Lazarus (Anon.)
    (In Medieval Church Music-Dramas)
Raising the Devil (see Sachs, Hans)
Raising the Wind (see Kenney, James)
Rajk, Laszlo, Hungarian Foreign Minister, d. 1949
  *Shadow of Heroes (see Ardrey, Robert)
Ralph Roister Doister (see Udall, Nicholas)
Rama's Later History (see Bhavabhuti)
RAMIREZ, Frank
  La Bolsa Negra
    (In El Teatro de la Esperanza)
RAMOS, José Antonio, 1885-
  Tembladera
    (In Teatro Cubano Contemporaneo)
RAMUZ, Charles Ferdinand
  L'Histoire du Soldat; text de Charles Ferdinand Ramuz, adapta-
    tion de Devy Erlih; musique d'Igor Stravinsky
    (In L'Avant-Scène Théâtre, no. 574, Nov. 1, 1975)
Las Ranas y el Mar (see San Felix, Alvaro)
RANCK, Carty
  The Weakest Link
    (The Prize Plays of 1927-28, Vol. 1)
RANDOLPH, Clemence
  Rain (see Colton, John)
RANDOLPH, Thomas, 1605-1634
  Amyntas, or, The Impossible Dowry
    (In his Poetical & Dramatic Works, Vol. 1)

Aristippus, or, The Jovial Philosopher
    (In his Poetical & Dramatic Works, Vol. 1)
The Conceited Peddler
    (In his Poetical & Dramatic Works, Vol. 1)
Hey for Honesty
    (In his Poetical & Dramatic Works, Vol. 1)
The Muses' Looking-Glass
    (In his Poetical & Dramatic Works, Vol. 1)
RANGACHARYA, Adya, 1904-
    Mahabharatha, by Sriranga, pseud. (excerpts)
    (In Indian Writing Today, Vol. 4, 1970)
The Rape of Lucrece (see Heywood, Thomas)
RAPHAEL, Frederick, 1931-
    Darling; filmscript by Frederick Raphael, directed by John
      Schlesinger
    (In Film Scripts Four)
    Two for the Road; a screenplay for the film directed by Stanley
      Donen
    (A Jonathan Cape Screenplay, 1967)
RAPID TRANSIT GUERILLA COMMUNICATIONS, CHICAGO
    The Mad Bomber
    (In Guerilla Street Theater)
RAPPOPORT, Shloyme Zanvl, 1863-1920
    The Dybbuk (Between Two Worlds) by S. Anski, pseud.
    (In The Great Jewish Plays)
Rapto (see Neville, Edgar)
The Rat Trap (see Coward, Noël)
Les Rates (see Leonrmand, Henri R.)
Ratnavali of Harsa (see Harsha)
Ratnavali; or, The Necklace (see Harsha)
Rats (see Horovitz, Israel)
A Rat's Mass (see Kennedy, Adrienne)
The Rats of Norway (see Winter, John K.)
RATTIGAN, Sir Terence Mervyn, 1911-
    After Lydia; or, In Praise of Love
    (In Best Short Plays of 1975)
    The Browning Version
    (In The Mentor Book of Short Plays)
    El Chino de los Winslow
    (In Teatro Ingles Contemporaneo)
    High Summer
    (In The Best Short Plays 1973)
    Ross, a Dramatic Portrait
    (In his Collected Plays, Vol. 3)
Rauhweiler (see Jakobs, Karl-Heinz)
RAVEL, Aviva
    Black Dreams
    (In Contemporary Canadian Drama)
    Dispossessed
    (In Women Write for the Theatre Series, Vol. 3)
    Soft Voices
    (In A Collection of Canadian Plays, Vol. 3)

The Twisted Loaf
    (In <u>A Collection of Canadian Plays</u>, Vol. 3)
RAVENSCROFT, Edward, fl. 1671-1697
    The Anatomist; or, The Sham Doctor
        (In <u>A Collection of the Most Esteemed Farces ...</u>, Vol. 1)
    The London Cuckolds
        (In <u>Restoration Comedy</u>, Vol. 2)
Ravenswood (see McNally, Terrence)
Le Revissement de Scapin (see Claudel, Paul)
RAWLINSON, Arthur
    Jew Süss; screenplay by Arthur Rawlinson and Dorothy Farnum,
        adapted from Lion Feuchtwanger's novel; film directed by Lo-
        thar Mendes
        (In <u>Garland Classics of Film Literature Series</u>)
RAY, Nicholas, 1911-
    Johnny Guitar; screenplay, text in French; d'après une nouvelle
        de Roy Chanslor
        (In <u>L'Avant-Scène Cinéma</u>, no. 145, Mar. 1974)
La Raza Pura, or Racial Racial (see Sierra, Ruben)
The Real You; a compass scenario (see May, Elaine)
REANEY, James Crerar, 1926-
    Colours in the Dark
        (In <u>Talonplays Series</u>, 1969)
    The Easter Egg: Masks of Childhood
        (In <u>New Drama 2 Series</u>, Toronto)
    The Killdeer: Masks of Childhood
        (In <u>New Drama 2 Series</u>, Toronto)
    Listen to the Wind
        (In <u>Talonplays Series</u>, 1972)
    Three Desks: Masks of Childhood
        (In <u>New Drama 2 Series</u>, Toronto)
Reason (see Wilson, Snoo)
The Rebel Saint (see Kozlenko, William)
Rebelde (see Paso, Alfonso)
Rebellion (see Drinkwater, John)
REBELLO, Luiz Francisco
    Es Urgente el Amor
        (In <u>Teatro Portugues Contemporaneo</u>)
RECHANI AGRAIT, Luis
    Como Se llama Esta Flor?
        (In <u>Teatro Puertorriqueño: Octavo Festival</u>)
RECHY, John
    Momma As She Became-But Not As She Was
        (In <u>Collision Course</u>)
RECKFORD, Barry
    Shyvers
        (In <u>Calder & Boyars Playscript Series</u>, 1977)
        (In his <u>Shyvers & X</u>)
    X
        (In his <u>Shyvers & X</u>)
Reckless (see Riggs, Lynn)
Recklessness (see O'Neill, Eugene)
The Recluse (see Foster, Paul)

The Recruiting Officer (see Farquhar, George)
The Recruiting Sergeant (see Bickerstaff, Isaac)
Recruits (see Axenfeld, Israel)
The Rector (see Crothers, Rachel)
The Red Burning Light; or, Mission XO3 (see Fornes, Maria I.)
Red Carnations; radio script (see Hughes, Glenn)
Red Cross (see Shepard, Sam)
Red Desert; film script (see Antonioni, Michelangelo. Desert Rosso)
The Red Detachment of Women (see Chiang, Ching)
Red Head Baker; radio script (see Maltz, Albert)
The Red Lantern (see China. Peking Opera Troup)
Red Light (see Hodson, James L.)
Red Magic (see Ghelderode, Michel de)
The Red Morning (see Bisson, Jean-Pierre)
The Red Owl (see Gillette, William H.)
Red Roses for Me (see O'Casey, Sean)
The Red Shoes (see Powell, Michael)
REDGRAVE, Sir Michael, 1908-
    The Aspern Papers; a comedy of letters adapted for the theatre
      from Henry James' story
        (In Heinemann Drama Library, 1959)
Redl, Alfred Victor, 1864-1913
    *A Patriot for Me (see Osborne, John)
REED, Bill, 1939-
    Burke's Company
        (In Australian Theatre Workshop, no. 1, 1969)
    Mr. Siggie Morrison with His Comb and Paper
        (In Australian Theatre Workshop no. 10, 1972)
REED, Sir Carol, 1906-
    The Third Man; screenplay and original story by Graham Greene;
      film directed by Carol Reed
        (In Masterworks of the British Cinema)
REED, Dena
    A Penny Saved; a play edited for radio
        (In On the Air: 15 Plays for Broadcast)
REED, Joseph, 1723-1787
    The Register Office
        (In A Collection of the Most Esteemed Farces ..., Vol. 3)
        (In The London Stage, Vol. 4)
REED, Mark
    A Transfer of Property
        (In One-Act Plays for Stage and Study, 8th Series)
Reedy River (see Diamond, Dick)
REELY, Mary Katharine
    The Lean Years
        (In Types of Modern Dramatic Composition)
El Reencuentro (see Adamov, Arthur)
References (see Longnecker, Edna B.)
A Refined Look at Existence (see Milgate, Rodney)
The Refrigerator (see Quiles, Eduardo)
The Refugee (see Currimbhoy, Asif)
REGIO, José, 1901-
    Jacob y el Angel
        (In Teatro Portugues Contemporaneo)

The Register (see Howells, William Dean)
The Register Office (see Reed, Joseph)
REGNIER, Max
    Paddle Your Own Canoe, adapted by Lucienne Hill
        (In Plays of the Year, Vol. 17, 1957/58)
REGO, Luis
    Viens Chez Moi J'Habite Chez une Copine, de Luis Rego et Di-
        dier Kaminka
        (In L'Avant-Scène Théâtre, no. 564, May 15, 1975)
Regulus, Marcus Atilius, d.c. 250 B. C.
    *Regulus (see Crowne, John)
The Rehearsal (see Baring, Maurice)
The Rehearsal (see Buckingham, George V.)
Rehearsal (see Morley, Christopher)
The Rehearsal at Gotham (fragment) (see Gay, John)
The Rehearsal at Versailles (L'Impromptu de Versailles) (see Mo-
    liére, Jean Baptiste)
Rei Momo (see Vieira, Cesar)
REICHMAN, Claude
    La Balànce
        (In L'Avant-Scène Théâtre, no. 586, May 1, 1976)
REID, Arthur
    People in Love
        (In Famous Plays of 1937)
REID, Ben
    The Fourth Room
        (In New Directions, Vol. 8, 1944)
La Reine de Césaree (see Brasillach, Robert)
La Reine de la Nuit (see Guidicelli, Christian)
La Reine Morte (see Montherlant, Henry de)
REINES, Bernard
    His Name Shall Be: Remember
        (In 100 Non-Royalty Radio Plays)
REINSHAGEN, Gerlind
    Himmel und Erde
        (In Theater Heute, no. 10, October, 1974)
    Sonntagkinder
        (In Theater Heute, no. 7, July 1976)
REISCH, Walter, 1900-
    Ninotchka; screenplay (see Lubitsch, Ernst)
Die Reise des Eugin Ozkartal von Nevsehir nach Herne und Zurück
    (see Korn, Reneke)
Reise mit Joujou (see Hanell, Robert)
REISZ, Karel, 1926-
    Saturday Night and Sunday Morning; screenplay adapted by Alan
        Sillitoe from his novel; film directed by Karel Reisz
        (In Masterworks of the British Cinema)
Reiter der Nacht; oper (see Meyer, Ernst H.)
Rektor Kleist (see Kaiser, Georg)
The Relapse; or, Virtue in Danger (see Vanbrugh, Sir John)
Relative Values (see Coward, Noël)
RELLAN, Miguel Angel
    The Blind Warrior
        (In New Generation Spanish Drama)

Remembrance of Things Past; screenplay (see Pinter, Harold)
REMINGTON, Erle, 1896-
    The Idlings of the King
      (In The Play Book)
Remington 22 (see Andrade Rivera, Gustave)
RENARD, Jules, 1864-1910
    La Bigote
      (In his Théâtre Complet)
    Le Cousin de Rose
      (In his Théâtre Complet)
    La Demande
      (In his Théâtre Complet)
    Household Bread
      (In his Poil de Carotte and Other Plays)
    Huit Jours a la Campagne
      (In his Théâtre Complet)
    Monsieur Vernet
      (In his Théâtre Complet)
    Le Pain de Ménage
      (In his Théâtre Complet)
    Le Plaisir de Rompre
      (In his Théâtre Complet)
    The Pleasure of Parting
      (In his Poil de Carotte and Other Plays)
    Poil de Carotte; text in English
      (In his Poil de Carotte and Other Plays)
    Poil de Carotte; text in French
      (In his Théâtre Complet)
Le Rendez-vous de Senlis (see Anouilh, Jean)
Rendez-vous du Lendemain (see Dubé, Marcel)
Renee (see Zola, Emile)
The Renegado (see Massinger, Philip)
RENE-GEORGES, 1924-
    Les Berlingots
      (In L-Avant-Scène Théâtre, no. 556, Jan. 15, 1975)
RENGIFO, Cesar, 1916-
    Lo Que Dejo la Tempestad
      (In El Teatro Hispanoamericano Contemporaneo, Vol. 2)
    Las Torres y el Viento
      (In Teatro Contemporaneo Hispanoamericano, Vol. 2)
RENOIR, Jean, 1894-
    Carola
      (In L'Avant-Scène Théâtre, no. 597, Nov. 1, 1976)
    La Chienne; réalisation, Jean Renoir; scénario, Jean Renoir et
    Andre Girard, d'après le roman de Georges de la Fourchar-
    diere
      (In L'Avant-Scène Cinéma, no. 162, Oct. 1975)
    Grand Illusion; scenario and adaptation by Charles Spaak and
    Jean Renoir; film directed by Jean Renoir
      (In Masterworks of the French Cinema)
Renzo e Luciana; screenplay (see Monicelli, Mario)
Le Repas du Lion (see Curel, François)
Repeat Performance (see Mrozek, Slawomir)

La Répeticion (see Arrufat, Anton)
La Répetition; ou, L'Amour Puni (see Anouilh, Jean)
Le Repos du Septième Jour (see Claudel, Paul)
The Reprisal; or, The Tars of Old England (see Smollet, Tobias)
The Prerobate (see James, Henry)
Repulsion; filmscript (see Polanski, Roman)
Request Concert (see Kroetz, Franz X.)
Requiem for a Heavyweight; television script (see Serling, Rod)
Requiem for Brother X (see Mackey, William W.)
Rescue (see Shaw, David)
The Rescue of Cynthia Ann (see Rogers, John W.)
The Rescuing Angel (see Kummer, Mrs. Clare)
Reserve Liberal Training Corps (see Radical Arts Troupe of Berkeley)
Resident of Nowhere (see Curnow, Allen)
RESNAIS, Alain, 1922-
    Hiroshima Mon Amour; screenplay (see Duras, Marguerite)
    Providence; scénario original David Mercer
        (In L'Avant-Scène Cinéma, no. 195, Nov. 1, 1977)
    Stavisky ...; screenplay by Jorge Semprun for the film by Alain
    Resnais
        (In Lorrimer Screenplay Series, 1975)
        (A Viking/Compass Book Screenplay, 1975)
    Le Stavisky ...; screenplay, text in French
        (In L'Avant-Scène Cinéma, no. 156, Mar. 1975)
A Resounding Tinkle (see Simpson, Norman F.)
The Resources of Quinola (see Balzac, Honoré de)
The Respectful Prostitute (see Sartre, Jean-Paul)
Les Ressources de Quinola (see Balzac, Honore de)
The Rest I'll Whistle (see Powell, Anthony)
Restless Heart (see Anouilh, Jean)
The Restoration of Arnold Middleton (see Storey, David)
The Resurrection (see Yeats, William Butler)
Retablillo de Don Cristobal (see Garcia Lorca, Federico)
Retablo (see Menen Desleal, Alvaro)
RETES, Ignacio, 1918-
    Una Ciudad Para Vivir
        (In Teatro Méxicano del Siglo XX, Vol. 3)
Le Retour de Jerusalem (see Donnay, Maurice C.)
Le Retour du Calvaire (see Silvain, Jean)
Retreat (see Ruthenburg, Grace D.)
The Return (see Boland, Bridget)
The Return (see Finch, Robert V.)
The Return (see Fratti, Mario)
The Return (see Ngunjiri, Julius)
The Return of Peter Grimm (see Belasco, David)
The Return of the Druses (see Browning, Robert)
Return of the Prodigal (see Hankin, St. John)
The Return of the Warrior (see Buenafe, Manuel E.)
Return to a City (see Saunders, James)
Return to Dust; radio script (see Bamber, George)
Returned "Killed" (see Planché, James R.)

REUBEN, William, 1947-
    Teofilo Amadeo: Una Biografia
        (In El Teatro de Hoy en Costa Rica)
La Réunion des Amours (see Marivaux, Pierre C.)
Le Réveil (see Hervieu, Paul E.)
Ne Réveillez pas Madame (see Anouilh, Jean)
Revenge (see Brenton, Howard)
Revenge for Honour (see Chapman, George)
The Revenge of Bussy d'Ambois (see Chapman, George)
Revision (see Biro, Lajos)
Revolt (see Biro, Lajos)
Revolt in Orthoepy; radio script (see Wyman, Justus E.)
Revolte auf Côte 3018 (see Horvath, Odön von)
La Révolte des Fleurs (see Mace, Jean)
Die Revolution (see Heym, Georg)
REXROTH, Kenneth, 1915-
    Iphigenia at Aulis; a dance play
        (In New Directions, Vol. 11, 1949)
    Phaedra
        (In New Directions, Vol. 9, 1946)
El Rey (see Lagerkvist, Pär F.)
REYES, Alfonso, 1889-
    Ifigenia Cruel
        (In Teatro Méxicano del Siglo XX, Vol. 2)
REYES, Carlos José, 1941-
    Metamorfosis; variaciones escenicas en partes, sobre un tema
        original de Franz Kafka
        (In Teatro Contemporaneo Hispanoamericano, Vol. 1)
Los Reyes del Mundo (see Basurto, Luis G.)
REYNOLDS, Jonathan
    Rubbers
        (In Best Short Plays, 1977)
    Yanks 3 Detroit 0 Top of the Seventh
        (In Best Short Plays, 1977)
REZMIK, Lipe, 1890-c. 1943
    Recruits (see Axenfeld, Israel)
REZVANI, 1928-
    Body
        (In Contemporary French Theater)
Rhadamiste et Zenobie (see Crebillon, Prosper)
Rheinpromenade (see Mühl, Karl O.)
Rhinoceros (see Ionesco, Eugene)
Rhoda in Potatoland (Her Fall-Starts) (see Foreman, Richard)
The Rhythm of Violence (see Nkosi, Lewis)
RIALTO-FILM PREBEN PHILLIPSEN & JARDRAN-FILM
    Winnetou; the motion picture trilogy, based on K. F. May's
        "Winnetou, " text in German
        (In Winnetou, Film-Bildbuch, 1964-66)
The Rib of the Man (see Kennedy, Charles R.)
RIBES, Jean-Michel
    Il Faut Que le Sycomore
        (In L'Avant-Scène Théâtre, no. 595, Oct. 1, 1976)

Les Fraises Musclées (extracts)
(In L'Avant-Scène du Théâtre, no. 513, Mar. 1, 1973)
Omphalos Hôtel
(In L'Avant-Scène Théâtre, no. 575, Nov. 15, 1975)
On Loge la Nuit--Café a l'Eau
(In L'Avant-Scène Théâtre, no. 575 Nov. 15, 1975)
Par delà les Marroniers
(In L'Avant-Scène du Théâtre, no. 513, Mar. 1, 1973)
Le Suis un Steak
(In L'Avant-Scène du Théâtre, no. 513, Mar. 1, 1973)
Tout Contre un Petit Bois
(In L'Avant-Scène Théâtre, no. 595, Oct. 1, 1976)
RIBMAN, Ronald Burt, 1932-
The Final War of Olly Winter
(In Great Television Plays)
The Journey of the Fifth Horse
(In The Off Off Broadway Book)
La Ricahembra (see Tamayo y Baus, Manuel)
Rice (see Alfon, Estrella D.)
RICE, Elmer L. , (Elmer Reizenstein), 1892-1967
The Adding Machine
(In The Disinherited: Plays)
(In Representative American Dramas)
(In his Seven Plays)
(In This Is My Best)
(In 20th Century American Writing)
Counsellor-at-law
(In his Seven Plays)
A Diadem of Snow
(In One-Act Plays for Stage and Study, 5th Series)
Dream Girl
(In 50 Best Plays of the American Theatre, Vol. 3)
(In his Seven Plays)
Exterior
(In his Three Plays Without Words)
The Gay White Way
(In One-Act Plays for Stage and Study, 8th Series)
Judgment Day
(In Famous Plays of 1937)
(In his Seven Plays)
Landscape with Figures
(In his Three Plays Without Words)
On Trial
(In his Seven Plays)
The Passing of Chow-Chow
(In One-Act Plays for Stage and Study, 2nd Series)
Rus in Urbe
(In his Three Plays Without Words)
Street Scene
(In 50 Best Plays of the American Theatre, Vol. 1)
(In his Seven Plays)
(In Six Plays: Famous Plays Series, 1930)

(In 20th Century Plays)
Two on an Island
    (In his Seven Plays)
RICH, John, 1692-1761
    The Spirit of Contradiction, by a Gentleman from Cambridge,
    pseud.
        (In A Collection of the Most Esteemed Farces ..., Vol. 4)
Richard I (Coeur de Lion) King of England, 1157-1199
    *The Foresters, Robin Hood and Maid Marian (see Tennyson, Al-
    fred Lord)
    *Richard Coeur de Lion (see Sedaine, Michel J.)
Richard Gamba di Sughero (see Behan, Brendan)
RICHARDS, Ivor Armstrong, 1893-
    The Eddying Ford
        (In Internal Colloquies)
    Job's Comforting
        (In Internal Colloquies)
    A Leak in the Universe
        (In Playbook; Five Plays for a New Theatre)
    Posada
        (In Internal Colloquies)
    Theodicy
        (In Internal Colloquies)
    Tomorrow Morning, Faustus!
        (In Internal Colloquies)
RICHARDS, Laura Elizabeth (Howe), 1850-1943
    **Chop-Chin and the Golden Dragon (see Smith, Moyne Rice)
    **With All My Heart (see Smith, Moyne Rice)
RICHARDS, Max, 1942-
    Cripple Play
        (In Landfall, Vol. 29, no.4, December 1975)
RICHARDS, Stanley, 1918-
    District of Columbia
        (In Black Theater U.S.A., 1847-1974)
Richard's Cork Leg (see Behan, Brendan)
Richards Korkbein (see Simpson, Alan)
RICHARDSON, Howard
    Dark of the Moon, written by Howard Richardson and William
    Berney
        (In Plays of the Year, Vol. 2, 1949)
RICHARDSON, Jack, 1935-
    Gallows Humor
        (In Themes of Drama)
RICHARDSON, Willis, 1889-
    The Black Horseman
        (In Plays and Pageants from the Life of the Negro)
    The Broken Banjo
        (In Black Writers of America)
    The Chip Woman's Fortune
        (In Anthology of the American Negro in the Theatre)
    The Flight of the Natives
        (In Black Theatre U.S.A., 1847-1974)

The House of Sham
    (In <u>Plays and Pageants from the Life of the Negro</u>)
The Idle Head
    (In <u>Black Theater U.S.A.</u>, 1847-1974)
The King's Dilemma
    (In <u>Plays and Pageants from the Life of the Negro</u>)
Mortgaged
    (In <u>The New Negro Renaissance</u>)
Richelieu, Armand Jean Duplessis, Cardinal, Duc de, 1585-1642
   *Richelieu; or, The Conspiracy (see Lytton, Edward George)
The Richest Girl in the World Finds Happiness (see Patrick, Robert)
Les Ricochets (see Mace, Jean)
Ride a Cock Horse (see Mercer, David)
The Ride Across Lake Constance (see Handke, Peter)
Riders to the Sea (see Synge, John M.)
Riding the Goat (see Miller, May)
RIDLER, Anne (Bradby), 1912-
   How Bitter the Bread
    (In her <u>Who Is My Neighbour? and How Bitter the Bread</u>)
   The Shadow Factory; a Nativity play
    (In <u>Faber & Faber Plays</u>, 1946)
   Who Is My Neighbour?
    (In her <u>Who Is My Neighbour? and How Bitter the Bread</u>)
RIFBJERG, Klaus
   Developments
    (In <u>Modern Nordic Plays: Denmark</u>)
La Riffa (see De Sica, Vittorio)
RIGGS, Lynn, 1899-1954
   The Hunger I Got
    (In <u>One-Act Plays for Stage and Study</u>, 10th Series)
   Knives from Syria
    (In <u>On the High Road</u>)
    (In <u>One-Act Plays for Stage and Study</u>, 3rd Series)
  **Oklahoma! (see Rodgers, Richard)
   Reckless
    (In <u>One-Act Plays for Stage and Study</u>, 4th Series)
The Right Prospectus (see Osborne, John)
Right You Are! (If You Think So) (see Pirandello, Luigi)
The Rights of Man (see Johnson, Greer)
RIGOIR, Vincent, 1935-
   Le Grand Autobus
    (In <u>L'Avant-Scène du Théâtre</u>, no. 509, Jan. 1, 1973)
RILEY, Mrs. Alice Cushing (Donaldson), 1867-?
   The Black Suitcase
    (In her <u>The Mandarin Coat and Five Other One-Act Plays</u>)
   The Blue Prince
    (In her <u>Ten Minutes by the Clock and Three Other Plays</u>)
   The Mandarin Coat
    (In her <u>The Mandarin Coat and Five Other One-Act Plays</u>)
   The Poet's Well
    (In her <u>Ten Minutes by the Clock and Three Other Plays</u>)
   Radio
    (In her <u>The Mandarin Coat and Five Other One-Act Plays</u>)

Skim-Milk
    (In her The Mandarin Coat and Five Other One-Act Plays)
The Sponge
    (In her The Mandarin Coat and Five Other One-Act Plays)
Taxi; a play edited for radio
    (In On the Air: 15 Plays for Broadcast)
Ten Minutes by the Clock
    (In her Ten Minutes by the Clock and Three Other Plays)
Their Anniversary
    (In her The Mandarin Coat and Five Other One-Act Plays)
Tom Piper and the Pig
    (In her Ten Minutes by the Clock and Three Other Plays)
The Weathervane Elopes
    (In One-Act Plays for Stage and Study, 3rd Series)
The Rimers of Eldritch (see Wilson, Lanford E.)
Ring Round the Moon (see Anouilh, Jean)
RINGWOOD, Gwen Pharis, 1910-
    The Courting of Marie Jenvrin
        (In Canada on Stage)
    Dark Harvest
        (In Canadian Theatre Review, Vol. 5, Winter 1975)
    Lament for Harmonica (Maya)
        (In Ten Canadian Short Plays)
RIOS, Juan, 1914
    Ayar Manko
        (In Teatro Peruano Contemporaneo)
Rip Van Winkle (see Jefferson, Joseph)
Rip Van Winkle, a Legend of the Catskills (see Burke, Charles)
RIPLEY, Arthur, 1895-1961
    The Barber Shop (see Fields, W.C.)
    The Pharmacist (see Fields, W.C.)
The Rise of Silas Lapham (see Howells, William Dean)
RISI, Dino
    Une Vie Difficile; un film titre original "Una Vita Difficile."
        (In L'Avant-Scène Cinéma, no. 182, Feb. 15, 1977)
The Rising of the Moon (see Gregory, Isabella A.)
RITCHIE, Paul
    Oh David, Are You There?
        (In Calder & Boyars Playscript Series, no. 6)
    Saint Honey
        (In Calder & Boyars Playscript Series, no. 6)
Rites (see Duffy, Maureen)
Il Ritorno del Cospiratore (see Taviani, Vittorio)
RITT, Martin, 1920-
    Jovanka e le Altre
        (In Dal Soggetto al Film Series, no. 14, 1960)
The Ritual (see Ibbitson, John)
The Ritz (see McNally, Terrence)
The Rival Candidates (see Dudley, Sir Henry)
The Rival Ladies (see Dryden, John)
The Rival Queens, or The Death of Alexander the Great (see Lee, Nathaniel)
The Rivals (see D'Avenant, Sir William)

The Rivals (see Sheridan, Richard Brinsley)
RIVAS, Angel Pérez de Saavedra Ramirez de Madrid Ramirez de
    Baquedano, 3, Duque de, 1791-1865
    Don Alvaro
        (In Tres Dramas Romanticos)
    Don Alvaro o La Fuerza del Sino
        (In Clásicos Castellanos, Vol. 206)
RIVERA, Vicente, Jr., 1920-
    The Four Freedoms
        (In Philippine Harvest)
RIVERS, Lou
    This Piece of Land
        (In Best Short Plays, 1977)
Riviera (see Molnar, Ferenc)
RIZZO, Frank
    Do You Like Me? Say You Like Me
        (In Story: The Yearbook of Discovery, 4th Series, 1971)
The Road (see Soyinka, Wole)
The Road to Ruin (see Mitchell, Ronald)
Roaring All Day Long, an epilogue (see Bentley, Eric Russell)
The Roaring Girl (see Middleton, Thomas)
ROBBE-GRILLET, Alain, 1922-
    L'Année Dernière à Marienbad
        (In Editions de Minuit Cinè Series, 1961)
    Glissements Progressifs du Plaisir
        (In Editions de Minuit Cinè Series, 1973)
    The Immortal One
        (In Calder & Boyars Playscripts, 1971)
    L'Immortelle
        (In Editions de Minuit Cinè Series, 1963)
The Robbers (see Schiller, Johann C.)
The Robbery (see Kummer, Mrs. Clare)
ROBBINS, Clarence Aaron "Tod," 1888-
  **Freaks; filmscript (see Browning, Tod)
ROBBINS, Jerome, 1918-
    West Side Story (see Bernstein, Leonard)
ROBERT, Yves, 1920-
    Salut l'Artiste
        (In L'Avant-Scène Cinéma, no. 146, April 1974)
Robert E. Lee (see Drinkwater, John)
Robert Macaire (see Neveux, Georges)
ROBERTSON, Thomas William, 1829-1871
    Caste
        (In Representative British Dramas)
Robin and Marian; screenplay (see Goldman, James)
Robin, Bachelor of Love (see Marivaux, Pierre C.)
Robin Hood
    *The Foresters, Robin Hood and Maid Marian (see Tennyson, Al-
        fred Lord)
    *George A Green, The Pinner of Wakefield (see Greene, Robert)
    *Robin and Marian; screenplay (see Goldman, James)
    Robin Hood: A Story of the Forest (see Mason, Timothy)
    *Robin Hood and the Pedlar (see Drinkwater, John)

The Sad Shepherd; or, A Tale of Robin Hood (see Jonson, Ben)
The Silver Arrow of Robin Hood (see Benton, Rita)
Robin Redbreast; television script (see Bowen, John)
Robin's Post (see Milligan, Spike)
ROBINSON, Lennox, 1886-1958
    The Far-Off Hills
        (In 20th Century Plays)
ROBINSON, Thelma
    The Visitor; television script by Thelma Robinson based on a
        story by Warren Wilson and Claire Kennedy, for the "Lassie"
        television program, Oct. 9, 1955
        (In Prize Plays of Television and Radio, 1956)
Robinson, Venerdi e Domenica (see Donati, Paolo L.)
ROBLES, Emmanuel
    Case for a Rebel
        (In his Three Plays)
    The Clock
        (In his Three Plays)
  **Montserrat (see Hellman, Lillian)
    Porfirio
        (In his Three Plays)
ROBLES, J. Humberto, 1921-
    Los Desarraigados
        (In Teatro Méxicano del Siglo XX, Vol. 4)
El Robo del Cochino (see Estorino, Abelardo)
Robsart, Amy, 1532?-1560
    *Amy Robsart (see Hugo, Victor)
ROBSON, Mark, 1913-
    Earthquake; filmscript (see Fox, George)
ROBSON, William N.
    No Help Wanted; radio script
        (In Best Broadcasts of 1938-39)
ROCA TEY, Bernardo, 1918-
    La Muerte de Atahualpa
        (In Teatro Peruano Contemporaneo)
Rocco e i Suoi Fratelli (Rocco and His Brothers); filmscript (see
    Visconti, Luchino)
ROCHA, Aurimar
    O Jogo da Verdade
        (In Revista de Teatro, no. 409, Jan./Feb. 1976)
ROCHA MIRANDA, Edgard da
    O Estranho
        (In Revista de Teatro, no. 402, Nov./Dec. 1974)
The Rock Garden (see Shepard, Sam)
Die Rockenstuben (see Sachs, Hans)
Rocket to the Moon (see Odets, Clifford)
Rocking Back and Forth (see Grass, Günter)
The Rocking-Horse Winner (see Fuller, Clark)
The Rocking-Horse Winner; screenplay (see Pelissier, Anthony)
Rocky; screenplay (see Stallone, Sylvester)
Rodeo (see Finch, Robert V.)
RODGERS, Richard, 1902-
    Allegro, by Richard Rodgers and Oscar Hammerstein II
        (In 6 Plays by Rodgers & Hammerstein)

Carousel, by Richard Rodgers and Oscar Hammerstein II; based
on Ferenc Molnar's "Liliom"
(In 6 Plays by Rodgers & Hammerstein)
The King and I, by Richard Rodgers and Oscar Hammerstein II;
based on "Anna and the King of Siam." by Margaret Landon
(In 6 Plays by Rodgers & Hammerstein)
Me and Juliet, by Richard Rodgers and Oscar Hammerstein II
(In 6 Plays by Rodgers & Hammerstein)
Oklahoma! by Richard Rodgers and Oscar Hammerstein II; based
on Lynn Riggs' "Green Grow the Lilacs"
(In 6 Plays by Rodgers & Hammerstein)
South Pacific; music by Richard Rodgers, lyrics by Oscar Ham-
merstein II, book by Joshua Logan, adapted from James A.
Michener's "Tales of the South Pacific"
(In Representative American Plays, 1792-1949)
(In 6 Plays by Rodgers & Hammerstein)
RODMAN, Howard
The Faith Hawker; television script, originally broadcast July
28, 1957 on the "Look Up and Live" series, CBS
(In The Seeking Years)
A Thing of Beauty; television script, originally broadcast July
7, 1957 on the "Look Up and Live" series, CBS
(In The Seeking Years)
The Will to Win; television script, originally broadcast June 2,
1957 on the "Look Up and Live" series, CBS
(In The Seeking Years)
Rodogune, or Rhodogune, Parthian princess, fl. 2nd Cent. B.C.
*Rodogune (see Corneille, Pierre)
RODRIGUEZ, Yamandu
1810
(In Teatro Uruguauo Contemporaneo)
RODRIGUEZ ALBERT, Rafael
El Concierto de San Ovidio (see Buero Vallejo, Antonio)
RODRIGUEZ ALVAREZ, Alejandro, 1903-1965
Los Arboles Mueren de Pie
(In his Teatro, Vol. 1)
(In his Teatro Español, 1962-63)
(In his Teatro Selecto)
La Barca Sin Pescador
(In Teatro Español, 1962-63)
The Boat Without a Fisherman, by Alejandro Casona, pseud.
(In The Modern Spanish Stage: Four Plays)
El Caballero de las Espuelas de Oro
(In Teatro Español, 1964-65)
(In his Teatro Selecto)
La Casa de los Siete Balcones
(In his Teatro Selecto)
Corona de Amor y Muerte, by Alejandro Casona, pseud.
(In his Teatro, Vol. 2)
(In Teatro Español, 1966-67)
Nuestra Natacha
(In his Teatro Selecto)

Prohibido Suicidarse en Primavera
    (In his Teatro, Vol. 2)
    (In his Teatro Selecto)
Siete Gritos en el Mar
    (In his Teatro, Vol. 2)
La Sirena Varada
    (In his Teatro, Vol. 1)
    (In his Teatro Selecto)
Las Tres Perfectas Casadas, by Alejandro Casona, pseud.
    (In Teatro Español, 1965-66)
RODRIGUEZ BUDED, Ricardo
    El Charlatan
    (In Teatro Español, 1961-62)
    La Madriguera
    (In Teatro Español, 1960-61)
RODRIGUEZ GALVAN, Ignacio, 1816-1842
    Muñoz, Visitador de México
    (In Teatro Méxicano del Siglo XIX, Vol. 1)
ROFFEY, Jack
    Hostile Witness
    (In 10 Classic Mystery and Suspense Plays of the Modern
        Theatre)
Roger (see Bowen, John)
ROGERS, James Webb
    Madame Surratt
    (In Magazine of History, Extra no. 20, 1912)
ROGERS, John William Jr., 1894-
    Judge Lynch
    (In Five Plays from the Other Side)
    (In One-Act Plays for Stage and Study, 1st Series)
    Mary Means What She Says
    (In One-Act Plays for Stage and Study, 3rd Series)
    The Rescue of Cynthia Ann
    (In One-Act Plays for Stage and Study, 5th Series)
    Saved
    (In One-Act Plays for Stage and Study, 2nd Series)
ROGERS, Merrill
    The Book of Job
    (In One-Act Plays for Stage and Study, 10th Series)
    Gramps; a play edited for radio
    (In On the Air: 15 Plays for Broadcast)
ROGERS, Robert, 1731-1795
    Ponteach; or, The Savages of America
    (In Representative Plays by American Dramatists, Vol. 1)
ROGERS, Robert Emmons, 1888-
    The Boy Will
    (In One-Act Plays by Modern Authors)
The Rogueries of Scapin (see Molière, Jean Baptiste)
ROHMER, Eric, 1920 or 1923-
    Faust; film directed by Friedrich-Wilhelm Murnau; based on the
        work of Goethe
    (In L'Avant-Scène Cinéma, no. 190-191, July/Sept., 1977)

La Marquise d'O ...; titre original "Die Marquise Von O ..."
   (In L'Avant-Scène Cinéma, no. 173, Oct. 1, 1976)
Le Roi des Cons (see Wolinski)
Le Roi S'Amuse (see Hugo, Victor)
Le Roi se Meurt (see Ionesco, Eugene)
ROINARD, Paul Napoleon
   The Song of Songs of Solomon, adapted by Paul Napoleon Roinard,
     musical adaptations by Flamen de Labrely
     (In The Drama Review, Vol. 20, no. 3, Sept. 1976)
ROKK, Vsevolod
   Engineer Sergeyev
     (In Seven Soviet Plays)
ROLFE, Frederick, 1860-1913
  **Hadrian VII (see Luke, Peter)
ROLLAND, Romain, 1866-1944
   Liluli
     (In his Plays)
   The Montespan
     (In his Plays)
ROLT, Richard, 1725?-1770
   Amintas; an alteration of Rolt's "Royal Shepherd" by Tenducci
     and music by George Ruch
     (In A Collection of the Most Esteemed Farces ..., Vol. 6)
Rom oder Die Zweite Erschaffung der Welt (see Hammel, Claus)
Roma, Città Aperta (Rome, Open City); filmscript (see Rossellini,
   Roberto)
ROMAINS, Jules (born Louis Farigoule), 1885-
   Amedee et les Messieurs en Rang
     (In his Pièces en un Acte)
   Le Déjeuner Marocain
     (In his Pièces en un Acte)
   Démétrios
     (In his Pièces en un Acte)
   Knock
     (In L'Avant-Scène du Théâtre, no. 521-522, July 1973)
   The Peach
     (In Modern One-Act Plays from the French)
   La Scintillante
     (In L'Avant-Scène du Théâtre, no. 521-522, July 1973)
     (In his Pièces en un Acte)
  **Volpone (see Tourneur, Maurice)
ROMAN A., Sergio
   Un Extrano en la Niebla
     (In Teatro Ecuatoriano Contemporaneo, Vol. 2)
The Roman Actor (see Massinger, Philip)
The Roman Father (see Whitehead, William)
Romance de Lobos (see Valle-Inclan, Ramon del)
The Romance of an Hour (see Kelly, Hugh)
The Romance of Red-Riding-Hood (see Daudet, Alphonse)
The Romancers (see Rostand, Edmond)
Romanoff and Juliet (see Ustinov, Peter)
ROMASHOV, Boris Sergueievich, 1895-
   El Pastel
     (In Teatro Comico Sovietico)

Romeo and Jeanette (see Anouilh, Jean)
Romeo and Juliet (see Garrick, David)
Romeo Before the Corpse of Juliet (see Denevi, Marco)
Romeo et Jeannette; text in French (see Anouilh, Jean)
The Romp (see Bickerstaff, Isaac)
The Roncarelli Affair (see Moore, Mavor)
RONCHI, Teresa
    Es 1st Krieg!
        (In Sipario, no. 347, April 1975)
RONCORONI, Jean-Louis
    La Petite Bête
        (In L'Avant-Scène Théâtre, no. 563, May 1, 1975)
La Ronda de la Hechizada (see Argulles, Hugo)
La Ronde; screenplay (see Ophuls, Max)
La Ronde (Reigen) (see Schnitzler, Arthur)
RONILD, Peter
    Boxing for One
        (In Modern Nordic Plays: Denmark)
The Roof (see Galsworthy, John)
The Roof; screenplay (see De Sica, Vittorio. Il Tetto)
The Roof Garden (see Kishida, Kunio)
Rook (see Osgood, Lawrence)
The Room (see Pedrolo, Manuel de)
The Room (see Pinter, Harold)
Room Forty-Five (see Howells, William Dean)
ROOSEVELT, Theodore, Pres. U.S., 1858-1919
    *Two Administrations (see Bierce, Ambrose)
Rooster Cogburn; screenplay (see Julien, Martin)
Root, Elihu, U.S. Sec'ty of War, 1845-1937
    *Two Administrations (see Bierce, Ambrose)
Roots (see Wesker, Arnold)
Roots in a Parched Ground; television script (see Foote, Horton)
The Rope (see O'Neill, Eugene)
La Rosa de Carta (see Valle-Inclan, Ramon M.)
Rosalee Pritchett (see Molette, Carlton W., II)
Rosalind (see Barrie, James M.)
Rosamond (see Swinburne, Algernon Charles)
Rosamunda (see Alfieri, Vittorio)
Rosamunde Floris (see Kaiser, Georg)
ROSE, Reginald, 1920-
    Blacklist; television script (see Kinoy, Ernest)
    Dino
        (In Eight American Ethnic Plays)
    Thunder on Sycamore Street
        (In The Mentor Book of Short Plays)
    Twelve Angry Men; television script
        (In Great Television Plays)
        (In On the Air)
ROSE, Si
    The Edgar Bergen Show; CBS radio comedy, first presented on
    CBS, Nov. 27, 1955. Guests: Jack Benny and others
        (In Prize Plays of Television and Radio, 1956)
Une Rose au Petit Déjeuner (see Barillet, Pierre)
The Rose Garden (see Williams, Frayne)

The Rose Tattoo (see Williams, Tennessee)
ROSEN, Sheldon
   Love Mouse
     (In <u>A Collection of Canadian Plays</u>, Vol. 1)
   Meyer's Room
     (In <u>A Collection of Canadian Plays</u>, Vol. 1)
ROSENBERG, James L.
   Mel Says to Give You His Best
     (In <u>Best Short Plays</u>, 1976)
ROSENCOF, Mauricio, 1934-
   Los Caballos
     (In <u>Teatro Contemporaneo Hispanoamericano</u>, Vol. 2)
ROSENSTOCK, Sami, 1896-1963
   The Gas Heart, by Tristan Tzara (pseud.)
     (In <u>Modern French Theatre</u>)
   The Second Celestial Adventure of Mr. Excedrin, Fire Extinguisher, by Tristan Tzara (pseud.)
     (In <u>Yale/Theatre</u>, Vol. 4, no. 1, Winter 1973)
ROSENTHAL, Andrew
   Third Person
     (In <u>Plays of the Year</u>, Vol. 7, 1951/52)
ROSENTHAL, Jack, 1931-
   Another Sunday and Sweet F.A.
     (In <u>The Television Dramatist</u>)
ROSI, Francesco
   Main Basse sur la Ville
     (In <u>L'Avant-Scène Cinéma</u>, no. 169, May 1976)
   Uomini Contro
     (In <u>Dal Soggetto al Film Series</u>, no. 41, 1970)
Rosie at the Train; a radio monologue (see Clark, Sylvia)
ROSIMOND, Claude La Rose, sieur de, d. 1686
  **The Libertine (see Shadwell, Thomas)
ROSKAM, Clair
   Plenty of Rein; television script, originally broadcast June 9, 1957 on the "Look Up and Live" series, CBS
     (In <u>The Seeking Years</u>)
   The Puzzle; television script, originally broadcast June 16, 1957 on the "Look Up and Live" series, CBS
     (In <u>The Seeking Years</u>)
Rosmersholm (see Ibsen, Henrik)
Ross, a Dramatic Portrait (see Rattigan, Terence)
ROSS, Herbert, 1927-
   Play It Again, Sam; screenplay (see Allen, Woody)
ROSS, Michael
   Gloria Poses in the Nude; television script for an episode in "All in the Family," by Michael Ross, Bernie West, and Norman Lear
     (In <u>Samuel French's Tandem Library Series</u>)
   Mike's Appendix; television script for an episode in "All in the Family," by Michael Ross and Bernie West
     (In <u>Samuel French's Tandem Library Series</u>)
Der Rossdieb Zu Funsing mit den Tollen Diebischen Bauern (see Sachs, Hans)

ROSSELLINI, Roberto, 1906-1977
    Città Aperta
        (In Dal Soggetto al Film Series Retrospettiva, no. 2, 1972)
    Era Notte a Roma
        (In Dal Soggetto al Film Series, no. 16, 1960)
    Germania Anno Zero
        (In Dal Soggetto al Film Series Retrospettiva, no. 2, 1972)
    Germany--Year Zero
        (In Lorrimer Screenplay Series, 1973)
        (In his The War Trilogy)
    Open City (Roma, Città Aperta); screenplay by Fellini for the
    film by Rossellini
        (In Lorrimer Screenplay Series, 1973)
        (In his The War Trilogy)
    Paisà; screenplay by Fellini for the film by Rossellini; text in
    Italian
        (In Dal Soggetto al Film Series Retrospettiva, no. 2, 1972)
    Paisan; screenplay by Fellini for the film by Rossellini
        (In Lorrimer Screenplay Series, 1973)
        (In his The War Trilogy)
    Roma, Città Aperta (Rome, Open City); screenplay by Fellini
    for the film by Rossellini
        (In Dal Soggetto al Film Series, no. 45, 1972)
ROSSELSON, Leon
    Le Primitif
        (In L'Avant-Scène du Théâtre, no. 542, June 1, 1974)
ROSSI, Gherardo de
    Il Calzolajo Inglese in Roma
        (In Teatro Comico Moderno)
ROSSI, Jean-Baptiste, 1931-
    Odessea Nuda
        (In Dal Soggetto al Film Series, no. 19, 1961)
ROSSO DI SAN SECONDO, Piermaria, 1889-
    The Stairs
        (In Eight European Plays)
ROSTAND, Edmond, 1868-1918
    Cyrano de Bergerac
        (In Representative Continental Dramas)
    The Last Night of Don Juan
        (In The Theatre of Don Juan)
    The Romancers
        (In The Mentor Book of Short Plays)
        (In The Play Book)
    The Two Pierrots; or, The White Supper
        (In Modern One-Act Plays from the French)
ROSTAND, Maurice, 1891-
    He Who Did Not Kill; or, The Way to Be Loved
        (In Modern One-Act Plays from the French)
ROSTEN, Hedda
    The Happy Housewife
        (In Best Television Plays, 1954)
ROSTEN, Norman
    Prometheus in Granada, a verse play
        (In 100 Non-Royalty Radio Plays)

El Rostro Perdido (see Weisenborn, Günther)
ROSZKOWSKI, David
    Canvas
        (In Playwrights for Tomorrow, Vol. 11)
ROTH, Gerhard
    Sehnsucht
        (In Theater Heute, no. 11, Nov. 1977)
ROTHE, Hans, 1894-
    Llegada de Noche
        (In Teatro Aleman Contemporaneo)
ROTIMI, Ola
    The Gods Are Not to Blame; based on the theme of Sophocles'
    "Oedipus Rex"
        (In Oxford Three Crowns Book Series, 1971)
ROTROU, Jean, 1609-1650
    La Bague de l'Oubli
        (In Théâtre du XVIIe Siècle, Vol. 1)
    La Belle Aphrede
        (In Théâtre du XVIIe Siècle, Vol. 1)
    Cosroes (Chosroes)
        (In The Chief Rivals of Corneille and Racine)
    Cosroès
        (In his Théâtre Choisi)
        (In Théâtre du XVIIe Siècle, Vol. 1)
    Don Bernard de Cabère
        (In his Théâtre Choisi)
    Laure Persecutée
        (In his Théâtre Choisi)
        (In Théâtre du XVIIe Siècle, Vol. 1)
    Saint Geneste (Saint Genesius)
        (In More Plays by Rivals of Corneille and Racine)
    La Soeur
        (In his Théâtre Choisi)
    Les Sosies
        (In his Théâtre Choisi)
    Venceslas (Wenceslaus)
        (In The Chief Rivals of Corneille and Racine)
        (In his Théâtre Choisi)
        (In Théâtre du XVIIe Siècle, Vol. 1)
    Le Véritable Saint Genest
        (In his Théâtre Choisi)
        (In Théâtre du XVIIe Siècle, Vol. 1)
Rotter (see Brasch, Thomas)
ROUDY, Pierre
    Les Oeufs à la Moutarde
        (In L'Avant-Scène Théâtre, no. 561, April 1, 1975)
"Rouge!" (see Cortez, Alfredo)
ROUGERIE, Jean, 1929-
    Entretiens avec le Professeur Y (see Céline, Louis-Ferdinand)
Round Dance (see Schnitzler, Arthur)
The Roundheads; or, The Good Old Cause (see Behn, Mrs. Aphra)
ROUSSEL, Raymond
    The Dust of Suns
        (In Calder & Boyars Playscript Series, no. 17)

ROUSSIN, Andre
    L'Amour For; ou, La Premiere Surprise
        (In L'Avant-Scène Théâtre, no. 569, Aug. 1975)
    La Claque
        (In L'Avant-Scène du Théâtre, no. 525, Sept. 1973)
    Le Mari, la Femme et la Mort
        (In L'Avant-Scène Théâtre, no. 544, July 1, 1974)
The Rover; or, The Banished Cavaliers (see Behn, Mrs. Aphra)
ROVINSKI, Samuel, 1932-
    Gobierno de Alcoba
        (In Obras Breves del Teatro Costarricense, Vol. 2)
        (In Teatro Contemporaneo Hispanoamericano, Vol. 2)
    El Laberinto
        (In El Teatro de Hoy en Costa Rica)
ROWE, Nicholas, 1674-1718
    The Fair Penitent
        (In Five Restoration Tragedies)
        (In Plays of the Restoration and 18th Century)
    Jane Shore
        (In British Plays from the Restoration to 1820, Vol. 2)
        (In The London Stage, Vol. 1)
    Lady Jane Grey
        (In The London Stage, Vol. 3)
    Tamerlane
        (In The London Stage, Vol. 3)
Rowley, Anthony (see Guthrie, Arthur)
ROWLEY, William, 1585?-1642?
    The Changeling (see Middleton, Thomas)
    A Cure for a Cuckold (see Webster, John)
    A Fair Quarrel (see Middleton, Thomas)
    Fortune by Land and Sea (see Heywood, Thomas)
    The Maid in the Mill (see Fletcher, John)
    The Old Law (see Massinger, Philip)
    The Spanish Gipsy (see Middleton, Thomas)
    The World Lost at Tennis (see Middleton, Thomas)
ROY, Claude
    Honni Soit Qui Mal y Pense (see Barnes, Peter)
    Le Premier (Le 1er) (see Horovitz, Israel)
Royal Favour (see Housman, Laurence)
The Royal Hunt of the Sun (see Shaffer, Peter)
Royal March; radio script (see Latzko, Andreas)
The Royal Master (see Shirley, James)
The Royal Shepherdesse (see Shadwell, Thomas)
The Royal Slave (see Cartwright, William)
The Royall King, and the Loyall Subject (see Heywood, Thomas)
ROYAS, Fernando de
    **La Célestine (see Laville, Pierre)
ROZEWICZ, Tadeusz
    The Card Index
        (In Calder & Boyars Playscript Series, no. 8)
        (In Evergreen Original Plays Series, 1970)
    The Funny Old Man
        (In Calder & Boyars Playscript Series, no. 8)

Gone Out
(In <u>Calder & Boyars Playscript</u> Series, no. 8)
(In <u>Evergreen Original Plays</u> Series, 1970)
The Interrupted Act
(In <u>Calder & Boyars Playscript</u> Series, no. 8)
(In <u>Evergreen Original Plays</u> Series, 1970)
(In <u>Gambit</u>, Vol. 3, no. 12)
The Laocoon Group
(In <u>Calder & Boyars Playscripts</u> no. 11)
The Witness
(In <u>Calder & Boyars Playscripts</u> no. 11)
ROZHDESTVENSKY, Robert
The Young Guard (see Aleksin, Anatoly)
ROZLIER, Jacques, 1926-
Adieu Philippine
(In <u>Film Language</u>)
ROZOV, Victor Sergeyevich, 1913-
ABC--A Cinema Scenario for Reading
(In <u>The New Writing in Russia</u>)
Alive Forever
(In <u>Contemporary Russian Drama</u>)
The Young Graduates (V Dobryi Chas!)
(In <u>Russian Plays for Young Audiences</u>)
ROZSA, Jorge, 1923-
"Hambre"
(In <u>Teatro Contemporaneo Hispanoamericano</u>, Vol. 2)
Le Ruban (see Feydeau, Georges)
Rubbers (see Reynolds, Jonathan)
Rubezahl (see Lubiez-Milosz, Oscar V.)
Le Rubicon (see Bourdet, Edouard)
RUBINSTEIN, Harold Frederick, 1891-
First Corinthians
(In <u>Best One-Act Plays of 1938</u>, London)
Ohad's Woman
(In <u>Best One-Act Plays of 1941</u>, London)
On the Portsmouth Road
(In <u>One-Act Plays for Stage and Study</u>, 7th Series)
Ruddigore: or, The Witch's Curse (see Gilbert, William S.)
Rude Journée pour la Reine; screenplay (see Allio, Rene)
Rudimentary (see Stramm, August)
RUDKIN, David, 1935-
Afore Night Came
(In <u>Evergreen Playscript</u> Series, 1966)
Ashes: Parts 1 & 2
(In <u>Plays and Players</u>, Vol. 21, no. 6, March 1974)
Ashes: Part 3
(In <u>Plays and Players</u>, Vol. 21, no. 7, April 1974)
RUDOLPH, Alan
Buffalo Bill and the Indians; or, Sitting Bull's History Lesson,
screenplay by Alan Rudolph and Robert Altman, suggested by
the play "Indians," by Arthur Kopit
(A <u>Bantam Books Screenplay</u>, 1976)

La Rue Saint-Honoré (see Musset, Alfred de)
Rückkopplung (see Gelman, Alexander)
La Rueda (see Laiglesia, Juan A.)
RUEDA, Lope de, d. 1565
    Comedia Armelina
        (In Clásicos Castellanos, Vol. 59)
        (In his Teatro)
    Comedia Eufemia
        (In Clásicos Castellanos, Vol. 59)
        (In his Teatro)
    El Deleitoso
        (In Clásicos Castellanos, Vol. 59)
        (In his Teatro)
    Los Engañados
        (In Clásicos Castellanos, Vol. 181)
    Medora
        (In Clásicos Castellanos, Vol. 181)
    The Seventh Farce
        (In The Drama, Vol. 6)
Der Ruf des Lebens (see Schnitzler, Arthur)
The Ruffian on the Stair (see Orton, Joe)
RUIBAL, José
    The Begging Machine
        (In Modern International Drama, Vol. 9, no. 2, Spring 1976)
    The Jackass
        (In The New Wave Spanish Drama)
    The Man and the Fly
        (In The New Wave Spanish Drama)
        (In Themes of Drama)
Die Ruinen von Athen (see Hofmannsthal, Hugo von H.)
Ruiz de Alarcón, Juan (see Ruiz de Alarcón y Mendoza, Juan)
RUIZ DE ALARCON Y MENDOZA, Juan, 1581-1639
    El Examen de Maridos
        (In Clásicos Castellanos, Vol. 146)
    Ganar Amigos
        (In Clásicos Castellanos, Vol. 147)
    Las Paredes Oyen
        (In Clásicos Castellanos, Vol. 37)
    Los Pechos Privilegiados
        (In Clásicos Castellanos, Vol. 147)
    La Prueba de las Promesas
        (In Clásicos Castellanos, Vol. 146)
    La Verdad Sospechosa
        (In Clásicos Castellanos, Vol. 37)
RUIZ IRIARTE, Victor, 1912-
    El Carrusell
        (In Teatro Español, 1964-65)
        (In Teatro Selecto de Victor Ruiz Iriarte)
    Esta Noche es la Vispera
        (In Teatro Español, 1958-59)
        (In Teatro Selecto de Victor Ruiz Iriarte)
    El Gran Minue
        (In Teatro Español, 1950-51)

(In <u>Teatro Selecto de Victor Ruiz Iriarte</u>)
La Guerra Empieza en Cuba
   (In <u>Teatro Español,</u> 1955-56)
Juego de Niños
   (In <u>Teatro Español,</u> 1951-52)
El Lando de Seis Caballos
   (In <u>Teatro Español,</u> 1949-50)
   (In <u>Teatro Selecto de Victor Ruiz Iriarte</u>)
La Muchacha del Sombreito Rosa
   (In <u>Teatro Español,</u> 1966-67)
Un Paraguas Bajo la Lluvia
   (In <u>Teatro Español,</u> 1965-66)
   (In <u>Teatro Selecto de Victor Ruiz Iriarte</u>)
El Pobrecito Embustero
   (In <u>Teatro Español,</u> 1952-53)
La Señora Recibe una Carta
   (In <u>Teatro Español,</u> 1967-68)
Rule a Wife, and Have a Wife (see Fletcher, John)
The Ruling Class; a baroque comedy (see Barnes, Peter)
The Rump; or, The Mirrour of the Late Times (see Tatham, John)
Rund um den Kongress (see Horvath, Odön von)
La Ruptura (see Krog, Helge)
Rus in Urbe (see Rice, Elmer L.)
Rush television scripts
   Lament the Days That Are Gone By (see Borg, Sonia)
   Of All the Crowd That Assembled There (see Griffiths, Howard)
   There's a Change from the Old to the New (see Martin, John)
Rush television script, "There's a Change from the Old to the New"
   (see Martin, John)
RUSSELL, George William, 1867-1935
   Deirdre, By A E (pseud.)
      (In <u>Irish Drama Series,</u> Vol. 4)
The Russian People (see Simonov, Konstantin)
Rusty Bugles (see Elliott, Sumner L.)
RUTEBEUF, fl. 13th Cent.
   Le Miracle de Théophile; text in English
      (In <u>Medieval English Plays</u>)
RUTHENBURG, Grace Dorcas
   Moses Was an Oyster Man
      (In <u>One-Act Plays for Stage and Study,</u> 7th Series)
   Retreat
      (In <u>One-Act Plays for Stage and Study,</u> 8th Series)
Ruy Blas (see Hugo, Victor)
Il Ruzzante (see Beolco, Angelo)
RYERSON, Florence, 1894-
   Hot Lemonade, by Florence Ryerson and Colin Clements
      (In <u>One-Act Plays for Stage and Study,</u> 5th Series)
   The Willow Plate, by Florence Ryerson and Colin Clements
      (In <u>One-Act Plays for Stage and Study,</u> 6th Series)
RYGA, George, 1932-
   Captives of the Faceless Drummer
      (In <u>Talonplays Series,</u> 1971)
   The Ecstasy of Rita Joe
      (In his <u>The Ecstasy of Rita Joe and Other Plays,</u> New Drama

1 Series, 1971)
    (In Talonplays Series, 1969)
Grass and Wild Strawberries
    (In his The Ecstasy of Rita Joe and Other Plays, New Drama
    1 Series, 1971)
Indian
    (In his The Ecstasy of Rita Joe and Other Plays, New Drama
    1 Series, 1971)
    (In Ten Canadian Short Plays)
Sunrise on Sarah
    (In Talonplays Series, 1973)
RYSKIND, Morris, 1895 or 1899-
    Animal Crackers, screenplay by Morrie Ryskind, based on the
    musical play by George S. Kaufman, Morrie Ryskind, Bert
    Kalmar and Harry Ruby; film directed by Victor Heerman
    (In Hooray for Captain Spaulding!)
Of Thee I Sing (see Gershwin, George)
RYTON, Royse
    Crown Matrimonial
        (In Plays of the Year, Vol. 43, 1972-73)
    The Other Side of the Swamp
        (In Plays and Players, Vol. 23, nos. 9 & 10, June & July,
        1976)

Saavedra, Angel de (see Rivas, Angel Pérez de Saavedra Ramirez
    de Madrid Ramirez de Baquedano, 3, Duque de)
SABATIER, Pierre
    Fait Divers
        (In L'Avant-Scène Théâtre, no. 588, June 1, 1976)
The Sabine Women (see Andreev, Leonid N.)
SACHS, Hans, 1494-1576
    Der Baurenknecht Will Zwo Frauen Haben
        (In his Werke in Zwei Bänden, Vol. 2)
    Der Blind Mesner mit dem Pfarrer und Seim Weib
        (In his Werke in Zwei Bänden, Vol. 2)
    Ein Burger, Bauer und Edelmann, die Holen Krapfen
        (In his Werke in Zwei Bänden, Vol. 2)
    Der Doktor mit der Grossen Nasen
        (In his Werke in Zwei Bänden, Vol. 2)
    Der Fahrend Schuler im Paradeis
        (In his Werke in Zwei Bänden, Vol. 2)
    Frau Wahrheit Will Niemand Herbergen
        (In his Werke in Zwei Bänden, Vol. 2)
    Das Gespräch Alexandri Magni mit dem Philosopho Diogeni
        (In his Werke in Zwei Bänden, Vol. 2)
    Das Heiss Eisen
        (In his Werke in Zwei Bänden, Vol. 2)
    Der Henno
        (In his Werke in Zwei Bänden, Vol. 2)
    Das Kälberbrüten
        (In his Werke in Zwei Bänden, Vol. 2)
    Der Ketzermeister mit den Viel Kessel Suppen
        (In his Werke in Zwei Bänden, Vol. 2)

Der Krämerkorb
(In his <u>Werke in Zewi Bänden,</u> Vol. 2)
Das Narrenschneiden
(In his <u>Werke in Zwei Bänden,</u> Vol. 2)
Der Neidhart mit dem Feiel
(In his <u>Werke in Zwei Bänden,</u> Vol. 2)
Der Pfarrer mit Sein Ehbrecher-Bauern
(In his <u>Werke in Zwei Bänden,</u> Vol. 2)
Raising the Devil
(In <u>The Drama,</u> Vol. 10)
Die Rockenstuben
(In his <u>Werke in Zwei Bänden,</u> Vol. 2)
Der Rossdieb zu Funsing mit den Tollen Diebischen Bauern
(In his <u>Werke in Zwei Bänden,</u> Vol. 2)
Die Sechs Kämperfer
(In his <u>Werke in Zwei Bänden,</u> Vol. 2)
Tristant und Isald
(In his <u>Werke in Zwei Bänden,</u> Vol. 2)
The Wandering Scholar from Paradise
(In <u>World Drama,</u> Vol. 1)
Das Wildbad
(In his <u>Werke in Zwei Bänden,</u> Vol. 2)
Die Zween Ritter von Burgund
(In his <u>Werke in Zwei Bänden,</u> Vol. 2)
SACKLER, Howard, 1929-
The Great White Hope; a chronicle of the rise and fall of an
American boxer, based on the life and times of Jack Johnson
(In <u>Best American Plays,</u> 7th Series, 1967-1973)
(In <u>Best Plays of the Sixties</u>)
Nine O'Clock Mail
(In <u>New Theatre in America,</u> Vol. 1)
Sackville, Thomas (see Dorset, Thomas Sackville, 1st Earl of)
The Sacred Flame (see Maugham, William Somerset)
Le Sacrifice (see Daudet, Alphonse)
Sacrifice (see Duncan, Thelma M.)
Sad Are the Eyes of William Tell (see Sastre, Alfonso)
The Sad Shepherd; or, A Tale of Robin Hood (see Jonson, Ben)
SADA, Concepcion, 1899-
Un Mundo Para Mi
(In <u>Teatro Méxicano del Siglo XX,</u> Vol. 2)
The Saddest Summer of Samuel S (see Donleavy, James Patrick)
SADE, Donatien Alphonse François, comte, called Marquis de, 1740-
1814)
**Le 120 Giornate di Sodoma (see Vasilico, Giuliano)
The Safety Match (see Ginsbury, Norman)
Saga of the Black Man (see Fabio, Sarah W.)
SAGARRA, José Maria de, 1894-
La Herida Luminosa; version y adaptacion de José Maria Peman
(In <u>Teatro Español,</u> 1955-56)
Sagasta, Praxedes Mateo, Prime Minister, Spain, 1827-1903
*Two Administrations (see Bierce, Ambrose)
LE SAGE, Alain-Rene, 1668-1747
Crispin, Rival of His Master
(In <u>The Drama,</u> Vol. 8)

**Neck of Nothing; The Narrow Escape (see Garrick, David)
La Sagesse; ou, La Parabole du Festin (see Claudel, Paul)
Sagro del Signore della Nave (see Pirandello, Luigi)
Sailor, Beware! (see King, Philip)
Saint Cyprian and the Devil (see Van der Veer, Ethel)
SAINT-FOIX, Germain François Poullain de, 1698-1776
   **Daphne and Amintor (see Bickerstaff, Isaac)
Saint Genest (Saint Genesius) (see Rotrou, Jean)
St. Helena (see Sheriff, Robert C.)
Saint Honey (see Ritchie, Paul)
Saint Joan (see Shaw, George Bernard)
Saint Joan of the Stockyards (see Brecht, Bertolt)
St. John's Night (see Ibsen, Henrik)
St. Louis Woman (see Bontemps, Arna)
Saint Narukami and the God Fudō (see Hanjurō, Tsuuchi)
St. Patrick for Ireland (see Shirley, James)
St. Patrick's Day; or, The Scheming Lieutenant (see Sheridan, Rich-
   ard Brinsley)
Saint Valentin (see Miracles de Nostra Dame par Personnages)
Sainte Nuevo (see Alarcón, Pedro Antonio de)
Saint's Day (see Whiting, John)
SAK, Norman
   John Whiffle Concentrates
      (In 100 Non-Royalty Radio Plays)
Saki (see Munro, Hector Hugh)
Sakoontalá (see Kálidása)
SAKS, Sol
   $100,000 for a Wife
      (In 100 Non-Royalty Radio Plays)
SALACROU, Armand, 1899-
   Atlas-Hôtel; text in French
      (In his Théâtre II)
   Le Casseur d'Assiettes
      (In his Théâtre I)
   A Circus Story
      (In Modern French Theatre)
   La Desconocida de Arras
      (In his Teatro)
   Une Femme Libre
      (In his Théâtre III)
   Les Fiancés du Havre
      (In his Théâtre V)
   Les Frénétiques
      (In his Théâtre II)
   Histoire de Rire
      (In his Théâtre IV)
   Un Hombre Como los Demas
      (In his Teatro)
   Un Homme Comme les Autres
      (In his Théâtre III)
   L'Inconnue d'Arras
      (In his Théâtre III)

Marguerite
  (In <u>Best Short Plays of the World Theatre</u>, 1968-1973)
Marguerite; English version by Norman Stokle
  (In <u>Minnesota Drama Editions</u>, no. 4)
La Marguerite; text in French
  (In his <u>Théâtre IV</u>)
Les Nuits de la Colère
  (In his <u>Théâtre V</u>)
Patchouli
  (In his <u>Théâtre I</u>)
Le Pont de l'Europe
  (In his <u>Théâtre I</u>)
Le Soldat et la Sorcière
  (In his <u>Théâtre V</u>)
La Terre est Ronde
  (In his <u>Théâtre IV</u>)
La Tierra es Redonda
  (In his <u>Teatro</u>)
Tour a Terre
  (In his <u>Théâtre I</u>)
La Vie en Rose
  (In his <u>Théâtre II</u>)
When the Music Stops; English version by Norman Stokle
  (In <u>Minnesota Drama Editions</u>, no. 4)
The World Is Round; English version by Norman Stokle
  (In <u>Minnesota Drama Editions</u>, no. 4)
Saladin (Salah-al-Din, Yusuf ibn-Ayyub), Sultan of Egypt and Syria,
  1138-1193
  *Nathan le Sage (see Chénier, Marie-Joseph B.)
SALAZAR BONDY, Sebastian, 1924-
  El Fabricante de Deudas
    (In <u>El Teatro Hispanoamericano Contemporaneo</u>, Vol. 1)
  No Hay Isla Feliz
    (In <u>Teatro Peruano Contemporaneo</u>)
SALAZAR TAMARIZ, Hugo
  Por un Plato de Arroz
    (In <u>Teatro Ecuatoriano Contemporaneo</u>, Vol. 2)
SALERNO, Henry F.
  The Trap
    (In <u>Drama and Theatre</u>, Vol. 11, no. 1, Fall 1972)
Salesman; filmscript (see Maysles, Albert)
The Salesmen (see Ward, Edmund)
Salieri, Antonio, 1750-1825
  *Mozart and Salieri (see Pushkin, Alexandr S.)
SALINAS, Marcelo, 1889-
  Alma Guajira
    (In <u>Teatro Cubano Contemporaneo</u>)
Salle d'Attente (see Praga, Andre)
Salmacida Spolia (see D'Avenant, Sir William)
SALMON, Raul
  La Calle del Pecado
    (In his <u>Teatro Boliviano</u>)

Escuela de Pillos
    (In his Teatro Boliviano)
El Estano Era Limachi
    (In his Teatro Boliviano)
Los Hijos del Alcohol
    (In his Teatro Boliviano)
Joven, Rica 7 Plebeya
    (In his Teatro Boliviano)
Juana Sanchez
    (In his Teatro Boliviano)
Mi Compadre, el Ministro
    (In his Teatro Boliviano)
Miss Chijini
    (In his Teatro Boliviano)
El Partido de la Contrapartida
    (In his Teatro Boliviano)
Plato Paceno
    (In his Teatro Boliviano)
Tres Generales
    (In his Teatro Boliviano)
Viva Belzu
    (In his Teatro Boliviano)
SALOM, Jaime
    El Baul de los Disfraces
        (In Teatro Español, 1963-64)
    La Casa de las Chivas
        (In Teatro Español, 1967-68)
    La Playa Vacia
        (In Teatro Español, 1970-71)
    Tiempo de Espadas
        (In Teatro Español, 1972-73)
Salome, 14? A.D.-before 62 A.D.
    *Mariamne (see Voltaire)
    *Salome (see Wilde, Oscar)
    *Salome's Head (see Ortiz de Montellano, Bernardo)
The Saloon (see James, Henry)
Salt of the Earth; screenplay (see Wilson, Michael)
El Saltimbanqui del Mundo Occidental (see Synge, John M.)
SALTYKOV-SHCHEDRIN, Mikhail
    Pazukhin's Death
        (In Russian Literature Triquarterly, no. 14, Winter 1976)
Salut an Alle, Marx (see Kaltofen, Gunter)
Salut l'Artiste; filmscript (see Robert, Yves)
The Salutation (see Kennedy, Charles R.)
Salutations (see Ionesco, Eugene)
SALUTIN, Rick
    1837: The Farmers' Revolt
        (In Canadian Theatre Review, Vol. 6, Spring 1975)
Las Salvajes en Puente San Gil (see Martin Recuerda, José)
Salvation (see Howard, Sidney C.)
Salvation Nell (see Sheldon, Edward)
SALVATORE, Gaston
    Freibrief
        (In Theater Heute, no. 9, Sept. 1977)

The Salvia Milkshake (see Brenton, Howard)
The Salzburg Great Theatre of the World (see Hofmannsthal, Hugo von H.)
Das Salzburger Grosse Welttheater (see Hofmannsthal, Hugo von H.)
Sam 'n' Ella (see Felton, Norman)
Sam Slade Is Missing (see Morrison, Bill)
The Same Old Thing (see Megrue, Roi C.)
Sammi (see Joselovitz, Ernest A.)
Sammuramat, Queen of Assyria, fl. at end of the 9th Cent. B.C.
   *Semiramis (see Crebillon, Prosper J.)
   *Semiramis (see Voltaire)
   *Semiramis; both French and English texts are given (see Valery, Paul)
SAMPAIO, Silveira
   The Need for Polygamy
      (In Modern International Drama, Vol. 9, no. 2, Spring 1976)
Sampson (see Selbourne, David)
Samson (see Howells, William Dean)
SAN FELIX, Alavaro
   Las Ranas y el Mar
      (In Teatro Ecuatoriano Contemporaneo, Vol. 2)
SAN FRANCISCO MIME TROUP
   L'Amant Militaire, adapted from a play by Carlo Goldoni, adapted by Joan Holden
      (In The New Consciousness)
   Eco-man
      (In Guerilla Street Theater)
   Meter Maid
      (In Break Out!)
   The Mother (see Brecht, Bertolt)
SAN FRANCISCO RED THEATRE
   Lay the Bosses Off--Not the Workers
      (In Guerilla Street Theater)
   One Day at Nixon High School
      (In Guerilla Street Theater)
   The Story of the Three Big Pigs!
      (In Guerilla Street Theater)
SAN FRANCISCO WOMEN'S STREET THEATER
   This Is a Cranky
      (In Guerilla Street Theater)
   This Is a Flippy
      (In Guerilla Street Theater)
San Juan de las Manzanas (see Villasis Endara, Carlos)
San Michele Aveva un Gallo Allonsanfan; filmscript (see Taviani, Paolo)
San Miguel de las Espinas (see Bustillo Oro, Juan)
SANCHEZ, Florencio, 1875-1910
   Barranca Abajo
      (In Teatro Uruguayo Contemporaneo)
Sanchez, Juana
   *Juana Sanchez (see Salmon, Raul)
SANCHEZ, Sonia, 1935-
   The Bronx Is Next
      (In Cavalcade)

Dirty Hearts
  (In Break Out!)
Uh, Uh; But How Do It Free Us?
  (In The New Lafayette Theatre Presents)
SANCHEZ MAYANS, Fernando, 1924-
  Las Alas del Pez
    (In Teatro Méxicano del Siglo XX, Vol. 4)
  El Pequeño Juicio
    (In 12 Obras en un Acto)
Sancho's Master (see Cervantes Saavedra, Miguel de)
Sancta Susanna (see Stramm, August)
Sancticity (see Head, Robert)
Sandcastle (see Hite, Barbara A.)
The Sand Castle (see Wilson, Lanford)
Sandhogs; radio script (see Lewerth, Margaret)
Sandra; screenplay (see Visconti, Luchino. Vaghe Stelle dell 'Orsa)
The Sandwiching (see Göring, Lars)
Sandford and Son television scripts
  The Engagement (see Stein, James R.)
  A House Is Not a Poolroom (see Moss, Winston)
  Superflyer (see Williams, Charles T.)
  This Land Is Whose Land? (see Farmer, Gene)
  Tooth or Consequences (see Stevenson, Adell)
La Sangre de Dios (see Sastre, Alfonso)
Sangre Gorda (see Alvarez Quintero, Serafin)
SANGSTER, Jimmy
  Le Cauchemar de Dracula; filmscript (see Fisher, Terence)
Sanibel and Captiva (see Terry, Megan)
Sanshiro Sugata; filmscript (see Kurosawa, Akira)
Santa Cruz (see Frisch, Max)
SANTANDER, Felipe, 1924-
  Luna de Miel
    (In Teatro Méxicano, 1959)
SANTAREÑO, Bernardo, 1924-
  La Promesa
    (In Teatro Portugues Contemporaneo)
SANTIS, Omar Saavedra, 1944-
  Szenen Wider die Nacht; original titel, "Historias Posibles
    Escenas Contra la Noche"
    (In Theater der Zeit, no. 8, 1977)
SANTOS, Vital, 1949-
  Os Martirios de Jorge e de Rosa, fantasia mágica musical de
    Cores Nordestinas
    (In Revista de Teatro, no. 419, Sept./Oct. 1977)
Sapho (see Daudet, Alphonse)
SAPINSLEY, Alvin
  Lee at Gettysburg
    (In Great Television Plays)
Sara B. Divine! (see Eyen, Tom)
Sardanapale; opéra imité de Lord Byron (see Becque, Henri)
SARDOU, Victorien, 1831-1908
  Let's Get a Divorce! by Victorien Sardou and Emile de Najac
    (In Three French Farces)

A Scrap of Paper
    (In <u>Camille and Other Plays</u>)
Tosca; opera (see Puccini, Giacomo)
SAROSSY, Via
    Dinner Party
      (In <u>Women Write for the Theatre Series</u>, Vol. 1)
SAROYAN, William, 1908-
    Coming Through the Rye
      (In <u>10 Short Plays</u>)
    The Man with the Heart in the Highlands
      (In <u>All the World's a Stage</u>)
    El Momento de Tu Vida
      (In <u>Teatro Norteamericano Contemporaneo</u>)
    The Slaughter of the Innocents
      (In <u>The William Saroyan Reader</u>)
    A Special Announcement
      (In <u>100 Non-Royalty Radio Plays</u>)
    The Time of Your Life
      (In <u>50 Best Plays of the American Theatre</u>, Vol. 3)
      (In <u>The William Saroyan Reader</u>)
SARRAUTE, Nathalie
    C'Est Beau
      (In <u>L'Avant-Scène Théâtre</u>, no. 582, Mar. 1, 1976)
    Isma; ou, Ce Qui s'Appelle Rien
      (In <u>Isma</u>)
    The Lie
      (In <u>Calder & Boyars Playscript</u> Series, no. 10)
    Le Mensonge
      (In <u>Isma</u>)
    Silence
      (In <u>Calder & Boyars Playscript</u> Series, no. 10)
    Le Silence
      (In <u>Isma</u>)
SARTORIS, Ramon
    The Clue of the Wrong Thing
      (In his <u>Three Plays</u>)
    From Core to Rind
      (In his <u>Three Plays</u>)
    If Caesar Be
      (In his <u>Three Plays</u>)
SARTRE, Jean-Paul, 1905-
    The Devil and the Good Lord
      (In <u>The Devil and the Good Lord</u>)
    Le Diable et le Bon Dieu
      (In <u>Le Théâtre d'Aujourd'hui</u>)
    Dirty Hands
      (In his <u>No Exit and Three Other Plays</u>)
    The Flies
      (In his <u>No Exit and Three Other Plays</u>)
    In Camera
      (In <u>Three European Plays</u>)
    Kean, based on the play by Alexandre Dumas
      (In <u>The Devil and the Good Lord</u>)

Les Mains Sales
    (In The French Theater Since 1930)
Nekrassov
    (In The Devil and the Good Lord)
No Exit
    (In his No Exit and Three Other Plays)
The Respectful Prostitute
    (In his No Exit and Three Other Plays)
Les Séquestres d'Altona
    (In Le Théâtre d'Aujourd'hui)
SASLAWSKI, Luis
    El Amor es un Potro Desbocado (see Escobar, Luis)
SASSONE, Felipe, 1884-
    Yo Tengo Veinte Años!
        (In Teatro Español, 1950-51)
SASTRE, Alfonso, 1926-
    Ana Kleiber
        (In Teatro Selecto de Alfonso Sastre)
    Condemned Squad
        (In The Modern Spanish Stage: Four Plays)
    La Cornada
        (In Teatro Selecto de Alfonso Sastre)
    Death Thrust
        (In Masterpieces of the Modern Spanish Theatre)
    En la Red
        (In Teatro Español, 1960-61)
        (In Teatro Selecto de Alfonso Sastre)
    Escuradra Hacia la Muerte
        (In Teatro Selecto de Alfonso Sastre)
    Guillermo Tell Tiene los Ojos Tristes
        (In Teatro Selecto de Alfonso Sastre)
    In the Net
        (In Modern International Drama, Vol. 8, no. 2, 1975)
    La Mordaza
        (In Teatro Español, 1954-55)
        (In Teatro Selecto de Alfonso Sastre)
    Oficio de Tinieblas
        (In Teatro Español, 1966-67)
    Sad Are the Eyes of William Tell
        (In The New Wave Spanish Drama)
    La Sangre de Dios
        (In Teatro Selecto de Alfonso Sastre)
    Il Vampiro di Uppsala
        (In Sipario, no. 325, June 1973)
"Saturday Morning"; filmscript (see Mackenzie, Kent)
Saturday Night and Sunday Morning; filmscript (see Reisz, Karel)
Saturday Night at the Movies (see Hoffman, William M.)
Saturday Night Live; television script (see Ackroyd, Dan)
Satyr of La Villette (see Obaldia, Rene de)
Satyricon (see Foster, Paul)
Saul, 1st King of Israel, 11th Cent. B.C.
    *King David and His Wives (see Pinski, David)
    *Saul (see Du Ryer, Pierre)

*Saul (see Goodman, Paul)
*Saul; text in English (see Alfieri, Vittorio)
*Saul; text in French (see Lamartine, Alphonse M.)
*Saul; text in Italian (see Alfieri, Vittorio)
*Saul le Furieux (see Taille, Jean de la)
SAUNDERS, James, 1925-
    Alas, Poor Fred
      (In his Neighbours and Other Plays)
    Neighbours
      (In Best Short Plays, 1976)
      (In his Neighbours and Other Plays)
    The Pedagogue
      (In his Neighbours and Other Plays)
    Return to a City
      (In his Neighbours and Other Plays)
    A Slight Accident
      (In his Neighbours and Other Plays)
    Triangle
      (In his Neighbours and Other Plays)
    Trio
      (In his Neighbours and Other Plays)
    Les Voisins; pièce de James Saunders, adaptation de Suzanne
      Lombard
      (In L'Avant-Scène du Théâtre, no. 534, Feb. 1974)
SAUNDERS, John Monk
    Love in a French Kitchen (see Clements, Colin C.)
SAURA, Carlos, 1932-
    Anne et les Loups; titre original "Ana y los Lobos"
      (In L'Avant-Scène Cinéma, no. 152, Nov. 1974)
SAUREL, Renée
    La Foi, l'Esperance et la Charite (see Horvath, Odön von)
Das Sauspiel (see Walser, Martin)
SAUTET, Claude
    Mado
      (In L'Avant-Scène Cinéma, no. 180, Jan. 15, 1977)
    Vincent, François, Paul et les Autres ... d'après le roman
      "La Grande Marrade, " de Claude Neron
      (In L'Avant-Scène Cinéma, no. 153, Dec. 1974)
SAUTI, Insan
    The Installment Plan
      (In Drama and Theatre, Vol. 11, no. 1, Fall 1972)
SAUVAJON, Marc-Gilbert
    Dear Charles (Les Enfants d'Edouard) by Marc-Gilbert Sauvajon
      and Frederick Jackson, adapted by Alan Melville, pseud.
      (In Plays of the Year, Vol. 8, 1952-53)
Savages; filmscript (see Trow, George S.)
Saved (see Bond, Edward)
Saved (see Howells, William Dean)
Saved (see Rogers, John W.)
The Savior of the Moment (see Kikuchi, Kwan)
SAVOIR, Alfred (born Posznanski), 1883-1934
    Going to the Dogs
      (In Modern One-Act Plays from the French)

SAYERS, Dorothy Leigh, 1893-1957
    Busman's Honeymoon, by Dorothy L. Sayers and M. St. Clare
    Byrne
        (In Famous Plays of 1937)
    The Zeal of Thy House
        (In Famous Plays of 1938-39)
SAYERS, Gale, 1943-
    Brian's Song (see Blinn, William)
SCALA, Flaminio, fl. 1620
    The Faithful Friend; a Commedia dell'Art play
        (In The Drama, Vol. 5)
    The Portrait
        (In World Drama, Vol. 2)
Scandal in the House of Zeus (see Biro, Lajos)
The Scape-Goat (see Poole, John)
The Scarecrow; a tragedy of the ludicrous (see MacKaye, Percy)
Scarface; filmscript, text in French (see Hecht, Ben)
The Scarlet Letter; filmscript (see Marion, Frances)
The Scarlet Princess of Edo (see Namboku, Tsuruya IV)
Scédase; ou, l'Hospitalité Violée (see Hardy, Alexandre)
Lo Sceicco Bianco (see Fellini, Federico)
Le Scenario (see Anouilh, Jean)
Scène a Quatre (see Ionesco, Eugene)
Scene di Caccia in Bassa Baviera (see Sperr, Martin)
Scene from an Unfinished Play (see Hellman, Lillian)
Scenes from a Marriage; screenplay (see Bergman, Ingmar)
Scent of Fear (see Peralta, Jesus T.)
Scevole (Scaevola) (see Du Ryer, Pierre)
SCHAFFNER, Franklin, 1920-
    The Best Man; filmscript (see Vidal, Gore)
SCHALLUCH, Paul, 1922-
    Lickrish; a radio tale. Both German and English texts are given
        (In Dimension, Vol. 1, no. 3, 1968)
SCHATROW, Michail
    Campanella und der Kommandeur
        (In Theater der Zeit, no. 7, 1973)
SCHATZBERG, Jerry, 1927-
    L'Epouvantail; titre original "Scarecrow"
        (In L'Avant-Scène du Cinéma, no. 140, Oct. 1973)
SCHECTER, Joel
    The Marx Brothers Meet Karl
        (In Yale/Theatre, Vol. 5, no. 1, Fall 1973)
SCHEHADE, Georges, 1910-
    L'Emigre de Brisbane
        (In Le Théâtre d'Aujourd'hui)
    Histoire de Vasco; text in French
        (In Le Théâtre d'Aujourd'hui)
    Historia de Vasco; text in Italian
        (In Teatro Frances de Vanguardia)
    Vasco; text in English
        (In Gambit, no. 1)
Schellenkönig, Eine Blutige Groteske (see Kaiser, Georg)

SCHEVILL, James
   The Pilots
     (In Break Out!)
SCHILDT, Runar, 1888-1925
   A Midwinter Story
     (In Scandinavian Plays of the 20th Century, Series 1)
SCHILLER, Bob
   The Convention; television script for an episode in "Maude," by
     Bob Schiller and Bob Weiskopf
     (In Samuel French's Tandem Library Series)
SCHILLER, Johann Christoph Friedrich von, 1759-1805
   The Bride of Messina
     (In his Works, Vol. 3)
   The Camp of Wallenstein
     (In The Drama, Vol. 10)
   The Death of Wallenstein
     (In his Works, Vol. 2)
   Demetrius; or, The Blood Wedding in Moscow
     (In his Works, Vol. 3)
   Don Carlos: A Dramatic History
     (In his Works, Vol. 2)
   Fiesco; or, The Genoese Conspiracy
     (In his Works, Vol. 1)
   The Homage of the Arts
     (In his Works, Vol. 3)
   Love and Intrigue
     (In his Works, Vol. 1)
   Macbeth; ein transerspiel; (see Shakespeare, William)
   The Maid of Orleans
     (In his Works, Vol. 2)
   The Maltese
     (In his Works, Vol. 3)
   Mary Stuart
     (In his Works, Vol. 2)
   The Misanthrope
     (In his Works, Vol. 2)
   Phädra; ein transerspiel (see Racine, Jean)
   The Piccolomini
     (In his Works, Vol. 2)
   The Robbers
     (In his Works, Vol. 1)
   Semele
     (In his Works, Vol. 1)
   Turandot, Prinzess in von China (see Gozzi, Carlo)
   Wallenstein's Camp
     (In his Works, Vol. 2)
   Warbeck
     (In his Works, Vol. 3)
   Wilhelm Tell, translated by John Prudhoe
     (In Classics of Drama in English Translation Series, 1970)
   William Tell
     (In his Works, Vol. 3)
     (In World Drama, Vol. 2)

SCHISGAL, Murray, 1929-
   The Chinese
      (In Best Short Plays of the World Theatre, 1968-1973)
Die Schlacht (see Muller, Heiner)
Die Schlacht der Heilande (see Brust, Alfred)
Der Schleier der Beatrice (see Schnitzler, Arthur)
SCHLESINGER, John, 1926-
   Darling; filmscript (see Raphael, Frederick)
SCHLONDORFF, Volker
   Le Coup de Grâce; un film titre original "Der Fangschuss."
   d'après le roman de Marguerite Yourcenar
      (In L'Avant-Scène Cinéma, no. 181, Feb. 1, 1977)
SCHMIDT, Harvey
   Celebration (see Jones, Tom)
   The Fantastics (see Jones, Tom)
SCHNEIDEMAN, Rose
   Dvořák's Song of the New World, a musical drama adapted for
   radio
      (In 100 Non-Royalty Radio Plays)
SCHNEIDER, Hansjörg, 1938-
   Der Erfinder
      (In Theater Heute, Jan. 1974)
SCHNITZLER, Arthur, 1862-1931
   Anatol; text in German
      (In his Theaterstücke, 1)
   The Big Scene
      (In his Comedies of Words)
   Der Einsame Weg
      (In his Theaterstücke, 3)
   The Festival of Bacchus
      (In his Comedies of Words)
   Die Frau mit dem Dolche
      (In his Theaterstücke, 2)
   Freiwild
      (In his Theaterstücke, 1)
   The Game of Love (Liebelei)
      (In Masterpieces of the Modern Central European Theatre)
   Die Gefährtin
      (In his Theaterstücke, 2)
   Der Grüne Kakadu
      (In his Theaterstücke, 2)
   His Helpmate
      (In his Comedies of Words)
   The Hour of Recognition
      (In his Comedies of Words)
   Der Junge Medardus
      (In his Theaterstücke, 4)
   Komtesse Mizzi; oder, Der Familientag
      (In his Theaterstücke, 4)
   Lebendige Stunden
      (In his Theaterstücke, 2)
   Die Letzten Masken
      (In his Theaterstücke, 2)

Liebelei
  (In his Theaterstücke, 1)
Literatur; text in German
  (In his Theaterstücke, 2)
Literature; text in English
  (In his Comedies of Words)
The Lonely Way
  (In Representative Continental Dramas)
Das Märchen
  (In his Theaterstücke, 1)
Paracelsus; text in German
  (In his Theaterstücke, 2)
Der Puppenspieler
  (In his Theaterstücke, 3)
Questioning the Irrevocable
  (In The Drama, Vol. 12)
La Ronde (Reigen)
  (In Masterpieces of the Modern Central European Theatre)
Round Dance
  (In Themes of Drama)
Der Ruf des Lebens
  (In his Theaterstücke, 3)
Der Schleier der Beatrice
  (In his Theaterstücke, 2)
Der Tapfere Cassian
  (In his Theaterstücke, 3)
Das Vermächtnis
  (In his Theaterstücke, 1)
Das Weite Land
  (In his Theaterstücke, 4)
Zum Grossen Wurstel
  (In his Theaterstücke, 3)
Zwischenspiel
  (In his Theaterstücke, 3)
SCHOENFELD, Bernard C.
  Independence Hall; radio script
    (In 100 Non-Royalty Radio Plays)
  We Became a Nation; radio script from "What Price America"
    Feb. 11, 1939
    (In Best Broadcasts of 1938-39)
  What We Defend; radio script
    (In 100 Non-Royalty Radio Plays)
The Scholastics (La Scholastica) (see Ariosto, Lodovico)
The School Act; a vaudeville skit
  (In The Disinherited: Plays)
The School for Arrogance (see Holcroft, Thomas)
The School for Guardians (see Murphy, Arthur)
The School for Husbands (see Macklin, Charles)
The School for Husbands (see Molière, Jean Baptiste)
The School for Scandal (see Sheridan, Richard Brinsley)
The School for Wives (see Kelly, Hugh)
The School for Wives (see Molière, Jean Baptiste)
A School for Women (L'Ecole des Femmes) (see Molière, Jean
  Baptiste)

The School for Women Criticised (La Critique de L'Ecole des Fem-
mes) (see Molière, Jean Baptiste)
The Schoolmaster (see Hyde, Douglas)
The Schoolteacher (see Buenaventura, Enrique)
SCHROCK, Gladden
 Goatsong for Glutt
  (In Guthrie New Theater, Vol. 1)
 Madam Popov
  (In Playwrights for Tomorrow, Vol. 9)
 Taps
  (In Guthrie New Theater, Vol. 1)
SCHUBERT, Franz Peter, 1797-1828
 *Schubert's Last Serenade (see Bovasso, Julie)
SCHULBERG, Budd, 1914-
 Across the Everglades; a play for the screen
  (A Random House Play, 1958)
Der Schüler (see Hofmannsthal, Hugo von H.)
Die Schüler (see Jahnn, Hans H.)
SCHÜTZ, Stefan, 1944-
 Fabrik im Walde
  (In Theater der Zeit, no. 12, 1975)
Die Schule der Diktatoren (see Kästner, Erich)
SCHULL, Joseph
 The Vice President
  (In A Collection of Canadian Plays, Vol. 3)
SCHUMAN, Howard
 Censored Scenes from King Kong
  (In Gambit, Vol. 7, nos. 26 & 27)
Der Schuss in die Offentlichkeit (see Kaiser, Georg)
SCHUSTER, Uwe
 Karl Damerow 1st Tot
  (In Theater der Zeit, no. 2, 1976)
Der Schuster und der Hahn (see Stolper, Armin)
SCHWARTZ, Delmore
 Paris and Helen; an entertainment inscribed to Metro-Goldwyn-
  Mayer
  (In New Directions, Vol. 6, 1941)
 Shenandoah
  (In New Directions in Prose and Poetry, Vol. 32)
Schwartz, Eugene (see Shvarts, Evgenii L'vovich)
SCHWARTZ, Joel
 Psalms of Two Davids
  (In Playwrights for Tomorrow, Vol. 9)
 Tilt
  (In New Theatre in America, Vol. 2)
SCHWEID, Mark
 A Miserable Day; or, Honesty Is the Best Soviet Policy, from
  the Russian of M. Zoschenko
  (In One-Act Plays for Stage and Study, 9th Series)
Schweyk in the Second World War (see Brecht, Bertolt)
La Scintillante (see Romains, Jules)
La Sconosciuta (see Blok, Aleksàndr)
The Scornful Lady (see Beaumont, Francis)

The Scorpion (see Bellido, José M.)
The Scotch Figgaries; or, A Knot of Knaves (see Tatham, John)
The Scotch Woman (see Voltaire)
SCOTT, F.R.
  **The Roncarelli Affair (see Moore, Mavor)
SCOTT, Munroe
    Wu-Feng
      (In A Collection of Canadian Plays, Vol. 1)
Scott, Robert Falcon, 1868-1912
  *Scott and the Antarctic (see Brenton, Howard)
The Scottish Hystorie of James the Fourth, Slaine at Flodden (see
    Greene, Robert)
The Scoundrel (see Ostrovskii, Alexandr N.)
The Scowrers (see Shadwell, Thomas)
A Scrap of Paper (see Sardou, Victorien)
SCRIBE, Augustin-Eugène, 1791-1861
    The Glass of Water
      (In Camille and Other Plays)
    A Peculiar Position
      (In Camille and Other Plays)
    Le Verre d'Eau, ou Les Effets et les Causes
      (In L'Avant-Scène Théâtre, no. 591, July 15, 1976)
Scuba Duba (see Friedman, Bruce J.)
Scyklon Z, But What Have You Done for Me Lately? or, Pure Pole-
    mic (see Lamb, Myrna)
The Scythe and the Sunset (see Johnston, Denis)
Se Vuelve a Llevar la Guerra Larga (see Millan, Juan J.)
The Sea (see Bond, Edward)
The Sea at Dauphin (see Walcott, Derek)
A Sea Change or Love's Stowaway (see Howells, William Dean)
Sea Usted Breve (see Villaurrutia, Xavier)
The Sea Voyage, (see Beaumont, Francis)
A Seacoast in Bohemia (see Radin, Ben)
The Seagull (see Chekhov, Anton)
Seagulls over Sorrento (see Hastings, Hugh)
SEAMI MOTOKIYO
    Nakamitsu
      (In World Drama, Vol. 1)
    Structure of Hagoromo, a Nō Play
      (In Harvard Journal of Asiatic Studies, Vol. 33, 1973)
Seance de Nuit (see Feydeau, Georges)
The Searching Sun (see O'Hara, John)
The Searching Wind (see Hellman, Lillian)
A Season in the Congo (see Cesaire, Aime)
Seastrom, Victor (see Sjostrom, Victor)
The Seaway to Baghdad (see Jakobsson, Jökull)
Seaweed (see Gerstenberg, Alice)
Sebastian, King of Portugal, 1554-1578
  *Don Sebastian, King of Portugal (see Dryden, John)
SEBREE, Charles, 1914-
    The Dry August
      (In Black Theater U.S.A., 1847-1974)

Die Sechs Kampfer (see Sachs, Hans)
The Second Celestial Adventure of Mr. Excedrin, Fire Extinguisher
        (see Rosenstock, Sami)
The Second Kiss (see Clarke, Austin)
The Second Man (see Behrman, Samuel N.)
The Second Mrs. Tanqueray (see Pinero, Arthur Wing)
The Second Shepherds' Play (Anon.)
        (In World Drama, Vol. 1)
Second Threshold (see Barry, Philip)
La Seconde Surprise de l'Amour (see Marivaux, Pierre C.)
The Secret Agent (see Conrad, Joseph)
Secret Love; or, The Maiden Queen (see Dryden, John)
Secret Service; a Drama of the Southern Confederacy (see Gillette,
        William H.)
Secret Transactions (see Musset, Alfred de)
El Secreto (see Pagano, José L.)
A Secreto Agravio, Secreta Venganza (see Calderon de la Barca,
        Pedro)
Les Secrets de la Comédie Humaine (see Marceau, Félicien)
The Secular Masque (see Dryden, John)
SEDAINE, Michel Jean, 1719-1797
        Richard Coeur de Lion
            (In The London Stage, Vol. 3)
SEDLEY, Sir Thomas, 1639?-1701
        The Mulberry Garden
            (In Restoration Comedy, Vol. 1)
SEDLEY, William Henry, 1806-1872
        The Drunkard
            (In Victorian Melodramas)
Seduced and Abandoned; screenplay (see Germi, Pietro. Sedotta e
        Abbandonata)
Seduction (see Holcroft, Thomas)
The Seduction of Mimi (see Wertmüller, Lina)
The Seductive Countess (La Comtesse d'Escarbagnas) (see Molière,
        Jean Baptiste)
Die See (see Bond, Edward)
SEE, Edmond, 1875-1959
        An Old Friend
            (In Modern One-Act Plays from the French)
Seems Radio Is Here to Stay; radio script (see Corwin, Norman L.)
The Seer (see Butcher, James W. , Jr.)
SEGHERS, Anna, 1900-
        **The Trial of Joan of Arc at Rouen, 1431 (see Brecht, Bertolt)
Il Segreto (see Lopez, Sabatino)
Segundo Asalto (see Martinez, José de Jesus)
Sehnsucht (see Roth, Gerhard)
Sei Personaggi in Cerca d'Autore (see Pirandello, Luigi)
SEILER, Conrad
        Why I Am a Bachelor
            (In New Fields for the Writer)
La Seinte Résureccion; text in English (Anon).
            (In Medieval French Plays)

Sejanus: His Fall (see Jonson, Ben)
SEJOUR, Victor, 1817-1874
    The Brown Overcoat
      (In Black Theater U.S.A., 1847-1974)
SELBOURNE, David, 1937-
    Alison Mary Fagan
      (In Calder & Boyars Playscript Series, 1971)
    The Damned
      (In Methuen Playscript Series, 1971)
    Dorabella
      (In Methuen Playscript Series, 1970)
    The Play of William Cooper and Edmund Dew-Nevett
      (In Methuen Playscript Series, 1968)
    Sampson
      (In Calder & Boyars Playscript no. 47, 1971)
    The Two-Backed Beast
      (In Methuen Playscript Series, 1969)
Self (see Bateman, Mrs. Sidney F.)
Self-Accusation (see Kandke, Peter)
Self-Sacrifice; a farce tragedy (see Howells, William Dean)
Semele (see Schiller, Johann C.)
Semilla del Aire (see Magana-Esquivel, Antonio)
Sémiramis (see Crebillon, Prosper)
Sémiramis (see Voltaire)
Sémiramis; both French and English texts are given (see Valery,
    Paul)
Sémiramis legend (see Sammuramat, Queen of Assyria)
Sempronio (see Cuzzani, Agustin)
SEMPRUN, Jorge
    Stavisky ...; screenplay (see Resnais, Alain)
S'en Debarrasser (see Ionesco, Eugene)
SENECA, Lucius Annaeus, c. 4 B.C.- 65 A.D.
    Medea
      (In World Drama, Vol. 1)
   *La Mort de Sénèque (The Death of Seneca) (see Tristan L'Her-
    mite, François)
  **Oedipus (see Dryden, John)
  **Phaedra (see Rexroth, Kenneth)
  **Tyestes (see Peman, José M.)
SENECAL, Jean Michel
    Angelo (see Jacquemard, Yves)
SENNETT, Mack, 1880-1960
    The Dentist; a Mack Sennett comedy (see Fields, W.C.)
El Señor de Pigmalion (see Grau, Jacinto)
El Señor Perro (see Urueta, Margarita)
La Señora en Su Balcon (see Garro, Elena)
La Señora Recibe una Carta (see Ruiz Iriarte, Victor)
La Señorita Voluntad (see Noriega Hope, Carlos)
Señoritas a Disgusto (see Gonzalez Caballero, Antonio)
A Sensational Novel (see Gilbert, William S.)
A Sense of Detachment (see Osborne, John)
La Sensitive (see Labiche, Eugene)
Senso; filmscript (see Visconti, Luchino)

Sentencia Provisional (see Hoeck, Josef van)
A Separate Peace (see Stoppard, Tom)
September Song (see Gottlieb, Alex)
A Sequelula to "The Synasts" (see Hardy, Thomas)
Les Sequestres d'Altona (see Sartre, Jean-Paul)
The Serenade (see Jullien, Jean)
Serie Bleme (see Vian, Boris)
SERLING, Rod, 1924-1975
    Back There; Twilight Zone television script
        (In On the Air)
    Requiem for a Heavyweight; television script presented on "Play-
      house 90," Oct. 11, 1956
        (In Great Television Plays)
        (In Prize Plays of Television and Radio, 1956)
    A Storm in Summer
        (In Great Television Plays, Vol. 2)
Les Serments Indiscrets (see Marivaux, Pierre C.)
The Serpent (see Van Itallie, Jean-Claude)
The Serpent's Egg; screenplay (see Bergman, Ingmar)
Sertorius, Quintus, d. 72 B.C.
   *Sertorius (see Corneille, Pierre)
   *Sertorius; or, The Roman Patriot (see Brown, David P.)
The Servant in the House (see Kennedy, Charles R.)
The Servant of the King (see Musset, Alfred de)
La Servante du Roi (see Musset, Alfred de)
Servants of the People (see Ferlinghetti, Lawrence)
I Servi (see Cankar, Ivan)
Servidumbre (see Martinez Cuitino, Vincente)
Servitude (see O'Neill, Eugene)
La Sesion (see Poblacion, Pablo)
The Set of Turquoise (see Aldrich, Thomas B.)
SETTLE, Elkanah, 1648-1724
    The Empress of Morocco
        (In The Empress of Morocco & Its Critics)
        (In Five Heroic Plays)
Seven Beauties (see Wertmüller, Lina)
The Seven Dull-Hearing Ones (see Turkish Theatre. Meddah)
Seven Impromptus for Leisure (see Obaldia, Rene de)
Seven Keys to Baldpate (see Cohan, George M.)
The Seven Kings and the Wind (see Young, Stark)
The Seven Princesses (see Maeterlinck, Maurice)
Seven Stations on the Road to Exile (see Howard, Roger)
Seven Women (see Barrie, James M.)
The Seven Year Itch (see Axelrod, George)
1789/1793 (see Theatre du Soleil)
1776 (see Edwards, Sherman)
The Seventh Farce (see Rueda, Lope de)
The Seventh Seal; screenplay (see Bergman, Ingmar)
Le Sexe Faible (see Bourder, Edward)
Seymour, Jane, 2nd wife of Henry VIII, King of England, 1509?-1536
    *Henry VIII (see Chénier, Marie-Joseph B.)
    *Henri VIII; text in French (see Chénier, Marie-Joseph B.)

Sganarelle; or, The Imaginary Cuckold (Sganarelle; ou, Le Cocu Im-
aginaire) (see Molière, Jean Baptiste)
Sganarel's Journey to the Land of the Philosophers (see Holberg,
Ludvig von)
Shade (see Udoff, Yale M.)
The Shadow (see Shvarts, Evgeny L.)
The Shadow Factory; a Nativity play (see Ridler, Anne B.)
Shadow Laurels (see Fitzgerald, F. Scott)
The Shadow of a Gunman (see O'Casey, Sean)
The Shadow of Doubt (see King, Norman)
Shadow of Heroes (see Ardrey, Robert)
The Shadow radio script
    The Final Hour (see McGill, Jerry)
Shadows; screenplay; text in French (see Cassavetes, John)
The Shadowy Waters (see Yeats, William Butler)
SHADWELL, Thomas, 1642?-1692
    The Amorous Bigotte, with the second part of Tegue O Divelly
        (In his Complete Works, Vol. 5)
    Bury-Fair
        (In his Complete Works, Vol. 4)
    Epsom-Wells
        (In his Complete Works, Vol. 2)
    The History of Timon of Athens, the Man-Hater, greatly altered
    from Shakespeare
        (In his Complete Works, Vol. 3)
    The Humorists
        (In his Complete Works, Vol. 1)
    The Lancashire Witches and Tegue O Divelly the Irish Priest
        (In his Complete Works, Vol. 4)
        (In The Drama, Vol. 22)
    The Libertine, adaptation of Rosimond's "Nouveau Festin de
    Pierre; or, L'Athee Foudroye"
        (In his Complete Works, Vol. 3)
        (In The Theatre of Don Juan)
    The Miser, based on Mòliere's "L'Avare"
        (In his Complete Works, Vol. 2)
    The Miser; plot based on Molière's play but with many new
    characters added
        (In The London Stage, Vol. 1)
    Psyche, adaptation of the French Psyche by Molière and Cor-
    neille, with the music by Matthew Locke and Draghi
        (In his Complete Works, Vol. 2)
    The Royal Shepherdesse, an adaptation of John Fountain's "The
    Rewards of Virtue"
        (In his Complete Works, Vol. 1)
    The Scowrers
        (In his Complete Works, Vol. 5)
    The Squire of Alsatia
        (In his Complete Works, Vol, 4)
        (In Plays of the Restoration and 18th Century)
        (In Restoration Comedy, Vol. 3)
    The Sullen Lovers; or, The Impertinents, based on Molière's
    "Les Facheus" and "Le Misanthrope"
        (In his Complete Works, Vol. 1)

The Tempest, altered from the work of Shakespeare
   (In his Complete Works, Vol. 2)
The True Widow, with a prologue by John Dryden
   (In his Complete Works, Vol. 3)
The Virtuoso
   (In his Complete Works, Vol. 3)
The Volunteers; or, The Stock-Jobbers
   (In his Complete Works, Vol. 5)
The Woman-Captain
   (In his Complete Works, Vol. 4)
SHAFFER, Anthony, 1926-
  Sleuth
    (In Best Mystery and Suspense Plays of the Modern Theatre)
    (In Contact with Drama)
SHAFFER, Peter, 1926-
  Black Comedy
    (In his Black Comedy, including White Lies)
    (In Contact with Drama)
  Equus
    (In his Three Plays)
    (In his Two Plays, 1974)
  Equus; text in German
    (In Theater Heute, no. 3, March 1974)
  Five Finger Exercise
    (In his Three Plays)
  The Private Ear
    (In his The Private Ear and The Public Eye)
  The Public Eye
    (In his The Private Ear and The Public Eye)
  The Royal Hunt of the Sun; a play concerning the conquest of
    Peru
    (In Best Plays of the Sixties)
    (In Stein & Day's Play Series, 1965)
  Shrivings
    (In his Three Plays)
    (In his Two Plays, 1974)
  White Lies
    (In his Black Comedies, including White Lies)
Shakes Versus Shav; a puppet play (see Shaw, George Bernard)
SHAKESPEARE, William, 1564-1616
  **All for Love; or, The World Well Lost (see Dryden, John)
  **Amleto Principe de Danimarca (see Brecht, Bertolt)
  Antony and Cleopatra
    (In Themes of Drama)
  *Bingo: Scenes of Money and Death (see Bond, Edward)
  **Capuletta; or, Romeo and Juliet Restored; an operatic burlesque
    (see Baker, George M.)
  **Catherine and Petruchio (see Garrick, David)
  Coriolanus
    (In Revolution: A Collection of Plays)
  **Coriolanus; adaptation (see Brecht, Bertolt)
  **Cymbeline; adaptation (see Garrick, David)
  *The Dark Lady of Sonnets (see Shaw, George Bernard)

**The Fairies (see Garrick, David)
**Florizel and Perdita (see Garrick David)
**Fragments de Romeo et Juliette (see Vigny, Alfred V.)
**Un Hamlet de Moins (see Bene, Carmelo)
**Hamlet em Brasilia (see Laura, Ida)
**Die Hamletmaschine (see Muller, Heiner)
**The History of King Lear (see Tate, Nahum)
**The History of King Richard III (see Cibber, Colley)
**The History of Timon of Athens, the Man-Hater (see Shadwell, Thomas)
**The Jew of Venice (see Lansdowne, George G.)
 *The Jubilee (see Garrick, David)
 Julius Caesar
   (In On the High Road)
**Kiss Me, Kate (see Porter, Cole)
**Lear; adaptation (see Bond, Edward)
**Macbeth; adaptation (see D'Avenant, Sir William)
**Macbeth; ein trauerspiel von Shakespeare von Schiller; fragment
   (In Schiller's Works, Vol. 4)
**Macbeth Skit (see Shaw, George Bernard)
**Macbett (see Ionesco, Eugene)
 Measure for Measure; adapted by Charles Marowitz
   (In Plays and Players, Vol. 22, no. 9, June 1975)
**The Mock-Tempest (see Duffet, Thomas)
**Le More de Venise (see Vigny, Alfred V.)
**The New Wing at Elsinore. A dramatic sequel to Hamlet by 'Mr. Punch"
   (In The Drama, Vol. 22)
**L'Ombra di Banquo ossia La Lezione di Potere (see Cagli, Bruno) Othello
   (In Contact with Drama)
**A Place Calling Itself Rome (see Osborne, John)
**A Prologue to "King Lear" (see Molnar, Ferenc)
**The Rehearsal (see Baring, Maurice)
**Romeo and Juliet; adaptation (see Garrick, David)
**Romeo Before the Corpse of Juliet (see Denevi, Marco)
**Shakes Versus Shav; a puppet play (see Shaw, George Bernard)
**Shylock, le Marchand de Venise (see Vigny, Alfred V.)
**The Tempest; adaptation (see Shadwell, Thomas)
**The Tempest; or, The Enchanted Island (see Dryden, John)
**Troilus and Cressida; or, Truth Found Too Late (see Dryden, John)
**The Twins; or, Which Is Which? (see Woods, William)
**Two Gentlemen of Soho (see Herbert, Alan P.)
 *William Ireland's Confession (see Miller, Arthur)
**Your Own Thing (see Driver, Donald)
Shakespeare Wallah (see Jhabvala, R. Prawer)
Shakuntala; or, The Recovered Ring (see Kalidasa)
Shall We Dance? (see Parker, Kenneth T.)
Shall We Join the Ladies? (see Barrie, James M.)
Shame; screenplay (see Bergman, Ingmar)
Shanwalla (see Gregory, Isabella A.)

SHARMA, Pratap
    A Touch of Brightness
        (In <u>Gambit,</u> no. 9)
Sharon's Grave (see Keane, John B.)
SHARP, Anthony
    Nightmare Abbey, based on Thomas Love Peacock's novel
        (In <u>Plays of the Year,</u> Vol. 7, 1951/52)
Shattered (see Bordeaux, Henry)
SHATZKY, Joel, 1943-
    The Emperor of the West End
        (In <u>Modern International Drama,</u> Vol. 7, no. 1B, Spring 1976)
The Shaughraun (see Boucicault, Dion)
Shaved Splits (see Shepard, Sam)
SHAW, David
    Native Dancer, NBC Goodyear Television Playhouse script, Mar.
    28, 1954
        (In <u>Top TV Shows of the Year,</u> 1954-55)
    Rescue; television script
        (In <u>Best Television Plays,</u> 1954)
SHAW, George Bernard 1856-1950
    The Admirable Bashville; or, Constancy Unrewarded
        (In his <u>Collected Plays,</u> Vol. 2)
    Androcles and the Lion: A Fable Play
        (In his <u>Collected Plays,</u> Vol. 4)
    Annajanska, the Bolshevik Empress: A Revolutionary Romance-
    let
        (In his <u>Collected Plays,</u> Vol. 5)
    The Apple Cart: A Political Extravaganza
        (In his <u>Collected Plays,</u> Vol. 6)
    Arms and the Man
        (In his <u>Collected Plays,</u> Vol. 1)
    Arthur and the Acetone
        (In his <u>Collected Plays,</u> Vol. 7)
    Augustus Does His Bit: A True-to-Life Farce
        (In his <u>Collected Plays,</u> Vol. 5)
    Back to Methuselah: A Metabiological Pentateuch
        (In his <u>Collected Plays,</u> Vol. 5)
    Beauty's Duty
        (In his <u>Collected Plays,</u> Vol. 7)
    Buoyant Billions: A Comedy of No Manners
        (In his <u>Collected Plays,</u> Vol. 7)
    Caesar and Cleopatra: A History
        (In his <u>Collected Plays,</u> Vol. 2)
    Candida
        (In his <u>Collected Plays,</u> Vol. 1)
    Captain Brassbound's Conversion: An Adventure
        (In his <u>Collected Plays,</u> Vol. 2)
    The Cassone
        (In his <u>Collected Plays,</u> Vol. 7)
    Cousin Muriel; a new ending for the play by Clemence Dane,
    pseud.
        (In his <u>Collected Plays,</u> Vol. 7)

Cymbeline Refinished: A Variation on Shakespear's Ending
   (In his Collected Plays, Vol. 7)
The Dark Lady of the Sonnets
   (In his Collected Plays, Vol. 4)
The Devil's Disciple
   (In his Collected Plays, Vol. 2)
   (In Contemporary Drama: 13 Plays)
The Doctor's Dilemma
   (In his Collected Plays, Vol. 3)
Fanny's First Play
   (In his Collected Plays, Vol. 4)
Farfetched Fables
   (In his Collected Plays, Vol. 7)
The Fascinating Foundling
   (In his Collected Plays, Vol. 3)
The Gadfly; or, The Son of the General; an adaptation of the
novel by Ethel Voynich
   (In his Collected Plays, Vol. 7)
The Garden of the Hesperides
   (In his Collected Plays, Vol. 7)
Geneva: Another Political Extravaganza
   (In his Collected Plays, Vol. 7)
Getting Married
   (In his Collected Plays, Vol. 3)
   (In Edwardian Plays)
The Girl with the Golden Voice
   (In his Collected Plays, Vol. 7)
Glastonbury Skit; an interpolation in Frederick Austin's "The
Glastonbury Travesty," by Walter Wombwell, pseud.
   (In his Collected Plays, Vol. 7)
The Glimpse of Reality
   (In his Collected Plays, Vol. 3)
Great Catherine (Whom Glory Still Adores)
   (In his Collected Plays, Vol. 4)
Heartbreak House: A Fantasia in the Russian Manner on Eng-
lish Themes
   (In his Collected Plays, Vol. 5)
How He Lied to Her Husband
   (In his Collected Plays, Vol. 2)
"In Good King Charles's Golden Days": A True History That
Never Happened
   (In his Collected Plays, Vol. 7)
The Inauguration Speech: An Interlude
   (In his Collected Plays, Vol. 7)
The Inca of Perusalem: An Almost Historical Comedietta
   (In his Collected Plays, Vol. 4)
**Jitta's Atonement (see Trebitsch, Siegfried)
John Bull's Other Island
   (In his Collected Plays, Vol. 2)
The King's People; sequence for John Drinkwater's Coronation
film
   (In his Collected Plays, Vol. 7)

Macbeth Skit
  (In his <u>Collected Plays,</u> Vol. 7)
The Madras House; suggested Act III for Barker's play
  (In his Collected Plays, Vol. 7)
Major Barbara
  (In his <u>Collected Plays</u>, Vol. 3)
  (In <u>Masterpieces of the Modern English Theatre</u>)
Man and Superman: A Comedy and a Philosophy
  (In his <u>Collected Plays</u>, Vol. 2)
Man and Superman; extract from Act III
  (In <u>The Theatre of Don Juan</u>)
The Man of Destiny
  (In his <u>Collected Plays</u>, Vol. 1)
The Millionairess
  (In his <u>Collected Plays</u>, Vol. 6)
Misalliance
  (In his <u>Collected Plays</u>, Vol. 4)
Mrs. Warren's Profession
  (In his <u>Collected Plays</u>, Vol. 1)
  (In <u>Themes of Drama</u>)
The Music-Cure: A Piece of Utter Nonsense
  (In his <u>Collected Plays,</u> Vol. 4)
O'Flaherty, V.C.: A Recruiting Pamphlet
  (In his <u>Collected Plays</u>, Vol. 4)
On the Rocks: A Political Comedy
  (In his <u>Collected Plays,</u> Vol. 6)
Overruled
  (In his <u>Collected Plays</u>, Vol. 4)
A Pageant of Plays and Players; sequence
  (In his <u>Collected Plays</u>, Vol. 7)
Passion Play
  (In his <u>Collected Plays</u>, Vol. 7)
Passion, Poison, and Petrification; or, The Fatal Gazogene
  (In his <u>Collected Plays</u>, Vol. 3)
Un Petit Drame; text in English
  (In his <u>Collected Plays</u>, Vol. 7)
The Philanderer
  (In his <u>Collected Plays,</u> Vol. 1)
Press Cuttings
  (In his <u>Collected Plays,</u> Vol. 3)
Pygmalion: Romance in Five Acts
  (In his <u>Collected Plays,</u> Vol. 4)
Saint Joan: Chronicle Play in Six Scenes and an Epilogue
  (In his <u>Collected Plays</u>, Vol. 6)
Shakes Versus Shav; puppet play
  (In his <u>Collected Plays</u>, Vol. 7)
The Shewing-Up of Blanco Posnet
  (In his <u>Collected Plays</u>, Vol. 3)
The Simpleton of the Unexpected Isles: Vision of Judgment
  (In his <u>Collected Plays</u>, Vol. 6)
The Six of Calais: A Medieval War Story
  (In his <u>Collected Plays</u>, Vol. 6)

The Tiptaft Revue Skit
    (In his Collected Plays, Vol. 7)
Too True to Be Good: A Political Extravaganza
    (In his Collected Plays, Vol. 6)
Village Wooing: A Comedietta for Two Voices
    (In his Collected Plays, Vol. 6)
The War Indemnities
    (In his Collected Plays, Vol. 7)
Why She Would Not
    (In his Collected Plays, Vol. 7)
Widower's Houses
    (In his Collected Plays, Vol. 1)
The Yahoos
    (In his Collected Plays, Vol. 7)
You Never Can Tell
    (In his Collected Plays, Vol. 1)
SHAW, Irwin, 1913
Bury the Dead
    (In 50 Best Plays of the American Theatre, Vol. 2)
SHAW, Richard
Sleeping Beauty
    (In Five Plays from the Children's Theatre Company of Minne-
    apolis)
SHAWN, Wallace
Summer Evening
    (In Plays and Players, Vol. 24, no. 7, Apr. 1977)
She Stoops to Conquer; or, The Mistakes of a Night (see Goldsmith,
    Oliver)
She Walks in Beauty; television script (see Koln, Kenneth)
She Would and She Would Not (see Cibber, Colley)
She Would Be a Soldier; or, The Plains of Chippewa (see Moah, Mor-
    decai M.)
She Would If She Could (see Etherege, Sir George)
SHEARER, Marjorie, 1915-1963
Charity in Two Keys
    (In her Four Short Plays for Introducing Discussions)
Façades
    (In her Four Short Plays for Introducing Discussions)
No Thank You, Mr. Smart
    (In her Four Short Plays for Introducing Discussions)
Were You There
    (In her Four Short Plays for Introducing Discussions)
Shearwater (see Hauptman, William)
Sheep on the Runway (see Buchwald, Art)
SHEHADE, Georges, 1910-
Le Voyage
    (In Le Théâtre d'Aujourd'hui)
SHEININ, Leo Romanovich, 1905-
Smoke of the Fatherland (see Tur, Leonid D.)
SHELDON, Edward, 1886-1946
The Boss
    (In Representative American Plays, 1792-1949)

Lulu Belle, by Edward Sheldon and Charles MacArthur
    (In The Stage Works of Charles MacArthur)
Salvation Nell
    (In 50 Best Plays of the American Theatre, Vol. 1)
SHELLAN, David
  Pistols for Two
    (In The Best One-Act Plays of 1958-59, London)
SHELLEY, Mary Wollstonecraft, 1797-1851
  **Frankenstein; screenplay (see Whale, James)
  **Frankenstein: The True Story; teleplay (see Isherwood, Chris-
    topher)
SHELLEY, Percy Bysshe, 1792-1822
   The Cenci
     (In British Plays from the Restoration to 1820, Vol. 2)
  *Shelley; or, The Idealist (see Jellicoe, Ann)
Shenandoah (see Howard, Bronson C.)
Shenandoah (see Schwartz, Delmore)
SHEPARD, Sam, 1943-
  Black Bog Beast Bait
    (In his The Unseen Hand and Other Plays)
  Chicago
    (In his Five Plays)
  Cowboy Mouth
    (In Winter Repertory no 4, 1972)
  Cowboys #2
    (In Collision Course)
    (In Winter Repertory no. 4, 1972)
  Forensic and the Navigators
    (In his The Unseen Hand and Other Plays)
  4-H Club.
    (In his The Unseen Hand and Other Plays)
  Fourteen Hundred Thousand
    (In his Five Plays)
  Geography of a Horse Dreamer
    (In Evergreen Playscript Series, 1974)
  The Holy Ghostly
    (In Best Short Plays of the World Theatre, 1968-1973)
    (In his The Unseen Hand and Other Plays)
  Icarus's Mother
    (In his Five Plays)
  Mad Dog Blues
    (In his Five Plays)
  Melodrama Play
    (In his Five Plays)
  Operation Sidewinder
    (In The Great American Life Show)
  Red Cross
    (In his Five Plays)
    (In Off-Broadway Plays, Vol. 2)
  The Rock Garden
    (In Winter Repertory no. 4, 1972)
  Shaved Splits
    (In his The Unseen Hand and Other Plays)

The Tooth of Crime
(In Evergreen Playscript Series, 1974)
(In Performance, Vol. 1, no. 5, Mar./Apr. 1973)
The Unseen Hand
(In The Off Off Broadway Book)
(In Plays and Players, Vol. 20, no. 8, May 1973)
(In his The Unseen Hand and Other Plays)
The Shepherds (Anon.)
(In Medieval Church Music-Dramas)
SHEPP, Archie
Junebug Graduates Tonight
(In Black Drama Anthology)
SHEPPEY (see Maugham, William Somerset)
SHERIDAN, Richard Brinsley Butler, 1751-1816
The Camp
(In his Dramatic Works, Vol. 2)
The Critic
(In his Dramatic Works, Vol. 1)
The Duenna, with music by Thomas Linley and his son
(In his Dramatic Works, Vol. 1)
(In The London Stage, Vol. 1)
The Glorious First of June
(In his Dramatic Works, Vol. 2)
Pizarro, adapted from Kotzebue's "Die Spanier in Peru"
(In his Dramatic Works, Vol. 2)
(In The London Stage, Vol. 1)
The Rivals
(In his Dramatic Works, Vol. 1)
(In On the High Road)
St. Patrick's Day; or, The Scheming Lieutenant
(In A Book of Short Plays, XV-XX Centuries)
(In his Dramatic Works, Vol. 1)
The School for Scandal
(In British Plays from the Restoration to 1820, Vol. 2)
(In his Dramatic Works, Vol. 1)
(In The London Stage, Vol. 4)
(In Plays of the Restoration and 18th Century)
(In World Drama, Vol. 1)
A Trip to Scarborough, altered from Sir John Vanbrugh's "The
Relapse"
(In his Dramatic Works, Vol. 2)
SHERIDAN, Thomas, 1719-1788
Captain O'Blunder
(In A Collection of the Most Esteemed Farces ..., Vol. 3)
Sherlock Holmes (see Gillette, William H.)
Sherlock Jr. (see Keaton, Buster)
SHERRIFF, Robert Cedric, 1896-
Badger's Green
(In Six Plays: Famous Plays Series, 1930)
Journey's End
(In 20th Century Plays)
The Long Sunset
(In Plays of the Year, Vol. 12, 1954-55)

St. Helena, by R.C. Sherriff and Jeanne De Casalis
 (In <u>Famous Plays of 1935-36</u>)
The Telescope
 (In <u>Plays of the Year</u>, Vol. 15, 1956)
Sherrill; adapted for radio (see Burnett, Whit)
SHERWOOD, Robert Emmet, 1896-1955
 Abe Lincoln in Illinois
  (In <u>50 Best Plays of the American Theatre</u>, Vol. 2)
 Abe Lincoln in Illinois (selection)
  (In <u>This Is My Best</u>)
 The Petrified Forest
  (In <u>Representative American Dramas</u>)
 There Shall Be No Night
  (In <u>The Ordeal of a Playwright</u>)
The Shewing-Up of Blanco Posnet (see Shaw, George Bernard)
SHINE, Ted, 1931-
 Herbert III
  (In <u>Black Theater U.S.A.</u>, 1847-1974)
The Ship (see Benet i Jornet, Josep)
The Ship of Dreams (see Hughes, John)
The Ship of the Righteous; a Dramatic Epopee in Three Acts (see
 Evreinov, Nikolai N.)
SHIRLEY, Henry, d. 1627
 **The Lucky Chance; or, An Alderman's Bargain (see Behn, Mrs.
 Aphra)
SHIRLEY, James, 1596-1666
 The Arcadia, a Pastoral
  (In his <u>Dramatic Works & Poems</u>, Vol. 6)
 The Ball (see Chapman, George)
 The Bird in a Cage
  (In his <u>Dramatic Works & Poems</u>, Vol. 2)
 The Brothers
  (In his <u>Dramatic Works & Poems</u>, Vol. 1)
 The Cardinal
  (In his <u>Dramatic Works & Poems</u>, Vol. 5)
 Changes; or, Love in a Maze
  (In his <u>Dramatic Works & Poems</u>, Vol. 2)
 The Constant Maid
  (In his <u>Dramatic Works & Poems</u>, Vol. 4)
 A Contention for Honour and Riches
  (In his <u>Dramatic Works & Poems</u>, Vol. 6)
 The Contention of Ajax and Ulysses for the Armour of Achilles,
 founded on the 13th book of Ovid's "Metamorphoses"
  (In his <u>Dramatic Works & Poems</u>, Vol. 6)
 The Coronation
  (In his <u>Dramatic Works & Poems</u>, Vol. 3)
 The Court Secret
  (In his <u>Dramatic Works & Poems</u>, Vol. 5)
 Cupid and Death
  (In his <u>Dramatic Works & Poems</u>, Vol. 6)
 The Doubtful Heir
  (In his <u>Dramatic Works & Poems</u>, Vol. 4)

The Duke's Mistress
(In his <u>Dramatic Works & Poems</u>, Vol. 4)
The Example
(In his <u>Dramatic Works & Poems</u>, Vol. 3)
The Gamester
(In his <u>Dramatic Works & Poems</u>, Vol. 3)
The Gentleman of Venice
(In his <u>Dramatic Works & Poems</u>, Vol. 5)
The Grateful Servant
(In his <u>Dramatic Works & Poems</u>, Vol. 2)
Honoria and Mammon
(In his <u>Dramatic Works & Poems</u>, Vol. 6)
The Humorous Courtier
(In his <u>Dramatic Works & Poems</u>, Vol. 4)
Hyde Park
(In his <u>Dramatic Works & Poems</u>, Vol. 2)
The Imposture
(In his <u>Dramatic Works & Poems</u>, Vol. 5)
The Lady of Pleasure
(In his <u>Dramatic Works & Poems</u>, Vol. 4)
(In <u>Six Caroline Plays</u>)
Love Tricks; or, The School of Complement
(In his <u>Dramatic Works & Poems</u>, Vol. 1)
Love's Cruelty
(In his <u>Dramatic Works & Poems</u>, Vol. 2)
The Maid's Revenge
(In his <u>Dramatic Works & Poems</u>, Vol. 1)
The Opportunity
(In his <u>Dramatic Works & Poems</u>, Vol. 3)
The Politician
(In his <u>Dramatic Works & Poems</u>, Vol. 5)
The Royal Master
(In his <u>Dramatic Works & Poems</u>, Vol. 4)
St. Patrick for Ireland
(In his <u>Dramatic Works & Poems</u>, Vol. 4)
The Sisters
(In his <u>Dramatic Works & Poems</u>, Vol. 5)
The Tragedy of Chabot Admiral of France (see Chapman, George)
The Traitor
(In his <u>Dramatic Works & Poems</u>, Vol. 2)
The Triumph of Beauty
(In his <u>Dramatic Works & Poems</u>, Vol. 6)
The Triumph of Peace
(In his <u>Dramatic Works & Poems</u>, Vol. 6)
The Wedding
(In his <u>Dramatic Works & Poems</u>, Vol. 1)
(In <u>Six Caroline Plays</u>)
The Witty Fair One
(In his <u>Dramatic Works & Poems</u>, Vol. 1)
The Young Admiral
(In his <u>Dramatic Works & Poems</u>, Vol. 3)
SHIRLEY, William, fl. 1739-1780
Edward, the Black Prince
(In <u>The London Stage</u>, Vol. 4)

Shivaree (see O'Dea, Mark L.)
SHKVARKIN, Vassily Vassilyevich, 1893-
    Father Unknown
        (In Soviet Scene)
The Shoelace (see Gregory, Isabella A.)
The Shoemakers (see Witkiewicz, Stanislaw I.)
The Shoemaker's Prodigious Wife (see Garcia Lorca, Federico)
Shore Acres (see Herne, James A.)
Short Circuit (Korotkoye Zamykaniye) (see Tendrayakov, Vladimir
    F.)
A Short Play About Joseph Smith, Jr. (see Hutchins, Maude P.)
SHOUB, Mac
    Ashes in the Wind
        (In Best Television Plays, 1954)
SHOVELLER, Brock
    Westbound 12:01
        (In A Collection of Canadian Plays, Vol. 2)
The Show-Off (see Kelly, George E.)
Shower (see Tavel, Ronald)
Shrivings (see Shaffer, Peter)
Shudraka, King (see Sūdraka, Rajah of Magadha)
The Shuiler's Child (see O'Kelly, Seumas)
SHULMAN, Max, 1919-
    Love Is a Fallacy
        (In Readers Theatre Handbook)
SHULMAN, William E.
    The Magic Git-Flip
        (In 100 Non-Royalty Radio Plays)
SHVARTS, Evgenii L'vovich, 1904-1958
    Little Red Riding Hood
        (In All the World's a Stage)
    The Naked King
        (In Contemporary Russian Drama)
    The Shadow
        (In 20th Century Russian Plays)
    The Two Maples: A Fairy-Tale Play (Dva Klyona)
        (In Russian Plays for Young Audiences)
Shylock, le Marchand de Venise (see Vigny, Alfred V.)
Shyvers (see Reckford, Barry)
El Si de las Niñas (see Moratin, Leandro F.)
Si Jamais Je Te Pince! (see Labiche, Eugene)
The Sicilian; or, Love Makes a Painter (Le Sicilien; ou, L'Amour
    Peintre) (see Molière, Jean Baptiste)
Sicilian Limes (see Pirandello, Luigi)
Sieben Wünsche (see Müller, Armin)
Le Siècle des Lumières (see Brule, Claude)
The Siedge; or, Love's Convert (see Cartwright, William)
The Siege (see Clements, Colin C.)
The Siege (see D'Avenant, Sir William)
The Siege of Belgrade (see Cobb, James)
The Siege of Damascus (see Hughes, John)
The Siege of Rhodes (see D'Avenant, Sir William)
Siegfried (see Wagner, Richard)
Siegfried; text in French (see Giraudoux, Jean)

SIERRA, Ruben
  La Raza Pura, or Racial, Racial
    (In Contemporary Chicano Theatre)
Siete Gritos en el Mar (see Rodriguez Alvarez, Alejandro)
SIEVEKING, Alejandro
  Animas de Dia Claro
    (In Teatro Contemporaneo Chileno)
SIEVEKING, Lance
  The Strange Case of Dr. Jekyll and Mr. Hyde, adapted from
    Robert Louis Stevenson's novel
    (In Plays of the Year, Vol. 15, 1956)
SIEVERS, Wieder David
  Doors That Slam, by Wieder David Sievers, with additional dia-
    logue by Betty Smith; radio version
    (In On the Air: 15 Plays for Broadcast)
SIGAUX, Gilbert, 1918-
  La Dame de la Mer (see Ibsen, Henrik)
Sigismond (see Moinaux, Georges)
The Sign of the Prophet Jonah; radio play (see Mavor, Osborne H.)
The Sign of the Sea Gulls (see Peralta, Jesus T.)
The Signet Ring of Rakshasa (see Visakha-Datta)
La Signora Morli, Una e Due (see Pirandello, Luigi)
La Signora Senza Camelie; screenplay (see Antonioni, Michelangelo)
Los Signos de Zodiaco (see Magana, Sergio)
SIGURD, Jacques
  Un Pape a New-York (see Guare, John)
Sigurd der Schlimme (see Bjørnson, Bjørnstjerne)
Der Silbersee (see Kaiser, Georg)
Silence (see Pinter, Harold)
Silence (see Sarraute, Nathalie)
Silencio, Pollos Pelones, Ya Les Van a Echar Su Maíz (see Carbal-
    lido, Emilio)
Silent Movie; screenplay (see Brooks, Mel)
Silent Snow, Secret Snow; screenplay (see Kearney, Gene)
Las Sillas (Les Chaises) (see Ionesco, Eugene)
SILLITOE, Alan
  Saturday Night and Sunday Morning; screenplay (see Reisz, Karel)
Silly Willy (see Bax, Clifford)
La Silueta de Humo (see Jimenez Rueda, Julio)
SILVA VALDES, Fernan
  El Burlador de la Pampa
    (In Teatro Uruguayo Contemporaneo)
SILVAIN, Jean
  Le Retour du Calvaire
    (In L'Avant-Scène Théâtre, no. 611, June 1, 1977)
La Silvanaire; ou, La Morte Vive (see Mairet, Jean de)
The Silver Age (see Heywood, Thomas)
The Silver Arrow of Robin Hood (see Benton, Rita)
The Silver Box (see Galsworthy, John)
The Silver Cord (see Howard, Sidney Coe)
The Silver Coronet; radio script (see Pettitt, Wilfrid H.)
The Silver Foxes Are Dead (see Lind, Jakov)
The Silver Queen (see Foster, Paul)

The Silver Tassie (see O'Casey, Sean)
The Silver Theatre radio script
    Expert Opinion (see Boardman, Ture)
SIMENON, Georges
    **L'Horloger de Saint-Paul (see Tavernier, Bertrand)
SIMMONS, Pip
    Superman
        (In New Short Plays: 3)
Simnel, Lambert, 1477?-1534
    *Warbeck (see Schiller, Johann C.)
SIMON, Neil, 1927-
    The Odd Couple
        (In Best Plays of the Sixties)
        (In 50 Best Plays of the American Theatre, Vol. 4)
    The Prisoner of Second Avenue
        (In Best American Plays, 7th Series, 1967-1973)
    Visitor from Forest Hills
        (In Best Short Plays of the World Theatre, 1968-1973)
SIMONOV, Konstantin, 1915-
    The Russian People
        (In Seven Soviet Plays)
SIMONS, Beverley
    Crabdance
        (In Talonplays Series, 1972)
    Preparing
        (In Talonplays Series, 1975)
Le Simoun (see Lenormand, Henri R.)
SIMPLE, Lorenzo, Jr.
    King Kong; screenplay by Lorenzo Simple, Jr., based on a
    story by Edgar Wallace and Merian C. Cooper; film produced
    by Dino De Laurentiis, directed by John Guillermin
        (An Ace Books Film Book, 1976)
The Simpleton of the Unexpected Isles: A Vision of Judgment (see
    Shaw, George Bernard)
Simply Heavenly (see Hughes, Langston)
SIMPSON, Alan
    Richards Korkbein; Deutsch von Jürgen und Astrid Fischer
        (In Theater Heute, no. 1, Dec. 1974)
SIMPSON, Norman Frederick, 1919-
    The Form
        (In The Hole and Other Plays and Sketches)
    Gladly Otherwise
        (In The Hole and Other Plays and Sketches)
    The Hole
        (In The Hole and Other Plays and Sketches)
    Oh
        (In The Hole and Other Plays and Sketches)
    One Blast and Have Done
        (In The Hole and Other Plays and Sketches)
    One Way Pendulum
        (In Evergreen Playscripts Series, 1961)
    A Resounding Tinkle
        (In The Hole and Other Plays and Sketches)

Was He Anyone?
(In <u>Faber & Faber Plays</u>, 1973)
Les Sinceres (see Marivaux, Pierre C.)
SINCLAIR, Andrew
Under Milk Wood; screenplay by Andrew Sinclair, based on the
play by Dylan Thomas
(In <u>Lorrimer Screenplay Series</u>, 1971)
(In <u>Modern Filmscripts Series</u>, 1972)
Der Singende Fisch (see Brust, Alfred)
The Singer (see Wedekind, Frank)
Singspiel zum Weihnachtsball (see Kaiser, Georg)
A Singular Man (see Donleavy, James P.)
Sir Courtly Nice; or, It Cannot Be (see Crowne, John)
Sir Giles Goosecap, Knight (see Chapman, George)
Sir Henry Wildair (see Farquhar, George)
Sir Martin Mar-All (L'Estourdi) (see Molière, Jean Baptiste)
Sir Martin Mar-All; or, The Feign'd Innocence (see Dryden, John)
Sir Patient Fancy (see Behn, Mrs. Aphra)
La Sirena Varada (see Rodriguez Alvarez, Alejandro)
Sirocco (see Coward, Nöel)
Sister Eucharia (see Clarke, Austin)
The Sisters (see Chorell, Walentin)
The Sisters (see Shirley, James)
The Sisters (see Swinburne, Algernon Charles)
Sisters Under the Skin (see Hughes, Babette)
Sitting (see Tobias, John)
Sitting Bull, American Indian Leader, 1834-1890
*Buffalo Bill and the Indians; or, Sitting Bull's History Lesson;
screenplay (see Rudolph, Alan)
*Indians (see Kopit, Arthur L.)
Siwan (see Lewis, Saunders)
Six Characters in Search of an Author (see Pirandello, Luigi)
Six Men of Dorset (see Malleson, Miles)
The Six of Calais: A Medieval War Story (see Shaw, George Ber-
nard)
Six Public Acts (see The Living Theatre)
Sizwe Bansi Is Dead (see Fugard, Athol)
Sizwe Bansi Ist Tot; text in German (see Fugard, Athol)
SJÖSTRÖM, Victor, 1879-1960
The Scarlet Letter; screenplay (see Marion, Frances)
Skim-Milk (see Riley Mrs. Alice C.)
The Skin Game (see Galsworthy, John)
The Skin of Our Teeth (see Wilder, Thornton)
Ein Sklavenball (see Horvath, Odön von)
SKOLIMSKI, Jerzy, 1938-
Knife in the Water; screenplay (see Polanski, Roman)
Skywriting (see Drexler, Rosalyn)
Sladek oder Die Schwarze Armee (see Horvath, Odön von)
SLADEN-SMITH, Francis, 1886-
Westbury Fair
(In <u>Best One-Act Plays of 1939</u>, London)
The Slaughter of the Innocents (Anon.)
(In <u>Medieval Church Music-Dramas</u>)

The Slaughter of the Innocents (see Saroyan, William)
The Slave (see Jones, LeRoi)
Slaveship (see Jones, LeRoi)
The Sleep of the King (see Cousins, James)
Sleeping Beauty (see Shaw, Richard)
The Sleeping Car (see Howells, William Dean)
A Sleeping Clergyman (see Mavor, Osborne Henry)
Sleeping Dog; a play for television (see Gray, Simon)
Sleuth (see Shaffer, Anthony)
A Slight Accident (see Saunders, James)
A Slight Ache (see Pinter, Harold)
The Slippers of Aphrodite (see Weyl, Fernand)
SLOANE, Allan
    Bring on the Angels; radio dramatization from H. L. Mencken's
      "Newspaper Days" and other material. CBS Radio Workshop,
      June 8, 1956
        (In Prize Plays of Television and Radio, 1956)
SLOVES, Chaim, 1905-
    Haman's Downfall
        (In Epic and Folk Plays of the Yiddish Theatre)
Slowly Comes the Wind (see Casale, Michael)
Small Change (see Gill, Peter)
Small Craft Warnings (see Williams, Tennessee)
Small Hotel (see Frost, Rex)
Small Town Editor; radio script (see Wayne, Anthony)
Smiles of a Summer Night; screenplay (see Bergman, Ingmar)
Smith (see Maugham, William Somerset)
SMITH, Betty, 1904-1972
    The Desert Shall Rejoice; radio script (see Finch, Robert V.)
    Doors That Slam; radio script (see Sievers, Wieder D.)
    Ghost Town (see Finch, Robert V.)
    Johnny (see Finch, Robert V.)
    Murder in the Snow (see Finch, Robert V.)
    Summer Comes to the Diamond O (see Finch, Robert V.)
    Western Night, by Betty Smith and Robert Finch
        (In Plays of the American West)
Smith, Dodie (pseud.) (see Smith, Dorothy Gladys)
SMITH, Dorothy Gladys, 1896-
    Call It a Day, by C. L. Anthony (Dodie Smith), pseud.
        (In Famous Plays of 1935-36)
    Touch Wood, by C. L. Anthony, pseud.
        (In Famous Plays of 1934)
SMITH, Edgar Valentine
    'Lijah
        (In Types of Modern Dramatic Compositions)
SMITH, Edward Percy, 1891-
    Ladies in Retirement, by Edward Percy and Reginald Denham
        (In 10 Classic Mystery and Suspense Plays of the Modern
        Theatre)
SMITH, Harry James, 1880-1918
    Mrs. Bumpstead-Leigh
        (In Representative American Dramas)

SMITH, Henry Nash
    Facing Westward; radio script (see Guaedinger, Arthur)
SMITH, John, 1752-1809
    A Dialogue Between an Englishman and an Indian
       (In <u>Dramas from the American Theatre</u>, 1762-1909)
    A Little Teatable Chitchat, Alamode; or, An Ancient Discovery
    Reduced to Modern Practice;--Being a Dialogue, and a Dish of
    Tea
       (In <u>Dramas from the American Theatre</u>, 1762-1909)
Smith, Joseph, 1805-1844
    *A Short Play About Joseph Smith, Jr. (see Hutchins, Maude P.)
SMITH, Kate
    The Kate Smith Hour; radio script, Dec. 22, 1938. Guests:
    The Aldrich Family and Abbott and Costello: Christmas 1938
       (In <u>Best Broadcasts of 1938-39</u>)
SMITH, Michael Townsend, 1935-
    Country Music
       (In <u>The Off Off Broadway Book</u>)
SMITH, Moyne Rice
    Chop-Chin and the Golden Dragon; dramatized from a story by
    Laura E. Richards
       (In <u>7 Plays and How to Produce Them</u>)
    The Lady Who Put Salt in Her Coffee, a dramatization of Lu-
    cretia P. Hale's story
       (In <u>7 Plays and How to Produce Them</u>)
    Long and Short Division, a dramatization based on the story,
    "Melisande," by E. Nesbit
       (In <u>7 Plays and How to Produce Them</u>)
    The Miniature Darzis, adapted from Grimm's story
       (In <u>7 Plays and How to Produce Them</u>)
    Old Pipes, a dramatization from the story "Old Pipes and the
    Dryad," by Frank R. Stockton
       (In <u>7 Plays and How to Produce Them</u>)
    The Swineherd, a dramatization of a story by Hans Christian
    Andersen
       (In <u>7 Plays and How to Produce Them</u>)
    With All My Heart, based in part on "The Three Remarks," a
    story by Laura E. Richards
       (In <u>7 Plays and How to Produce Them</u>)
SMITH, Robert Kimmel
    A Little Dancing
       (In <u>Best Short Plays of 1975</u>)
Smith, Sydney, 1771-1845
    *Mr. Sydney Smith Coming Upstairs
       (In <u>Plays of the Year</u>, Vol. 42, 1972)
SMITH, Sydney Goodsir
    Colickie Meg
       (In <u>Calder & Boyars Scottish Library Series</u>, 1977)
SMITH, Victor
    Surprise for the Boys, a radio script, adapted by Victor Smith
    from the story by Herbert Lewis, Mar. 6, 1938
       (In <u>Best Broadcasts of 1938-39</u>)

SMITH, W.H., 1806-?
    The Drunkard; or, The Fallen Saved
        (In Dramas from the American Theatre, 1762-1909)
Smoke of the Fatherland (see Tur, Leonid D.)
Smoke-Screens (see Brighouse, Harold)
The Smoking Car (see Howells, William Dean)
Smoking Is Bad for You (see Chekhov, Anton)
SMOLLET, Tobias George, 1721-1771
    The Reprisal; or, The Tars of Old England
        (In A Collection of the Most Esteemed Farces ..., Vol. 2)
SMYTHE, Norman
    The Ragpickers
        (In The Best Short Plays 1973)
The Snake Charmer (see Bennet, Arnold)
Snake Chief (see Brown, Beverly S.)
The Snake Eater (see Nicholson, Kenyon)
The Snakeskin; screenplay (see Bergman, Ingmar)
Snare-That-Lures-a-Far-Flung-Bird (see Charlot, Jean)
The Sniper (see O'Neill, Eugene)
The Snob (see Sternheim, Carl)
Snow Birds (see Tipe, David)
Snow in May (see Manner, Eeva-Liisa)
The Snowstorm (see Hirschbein, Perez)
So Long (see Atlas, Leopold)
So Why Does That Weirdo Prophet Keep Watching the Water? (see
    Bennett, Gordon C.)
Las Sobras Para el Gusano (see Tobar-Garcia, Francisco)
Social Service; or, All Creatures Great and Small (see Cotterell, A.
    F.)
Socrates, 469-399 B.C.
    *L'Ame et la Danse (see Valery, Paul)
    *Callados Como Muertos (see Peman, José M.)
    *Eupalinos; ou, L'Architecte (see Valery, Paul)
    *Socrates (see Bax, Clifford)
    *Socrates (see Llovet, Enrique)
    *Socrates (see Voltaire)
Sodome et Gomorrhe (see Giraudoux, Jean)
La Soeur (see Rotrou, Jean)
Soeur Beatrice (see Maeterlinck, Maurice)
La Soeur du Cadre; screenplay (see Biette, Jean-Claude)
Sofonisba (see Alfieri, Vittorio)
Soft Voices (see Ravel, Aviva)
Softly, and Consider the Nearness (see Drexler, Rosalyn)
Sogno (Ma Forse No) (see Pirandello, Luigi)
Le Soir des Diplomates (see Bouteille, Romain)
El Sol y los Macdonald (see Marques, Rene)
SOLANA, Rafael, 1915-
    Debiera Haber Obispas
        (In Teatro Méxicano del Siglo XX, Vol. 3)
    Ensalada de Nochebuena
        (In Teatro Méxicano, 1963)
    No Se Culpe a Nadie
        (In 12 Obras en un Acto)

SOLARI SWAYNE, Enrique
     Collacocha
          (In Teatro Peruano Contemporaneo)
Le Soldat Diocles (see Audiberti, Jacques)
Le Soldat et la Sorciere (see Salacrou, Armand)
Der Soldat Tanaka (see Kaiser, Georg)
Soldier, Soldier (see Arden, John)
The Soldier's Daughter (see Cherry, Andrew)
The Soldiers of Fortune (see Norris, June)
The Solemn Communion (see Arrabal, Fernando)
Solico en el Mundo (see Alvarez Quintero, Serafin)
SOLINAS, Franco
     State of Siege, screenplay of the film directed by Costa-Gavras
          (A Ballantine Books Screenplay, 1973)
Le Solitaire; ou, Les Maledictions d'Univers (see Valéry, Paul)
Solomon, King of Israel, c. 1015-977 B.C.
     *The Song of Solomon (see O'Dea, Mark L.)
     **The Song of Songs of Solomon; adaptation (see Roinard, Paul N.)
     *The Wisdom of Solomon Paraphrased (see Middleton, Thomas)
Solon Shingle (see Jones, Joseph S.)
SOLORZANO, Carlos, 1922-
     Cruce de Vias
          (In 12 Obras en un Acto)
     The Crucifixion
          (In The Orgy)
     Doña Beatriz (La Sin Ventura)
          (In Teatro Guatemalteco Contemporaneo)
     Los Fantoches
          (In Teatro Breve Hispanoamericano Contemporaneo)
     Las Manos de Dios
          (In El Teatro Hispanoamericano Contemporaneo, Vol. 2)
     The Puppets
          (In Modern International Drama, Vol. 7, no. 2, Spring 1974)
SOLOVYOV, Vladimir Alexandrovich, 1907-
     Field Marshal Kutuzov
          (In Seven Soviet Plays)
Solsado Razo (see Valdez, Luis)
Soluna (see Asturias, Miguel A.)
SOLZHENITSYN, Aleksandr Isaevich, 1918-
     The Love-Girl and the Innocent, translated by Nicholas Bethell
          (In Noonday Plays Series, 1969)
     One Day in the Life of Ivan Denisovich; screenplay (see Harwood
          Ronald)
La Sombra Pasa (see Fernandez Ardavin, Luis)
Sombras de Sueño (see Unamuno y Jugo, Don Miguel)
Some Angry Summer Songs (see Herbert, John)
Some Are So Lucky (see Garner, Hugh)
Some Words in Edgewise (see Kennedy, Charles O'Brien)
Someone Waiting (see Williams, Emlyn)
Something I'll Tell You Tuesday (see Guare, John E.)
Der Sommerbürger (see Baierl, Helmut)
A Son, Come Home (see Bullins, Edward A.)
The Son of Getron (Anon.)
          (In Medieval Church Music-Dramas)

The Son of Learning (see Clarke, Austin)
Un Sonador Para un Pueblo (see Cuero Vallejo, Antonio)
Sonar Bangla (see Currimbhoy, Asif)
Sonata for Mott Street (see Hart, Joseph)
SONDHEIM, Stephen, 1930-
    Company; book by George Furth; music and lyrics by Stephen
    Sondheim
      (In Ten Great Musicals of the American Theatre)
    Gypsy (see Styne, Jule)
    A Little Night Music; book by Hugh Wheeler, suggested by the
    film "Smiles of a Summer Night, " by Ingmar Bergman; music
    and lyrics by Ingmar Bergman
      (In Ten Great Musicals of the American Theatre, Vol. 2)
Song at Twilight (see Coward, Noël)
Song of a Goat (see Clark, John P.)
The Song of Death (see Al Hakim, Tewfik)
The Song of Solomon (see O'Dea, Mark L.)
The Song of Songs of Solomon; adaptation (see Roinard, Paul N.)
Song of the Anvil (see MacMahon, Bryan)
Song of the Mighty B-52 (see People's Street Theater, N. Y.)
Le Songe d'Auguste (see Musset, Alfred de)
Il Sonno dei Carnefici (see Celli, Giorgio)
Sonntagkinder (see Reinshagen, Gerlind)
SONTAG, Susan
    Brother Carl
      (A Farrar, Straus & Giroux Filmscript, 1974)
Sophia= (Wisdom) Part 3: The Cliffs (see Foreman, Richard)
SOPHOCLES, 496-401 B. C.
    Antigone
      (In Contact with Drama)
      (In The Drama, Vol. 1)
      (In World Drama, Vol. 1)
    **Antigone; adaptation (see Alfieri, Vittorio)
    **Antigone; adaptation (see Anouilh, Jean)
    **Edipo; adaptation; text in Spanish (see Peman, José M.)
    **Electra, a tragedy in one act freely rendered after Sophocles
      (see Hofmannsthal, Hugo von H.)
    **Electre; adaptation, text in French (see Chénier, Marie-Joseph
      B.)
    **Electre; adaptation, text in French (see Crebillon, Prosper)
    **Elektra; adaptation, text in German (see Hofmannsthal, Hugo
      von H.)
    **The Gods Are Not to Blame (see Rotimi, Ola)
    **König Ödipus; adaptation, text in German (see Hofmannsthal, Hugo
      von H.)
    **Oedipe; adaptation, text in French (see Corneille, Pierre)
    **Oedipe; adaptation, text in French (see Voltaire)
    **Oedipe a Colone; adaptation (see Chénier, Marie-Joseph B.)
    **Oedipe ou le Silence des Dieux; adaptation (see Kihm, Jean-
      Jacques)
    **Oedipe-Roi; adaptation (see Chénier, Marie-Joseph B.)
    **Oedipus; adaptation (see Dryden, John)
    **Oedipus; adaptation (see Voltaire)

**Oedipus Rex; adaptation, filmscript, text in English (see Pasolini, Pier P.)

Oedipus the King, edited and adapted by Anthony Burgess
(In <u>Minnesota Drama Editions</u>, no. 8)

**Ödipus und die Sphinx; adaptation; text in German (see Hofmannsthal, Hugo von H.)

**Orestes; adaptation (see Voltaire)

**Sophocles' King Oedipus (see Yeats, William Butler)

**Sophocles' Oedipus at Colonus (see Yeats, William Butler)

**Vorspiel zur "Antigone" des Sophokles (prologue to the "Antigone" of Sophocles); both German and English texts are included (see Hofmannsthal, Hugo von H.)

Sophonisba, or Sophoniba, Daughter of Hasdrubal of Carthage, d. c. 204 B. C.

*Sofonisba; text in Italian (see Alfieri, Vittorio)

*Sophonisba; or, Hannibal's Overthrow (see Lee, Nathaniel)

*Sophonisbe; text in English (see Mairet, Jean de)

*Sophonisbe; text in French (see Corneille, Pierre)

*La Sophonisbe; text in French (see Mairet, Jean de)

*The Wonder of Women; or, The Tragedie of Sophonisba (see Marston, John)

The Sorcerer (see Gilbert, William S.)

Sorcery (see Biro, Laios)

The Sorcery (see Turkish Theatre.   Orta Oinuu)

SORIANO DE ANDIA, Vincente

Ayer ... Sera Mañana
(In <u>Teatro Español</u>, 1951-52)

Die Sorina (see Kaiser, Georg)

The Sorrows of Frederick (see Linney, Romulus)

So's Your Old Antique! (see Kummer, Mrs. Clare)

Les Sosies (see Rotrou, Jean)

SOSUKE, Namiki

Chronicle of the Battle of Ichinotani, by Namiki Sōsuke, Namiki Shōzō I, Namiki Geiji, and Asada Itcho
(In <u>Kabuki: Five Classic Plays</u>)

Soul Gone Home (see Hughes, Langston)

The Soul of Ch'ien-nü Leaves Her Body (see Cheng Teh-hui)

Le Soulier de Satin (see Claudel, Paul)

The Soul's Tragedy (see Browning, Robert)

The Sounding Shell (see Krog, Helge)

SOUPAULT, Philippe, 1897-

If You Please (see Breton, André)

Sous le Rempart d'Athènes (see Claudel, Paul)

South (see Green, Julien)

South Pacific (see Rodgers, Richard)

South Sea Bubble (see Coward, Noël)

The Southern Cross (see Green, Paul)

SOUTHERNE, Thomas, 1660-1746

Cleomenes, The Spartan Heroe (see Dryden, John)

Oroonoko
(In <u>Five Restoration Tragedies</u>)

SOUTO, Alexandrino de
    A Bomba
        (In <u>Revista de Teatro</u>, no. 420, Nov. /Dec. 1977)
Souvenirs de Pension (see Mace, Jean)
Souvenirs d'en France (see Téchiné, André)
The Sovereign State of Boogedy Boogedy (see Carter, Lonnie)
SOYA, Carl Erik, 1896-
    Lion with Corset
        (In <u>Five Modern Scandinavian Plays</u>)
    Quien Soy Yo?
        (In <u>Teatro Danes Contemporaneo</u>)
SOYINKA, Wole, 1934-
    The Bacchae of Euripides
        (In his <u>Collected Plays</u>, Vol. 1)
    A Dance of the Forests
        (In his <u>Collected Plays</u>, Vol. 1)
    The Lion and the Jewel; excerpt
        (In <u>African English Literature</u>)
    Madmen and Specialists
        (In <u>Methuen Modern Plays Series</u>, 1971)
    The Road
        (In his <u>Collected Plays</u>, Vol. 1)
        (In <u>Gambit,</u> no. 4)
    The Strong Breed
        (In his <u>Collected Plays</u>, Vol. 1)
    The Swamp Dwellers
        (In his <u>Collected Plays</u>, Vol. 1)
The Spanish Curate (see Beaumont, Francis)
The Spanish Fryar; or, The Double Discovery (see Dryden, John)
The Spanish Gipsy (see Middleton, Thomas)
The Spanish Student (see Longfellow, Henry Wadsworth)
The Spanish Tragedic; or, Hicronimo Is Mad Againe (see Kyd, Tho-
    mas)
The Sparagus Garden (see Brome, Richard)
Spare (see Wood, Charles)
Spared (see Horovitz, Israel)
The Sparrow (see Lopez, Sabatino)
Spartacus (see Heym, Georg)
Speak o' the Devil; a modern miracle play (see Grubb, Davis)
The Speakers (see Gaskill, William)
The Speakers (see Williams, Heathcote)
Speaking Terms (see Pertwee, Roland)
A Special Announcement (see Saroyan, William)
SPEIRS, Russell, 1901-
    A Change of Mind
        (In <u>One-Act Plays for Stage and Study</u>, 6th Series)
The Spelling Mistakes (see Labiche, Eugene)
SPENCE, Eulalie, 1894-
    Undertow
        (In <u>Black Theater U.S.A.</u>, 1847-1974)
SPENCER, James
    A Bunch of the Gods Were Sitting Around One Day
        (In <u>Playwrights for Tomorrow</u>, Vol. 12)

SPERR, Martin
    Amleto Principe di Danimarca (see Brecht, Bertolt)
    Hunting Scenes from Lower Bavaria
        (In Contemporary German Theater)
    Scene di Caccia in Bassa Baviera
        (In Sipario, no. 309, Feb. 1972)
    Tales from Landshut
        (A Methuen Playscript, 1969)
SPEWACK, Bella (Cohen), 1899-
    Kiss Me, Kate (see Porter, Cole)
    Leave It to Me! (see Porter, Cole)
SPEWACK, Samuel, 1899-
    Kiss Me, Kate (see Porter, Cole)
    Leave It to Me! (see Porter, Cole)
    Under the Sycamore Tree
        (In Plays of the Year, Vol. 7, 1951/52)
Das Spiel Christa vom Schmerz der Schoenheit des Weibes (see Brust,
    Alfred)
SPIELBERG, Peter
    Back to Back; a short view of the long of marriage in one act
        or three scenes, without intermission
        (In Modern Occasions)
Die Spieldose (see Kaiser, Georg)
The Spirit of Contradiction (see Rich, John)
Spirochete: A History (see Sundgaard, Arnold)
Spoiled (see Gray, Simon)
The Spoiled Child (see Bickerstaffe, Isaac)
Spokesong; or, The Common Wheel (see Parker, Stewart)
The Spon Plague (see Milligan, Spike)
The Sponge (see Riley, Mrs. Alice C.)
The Sport Model; vaudeville script (see Fields, W.C.)
Spreading the News (see Gregory, Isabella A.)
Spring Awakening (see Wedekind, Frank)
Spring, 1600 (see Williams, Emlyn)
SPUNDE, Walter G.
    The Mercenary
        (In Contemporary Canadian Drama)
Spur des Dunklen Engels (see Jahnn, Hans H.)
SPURLING, John
    Macrune's Guevara
        (In Calder & Boyars Playscript Series, no. 33)
The Square of Flowers (see Ilyenkov, Vassily P.)
Square Pegs (see Bax, Clifford)
Squaring the Circle (see Katayev, Valentine)
Squire Blue Boll (see Barlach, Ernst)
The Squire of Alsatia (see Shadwell, Thomas)
Sriranga (pseud.) (see Rangacharya, Adya)
Stag at Bay (see Johnson, Nunnally)
Stage Directions (see Horovitz, Israel)
The Stage-Coach (see Farquhar, George)
Stagecoach; screenplay (see Ford, John)
Staircase (see Dyer, Charles)
The Stairs (see Rosso di San Secondo, Piermaria)
Stallerhof (see Kroetz, Franz X.)

STALLINGS, Lawrence, 1894-1968
 What Price Glory? (see Anderson, Maxwell)
STALLONE, Sylvester
 Rocky; screenplay (excerpts) written by Sylvester Stallone for
  the film directed by John G. Avildsen
   (In The Official Rocky Scrapbook)
Stan McAllister's Heir; scenario (see Sullivan, C. Gardner)
Stand Up to Death (see Parker, Kenneth T.)
Standard Safety (see Bovasso, Julie)
The Staple of News (see Jonson, Ben)
The Star in the Trees (see Young, Stark)
Star Minded (see Parker, Kenneth T.)
Star of the Morning (see Mitchell, Loften)
Star Trek television scripts
  City on the Edge of Forever (see Eillison, Harlan)
  Trouble with Tribbles (see Gerrold, David)
The Star Turns Red (see O'Casey, Sean)
Der Starke Stamm (see Fleisser, Marieluise)
Starkodder (see Oehlenschläger, Adam G.)
STARKWEATHER, David, 1935-
 You May Go Home Again
  (In The Off Off Broadway Book)
Stars and Stripes (see Melfi, Leonard)
The State of Innocence and Fall of Man (see Dryden, John)
State of Siege; screenplay (see Solinas, Franco)
State of the Union (see Lindsay, Howard)
Statement After an Arrest Under the Immortality Act (see Fugard,
 Athol)
La Station Champbaudet (see Labiche, Eugene)
The Statue's Daughter (see O'Connor, Frank)
Stavisky ... ; screenplay (see Resnais, Alain)
Steal Away Home (see Harris, Aurand)
The Steel Worker; radio script (see Oboler, Arch)
STEELE, Sir Richard, 1672-1729
 The Conscious Lovers
  (In British Plays from the Restoration to 1820, Vol. 1)
  (In The London Stage, Vol. 2)
  (In his Plays)
  (In Plays of the Restoration and 18th Century)
  (In Restoration Comedy, Vol. 4)
 The Funeral; or, Grief A-la-Mode
  (In his Plays)
 The Lying Lover; or, The Ladies Friendship
  (In his Plays)
 The Tender Husband; or, The Accomplish'd Fools
  (In his Plays)
  (In The London Stage, Vol. 3)
STEELE, Wilbur Daniel, 1886-
 Luck, an adaptation for radio of the prize-winning story by
  Margaret Lewerth
  (In 100 Non-Royalty Radio Plays)
STEFANSSON, Davio, 1895-1964
 The Golden Gate
  (In Five Modern Scandinavian Plays)

STEIN, Gertrude, 1874-1946
    Daniel Webster: Eighteen in America
      (In New Directions, Vol. 2, 1937)
    Four Saints in Three Acts: An Opera to Be Sung
      (In Transition, no. 16-17, Spring-Summer 1929)
    Look and Long
      (In All the World's a Stage)
    What Happened
      (In The Off Off Broadway Book)
STEIN, James R.
    The Engagement; television script for an episode in "Sanford
    and Son, " by James R. Stein and Robert Illes
      (In Samuel French's Tandem Library Series)
STEIN, Joseph, 1912-
    Fiddler on the Roof (see Bock, Jerry)
STEINBECK, John, 1902-1968
    **A l'Est D'Eden; scenario (see Kazan, Elia)
    Des Souris et des Hommes; adaptation Marcel Duhamel
      (In L'Avant-Scène Théâtre, no. 589, June 15, 1976)
    Viva Zapata; screenplay by John Steinbeck, based on the novel
    "Zapata, the Unconquerable, " by Edgcumb Pinchon and O. B.
    Stade; film directed by Elia Kazan
      (A Viking/Compass Book Screenplay, 1975)
STEINER, Rolando, 1936-
    La Trilogia del Matrimonia: Judit; Un Drama Corriente; La
    Puerta
      (In Teatro Contemporaneo Hispanoamericano, Vol. 2)
Stella (see Goethe, Johann Wolfgang von)
Step-in-the-Hollow (see MacDonagh, Donagh)
STEPHENS, James
    The Demi-Gods
      (In The Journal of Irish Literature, Vol. 4, no. 3, Sept. 1975)
The Stepmother (see Balzac, Honoré de)
La Steppa; filmscript (see Lattuada, Alberto)
STERN, Leonard
    The Honeymooners: 'The $99, 000 Answer, " television script by
    Leonard Stern and Sydney Zelinka. Jackie Gleason Enterprises,
    CBS, Jan. 28, 1956
      (In Prize Plays of Television and Radio, 1956)
STERNHEIM, Carl, 1878-1943
    The Bloomers
      (In his Scenes from the Heroic Life of the Middle Classes:
        5 Plays)
    The Fossil
      (In his Scenes from the Heroic Life of the Middle Classes:
        5 Plays)
    1913
      (In his Scenes from the Heroic Life of the Middle Classes:
        5 Plays)
    A Pair of Drawers
      (In Transition, Vol. 1, nos. 6-9, Sept. -Dec. 1927)
    Paul Schippel Esq.
      (In his Scenes from the Heroic Life of the Middle Classes:
        5 Plays)

A Place in the World
  (In Eight European Plays)
The Snob
  (In his Scenes from the Heroic Life of the Middle Classes:
     5 Plays)
STEVENS, Gould, 1927-
  The Good and Obedient Young Man (see Barr, Betty)
STEVENS, Thomas Wood, 1880-1942
     Drum Head
        (In One-Act Plays for Stage and Study, 10th Series)
STEVENSON, Adell
     Tooth or Consequences; television script for an episode in "San-
     ford and Son"
        (In Samuel French's Tandem Library Series)
STEVENSON, Robert Louis Balfour, 1850-1894
  **The Bottle Imp; adapted for radio (see Koopman, Romance C.)
  **Dr. Jekyll and Mr. Hyde; screenplay (see Mamoulian, Rouben)
  **The Strange Case of Dr. Jekyll and Mr. Hyde; adaptation (see
     Sieveking, Lance)
Sticks and Bones (see Rabe, David)
The Still Alarm (see Kaufman, George S.)
Still Fires (see Quackenbush, Jan)
Still Life (see Molnar, Ferenc)
Still-Love (see Patrick, Robert)
Still Waters (see James, Henry)
STOCKTON, Frank Richard, 1834-1902
  **The Lady or the Tiger? a radio script (see Olfson, Lewy)
  **Old Pipes (see Smith, Moyne Rice)
The Stoker (see Brighouse, Harold)
STOKER, Bram, 1847-1912
  **Le Cauchemar de Dracula; screenplay (see Fisher, Terence)
  **Dracula (see Deane, Hamilton)
  **Dracula: Sabbat (see Katz, Leon)
  **Nosferatu: A Symphony of Horror; screenplay (see Murnau,
     Friedrich W.)
STOKLE, Norman
     Marguerite; English version (see Salacrou, Armand)
     When the Music Stops; English version (see Salacrou, Armand)
     The World Is Round; English version (see Salacrou, Armand)
Stolen Kisses; screenplay (see Truffaut, François)
The Stolen Prince (see Totheroh, Dan)
STOLPER, Armin
     Klara und der Gänserich
        (In Theater der Zeit, no. 10, 1973)
     Der Schuster und der Hahn
        (In Theater der Zeit, no. 1, 1976)
     ... stolz auf 18 Stunden (see Baierl, Helmut)
Stone (see Bond, Edward)
STONE, John Augustus, 1800-1834
     Metamora; or, The Last of the Wampanoags
        (In Dramas from the American Theatre, 1762-1909)
        (In Favorite American Plays of the 19th Century)

STONE, Peter, 1930-
    Charade; screenplay by Peter Stone, based on the unpublished
        story "The Unsuspecting Wife, " by Peter Stone and Marc Behm;
        film directed by Stanley Donen
        (In Film Scripts Three)
    1776 (see Edwards, Sherman)
STONE, Weldon
    Here's a Howdy-do
        (In One-Act Plays for Stage and Study, 10th Series)
    Mammon and the Whittler
        (In One-Act Plays for Stage and Study, 9th Series)
A Stone Flower (see Hanley, James)
STOPPARD, Tom, 1937-
    Albert's Bridge
        (In Albert's Bridge and Other Plays)
    Artist Descending a Staircase
        (In Albert's Bridge and Other Plays)
        (In Artist Descending a Staircase and Where Are They Now?)
    Dirty Linen
        (In his Dirty Linen and New-Found Land)
    Enter a Free Man
        (In Evergreen Playscripts, 1972)
    If You're Glad I'll Be Frank
        (In Albert's Bridge and Other Plays)
    Jumpers
        (In Evergreen Play Series, 1972)
    New-Found Land
        (In his Dirty Linen and New-Found Land)
    A Separate Peace
        (In Albert's Bridge and Other Plays)
    Travesties
        (In Evergreen Playscript Series, 1975)
        (A Faber & Faber Play, 1975)
    Where Are They Now?
        (In Albert's Bridge and Other Plays)
        (In Artist Descending a Staircase and Where Are They Now?)
Stops (see Auletta, Robert)
The Store (see Moore, Mavor)
STOREY, David
    The Changing Room
        (In Plays of the Year, Vol. 44, 1975)
        (In Sports Illustrated, Vol. 38, no. 9, March 1973)
    The Contractor
        (In Cape Plays Series, 1970)
    Cromwell
        (In Cape Plays Series, 1973)
    The Farm
        (In Cape Plays Series, 1973)
    The Restoration of Arnold Middleton
        (Jonathan Cape Plays, 1967)
Storia di Giovanni (see Cuomo, Franco)
STORM, Lesley
    Black Chiffon
        (In Plays of the Year, Vol. 2, 1949)

The Storm (see Drinkwater, John)
The Storm (see Ostrovskii, Alexandr N.)
A Storm in Summer; television script (see Serling, Rod)
Storm Song (see Johnston, Denis)
Storm Warning (see Kao Hung)
Storm Weather (see Strindberg, August)
The Story Brought by Brigit (see Gregory, Isabella A.)
Story in Dogtown Common; a poetic play (see Liss, Joseph)
Story of a Kidnapping (see Diament, Mario)
The Story of Adele H.; filmscript (see Truffaut, François)
The Story of John Milton; radio script (see Walpole, Helen)
The Story of Mrs. Surratt (see Goggan, John Patrick)
The Story of Panchito González (see Dragún, Osvaldo)
The Story of Silent Night (see Watts, William)
The Story of the Little White Bull (see Amalrik, Andrei)
The Story of the Man Who Turned into a Dog (see Dragún, Oscaldo)
The Story of the Three Big Pigs! (see San Francisco Red Theatre)
STOTT, Mike
    Funny Peculiar
        (In Plays and Players, Vol. 23, nos. 7-8, April-May, 1976)
STOWE, Harriet Beecher, 1811-1895
    **Uncle Tom's Cabin; adaptation (see Aiken, George L.)
STRACHAN, Edna Higgins
    The Chinese Water Wheel
        (In One-Act Plays for Stage and Study, 6th Series)
La Strada; filmscript (see Fellini, Federico)
Strafford, 1st Earl of, Sir Thomas Wentworth, 1593-1641
    *Strafford (see Browning, Robert)
The Straight and the Jew; a vaudeville skit
        (In The Disinherited: Plays)
STRAKL, Rudi
    Arno Prinz von Wolkenstein oder Kader Entscheinden Alled
        (In Theater der Zeit, no. 7, 1977)
STRAMM, August, 1874-1915
    Awakening
        (In Seven Expressionists Plays)
    Rudimentary
        (In The Drama Review, Vol. 19, no. 3, Sept. 1975)
    Sancta Susanna
        (In The Drama Review, Vol. 19, no. 3, Sept. 1975)
        (In Sipario, no. 326, July 1973)
The Strange Case of Dr. Jekyll and Mr. Hyde (see Sieveking, Lance)
The Strange Case of Martin Richter (see Eveling, Stanley)
Strange Interlude (see O'Neill, Eugene)
Strange Occurrence on Ireland's Eye (see Johnston, Denis)
The Strange Rider (see Ghelderode, Michel de)
The Stranger (see Hirschbein, Perez)
The Stranger (see Kotzebue, August R.)
Stranger with Roses (see Jakes, John)
Strassenecke (see Jahnn, Hans H.)
A Stratagem of Interlocking Rings (Anon.)
        (In Six Yüan Plays)

STRAUB, Jean-Marie
    Fortini /Cani; texte du film de Jean-Marie Straub et Danièle
    Huillet, couverture du livre Franco Fortini, "I Cani del Sinai"
       (In Cahiers du Cinéma, no. 275, April 1977)
    Moise et Aaron; texte du film, Jean-Marie Straub et Danièle
    Huillet
       (In Cahiers du Cinéma, nos 258-259, July /Aug., nos. 260-261,
        Oct. /Nov. 1975, nos. 262-263, Jan. 1976)
STRAUSS, Botho
    Bekannte Gesichter, Gemischte Gefühle
       (In Theater: Chronik und Bilanz des Bühenjahres, 1974)
    Die Hypochonder
       (In Theater Heute, no. 1, Jan. 1973)
    Trilogie des Wiedersehens
       (In Theater: Chronik und Bilanz des Bühenjahres, 1976)
STRAVINSKY, Igor, 1882-1971
    L'Histoire du Soldat (see Ramuz, Charles F.)
The Straw (see O'Neill, Eugene)
Strawberry Fields (see Hollingsworth, Michael)
Strawberry Fields (see Poliakoff, Stephen)
Stray Dog; screenplay (see Kurosawa, Akira)
Street Scene (see Rice, Elmer L.)
Street Sounds (see Bullins, Edward A.)
A Streetcar Named Desire (see Williams, Tennessee)
Der Streit (see Marivaux, Pierre C.)
Der Strick (see Bartsch, Kurt)
STRICKLAND, Dwight
    Legend of Dust, a verse play for women
       (In 100 Non-Royalty Radio Plays)
Strictly Matrimony (see Hill, Errol)
Strife (see Galsworthy, John)
STRIKER, Fran
    The Lone Ranger; radio script no. 1, 000, June 30, 1940
       (In Best Broadcasts of 1939-40)
STRINDBERG, August, 1849-1912
    Advent
       (In his Dramas of Testimony)
    The Bond
       (In Pre-Inferno Plays)
    The Burned House
       (In The Chamber Plays)
    Creditors
       (In Pre-Inferno Plays)
    Creditors, translated by Elizabeth Sprigge
       (In Plays of the Year, Vol. 21, 1959/60)
    The Dance of Death I and II
       (In his Dramas of Testimony)
    A Dream Play
       (In Eight Expressionists Plays)
    Easter
       (In his Dramas of Testimony)
    The Father
       (In Pre-Inferno Plays)

The Ghost Sonata
   (In The Chamber Plays)
   (In Eight Expressionists Plays)
   (In Masterpieces of the Modern Scandinavian Theatre)
The Great Highway
   (In Eight Expressionists Plays)
   (In Modern Scandinavian Plays)
The Keys of Heaven
   (In Eight Expressionists Plays)
Lady Julie
   (In Pre-Inferno Plays)
Lucky Per's Journey
   (In Eight Expressionists Plays)
Miss Julie
   (In Contemporary Drama: 13 Plays)
   (In Masterpieces of the Modern Scandinavian Theatre)
The Pelican
   (In The Chamber Plays)
**Play Strindberg; the Dance of Death (see Dürrenmatt, Friedrich)
Storm Weather
   (In The Chamber Plays)
The Stronger
   (In Pre-Inferno Plays)
Swanwhite
   (In All the World's a Stage)
There Are Crimes and Crimes
   (In Dramas of Modernism)
   (In his Dramas of Testimony)
To Damascus I, II, III
   (In Eight Expressionists Plays)
*Strindberg (see Wilson, Colin)
The Strings, My Lord, Are False (see Carroll, Paul Vincent)
Striptease (see Mrozek, Slawomir)
Strip-Tease de la Jalousie (see Arrabal, Fernando)
Stripwell (see Barker, Howard)
A Stroll in the Air (see Ionesco, Eugene)
STRONG, Austin, 1881-1952
   The Drums of Oude
     (In One-Act Plays for Stage and Study, 2nd Series)
   The Little Father of the Wilderness, by Austin Strong and Lloyd
    Osbourne
     (In Five Plays from the Other Side)
     (In More One-Act Plays by Modern Authors)
     (In One-Act Plays for Stage and Study, 1st Series)
The Strong Are Lonely (see Hochwalder, Fritz)
The Strong Breed (see Soyinka, Wole)
The Stronger (see Strindberg, August)
STROUSE, Charles, 1928-
   Applause; book by Betty Comden and Adolph Green, based on
   the film "All About Eve," by Joseph L. Mankiewicz and the
   original story by Mary Orr; lyrics by Lee Adams; music by
   Charles Strouse
     (A Random House Play, 1970)
     (In Ten Great Musicals of the American Theatre, Vol. 2)

Südseespiel (see Brust, Alfred)
Sueño de Día (see Usigli, Rudolfo)
El Sueño de la Razón (see Buero Vallejo, Antonio)
Los Sueños Encendidos (see Moreno, Luis)
Il Suffit d'un Bâton (see Jugand, Jean-Philippe)
The Suicide (see Erdman, Nikolai)
The Suicide (see Freeman, Carol)
Le Suicide (see Hugo, Victor)
The Suicide; a radio play (see Campbell, Alistair)
Le Suis un Steak (see Ribes, Jean-Michel)
A Suitable Case for Treatment (see Mercer, David)
La Suite du Menteur (see Corneille, Pierre)
Les Suites d'un Premier Lit (see Labiche, Eugene)
La Suivante (see Corneille, Pierre)
Sukeroki: Flower of Edo (see Jihei, Tsuuchi II)
SUKHOVO-KOBYLIN, Aleksandr Vasil'evich, 1817-1903
    The Case
        (In his Trilogy)
    The Death of Tarelkin
        (In his Trilogy)
    Krechinsky's Wedding
        (In his Trilogy)
SULLIVAN, Arthur, 1842-1900
    The Gondoliers; pr, The King of Barataria (see Gilbert, William
        S.)
    The Grand Duke; or, The Statutory Duel (see Gilbert, William S.)
    H.M.S. Pinafore; or, The Lass That Loved a Sailor (see Gilbert,
        William S.)
    Iolanthe; or, The Peer and the Peri (see Gilbert, William S.)
    The Mikado; or, The Town of Titipu (see Gilbert, William S.)
    Patience; or, Bunthorne's Bride (see Gilbert, William S.)
    The Pirates of Penzance; or, The Slave of Duty (see Gilbert,
        William S.)
    Princess Ida; or, Castle Adamant (see Gilbert, William S.)
    Ruddigore; or, The Witch's Curse (see Gilbert, William S.)
    The Sorcerer (see Gilbert, William S.)
    Thespis; or, The Gods Grown Old (see Gilbert, William S.)
    Trial by Jury (see Gilbert, William S.)
    Utopia, Limited; or, The Flowers of Progress (see Gilbert, Wil-
        liam S.)
    The Yeomen of the Guard; or, The Merryman and His Maid (see
        Gilbert, William S.)
SULLIVAN, C. Garnder
    Stan McAllister's Heir; scenario of the film by C. Gardner Sul-
        livan and Thomas H. Ince
        (In Spellbound in Darkness)
The Sultan; or, A Peep into the Seraglio (see Bickerstaff, Isaac)
The Sultan's Dilemma (see Al Hakim, Tewfik)
SUMAROKOV, Aleksandr Petrovich, 1718-1777
    Dimitrii the Imposter
        (In The Literature of 18th Century Russia, Vol. 2)
Summer and Smoke (see Williams, Tennessee)
Summer Comes to the Diamond O (see Finch, Robert V.)

Summer Day's Dream (see Priestley, John B.)
Summer Evening (see Shawn, Wallace)
Summersoft (see James, Henry)
Summertime (see Betti, Ugo)
Sun (see Kennedy, Adrienne)
Sun-Up (see Vollmer, Lula)
Sundance Kid (see Longbaugh, Harry)
Sunday Costs Five Pesos (see Niggli, Josephina)
A Sunday Morning in the South (see Johnson, Georgia D.)
Sunday News (see McVeigh, Christopher)
Sunday Promenade (see Forsell, Lars)
Sunday They'll Make Me a Saint (see Toteras, Demetrius)
The Sunday Walk (see Michel, Georges)
SUNDGAARD, Arnold
     Spirochete: A History
          (In Federal Theatre Plays)
The Sundial (see Pillot, Joseph E.)
Die Sundflut (see Barlach, Ernst)
The Sunken Bell (see Hauptmann, Gerhart J.)
Sunrise; screenplay (see Murnau, F.W. L'Aurore)
Sunrise on Sarah (see Ryga, George)
Superintendent (see Haavikko, Paavo)
Superman (see Simmons, Pip)
Superstition (see Barker, James N.)
A Supper at the House of Mademoiselle Rachel (see Musset, Alfred
     de)
Supper for the Dead (see Green, Paul)
Supplément; ou, Voyage de Cook (see Giraudoux, Jean)
Suppressed Desires (see Glaspell, Susan)
Sur la Lisière d'un Bois (see Hugo, Victor)
Surenas (see Corneille, Pierre)
La Surprise de l'Amour (see Marivaux, Pierre C.)
Surprise for the Boys; radio script (see Smith, Victor)
Surratt, Mary Eugenia (Jenkins), 1820-1865
     *Madame Surratt (see Rogers, James W.)
     *The Story of Mrs. Surratt (see Goggan, John Patrick)
Susana y los Jovenes (see Ibargüengoitia, Jorge)
Susannah and the Elders (see Mavor, Osborne Henry)
Suspense radio script
     Return to Dust (see Bamber, George)
Sutter, John Augustus, 1803-1880
     *Sutter's Gold; scenario (see Eisenstein, Sergei M.)
SUZUKI, Sensaburo
     Living Koheiji
          (In The Passion)
SVEINBJÖRNSSON, Tryggvi
     Bishop Jon Arason
          (In Modern Scandinavian Plays)
SVEVO, Italo, 1861-1928
     La Comédie sans Titre; ou, La Régénération, adaptation Fran-
     çaise de Ginette Herry
          (In L'Avant-Scène Théâtre, no. 585, April 15, 1976)

Ein Mann Wird Jünger
      (In Theater Heute, no. 11, Nov. 1975)
The Swallows (see Dubillard, Roland)
The Swamp Dwellers (see Soyinka, Wole)
The Swan (see Molnar, Ferenc)
Swan Song (see Chekhov, Anton)
Swan Song (see Hecht, Ben)
SWANSON, Bud
      The Lion Roars
            (In 100 Non-Royalty Radio Plays)
Swanwhite (see Strindberg, August)
Swedenhielmas (see Bergman, Hjalmar F.)
The Sweeps of Ninety-Eight (see Masefield, John)
SWEET, Jeffrey
      Porch
            (In Best Short Plays, 1976)
Sweet Bird of Youth (see Williams, Tennessee)
Sweet Bird of Youth; screenplay (see Brooks, Richard)
Sweet Eros (see McNally, Terrence)
Sweet of You to Say So (see Johnson, Page)
Sweet Sweetback's Baadasssss; screenplay (see Van Peebles, Melvin)
Sweet Talk (see Abbensetts, Michael)
Sweethearts (see Gilbert, William S.)
The Sweethearts (see Taylor, Peter H.)
Swept Away (see Wertmüller, Lina)
SWET, Peter
      The Interview
            (In Best Short Plays of 1975)
SWIFT, Jonathan, 1667-1745
      *Farewell to Greatness! (see Carroll, Paul Vincent)
      **Lilliput (see Garrick, David)
SWINBURNE, Algernon Charles, 1837-1909
      Atalanta in Calydon
            (In his Complete Works, Vol. 7)
      Bothwell
            (In his Complete Works, Vols. 8 & 9)
      Chaslelard
            (In his Complete Works, Vol. 8)
      The Duke of Gandia
            (In his Complete Works, Vol. 10)
      Erechtheus
            (In his Complete Works, Vol. 7)
      Locrine
            (In his Complete Works, Vol. 10)
      Marino Faliero
            (In his Complete Works, Vol. 10)
      Mary Stuart
            (In his Complete Works, Vol. 9)
      The Queen-Mother
            (In his Complete Works, Vol. 7)
      Rosamond
            (In his Complete Works, Vol. 7)

The Sisters
  (In his Complete Works, Vol. 10)
The Swineherd (see Smith, Moyne Rice)
The Swing (see Bond, Edward)
The Sword of Dermot (see Cousins, James)
SYLVAINE, Vernon
  As Long as They're Happy
    (In Plays of the Year, Vol. 9, 1953)
Sylvanire (see Zola, Emile)
SYLVANUS, Erwin, 1917-
  Dr. Korczak and the Children
    (In Postwar German Theatre)
Sylvia Hears a Secret (see Marivaux, Pierre C.)
La Sylvie (see Mairet, Jean de)
Symphonie; ein film (see Kaiser, Georg)
SYNGE, John Millington, 1871-1909
  Playboy of the Western World
    (In his Collected Works, Vol. 4)
    (In Masterpieces of the Modern Irish Theatre)
  Riders to the Sea
    (In A Book of Short Plays, XV-XX Centuries)
    (In his Collected Works, Vol. 3)
    (In Contact with Drama)
    (In Masterpieces of the Modern Irish Theatre)
    (In The Mentor Book of Short Plays)
    (In One-Act Plays by Modern Authors)
    (In Representative British Dramas)
  El Saltimbanqui del Mundo Occidental
    (In Teatro Irlandes Contemporaneo)
  The Tinker's Wedding
    (In his Collected Works, Vol. 4)
  The Well of the Saints
    (In his Collected Works, Vol. 3)
  When the Moon Has Set
    (In his Collected Works, Vol. 3)
Syphax, Numidian king, d. about 201 B.C.
  *Sophonisbe (Sophonisba) (see Mairet, Jean de)
The System of Doctor Goudron and Professor Plume (see Lorde, An-
  dre de)
Le Système Ribadier (see Feydeau, Georges)
Szenen Wider die Nacht (see Santis, Omar S.)

Ta Ch'eng Huang (Beating the Tutelar Deity)
    (In Famous Chinese Plays)
Le Tableau (see Ionesco, Eugene)
Tables and Chairs (see Davies, Mary C.)
TACCHELLA, Jean-Charles, 1925-
  Cousin, Cousine
    (In L'Avant-Scène Cinéma, no. 184, Mar. 15, 1977)
Der Tag des Zorns (see Brust, Alfred)
I Tagliatori di Teste (see Caleffi, Fabrizio)

TAGORE, Sir Rabindranath, 1861-1941
    The Post Office
        (In All the World's a Stage)
TAILLE, Jean de la, 1533?-1608?
    Saul le Furieux
        (In Four Renaissance Tragedies)
Tailleur pour Dames (see Feydeau, Georges)
Take a Giant Step (see Peterson, Louis)
TAKEDA, Izumo, 1691-1756
    The Village School
        (In One-Act Plays for Stage and Study, 8th Series)
Taking the Bandits' Stronghold (see China Peking Opera Troup)
Taking Tiger Mountain by Strategy (see Taking the Bandits' Strong-
    hold)
A Tale of a Tub (see Jonson, Ben)
A Tale of Two Cities (see Radical Arts Troupe, Chicago)
The Tale of the Wolf (see Molnar, Ferenc)
Tales from Landshut (see Sperr, Martin)
Tales of Beatrix Potter; filmscript (see Lanchbery, John)
Tales of Hoffman, filmscript (see Powell, Michael)
Talk to Me Like the Rain and Let Me Listen ... (see Williams, Ten-
    nessee)
The Talkative Barber (see Holberg, Ludvig von. Master Gert West-
    phaler; or, The Talkative Barber)
Talking of Michaelangelo (see Quackenbush, Jan)
Talleyrand (see Guitry, Sacha)
TALLMAN, James, 1947-
    Trans-Canada Highway
        (In Contemporary Canadian Drama)
TAMAYO Y BAUS, Manuel, 1829-1898
    Angela
        (In Obras Completas)
    Una Apuesta
        (In Obras Completas)
    La Bola de Nieve
        (In Obras Completas)
    Del Dicho al Hecho
        (In Obras Completas)
    Un Drama Nuevo
        (In Obras Completas)
    La Esperanza de la Patria
        (In Obras Completas)
    Hija y Madre
        (In Obras Completas)
    Los Hombres de Bien
        (In Obras Completas)
    Huyendo del Perejil
        (In Obras Completas)
    Juana de Arco
        (In Obras Completas)
    Lances de Honor
        (In Obras Completas)

La Locura de Amor
 (In Obras Completas)
Mas Vale Mana que Fuerza
 (In Obras Completas)
No Hay Mal que por Bien No Venga
 (In Obras Completas)
Lo Positivo
 (In Obras Completas)
La Ricahembra
 (In Obras Completas)
Virginia
 (In Obras Completas)
Virginia (segunda edicion)
 (In Obras Completas)
Tamburlaine the Great, pts, 1 & 2 (see Marlowe, Christopher)
Tamerlane (see Rowe, Nicholas)
Tamerlane, the Great (see Timur, the Great)
TANAKA, Chikao
 Historia de Hizen
  (In Teatro Japones Contemporaneo)
TANAKA, M. Magdalena Sumie
 La Mujer del Tambor
  (In Teatro Japones Contemporaneo)
Tancred and Sigismunda (see Thompson, James)
Tango (see Mrozek, Slawomir)
Tango Palace (see Fornes, Maria, I.)
TANIZAKI, Junichiro, 1886-1965
 The Man with the Mandoline
  (In New Directions, Vol. 24, 1972)
Der Tapfere Cassian (see Schnitzler, Arthur)
TAPIA Y RIVERA, Alejandro, 1826-1882
 Bernardo de Palissy
  (In his Obras Completas, Volumen II: Teatro)
 Camoens
  (In his Obras Completas, Volumen II: Teatro)
 La Cuarterona
  (In his Obras Completas, Volumen II: Teatro)
 Vasco Nuñez de Balboa
  (In his Obras Completas, Volumen II: Teatro)
Taps (see Schrock, Gladden)
TARABIN, Jean Salomon (known as) C. 1584-1633
 Les Deux Pourceaux
  (In Théâtre du XVIIe Siècle, Vol. 1)
 Le Voyage aux Indes
  (In Théâtre du XVIIe Siècle, Vol. 1)
Tarare (see Beaumarchais, Pierre A.)
TARDIEU, Jean, 1903-
 Le Guichet
  (In Le Théâtre d'Aujourd'hui)
 Un Mot pour un Autre
  (In Le Théâtre d'Aujourd'hui)
 One Way for Another
  (In Modern French Theatre)

TARKINGTON, Booth, 1869-1946
    Beauty and the Jacobin
        (In One-Act Plays by Modern Authors)
Tarquinius, Lucius Tarquinius Superbus, king of Rome, 6th Cent. B. C.
    *Scevole (Scaevola) (see Du Ryer, Pierre)
Tartuffe; filmscript (see Mayer, Carl)
Tartuffe; or, The Hypocrite (Tartuffe; ou, L'Imposteur) (see Molière,
    Jean Baptiste)
Taste (see Foote, Samuel)
TATE, Nahum, 1652-1715
    Duke or No Duke; or, Trapolin's Vagaries, altered from "Trap-
        polin Creduto Principe" by Sir Aston Cokayne
        (In A Collection of the Most Esteemed Farces ..., Vol. 5)
    The History of King Lear
        (In Shakespeare Adaptations)
TATHAM, John, fl. 1632-1664
    The Distracted State
        (In his Dramatic Works)
    Love Crowns the End
        (In his Dramatic Works)
 ** The Roundheads; or, The Good Old Cause (see Behn, Mrs. Aphra)
    The Rump; or, The Mirrour of the Late Times
        (In his Dramatic Works)
    The Scotch Figgaries; or, A Knot of Knaves
        (In his Dramatic Works)
The Tatier (see Voltaire)
Tatyana Repin (see Chekhov, Anton)
Tausk (see Harris, Andrew B.)
TAVEL, Ronald, 1941-
    Gorilla Queen
        (In The Off Off Broadway Book)
    Shower
        (In The Young American Writers)
TAVERNIER, Bertrand, 1941-
    L'Horloger de Saint-Paul; d'après le roman "L'Horloger d'Ever-
        ton, " de Georges Simenon
        (In L'Avant-Scène Cinéma, no. 147, May 1974)
    Le Juge et l'Assassin; scénario et dialogue, Jean Aurenche, Ber-
        trand Tavernier
        (In L'Avant-Scène Cinéma, no. 170, June 1976)
TAVIANI, Paolo, 1931-
    Il Ritorno del Cospiratore, di Paolo e Vittorio Taviani (Scena
        8-12)
        (In Sipario, no. 330, Nov. 1973)
    San Michele Aveva un Gallo Allonsanfan; Paolo e Vittorio Taviani
        (In Dal Soggetto al Film Series, no. 50, 1975)
TAVIANI, Vittorio, 1929-
    Il Ritorno del Cospiratore (see Taviani, Paolo)
    San Michele Aveva un Gallo Allonsanfan (see Taviani, Paolo)
Taxi; radio script (see Riley, Mrs. Alice C.)
TAYLEURE, Clifton W.
    Horse-shoe Robinson
        (In Representative Plays by American Dramatists, Vol. 2)

TAYLOR, Donald Fraser
  **The Doctor and the Devil (see Thomas, Dylan)
TAYLOR, Helen Louise, 1908-
    Angelus
        (In One-Act Plays for Stage and Study, 5th Series)
TAYLOR, Laurette, 1884-1946
    The Dying Wife
        (In One-Act Plays for Stage and Study, 1st Series)
TAYLOR, Peter Hillsman, 1917-
    Arson
        (In Presences)
    A Father and a Son
        (In Presences)
    Missing Person
        (In Presences)
    The Sweethearts
        (In Presences)
    Two Images
        (In Presences)
    A Voice Through the Door
        (In Presences)
    The Whistler
        (In Presences)
TAYLOR, Ron
    The Unreasonable Act of Julian Waterman
        (In A Collection of Canadian Plays, Vol. 3)
TAYLOR, Tom, 1817-1880
    New Men and Old Acres; by Tom Taylor and Augustus William
      Dubourg
        (In English Plays of the 19th Century, Vol. III: Comedies)
    The Ticket-of-Leave Man
        (In English Plays of the 19th Century, Vol. II: Dramas 1850-
          1900)
        (In Representative British Dramas)
TAZEWELL, Charles
    Can Long Endure
        (In One-Act Plays for Stage and Study, 10th Series)
Tchaikovsky, Peter Ilyich, 1840-1893
    *This Lonely Heart; radio script (see Obler, Arch)
Tchekhoff, Anton (see Chekhov, Anton Pavlovich)
Tchin-Tchin (see Billetdoux, François P.)
Tea and Sympathy (see Anderson, Robert W.)
The Tea-pot on the Rocks (see Kirkpatrick, John)
Teacher, Teacher; television script (see Carroll, Ellison)
The Teahouse of the August Moon (see Goggan, John Patrick)
El Teatro Campesino scripts
    La Conquista de Mexico (see Valdez, Luis)
    Las Dos Caras del Patroncito (see Valdez, Luis)
    Hueguistas (see Valdez, Luis)
    The Militants (see Valdez, Luis)
    No Saco Nada de la Escuela (see Valdez, Luis)
    La Quinta Temporada (see Valdez, Luis)
    Solsado Razo (see Valdez, Luis)

Los Vendidos (see Valdez, Luis)
Vietnam Campesino (see Valdez, Luis)
EL TEATRO DE LA ESPERANZA
     Pánfila la Curandera
          (In El Teatro de la Esperanza)
TECHINE, André, 1943-
     Souvenirs d'en France
          (In L'Avant-Scène Cinéma, no. 166, Feb. 1976)
TEIRLINCK, Herman, 1879-
     El Hombre Sin Cuerpo
          (In Teatro Flamenco Contemporaneo)
TEIXIDOR, Jordi
     The Legend of the Piper
          (In 3 Catalan Dramatists)
Teja (see Sudermann, Hermann)
La Tejedora de Sueños (see Buero Vallejo, Antonio)
Telegram from Heaven; radio script (see Manoff, Arnold)
The Telescope (see Sherriff, Robert C.)
Tell, William
     *Guillermo Tell Tiene los Ojos Tristes (see Sastre, Alfonso)
     *The Sad Eyes of William Tell (see Sastre, Alfonso)
     *William Tell (see Schiller, Johann C.)
Tell Me Lies (see Brook, Peter. US)
TELLES, Carlos Queiroz, 1936-
     Frei Caneca
          (In Revista de Teatro, no. 396, Nov. /Dec. 1973)
     Muro de Arrimo
          (In Revista de Teatro, no. 412, July /Aug. 1976)
TELLEZ, Gabriel, 1570?-1648
     El Amour Medico; Tirso de Molina, pseud.
          (In Clásicos Castellanos, Vol. 131)
     Averigüelo Vargas
          (In Clásicos Castellanos, Vol. 131)
     El Burlador de Sevilla
          (In Clásicos Castellanos, Vol. 2)
     The Playboy of Seville; or, Supper with a Statue, by Tirso de
     Molina, pseud.
          (In The Theatre of Don Juan)
     El Vergonzoso en Palacio
          (In Clásicos Castellanos, Vol. 2)
Telltale Heart; adaptation (see Holland, Norman)
TEMBECK, Robert, 1940-
     Baptism
          (In Contemporary Canadian Drama)
Tembladera (see Ramos, José A.)
Temperament (see Aldis, Mrs. Mary)
A Temperance Town (see Hoyt, Charles H.)
The Tempest (see Shadwell, Thomas)
The Tempest; or, The Enchanted Island (see Dryden, John)
La Tempesta; filmscript (see Lattuada, Alberto)
The Temple of Love (see D'Avenant, Sir William)
Tempo (see Pogodin, Nikolai F.)
Le Temps des Lilas (see Dubé, Marcel)

Les Temps Difficiles (see Bourdet, Edouard)
Le Temps Est un Songe (see Lenormand, Henri R.)
The Ten Days That Shook the World; screenplay (see Eisenstein,
   Sergi. October)
Ten Little Indians (see Christie, Agatha)
Ten Minutes by the Clock (see Riley, Mrs. Alice C.)
Ten Thousand People Killed; a musical review and vaudeville sketch
   (see Fields, W.C.)
Ten Variations (see Björnsson, Oddur)
The Ten Worst Things About a Man (see Kerr, Jean)
Les Tenailles (see Hervieu, Paul E.)
Tenants (see James, Henry)
The Tender Husband; or, The Accomplish'd Fools (see Steele, Rich-
   ard)
TENDRYAKOV, Vladimir Fedorovich, 1923-
   Die Nacht Nach der Abschlussfeier
      (In Theater der Zeit, no. 2, 1977)
   Short Circuit (Korotkoye Zamykaniye)
      (In The New Writing in Russia)
TENDUCCI, Giusto Ferdinando, fl. 1760-1790
   **Amintas (see Rolt, Richard)
TENNYSON, Alfred Tennyson, 1st baron, 1809-1892
   Becket
      (In Poems and Plays)
      (In Representative British Dramas)
   The Cup
      (In Poems and Plays)
   The Falcon; based on the ninth story of the fifth day of Boccac-
   cio's "Decamerone"
      (In A Book of Short Plays: XV-XX Centuries)
      (In Poems and Plays)
   The Foresters, Robin Hood and Maid Marian
      (In Poems and Plays)
   Harold
      (In Poems and Plays)
   The Promise of May
      (In Poems and Plays)
   Queen Mary
      (In Poems and Plays)
Tentato Suicidio; screenplay (see Antonioni, Michelangelo)
La Tentazioni del Dottor Antonio; screenplay (see Fellini, Federico)
The Tenth Man (see Chayefsky, Paddy)
Teofilo Amadeo: Una Biografia (see Reuben, William)
Teregalu; excerpts (see Lankesh, P.)
TERENCE (Publius Terentius Afer), 185-159 B.C.
   The Eunuch
      (In The Drama, Vol. 2)
   Phormio
      (In World Drama, Vol. 1)
TERKEL, Louis "Studs," 1912-
   Monologues from Division Street
      (In The Disinherited: Plays)
Terminal (see Yankowitz, Susan)

Ternura (see Menen Desleal, Alvaro)
Terra Adorada (see Oliveira, Vlademar de)
La Terra Trema (1 e 2 edizione); filmscript (see Visconti, Luchino)
La Terrasse de Midi (see Clavel, Maurice)
La Terre est Ronde (see Salacrou, Armand)
The Terrible Revenge of Fred Fumanchu (see Milligan, Spike)
TERRY, Megan, 1932-
    Calm Down Mother
       (In Plays By and About Women)
    Massachusetts Trust
       (In The Off Off Broadway Book)
    Sanibel and Captiva
       (In Spontaneous Combustion; The Winter Repertory, Vol. 6)
TESHIGAHARA, Hiroshi, 1927-
    Woman in the Dunes; original story and script by Kobo Abe; di-
    rected by Hiroshi Teshigahara
       (A Phaedra Screenplay, 1971)
Tessa; text in French (see Giraudoux, Jean)
The Test (see Marivaux, Pierre C.)
The Testament (see López Mozo, Jerónimo)
Tests (see Ableman, Paul)
Tête de Méduse (see Vian, Boris)
La Tête des Autres (see Ayme, Marcel)
Tête d'Or (see Claudel, Paul)
Il Tetto; screenplay (see De Sica, Vittorio)
TEWKESBURY, Joan
    Nashville; screenplay of the film, directed by Robert Altman
       (A Bantam Books Screenplay, 1976)
A Texas Steer; or, "Money Makes the Mare Go" (see Hoyt, Charles
    H.)
TEYSSANDIER, François, 1944-
    Des Voix dans la Ville
       (In L'Avant-Scène du Théâtre, no. 512, Feb. 15, 1973)
Thanksgiving in Detroit (see Pomerance, Bernard)
That Boy, Call Him Back (see Hendry, Thomas)
That Good Between Us (see Barker, Howard)
That Time (see Beckett, Samuel)
THATCHER, George, 1929-
    The Only Way Out
       (In New Plays, First Series, no. 3, 1977)
That's Where the Town's Going! television script (see Mosel, Tad)
The Theater of the Soul; a one-act monologue with prologue (see
    Evreinov, Nikolai N.)
THEATRE DU SOLEIL
    1789/1793
       (In L'Avant-Scène du Théâtre, no. 526/527, Oct. 1973)
Theatre I & Theatre II (see Beckett, Samuel)
THEATRE WORKSHOP, LONDON
    Oh What a Lovely War
       (In Methuen's Modern Plays Series, 1965)
The Theban Brothers (see Racine, Jean Baptiste)
Their Anniversary (see Riley, Mrs. Alice C.)

Their First Anniversary (see Morrison, Anne)
Their Husband (see Gerstenberg, Alice)
Theodicy (see Richards, Ivor A.)
THEODORAKIS, Mikis
    Das Sauspiel (see Walser, Martin)
Theodore I, Fyodor Ioannovich, Czar of Russia, 1557-1598
    *Tsar Fyodor Ivanovich (see Tolstoi, Aleksiei K.)
Theodore Cherche des Allumettes (see Moinaux, Georges)
Theodore, Vierge et Martyre (see Corneille, Pierre)
Theodosius II, "The Younger," Emperor of the Eastern Roman Empire, 401-450
    *The Emperor of the East (see Massinger, Philip)
    *Pulcheria (see Corneille, Pierre)
    *Theodosius; or, The Force of Love (see Lee, Nathaniel)
Theophile de Vian (see Vian, Theophile de)
There Are Crimes and Crimes (see Strindberg, August)
There Shall Be No Night (see Sherwood, Robert E.)
There Was a Father; filmscript (excerpt) (see Ozu, Yasujiro)
There's a Change from the Old to the New; television script (see Martin, John)
There's No Point in Arguing the Toss (see Haworth, Don)
There's No Room for You Here for a Start (see Livings, Henry)
Thérèse Raquin (see Zola, Emile)
Therese, the Orphan of Geneva (see Payne, John H.)
Thermopylae (see Branner, H.C.)
Theroigne de Mericourt (see Hervieu, Paul E.)
These Honored Dead (see Algyer, Harold C.)
Theseus (see Carballido, Emilio)
Thespis; or, The Gods Grown Old (see Gilbert, William S.)
They (see Witkiewicz, Stanislaw I.)
They Are Dying Out (see Handke, Peter)
They Came to a City (see Priestley, John B.)
They Shall Not Die (see Wexley, John)
They That Sit in Darkness (see Burrill, Mary)
THIE, Sharon
    Thoughts on the Instant of Greeting a Friend on the Street (see Van Itallie, Jean-Claude)
Thierry and Theodoret (see Beaumont, Francis)
THIESSEN, Cherie Stewart
    Elevator
        (In The Malahat Review, Vol. 39, July 1976)
Thieves (see Jones, LeRoi)
The Thieves (see Kawatake, Mokuami)
Thieves' Carnival (see Anouilh, Jean)
A Thing of Beauty; television script (see Rodman, Howard)
Things Is That-a-Way (see Conkle, Ellsworth P.)
Things That Are Caesar's (see Carroll, Paul Vincent)
The Thinking Heart; television script (see Faulkner, George H.)
The Third Floor Front (see Larrimore, Lida)
The Third Man; screenplay (see Reed, Sir Carol)
Third Person (see Rosenthal, Andrew)
Thirst (see O'Neill, Eugene)
Thirst (see O'Nolan, Brian)

39 East (see Crothers, Rachel)
This Bird of Dawning Singeth All Night Long (see Dean, Philip H.)
This Happy Breed (see Coward, Noël)
This Is a Cranky (see San Francisco Women's Street Theater)
This Is a Flippy (see San Francisco Women's Street Theater)
This Is the Rill Speaking (see Wilson, Lanford)
This Jockey Drives Late Nights (see Livings, Henry)
This Lonely Heart; radio script (see Obler, Arch)
This Obscene Pomp (see Morgan, Albert E.)
This Piece of Land (see Rivers, Lou)
This Room and This Gin and These Sandwiches (see Wilson, Edmund)
This Story of Yours (see Hopkins, John R.)
This Train (see Mitchell, Ken)
"This Was a Man" (see Coward, Noël)
This Year of Grace (see Coward, Noël)
The Thistle and the Rose (see Home, William D.)
THOLY, René
    L'Air des Bijoux
        (In L'Avant-Scène Théâtre, no. 554, Dec. 15, 1974)
    Pollution; text in French
        (In L'Avant-Scène Théâtre, no. 587, May 15, 1976)
THOMAS, Augustus, 1857-1934
    In Mizzoura
        (In Representative Plays by American Dramatists, Vol. 3)
    The Witching Hour
        (In Representative American Dramas)
        (In Representative American Plays, 1792-1949)
THOMAS, Dylan, 1914-1953
    The Doctor and the Devil; filmscript, from a story by Donald
      Taylor
        (In his The Doctor and the Devil and Other Scripts)
    A Dream in Winter; filmscript
        (In his The Doctor and the Devil and Other Scripts)
    The Londoner; filmscript
        (In his The Doctor and the Devil and Other Scripts)
    Twenty Years a-Growing Up; filmscript, from a story by Mau-
      rice O'Sullivan
        (A Dent-Aldine Press Film Script, 1964)
        (In his The Doctor and the Devil and Other Scripts)
    Under Milk Wood; screenplay (see Sinclair, Andrew)
THOMAS, Pascal
    Le Poème de l'Elève Mikovsky; filmscript
        (In L'Avant-Scène Cinéma, no. 198, Dec. 15, 1977)
THOMAS, Robert, 1930-
    La Chambre Mandarine
        (In L'Avant-Scène Théâtre, no. 553, Dec. 1, 1974)
    Le Corbeau et la Grue
        (In L'Avant-Scène Théâtre, no. 606, May 1, 1977)
    La Louve
        (In L'Avant-Scène Théâtre, no. 592, Aug. 1976)
Thomas a Becket, Saint, Abp. of Canterbury, 1118?-1170
    *Becket (see Tennyson, Alfred Lord)
    *Becket; ou, l'Honneur de Dieu (see Anouilh, Jean)

Thomas and Sally; or, The Sailor's Return (see Bickerstaff, Isaac)
Thomas Chatterton (see Jahnn, Hans H.)
Thomas Cranmer of Canterbury (see Williams, Charles)
Thomas Muntzer (see Pfeiffer, Hans)
Thomas Muskerry (see Colum, Padraic)
Thomaso; or, The Wanderer (see Killigrew, Thomas)
Thompson (see Hankin, St. John)
THOMPSON, James, 1700-1748
    Tancred and Sigismunda
        (In The London Stage, Vol. 4)
THOMPSON, Palmer
    Our Love: A Radio Romance
        (In On the Air: 15 Plays for Broadcast)
THORBURN, John
    The Woman
        (In Best One-Act Plays of 1941, London)
Thoreau, Henry David, 1817-1862
    *The Night Thoreau Spent in Jail (see Lawrence, Jerome)
Those Golden Gates Fall Down (see Watson, Harmon C.)
Thoughts on the Instant of Greeting a Friend on the Street (see Van
    Itallie, Jean-Claude)
Three Actors and Their Drama (see Ghelderode, Michel de)
Three Bad Men in a Hidden Fortress; screenplay (see Kurosawa,
    Akira)
The Three Clerks (Anon.)
        (In Medieval Church Music-Dramas)
The Three Daughters (Anon.)
        (In Medieval Church Music-Dramas)
Three Desks (see Reaney, James C.)
3 Filosofers in a Firetower (see Collins, Margaret)
Three Hours After Marriage (see Gay, John)
Three Men for Colverton (see Cregan, David)
3 Miles to Poley (see Lynch, Hal)
Three Months Gone (see Howarth, Donald)
Three Players, a Fop and a Duchess (see Hughes, Babette)
The Three Sisters (see Chekhov, Anton)
The Three Sisters from Springfield, Illinois (see Eyen, Tom)
Three Strikes You're Out; radio script (see Delston, Vernon)
Three Suitors: One Husband (see Oyono-Mbia, Guillaume)
Three Top Hats (see Mihura, Miguel)
Three Verse Plays: Three Wars, The Market, The Removal of the
    Academy (see Cahoon, Herbert)
Three Weeks After Marriage; or, What We Must All Come To (see
    Murphy, Arthur)
Three X Love (see Zuber, Ron)
The Threepenny Opera; screenplay (see Lania, Leo)
Through the Night; television script (see Griffiths, Trevor)
The Thumping Process; a minstrel show (see Leavitt, A.J.)
Thunder in the Night (see Dean, Phillip H.)
Thunder on Sycamore Street (see Rose, Reginald)
The Thunderbolt (see Pinero, Arthur Wing)
The Thunderstorm (see Ostrovskii, Aleksandr N.)

THURBER, James, 1894-1961
    The Last Clock
        (In <u>Readers Theatre Handbook</u>)
Thursday Evening (see Morley, Christopher D.)
Thus Spake Zarathustra (see Nietzsche, Friedrich)
The Thwarting of Baron Bollingrew (see Bolt, Robert)
Ti-Jean and His Brothers (see Walcott, Derek)
Ti Yette (see Matheus, John)
Tiao Ch'an (Sable Cicada)
        (In <u>Famous Chinese Plays</u>)
Tiberius (Tiberius Claudio Nero), 2nd Emperor of Rome, 42 B.C.-
    A.D. 37
    *Tibère (see Chénier, Marie-Joseph B.)
The Ticket-of-Leave Man (see Taylor, Tom)
The Ticklish Acrobat (see Hivnor, Robert)
Tiempo de Espadas (see Salom, Jaime)
Tiempo Muerto (see Méndez Ballester, Manuel)
El Tiempo y los Conway (see Priestly, John B.)
T'ien Ho P'ei (The Mating at Heaven's Bridge)
        (In <u>Famous Chinese Plays</u>)
La Tierra es Redonda (see Salacrou, Armand)
El Tifon Kitty (see Fukuda, Tsuneari)
A Tiger Is Loose in Our Community (see Dorall, Edward)
Tigers (see Lascelles, Kendrew)
El Tigre (see Aguilera Malta, Demetrio)
Till the Day I Die (see Odets, Clifford)
Tilly Tutweiler's Silly Trip to the Moon (Dietz, Norman D.)
Tilt (see Schwartz, Joel)
Time and the Conways (see Priestley, John B.)
The Time and the Place (see Carballido, Emilio)
Time Is a Thief (see Carroll, Robert F.)
The Time of Your Life (see Saroyan, William)
Time Present (see Osborne, John)
Time Remembered (see Anouilh, Jean)
A Time to Die (see Bentley, Eric Russell)
Time to Go (see O'Casey, Sean)
A Time to Live (see Bentley, Eric Russell)
Timewatch (see Godlovitch, Charles Z.)
Timocrate (Timocrates) (see Corneille, Thomas)
Timoleon, d. ca. 337 B.C.
    *Timoléon (see Chénier, Marie-Joseph B.)
    *Timoleone (see Alfieri, Vittorio)
Timur the Great, Eastern Conqueror, 1336?-1405
    *Tamburlaine the Great, pts. 1 & 2 (see Marlowe, Christopher)
    *Tamerlane (see Rowe, Nicholas)
The Tin Soldier and the Paper Dancer (see Magre, Maurice)
Tina (see Cregan, David)
The Tingalary Bird (see Melwood, Mary)
Tinka (see Braun, Volker)
The Tinker and the Sheeog (see Hyde, Douglas)
The Tinker's Wedding (see Synge, John M.)
TIPE, David
    Snow Birds
        (In <u>Performing Arts in Canada</u>, Vol. 9, no. 1, Spring 1972)

The Tiptaft Revue Skit (see Shaw, George Bernard)
Tira Tells Everything There Is to Know About Herself (see Weller,
    Michael)
Tiridate (Tiridates) (see Campistron, Jean-Galbert de)
Tirso de Molina (pseud.) (see Téllez, Gabriel)
Los Titeres de Cachiporra (see Garcia Lorca, Federico)
Tituba's Children (see Williams, William Carlos)
Titus Flavius Sabinus Vespasianus, Emperor of Rome, 40?-81 A.D.
    *Berenice (see Racine, Jean)
To Be Radical Is to Get to the Root of Things (see People's Street
    Theater, N.Y.)
To Bobolink, for Her Spirit (see Inge, William M.)
To Damascus I, II, III (see Strindberg, August)
To Dorothy, a Son (see MacDougall, Roger)
To Love and to Cherish (see Egan, Michael)
To the Chicago Abyss (see Bradbury, Ray)
Tobacco Road (see Kirkland, Jack)
The Tobacconist (see Jonson, Ben)
TOBAR-GARCIA, Francisco, 1928-
    Las Sobras Para el Gusano
        (In Teatro Breve Hispanoamericano Contemporaneo)
TOBIAS, John
    Sitting
        (In Best Short Plays, 1974)
Tobias and Sara (l'Histoire de Tobie et de Sara) (see Claudel, Paul)
Tobias and the Angel (see Mavor, Osborne Henry)
TOBIN, John, 1770-1804
    The Curfew
        (In The London Stage, Vol. 4)
    The Honeymoon
        (In The Drama, Vol. 16)
Toby Dammit; filmscript; text in Italian (see Fellini, Federico)
Der Tod (see Jahnn, Hans H.)
Der Tod des Helden (see Heym, Georg)
Todo Acaba Bien ... a Veces (see Baroja y Nessi, Pio)
Todos Contra el Payo Contra Todos, o La Visita del Payo en el Hos-
    pital de Locos (see Fernandez de Lizardi, José J.)
Todos Contra Todos (see Adamov, Arthur)
Toe Jam (see Jackson, Elaine)
TOEPLITZ, Krysztof T., 1933-
    Aquarium 2 (see Gruza, Jerzy)
Together Tonite... (see Vilalta, Maruxa)
La Toison d'Or (see Corneille, Pierre)
Tokayo Story; filmscript (excerpt) (see Ozu, Yasujiro)
Tolkening (see Brust, Alfred)
TOLKIEN, John Ronald Reuel, 1892-1973
    The Homecoming of Beorhtnoth, Beorhthelm's Son, based on an
    anonymous fragment, "The Battle of Maldon"
        (In The Tolkien Reader)
TOLLER, Ernst, 1893-1939
    Hinkemann
        (In Vision and Aftermath: Four Expressionist War Plays)

Hinkemann; text in French
   (In L'Avant-Scène Théâtre, no. 580, Feb. 1, 1976)
The Machine-Wreckers; English version by Ashley Dukes
   (In Dramas of Modernism)
No More Peace!
   (In German Drama Between the Wars)
TOLSTOI, Aleksiei Konstaninovich, graf, 1817-1875
   The Death of Ivan the Terrible
      (In Masterpieces of the Russian Drama, Vol. 2)
   Tsar Fyodor Ivanovitch
      (In The Moscow Art Theatre Series of Russian Plays)
TOLSTOI, Lev Nikalawich, graf, 1828-1910
   The Cause of It All
      (In his Plays)
   The First Distiller
      (In his Plays)
   The Fruits of Enlightenment
      (In his Plays)
 **Ivan the Fool (see Benton, Rita)
   The Light Shine in Darkness
      (In his Plays)
   The Live Corpse (The Man Who Was Dead)
      (In his Plays)
      (In 20th Century Plays)
 **La Passion d'Anna Karénini (see Arout, Gabriel)
   The Power of Darkness
      (In Masterpieces of the Russian Drama, Vol. 2)
      (In Nineteenth-Century Russian Plays)
      (In The Storm and Other Russian Plays)
 **This Jockey Drives Late Nights (see Livings, Henry)
 **What Men Live By; adapted for radio (see Shipman, Karyl K.)
 **What Men Live By; adapted for the stage (see Benton, Rita)
   The Wisdom of Children
      (In A Treasury of Classic Russian Literature)
Tolstoy, Count Alexey (see Tolstoi, Aleksiei Konstaninovich, graf)
Tolstoy, Count Leo (see Tolstoi, Lev Nikalawich, graf)
Tom Cob; or, Fortune's Toy (see Gilbert, William S.)
Tom Paine (see Foster, Paul)
Tom Piper and the Pig (see Riley, Mrs. Alice C.)
TOMASI DI LAMPEGUSA, Giuseppe, 1896-1957
   Il Gattopardo; screenplay (see Visconti, Luchino)
Tomorrow (see Foote, Horton)
The Tomorrow Business (see Ward, Edmund)
Tomorrow Morning, Faustus! (see Richards, Ivor A.)
Tonight at 8:30 (see Coward, Noël)
Tonight We Shall Pray to My Gods (see Kariara, Jonathan)
Too True to Be Good: A Political Extravaganza (see Shaw, George
   Bernard)
TOOMER, Jean, 1894-1967
   Balo
      (In Black Theater U.S.A., 1847-1974)
   Kabnis
      (In Kuntu Drama)

The Tooth of Crime (see Shepard, Sam)
Top of the Ladder (see Guthrie, Sir Tyrone)
TOPOR, Roland
    La Planète Sauvage; filmscript (see Laloux, René)
Der Tor und der Tod (see Hofmannsthal, Hugo von H.)
Tordenskiold (see Oehlenschläger, Adam G.)
TORPHY, William
    Brandywine
        (In Drama & Theatre, Vol. 12, no. 2, Spring 1975)
Torquemada, Juan de, 1545?-after 1617
    *Torquemada (see Hugo, Victor)
TORRE, Claudio de la
    La Cana de Pescar
        (In Teatro Español, 1958-59)
Le Torrent (see Donnay, Maurice C.)
TORRES NAHARRO, Bartolomé de, fl. 1517
    Hymen
        (In The Drama, Vol. 6)
Las Torres y el Viento (see Rengifo, Cesar)
Tortesa the Usurer (see Willis, Nathaniel P.)
Une Tortur Nommée Dostoievsky (see Arrabal, Fernando)
Tosca (see Puccini, Giacomo)
Total Recall (Sophia-Wisdom): Part 2 (see Foreman, Richard)
Der Tote Tag (see Barlach, Ernst)
TOTERAS, Demetrius K.
    Sunday They'll Make Me a Saint; two scenes
        (In New Directions in Prose and Poetry, Vol. 22)
TOTH, Sandor Somogyi
    Wie Gehts, Junger Mann?
        (In Theater der Zeit, no. 2, Jan. 1974)
TOTHEROH, Dan
    The Breaking of the Calm
        (In his One-Act Plays for Everybody)
    Dark Comet
        (In One-Act Plays for Stage and Study, 9th Series)
    Good Vintage
        (In his One-Act Plays for Everybody)
    The Great Dark
        (In his One-Act Plays for Everybody)
    In the Darkness
        (In his One-Act Plays for Everybody)
    The Kelly Kid (see Norris, Kathleen)
    The Lost Princess
        (In his One-Act Plays for Everybody)
        (In his One-Act Plays for Stage and Study, 6th Series)
    Mirthful Marionettes
        (In his One-Act Plays for Everybody)
    Pearls
        (In More One-Act Plays by Modern Authors)
        (In his One-Act Plays for Everybody)
    The Stolen Prince
        (In his One-Act Plays for Everybody)

A Tune of a Tune
    (In his <u>One-Act Plays for Everybody</u>)
    (In <u>One-Act Plays for Stage and Study</u>, 4th Series)
While the Mushrooms Bubble
    (In his <u>One-Act Plays for Everybody</u>)
The Widdy's Mite
    (In his <u>One-Act Plays for Everybody</u>)
    (In <u>One-Act Plays for Stage and Study</u>, 5th Series)
A Touch of Brightness (see Sharma, Partap)
Touch Wood (see Smith, Dorothy G.)
Touched (see Lowe, Stephen)
Tour (see McNally, Terrence)
Tour à Terre (see Salacrou, Armand)
Le Tournant (see Dorin, Françoise)
TOURNEUE, Maurice
    Volpone; d'après la pièce de Jules Romains, "L'Amour de l'Or"
       (In <u>L'Avant-Scène Cinéma,</u> no. 189, June 15, 1977)
Toussaint Louverture (see Lamartine, Alphonse)
Tout Contre un Petit Bois (see Ribes, Jean-Michel)
Tout un Dimanche Ensemble... (see Boucher, Pierre)
The Tower (see Hofmannsthal, Hugo von H.)
The Tower (see Weiss, Peter)
The Tower of Babel; a puppet show (see Goodman, Paul)
The Town-Fop; or, Sir Timothy Tawdrey (see Behn, Mrs. Aphra)
Town Hall Tonight; radio script (see Allen, Fred)
The Townland of Tamney (see MacManus, Seumas)
TOWNLEY, James, 1714-1778
    High Life Below Stairs, by James Townley and David Garrick
       (In <u>A Collection of the Most Esteemed Farces...</u>, Vol. 1)
       (In <u>The Drama</u>, Vol. 16)
       (In <u>Garrick's Dramatic Works</u>, Vol. 3)
The Toy Cart (see Südraka, Rajah of Magadha)
The Toy-Shop (see Dodsley, Robert)
Toys in the Attic (see Hellman, Lillian)
The Trafalgar Coup (see Vitrac, Roger)
Traffic Signals (see Drummond, Alexander M.)
El Tragaluz (see Buero Vallejo, Antonio)
Tragedia ... (see Kyd, Thomas)
Tragedia Indiano (see Baralt, Luis A.)
The Tragedy of Alphonsus Emperor of Germany (see Chapman, George)
The Tragedy of Caesar and Pompey (see Chapman, George)
The Tragedy of Chabot Admiral of France (see Chapman, George)
The Tragedy of Charles Duke of Byron (see Chapman, George)
The Tragedy of Mustapha (see Boyle, Robert)
The Tragedy of Nan (see Masefield, John)
The Tragedy of Nero, Emperour of Rome (see Lee, Nathaniel)
The Tragedy of Ovid (see Cokayne, Sir Aston)
The Tragedy of Pompey the Great (see Masefield, John)
The Tragedye of Solyman and Perseda (see Kyd, Thomas)
Tragic Christening (see Lisle, William de)
A Tragic Role (see Chekhov, Anton)
The Tragical History of Dr. Faustus (see Marlowe, Christopher)

Tragicomedia de Amadis de Gaula (see Vincente, Gill)
Trail Horse No. 1 (Many Loves) (see Williams, William Carlos)
Train to H ... (see Bellido, José M.)
TRAINER, David
    Mr. Curator's Proposal
       (In Best Short Plays of 1975)
The Traitor (see Shirley, James)
Le Trajet (see Kattan, Naim)
Traktor (see Müller, Heiner)
Trampa sin Salida (see Verdugo, Jaime)
Trans-Canada Highway (see Tallman, James)
Transcending (see Cregan, David)
A Transfer of Property (see Reed, Mark)
The Transfiguration of Benno Blimpie (see Innaurato, Albert)
The Transformed Peasant (see Holberg, Ludvig von)
Un Tranvia Llamado Deseo (see Williams, Tennessee)
The Trap (see Salerno, Henry F.)
The Trap of Solid Gold; television script (see Violett, Ellen M.)
Trappolin (see Cokayne, Sir Aston)
Traumstück (see Kraus, Karl)
Traumtheater (see Kraus, Karl)
The Traveling Lady (see Foote, Horton)
Traveller Without Luggage (see Anouilh, Jean)
The Travelling Man (see Gregory, Isabella A.)
Travesties (see Stoppard, Tom)
El Travieso Jimmy (see Felipe, Carlos)
TREASE, Geoffrey
    After the Tempest
       (In Best One-Act Plays of 1938, London)
TREBITSCH, Siegfried, 1869-1956
    Jitta's Atonement; a free adaptation of Siegfried's "Frau Gittas
    Sühne," by Bernard Shaw
       (In Shaw, Collected Plays, Vol. 5)
The Tree Climber (see Al Hakim, Tewfik)
TREMBLAY, Michel, 1943-
    Les Belles Soeurs
       (In Talonplays Series, 1974)
    Bonjour la Bonjour
       (In Talonplays Series, 1975)
    La Duchesse de Langeais
       (In Deux Pièces)
    Forever Yours, Marie-Lou
       (In Talonplays Series, 1975)
    Hosanna
       (In Talonplays Series, 1974)
    En Pièces Détachées
       (In Deux Pièces)
    En Pièces Détachées; text in English
       (In Talonplays Series, 1975)
Les Trente Millions de Gladiator (see Labiche, Eugene)
Les 37 Sous de M. Montandoin (see Labiche, Eugene)
TRENYOV, Konstantin, 1878-1945
    Lyubov Yarovaya
       (In Soviet Scene)

Los Tres Etceteras de Don Simon (see Peman, José M.)
Tres Generales (see Salmon, Raul)
Las Tres Perfectas Casadas (see Rodriguez Alvarez, Alejandro)
Tres Sombreros de Copa (see Mihura, Miguel)
Tres Testigos (see Peman, José M.)
Trespass (see Williams, Emlyn)
TREVES, Luisa
    La Carta de Don Juan
        (In Teatro Neerlandes Contemporaneo)
Trial and Error (see Horne, Kenneth)
Trial by Jury (see Gilbert, William S.)
The Trial of Jean-Baptiste M. (see Gurik, Robert)
The Trial of Joan of Arc at Rouen, 1431 (see Brecht, Bertolt)
The Trial of Lucullus (see Brecht, Bertolt)
Triangle (see Saunders, James)
Le Triangle Immortel (see Evreinov, Nicolas)
A Trick to Catch the Old One (see Middleton, Thomas)
Trick upon Trick; or, The Vintner in the Suds (see Yarrow, Joseph)
The Tricolor Suite (see Preston, Peter S.)
The Tricycle (see Arrabal, Fernando)
Trifles (see Glaspell, Susan)
TRILLING, Ossia
    Ka Mountain and Guardenia Terrace
        (In The Drama Review, Vol. 17, no. 2, June 1973)
La Trilogia del Matrimonio: Judit; Un Drama Corriente; La Puerta
    (see Steiner, Rolando)
Trilogie des Wiedersehens (see Strauss, Botho)
Trio (see Saunders, James)
Le Triomphe de l'Amour (see Marivaux, Pierre C.)
Le Triomphe de Plutus (see Marivaux, Pierre C.)
The Trip (see Harris, Clarence)
A Trip for Mrs. Taylor (see Garner, Hugh)
Trip to Bountiful (see Foote, Horton)
A Trip to Calais (see Foote, Samuel)
A Trip to Chinatown (see Hoyt, Charles H.)
A Trip to Czardis (see Granberry, Edwin)
A Trip to Czardis; adapted for radio (see Hart, Elizabeth)
A Trip to Jubliee (see Farquhar, George. The Constant Couple; or,
    A Trip to Jubilee, and Sir Henry Wildair; being a sequel to A
    Trip to Jubilee)
A Trip to Niagara; or, Travellers in America (see Dunlap, William)
A Trip to Scarborough (see Sheridan, Richard Brinsley)
A Trip to Scotland (see Whitehead, William)
Tripe (see Micallef, Lexie)
Triple-A Plowed Under (see Living Newspaper. Editorial Staff)
Tripstych: Three Short Plays for Dummies (see Gerould, Daniel)
TRISTAN L'HERMITE, François, 1601-1655
    La Mariane (Mariamne)
        (In The Chief Rivals of Corneille and Racine)
    La Mort de Sénèque (The Death of Seneca)
        (In More Plays by Rivals of Corneille and Racine)
    Osman
        (In More Plays by Rivals of Corneille and Racine)

Tristant und Isald (see Sachs, Hans)
Tritte (see Beckett, Samuel)
Der Triumph der Zeit (see Hofmannsthal, Hugo von H.)
The Triumph of Beauty (see Shirley, James)
The Triumph of Peace (see Shirley, James)
The Triumph of the Egg (see Anderson, Sherwood)
Le Triumvirat (see Crebillon, Prosper J.)
Trixie & Baba (see Antrobus, John)
Troilus and Cressida; or, Truth Found Too Late (see Dryden, John)
Trois Couverts (see Oulmont, Charles)
Trois Mois de Prison (see Vildrac, Charles)
The Trojan Women; radio script (see Euripides)
Trompette (see Calvet, Aldo)
Trouble in Mind (see Childress, Alice)
The Trouble with Reason (see Griboyedov, Aleksandr S.)
Trouble with Tribbles; television script (see Gerrold, David)
El Trovador (see Gutierrez, Antonio G.)
Trovarsi (see Pirandello, Luigi)
TROW, George Swift
    Savages; a film by James Ivory from a screenplay by George
      Swift Trow and Michael Donoghue
        (In Savages & Shakespeare Wallah)
True (see Purdy, James)
The True-Born Irishman (see Macklin, Charles)
A True Hero: Melodrama (see Howells, William Dean)
The True History of Squire Jonathan and His Unfortunate Treasure
    (see Arden, John)
The True Widow (see Shadwell, Thomas)
Die Trümmer des Gewissens (see Jahnn, Hans H.)
TRUFFAUT, François, 1932-
    Bed and Board; screenplay
        (In The Adventures of Antoine Doinel)
        (In 4 by Truffaut)
    Day for Night; screenplay
        (In Evergreen Filmscript Series, 1975)
    The 400 Blows; screenplay
        (In The Adventures of Antoine Doinel)
        (In 4 by Truffaut)
    L'Histoire d'Adele H.; screenplay; avec la collaboration de Fran-
      ces V. Guille, auteur du libre "Le Journal d'Adele Hugo"
        (In L'Avant-Scène Cinéma, no. 165, Jan. 1976)
    Love at Twenty; screenplay
        (In The Adventures of Antoine Doinel)
        (In 4 by Truffaut)
    Stolen Kisses; screenplay
        (In The Adventures of Antoine Doinel)
        (In 4 by Truffaut)
    The Story of Adele H.; screenplay
        (In Grove Press Filmscript Series, 1976)
    The Wild Child; screenplay for the film by François Truffaut
      and Jean Gruault
        (A Pocket Books Screenplay, 1973)

Truman, Harry S, Pres. U.S., 1884-1972
    "Give 'em Hell, Harry," play presented on stage and screen,
      about Harry S Truman
        (An Avon Books Playscript, 1976)
The Trumpet and the Trumpeter (see Daudet, Alphonse)
Trumpets and Drums (see Brecht, Bertolt)
The Truth (see Fitch, Clyde)
The Truth About Blayds (see Milne, Alan A.)
TRZEBINSKI, Andrzej, 1922-1943
    To Pick Up the Rose
        (In Twentieth-Century Polish Avant-Garde Drama)
Tsar Fyodor Ivanovich (see Tolstoi, Aleksiei K.)
Tschapai ... Tschapai ... Tschapajew (see Hawemann, Horst)
Ts'ui P'ing Shan (Jade Screen Mountain)
        (In Famous Chinese Plays)
TUCHOLSKY, Kurt
    Christopher Columbus; by Kurt Tucholsky and Walter Hasenclever
        (In German Drama Between the Wars)
Tueur sans Gages (see Ionesco, Eugene)
Tuglakh (see Karnad, Girish)
Tullus Hostilius, 3rd legendary king of early Romans, 673-641 B.C.
    *Horace (The Horatii) (see Corneille, Pierre)
Tumble-Down Dick; or, Phaeton in the Suds (see Fielding, Henry)
The Tumult and the Shouting (see Pawley, Thomas)
Il Tumulto dei Ciompi (see Dursi, Massimo)
A Tune of a Tune (see Totheroh, Dan)
The Tunes of Chicken Little (see Gordon, Robert)
T'ung Wang Chen (The Brass Net Plan)
        (In Famous Chinese Plays)
TUOTTI, Joseph Dolan
    Big Time Buck White
        (In Evergreen Playscript Series, 1969)
TUR, Leonid Davidovich, 1905-
    Smoke of the Fatherland, by the Tur Brothers and L. Sheinin
        (In Seven Soviet Plays)
TUR, Peter Davidovich, 1907-
    Smoke of the Fatherland (see Tur, Leonid D.)
Turandot, Prinzessin von China (see Gozzi, Carlo)
Turcaret (see Lesage, Alain-Rene)
TURGENEV, Ivan Sergeyevich, 1818-1883
    An Amicable Settlement
        (In The Plays of Turgenev, Vol. 2)
    The Bachelor
        (In The Plays of Turgenev, Vol. 1)
    Broke
        (In The Plays of Turgenev, Vol. 1)
    Carelessness
        (In The Plays of Turgenev, Vol. 1)
    A Conversation on the Highway
        (In The Plays of Turgenev, Vol. 2)
    The Country Woman
        (In The Plays of Turgenev, Vol. 2)

An Evening in Sorrento
   (In The Plays of Turgenev, Vol. 2)
The Family Charge
   (In The Plays of Turgenev, Vol. 1)
A Month in the Country
   (In Famous Plays of 1937)
   (In Masterpieces of the Modern Russian Theatre)
   (In Masterpieces of the Russian Drama, Vol. 1)
   (In The Plays of Turgenev, Vol. 2)
A Month in the Country, translated by Ariadne Nicolaeff
   (In Plays of the Year, Vol. 45, 1976)
Where It Is Thin, There It Breaks
   (In The Plays of Turgenev, Vol. 1)
TURKISH THEATRE. KARAGÖZ
The Bloody Poplar
   (In The Turkish Theatre)
A Picnic to Ialova
   (In The Turkish Theatre)
TURKISH THEATRE. MEDDAH
A Dream of a Türk
   (In The Turkish Theatre)
Hamal the Porter
   (In The Turkish Theatre)
The Quest of the Bride
   (In The Turkish Theatre)
The Seven Dull-Hearing Ones
   (In The Turkish Theatre)
TURKISH THEATRE. ORTA OIUNU
The Sorcery
   (In The Turkish Theatre)
Der Turm (see Hofmannsthal, Hugo von H.)
The Turn of the Screw (see Radical Arts Troupe, University of Cali-
   fornia, Davis)
TURNBALL, Margaret
At the Mitre
   (In One-Act Plays for Stage and Study, 8th Series)
TURNER, Lloyd
Archie and the Computer; television script for an episode in "All
   in the Family, " by Lloyd Turner and Gordon Mitchell, and Don
   Nicholl
   (In Samuel French's Tandem Library Series)
Turner, Nat, 1800-1831
   *Nat Turner (see Edmonds, Randolph)
Turning the Earth (see The Living Theatre)
The Turnpike Gate (see Knight, Thomas)
The Tutor (see Brecht, Bertolt)
Tutto per Bene (see Pirandello, Luigi)
Twain, Mark (pseud.) (see Clemens, Samuel Langhorne)
Twelve Angry Men; television script (see Rose, Reginald)
Twelve Months (see Marshak, Samuel Y.)
The Twelve-Pound Look (see Barrie, James M.)
Twentieth Century (see Hecht, Ben)
Twenty Five (see Gregory, Isabella A.)

Uber die Kraft (see Bjørnson, Bjørnstjerne)
Ubu Cocu (Ubu Cuckolded) (see Jarry, Alfred)
Ubu, Colonialist (see Jarry, Alfred)
Ubu Enchained (see Jarry, Alfred)
Ubu Rex (Ubu Roi) (see Jarry, Alfred)
UConn GE Varsity Quiz (see Radical Arts Troupe, University of
    Connecticut)
UDALL, Nicholas, 1505-1556
    Ralph Roister Doister
        (In The Drama, Vol. 13)
Udienza (see Havel, Václav)
UDOFF, Yale M.
    A Gun Play
        (In Playwrights for Tomorrow, Vol. 8)
    Shade
        (In Mademoiselle, Vol. 74, April 1972)
Uh, Uh; But How Do It Free Us? (see Sanchez, Sonia)
U'l a U'i, Beauty Meets Beauty (see Charlot, Jean)
ULISES, Estrella
    Apenas de Este Mundo
        (In Teatro Ecuatoriano Contemporaneo, Vol. 2)
A Ultima Lingada (see Alencar Pimentel, Altimar de)
La Ultima Noche con Laura (see Inclan, Federico S.)
La Ultima Puerta (see Usigli, Rudolfo)
The Ultimate Pendejada (see Marcus, Ysidro, R.)
El Ultimo Capitulo (see Othon, Manuel J.)
UNAMUNO Y JUGO, Don Miguel, 1864-1936
    Sombras de Sueño
        (In Teatro Inquieto Español)
The Unattainable (see Maugham, William Somerset)
Die Unbekannte aus der Sein (see Horvath, Odön von)
Uncertain Joy (see Hastings, Charlotte)
Uncle Jimmy (see Gale, Zona)
Uncle Tom's Cabin (see Aiken, George L.)
Uncle Vanya (see Chekhov, Anton)
Uncle's Been Dreaming (see Vollmöller, Karl G.)
Und Wenn du König, und Wenn du Henker Bist (see Nowak, Tadeusz)
Under Milk Wood; screenplay (see Sinclair, Andrew)
Under Plain Cover (see Osborne, John)
Under the Pylon (see Brighouse, Harold)
Under the Sycamore Tree (see Spewack, Samuel)
The Undertaker (see Hawkes, John)
Undertow (see Spence, Eulalie)
The Unexpected Guests (see Howells, William Dean)
The Unexpurgated Memoirs of Bernard Mergendeiler (see Feiffer,
    Jules)
Unfinished Symphony (see Morgan, Albert)
The Unfortunate Lovers (see D'Avenant, Sir William)
The Unicorn from the Stars (see Yeats, William Butler)
Unidentified (see Moore, Eugene W.)
The Universal Gallant; or, The Different Husbands (see Fielding, Henry)
The University Today, 1: The Rise of the University (see Clisham,
    Stephen)

The University Today, 2: The Library (see McMenamin, Elizabeth)
The University Today, 3: The Freshman (see Kelly, Thomas)
The University Today, 4: The University Social Life (see McMenamin, Elizabeth)
The Unknown (see Maugham, William Somerset)
The Unknown Chinaman (see Bernard, Kenneth)
The Unknown General (see Obaldia, Rene de)
The Unknown Hand (see Bax, Clifford)
The Unknown Woman (see Blok, Alexandr A.)
The Unmasked Ball (The Theater of Eternal War) (see Evreinov, Nikolai N.)
The Unnatural Combat (see Massinger, Philip)
Los Unos Vrs. los Otros (see Martinez Queirolo, José)
Unpublished Story (see Levi, Paolo)
The Unreasonable Act of Julian Waterman (see Taylor, Ron)
UNRUH, Fritz von, 1885-1970
    Bismarck; oder, Warum Steht der Soldat Da?
        (In his _Dramen_)
    Bonaparte
        (In his _Dramen_)
    Louis Ferdinand Prinz von Preussen
        (In his _Dramen_)
    Offiziere
        (In his _Dramen_)
    Phaea
        (In his _Dramen_)
Der Unschuldige (see Hochwälder, Fritz)
The Unseen (see Gerstenberg, Alice)
The Unseen Hand (see Shepard, Sam)
UNT, Mati
    Doomsday
        (In _Modern International Drama_, Vol. 10, no. 2, Spring 1977)
Der Untergang des Egoisten Fatzer (see Brecht, Bertolt)
Until Further Notice (see Oyono-Mbia, Guillaume)
Unto Such Glory (see Green, Paul)
Die Unüberwindlichen (see Kraus, Karl)
Die Unvernünftigen Sterben aus (see Handke, Peter)
Uomini Contro; filmscript (see Rosi, Francesco)
L'Uomo dal Fore in Bocca (see Pirandello, Luigi)
L'Uomo di Paglia (see Germi, Pietro)
L'Uomo, la Bestia e la Virtu (see Pirandello, Luigi)
L'Uomo Malato (see Benco, Silvio)
Up She Rises (see Donahue, Patricia M.)
UPDIKE, John, 1932-
    Amor Vincit Omnia ad Nauseam
        (In _Readers Theatre Handbook_)
The Upholsterer; or, What News? (see Murphy, Arthur)
Upstairs Sleeping (see Perr, Harvey)
Uptight (see Grass, Günter)
URETA, Margarita, 1918-
    El Hombre y Su Máscara
        (In _Teatro Mexicano_, 1964)

URSELL, Geoffrey
   The Park
     (In Performing Arts in Canada, Vol. 9, no. 3, Fall 1972)
Ursula Underdog vs. The Money Grabbers; or, Tenant Go Round
   (see Mass Transit Street Theater)
URETA, Margarita, 1918-
   El Señor Perro
     (In Teatro Méxicano del Siglo XX, Vol. 5)
Urvashi (see Kalidasa)
US; The Book of the Royal Shakespeare Theatre Production (see Brook, Peter)
USIGLI, Rudolfo, 1905-
   Aguas Estancadas
     (In his Teatro Completo I)
   Alcestes; trasposición de "Le Misanthrope," de Molière
     (In his Teatro Completo I)
   El Apostol
     (In his Teatro Completo I)
   Buenos Días, Señor Presidente!
     (In Teatro del Volador Serie, 1972)
   Corona de Fuego; Tragedia Antihistórica Americana
     (In his Teatro Completo II)
   Corona de Luz: La Virgen: Comedia Antihistórica
     (In his Teatro Completo II)
     (In Teatro Méxicano del Siglo XX, Vol. 4)
   Corona de Sombra: Pieza Antihistórica
     (In his Teatro Completo II)
   La Critica de "La Mujer No Hace Milagros"
     (In his Teatro Completo I)
   Crown of Light: The Virgin: An Antihistorical Comedy; translated by Thomas Bledsoe
     (In his Two Plays)
   Crown of Shadows: An Antihistorical Play, translated by William F. Stirling
     (An A. Wingate Drama Publication, London, 1946)
   Un Día de Estos ...
     (In his Teatro Completo II)
   La Diadema
     (In his Teatro Completo II)
   Dios, Batdillo y la Mujer
     (In his Teatro Completo II)
   Estado de Secreto
     (In his Teatro Completo I)
   La Exposicion
     (In his Teatro Completo II)
   Falso Drama
     (In his Teatro Completo I)
   La Familia Cena en Casa
     (In his Teatro Completo II)
   Los Fugitivos
     (In his Teatro Completo II)
   La Función de Despedida
     (In his Teatro Completo II)
   El Gesticulador

(In his Teatro Completo I)
(In Teatro Méxicano Contemporaneo)
(In Teatro Méxicano del Siglo XX, Vol. 2)
Jano es una Muchacha
    (In his Teatro Completo II)
Las Madres
    (In his Teatro Completo II)
Medio Tono
    (In his Teatro Completo I)
Mientras Anemos
    (In his Teatro Completo I)
La Mujer No Hace Milagros
    (In his Teatro Completo I)
El Niño y la Niebla
    (In his Teatro Completo I)
Noche de Estio
    (In his Teatro Completo I)
One of These Days: A Nonpolitical Fantasy, translated by Thomas Bledsoe
    (In his Two Plays)
Otra Primavera
    (In his Teatro Completo I)
El Presidente y el Ideal
    (In his Teatro Completo I)
4 Chemins 4
    (In his Teatro Completo I)
Sueño de Día
    (In his Teatro Completo II)
La Ultima Puerta
    (In his Teatro Completo I)
Vacaciones I & II
    (In his Teatro Completo II)
Vacaciones II
    (In 12 Obras en un Acto)
Usted Puede Ser un Asesino (see Paso, Alfonso)
Usted Tambien Podra Disfrutar de Ella (see Diosdado, Ana)
USTINOV, Lev
    The City Without Love: A Fantasy. (Gorod Bez Liubvi)
    (In Russian Plays for Young Audiences)
USTINOV, Peter, 1921-
    El Amor de los Cuatro Coroneles
    (In Teatro Ingles Contemporaneo)
    Beyond
    (In his Five Plays)
    The Love of Four Colonels
    (In his Five Plays)
    The Moment of Truth
    (In his Five Plays)
    No Sign of the Dove
    (In his Five Plays)
    Romanoff and Juliet
    (In his Five Plays)
L'Utilité de la Douleur (see Mace, Jean)
Utopia, Limited; or, The Flowers of Progress (see Gilbert, William S.)

Vacaciones I & II (see Usigli, Rudolfo)
VADIM, Roger (full name Roger Vadim Plemiannikov), 1928-
    Les Liaisons Dangereuses; screenplay (see Vailland, Roger)
    Metzengerstein; screenplay based on the story by Edgar Allan
    Poe; an episode from the film "Histoires Extraordinaires, "
    scripted and directed by Roger Vadim
      (In Dal Soggetto al Film Series, no. 37, 1968)
Vaeingerne i Miklagard (see Oehlenschläger, Adam G.)
Vaghe Stelle dell'Orsa . . . (see Visconti, Luchino)
Vailland, Roger, 1907-1965
    Les Liaisons Dangereuses; screenplay by Roger Vailland, Roger
    Vadim and Claude Brulé, film directed by Roger Vadim, in-
    spired by the novel by Choderlos Laclos
      (A Ballantine Books Screenplay, 1962)
VAJDA, Ladislaus, 1906-
    The Threepenny Opera; screenplay (see Lania, Leo)
VALDEZ, Luis M.
    Bernabé
      (In Contemporary Chicano Theatre)
    La Conquista de México
      (In Actos)
    Las Dos Caras del Patroncito
      (In Actos)
    Huelguistas
      (In Actos)
    The Militants
      (In Actos)
    No Saco Nada de la Escuela
      (In Actos)
    Quinta Temporada, by Luis Valdez and El Teatro Campesino
      (In Actos)
      (In Guerilla Street Theater)
    Solsado Razo
      (In Actos)
    Los Vendidos, by Luis Valdez and El Teatro Campesino
      (In Actos)
      (In Guerilla Street Theater)
    Vietnam Campesino, by Luis Valdez and El Teatro Campesino
      (In Actos)
      (In Guerilla Street Theater)
VALDIVIELSO, José de, 1560-1738
    The Bandit Queen
      (In Three Spanish Sacramental Plays)
Valentine, Saint, d. c. 270 A. D.
    *Saint Valentin (see Miracles de Nostra Dame par Personnages)
Valentinian (see Fletcher, John)
VALERY, Paul, 1871-1945
    L'Ame et la Danse
      (In his Oeuvres II)
    Amphion
      (In his Oeuvres I)
    Amphion; text in English
      (In his Collected Works, Vol. 3: Plays)

Cantate du Narcisse
  (In his Oeuvres I)
Dialogue de l'Arbre
  (In his Oeuvres II)
Eupalinos; ou, L'Architecte
  (In his Oeuvres II)
Lust, La Demoiselle de Cristal ("Mon Faust")
  (In his Oeuvres II)
Luste; or, The Crystal Girl; both French and English texts are
  given
  (In his Collected Works, Vol. 3: Plays)
Monsieur Teste, d'après l'oeuvre de Paul Valery, adaptation de
  Pierre Franck
  (In L'Avant-Scène Théâtre, no. 558, Feb. 15, 1975)
The Narcissus Cantata; both French and English texts are given
  (In his Collected Works, Vol. 3: Plays)
The Only One; or, The Curses of the Cosmos; both French and
  English texts are given
  (In his Collected Works, Vol. 3: Plays)
Sémiramis; both French and English texts are given
  (In his Collected Works, Vol. 3: Plays)
Le Solitaire; ou, Les Malédictions d'Univers ("Mon Faust")
  (In his Oeuvres II)
VALLE-INCLAN, Ramon del, 1866-1936
Divinas Palabras
  (In Teatro Selecto de Ramon del Valle-Inclan)
Divine Words
  (In Modern Spanish Theatre)
Farsa Infantil de la Cabeza del Dragon
  (In Teatro Selecto de Ramon del Valle-Inclan)
Farsa y Licencia de la Reina Castiza
  (In Teatro Selecto de Ramon del Valle-Inclan)
Lichter der Boheme
  (In Theater Heute, no. 6, June 1974)
Luces de Bohemia
  (In Clásicos Castellanos, Vol. 180)
Romance de Lobos
  (In Teatro Español, 1970-71)
  (In Teatro Selecto de Ramon del Valle-Inclan)
La Rosa di Carta
  (In Sipario, no. 314, July 1972)
Vallejo, Antonio Buero (see Buero Vallejo, Antonio)
La Valse des Toréadors (see Anouilh, Jean)
Il Vampiro di Uppsala (see Sastre, Alfonso)
VANBRUGH, Sir John, 1664-1726
Aesop, pts. 1 & 2
  (In his Plays, Vol. 1)
The Confederacy
  (In The London Stage, Vol. 3)
  (In his Plays, Vol. 2)
The Country House
  (In his Plays, Vol. 2)

The False Friend
  (In his Plays, Vol. 1)
A Journey to London
  (In his Plays, Vol. 2)
Lovers' Quarrels
  (In The London Stage, Vol. 3)
The Mistake, by John Vanbrugh and Thomas Betterton, adapted
  from Molière's "Dépit Amoureux"
  (In his Plays, Vol. 1)
  (In Plays from Molière)
The Provok'd Husband, completed by Colley Cibber
  (In The Drama, Vol. 15)
  (In his Plays, Vol. 2)
The Provok'd Wife
  (In British Plays from the Restoration to 1820, Vol. 1)
  (In The London Stage, Vol. 3)
  (In his Plays, Vol. 1)
  (In Restoration Comedy, Vol. 3)
The Relapse; or, Virtue in Danger
  (In his Plays, Vol. 1)
  (In Plays of the Restoration and 18th Century)
  (In Restoration Comedy, Vol. 3)
**A Trip to Scarborough (see Sheridan, Richard Brinsley)
VANCINI, Florestano, 1926-
  La Banda Casaroli
  (In Dal Soggetto al Film Series, no. 24, 1962)
VAN DER VEER, Ethel
  As the Tumbrils Pass, by Ethel Van der Veer and Franklyn Bi-
  gelow
  (In One-Act Plays for Stage and Study, 7th Series)
Babouscka
  (In One-Act Plays for Stage and Study, 5th Series)
The Chalk Circle (Anon.), translated by Ethel Van der Veer
  (In World Drama, Vol. 1)
The Emperor's Doll, by Ethel Van der Veer and Franklyn Bi-
  gelow; based upon a legend of old Japan and done after the Ja-
  panese manner
  (In One-Act Plays for Stage and Study, 8th Series)
The Feast of Barking Women
  (In One-Act Plays for Stage and Study, 9th Series)
Saint Cyprian and the Devil
  (In One-Act Plays for Stage and Study, 6th Series)
VAN DRUTEN, John, 1901-1957
  **Cabaret (see Kander, John)
  Flowers of the Forest
  (In Famous Plays of 1934-35)
  I Remember Mama; adapted from Kathryn Forbes' "Mama's Bank
  Account"
  (In Eight American Ethnic Plays)
Il Vangelo Secondo Matteo ("The Gospel According to St. Matthew")
  (see Pasolini, Pier P.)
Vanilla Crescents (see Ingrisch, Lotte)

VAN ITALLIE, Jean-Claude, 1935
    Almost Like Being
        (In his American Hurrah & Other Plays)
    American Hurrah
        (In his American Hurrah & Other Plays)
        (In Contemporary Drama: 13 Plays)
    Eat Cake!
        (In Performance, Vol. 1, no. 5, Mar./Apr. 1973)
    A Fable
        (In his American Hurrah & Other Plays)
        (In Performing Arts Journal, Vol. 1, no. 3, Winter 1977)
    The Hunter and the Bird
        (In his American Hurrah & Other Plays)
    Motel
        (In The Off Off Broadway Book)
    Motel: A Masque for Three Dolls
        (In The Disinherited: Plays)
    Motel from American Hurrah
        (In Contact with Drama)
    The Serpent
        (In his American Hurrah & Other Plays)
        (In The Great American Life Show)
    Thoughts on the Instant of Greeting a Friend on the Street; by
        Jean-Claude Van Itallie and Sharon Thie
        (In Collision Course)
VAN PEEBLES, Melvin
    Sweet Sweetback's Baadasssss; screenplay, written and directed
        by Melvin Van Peebles
        (A Lancer Books Screenplay, 1971)
Vasco (see Schehade, Georges)
Vasco Nuñez de Balboa (see Gonzalez Bocanegra, Francisco)
Vasco Nuñez de Balboa (see Tapia y Rivera, Alejandro)
VASILICO, Giuliano, 1940-
    Le 120 Giornate di Sodoma; dal romanzo del Marchese De Sade
        (In Sipario, no. 324, May 1973)
Vassa Zheleznova (Mother) (see Gor'kii, Maksim)
Vatzlav (see Mrozek, Slawomir)
VAUTHIER, Jean, 1910-
    Capitane Bada
        (In Le Théâtre d'Aujourd'hui)
    The Character Against Himself
        (In Contemporary French Theater)
    Le Personnage Combattant
        (In Le Théâtre d'Aujourd'hui)
Vautrin (see Balzac, Honoré de)
VEBER, Pierre, 1869-1942
    Happiness
        (In Modern One-Act Plays from the French)
VEGA CARPIO, Lope Felix de, 1562-1635
    The Dog in the Manger
        (In The Drama, Vol. 6)
    For Our Sake
        (In Three Spanish Sacramental Plays)

Vernissage (see Havel, Václav)
Véronique (see O'Hara, John)
Le Verre d'Eau, ou Les Effets et les Causes (see Scribe, Augustin-
    Eugène)
Die Versuchung (see Kaiser, Georg)
Vertical Mobility (see Sophia = (Wisdom): Part 4 (see Foreman,
    Richard)
La Vertu des Chattes (see Laurendeau, André)
Very Like a Whale (see Osborne, John)
A Very Woman; or, The Prince of Tarent (see Massinger, Philip)
VESAAS, Tarjei
    The Bleaching Yard
        (In Modern Nordic Plays: Norway)
Vespasian (Titus Flavius Sabinus Vespasianus), Emperor of Rome,
    9-79 A. D.
    *The Destruction of Jerusalem, pts 1 & 2 (see Crowne, John)
Vestire Gli Ignudi (see Pirandello, Luigi)
La Veuve (see Corneille, Pierre)
Les Veuves (see Billetdoux, François)
Via Crucis (see Gamboa, José J.)
La Viaccia (see Bolognini, Mauro)
Un Viaje en la Noche (see Christiansen, Sigurd)
VIAN, Boris, 1920-1959
    Les Bâtisseurs d'Empire
        (In Le Théâtre d'Aujourd'hui)
        (In his Théâtre I)
    Le Chasseur Français
        (In his Théâtre Inédit)
    Le Dernier des Métiers
        (In his Théâtre I)
    The Empire Builders
        (In Evergreen Playscript Series, 1967)
    L'Equarrissage pour Tous
        (In his Théâtre I)
    Le Goûter des Généraux
        (In Le Théâtre d'Aujourd'hui)
        (In his Théâtre I)
    The Knacker's ABC: A Para-Military Vaudeville in One Long
    Act
        (In Grove Evergreen Playscript Series, 1968)
    Mood Indigo
        (In Grove Evergreen Playscript Series, 1968)
    Série Blême
        (In his Théâtre Inédit)
    Tête de Méduse
        (In his Théâtre Inédit)
VIAN, Theophile de, 1590-1626
    Les Amours Tragique de Pyrame et Thisbé
        (In Théâtre du XVIIᵉ Siècle, Vol. 1)
VIANA, Oduvaldo
    Cuatro Cuadras de Tierra
        (In El Teatro Actual Latinoamericano)

Vibrations (see Eveling, Stanley)
The Vice President (see Schull, Joseph)
VICENTE, Gill, 1470-1536
    Auto de la Barca de la Gloria
        (In Clásicos Castellanos, Vol. 156)
    Auto de la Sibila Casandra
        (In Clásicos Castellanos, Vol. 156)
    Auto de la Visitación
        (In Clásicos Castellanos, Vol. 156)
    Auto de las Gitanas
        (In Clásicos Castellanos, Vol. 156)
    Auto de los Cuatro Tiempos
        (In Clásicos Castellanos, Vol. 156)
    Auto de los Reyes Magos
        (In Clásicos Castellanos, Vol. 156)
    Auto de San Martin
        (In Clásicos Castellanos, Vol. 156)
    Auto Pastoril Castellano
        (In Clásicos Castellanos, Vol. 156)
    Comedia del Viudo
        (In Clásicos Castellanos, Vol. 156)
    Tragicomedia de Amadis de Gaula
        (In Clásicos Castellanos, Vol. 156)
Viceroy Sarah (see Ginsbury, Norman)
Vicky (see Woods, Grahame)
Victimes du Devoir (see Ionesco, Eugene)
Victims (see Havard, Lezley)
Victims of Duty (see Ionesco, Eugene)
Victor (see Vitrac, Roger)
Victor Amadeus II, 1st King of Sardinia, 1666-1732
    *King Victor and King Charles (see Browning, Robert)
Victoria, Queen of Great Britain, 1819-1901
    *Royal Favour (see Housman, Laurence)
Victory at Trafalgar (see Hickey, E. and D. E.)
La Vida en un Hilo (see Neville, Edgar)
La Vida Es Sueño (see Calderon de la Barca, Pedro)
VIDAL, Gore, 1925-
    The Best Man; filmscript by Gore Vidal, directed by Franklin
        Schaffner
        (In Film Scripts Four)
    Le Gaucher (see Penn, Arthur)
    Visit to a Small Planet
        (In The Mentor Book of Short Plays)
        (In 10 Short Plays)
VIDOR, Charles
    An Occurrence at Owl Creek Bridge, screenplay adapted and
        directed by Charles Vidor from the story by Ambrose Bierce
        (In Dickenson Literature and Film Series: From Fiction to
          Film: Ambrose Bierce's "An Occurrence at Owl Creek
          Bridge")
VIDOR, King, 1894-
    Guerra e Pace; screenplay
        (In Dal Soggetto al Film Series, no. 3, 1955)

Notre Pain Quotidien; titre original "Our Daily Bread" d'après
un sujet de King Vidor, dialogue Joseph L. Mankiewicz
  (In L'Avant-Scène Cinéma, no. 187, May 1, 1977)
Une Vie Difficile; filmscript (see Risi, Dino)
La Vie en Rose (see Salacrou, Armand)
Une Vie Secrète (see Lenormand, Henri R.)
Le Vieil Homme (see Porto-Riche, Georges de)
VIEIRA, Cesar
    "O Evangelho Segundo Zebedeu"
        (In Revista de Teatro, no. 404, March-April 1975)
    Rei Momo
        (In Revista de Teatro, no. 411, May/June 1976)
El Viejo y las Niñas (see Peman, José M.)
Viens Chez Moi J'Habite Chez une Copine (see Rego, Luis)
Vient de Paraître (see Bourdet, Edouard)
Der Vierzehnte Somme (see Kerndl, Rainer)
Vietnam Campesino (see Valdez, Luis)
A Vietnamese Wedding (see Fornes, Maria I.)
A View from the Bridge (see Miller, Arthur)
VIGNY, Alfred Victor, comte de, 1797-1863
    Chatterton; text in French
        (In his Oeuvres Complètes I)
    Fragments de Romeo et Juliette
        (In his Oeuvres Complètes I)
    La Maréchale d'Ancre
        (In his Oeuvres Complètes II)
    Le More de Venise
        (In his Oeuvres Complètes I)
    Quitte pour la Peur
        (In his Oeuvres Complètes II)
    Shylock, le Marchand de Venise
        (In his Oeuvres Complètes I)
The Vikings of Helgeland (see Ibsen, Henrik)
Vikramorvacie; or, The Hero and the Nymph (see Kalidasa)
Les Vilains (see Gille, André)
VILALTA, Maruxa, 1932-
    Cuestion de Narices
        (In Teatro Mexicano del Siglo XX, Vol. 5)
        (In Teatro Contemporaneo Hispanoamericano, Vol. 1)
    Number 9
        (In The Best Short Plays 1973)
    Un Pais Feliz
        (In Teatro Mexicano, 1964)
    Together Tonite ...
        (In Modern International Drama, Vol. 6, no. 2, Spring 1973)
VILDRAC, Charles Messager, 1882-
    L'Air du Temps
        (In his Théâtre II)
    The Art of Making Friends
        (In Modern One-Act Plays from the French)
    Michel Auclair
        (In his Théâtre II)

Le Pacquebot Tenacity
(In his Théâtre I)
Le Pèlerin
(In his Théâtre II)
Poucette
(In his Théâtre I)
Trois Mois de Prison
(In his Théâtre I)
Villa, Francisco (Pancho), 1877-1923
*Viva Zapata; screenplay (see Steinbeck, John)
Villa for Sale (see Guitry, Sacha)
The Village School (see Takeda, Izumo)
Village Wooing: A Comedietta for Two Voices (see Shaw, George
Bernard)
VILLASIS ENDARA, Carlos
San Juan de las Manzanas
(In Teatro Ecuatoriano Contemporaneo, Vol. 2)
VILLAURRUTIA, Xavier, 1903-1950
En Qué Piensas?
(In Teatro Mexicano Contemporaneo)
Parece Mentira
(In Teatro Mexicano Contemporaneo)
Sea Usted Breve
(In Teatro Mexicano Contemporaneo)
(In 12 Obras en un Acto)
El Yerro Candente
(In Teatro Mexicano del Siglo XX, Vol. 2)
La Ville (see Caludel, Paul)
La Ville Dont le Prince est un Enfant (see Montherlant, Henry de)
Villiers, George (see Buckingham, George Villiers, 2nd Duke of)
Vina (see Vodanovic, Sergio)
Vincent, François, Paul et les Autres ... (see Sautet, Claude)
Vincent Verkauft ein Bild (see Kaiser, Georg)
VINING, Donald
Delayed Glory
(In 100 Non-Royalty Radio Plays)
I Vinti; filmscript (see Antonioni, Michelangelo)
Violaine la Chevelue (see Zola, Emile)
Violence et Passion; filmscript (see Visconti, Luchino)
The Violet (see Molnar, Ferenc)
VIOLETT, Ellen M.
The Trap of Solid Gold; television script from the story by John
D. MacDonald, ABC, Jan. 4, 1967
(In Electronic Drama)
The Virgin, the Lizard, and the Lamb (see Feldhaus-Weber, Mary)
The Virgin-Martyr (see Massinger, Philip)
The Virgin Unmasked (see Fielding, Henry)
The Virgin Unmask'd (see also Fielding, Henry. The Old Man Taught
Wisdom; or, The Virgin Unmask'd. Miss Lucy in Town; a se-
quel to The Virgin Unmask'd)
Virginia, Daughter of Virginius
*Appius and Virginia (see Webster, John)
*Virginia; text in Italian (see Alfieri, Vittorio)

*Virginia; text in Spanish (see Tamayo y Baus, Manuel)
*Virginius (see Knowles, Ames S.)
Virginia's Letter to Santa Claus (see Yankanin, Frank)
The Virtuoso (see Shadwell, Thomas)
VISAKHA-DATTA, Prince
    The Minister's Seal, ascribed to Prince Visakhadatta
        (In Two Plays from Ancient India)
    The Signet Ring of Rakshasa, by Vishakadatta
        (In Great Sanskrit Plays)
VISCONTI, Luchino, 1906-
    Bellissima
        (In Dal Soggetto al Film Series Retrospettiva, no. 4)
    La Caduta Degli Dei (Götterdämmerung); a cura di Stefano Ron-
    coroni
        (In Dal Soggetto al Film Series, no. 39, 1969)
    Il Gattopardo; screenplay, based on the novel by Giuseppe To-
    masi di Lampedusa
        (In Dal Soggetto al Film Series, no. 29, 1963)
    Gruppo di Famiglia in un Interno
        (In Dal Soggetto al Film Series, no. 51, 1975)
    Il Lavora
        (In Dal Soggetto al Film Series, no. 22, 1962)
    Ludwig
        (In Dal Soggetto al Film Series, no. 47, 1973)
    Le Notti Bianche; screenplay, based on a story by Dostoevsky
        (In Dal Soggetto al Film Series, no. 6, 1957)
    Ossessione; screenplay, based on James Cain's novel "The Post-
    man Always Rings Twice"
        (In Dal Soggetto al Film Series Retrospettiva, no. 4)
    Rocco e i Suoi Fratelli
        (In Dal Soggetto al Film Series, no. 17, 1960)
    Senso; screenplay based on a novella by Camillo Boito
        (In Dal Soggetto al Film Series, no. 2, 1956)
    La Terra Trema (1 e 2 edizione); screenplay based on a story
    by Zavattini
        (In Dal Soggetto al Film Series Retrospettiva, no. 4)
    Vaghe Stelle dell'Orsa ...
        (In Dal Soggetto al Film Series, no. 34, 1965)
    Violence et Passion; titres originaux "Conversation Piece, " "Rup-
    po di Famiglia in un Interno"
        (In L'Avant-Scène Cinéma, no. 159, June 1975)
The Viscount of Blarney (see Clarke, Austin)
The Vise (see Pirandello, Luigi)
Vishakadatta (see Visākha-Datta)
The Vision of Vasavadatta (see Bhasa)
The Visions of Simone Marchard (see Brecht, Bertolt)
Visit to a Small Planet (see Vidal, Gore)
The Visit to the Sepulcher (Anon.)
        (In Medieval Church Music-Dramas)
"Uma Visita" (see Walser, Martin)
Visitation; radio script (see Kanigher, Robert)
La Visite (see Haim, Victor)
Une Visite de Noces (see Dumas, Alexandre, Fils)

Le Visiteur (see Dube, Marcel)
Les Visiteurs du Soir; filmscript (see Prevert, Jacques)
The Visiting House (see Molly, Michael J.)
The Visitor; television script (see Robinson, Thelma)
Visitor from Forest Hills (see Simon, Neil)
La Vista Que No Toco el Timbre (see Calvo-Sotelo, Joaquin)
La Vita Che Ti Diedi (see Pirandello, Luigi)
I Vitelloni (see Fellini, Federico)
VITRAC, Roger
    Médor
       (In his Victor and Other Plays)
    The Mysteries of Love
       (In Modern French Theatre)
    The Trafalgar Coup
       (In his Victor and Other Plays)
    Victor
       (In his Victor and Other Plays)
La Viuda de Padilla (see Martinez de la Rosa, Francisco)
Viva Belzu (see Salmon, Raul)
Viva Zapata; screenplay (see Steinbeck, John)
Les Vivacités du Capitaine Tic (see Labiche, Eugene)
Vivat! Vivat Regina! (see Bolt, Robert)
VODANOVIC, Sergio
    Vina
       (In Teatro Contemporaneo Chileño)
Voice of the Machines (see Parker, Kenneth T.)
The Voice of the People (see Davies, William R.)
The Voice of the Snake (see Halman, Doris F.)
A Voice Through the Door (see Taylor, Peter H.)
Voices of Desire (see Procunier, Edwin R.)
Les Voisins (see Saunders, James)
La Voiture Versee (see Moinaux, Georges)
Des Voix dans la Ville (see Teyssandier, François)
The Volcanic Island (see Bax, Clifford)
Vollkommenheit Sind Zwei; film exposé (see Kaiser, Georg)
VOLLMER, Lula
    Sun-Up
       (In Representative American Plays, 1792-1949)
VOLLMOLLER, Karl Gustav, 1848-1922
    Uncle's Been Dreaming
       (In Eight European Plays)
VOLODIN, Aleksandr Moiseevich (pseud.), 1919-
    Le Due Frecce
       (In Sipario, no. 331, Dec. 1973)
    Five Evenings, translated and adapted by Ariadne Nicolaeff
       (In Minnesota Drama Editions, no. 3)
Volpone; or, The Fox (see Jonson, Ben)
Volpone; screenplay (see Tourneur, Maurice)
VOLTAIRE, François Marie Arouet de, 1694-1778
    Alzaire
       (In his Works: Dramatic Works, Vol. 9, pt. 1)
    Amelia
       (In his Works: Dramatic Works, Vol. 8, pt. 2)

Brutus
    (In his <u>Works:</u> Dramatic Works, Vol. 8, pt. 1)
Caesar
    (In his <u>Works:</u> Dramatic Works, Vol. 10, pt. 1)
**Candide (see Ganzl, Serge)
**Candide; a comic operetta (see Hellman, Lillian)
Catiline
    (In his <u>Works:</u> Dramatic Works, Vol. 9, pt. 1)
Le Fanatisme ou, Mahomet le Prophete
    (In <u>Théâtre de XVIIIe Siècle,</u> Vol. 1)
La Femme Qui a Raison
    (In <u>Théâtre de XVIIIe Siècle,</u> Vol. 1)
Mahomet
    (In <u>The Drama,</u> Vol. 8)
    (In his <u>Works:</u> Dramatic Works, Vol. 8, pt. 2)
Marianne
    (In his <u>Works:</u> Dramatic Works, Vol. 8, pt. 2)
Mérope; based on the works of Hyginus and Maffei
    (In his <u>Works:</u> Dramatic Works, Vol. 8, pt. 1)
Mérope; text in French
    (In <u>Théâtre de XVIIIe Siècle,</u> Vol. 1)
Nanine
    (In his <u>Works:</u> Dramatic Works, Vol. 9, pt. 2)
Nanine; ou, Le Prejuge Vaincu
    (In <u>Théâtre de XVIIIe Siècle,</u> Vol. 1)
**No One's Enemy but His Own (see Murphy, Arthur)
Oedipe
    (In <u>Théâtre du XVIIIe Siècle,</u> Vol. 1)
Oedipus
    (In his <u>Works:</u> Dramatic Works, Vol. 8, pt. 2)
Olympia
    (In his <u>Works:</u> Dramatic Works, Vol. 9, pt. 1)
Orestes
    (In his <u>Works:</u> Dramatic Works, Vol. 9, pt. 1)
The Orphan of China
    (In his <u>Works:</u> Dramatic Works, Vol. 8, pt. 1)
**The Orphan of China; adaptation (see Murphy, Arthur)
Pandora
    (In his <u>Works:</u> Dramatic Works, Vol. 9, pt. 1)
The Prodigal
    (In his <u>Works:</u> Dramatic Works, Vol. 10, pt. 1)
The Prude
    (In his <u>Works:</u> Dramatic Works, Vol. 9, pt. 2)
The Scotch Woman
    (In his <u>Works:</u> Dramatic Works, Vol. 9, pt. 2)
Sémiramis
    (In his <u>Works:</u> Dramatic Works, Vol. 9, pt. 1)
Socrates
    (In <u>The Drama,</u> Vol. 8)
    (In his <u>Works:</u> Dramatic Works, Vol. 8, pt. 2)
The Tatler
    (In his <u>Works:</u> Dramatic Works, Vol. 9, pt. 2)

Zaire
  (In The Chief Rivals of Corneille and Racine)
  (In his Works: Dramatic Works, Vol. 10, pt. 1)
Zaire; text in French
  (In Théâtre du XVIIIe Siècle, Vol. 1)
The Volunteers; or, The Stock-Jobbers (see Shadwell, Thomas)
Von Morgens Bis Mitternachts (see Kaiser, Georg)
VON STERNBERG, Josef, 1894-1969
  The Last Command; screenplay (see Goodrich, John F.)
VON STROHEIM, Erich, 1885-1957
  Greed; a reconstruction of the film following the original screen-
  play; based on the novel "MacTeague" by Frank Norris
  (In The Complete Greed)
VONNEGUT, Kurt, Jr.
  Happy Birthday, Wanda June
  (A Delta Play, 1971)
Vorspiel für ein Puppentheater (see Hofmannsthal, Hugo von H.)
Vorspiel zur Antigone des Sophokles (see Hofmannsthal, Hugo von H.)
The Vortex (see Coward, Noël)
Vortigern (see Ireland, William H.)
The Votary of Wealth (see Holman, Joseph G.)
Vote Communist: An Election Play for Street Performances (see
  Workers Theater, 1930s)
VOULET, Jacqueline
  L'Arret
  (In L'Avant-Scène du Théâtre, no. 514, Mar. 15, 1973)
Voulez-vous Jouer avec Môa? (see Achard, Marcel)
Le Voyage (see Schehade, Georges)
Voyage Autour de Ma Marmite (see Labiche, Eugene)
Le Voyage aux Indes (see Tarabin, Jean S.)
Le Voyage de Monsieur Perrichon (see Labiche, Eugene)
Le Voyage des Comediens; filmscript (see Angelopoulos, Theo)
Le Voyageur sans Bagage (see Anouilh, Jean)
VOYNICH, Mrs. Ethel Lillian (Boole), 1864-1960
  **The Gadfly: or, The Son of the General (see Shaw, George Ber-
  nard)
La Voz (see Naranjo, Carmen)
Vuelta a la Tierra (see Lira, Miguel N.)
VULGARIN M. , Agustin
  Los Negocios Registrados
  (In Teatro Ecuatoriano Contemporaneo, Vol. 2)
VVEDENSKY, Alexander, 1904-1942?
  Christmas at the Ivanovs'
  (In Russia's Lost Literature of the Absurd)

WABEI, Turuk
  Kulubob
  (In Australian Theatre Workshop, no. 3, 1970)
The Wages of War; filmscript (see Clouzot, Henri-Georges)
WAGNER, Richard, 1813-1883
  *Faust; text in German (see Kaiser, Georg)
  L'Or du Rhin
  (In L'Avant-Scène Opéra, nos. 6-7, Nov. -Dec. 1976)

"Uma Visita"
(In <u>Revista de Teatro</u>, numero especial, Dec. 1973)
Walsh (see Pollock, Sharon)
WALSH, Raoul, 1889-
Gentleman Jim; scénario Vincent Lawrence et Horace McCoy
base sur la vie de James J. Corbett et son autobiographie
"The Roar of the Crowd"
(In <u>L'Avant-Scène Cinéma</u>, no. 167, Mar. 1976)
Walt (see Morley, Christopher D.)
WALTER, Eugene, 1874-1941
The Easiest Way
(In <u>Representative Plays by American Dramatists</u>, Vol. 3)
WALTER, Otto F.
The Cat
(In <u>Gambit</u>, Vol. 4, no. 15)
WALTON, Izaak, 1593-1683
**A Piscatorial Eclogue: Vel Isaacus Walton in Novam Scalam
Redivivus (see Geist, Peter von)
The Waltons television script
The Foundling (see McGreevy, John)
The Waltz Invention (Izobretenie Val'sa) (see Nabakov, Vladimir)
Waltz of the Toreadors (see Anouilh, Jean)
WAMPILOW, Alexander
Provinzanekdoten (Original titel: "Provincial 'nye Anekdoty")
(In <u>Theater Heute</u>, no. 4, April 1977)
WANDER, Fred, 1917-
Josua Lässt Grüssen
(In <u>Theater der Zeit</u>, no. 1, 1977)
Wandering (see Wilson, Lanford)
The Wandering Jew (see Hutchins, Maude P.)
The Wandering Scholar from Paradise (see Sachs, Hans)
Wanderlust (see Nicholson, Kenyon)
WANG, Fa
One Big Family, a short stage show by Fa Wang and Ya-nan
Chu
(In <u>Chinese Literature</u>, no. 2, 1973)
WANG, William Howard
The Girl from Kavalla: An Historical Romance
(In <u>100 Non-Royalty Radio Plays</u>)
Wang Hua Mai Fu (Wang Hua Buys a Father)
(In <u>Famous Chinese Plays</u>)
WANG SHU-YUAN
Azalea Mountain (see China Peking Opera Troupe)
Wann Kommst'n Wieder Roter Reiter? (see Medoff, Mark)
The Wanton Countess; screenplay (see Visconti, Luchino. Senso)
War, A Te Deum (see Hauptmann, Carl)
The War Indemnities (see Shaw, George Bernard)
Warbeck, Perkin, Pretender to the Crown of England, 1477?-1534
*Warbeck (see Schiller, Johann C.)
WARD, Douglas Turner, 1930-
Brotherhood
(In <u>Black Drama Anthology</u>)
Day of Absence
(In <u>Best Short Plays of the World Theater</u>, 1968-1973)

        (In <u>Black Theater U.S.A.</u>, 1847-1974)
        (In <u>Blackamerican Literature 1760-Present</u>)
        (In <u>Contemporary Black Drama</u>)
        (In <u>Eight American Ethnic Plays</u>)
        (In his <u>Two Plays</u>)
    Happy Ending
        (In <u>Contemporary Black Drama</u>)
        (In his <u>Two Plays</u>)
WARD, Edmund
    History Doesn't Pay the Rent
        (In <u>The Challengers</u>)
    The Salesmen
        (In <u>The Challengers</u>)
    The Tomorrow Business
        (In <u>The Challengers</u>)
    What About England?
        (In <u>The Challengers</u>)
    Who's Been Eating My Porridge?
        (In <u>The Challengers</u>)
    Whose Law? Whose Order?
        (In <u>The Challengers</u>)
WARD, Monica
    Away From It All
        (In <u>100 Non-Royalty Radio Plays</u>)
WARD, Theodore, 1902-
    Big White Fog
        (In <u>Black Theater U.S.A.</u>, 1847-1974)
    Big White Fog (selection)
        (In <u>The Negro Caravan</u>)
WARHOL, Andy, 1928-
    Blue Movie
        (A <u>Grove Press Filmscript,</u> 1970)
The Warning--A Theme for Linda (see Milner, Ronald)
Warnings (see O'Neill, Eugene)
WARREN, Mrs. Mercy (Otis), 1728-1814
    The Group
        (In <u>Representative Plays by American Dramatists</u>, Vol. 1)
A Warsaw Melody (see Zorin, Leonid G.)
Warwick, Richard Neville, Earl of, 1428-1471
    *L'Alouette (see Anouilh, Jean)
Was He Anyone? (see Simpson, Norman F.)
Washington, George, Pres. U.S., 1732-1799
    *Daniel Webster: Eighteen in America (see Stein, Gertrude)
    *The First President (see Williams, William Carlos)
    *Mount Vernon Interlude (see Meyer, Lewis)
    *Valley Forge (see Anderson, Maxwell)
    *The Widow and the Colonel (see Owens, Rochelle)
Washington, Martha Dandridge (Custis), 1731-1802
    *The First President (see Williams, William Carlos)
    *The Widow and the Colonel (see Owens, Rochelle)
The Washtub (Le Cuvier) (Anon.)
        (In <u>Five Comedies of Medieval France</u>)

WASLEY, Richard
    The Past Is Past
        (In Best Short Plays of 1975)
The Wasps (see Aristophanes)
WASSERMAN, Dale
    Elisha and the Long Knives, NBC Kraft Television Theatre script
        by Dale Wasserman and Jack Balch, Feb. 4, 1954
        (In Top TV Shows of the Year, 1954-55)
    Man of La Mancha (see Leigh, Mitch)
Watch It Come Down (see Osborne, John)
Watch on the Rhine (see Hellman, Lillian)
The Water Baby (see Raban, Jonathan)
The Water Hen (see Witkiewicz, Stanislaw I.)
Water Upon Fire (see Morselli, Ercole L.)
WATERHOUSE, Keith, 1929-
    Qui Est Qui? une comédie de Keith Waterhouse et Willis Hall;
        adaptation de Albert Husson
        (In L'Avant-Scène Théatre, no. 608, Apr. 15, 1977)
    Who's Who?
        (In Plays and Players, Vol. 20, no. 12, Sept. 1973)
The Waterman (see Dibdin, Charles, The Elder)
WATKYN, Arthur
    For Better, for Worse
        (In Plays of the Year, Vol. 8, 1952/53)
    Not in the Book
        (In Plays of the Year, Vol. 17, 1957/58)
WATSON, Harmon C. , 1943-
    Those Golden Gates Fall Down
        (In Black Insights)
WATTS, William
    The Story of Silent Night
        (In 100 Non-Royalty Radio Plays)
The Wax Museum (see Hawkes, John)
Waxworks (see Molnar, Ferenc)
The Way It Was (see O'Hara, John)
The Way of the World (see Congreve, William)
A Way Out (see Frost, Robert)
The Way Out (see Giorloff, Ruth)
The Way to Keep Him (see Murphy, Arthur)
WAYNE, Anthony
    Small Town Editor; a play edited for radio
        (In On the Air: 15 Plays for Broadcast)
Ways and Means (see Colman, George, The Younger)
We Are God (see Canton, Wilberto)
We Are the History of the U.S. (see Wheatcroft, John)
We Are the Rising Wing; radio script (see Lechlitner, Ruth)
We Become a Nation; radio script (see Schoenfeld, Bernard)
We Can't All Be Martin Luther King (see Nkosi, Lewis)
We Find the Bunyip (see Mathew, Ray)
We Need Another Man (see Press, Steve)
We Own the Night (see Garrett, Jimmy)
We Three, You and I (see Greenland, Bill)
The Weakest Link (see Ranck, Carty)

Pandora's Box
(In his <u>The Lulu Plays and Other Sex Tragedies</u>)
The Singer, adapted by Peter Barnes
(In <u>The Frontiers of Farce</u>)
Spring Awakening
(In <u>Calder & Boyars Playscript</u> Series, no. 23)
Wege (see Haitow, Einakter von N.)
WEGENER, Paul, 1874-1948
The Golem; scenario of the film by Henrik Galeen, adapted from
Gustav Meyrink, directed by Paul Wegener
(In <u>Masterworks of the German Cinema</u>)
WEHBI, Timochenco
A Drama de Copas e o Rei de Cuba
(In <u>Revista de Teatro</u>, no. 399, May/June 1974)
WEIDMAN, Jerome, 1913-
Fiorello! (see Bock, Jerry)
WEIL, Rene, 1868-1952
Love and Learning, by Romain Coolus (pseud.)
(In <u>Modern One-Act Plays from the French</u>)
WEILL, Kurt, 1900-1950
He Who Says Yes and He Who Says No (see Brecht, Bertolt)
Der Jasager (see Brecht, Bertolt)
Lady in the Dark. Book by Moss Hart; lyrics by Ira Gershwin;
music by Kurt Weill
(In <u>Ten Great Musicals of the American Theatre</u>, Vol. 2)
(A <u>Random House Play</u>, 1941)
Lost in the Stars. Book and lyrics by Maxwell Anderson, based
on the novel "Cry, the Beloved Country, " by Alan Paton; music
by Kurt Weill
(In <u>Ten Great Musicals of the American Theatre</u>, Vol. 2)
One Touch of Venus; book by S. J. Perelman and Ogden Nash;
music by Kurt Weill; lyrics by Ogden Nash; suggested by F.
Anstey's story "The Tinted Venus. "
(In <u>Ten Great Musicals of the American Theatre</u>)
L'Opéra de Quat'sous (Die Dreigroschenoper) (see Pabst, Georg
W.)
The Threepenny Opera; screenplay (see Lania, Leo)
WEINBERG, Dan
The Land of Laughingstock
(In <u>Yale/Theatre</u>, Vol. 5, no. 1, Fall 1973)
WEINGARTEN, Romain
Akara
(In <u>Le Théâtre d'Aujourd'hui</u>)
L'Eté
(In <u>Le Théâtre d'Aujourd'hui</u>)
WEISENBORN, Günther, 1902-
El Rostro Perdido
(In <u>Teatro Aleman Contemporaneo</u>)
WEISS, Morton Jerry
Parents Are People
(In <u>10 Short Plays</u>)
WEISS, Peter, 1916-
Amleto Principe di Danimarca (see Brecht, Bertolt)

Come il Signor Mockinpott Fu Liberato Dai Suoi Tormenti
        (In Sipario, no. 327-328, Aug. /Sept. 1973)
Discourse on Vietnam
        (In Calder & Boyars Playscripts Series, no. 38)
Hölderlin; traduction Française de Philippe Ivernel
        (In L'Avant-Scène Théâtre, no. 550, Oct. 15, 1974)
How Mr. Mockinpott Was Cured of His Sufferings
        (In Contemporary German Theater)
Der Prozesc
        (In Theater Heute, no. 7, July 1975)
The Tower
        (In Postwar German Theatre)
Das Weite Land (see Schnitzler, Arthur)
WEITZ, Elissa-Raquel
    The Lansky Soliloquies
        (In Modern International Drama, Vol. 7, no. 1A, Oct. 1973)
WELBURN, Vivienne C.
    Clearway
        (In Calder & Boyars Playscript Series, no. 4)
    The Drag
        (In Calder & Boyars Playscript Series, no. 5)
    Johnny So Long
        (In Calder & Boyars Playscript Series, no. 5)
        (In Gambit, no. 8)
Welcome to Andromeda (see Whyte, Ron)
"Welcome to Dallas, Mr. Kennedy" (see Himmelstrup, Kaj)
Welded (see O'Neill, Eugene)
The Well (see McKinney, Jack)
The Well of the Saints (see Synge, John M.)
A Well-Remembered Voice (see Barrie, James M.)
The Well Wherein a Deer's Head Bleeds (see Kelly, Robert)
WELLER, Michael, 1942-
    The Bodybuilders
        (In Off-Broadway Plays, Vol. 2)
    Fishing
        (In Plays and Players, nos. 10-11, Vol. 22, July-August,
        1975)
    Now There's Just the Three of Us
        (In Off-Broadway Plays, Vol. 2)
    Tira Tells Everything There Is to Know About Herself
        (In The Best Short Plays, 1973)
WELLS, Herbert George, 1866-1946
    **Ann Veronica (see Gow, Ronald)
    The Man Who Could Work Miracles; scenario and dialogue by
        H. G. Wells, film directed by Lothar Mendes
        (In A Film by H. G. Wells)
Welsh Honeymoon (see Marks, Jeannette A.)
Wenceslaus II, King of Poland, 1271-1305
        Venceslas (Wenceslaus) (see Rotrou, Jean)
Wenn der Neue Wein Blüht (see Bjørnson, Bjørnstjerne)
Wenn Er Nicht Da Ist (see Peiper, Tadeusz)
The Wept of the Wish-Ton-Wish, from the novel by James Fenimore
    Cooper
        (In The Drama, Vol. 19)

Were You There (see Shearer, Marjorie)
Werner, Friedrich Ludwig Zacharias (see Werner, Zacharias)
WERNER, Zacharias, 1768-1823
    The Twenty-Fourth of February
        (In The Drama, Vol. 10)
WERRY, Wilfrid, 1897-
    Breakdown
        (In Canada on Stage)
        (In Ten Canadian Short Plays)
WERTMÜLLER, Lina (Arcangela Wertmüller von Elgg)
    Amore e Magia Nella Cucina di Manna
        (In Sipario, no. 329, Oct. 1973)
    Love and Anarchy
        (In her Screenplays)
    The Seduction of Mimi
        (In her Screenplays)
    Seven Beauties
        (In her Screenplays)
    Swept Away
        (In her Screenplays)
WERZLAU, Joachim
    Meister Röckle; oper für grosse und kleine Leute nach Motiven
        des Kinderbuches "Meister Hans Röckle und Meister Flammfus, "
        von Ilse und Vilmos Korn.   Libretto: Günther Deicke; Musik:
        Joachim Werzlau
        (In Theater der Zeit, no. 11, Jan. 1976)
WESKER, Arnold, 1932-
    Chicken Soup with Barley
        (In his Plays, Vol. 1)
        (In The Wesker Trilogy)
    Chips with Everything
        (In his Plays, Vol. 1)
    I'm Talking About Jerusalem
        (In his Plays, Vol. 1)
        (In The Wesker Trilogy)
    The Kitchen
        (In his Plays, Vol. 1)
    Roots
        (In his Plays, Vol. 1)
        (In The Wesker Trilogy)
    I Vecchi
        (In Sipario, no. 320, Jan. 1973)
    The Wedding Feast, adapted from the story "An Unpleasant Pre-
        dicament, " by Fyodor Dostoevsky
        (In Plays and Players, Vol. 24, nos. 7-8, Apr. -May 1977)
Wesley (see Brenton, Howard)
WESLEY, Richard
    Black Terror
        (In The New Lafayette Theatre Presents)
The West Indian (see Cumberland, Richard)
West of Suez (see Osborne, John)
West Side Story (see Bernstein, Leonard)
Westbound 12:01 (see Shoveller, Brock)

Westbury Fair (see Sladen-Smith, Francis)
Western Night (see Smith, Betty)
WESTHEIMER, David
   **My Sweet Charlie; television script (see Levinson, Richard)
WESTPHAL, Eric, 1929-
   Mozartement Votre
         (In L'Avant-Scène Théâtre, no. 570, 1975)
Wet Fish (see Arden, John)
Wetback Run (see Apstein, Theodore E.)
WEXLER, Norman
   Joe; screenplay, film directed by John G. Avildsen
         (An Avon Books Filmscript, 1970)
WEXLEY, John
   They Shall Not Die (selection)
         (In The Anxious Years)
WEYL, Fernand, 1874-1931
   Beauty and the Beast
         (In his Three Gallant Plays)
   A Byzantine Afternoon
         (In his Three Gallant Plays)
   The Slippers of Aphrodite
         (In his Three Gallant Plays)
WEYRAUNCH, Wolfgang, 1907-
   I'm Somebody, I'm Nobody: A Stereo Radio Play; both German
      and English texts are given
         (In Dimension, Vol. 1, no. 1, 1968)
WHALE, James, 1889-1957
   Frankenstein; screenplay by Garrett Fort and Francis Edwards
      Faragoh, based upon the composition of John L. Balderston
      from the novel by Mrs. Percy B. Shelley, adapted from the
      play by Peggy Webling, directed by James Whale. Pictures
      and complete dialogue edited by Richard J. Anobile
         (In The Film Classics Library, 1974)
What? screenplay (see Polanski, Roman)
What a Night! vaudeville script (see Fields, W. C.)
What About England? (see Ward, Edmund)
What Does Greta Garbo Mean to You? (see Parlakian, Nishan)
The What D'Ye Call It (see Gay, John)
What Every Woman Knows (see Barrie, James M.)
What Happened (see Stein, Gertrude)
What If It Had Turned Up Heads (see Gaines, J. E.)
What Is It, Mrs. Perkins? (see Buchwald, Art)
What Is Hys Lyflode? (see Foy, Helen)
What It Is to Be Young (see Mavor, Osborne Henry)
What Men Live By (see Benton, Rita)
What Men Live By; adapted for radio (see Chipman, Karyl K.)
What Next? (see Dibdin, Thomas F.)
What Price Glory? (see Anderson, Maxwell)
What Say They? (see Mavor, Osborne Henry)
What Shall We Tell Caroline? (see Mortimer, John C.)
What the Butler Saw (see Orton, Joe)
What the Twilight Says: An Overture (see Walcott, Derek)
What They Think (see Crothers, Rachel)

What Time Is It? (see Frederic, Phyllis)
What Use Are Flowers? (see Hansberry, Lorraine)
What W. C. Fields Thinks He Heard on the Quiz Kids Hour; radio
    script (see Fields, W. C.)
What We Defend (see Schoenfeld, Bernard C.)
What You Will (see Marston, John)
What's in a Word? radio script (see Berlin, Nathan)
What's Your Name, Dear? (see Barry, Spranger)
WHEATCROFT, John
    We Are the History of the U.S.
        (In Drama & Theatre, Vol. 12, no. 2, Spring 1975)
Wheelchair (see Penman, Margaret)
Wheelchair Willie (see Brown, Alan)
WHEELER, A. C.
    The Great Diamond Robbery (see Alfriend, Edward M.)
WHEELER, Hugh, 1916-
    A Little Night Music (see Sondheim, Stephen)
When Did They Meet Again? (see Brighouse, Harold)
When the Dew Falleth (see Hirschbein, Perez)
When the Moon Has Set (see Synge, John M.)
When the Music Stops (see Salacrou, Armand)
When the Sun Sits on the Branches of That Jambu Tree (see Jo For,
    Lee)
When We Are Married (see Priestley, John B.)
When We Dead Awaken (see Ibsen, Henrik)
Where Are They Now? (see Stoppard, Tom)
Where E'er We Go (see O'Dea, John B.)
Where Has Tommy Flowers Gone? (see McNally, Terrence)
Where Is a Door Not a Door? (see Arden, John)
Where It Is Thin, There It Breaks (see Turgenev, Ivan S.)
Where the Cross Is Made (see O'Neill, Eugene)
Where the Difference Begins (see Mercer, David)
Where's Peter? (see Loring, Emilie)
While the Mushrooms Bubble (see Totheroh, Dan)
Whiskey (see McNally, Terrence)
WHISKIN, Nigel
    Come to the Front; a documentary play based on a series of
        interviews. National Association for the Care and Resettle-
        ment of Offenders, Bristol
        (In New Theatre Magazine, Vol. 12, no. 3, 1st series, 1971-
        72)
The Whistler (see Taylor, Peter H.)
WHITE, Bessie F.
    Family
        (In One-Act Plays for Stage and Study, 7th Series)
WHITE, Edgar, 1947-
    The Burghers of Calais
        (In Underground)
    The Crucificado
        (In The Crucificado)
    Fun in Lethe; or, The Feast of Misrule
        (In Underground)

The Life and Times of J. Walter Smintheus
    (In The Crucificado)
The Mummer's Play
    (In Underground)
The Wonderful Years
    (In Underground)
WHITE, Joseph, 1935
    The Leader
        (In Black Fire)
WHITE, Lionel
    **Pierrot le Fou; filmscript (see Godard, Jean-Luc)
WHITE, Terence Hanbury, 1906-1964
    **Camelot (see Loewe, Frederick)
The White Cloud (see Molnar, Ferenc)
The White Cockade (see Gregory, Isabella A.)
The White Devil; or, The Tragedy of Paulo Giordano (see Webster,
    John)
The White Geese (see Dubé, Marcel)
The White-Haired Girl (see China Peking Opera Troup)
The White House Murder Case (see Feiffer, Jules)
White Lies (see Shaffer, Peter)
White Nights; screenplay (see Visconti, Luchino. Le Bianche)
The White Steed (see Carroll, Paul Vincent)
The White Whore and the Bit Player (see Eyen, Tom)
White Wings (see Barry, Philip)
WHITEHAND, Robert
    Derricks on a Hill
        (In 100 Non-Royalty Radio Plays)
WHITEHEAD, William, 1715-1785
    The Roman Father
        (In The London Stage, Vol. 3)
    A Trip to Scotland
        (In A Collection of the Most Esteemed Farces ..., Vol. 6)
WHITING, John, 1917-
    Conditions of Agreement
        (In his Collected Plays, Vol. 1)
    The Devils
        (In his Collected Plays, Vol. 2)
        (In Hill & Wang Spotlight Drama Series, 1961)
    The Gates of Summer
        (In his Collected Plays, Vol. 2)
    Marching Song
        (In his Collected Plays, Vol. 1)
        (In Heineman Drama Library, 1962)
    No Why
        (In his Collected Plays, Vol. 2)
    Noman and the Nomads
        (In his Collected Plays, Vol. 2)
    A Penny for a Song
        (In his Collected Plays, Vol. 1)
        (In Heinemann Drama Library, 1964)
    Saint's Day
        (In his Collected Plays, Vol. 1)
        (In Heinemann Drama Library, 1963)

Who Called You Here? adapted for radio (see Petersen, Eric J.)
Who Do You Kill? television script (see Perl, Arnold)
Who Is My Neighbour (see Ridler, Anne B.)
Who Killed Me? (see Chantel, Lucien)
The Whole Town's Talking (see Emerson, John)
The Whole Truth (see Mackie, Philip)
Who's Afraid of Virginia Woolf? (see Albee, Edward)
Who's Been Eating My Porridge? (see Ward, Edmund)
Who's Got His Own (see Milner, Ron)
Who's Who? (see Waterhouse, Keith)
Whose Law? Whose Order? (see Ward, Edmund)
Why Bournemouth? (see Antrobus, John)
Why Hannah's Skirt Won't Stay Down (see Eyen, Thomas L.)
Why I Am a Bachelor (see Seiler, Conrad)
Why She Would Not (see Shaw, George Bernard)
WHYTE, Ron
    Welcome to Andromeda
        (In Best Short Plays, 1974)
WICKER, Mrs. Irene (Seaton)
    Alice in Wonderland; radio script, Jan. 1, 1939
        (In Best Broadcasts of 1938-39)
The Widdy's Mite (see Totheroh, Dan)
Wide Open Spaces (see Obaldia, Rene de)
WIDMER, Urs
    Nepal
        (In Theater Heute, no. 10, Oct. 1977)
The Widow (see Middleton, Thomas)
The Widow and the Colonel (see Owens, Rochelle)
The Widow of Wasdale Head (see Pinero, Sir Arthur Wing)
The Widow Ranter; or, The History of Bacon in Virginia (see Behn,
    Mrs. Aphra)
Widowers' Houses (see Shaw, George Bernard)
The Widow's Marriage (see Boker, George Henry)
Widows Shouldn't Weep (see Grey, Bernice G.)
The Widow's Tears (see Chapman, George)
Wie Gehts, Junger Mann? (see Toth, Sandor S.)
WIELAND, Christoph Martin, 1733-1813
    Alceste
        (In his Werke, Vol. 3: Dramen, Essays, Dialoge)
    Lady Johanna Gray
        (In his Werke, Vol. 3: Dramen, Essays, Dialoge)
    Neue Götter-Gespräche
        (In his Werke, Vol. 3: Dramen, Essays, Dialoge)
WIENE, Robert, 1881-1938
    Le Cabinet du Docteur Caligari; titre original "Das Kabinett des
        Docktors Caligari" scenario Carl Mayer, Hans Janowitz
        (In L'Avant-Scène Cinéma, no. 160-161, July/Sept. 1975)
WIENER, Frantz, 1877-1937
    On with the New, by Francis de Croisset (pseud.)
        (In Modern One-Act Plays from the French)
The Wife for a Life (see O'Neill, Eugene)
A Wife for a Month (see Beaumont, Francis)
The Wife of Bath (see Gay, John)

WILBUR, Richard
    Candide (see Hellman, Lillian)
The Wild Child; screenplay (see Truffaut, François)
Wild Decembers (see Ashton, Winifred)
The Wild Duck (see Ibsen, Henrik)
Wild for to Hold (see Morris, Thomas B.)
The Wild Gallant (see Dryden, John)
The Wild-Goose Chase (see Fletcher, John)
Wild Strawberries; screenplay (see Bergman, Ingmar)
Das Wildbad (see Sachs, Hans)
WILDE, Oscar, 1854-1900
    The Duchess of Padua
        (In his Plays)
  **The Happy Prince (see Benton, Rita)
    An Ideal Husband
        (In his Plays)
    The Importance of Being Earnest
        (In Masterpieces of the Modern English Theatre)
        (In his Plays)
        (In Representative British Dramas)
    Lady Windemere's Fan
        (In his Plays)
  **The Picture of Dorian Gray (see Osborne, John)
  **Le Portrait de Dorian Gray (see Boutron, Pierre)
    Salome
        (In his Plays)
    Vera; or, The Nihilists
        (In his Plays)
    A Woman of No Importance
        (In his Plays)
WILDE, Percival, 1887-1953
  **Blood of the Martyrs; radio script (see Macfarlane, Donald)
    Confessional
        (In On the High Road)
    Dawn
        (In Types of Modern Dramatic Composition)
    Mr. F.
        (In Best One-Act Plays of 1941, London)
Die Wilde Rotte (see Kerndl, Rainer)
Die Wilden (see Hampton, Christopher)
WILDER, Billy
    The Apartment, script by Billy Wilder and I. A. L. Diamond
        (In Film Scripts Three)
    Ninotchka; screenplay (see Lubitsch, Ernst)
WILDER, Thornton Niven, 1897-
    Childhood
        (In All the World's a Stage)
    The Drunken Sisters
        (In This Is My Best in the Third Quarter Century)
    The Happy Journey
        (In The Mentor Book of Short Plays)
    The Happy Journey to Trenton and Camden
        (In 10 Short Plays)
        (In This Is My Best)

The Matchmaker
(In <u>50 Best Plays of the American Theatre</u>, Vol. 2)
(In his <u>Three Plays</u>)
Nuestro Pueblo
(In <u>Teatro Norteamericano Contemporaneo</u>)
Our Town; revised from previously published version
(In his <u>Three Plays</u>)
The Skin of Our Teeth
(In his <u>Three Plays</u>)
The Wiles of Love (see Marivaux, Pierre C.)
Wilhelm Tell (see Schiller, Johann C.)
WILKINS, George, fl. 1607
**The Town-Fop; or, Sir Timothy Tawdrey (see Behn, Mrs. Aphra)
The Will (see Barrie, James M.)
A Will and No Will (see Macklin, Charles)
The Will to Win; television script (see Rodman, Howard)
William Ireland's Confession (see Miller, Arthur)
William Tell (see Schiller, Johann C.)
William III, called William of Orange, King of Great Britain, 1650-1702
*Egmont (see Goethe, Johann Wolfgang von)
William Wilson; screenplay (see Malle, Louis)
WILLIAMS, Albert N.
Festival; radio script
(In <u>New Fields for the Writer</u>)
Williams, Bert, 1876?-1922
*Star of the Morning (see Mitchell, Loften)
WILLIAMS, Charles, 1886-1945
Thomas Cranmer of Canterbury
(In <u>Four Modern Verse Plays</u>)
WILLIAMS, Charles T.
Superflyer; television script for an episode in "Sanford and Son,"
by Charles T. Williams and Ilunga Adell
(In <u>Samuel French's Tandem Library Series</u>)
WILLIAMS, Emlyn, 1905-
Beth
(In <u>Heinemann Drama Library</u>, 1959)
The Corn Is Green
(In <u>Heinemann Drama Library</u>, 1956)
The Light of Heart
(In <u>Heinemann Drama Library</u>, 1957)
Night Must Fall
(In <u>Heinemann Drama Library</u>, 1961)
(In <u>10 Classic Mystery and Suspense Plays of the Modern Theatre</u>)
Someone Waiting
(In <u>Heinemann Drama Library</u>, 1955)
Spring, 1600
(In <u>Heinemann Drama Library</u>, 1953)
Trespass
(In <u>Heinemann Drama Library</u>, 1954)
The Wind of Heaven
(In <u>Heinemann Drama Library</u>, 1945)

WILLIAMS, Frayne
    The Blue Vase
        (In Three Oriental Plays)
    The Man with the Bundle
        (In Three Oriental Plays)
    The Rose Garden
        (In Three Oriental Plays)
WILLIAMS, Heathcote, 1941-
    AC/DC
        (In AC/DC & The Local Stigmatic)
        (In his Collected Plays, Vol. 1)
        (In Gambit, Vol. 5, nos. 18 & 19)
        (In The Great American Life Show)
        (In Guthrie New Theater, Vol. 1)
    The Local Stigmatic
        (In AC/DC & The Local Stigmatic)
        (In his Collected Plays, Vol. 1)
    The Speakers
        (In his Collected Plays, Vol. 1)
  **The Speakers; adaptation (see Gaskill, William)
WILLIAMS, Hugh
    Double Yolk, by Hugh and Margaret Williams
        (In Plays of the Year, Vol. 21, 1959/60)
    The Happy Man, by Hugh and Margaret Williams
        (In Plays of the Year, Vol. 17, 1957/58)
    Plaintiff in a Pretty Hat, by Hugh and Margaret Williams
        (In Plays of the Year, Vol. 15, 1956)
WILLIAMS, Norman, 1923-
    Protest
        (In Ten Canadian Short Plays)
WILLIAMS, Tennessee, 1911-
    Battle of Angels
        (In The Theatre of Tennessee Williams, Vol. 1)
    Camino Real
        (In The Theatre of Tennessee Williams, Vol. 2)
    Camino Real (selection)
        (In This Is My Best in the Third Quarter Century)
    The Case of the Crushed Petunias
        (In 10 Short Plays)
    Cat on a Hot Tin Roof
        (In The Theatre of Tennessee Williams, Vol. 3)
    Confessional
        (In Best Short Plays of the World Theatre, 1968-1973)
    Dos Ranchos; or, The Purification
        (In New Directions, Vol. 8, 1944)
    The Eccentricities of a Nightingale
        (In The Theatre of Tennessee Williams, Vol. 2)
    The Glass Menagerie
        (In 50 Best Plays of the American Theatre, Vol. 3)
        (In The Theatre of Tennessee Williams, Vol. 1)
        (In 20th Century American Writing)
    Hello from Bertha
        (In The Disinherited: Plays)

Kingdom of Earth
    (In <u>The Theatre of Tennessee Williams</u>, Vol. 5)
Lo Que No Se Dice
    (In his <u>Teatro 2</u>)
Lord Byron's Love Letter
    (In <u>The Mentor Book of Short Plays</u>)
The Milk Train Doesn't Stop Here Anymore
    (In <u>The Theatre of Tennessee Williams</u>, Vol. 5)
The Night of the Iguana
    (In <u>Best Plays of the Sixties</u>)
    (In <u>Theatre of Tennessee Williams</u>, Vol. 4)
La Noche de la Iguana
    (In his <u>Teatro 2</u>)
Orpheus Descending
    (In <u>The Theatre of Tennessee Williams</u>, Vol. 3)
Period of Adjustment
    (In <u>The Theatre of Tennessee Williams</u>, Vol. 4)
Período de Ajuste
    (In his <u>Teatro 2</u>)
The Rose Tattoo
    (In <u>Contemporary Drama: 13 Plays</u>)
    (In <u>The Theatre of Tennessee Williams</u>, Vol. 2)
Senso; screenplay (see Visconti, Luchino)
Small Craft Warnings
    (In <u>Plays and Players</u>, Vol. 20, no. 7)
Small Craft Warnings (revised edition)
    (In <u>The Theatre of Tennessee Williams</u>, Vol. 5)
A Streetcar Named Desire
    (In <u>50 Best Plays of the American Theatre</u>, Vol. 3)
    (In <u>The Theatre of Tennessee Williams</u>, Vol. 1)
Subitamente el Ultimo Verano
    (In his <u>Teatro 2</u>)
Suddenly Last Summer
    (In <u>The Theatre of Tennessee Williams</u>, Vol. 3)
Summer and Smoke
    (In <u>The Theatre of Tennessee Williams</u>, Vol. 2)
Sweet Bird of Youth
    (In <u>The Theatre of Tennessee Williams</u>, Vol. 4)
**Sweet Bird of Youth; screenplay (see Brooks, Richard)
Talk to Me Like the Rain and Let Me Listen ...
    (In <u>The Disinherited: Plays</u>)
Un Tranvia Lamado Deseo
    (In <u>Teatro Norteamericano Contemporaneo</u>)
    (In his <u>Teatro I</u>)
The Two-Character Play (revised edition)
    (In <u>The Theatre of Tennessee Williams</u>, Vol. 5)
Verano y Humo
    (In his <u>Teatro 1</u>)
El Zoológico de Cristal
    (In his <u>Teatro 1</u>)
WILLIAMS, William Carlos, 1883-1963
    The Cure
        (In his <u>Many Loves and Other Plays</u>)

A Dream of Love
   (In Direction Series, no. 6, 1948)
   (In his Many Loves and Other Plays)
   (In William Carlos Williams Reader)
The First President
   (In The New Caravan)
The First President; libretto for an opera and ballet
   (In his Many Loves and Other Plays)
Many Loves
   (In his Many Loves and Other Plays)
Tituba's Children
   (In his Many Loves and Other Plays)
Trail Horse No. 1 (Many Loves): An Entertainment
   (In New Directions in Prose and Poetry, Vol. 7, 1942)
WILLIAMSON, Hugh Ross
   Diamond Cut Diamond
     (In Plays of the Year, Vol. 7, 1951/52)
Willie Rough (see Bryden, Bill)
WILLIS, Nathaniel Parker, 1806-1867
   Tortesa the Usurer
     (In Representative American Plays, 1792-1949)
     (In Representative Plays by American Dramatists, Vol. 2)
The Willow Plate (see Ryerson, Florence)
Wilson (see Greanias, George)
WILSON, Colin
   Strindberg
     (In Calder & Boyars Playscript Series, no. 31, 1970)
WILSON, Dave
   Saturday Night Live; television script (see Aykroyd, Dan and
   others)
WILSON, Edmund, 1895-
   Beppo and Beth
     (In his Five Plays)
   The Crime in the Whistler Room
     (In his Five Plays)
   Cyprian's Prayer
     (In his Five Plays)
   The Little Blue Light
     (In his Five Plays)
   This Room and This Gin and These Sandwiches
     (In his Five Plays)
WILSON, John, 1626-1696
   Andronicus Comnenius
     (In his Dramatic Works)
   Belphegor; or, The Marriage of the Devil
     (In his Dramatic Works)
   The Cheats
     (In his Dramatic Works)
   The Projectors
     (In his Dramatic Works)
WILSON, John Anthony Burgess, 1917-
   Oedipus the King (see Sophocles)

WILSON, Lanford, 1938-
   Days Ahead
     (In The Rimers of Eldritch and Other Plays)
   Lemon Sky
     (In Best American Plays, 7th Series, 1967-1973)
   The Madness of Lady Bright
     (In The Rimers of Eldritch and Other Plays)
   The Rimers of Eldritch
     (In The Off Off Broadway Book)
     (In The Rimers of Eldritch and Other Plays)
   The Sand Castle
     (In Best Short Plays of 1975)
   This Is the Rill Speaking
     (In The Rimers of Eldritch and Other Plays)
   Wandering
     (In Collision Course)
     (In The Rimers of Eldritch and Other Plays)
WILSON, Michael
   Salt of the Earth; screenplay
     (In Salt of the Earth: The Story of a Film)
WILSON, Snoo
   The Beast
     (In Plays and Players, Vol. 22, nos. 3 & 4, Dec. 1974 and
      Jan. 1975)
   The Everest Hotel
     (In Plays and Players, Vol. 23, no. 6, March 1976)
   Reason
     (In Gambit, Vol. 8, no. 29, 1976)
Wilson, Woodrow, Pres. U. S. , 1856-1924
   *Wilson (see Greanias, George)
The Wily One (see Monkhouse, Allan N.)
WIMPERIS, Arthur
   The Private Life of Henry VIII; screenplay (see Biro, Lajos)
WINCELBERG, Shimon
   Kataki
     (In Gambit, no. 5)
   The Windows of Heaven, based on "A Cat in the Ghetto, " by
     Rachmil Bryks
     (In Gambit, no. 3)
Wind in the Branches of the Sassafras (see Obaldia, Rene de)
The Wind of Heaven (see Williams, Emlyn)
The Window (see Lowe, Allen D.)
Windows (see Galsworthy, John)
The Windows of Heaven (see Wincelberg, Shimon)
Wine in the Wilderness (see Childress, Alice)
Wings over Europe (see Nichols, Robert M.)
Winners (see Friel, Brian)
Winnetou; filmscript (see Rialto-Film Preben Phillipsen & Jardran-
   Film)
WINTER, John Keith, 1906-
   The Rats of Norway
     (In Six Plays)
Winter, Keith (see Winter, John Keith)

The Winterfeast (see Kennedy, Charles Rann)
Winterset (see Anderson, Maxwell)
The Wisdom of Children (see Tolstoi, Lev N.)
The Wisdom of Solomon Paraphrased (see Middleton, Thomas)
WISE, Ernest George, 1894-
    Down Our Street, by Ernest George (pseud.)
        (In Six Plays: Famous Plays Series, 1930)
The Wise and Foolish Maidens (Anon.)
        (In Medieval Church Music-Dramas)
The Wise Virgins and the Foolish Virgins (Anon.); translated by
    Babette and Glenn Hughes
        (In World Drama, Vol. 1)
The Wise-Woman of Hogsdon (see Heywood, Thomas)
Wit at Several Weapons (see Beaumont, Francis)
Wit Without Money (see Fletcher, John)
Wit Works Woe (see Griboyedov, Alexander S.)
The Witch (see Middleton, Thomas)
The Witch (see Molnar, Ferenc)
A Witch in My Heart: A Play About the Swazi People (see Kuper,
    Hilda)
The Witches of Lancashire (see Heywood, Thomas)
The Witches' Sabbath (see Benavente y Martinez, Jacinto)
The Witching Hour (see Thomas, Augustus)
The Witch's Daughter (see Brighouse, Harold)
With All My Heart (see Smith, Moyne Rice)
Within the Family (see Parker, Kenneth T.)
Within the Gates (see O'Casey, Sean)
Witkacy (pseud.) (see Witkiewicz, Stanislaw Ignacy)
WITKIEWICZ, Stanislaw Ignacy, 1885-1939
    The Anonymous Work: Four Acts of a Rather Nasty Nightmare
        (In Drama & Theatre, Vol. 12, no. 1, Fall 1974)
        (In Twentieth-Century Polish Avant-Garde Drama)
    Cockroaches
        (In Yale/Theatre, Vol. 5, no. 3, 1974)
    Comedies of Family Life
        (In Yale/Theatre, Vol. 5, no. 3, 1974)
    Courageous Princess
        (In Yale/Theatre, Vol. 5, no. 3, 1974)
    The Crazy Locomotive
        (In his The Madman and the Nun & Other Plays)
    Gyubal Wahazar; or, Along the Cliffs of the Absurd
        (In Tropical Madness, The Winter Repertory # 7)
    The Madman and the Nun; or, There Is Nothing Which Could Not
    Turn into Something Worse
        (In his The Madman and the Nun & Other Plays)
    Menagerie; or, The Elephant's Escapades
        (In Yale/Theatre, Vol. 5, no. 3, 1974)
    La Metafisica di un Vitello a Due Teste
        (In Sipario, no. 312, May 1972)
    Metaphysics of a Two-Headed Calf
        (In Tropical Madness, The Winter Repertory # 7)
    The Mother
        (In his The Madman and the Nun & Other Plays)

Mr. Price; or, Tropical Madness
  (In Tropical Madness, The Winter Repertory # 7)
The New Deliverance
  (In New Directions in Prose and Poetry, Vol. 30, 1975)
The Poor Boy
  (In Yale/Theatre, Vol. 5, no. 3, 1974)
The Pragmatists
  (In Tropical Madness, Winter Repertory # 7)
Princess Magdalena; or, The Importunate Prince
  (In Yale/Theatre, Vol. 5, no. 3, 1974)
The Shoemakers
  (In his The Madman and the Nun & Other Plays)
They
  (In his The Madman and the Nun & Other Plays)
The Water Hen
  (In his The Madman and the Nun & Other Plays)
The Witness (see Rozewicz, Tadeusz)
Witness for the Prosecution (see Christie, Agatha)
The Wits (see D'Avenant, Sir William)
The Witty Fair One (see Shirley, James)
Wives As They Were, and Maids As They Are (see Inchbald, Mrs.
  Elizabeth)
WODEHOUSE, Pelham Granville, 1881-1975
  The Play's the Thing (see Molnar, Ferenc)
WOHMANN, Gabriel
  Norwegian Wood; a radio play; both German and English texts
  are given
    (In Dimension, Vol. 6, no. 2, 1973)
WOLF, Gerhard
  Litauische Claviere (see Kunad, Rainer)
The Wolf at the Door (see Hanlon, Daniel E.)
The Wolf-Hunt (see Verga, Giovanni)
WOLFE, Thomas Clayton, 1900-1938
  **Look Homeward, Angel (see Frings, Ketti)
WOLFF, Egon, 1926-
  Flores de Papel
    (In Teatro Contemporaneo Hispanoamericano, Vol. 1)
  The Invaders
    (In Modern International Drama, Vol. 8, no. 2, 1975)
  Los Invasores
    (In Teatro Contemporaneo Chileño)
    (In El Teatro Hispanoamericano Contemporaneo, Vol. 1)
WOLFF, Pierre, 1965-1930
  Faithful! A Sentimental Fragment
    (In Modern One-Act Plays from the French)
WOLINSKI
  Le Roi des Cons
    (In L'Avant-Scène Théâtre, no. 582, Mar. 1, 1976)
Wolkenkuckucksheim (see Kraus, Karl)
Wolsey, Thomas, 1475?-1530
  *Cant: A Play of Henry VIII and Anne Boleyn (see Munk, Kaj H.)
  *The Life and Death of Thomas, Lord Cromwell (Anon.)
    (In Disputed Plays of William Shakespeare)
  *A Man for All Seasons (see Bolt, Robert)

The Wolves (see Brust, Alfred)
Wolves and Sheep (see Ostrovskii, Alexandr N.)
The Woman (see Thorburn, John)
The Woman-Captain (see Shadwell, Thomas)
The Woman-Hater (see Beaumont, Francis)
The Woman in the Case (see Fitch, Clyde)
Woman in the Dunes; screenplay (see Teshigahara, Hiroshi)
A Woman Is a Woman; filmscript (see Godard, Jean-Luc)
A Woman Kilde with Kindnesse (see Heywood, Thomas)
A Woman of No Importance (see Wilde, Oscar)
The Woman Who Understood Men (see Kirkpatrick, John)
Woman's Craze for Titles (see Dancourt, Florent C.)
The Woman's Prize; or, The Tamer Tam'd (see Beaumont, Francis)
The Women (see Luce, Clare Booth)
Women; a radio play (see Iredynski, Ireneusz)
The Women at the Tomb (see Ghelderode, Michel de)
Women Beware Women (see Middleton, Thomas)
The Women Have Their Way (see Alvarez Quintero, Serafin)
Women Pleas'd (see Beaumont, Francis)
The Wonder Hat (see Goodman, Kenneth S.)
The Wonder of Women; or, The Tragedie of Sophonisba (see Mars-
     ton, John)
The Wonderful Ice Cream Suit (see Bradbury, Ray)
Wonderful Town (see Bernstein, Leonard)
WOOD, Charles, 1932-
     Dingo
          (In Evergreen Playscripts Series, 1969)
     John Thomas
          (In his Cockade)
     Prisoner and Escort
          (In his Cockade)
     Spare
          (In his Cockade)
WOOD, Margaret
     Fool's Errand
          (In The Best One-Act Plays of 1958-59, London)
The Wood-Demon (see Chekhov, Anton)
The Woodman (see Dudley, Sir Henry B.)
WOODS, Grahame
     Vicky
          (In A Collection of Canadian Plays, Vol. 3)
WOODS, William, d. 1802
     The Twins; or, Which Is Which? based on Shakespeare's "Come-
     dy of Errors"
          (In A Collection of the Most Esteemed Farces ..., Vol. 4)
WOODWARD, Helen R.
     Ask Aunt Mary
          (In 100 Non-Royalty Radio Plays)
WOODWORTH, Samuel, 1785-1842
     The Forest Rose; or, American Farmers
          (In Dramas from the American Theatre, 1762-1909)
Wooed and Viewed (see Feydeau, Georges)
The Wooing of Lady Sunday (see Pezzulo, Ted)

WOOLF, Benjamin Edward, 1836-1901
    The Mighty Dollar
        (In Favorite American Plays of the 19th Century)
WOOLF, Douglas
    The Love Letter
        (In New Directions in Prose and Poetry, Vol. 19, 1966)
The Word (see Munk, Kaj H.)
A Word to the Wise (see Kelly, Hugh)
Words and Music (see Coward, Noël)
Words and Music (see Nicholson, Kenyon)
The Words upon the Window-Pane (see Yeats, William Butler)
The Work Out (see Bermel, Albert)
The Worked-Out Ward (see Gregory, Isabella A.)
WORKERS THEATER, 1930s
    Middleman
        (In Guerilla Street Theater)
    Vote Communist: An Election Play for Street Performances
        (In Guerilla Street Theater)
    Yoo-Hooey ...: An Election Play for Outdoor Performance
        (In Guerilla Street Theater)
The Workhouse Donkey: A Vulgar Melodrama (see Arden, John)
The Workhouse Ward (see Gregory, Isabella A.)
The World and His Wife (see Nirdlinger, Charles F.)
The World Is Round (see Salacrou, Armand)
The World Lost at Tennis (see Middleton, Thomas)
The World of Paul Slickey (see Osborne, John)
World Peace--a Dream (see Abelardo, Victoria)
WORMS, Jeannine
    La Boutique
        (In L'Avant-Scène Théâtre, no. 607, Apr. 1, 1977)
A Worthy Guest (see Bailey, Paul)
The Would-Be Gentleman (see Molière, Jean Baptiste)
Woyzeck (see Buechner, George)
Wreckers (see Edgar, David)
The Wrens (see Gregory, Isabella A.)
WRIGHT, Richard, 1908-1960
    Native Son; written by Richard Wright and Paul Green
        (In Black Theater U.S.A., 1847-1974)
Writer's Cramp (see Byrne, John)
Wu-Feng (see Scott, Munroe)
Wu Hua Tung (The Five Flower Grotto)
        (In Famous Chinese Plays)
WUL, Stefan
    **La Planète Sauvage; filmscript (see Lalous, Rene)
Die Wupper (see Lasker-Schüler, Else)
Wurzel-Flummery (see Milne, Alan A.)
WYCHERLEY, William, 1640?-1716
    The Country Wife
        (In his Complete Plays)
        (In his Complete Works, Vol. 2)
        (In Contact with Drama)
        (In Enclosure)
        (In Restoration Comedy, Vol. 1)

The Gentleman Dancing-Master
   (In his Complete Plays)
   (In his Complete Works, Vol. 1)
Love in a Wood
   (In his Complete Plays)
   (In his Complete Works, Vol. 1)
The Plaindealer; adapted from Molière's "Le Misanthrope"
   (In British Plays from the Restoration to 1820, Vol. 1)
   (In his Complete Plays)
   (In his Complete Works, Vol. 2)
   (In Plays from Molière)
   (In Restoration Comedy, Vol. 2)
WYMAN, Justus Edwin
   Revolt in Orthoepy, a comic opera without music for radio
      (In 100 Non-Royalty Radio Plays)
WYMARK, Olwen
   Coda
      (In Calder & Boyars Playscript Series, no. 3)
   The Inhabitants
      (In Calder & Boyars Playscript Series, no. 3)
   Lunchtime
      (In Best Short Plays of 1975)
   Lunchtime Concert
      (In Calder & Boyars Playscript Series, no. 3)
      (In Gambit, Vol. 3, no. 10)

X (see Reckford, Barry)
X= o: A Night of the Trojan War (see Drinkwater, John)
Xantippe, wife of Socrates
   *Socrates (see Voltaire)
XARDO, Franco
   Dopo una Giornata di Lavoro Chiunque Può Essere Brutale
      (In Sipario, no. 368, Jan. 1977)
Xenia; filmscript (see Kaiser, Georg)
Xerxes I, called "the Great," King of Persia, 519?-465 B. C.
   *Xerxes (see Crebillon, Prosper J.)
   *Esther (see Du Ryer, Pierre)

The Yahoos (see Shaw, George Bernard)
YANKANIN, Frank
   Virginia's Letter to Santa Claus
      (In 100 Non-Royalty Radio Plays)
Yankee Doodle (see Harris, Aurand)
Yankel Boyla (see Kobrin, Leon)
YANKOWITZ, Susan
   Boxes
      (In Playwrights for Tomorrow, Vol. 11)
   The Land of Milk and Funny; or, Portrait of a Scientist as a
   Dumb Broad; a film scenario
      (In Yale/Theatre, Vol. 6, no. 1, Fall 1974)
   Terminal; revised text, 1974
      (In Three Works by the Open Theater)

Yanks 3 Detroit 0 Top of the Seventh (see Reynolds, Jonathan)
YARROW, Joseph, fl. 1742
    Trick upon Trick; or, The Vintner in the Suds
       (In <u>A Collection of the Most Esteemed Farces ...</u>, Vol. 5)
YATES, J. Michael
    Night Freight
       (In <u>Performing Arts in Canada,</u> Vol. 8, no. 1, Spring 1971)
YAVIN, Naftali
    Precious Moments from the Family Album to Provide You with
      Comfort in the Long Years to Come
       (In <u>Calder & Boyars Playscript</u> Series, no. 24)
A Year-End Dialogue with Outer Space (see Ciardi, John)
YEATS, William Butler, 1865-1936
    At the Hawk's Well
       (In his <u>Collected Plays</u>)
    The Cat and the Moon
       (In his <u>Collected Plays</u>)
    Cathleen Ni Houlihan
       (In his <u>Collected Plays</u>)
       (In <u>Representative British Dramas</u>)
    Calvary
       (In his <u>Collected Plays</u>)
    La Condesa Catalina
       (In <u>Teatro Irlandes Contemporaneo</u>)
    The Countess Cathleen
       (In his <u>Collected Plays</u>)
       (In <u>Masterpieces of the Modern Irish Theatre</u>)
    The Death of Cuchulain
       (In his <u>Collected Plays</u>)
    Deirdre
       (In his <u>Collected Plays</u>)
    The Dreaming of the Bones
       (In his <u>Collected Plays</u>)
    A Full Moon in March
       (In his <u>Collected Plays</u>)
    The Green Helmet
       (In his <u>Collected Plays</u>)
    Heads or Harps, by William Butler Yeats and Lady Gregory
       (In <u>Complete Plays of Lady Gregory</u>, Vol. 4)
    The Herne's Egg
       (In his <u>Collected Plays</u>)
    The Hour-Glass
       (In his <u>Collected Plays</u>)
    The King of the Great Clock Tower
       (In his <u>Collected Plays</u>)
    The King's Threshold
       (In his <u>Collected Plays</u>)
    The Land of Heart's Desire
       (In his <u>Collected Plays</u>)
    On Baile's Strand
       (In his <u>Collected Plays</u>)
    The Only Jealousy of Emer
       (In his <u>Collected Plays</u>)

The Player Queen
 (In his Collected Plays)
The Pot of Broth
 (In his Collected Plays)
Purgatory
 (In his Collected Plays)
The Resurrection
 (In his Collected Plays)
The Shadowy Waters
 (In his Collected Plays)
Sophocles' King Oedipus; a version for the modern stage
 (In his Collected Plays)
Sophocles' Oedipus at Colonus; a version for the modern stage
 (In his Collected Plays)
The Unicorn from the Stars, by William Butler Yeats and Lady
 Gregory
 (In his Collected Plays)
 (In Complete Plays from Lady Gregory, Vol. 4)
The Words upon the Window-Pane
 (In his Collected Plays)
Yegor Bulichoff (see Gor'kii, Maksim)
Yegor Bulichoff and the Others (see Gor'kii, Maksim)
YEOH, Patrick
 The Need to Be
 (In New Drama Two: Oxford in Asia Modern Authors)
The Yeomen of the Guard; or, The Merryman and His Maid (see
 Gilbert, William S.)
Yerma (see Garcia Lorca, Federico)
El Yerro Candente (see Villaurrutia, Xavier)
Yesterday's Roses (see Larrimore, Lida)
Les Yeux sans Visage; filmscript (see Franju, Georges)
YGLESIAS, Antonia, 1943-
 Las Hormigas
 (In El Teatro de Hoy en Costa Rica)
Yo Tambien Hablo de la Rosa (see Carballido, Emilio)
Yo Tengo Viente Años! (see Sassone, Felipe)
The Yoke (see Guinon, Albert)
Yoo-Hooey ...: An Election Play for Outdoor Performance (see
 Workers Theater, 1930s)
Yorick's Love (see Howells, William Dean)
York-Life (see Björnsson, Oddur)
A Yorkshire Tragedy (Anon.)
 (In A Book of Short Plays, XV-XX Centuries)
 (In Disputed Plays of William Shakespeare)
YOSHOV, Valentin
 Ballad of a Soldier; screenplay (see Chukrai, Grigori)
You and I (see Barry, Philip)
You and Me and Him (see Mercer, David)
You Can't Cheat an Honest Man; scenario (see Fields, W. C.)
You Can't Take It with You (see Hart, Moss)
You Don't Have to Complicate Happiness (see Denevi, Marco)
You May Go Home Again (see Starkweather, David)
You Never Can Tell (see Shaw, George Bernard)

YOUNG, Stark, 1881-1963
  Addio
    (In his <u>Addio, Madretta & Other Plays</u>)
  The Dead Poet
    (In his <u>Addio, Madretta & Other Plays</u>)
  Madretta
    (In his <u>Addio, Madretta & Other Plays</u>)
  The Queen of Sheba
    (In his <u>Addio, Madretta & Other Plays</u>)
  The Seven Kings and the Wind
    (In his <u>Addio, Madretta & Other Plays</u>)
  The Star in the Trees
    (In his <u>Addio, Madretta & Other Plays</u>)
  The Twilight Saint
    (In his <u>Addio, Madretta & Other Plays</u>)
    (In <u>One-Act Plays by Modern Authors</u>)
The Young Admiral (see Shirley, James)
Young America (see Ballard, Fred)
The Young and the Damned; screenplay (see Buñuel, Luis. Los Olvidados)
The Young Elizabeth (see Letton, Jennette)
The Young Graduates (see Rozov, Victor)
The Young Guard (see Aleksin, Anatoly)
The Young Hopeful (see Fonvizin, Denis I.)
The Young Idea (see Coward, Noël)
The Young King; or, The Mistake (see Behn, Mrs. Aphra)
A Young Man's Fancy; radio script (see Manning, Hilda)
Young Winston; screenplay (see Foreman, Carl)
Young Wives' Tale (see Jeans, Ronald)
The Younger Brother; or, The Amorous Jilt (see Behn, Mrs. Aphra)
Your Five Gallants (see Middleton, Thomas)
Your Murderer: An Antialcoholic Comedy (see Aksyonov, Vasilii)
Your Own Thing (see Driver, Donald)
YOURCENAR, Marguerite
  Le Coup de Grâce; filmscript (see Schlöndorff, Volker)
You're Gonna Be Alright, Jamie Boy (see Freeman, David)
Youth Must Be Served (see Ford, Harriet)
Yu Pei T'ing (Pavilion of the Imperial Tablet)
    (In <u>Famous Chinese Plays</u>)
Yu T'ang Ch'un (The Happy Hall of Jade)
    (In <u>Famous Chinese Plays</u>)

Zabriskie Point; filmscript (see Antonioni, Michelangelo)
ZAGOREN, Marc Alan
  Knight of the Twelfth Saucer
    (In <u>Best Short Plays</u>, 1977)
Zaire (see Voltaire)
ZAMIATIN, Evgeni Ivanovich, 1844-1939
  La Pulga
    (In <u>Teatro Comico Sovietico</u>)
Zamore (see Neveux, Georges)
Zankar, Ivan (see Cankar, Ivan)

Zanorin (see Brickenden, Catherine)
Zapata, Emiliano, 1877?-1919
    *Viva Zapata; screenplay (see Steinbeck, John)
La Zapatera Prodigiosa (see Garcia Lorca, Federico)
Der Zar Lässt Sich Photographieren (see Kaiser, Georg)
Zara (see Hill, Aaron)
ZAVATTINI, Cesare, 1902-
    **I Misteri di Roma (Rocca San Casciano); screenplay (see Bolzoni,
    Francesco)
    **La Terra Trema; screenplay (see Visconti, Luchino)
The Zeal of Thy House (see Sayers, Dorothy L.)
Zee-Zee (see Murray, Anne)
Zement (see Müller, Heiner)
ZEMME, Oskar
    The Arrival
        (In Modern International Drama, Vol. 9, no. 1, Fall 1975)
ZIEGLEMAIER, Gregory
    The Archbishop
        (In Drama and Theatre, Vol. 10, no. 3, Spring 1972)
ZIMMERMAN, Armand L.
    A Dream
        (In One-Act Plays for Stage and Study, 10th Series)
ZINDEL, Paul, 1937-
    The Effect of Gamma Rays on Man-in-the-Moon Marigolds
        (In Contact with Drama)
    The Ladies Should Be in Bed
        (In Best Short Plays, 1974)
    Let Me Hear You Whisper
        (In Six Science Fiction Plays)
Zio Paperone (see Boal, Augusto)
ZOLA, Emile, 1840-1902
    Le Bouton de Rose
        (In his Oeuvres Complètes: Théâtre I, Vol. 42)
    Les Héritiers Rabourdin
        (In his Oeuvres Complètes: Théâtre I, Vol. 42)
    Lazare
        (In his Oeuvres Complètes: Théâtre II, Vol. 43)
    Madeleine
        (In his Oeuvres Complètes: Théâtre I, Vol. 42)
    L'Ouragan
        (In his Oeuvres Complètes: Théâtre II, Vol. 43)
    Renee
        (In his Oeuvres Complètes: Théâtre II, Vol. 43)
    Sylvanire
        (In his Oeuvres Complètes: Théâtre II, Vol. 43)
    Thérèsa Raquin
        (In his Oeuvres Complètes: Théâtre I, Vol. 42)
    Violaine la Chevelue
        (In his Oeuvres Complètes: Théâtre II, Vol. 43)
Zone (see Dubé, Marcel)
El Zoológico de Cristal (see Williams, Tennessee)
Zoraide (see Lamartine, Alphonse)

ZORIN, Leonid Genrikhovich, 1924-
  A Warsaw Melody
  (In Contemporary Russian Drama)
ZORRILLA Y MORAL, José, 1817-1893
  Don Juan Tenorio
  (In Clásicos Castellanos, Vol. 206)
  (In The Theatre of Don Juan)
  (In Tres Dramas Romanticos)
ZOSCHENKO, Mikhail Mikhailovich, 1895-
  **A Miserable Day; or, Honesty Is the Best Soviet Policy (see
    Schweid, Mark)
Zoya's Apartment (see Bulgakov, Mikhail A.)
Zu Treuen Händen (see Kastner, Erich)
ZUBER, Ron
  Three X Love
  (In Black Drama Anthology)
Zubiri (see Porto-Riche, Georges de)
ZUCKMAYER, Carl, 1896-
  The Captain of Köpenick
  (In German Drama Between the Wars)
  El General del Diablo
  (In Teatro Aleman Contemporaneo)
ZULAWSKI, Andrzej, 1940-
  L'Important c'Est d'Aimer; d'après le roman de Christopher
    Frank, "La Nuit Americaine"
  (In L'Avant-Scène Cinéma, no. 158, May 1975)
Zum Grossen Wurstel (see Schnitzler, Arthur)
Zur Schöne Aussicht (see Horvath, Odön von)
Zutik il Processo de Burgos (see Maffei, Mario)
Die Zween Ritter von Burgund (see Sachs, Hans)
Zwei Krawatten (see Kaiser, Georg)
Zweimal Amphitryon (see Kaiser, Georg)
Zweimal Oliver (see Kaiser, Georg)
Zwischen den Schlachten (see Bjørnson, Bjørnstjerne)
Zwischenspiel (see Schnitzler, Arthur)

AUTHOR LIST OF ANTHOLOGIES
INDEXED IN VOLUME 2

Abse, Dannie. Three Questor Plays. Lowestoft, Suffolk: Scorpion Press, 1967.

Achard, Marcel. Histoires d'Amour. Paris: La Table Ronde, 1959.

Adamov, Arthur. Teatro. Buenos Aires: Editorial Losada, 1961. 2 vols.

_____. Two Plays. London: John Calder, 1962.

Aiiieeeee! An Anthology of Asian-American Writers, edited by Frank Chin and others. Washington, D. C.: Howard University Press, 1974.

Aldis, Mary. Plays for Small Stages. New York: Duffield and Company, 1915. Reprint edition, Great Neck, N. Y.: Core Collection Books, 1976.

Alfieri, Vittorio. Tragedie. Firenze: Salani Editore, 1964. 3 vols.

Al-Hakim, Tewfik. Fate of a Cockroach: Four Plays of Freedom. London: Heinemann, 1973.

Alvarez Quintero, Serafin. Four Plays, by Serafin and Joaquin Alvarez Quintero, in English versions by Helen and Harley Granville-Barker. Boston: Little, Brown, 1928.

_____, Serafin y Joaquin. Teatro Selecto. Madrid: Escelicer, 1971.

Amalrik, Andrei. Nose! Nose? No-se! and Other Plays. New York: Harcourt Brace Jovanovich, 1973.

The American Caravan: A Yearbook of American Literature, edited by Van Wyck Brooks, Lewis Mumford, Alfred Kreymborg, Paul Rosenfeld. New York: Macauly Company, 1927.

Amiel, Denys. Theatre. Paris: Etablissements Pusson, 1938.

Amphitryon: Three Plays in New Verse Translations, Together with a Comprehensive Account of the Evolution of the Legend and Its Subsequent History on the Stage. Chapel Hill: University of North Carolina Press, 1974.

Andreev, Leonid Nikolaevich. Plays. New York: Scribner's, 1915.

Anobile, Richard J. , ed. The Best of Buster. The Classic Comedy
Scenes Direct from the Films of Buster Keaton. New York:
Darien House, 1976.

_____. The Film Classics Library. New York: Universe Books,
1974-75. 8 vols.

_____. "Godfrey Daniels!" Verbal and Visual Gems from the
Short Films of W. C. Fields. New York: Darien House, 1975.

_____. Hooray for Captain Spaulding! Verbal and Visual Gems
from "Animal Crackers. " New York: Darien House, 1974.

_____. Woody Allen's "Play It Again, Sam. " New York: Gros-
set & Dunlap, 1977.

Anouilh, Jean. Collected Plays. London: Methuen, 1966-67. 2
vols.

_____. Nouvelle Pièces Noires. Paris: La Table Ronde, 1958.

_____. Pièces Brillantês. Paris: La Table Ronde, 1954.

_____. Pièces Costumees. Paris: La Table Ronde, 1967.

_____. Pièces Grincantes. Paris: La Table Ronde, 1956.

_____. Pièces Roses. Paris: Calamann-Levy, 1942.

_____. Teatro: Piezas Rosas. Buenos Aires: Editorial Losada,
1959.

Antonioni, Michelangelo. Sei Film. Torino: Ei audi, 1964.

Arden, John. Soldier, Soldier and Other Plays. London: Methuen,
1967.

Ardrey, Robert. Plays of Three Decades. New York: Atheneum,
1968.

Ariosto, Lodovico. The Comedies of Ariosto, translated and edited
by Edmond M. Beame and Leonard G. Sbrocchi. Chicago:
University of Chicago Press, 1975.

Aristophanes. Five Comedies, translated by B. B. Rogers. New
York, Doubleday, 1955.

_____. Four Comedies. A new English version by Dudley Fitts.
New York: Harcourt, Brace & World, 1962.

Arlington, L. C. & Harold Action, tr. <u>Famous Chinese Plays.</u> New
York: Russell & Russell, 1963.

<u>The Army Play by Play: Five One-Act Plays</u>, with a foreword by
John Golden. New York: Random House, 1943.

Arrabal, Fernando. <u>The Automobile Graveyard and The Two Executioners.</u> New York: Grove Press, 1960.

_____. <u>Guernica and Other Plays.</u> New York: Grove Press,
1969.

_____. <u>Plays.</u> London: Calder & Boyars, 1966-1971.

_____. <u>Théâtre.</u> Paris: Christian Bourgois, 1968-1972.

Asturias, Miguel Angel. <u>Teatro 1.</u> Buenos Aires: Editorial Losada, 1964.

Auden, Wystan Hugh. <u>Two Great Plays by W. H. Auden and Christopher Isherwood.</u> New York, Modern Library, 1959.

Audiberti, Jacques. <u>Théâtre.</u> Paris: Gallimard, 1948-62. 5 vols.

<u>Australian Theatre Workshop.</u> Victoria: Heinemann Educational Aus-
tralia, 1969-1975. Vols. 1-13.

Averson, Richard and David Manning White, comp. <u>Electronic Drama: Television Plays of the Sixties.</u> Boston: Beacon Press,
1971.

Axton, Richard, and John Stevens, tr. <u>Medieval French Plays.</u>
Oxford: Basil Blackwell, 1971.

Ayckbourn, Alan. <u>Three Plays.</u> London: Chatto & Windus, 1977.

Bagnold, Enid. <u>Four Plays.</u> Boston: Little, Brown, 1970.

_____. <u>Theatre.</u> New York: Doubleday, 1951.

Baker, George M. <u>The Mimic Stage.</u> A Series of Dramas, Comedies, Burlesques, and Farces for Public Exhibitions and Private Theatricals. Boston: Lee and Shepard, 1869.

Bakshy, Alexander, tr. <u>Soviet Scene: Six Plays of Russian Life.</u>
Freeport, N. Y. : Books for Libraries Press, 1970.

Ballet, Arthur H. , ed. <u>Playwrights for Tomorrow: A Collective of
Plays.</u> Minneapolis: University of Minnesota Press, 1966-
75. Vols. 1-13.

Balzac, Honoré de. <u>Oeuvres Complètes.</u> Paris: Louis Conrad, 1929.
Theatre I, II, Vols. 34, 35.

Author List of Anthologies   590

──────. The Plays of Honoré de Balzac. New York: Howard
Fertig, 1976.

──────. Works. London: The Chesterfield Society, 1901.
Plays, Vols. 33-36.

Barker, Howard. Stripwell and Claw. London: Calder & Boyars,
1977.

Barksdale, Richard and Kenneth Kinnamon, eds. Black Writers of
America: A Comprehensive Anthology. New York: Macmillan,
1972.

Barlach, Ernst. Das Dichterische Werk: 1, Die Dramen. Munchen:
R. Piper, 1956.

──────. Three Plays, translated by Alex Page. Minneapolis:
University of Minnesota Press, 1964.

Barnes, Peter. The Frontiers of Farce. London: Heineman, 1977.

Barnes, R. G. , ed. Three Spanish Sacramental Plays. San Francisco:
Chandler Publishing Co. , 1969.

Baroja y Nessi, Pio. Obras Complètas. Madrid: Biblioteca Nueva,
1946.

Barrie, James M. Plays, ed. by A. E. Wilson. New York: Scribner's,
1956.

Barry, Philip. States of Grace: Eight Plays, edited by Brendan
Gill. New York: Harcourt Brace Jovanovich, 1975.

Bates, Alfred, ed. The Drama: Its History, Literature and Influence on Civilization. London: The Athenian Society, 1903.
22 vols.

Bauer, Wolfgang. Change and Other Plays. New York: Hill &
Wang, 1973.

Bax, Clifford. Polite Satires. London: The Medici Society, Ltd. ,
1922. Reprint edition, Great Neck, N. Y. : Core Collection
Books, 1976.

Beaumarchais, Pierre de. Théâtre Complet de Beaumarchais.
Geneve: Statkine Reprints, 1967. 4 vols.

Beaumont, Francis, and John Fletcher. Works. London: Cambridge University Press, 1905-12. 10 vols.

Beckett, Samuel. Ends and Odds: Eight New Dramatic Pieces.
New York: Grove Press, 1976.

_____. *First Love and Other Shorts.* New York: Grove Press, 1974.

Becque, Henri. *Théâtre Complet.* Paris: Bibliotheque-Charpentier, 1922. 2 vols.

Behn, Aphra. *Works.* New York: Blom, 1967. 6 vols.

Belasco, David. *Six Plays.* Boston: Little, Brown, 1928.

Benedikt, Michael and George E. Wellwarth, eds., tr. *Modern French Theatre.* New York: Dutton, 1964.

_____, and _____, eds. *Modern Spanish Theatre.* New York: Dutton, 1968.

_____, and _____. *Postwar German Theatre.* New York: Dutton, 1967.

Bennett, Gordon C. *From Nineveh to Now: Three Dramatic Fantasies Based on the Old Testament.* St. Louis: The Bethany Press, 1973.

Bennett, Henry Garland, comp. *On the High Road.* New York: American Book Company, 1935.

Bergman, Hjalmar. *Four Plays.* Seattle: University of Washington Press, 1968.

Bergman, Ingmar. *Four Screenplays,* translated by Lars Malmstrom and David Kushner. New York: Simon & Schuster, 1960.

Berkoff, Steven. *East and Other Plays.* London: Calder & Boyars, 1977.

Bernard, Kenneth. *Night Club and Other Plays.* Winter Repertory No. 1. New York: Winter House, 1971.

Best American Plays, ed. by Clive Barnes. Seventh Series, 1967-1973. New York: Crown, 1974.

Best One Act Plays, selected by J. W. Marriott. London: Harrap, 1931-59.

Best Short Plays (formerly *Best One Act Plays*), edited by Margaret Mayorga. New York: Dodd, Mead, 1937-1967/68; edited by Stanley Richards, 1968-76.

Best Television Plays, 1957, ed. by William I. Kaufman. New York: Harcourt, 1957.

Best Television Plays of the Year, 1949, 1950, 1950-51, 1954, edited by William I. Kaufman. New York: Merlin Press, 1950-54.

Betti, Ugo. Three Plays. New York: Grove Press, 1956.

_____. Three Plays on Justice. San Francisco: Chandler Publishing Co. , 1964.

Bevis, R. W. , ed. Eighteenth Century Drama: Afterpieces. London: Oxford University Press, 1970.

Biberman, Herbert. Salt of the Earth: The Story of a Film. Boston: Beacon Press, 1965.

Bierce, Ambrose. Collected Works. New York: Neale Publishing Co. , 1909-12. Vol. 12.

Biro, Lajos. Gods and Kings: Six Plays. London: George Allen & Unwin, 1945.

Bjørnson, Bjørnstjerne. Gesammekte Werke. Berlin: S. Ficher, 1911. Vols. 4-5.

_____. Plays, 1st and 2nd series. New York: Charles Scribner's, 1913-1914. 2 vols.

_____. Three Comedies. London: J. M. Dent, 1925.

_____. Three Dramas. London: J. M. Dent, 1925.

A Black Quartet: Four New Black Plays. New York: New American Library, 1970.

Block, Etta, tr. One-Act Plays from the Yiddish. Cincinnati: Stewart Kidd Co. , 1923.

Boker, George H. Plays and Poems. New York: AMS Press, 1967. 2 vols.

Bond, Edward. A-A-America! and Stone. London: Methuen, 1976.

A Book of Short Plays XV-XX Centuries. London: English Association, Oxford University Press, 1940.

Booth, M. R. , ed. Eighteenth Century Tragedy. London: Oxford University Press, 1965.

_____. English Plays of the 19th Century. London: Oxford University Press, 1969-73. 4 vols.

Bourdet, Edouard. Théâtre Complet. Paris: Librairie Stock, 1959. 5 vols.

Bowles, Jane. Feminine Wiles, with an introduction by Tennessee Williams. Santa Barbara, Calif. : Black Sparrow Press, 1976.

Bradbury, Ray. The Anthem Sprinters and Other Antics. New York: Dial Press, 1963.

_____. The Wonderful Ice Cream Suit and Other Plays. New York: Bantam, 1972.

Brecht, Bertolt. Collected Plays. New York: Random House, 1971-73. 4 vols.

_____. The Jewish Wife and Other Short Plays. New York: Grove Press, 1965.

_____. Seven Plays. New York: Grove Press, 1961.

Brenton, Howard. Christie in Love and Other Plays. London: Methuen, 1970.

_____. Plays for Public Places. London: Eyre Methuen, 1972.

Brissenden, Connie, ed. The Factory Lab Anthology. Vancouver: Talonbooks, 1974.

Brodkin, Sylvia Z. and Elizabeth J. Pearson, ed. On the Air: A Collection of Radio and TV Plays. New York: Scribner's, 1977.

Brome, Richard. Dramatic Works. New York: AMS Press, 1966. 3 vols.

Brown, Alan. Wheelchair Willie and Other Plays. London: Calder and Boyars, 1977.

Brown, John Mason. The Ordeal of a Playwright: Robert E. Sherwood and the Challenge of War. New York: Harper and Row, 1970.

Brown, Sterling Allen, ed. The Negro Caravan, writings by American Negroes, selected and edited by Sterling Allen Brown, Arthur P. Davis, and Ulysses Lee. New York: Dryden Press, 1941; reprint edition Arno Press, 1969.

Browne, Elliott Martin, ed. Three European Plays. Harmondsworth, Middlesex: Penguin Books, 1958.

_____. Three Irish Plays. Baltimore: Penguin Books, 1960.

_____. Four Modern Verse Plays. Harmondsworth, Middlesex: Penguin Books, 1958.

Browning, Robert. Works. New York: AMS Press, 1966. Vols. 1-4, 10.

Brust, Alfred. Dramen, 1917-1924. Hrsg. von Horst Denkler, Müchen: W. Fink, 1971.

Buchwald, Art. Counting Sheep; the log and the complete play: "Sheep on the Runway. " New York: Putnam, 1970.

Buero Vallejo, Antonio. Teatro Selecto. Madrid: Escelicer, 1966.

Buitenen, J. A. B. van, tr. Two Plays from Ancient India. New York: Columbia University Press, 1968.

Bulgakov, Mikhail. The Early Plays, edited by Ellendea Proffer. Bloomington: Indiana University Press, 1972.

Bullins, Ed. Four Dynamite Plays. New York: William Morrow, 1972.

_____. The Theme Is Blackness: The Corner and Other Plays. New York: William Morrow, 1972.

Burnett, Whit, ed. This Is My Best. New York: Dial, 1942.

_____. This Is My Best in the Third Quarter Century. New York: Doubleday, 1970.

Burns, George. I Love Her, That's Why! An autobiography with Cynthia Hobart Lindsay and prologue by Jack Benny. New York: Simon and Schuster, 1955.

_____. Living It Up; or, They Still Love Me in Altoona. New York: G. P. Putnam's Sons, 1976.

Calvet, Aldo. Teatro. Rio de Janeiro: Graf. do Livor, 1968.

Camus, Albert. Collected Plays. London: Hamish Hamilton, 1965.

Cantón, Wilberto, ed. 12 Obras en Un Acto. México; Ecuador: 0º0'0'', 1967.

Capote, Truman and Eleanor and Frank Perry. Trilogy. New York: Macmillan, 1969.

Carroll, Paul Vincent. Irish Stories and Plays. New York: Devin-Adair, 1958.

_____. Three Plays. London: Macmillan, 1943.

_____. The White Steed and Coggerers. New York: Random House, 1939.

Carter-Harrison, Paul, comp. Kuntu Drama: Plays of the African Continuum. New York: Grove Press, 1974.

Cartwright, William. Plays and Poems. Madison: University of Wisconsin Press, 1951.

Casey, Warren. Grease, a new 50's Rock 'n Roll musical; music, book and lyrics by Jim Jacobs and Warren Casey. Winter Repertory Special Number. New York: Winter House, 1972.

Casper, Leonard. New Writing from the Philippines. New York: Syracuse University Press, 1966.

Chandler, Frank W. and Richard A. Cordell, ed. Twentieth Century Plays. New York: Nelson, 1934.

Chandler, Raymond. The Blue Dahlia; a screenplay with a memoir by John Houseman, edited by Matthew H. Bruccoli. Carbondale: Southern Illinois University Press, 1976.

Chapman, George. Plays: Tragedies, I & II; Comedies, I & II, edited by T. M. Parrott. New York: Russell & Russell, 1961. 4 vols.

Charlot, Jean. Three Plays About Ancient Hawaii. Honolulu: University Press of Hawaii, 1963.

_____. Two Hawaiian Plays. Honolulu: University Press of Hawaii, 1976.

Chekhov, Anton. The Oxford Chekhov. London: Oxford University Press, 1964-68. Vols. 1-3.

Chénier, Marie Joseph Blaise. Théâtre. Paris: Foulon, 1818. 3 vols.

The Chicago Review Anthology, edited by David Ray. Chicago: University of Chicago Press, 1959.

Cibber, Colley. Three Sentimental Comedies. New Haven, Conn.: Yale University Press, 1973.

Clark, Barrett H. , ed. Favorite American Plays of the Nineteenth Century. Princeton, N. J.: Princeton University Press, 1943.

_____. Four Plays of the Free Theater. Cincinnati: Stewart & Kidd Co. , 1914.

_____. World Drama. New York: Appleton, 1933. 2 vols.

Clark, J. P. Three Plays. London: Oxford University Press, 1964.

Clarke, Austin. Collected Plays. Dublin: Dolmen Press, 1963.

Clásicos Castellanos. Madrid: Espasa-Caple, 1947-1975. 207 vols.: Vols. 2-3, 15, 20, 23, 32, 35, 37, 39, 50, 57-60, 65, 69-70, 74, 89, 92, 96, 106-107, 127, 131-32, 137-38, 141-42, 146-47, 152-53, 156-57, 159, 162, 171, 180-83, 200-01, 204, 206.

Claudel, Paul. Théâtre. Paris: Gallimard, 1956. 2 vols.

Clayes, Stanley and David Spencer, ed. Contemporary Drama: 13 Plays. New York: Scribner's 2nd edition, 1970.

Coger, Leslie Irene and Melvin R. White. Readers Theatre Handbook. Glenville, Ill.: Scott, Foresman, Revised edition, 1973.

Cohen, Helen Louise, ed. More One-Act Plays by Modern Authors. New York: Harcourt, Brace, 1927.

_____. One-Act Plays by Modern Authors. New York: Harcourt, Brace, 1921.

Cokayne, Sir Aston. Dramatic Works. New York: Benjamin Blom, 1967.

A Collection of the Most Esteemed Farces and Entertainments Performed on the British Stage. Edinburgh: S. Doig, 1792. 6 vols.

Collier, John. Milton's Paradise Lost: Screenplay for Cinema of the Mind. New York: Borzoi Books, Alfred A. Knopf, 1973.

Collins, Margaret, ed. Theatre Wagon Plays of Place and Any Place. Charlottsville: University Press of Virginia, 1973.

Colum, Padraic. Three Plays. Dublin: Allen Figgis, 1963.

Congreve, William. Complete Plays, edited by Herbert Davis. Chicago: University of Chicago Press, 1967.

Conn, Stewart. The Aquarium and Other Plays. London: Calder & Boyars, 1973.

Conrad, Joseph. Three Plays. London: Methuen, 1934.

Copi. Plays of Copi, translated by Anni Lee Taylor. London: John Calder, 1976. Vol. 1.

Corneille, Pierre. Chief Plays of Corneille, translated by Lucy Lockert. Princeton, N. J.: Princeton University Press, 1957.

_____. Moot Plays of Corneille, translated by Lucy Lockert. Nashville, Tenn.: Vanderbilt University Press, 1959.

_____. Théâtre Complet. Paris: Editions Garnier Freres, 1960. 3 vols.

Corrigan, Robert W., ed. Masterpieces of the Modern Central European Theatre. New York: Collier Books, 1967.

_____. Masterpieces of the Modern English Theatre. New York: Collier Books, 1967.

_____. Masterpieces of the Modern French Theatre. New York: Collier Books, 1967.

_____. Masterpieces of the Modern German Theatre. New York: Collier Books, 1967.

_____. Masterpieces of the Modern Irish Theatre. New York: Collier Books, 1967.

_____. Masterpieces of the Modern Italian Theatre. New York: Collier Books, 1967.

_____. Masterpieces of the Modern Russian Theatre. New York: Collier Books, 1967.

_____. Masterpieces of the Modern Scandinavian Theatre. New York: Collier Books, 1967.

_____. Masterpieces of the Modern Spanish Theatre. New York: Collier Books, 1967.

_____, and Martin Esslin, eds. New Theatre in Europe. New York: Delta, Dell Publishers, 1968, 1970. Vols. 3-4.

Cournos, John, ed. A Treasury of Classic Russian Literature. New York: Capricorn Books, 1962.

Coward, Noël. Play Parade. London: Heinemann, 1949-62. 6 vols.

_____. Suite in Three Keys. New York: Doubleday, 1967.

Craik, T. W., ed. Minor Elizabethan Tragedies. London: J. M. Dent & Sons, 1973.

Crébillon, Prosper Jolyot de. Théâtre Complet. Paris: Garnier Freres, 1923.

Cregan, David. The Land of the Palms and Other Plays. London: Methuen, 1973.

_____. Poor Tom/Tina. London: Methuen, 1976.

_____. Transcending and The Dancers. London: Methuen, 1967.

Crothers, Rachael. Six One-Act Plays. Boston: Walter H. Baker Co., 1925.

_____. Three Plays. New York: Brentano's, 1923.

_____. Three Plays. New York: Brentano's, 1924.

Crowne, John. Dramatic Works. New York: Benjamin Blom, 1967.

Curel, Francois de. Théâtre Complet. Paris: G. Crès et Cie,
1919. 5 vols.

Curnow, Allen. Four Plays. Wellington: A. H. & A. W. Reed, 1972.

Currimbhoy, Asif. Asif Currimbhoy's Plays. New Delhi: Oxford
and IBH Publishing Company, 1972.

Curry, George. Copperfield '70. New York: Ballantine Books,
1970.

Curteis, Ian. Long Voyage Out of War. Playscript 54. London:
Calder and Boyars, 1971.

Daudet, Alphonse. Théâtre. Paris: Bibliothèque-Charpentier, 1896-
1906. 4 vols.

————. Works. Boston: Little, Brown, 1899. Vols. 12, 15.

D'Avenant, Sir William. Dramatic Works. Edinburgh: W. Pater-
son, 1872-74. 5 vols.

Davies, William Robertson. Four Favorite Plays. Toronto: Clarke,
Irwin, 1949.

Davis, Arthur P. and Saunders Redding, ed. Cavalcade: Negro
American Writing from 1760 to the Present. Boston: Houghton Mifflin, 1971.

Dean, Phillip Hayes. The Sty of the Blind Pig and Other Plays.
Indianapolis: Bobbs-Merrill Company, 1973.

Dietz, Norman D. Fables & Vaudevilles & Plays: Theatre More-
or-Less at Random. Richmond, Va.: John Knox Press, 1966.

Dizenzo, Charles. Big Mother and Other Plays. New York: Grove
Press, 1970.

Dobrée, Bonamy, ed. Five Heroic Plays. London: Oxford University Press, 1960.

————. Five Restoration Tragedies. London: Oxford University
Press, 1928.

Donahue, John Clark. The Cookie Jar and Other Plays, edited by
Linda Walsh Jenkins. Minneapolis: University of Minnesota
Press, 1975.

Donleavy, James Patrick. The Plays of J. P. Donleavy. A Delta
Book. New York: Dell Publishing Co., 1972.

Donnay, Maurice. Théâtre. Paris: E. Fasquelle, 1908-1912.

Drexler, Rosalyn. The Investigation and Hot Buttered Roll. London: Methuen, 1969.

_____. The Line of Least Existence and Other Plays. New York: Random House, 1967.

Drinkwater, John. Collected Plays. London: Sidgwick & Jackson, 1925.

Dryden, John. Dramatic Works. New York: Gordian Press, 1968. 6 vols.

Dubé, Marcel. De L'Autre Cote du Mur Suivi de Cinq Courtes Pieces. Ottawa: Lemeac, 1973.

_____. Le Monde de Marcel Dubé. Ottawa: Lemeac. Nos. 1-2, 1971, 1973.

Duffet, Thomas. Three Burlesque Plays. Iowa City: University of Iowa Press, 1972.

Dumas, Alexandre (Fils). Théâtre Complet. Paris: Michel Levy, 1870-99. 8 vols.

D'Urfey, Thomas. Two Comedies, edited by Jack A. Vaughn. Cranbury, N. J.: Associated University Presses, 1976.

Ebon, Martin, ed. Five Chinese Communist Plays. New York: John Day, 1975.

Eckart, Dietrich. Eight Plays. Houston, Texas: William Gillespie, 1977. 35mm microfilm.

Edmonds, Randolph. Six Plays for a Negro Theatre. Boston: Walter H. Baker Co., 1934.

Edson, Russell. Falling Sickness: A Book of Plays. New York: New Directions, 1975.

Eisenstein, Sergi-Mikhailovitch. Three Films. New York: Harper, 1974.

Eisner, Lotte H. Murnau. Revised and enlarged edition. Berkeley: University of California Press, 1973.

Elwood, Roger, ed. Six Science Fiction Plays. New York: Pocket Books, 1976.

Emerson, John and Anita Loos. How to Write Photoplays. Philadelphia: George W. Jacobs and Company, 1923.

The Empress of Morocco and Its Critics, with an introduction by M.
    E. Novak. Augustan Reprint Society. Los Angeles: Uni-
    versity of Calif., 1968.

Euripides. Three Plays, translated by Paul Roche. New York:
    Norton, 1974.

_____. Three Plays, translated by Philip Vellacott. Harmonds-
    worth: Penguin, 1968.

Evreinov, Nikolai. Life as Theatre: Five Modern Plays. Ann Ar-
    bor, Mich.: Ardis, 1973.

Eyen Tom. Sarah B. Divine and Other Plays. Winter Repertory
    No. 3. New York: Winter House, 1971.

Famous Plays of Today, 1929-39, 1953-54. London: Gollancz.
    16 vols.

Farquhar, George. Complete Works, edited by Charles Stonehill.
    New York: Gordian Press, 1967. 2 vols.

Federal Theatre Project. Federal Theatre Plays, edited by Pierre
    De Rohan. New York: Random House, 1938; reprint edition,
    New York: Da Capo Press, 1973.

Fernando, Lloyd, ed. New Drama One. Oxford Asia Modern Authors.
    Melbourne: Oxford University Press, 1972.

Feydeau, Georges. Four Farces. Chicago: University of Chicago
    Press, 1970.

_____. Théâtre Complet. Paris: Le Belier, 1949.

Fielding, Henry. Works, edited by J. P. Brown. London: Bickers,
    1902. Vols. 2-4.

Fields, W. C. W. C. Fields by Himself, with a commentary by Ron-
    ald J. Fields. Englewood Cliffs, N. J.: Prentice-Hall, 1973.

50 Best Plays of the American Theatre, selected and introduced by
    Clive Barnes and John Gassner. New York: Crown, 1969.
    4 vols.

Filippo, Eduard de. Three Plays. London: Hamish Hamilton, 1976.

Filler, Louis, ed. The Anxious Years: America in the 1930s; a
    collection of contemporary writings. New York: Capricorn,
    1963.

Finch, Robert. Plays of the American West. New York: Green-
    berg, 1947.

Firesign Theatre Performing Group. The Firesign Theatre's Big
  Book of Plays. Radio plays. San Francisco: Straight Arrow
  Books, 1972.

Fitch, Clyde. Plays, edited by Montrose J. Moses and Virginia
  Gerson. Boston: Little, Brown, 1915.

Fitzgerald, Francis Scott Key. The Apprentice Fiction of F. Scott
  Fitzgerald, edited and introduction by John Kuehl. New Brunswick, N.J.: Rutgers University Press, 1965.

Five Plays from the Children's Theatre Company of Minneapolis, edited by John Clark Donahue and Linda Walsh Jenkins. Minneapolis: University of Minnesota Press, 1975.

Five Plays from the Other Side, 1912-1924. London: Samuel French,
  192-?

Five Modern Scandinavian Plays. New York: Twayne, 1971.

Flavin, Martin. Brains and Other One-Act Plays. New York:
  Samuel French, 1926.

Folsom, Marcia McClintock and Linda Heinlein Kirschner, ed. By
  Women: An Anthology of Literature. Boston: Houghton
  Mifflin, 1976.

Foote, Samuel. Dramatic Works. New York: Benjamin Blom,
  1968. 2 vols.

Ford, Alla T. The Musical Fantasies of L. Frank Baum, by Alla
  T. Ford and Dick Martin, with three unpublished scenarios.
  Hong Kong: Ford Press, 1969.

Ford, Nick Aaron, ed. Black Insights: Significant Literature by
  Black Americans, 1760 to the Present. Waltham, Mass.:
  Xerox College Publishing, 1971.

Foreman, Richard. Plays and Manifestoes, edited by Kate Davy.
  New York: New York University Press, 1976.

Fornes, Maria Irene. Promenade & Other Plays. Winter Repertory No. 2. New York: Winter House, 1971.

Foster, Paul. "Balls" and Other Plays. London: Calder & Boyars, 1967.

_____. Elizabeth I and Other Plays. London: Calder & Boy-
  ars, 1973.

_____. Marcus Brutus and The Silver Queen. London: Calder
  & Boyars, 1977.

4 Modern French Comedies. New York: Putnam, 1960.

Friel, Brian. Crystal and Fox and The Mundy Scheme. New York: Farrar, Straus and Giroux, 1970.

————. Lovers. Noonday Plays. New York: Farrar, Straus and Giroux, 1968.

Frisch, Max. Stücke. Frankfurt am Main: Suhrkamp Verlag, 1962. 2 vols.

————. Three Plays. London: Methuen, 1962.

Fugard, Athol. Statements, two workshop productions by Athol Fugard and others. London: Oxford University Press, 1974.

————. Three Port Elizabeth Plays. New York: Viking Press, 1974.

Galsworthy, John. Ten Famous Plays. London: Duckworth, 1941.

Garcia Lorca, Federico. Obras Completas. Madrid: Aguilar, 1963.

Garrett, George P., comp. Film Scripts Three and Four. New York: Appleton-Century-Crofts, 1972. 2 vols.

Garrick, David. Dramatic Works. London: A. Millar, Strand, 1798; reprint edition, Farnborough, England: Gregg International Publishers, 1969. 3 vols.

————. Three Plays, edited by Elizabeth P. Stein. New York: Benjamin Blom, 1967.

Garza, Roberto J., ed. Contemporary Chicano Theatre. Notre Dame, Ind.: University of Notre Dame, 1976.

Gay, John. Poetical Works. London: Oxford University Press, 1926.

Gerould, Daniel, ed. Twentieth-Century Polish Avant-Garde Drama, edited with an introduction by Daniel Gerould. Ithaca, N.Y.: Cornell University Press, 1977.

Gerstenberg, Alice. Four Plays for Women. New York: Brentano's, 1924.

————. Ten One-Act Plays. New York: Brentano's, 1921.

Ghelderode, Michel de. Seven Plays, with an introduction by George Hauger. New York: Hill & Wang, 1960, 1964. 2 vols.

Gibian, George, tr. Russia's Lost Literature of the Absurd: A Literary Discovery. Ithaca, N.Y.: Cornell University Press, 1971.

Gifford, Tony, ed. The Play's the Thing: Four Original Television Dramas. Toronto: Macmillan of Canada, 1976.

Gilbert, W. S. The Complete Plays of Gilbert and Sullivan. New York: Modern Library, 1936.

_____. Gilbert Before Sullivan: Six Comic Plays, edited by Jane W. Stedman. Chicago: University of Chicago Press, 1967.

Giraudoux, Jean. Théâtre. Paris: Editions Bernard Grasset, 1958, 1959. 4 vols.

Godard, Jean-Luc. Three Films. New York: Harper & Row, 1975.

Godden, Rumer. The Tale of the Tales. London: Frederick Warne, 1971.

Gogol, Nikolai. Collected Tales and Plays, edited by L. J. Kent. New York: Modern Library, 1969.

Goldberg, Isaac, tr. Plays of the Italian Theatre. Boston: J. W. Luce & Co., 1921; reprint edition, Great Neck, N. Y.: Core Collection Books, 1976.

Goldsmith, Oliver. Collected Works, ed. by Arthur Friedman. Oxford: Clarendon Press, 1966. Vol. 5.

Goldstone, Richard H. and Abraham H. Lass, ed. The Mentor Book of Short Plays. New York: New American Library, 1969.

Gor'kii, Maksim. The Last Plays of Maxim Gorki, adapted for the English stage by Gibson-Cowan. New York: International Publishers, 1937.

_____. Seven Plays. New Haven, Conn.: Yale University Press, 1945.

Goss, Clay. Homecookin': Five Plays. Washington, D. C.: Howard University Press, 1974.

Gray, Simon. Otherwise Engaged and Other Plays. New York: Viking Press, 1976.

The Great American Parade. New York: Doubleday, Doran, 1935.

Greene, Robert. Plays & Poems. Oxford: Clarendon Press, 1905.

Gregory, Isabella Augusta (Persse), Lady. Collected Plays of Lady Gregory, edited and with a foreword by Ann Saddlemyer. Gerrards Cross, Buckinghamshire: Colin Smythe, 1970. 4 vols.

_____. Poets and Dreamers: Studies from the Irish, including nine plays by Douglas Hyde, with a foreword by T. R. Henn. New York: Oxford University Press, 1974.

Griffith, Francis and Joseph Mersand, ed. Eight American Ethnic Plays. New York: Charles Scribner's Sons, 1974.

Gross, Theodore L., ed. The Literature of American Jews. New York: Free Press, 1973.

Guare, John. Cop Out, Muzeeka, Home Fires. New York: Grove Press, 1971.

Guitry, Sacha. Théâtre: Works. Paris: Libraire Academique Perrin, 1962. Vol. 12.

Guthrie New Theatre, edited by Eugene Lion. New York: Grove Press, 1975. Vol. 1.

Hammond, Robert M. & Marguerite, eds. Deux Films Français: Les Visiteurs du Soir and Le Feu Follet. New York: Harcourt, Brace and World, 1965.

Handke, Peter. The Ride Across Lake Constance and Other Plays. New York: Farrar, Straus and Giroux, 1976.

Hankin, St. John. Plays. London: Martin Secker, 1923. 2 vols.

Hanley, James. Plays One. London: Kaye & Ward, 1968.

Harris, Aurand. Six Plays for Children, with a biography and play analysis by Coleman A. Jennings. Austin: University of Texas Press, 1977.

Harsavardhana, King of Thanesar & Kanauj. Sri Harsa's Plays, translated by Bak Kun Bae; both Sanskrit and English texts are given. New Delhi: Indian Council for Cultural Relations. New York: Asia House, 1964.

Harwood, Ronald. Making of "One Day in the Life of Ivan Denisovich". New York: Ballantine Books, 1971.

Hatch, James V., ed. Black Theater, USA: 45 Plays by Black Americans, 1847-1974. New York: Free Press, 1974.

Hauptman, William. Comanche Cafe/Domino Courts. New York: Samuel French, 1977.

Hawkes, John. The Innocent Party: Four Short Plays, with a preface by Herbert Blau. New York: J. Laughlin, New Directions Publishing Corp., 1966.

Hay, David L.   Contact with Drama, by David L. Hay and James
    F. Howell.   Chicago: Science Research Associates, 1974.

Hayes, Richard, ed.   Port-Royal and Other Plays.   New York: Hill
    & Wang, 1962.

Hebbel, Friedrich.   Three Plays, translated by Marion W. Sonnen-
    feld. Cranbury, N. J.: Associated Universities Press, 1974.

_____. Werke: Dramen und Prosa.   Hamburg: Hoffmann und
    Campe Verlag, 1958?

Hellman, Lillian.   Collected Plays.   Boston: Little, Brown, 1972.

Hervieu, Paul Ernest.   Oeuvres: Théâtre.   Paris: Alphonse Le-
    merre, 1900-09. 4 vols.

Herzfeld, Anita and Teresa Cajiao Salas, ed.   El Teatro de Hoy en
    Costa Rica. San Jose: Editorial Costa Rica, 1974.

Heym, Georg.   Dichtungen und Schriften: 2, Prosa und Dramen.
    Hamburg: Verlag Heinrich Ellermann, 1962.

Hillhouse, James A.   Dramas, Discourses, and Other Pieces.   New
    York: Benjamin Blom, 1967. 2 vols. in 1.

Hochwälder, Fritz.   Dramen.   Wiesbaden: Styria Graz Wien Köln,
    1975. 2 vols.

Hofmannsthal, Hugo von.   Dramen.   Frankfurt am Main: S. Fischer
    Verlag, 1950. 4 vols.

_____. Poems and Verse Plays, edited and introduced by Michael
    Hamburger. New York: Pantheon Books, 1961.

_____. Selected Plays and Libretti, edited and introduced by
    Michael Hamburger. New York: Pantheon Books, 1963.

Hogan, Robert, ed.   Seven Irish Plays, 1946-1964.   Minneapolis:
    University of Minnesota Press, 1967.

Holberg, Ludvig von.   Four Plays, translated by Henry Alexander.
    Princeton, N. J.: Princeton University Press, 1946.

_____. Seven One-Act Plays, translated by Henry Alexander.
    Princeton, N. J.: Princeton University Press, 1950.

_____. Three Comedies; English text and introduction by Regin-
    ald Spink. London: Heinemann, 1957.

Holt, Marion, ed.   The Modern Spanish Stage: Four Plays.   New
    York, Hill & Wang, 1970.

Hoopes, Ned E. and Patricia Neale Gordon, ed. Great Television Plays, Vol. 2. Dell Publishing Co., 1975.

Hopkins, John Richard. Talking to a Stranger: Four Television Plays. Harmondsworth: Penguin, 1967.

Horvath, Odön von. Gesammelte Werke. Frankfurt am Main: Suhrkamp Verlag, 1972. 8 vols.

Horwitz, Simi. South of the Navel. New York: Crowell, 1973.

Howells, William Dean. Complete Plays, edited by Walter J. Meserve. New York: New York University Press, 1960.

Huerta, Jorge A., ed. El Teatro de la Esperanza, an Anthology of Chicano Drama. Goleta, Calif.: El Teatro de la Esperanza, 1973

Hugo, Victor. Dramas. Boston: Dana Estes, 1900. 4 vols.

_____. Théâtre Complet. Paris: Gallimard, 1969.

Ibsen, Henrik. Eleven Plays. New York: Modern Library, 1935.

_____. The Oxford Ibsen, edited and translated by James Walter McFarlane and Graham Orton. London: Oxford University Press, 1960-72. 7 vols.

_____. Works. New York: Scribner's, 1911-12. 13 vols.

Ionesco, Eugene. Plays, translated by Donald Watson. London: J. Calder, 1958-76. 10 vols.

_____. Théâtre. Paris: Gallimard, 1954. 4 vols.

Iriarte, Victor Ruiz. Teatro Selecto. Madrid: Escelicer, 1967.

Ivory, James. Savages and Shakespeare Wallah: Two Films. London: Plexus Publishers, 1973.

Iwasaki, Yozan T. Three Modern Japanese Plays, translated by Yozan T. Iwasaki and Glenn Hughes, with an introduction by Glenn Hughes. Cincinnati: Stewart Kidd Co., 1923.

Jahnn, Hans Henny. Dramen. Frankfurt am Main: Europäische Verlagsantalt, 1965. 2 vols.

James, Henry. Complete Plays, edited by Leon Edel. London: Rupert Hart-Davis, 1949.

_____. Theatricals. New York: Harper, 1894-95. 2 vols.

Jansen, Frederik Julius Billeskov and P. M. Mitchell, ed. Anthology of Danish Literature. Bilingual edition. Carbondale: Southern University Press, 1971.

Jardiel Poncela, Enrique. Teatro Selecto. Madrid: Escelicer, 1968.

Jarry, Alfred. Selected Works, edited by Roger Shattuck and Simon Watson Taylor. New York: Grove Press, 1965.

_____. The Ubu Plays, edited with an introduction by Simon Watson Taylor. New York: Grove Press, 1969.

Jeffares, A. Norman, ed. Restoration Comedy. London: The Folio Press, 1974. 4 vols.

John, Errol. Force Majeure, The Dispossessed, and Hasta Luego. London: Faber & Faber, 1967.

Johnston, Denis. The Old Lady Says "No!" and Other Plays. Boston: Little, Brown, 1960.

_____. Storm Song and A Bride for the Unicorn. London: J. Cape, 1935.

Jones, LeRoi, ed. The Moderns: An Anthology of New Writing in America. New York: Corinth Books, 1963.

_____, and Larry Neal, ed. Black Fire: An Anthology of Afro-American Writing. New York: William Morrow, 1968.

Jones, Tom. 2 Musicals, by Tom Jones and Harvey Schmidt. New York: Drama Book Specialists, 1973.

Jonson, Ben. Plays, with an introduction by F. E. Schelling. London: Dent, Everyman's Library, 1910. 2 vols.

Jupp, Kenneth. A Chelsea Trilogy. London: Calder and Boyars, 1969.

Kabuki: Five Classic Plays, translated by James R. Brandon. Cambridge: Harvard University Press, 1975.

Kästner, Erich. Gesammelte Schriften 4: Theater. Zurich: Atrium Verlag, 1959.

Kaiser, Georg. A Day in October and Other Plays. London: Calder and Boyars, 1977.

_____. Five Plays. London: Calder and Boyars, 1971.

_____. Stücke Erzählungen Aufsätze Gedichte. Berlin: Kiepenheuer and Witsch, 1966.

_____. Teatro. Buenos Aires: Editorial Losada, 1959.

_____. Werke. Frankfurt: Verlag Ullstein Gmbh, 1972.

Kalidasa. Shakuntala and Other Writings. New York: Dutton, 1959.

Kalman, Rolf, ed. A Collection of Canadian Plays. Toronto: Simon and Pierre Publishing Company, 1976. Vols. 1-3.

Katzin, Winifred, comp. Eight European Plays, with a preface by Barrett H. Clark. New York: Brentano's, 1927.

Kaufman, William I. , ed. Great Television Plays. New York: Dell Publishing Company, 1969.

Keene, Donald, ed. Modern Japanese Literature. New York: Grove Press, 1960.

Kelly, Hugh. Works. London: T. Cadell, 1778; reprint edition, Hildesheim, N. Y. : Georg Olms Verlag, 1973.

Kennedy, Charles Rann. A Repertory of Plays for a Company of Seven Players. Chicago: University of Chicago Press, 1930.

_____. A Repertory of Plays for a Company of Three Players. Chicago: University of Chicago Press, 1927-40. 3 vols.

Killigrew, Thomas. Comedies & Tragedies. New York: Benjamin Blom, 1967.

King, Woodie, ed. Black Drama Anthology, edited by Woodie King and Ron Milner. New York: Columbia University Press, 1972.

Knapp, Bettina. The Contemporary French Theater. New York: Avon, Equinox Books, 1973.

Knight, Etheridge. Black Voices from Prison. New York: Pathfinder Press, 1970.

Knowland, A. S. , ed. Six Caroline Plays. London: Oxford University Press, 1962.

Koch, Howard. Casablanca, Script and Legend. Woodstock, N. J. : Overlook Press, 1973.

Kostelanetz, Richard, ed. The Young American Writers. New York: Funk and Wagnall's, 1967.

Kozlenko, William, ed. Disputed Plays of Shakespeare. New York: Hawthorne Books, 1974.

_____. 100 Non-Royalty Radio Plays. New York: Greenberg, 1941.

Kraus, Karl. Dramen. Munchen: Wien, Albert Langen, 1967.

Kühner, Maria Helena. Teatro Popular: Uma Experienca. Rio de
Janiero: F. Alver, 1975.

Kummer, Mrs. Clare (Beecher). Selected Plays. New York:
Samuel French, 1934.

Kurosawa, Akira. Complete Works, in Japanese and English. Tokayo: Kinema Jumop Sha, 1970. Vols. 1-4, 6, 9.

Kyd, Thomas. Works. Oxford: Clarendon Press, 1955.

Labiche, Eugene. The Italian Straw Hat and The Spelling Mistakes,
translated and adapted by Frederick Davies. New York:
Theatre Arts Books, 1967.

_____. Théâtre Complet. Paris: Calmann Lévy, 1881-82. 10
vols.

_____. Two Plays. English version by Emanuel Wax. New
York: Dramatist Play Service, 1962.

Lahr, John and Jonathan Price. The Great American Life Show:
9 Plays from the Avant-Garde Theatre. New York: Bantam
Books, 1974.

Lal, P. , ed. Great Sanskrit Plays. New York: New Directions,
1959.

Lamarche, Gustave. Oeuvres Théâtrales. Quebéc: Les Presses
de l'Universite Laval, 1971. Vol. 1.

Lamartine, Alphonse. Oeuvres Póetiques Completes. Paris: Gallimard, 1963.

Landis, Joseph C. , ed. The Great Jewish Plays. New York: Horizon Press, 1972.

Lathrop, William Addison. Little Stories from the Screen, 1917.
New York: Garland Publishing, Inc. , 1977.

Laura, Ida. Hamlet em Brasília e Outras Oecas. São Paulo: Editora Franciscana, 1966.

Laurendeau, Andre. Théâtre. Montreal: L'Arbre, 1970.

La Valley, Albert J. The New Consciousness: an Anthology of the
New Literature. Cambridge: Winthrop, 1972.

Lee, Nathaniel. Works. Metuchen, N. J. : Scarecrow Reprint Corp. ,
1968. 2 vols.

Lenormand, H. R. Théâtre Complet. Paris: G. Cres, 1921-24.
3 vols.

_____. Three Plays. London: Gollancz, 1928.

Lesnick, Henry, ed. Guerilla Street Theatre. New York: Avon Books, 1973.

Leverton, Garrett H. On the Air: Fifteen Plays for Broadcast and for Classroom Use, collected and edited by Garrett H. Leverton. New York: Samuel French, 1944.

Lifson, David S., tr. and ed. Epic and Folk Plays of the Yiddish Theatre. London: Associated University Presses, 1975.

Lind, Jakov. The Silver Foxes Are Dead and Other Plays. New York: Hill and Wang, 1965.

Linney, Romulus. The Sorrows of Frederick/Holy Ghosts. New York: Harcourt Brace Jovanovich, 1977.

Liu Jung-en, tr. Six Yüan Plays. Harmondsworth, Middlesex: Penguin Books, 1972.

Livings, Henry. Kelly's Eye and Other Plays. New York: Hill and Wang, 1964.

Lockert, Lacy, ed. and tr. The Chief Rivals of Corneille and Racine. Nashville, Tenn.: Vanderbilt University Press, 1956.

_____, comp. More Plays by Rivals of Corneille and Racine. Nashville, Tenn.: Vanderbilt University Press, 1968.

Longfellow, Henry Wadsworth. Poetical Works. New York: AMS Press, 1966. Vols, 1, 3, 5-6, 19.

Lopez, Sabatino. Il Teatro. Torino: R. Streglio, 1905.

Lopez Rubio, Jose. Teatro Selecto. Madrid: Escelicer, 1969.

Lyons, Eugene, ed. Six Soviet Plays. Boston: Houghton Mifflin, 1934.

MacArthur, Charles. The Stage Works of Charles MacArthur. Tallahassee, Fla.: Florida State University, 1974.

McClelland, C. Kirk. On Making a Movie: "Brewster McCloud". New York: New American Library, 1971.

MacDonald, Dwight. Parodies: An Anthology from Chaucer to Beerbohm--and After. New York: Modern Library, 1965.

Mace, Jean. Théâtre du Château. Paris: J. Hetzel, 1861.

McNally, Terrence. The Ritz and Other Plays. New York: Dodd, Mead and Company, 1976.

Macklin, Charles. Four Comedies, edited by J. O. Bartley. London: Sidgwick and Jackson. Hamden, Conn.: Archon Books, 1968.

MacMillan, Dougald, ed. Plays of the Restoration and Eighteenth Century as They Were Acted at the Theatres-Royal by Their Majesties' Servants. New York: Holt, 1959.

Maeterlinck, Maurice. Plays, translated by Richard Hovey. Chicago: Stone and Kimball, 1894-96. 2 vols.

_____. Théâtre, edited by Eugene Fasquelle. Paris: Bibliothèque-Charpentier, 1925. 3 vols.

Magarshack, David, tr. The Storm and Other Russian Plays. New York: Hill and Wang, 1960.

Mandel, Oscar, ed. Five Comedies of Medieval France. New York: Dutton, 1970.

_____, ed. The Theatre of Don Juan: a Collection of Plays and Views, 1630-1963. Lincoln, Nebr.: University of Nebraska Press, 1963.

Mankiewicz, Joseph L. More About All About Eve. New York: Random House, 1972.

Mankowitz, Wolf. Five One-Act Plays. Boston: Baker's Plays, 1965.

Marcel, Gabriel. Théâtre Comique. Paris: A. Michel, 1947.

_____. Three Plays. New York: Hill and Wang, 1965.

Marivaux, Pierre Carlet de Chamblain de. Seven Comedies by Marivaux. Ithaca, N. Y.: Cornell University Press, 1968.

_____. Théâtre Complet. Paris: Aux Editions de Seuil, 1964.

Marlowe, Christopher. Complete Plays, edited by Irving Ribner. New York: Odyssey Press, 1963.

Marmion, Shakerly. Dramatic Works. New York: Benjamin Blom, 1967.

Marques, Rene. Teatro. Rio Piedras, Puerto Rico: Editorial Cultural, 1971. Vol. 2-3.

Marston, John. Plays, edited by H. H. Wood. London: Oliver and Boyd, 1934. 3 vols.

Martinovich, Nicholas N, ed. The Turkish Theatre. New York: Theatre Arts, 1933.

Massinger, Philip. Plays. New York: AMS Press, 1966.

Masterworks of the British Cinema, with an introduction by John Russell Taylor. New York: Harper and Row, 1974.

Masterworks of the French Cinema, with an introduction by John Weightman. New York: Harper and Row, 1974.

Masterworks of the German Cinema, with an introduction by Roger Manvell. New York: Harper and Row, 1973.

Maugham, William Somerset. Collected Plays. London: Heinemann, 1952. 3 vols.

_____. The Maugham Reader. New York: Doubleday, 1950.

_____. Six Comedies. New York: Doubleday, 1937.

Maupassant, Guy de. The Life Work of Henri René Guy de Maupassant. Akron, Ohio: The St. Dunstan Society, 1903.

Mavor, Osborne Henry. Colonel Wotherspoon and Other Plays. London: Constable, 1938.

_____. The King of Nowhere and Other Plays. London: Constable, 1938.

_____. Moral Plays. London: Constable, 1936.

_____. Plays for Plain People, by James Bridie, pseudonym. London: Constable, 1944.

_____. A Sleeping Clergyman and Other Plays. London: Constable, 1934.

_____. Susannah and the Elders and Other Plays. London: Constable, 1940.

Medieval Church Music-Dramas; a Repertory of Complete Plays, transcribed and edited by Fletcher Collins, Jr. Charlottesville, Va.: University Press of Virginia, 1976.

Mercer, David. The Bankrupt and Other Plays. London: Eyre Methuen, 1974.

_____. Generations: A Trilogy of Plays. London: Calder and Boyars, 1964.

_____. On the Eve of Publication and Other Plays. London: Methuen, 1970.

_____. The Parachute with Two More TV Plays. London: Calder and Boyars, 1967.

_____. Three TV Comedies. London: Calder and Boyars, 1966.

Mérimée, Prosper. Théâtre de Clara Gazul. Paris: Calmann-
     Lévy, 1925.

Metz, Christian. Film Language; a Semiotics of the Cinema. New
     York: Oxford University Press, 1974.

Middleton, Thomas. Works, edited by A. H. Bullen. London: J.
     C. Nimmo, 1885-86. 8 vols.

Mihura, Miguel. Teatro Selecto de Miguel Mihura. Madrid: Esceli-
     cer, 1967.

Mikasinovich, Branko, ed. Five Modern Yugoslav Plays. New
     York: Cyrco Press, 1977.

Miller, Arthur. Collected Plays. New York: Viking Press, 1957.

Miller, Ruth, ed. Blackamerican Literature 1760-Present. Beverly
     Hills, Calif.: Glencoe Press, 1971.

Miller, Wayne Charles, ed. A Gathering of Ghetto Writers: Irish,
     Italian, Jewish, Black and Puerto Rican. New York: N. Y.
     University Press, 1972.

Milligan, Terrence Allan. The Book of the Goons, by Spike Milligan.
     New York: St. Martin's Press, 1974.

_____. The Goon Show Scripts. New York: St. Martin's Press,
     1972.

Minnesota Showcase: Four Plays. Minnesota Drama Editions, no.
     9, edited by Michael Langham. Minneapolis: University of
     Minnesota Press, 1975.

Modern Italian One-Act Plays, edited by C. A. Swanson. Boston:
     D. C. Heath, 1948.

Modern Nordic Plays: Denmark. New York: Twayne, 1974.

Modern Nordic Plays: Finland. New York: Twayne, 1973.

Modern Nordic Plays: Iceland. New York: Twayne, 1974.

Modern Nordic Plays: Norway. New York: Twayne, 1974.

Modern Nordic Plays: Sweden. New York: Twayne, 1973.

Modern Scandinavian Plays. New York: Liveright Publishing Com-
     pany, 1954.

Moinaux, Georges. Plays, by Georges Courteline, pseudonym. New
     York: Theatre Arts Books, 1961.

_____. <u>Théâtre Complet</u>, by Georges Courteline, pseudonym. Paris: Flammarion, 1961.

Molière, Jean Baptiste Poquelin. <u>One-Act Comedies of Molière</u>, translated by Albert Bermel. 2d edition. New York: Ungar, 1975.

_____. <u>Works</u>. New York: Benjamin Blom, 1967. 6 vols. in 3.

Molnár, Ferenc. <u>Plays</u>. New York: Vanguard Press, 1929.

_____. <u>Romantic Comedies</u>. New York: Crown, 1952.

Montagu, Ivor. <u>With Eisenstein in Hollywood</u>. New York: International Publishers, 1969.

Montherlant, Henry de. <u>Théâtre</u>. Paris: Gallimard, 1972.

Moody, Richard, ed. <u>Dramas from the American Theatre, 1762-1909</u>. Cleveland: World Publishing Company, 1966.

Moore, Stephen, ed. <u>New Fields for the Writer</u>. New York: National Library Press, 1939.

Morley, Christopher Darlington. <u>One Act Plays</u>. Garden City, N. Y.: Doubleday, Page, 1924.

Morley, Henry, ed. <u>Plays from Molière by English Dramatists</u>. London: G. Routledge, 1883.

Morris, William. <u>Collected Works</u>. New York: Russell and Russell, 1966. Vol. 9.

Mortimer, John. <u>Five Plays</u>. London: Methuen, 1970.

_____. <u>Lunch Hour and Other Plays</u>. London: Methuen, 1960.

_____. <u>Three Plays</u>. New York: Grove Press, 1962.

Morton, Miriam, tr. & ed. <u>Russian Plays for Young Audiences: Five Contemporary Selections</u>. Rowayton, Conn.: New Plays Books, 1977.

Moses, Montrose J., ed. <u>British Plays from the Restoration to 1820</u>. Boston: Little, Brown, 1929. 2 vols.

_____. <u>Dramas of Modernism and Their Forerunners</u>. Boston: Little, Brown, 1931.

_____. <u>Representative American Dramas, National and Local</u>. Revised edition. Boston: Little, Brown, 1941.

_____. <u>Representative British Dramas: Victorian and Modern</u>. Boston: Little, Brown, 1918.

615   Author List of Anthologies

_____. Representative Continental Dramas. Boston: Little,
Brown, 1924.

_____. Representative Plays by American Dramatists. New York:
Dutton, 1918-1925. 3 vols.

Mrozek, Slawomir. Six Plays, translated by Nicholas Bethell. New
York: Grove Press, 1962.

_____. Three Plays. New York: Grove Press, 1973.

Muller, Robert, ed. The Television Dramatist. London: Paul Elek,
1973.

Munk, Kaj Harald Leininger. Five Plays, translated by R. P. Keig-
win. New York: American-Scandinavian Foundation, 1953.

Murphy, Arthur. Works. London: T. Cadell, 1786. Vols. 1-4.

Musset, Alfred de. Complete Writings. New York: J. L. Perkins
Company, 1908. Vols. 2-5, 10.

_____. Théâtre Complet. Paris: Gallimard, 1958.

Nelson, Robert James, ed. Enclosure: A Collection of Plays. New
York: D. McKay Company, 1975.

Neville, Edgar. Teatro Selecto de Edgar Neville. Madrid: Escelicer, 1968.

The New Caravan, edited by Alfred Kreymborg, Lewis Mumford,
Paul Rosenfeld. New York: W. W. Norton, 1936.

New Directions in Prose and Poetry. New York: New Directions,
1936-1977. Vols. 1-34.

The New Lafayette Theatre Presents: Plays with Aesthetic Comments
by 6 Black Playwrights, edited by Edward Bullins. New York:
Doubleday, 1974.

The New Negro Renaissance: An Anthology, edited by Arthur P.
Davis and Michael W. Peplow. New York: Holt, Rinehart
and Winston, 1975.

New Short Plays. London: Methuen, 1968-72. Vols, 1-3.

Nicol, Eric Patrick. Three Plays. Vancouver: Talonbooks, 1975.

Nobel Prize Library, published under the sponsorship of the Nobel
Foundation and the Swedish Academy. William Faulkner,
Eugene O'Neill, John Steinbeck. New York: Alexis Gregory,
1971.

Noyes, G. R., ed. Masterpieces of the Russian Drama. New York: Dover, 1960. 2 vols.

Obaldia, René de. Plays. London: Calder and Boyars, 1966-77. 4 vols.

Obey, Andre. Three Plays, translated from the French by Judith D. Suther and Earle D. Clowney. Fort Worth, Tex.: Texas Christian University Press, 1972.

Obras Breves del Teatro Costarricense. Coleccion la Propia. San Jose: Editorial Costa Rica, 1969, 1971. 2 vols.

O'Casey, Sean. Collected Plays. London: Macmillan, 1949-51. 4 vols.

O'Dea, Mark. Red Bud Women: Four Dramatic Episodes. Cincinnati: Stewart Kidd Company, 1922. Reprint edition, Great Neck, N. J.: Core Collection Books, 1976.

Odets, Clifford. Six Plays. New York: Modern Library, 1939.

Oehlenschläger, A. G. Tragoedier. Kjøbenhavn: Selskabet til udgivelse af Oehlenschlägers skrifter, 1879. 4 vols. in 2.

Off-Broadway Plays. Harmondsworth, Middlesex: Penguin, 1970, 1972. 2 vols.

Ogden, Jean. The Play Book, by Jean Carter and Jess Ogden. New York: Harcourt, Brace, 1937.

O'Hara, John. Five Plays. New York: Random House, 1961.

Oliver, Clinton F., ed. Contemporary Black Drama. New York: Scribner, 1971.

One-Act Plays for Stage and Study. New York: Samuel French, 1925-1949. Series 1-10.

O'Neill, Eugene. Plays. New York: Random House, 1951. 3 vols.

_____. Ten "Lost" Plays. New York: Random House, 1964.

O'Nolan, Brian. Stories and Plays, by Flann O'Brien, pseudonym. London: Hart-Davis, MacGibbon, 1973.

The Open Theater: Three Works by the Open Theater, edited by Karen Malpede. New York: Drama Book Specialists, 1974.

The Orgy: Modern One-Act Plays from Latin America, edited and translated by Gerardo Luzuriaga and Robert S. Rudder. Los Angeles: University of California Press, 1974.

Ortiz Guerrero, Manuel. Obras Completas. Asuncion: Patronato
de Leprosos del Paraguay, 1969.

Orton, Joe. Complete Plays. London: Methuen, 1976.

_____. Crimes of Passion. London: Methuen, 1967.

_____. Funeral Games and The Good and Faithful Servant. Lon-
don: Methuen, 1970.

Osborne, John. The End of Me Old Cigar and Jill and Jack. London: Faber and Faber, 1975.

_____. Four Plays. New York: Dodd, Mead, 1973.

_____. Plays for England. New York: Grove Press, 1966.

Ostrovskii, Alexandr Nikolaevich. Easy Money and Two Other Plays,
translated by David Magarshack. Westport, Conn.: Green-
wood Press, 1970.

_____. Five Plays, translated by E. K. Bristow. New York:
Pegasus, 1969.

Owen, Alun. Three TV Plays. New York: Hill and Wang, 1963.

Owen, Rochelle. The Karl Marx Play and Others. New York:
Drama Book Specialists, 1974.

_____, ed. Spontaneous Combustion: Eight New American Plays.
The Winter Repertory 6. New York: Winter House, 1972.

Oyono-Mbia, Guillaume. Three Suitors: One Husband & Until Further Notice. London: Methuen, 1974.

Parker, Kenneth T. Parker's Television Plays. Minneapolis: The
Northwestern Press, 1954.

Parone, Edward, ed. Collision Course. New York: Random House,
1968.

_____. New Theatre for Now. New York: Dell, 1970. Vol. 2
of "New Theatre in America."

_____. New Theatre in America. New York: Dell, 1965. Vol.
1 of 2.

Paso, Alfonso. Teatro Selecto de Alfonso Paso. Madrid: Escelicer, 1971.

Patrick, Robert. Cheep Theatricks. Winter Repertory no. 5. New
York: Winter House, 1972.

Patterson, Frances. Motion Picture Continuities, 1929. Reprint edition, New York: Garland Publishing, Incorporated, 1977.

Patterson, Lindsay, comp. Anthology of the American Negro in the Theatre; a Critical Approach. New York: Association for the Study of Negro Life and History, 1967.

_____. Black Theater. New York: Dodd, Mead, 1971.

Peele, George. Life and Works, edited by Charles Tyler Prouty. New Haven, Conn. : Yale University Press, 1952-70. 3 vols.

Peman, José Maria. Teatro Selecto de José Maria Peman. Madrid: Escelicer, 1968.

Phillips, Le Roy, ed. Types of Modern Dramatic Composition: an Anthology of One-Act Plays for Schools and Colleges, selected and edited by Le Roy Phillips and Theodore Johnson. Boston: Ginn, 1927.

Pillement, Georges, comp. Le Théâtre d'Aujourd'hui. Paris: Le Belier, 1970.

Pinero, Arthur Wing. Social Plays, edited by Clayton Hamilton. New York: Dutton, 1917-22. 4 vols.

Pinget, Robert. Plays. New York: Hill and Wang, 1966-68. 2 vols.

Pinter, Harold. Complete Works: One & Two. New York: Grove Press, 1977. 2 vols.

_____. Landscape and Silence and Night. New York: Grove Press, 1970.

Pirandello, Luigi. One-Act Plays, translated by William Murray. New York: Funk and Wagnalls, 1970.

_____. Teatro: Maschere Nude. Milano: A. Mondadori, 1930. 10 vols.

A Play and Two Poems, by Robert Kelly, Ron Loewinsohn, and Diane Wakoski. Los Angeles: Black Sparrow Press, 1968.

Playbook: Five Plays for a New Theatre. New York: New Directions, 1956.

Plays of the Year, edited by J. C. Trewin. London: P. Elek, 1948-76. Vols. 1-45.

Plays of the Year Special: Television Scripts of the Two Series "The Six Wives of Henry VIII" and "Elizabeth R", edited by J. C. Trewin. London: P. Elek, 1972. 2 vols.

Poland, Albert and Bruce Mailman. The Off Off Broadway Book. Indianapolis: Bobbs-Merrill, 1972.

Polanski, Roman. Polanski: 3 Filmscripts. New York: Harper and Row, 1975.

Porto-Riche, Georges de. Théâtre d'Amour. Paris: Ollendorff, 1922. 2 vols.

Powell, Anthony. Two Plays. Boston: Little, Brown, 1972.

Pratt, George C. Spellbound in Darkness: a History of the Silent Film. Revised edition, Greenwich, Conn.: New York Graphic Society, 1973.

Priestley, J. B. Plays. London: Heinemann, 1950. 3 vols.

Prize Plays of 1927-28. Philadelphia: Penn Publishing Company, 1930. 2 vols.

The Prize Plays of Television and Radio, 1956, foreword by Clifton Fadiman, New York: Random House, 1957.

Pucciani, Oreste F., ed. The French Theater Since 1930. Waltham, Mass: Blaisdell Publishing Company, 1954.

Pushkin, Alexander. Poems, Prose and Plays. New York: Modern Library, 1964.

Quinn, A. H., ed. Representative American Plays from 1767 to 1949. 7th edition, New York: Appleton-Century-Crofts, 1953.

Racine, Jean Baptiste. Complete Plays, translated by Samuel Solomon. New York: Random House, 1967.

Rahv, Philip, ed. Modern Occasions. New York: Farrar, Straus and Giroux, 1966.

Ramos, Maximo, ed. Philippine Harvest. Quezon City, Philippines: Phoenix Publishing House, 1964.

Randolph, Thomas. Poetical and Dramatic Works, collected and edited by W. Carew Hazlitt. New York: Benjamin Blom, 1968. 2 vols.

Ravitz, Abe C. The Disinherited: Plays. Encino, Calif.: Dickenson Publishing Company, 1974.

Reckford, Barry. Shyvers and X. London: Calder and Boyars, 1977.

Reed, Ishmael, ed. 19 Necromancers from Now. New York: Doubleday, 1970.

Reeve, F. D., tr. Contemporary Russian Drama. New York: Pegasus, 1968.

_____, ed. Nineteenth-Century Russian Plays. New York: Norton, 1961.

_____, ed. & tr. Twentieth Century Russian Plays: An Anthology. New York: Norton, 1963.

Renard, Jules. Poil de Carotte and Other Plays, edited by Stanley Hochman. New York: Frederick Ungar, 1977.

_____. Théâtre Complet. Paris: Gallimard, 1959.

Renzi, Renzo, ed. I Clowns, a Cura di Renzo Renzi. Rome: Cappelli Editore, 1970.

Rezvani, Medjid. Le Théâtre et la Danse en Iran. Paris: Maisonneuve et Larose, 1962.

Rialto-Film Preben Phillipsen & Jardran-Film. Winnetou, Film-Bildbuch. Hrsg. von Peter Korn. Bern: Phoenix Verlag, 1964-1966. 3 vols.

Rice, Elmer L. Seven Plays. New York: Viking Press, 1950.

_____. Three Plays Without Words. New York: Samuel French, 1934.

Richards, I. A. Internal Colloquies. New York: Harcourt Brace Jovanovich, 1971.

Richards, Stanley, ed. Best Mystery and Suspense Plays of the Modern Theatre. New York: Dood, Mead, 1971.

_____. Best Plays of the Sixties. New York: Doubleday, 1970.

_____, ed. Best Short Plays. New York: Chilton Book Company, 1968-1977. 10 vols.

_____, comp. Best Short Plays of the World Theatre, 1968-1973, edited with an introduction and prefaces to the plays. New York: Crown, 1973.

_____, ed. Canada on Stage. Toronto: Clarke, Irwin, 1960.

_____. 10 Classic Mystery and Suspense Plays of the Modern Theatre. New York: Dodd, Mead, 1973.

_____. Ten Great Musicals of the American Theatre. Radnor, Pa.: Chilton, 1973, 1976. 2 vols.

Richardson, Willis, ed. Plays and Pageants from the Life of the Negro. Washington, D. C.: Associated Publishers, 1930.

Richie, Donald. Ozu. Berkeley, Calif. : University of California Press, 1974.

Ridler, Anne. Who Is My Neighbour? and How Bitter the Bread. London: Faber and Faber, 1963.

Riley, Mrs. Alice Cushing (Donaldson). The Mandarin Coat and Five Other One-Act Plays for Little Theatres. New York: Brentano's, 1925.

_____. Ten Minutes by the Clock and Three Other Plays for Out-Door and In-Door Production. New York: George H. Doran Company, 1923.

Robinson, William H., Jr., ed. Early Black American Prose. Dubuque, Iowa: William C. Brown Company, 1971.

Roblès, Emmanuel. Three Plays. Carbondale: Southern Illinois University Press, 1977.

Rodgers, Richard and Oscar Hammerstein II. 6 Plays. New York: Modern Library, 1959.

Rodriguez Alvarez, Alejandro. Teatro. Buenos Aires: Editorial Losada, 1951-1965. 2 vols.

_____. Teatro Selecto de Alejandro Casona, pseudonym. Madrid: Escelicer, 1972.

Rolland, Romain. Plays. London: Jarrolds, 1927.

Roloff, Michael, ed. The Contemporary German Theater. New York: Avon, Equinox Books, 1972.

Romaines, Jules. Pièces en un Acte. Paris: Gallimard, 1930.

Rossellini, Roberto. The War Trilogy, translated by Judith Green. New York: Grossman, 1973.

Rotrou, Jean. Théâtre Choisi. Paris: Garnier Frères, 1928.

Rozewicz, Tadeusz. The Card Index and Other Plays. New York: Grove Press, 1970.

Rueda, Lope de. Teatro. Madrid: Espasa-Calpe, 1949.

Ryga, George. The Ecstasy of Rita Joe and Other Plays. New Drama 1. Toronto: New Press, 1971.

Sachs, Hans. Werke in Zwei Banden. Berlin: Aufbau, 1966. 2 vols.

Salacrou, Armand. Teatro. Buenos Aires: Losada, 1955.

————. Théâtre. Paris: Gallimard, 1943. 5 vols.

Salmon, Raul. Teatro Boliviano. La Paz, Bolivia: Los Amigos del Libro, 1969.

Saroyan, William. The William Saroyan Reader. New York: George Braziller, 1958.

Sarrante, Nathalie. Isma: ou, Ce Qui s'Appelle Rien. Paris: Gallimard, 1970.

Sartoris, Ramon. Three Plays. Washington, D. C.: The Black Sun Press, 1944.

Sartre, Jean-Paul. The Devil and the Good Lord and Two Other Plays. New York: Vintage, 1960.

————. No Exit and Three Other Plays. New York: Vintage, 1955.

Sastre, Alfonso. Teatro Selecto de Alfonso Sastre. Madrid: Escelicer, 1966.

Saunders, James. Neighbours and Other Plays. London: Deutsch, 1968.

Sayler, O. M., ed. The Moscow Art Theatre Series of Russian Plays. New York: Brentano's, 1923.

Schevill, James, ed. Break Out! In Search of New Theatrical Environments. Chicago: Swallow Press, 1973.

Schnitzler, Arthur. Comedies of Words and Other Plays, Englished from the German by Pierre Loving. Cincinnati: Stewart Kidd Company, 1917.

————. Theaterstücke, Berlin: S. Fischer Verlag, 1922. 4 vols.

Sedgwick, Ellery, comp. Atlantic Harvest: Memoirs of the Atlantic. Boston: Little, Brown, 1947.

The Seeking Years: Six Television Plays from CBS-TV Series "Look Up and Live, " edited by John M. Gunn. St. Louis, Mo.: The Bethany Press, 1959.

Segel, Harold B., tr. The Literature of 18th Century Russia. New York: Dutton, 1967. 2 vols.

Settel, Irving, ed. Top TV Shows of the Year, 1954-55. New York: Hastings House, 1955.

Seven Expressionist Plays: Kokoschka to Barlach, translated from the German by J. M. Ritchie and H. F. Garten. London: Calder and Boyars, 1968.

Seven Soviet Plays, with introductions by H. W. L. Dana. New York:
Macmillan, 1946.

Sforzosi, Luigi. Teatro Comico Moderno, Ossia Raccolta di Alcune
Commedie Italiane. Parigi: Truchy, 1836.

Shadwell, Thomas. Complete Works. London: Fortune Press, 1927.
5 vols.

Shaffer, Peter. The Private Ear and The Public Eye. London:
Hamilton, 1962.

_____. Three Plays. London: Penguin, 1976.

_____. Two Plays. New York: Atheneum, 1974.

Shakespeare, William. Five Restoration Adaptations of Shakespeare.
Urbana: University of Illinois Press, 1965.

_____. Shakespeare Adaptations, with notes by Montague Summers.
New York: B. Blom, 1966.

Shaver, Joseph L. , ed. Contemporary Canadian Drama. Ottawa:
Ottawa Press, Borealis Press, 1974.

Shaw, George Bernard. The Bodley Head Bernard Shaw, Collected
Plays with Their Prefaces. London: The Bodley Head, 1970-
1974. 7 vols.

Shearer, Marjorie. Four Short Plays for Introducing Discussions.
New York: Seabury Press, 1963.

Shepard, Sam. Five Plays. Indianapolis: Bobbs-Merrill, 1967.

_____. Mad Dog Blues and Other Plays. Winter Repertory no.
4. New York: Winter House, 1972.

_____. The Unseen Hand and Other Plays. Indianapolis: Bobbs-
Merrill, 1972.

Sheridan, Richard Brinsley. Dramatic Works. Oxford: Clarendon
Press, 1973. 2 vols.

Shirley, James. Dramatic Works & Poems. New York: Russell
and Russell, 1966. 6 vols.

Shuman, R. Baird, ed. A Galaxy of Black Writing. Durham, N. C. :
Moore Publishing Company, 1970.

Simpson, N. F. The Hole and Other Plays and Sketches. London:
Faber, 1946.

Six Plays. London: William Heinemann, 1934.

Smith, Moyne Rice. 7 Plays and How to Produce Them. New York: Walck, 1968.

Soyinka, Wole. Collected Plays. London: Oxford University Press, 1973. Vol. 1.

Spicer, Jack. The Collected Books of Jack Spicer, edited and with a commentary by Robin Blaser. Los Angeles: Black Sparrow Press, 1975.

Stafford, William T., ed. Twentieth Century American Writing. New York: Odyssey Press, 1965.

Stallone, Sylvester. The Official Rocky Scrapbook. New York: Grosset & Dunlap, 1977.

Stanton, Stephen S., ed. Camille and Other Plays. New York: Hill and Wang, 1957.

Steele, Richard. Plays. Oxford: Clarendon Press, 1971.

Sternheim, Carl. Scenes from the Heroic Life of the Middle Classes: 5 Plays. London: Calder and Boyars, 1970.

Stevens, John, ed. Ten Canadian Short Plays. New York: Dell Publishing Company, 1975.

Stone, Donald, Jr., ed. Four Renaissance Tragedies. Cambridge: Harvard University Press, 1966.

Stoppard, Tom. Albert's Bridge and Other Plays. New York: Grove Press, 1977.

_____. Artist Descending a Staircase and Where Are They Now? Two Plays for Radio. London: Faber and Faber, 1973.

_____. Dirty Linen and New-Found Land. London: Faber and Faber, 1976.

Story, the Yearbook of Discovery. New York: Four Winds Press, 1968-71.

Strindberg, August. The Chamber Plays, translated by Evert Sprinchorn, Seabury Quinn, Jr., and Kenneth Petersen. New York: Dutton, 1962.

_____. Eight Expressionist Plays. New York: New York University Press, 1972.

_____. Pre-Inferno Plays. Seattle: University of Washington Press, 1970.

Sukhovo-Kobylin, Alexander. The Trilogy, translated by H. B. Segel. New York: Dutton, 1969.

Sullivan, Victoria and James Hatch, ed. <u>Plays By and About Women.</u>
New York: Random House, 1973.

Swados, Harvey, ed. <u>The American Writer and the Great Depression.</u>
Indianapolis: Bobbs-Merrill, 1966.

Swinburne, Algernon Charles. <u>Complete Works,</u> edited by Edmund
Gosse and T. J. Wise. London: William Heinemann, 1926.
Vols. 7-10.

Swortzell, Lowell, ed. <u>All the World's a Stage: Modern Plays for
Young People.</u> New York: Delacorte Press, 1972.

Synge, John Millington. <u>Collected Works.</u> London: Oxford University Press, 1968.

Tamayo y Baus, Manuel. <u>Obras Completas.</u> Madrid: Ediciones
Fax, 1947.

Tapia y Rivera, Alejandro. <u>Obras Completas.</u> San Juan de Puerto
Rico: Instituto de Cultura Puertorriqueña, 1968. 2 vols.

Tatham, John. <u>Dramatic Works.</u> New York: Benjamin Blom, 1967.

Taylor, Peter. <u>Presences: Seven Dramatic Pieces.</u> Boston: Houghton Mifflin, 1973.

<u>El Teatro Actual Latinoamericano,</u> edited by Carlos Solorzano. Mé-
xico, D. F.: Ediciones de Andrea, 1972.

<u>Teatro Alemán Contemporáneo.</u> Madrid: Aguilar, 1965.

<u>Teatro Argentino Contemporáneo.</u> Madrid: Aguilar, 1962.

<u>Teatro Belga Contemporáneo.</u> Madrid: Aguilar, 1965.

<u>Teatro Breve Hispanoamericano Contemporáneo.</u> Madrid: Aguilar, 1969.

<u>Teatro Chileño Contemporáneo.</u> México, D. F.: Aguilar, 1970.

<u>Teatro Cómico Soviético.</u> Madrid: Aguilar, 1968.

<u>Teatro Contemporaneo Hispanoamericano,</u> prologo, seleccion y notas
de Orlando Rodriguez-Sardinas y Carlos Miguel Suarez Radillo. Madrid: Escelicer, 1971. Tomo I-II.

<u>Teatro Cubano Contemporáneo.</u> Madrid: Aguilar, 1959.

<u>Teatro Danes Contemporáneo.</u> Madrid: Aguilar, 1962.

<u>Teatro Ecuatoriano Contemporáneo.</u> Guayaquil, Ecuador: Casa de
la Cultura Ecuatoriana, 1971. Vol. 2.

Teatro Español. Madrid: Aguilar, 1949/50-1973/74.

Teatro Flamenco Contemporáneo. México, D. F.: Aguilar, 1962.

Teatro Frances de Vanguardia. Madrid: Aguilar, 1967.

Teatro Guatemalteco Contemporáneo. Madrid: Aguilar, 1964.

El Teatro Hispanoamericano Contemporáneo, edited by Carlos Solorzano. México, D. F.: Fonda de Cultura Economica, 1964. Vol. 1.

Teatro Inglés Contemporáneo. Madrid: Aguilar, 1965.

Teatro Inquieto Español. Madrid: Aguilar, 1967.

Teatro Irlandes Contemporáneo. Madrid: Aguilar, 1963.

Teatro Italian Contemporáneo. Madrid: Aguilar, 1961.

Teatro Japonés Contemporáneo. Madrid: Aguilar, 1964.

Teatro Méxicano. Madrid: Aguilar, 1958-59, 1963-64.

Teatro Méxicano Contemporáneo. Madrid: Aguilar, 1962.

Teatro Méxicano del Siglo XIX, prologo y notas de Antonio Magana-Esquivel. México, D. F.: Fonda de Cultura Economica, 1972. Vol. 1.

Teatro Méxicano del Siglo XX, seleccion, prologo y notas de Antonio Magana-Esquivel. México, D. F.: Fonda de Cultura Economica, 1956-70. Vols. 1-5.

Teatro Neerlands Contemporáneo. Madrid: Aguilar, 1959.

Teatro Norteamericano Contemporáneo. Madrid: Aguilar, 1968.

Teatro Noruego Contemporáneo. México, D. F.: Aguilar, 1960.

Teatro Peruano Contemporáneo. Madrid: Aguilar, 1959.

Teatro Portugués Contemporáneo. Madrid: Aguilar, 1961.

Teatro Puertorriqueño: Octavo Festival. San Juan de Puerto Rico: Instituto de Cultura Puertorriqueña, 1966.

Teatro Puertorriqueño: Quinto Festival. San Juan de Puerto Rico: Instituto de Cultura Puertorriqueña, 1963.

Teatro Sueco Contemporáneo. Madrid: Aguilar, 1967.

Teatro Uruguayo Contemporáneo. Madrid: Aguilar, 1960.

Tennyson, Alfred Tennyson, 1st Baron. <u>Poems and Plays.</u> London: Oxford University Press, 1967.

Théâtre du XVIIe Siècle, edited by Jacques Scherer. Paris: Gallimard, 1975. Vol. 1.

Théâtre du XVIIIe Siècle, edited by Jacques Truchet. Paris: Gallimard, 1972. 2 vols.

Thomas, Dylan. <u>The Doctor and the Devil and Other Scripts.</u> New York: New Directions, 1966.

Thompson, Laurence C., Willis Konick, & Vladimir Gross, eds. <u>Ballada o Soldate.</u> New York: Harcourt, Brace and World, 1966.

<u>Three Australian Plays,</u> edited by Eunice Hanger. Minneapolis: University of Minnesota Press, 1968.

<u>3 Filipino Playwrights.</u> Manila: Philippine Educational Theater Association, 1968.

<u>Three French Farces.</u> Baltimore, Md.: Penguin Books, 1973.

<u>Three Popular French Comedies,</u> translated by Albert Bermel. New York: Frederick Ungar, 1975.

Tibble, Anne, ed. <u>African English Literature.</u> New York: October House, 1965.

Tolkien, J. R. R. <u>The Tolkien Reader.</u> New York: Ballantine Books, 1966.

Tolstoi, Lev Nikalawich. <u>Plays,</u> translated by Louise and Aylmer Maude. London: Oxford University Press, 1928.

Totheroh, Dan. <u>One-Act Plays for Everybody.</u> New York: Samuel French, 1931.

Tremblay, Michel. <u>Deux Pièces.</u> Ottawa: Lemeac, 1970.

<u>Tres Dramas Romanticos.</u> Freeport, N. Y.: Books for Libraries Press, 1970.

Truffaut, François. <u>4 by Truffaut: The Adventures of Antoine Doinel.</u> New York: Simon and Schuster, 1972.

Turgenev, Ivan Sergeyevich. <u>The Plays of Ivan S. Turgenev,</u> translated by M. S. Mandell. New York: Macmillan, 1924. 2 vols.

<u>Two Great Belgian Plays About Love,</u> translated from the French by Marnix Gijsen. New York: Heinemann, 1966.

<u>Two Russian Film Classics.</u> Classic Film Scripts Series. New
    York: Simon and Schuster, 1973.

Unruh, Fritz von. <u>Dramen.</u> Nürnberg: Verlag Han Carl, 1960.

Usigli, Rudolfo. <u>Teatro Completo.</u> México, D. F.: Fondo de Cul-
    tura Economica, 1963, 1966. 2 vols.

Ustinov, Peter. <u>Five Plays.</u> Boston: Little, Brown, 1965.

Valdez, Luis. <u>Actos,</u> by Luis Valdez y El Teatro Campesino. San
    Juan Bautista, Calif.: Cucaracha Publications, 1971.

Valery, Paul. <u>Collected Works, Vol. 3: Plays.</u> New York: Pan-
    theon, 1960.

_____. <u>Oeuvres.</u> Paris: Gallimard, 1960. 2 vols.

Vanbrugh, Sir John. <u>Plays.</u> London: C. Hitch and L. Hawes,
    1759.

Van Itallie, Jean-Claude. <u>American Hurrah & Other Plays.</u> New
    York: Grove Press, 1978.

Verga, Giovanni. <u>Teatro di Giovanni Verga.</u> Milano: Fratelli Tre-
    ves, 1912.

Vernon, Virginia & Frank, comp. <u>Modern One-Act Plays from the
    French.</u> New York: Samuel French, 1933.

Vian, Boris. <u>Théâtre.</u> Paris: Jean-Jacques Pauvert, 1972.

_____. <u>Théâtre Inedit.</u> Paris: Christian Bourgois, 1970.

<u>Victorian Melodramas: Seven English, French and American Melo-
    dramas,</u> edited and introduced by James L. Smith. London:
    J. M. Dent, 1976.

Vigny, Alfred Victor. <u>Oeuvres Completes.</u> Paris: Gallimard, 1948.
    2 vols.

Vildrac, Charles. <u>Théâtre.</u> Paris: Gallimard, 1943. 2 vols.

<u>Vision and Aftermath: Four Expressionist War Plays,</u> translated
    from the German by J. M. Ritchie and J. D. Stowell. London:
    Calder and Boyars, 1969.

Vitrac, Roger. <u>Victor and Other Plays.</u> London: Calder and Boy-
    ars, 1977.

Voltaire, François Marie Arouet de. <u>Works: Dramatic Works.</u>
    New York: St. Hubert Guild, 1901. Vols. 8-10.

Walcott, Derek. Dream on Monkey Mountain & Other Plays. New York: Farrar, Straus and Giroux, 1970.

Ward, Edmund. The Challengers; a Series of Plays for Yorkshire Television. London: Elek, 1972.

Weales, Gerald Clifford, ed. Edwardian Plays. New York: Hill and Wang, 1962.

_____. Revolution: A Collection of Plays, edited by Gerald Clifford Weales and Robert J. Nelson. New York: D. McKay, 1975.

Webster, John. Complete Works, edited by F. L. Lucas. London: Chatto and Windus, 1927. 4 vols.

Wedekind, Frank. The Lulu Plays and Other Sex Tragedies, translated by Stephen Spender. London: Calder and Boyars, 1972.

Weinberg, Herman G., comp. The Complete Greed of Erich von Stroheim. New York: Dutton, 1973.

Weiss, M. Jerry, ed. 10 Short Plays. New York: Dell Publishing Company, 1963.

Wells, H. G. A Film by H. G. Wells: The Man Who Could Work Miracles. New York: Macmillan Company, 1936.

Wells, Henry W., ed. Six Sanskrit Plays. New York: Asia Publishing House, 1964.

Wellwarth, George E., ed. German Drama Between the Wars. New York: Dutton, 1972.

_____. New Generation Spanish Drama. Montreal: Engendra Press, 1976.

_____. The New Wave Spanish Drama. New York: New York University Press, 1970.

_____. Themes of Drama: An Anthology. New York: Crowell, 1973.

Wertmüller, Lina. The Screenplays of Lina Wertmüller. New York: Quadrangle/New York Times Book Company, 1977.

Wesker, Arnold. Plays. New York: Harper and Row, 1976. Vol. 1.

_____. The Wesker Trilogy. New York: Random House, 1960.

Weyl, Fernand. Three Gallant Plays, by Fernand Noziere, pseudonym. New York: William Edwin Rudge, 1929.

White, Edgar. The Crucificado: Two Plays. New York: William Morrow, 1973.

_____. Underground: 4 Plays. New York: William Morrow, 1970.

Whiting, John. The Collected Plays of John Whiting. New York: Theatre Arts Books, 1969. 2 vols.

Whitney, Thomas P., tr. The New Writing in Russia. Ann Arbor: University of Michigan Press, 1964.

Wieland, Christoph Martin. Werke: Dramen, Essays, Dialoge. München: Carl Hanser Verlag, 1967. Vol. 3.

Wilde, Oscar. Plays. New York: A. and C. Boni, 1935.

Wilder, Thornton. Three Plays. New York: Harper and Row, 1957.

Wilkins, Nigel, ed. Two Miracles. New York: Barnes and Noble, 1973.

The William Carlos Williams Reader, edited by M. L. Rosenthal. New York: New Directions Books, 1966.

Williams, Frayne, ed. Three Oriental Plays. Los Angeles: J. A. Alles Company, 1921.

Williams, Heathcote. AC/DC & The Local Stigmatic. New York: Viking, 1973.

_____. Collected Plays. London: Calder and Boyars, 1977. Vol. 1.

Williams, Tennessee. Teatro, traduccion de Manuel Barberá. Buenos Aires: Editorial Losada, 1966. 2 vols.

_____. The Theatre of Tennessee Williams. New York: New Directions, 1971-76. 5 vols.

Williams, William Carlos. Many Loves and Other Plays: The Collected Plays of William Carlos Williams. New York: New Directions Books, 1961.

Wilson, Edmund. Five Plays. New York: Farrar, Straus and Young, 1954.

Wilson, John. Dramatic Works, New York: Benjamin Blom, 1967.

Wilson, Lanford. The Rimers of Eldritch and Other Plays. New York: Hill and Wang, 1967.

Witkiewicz, Stanislaw Ignacy. The Madman and the Nun and Other Plays. Seattle: University of Washington Press, 1968.

_____. Tropical Madness: Four Plays. The Winter Repertory
7. New York: Winter House, 1972.

Wood, Charles. Cockade: Three One-Act Plays. New York: Grove
Press, 1967.

Wycherley, William. Complete Plays, edited by Gerald Weales.
New York: New York University Press, 1967.

_____. Complete Works, edited by Montague Summers. New
York: Russell and Russell, 1964, Vols. 1-2.

Wylie, Max, ed. Best Broadcasts of 1938-39; 1939-40. New York:
Whittlesey House, 1939, 1940. 2 vols.

Yeats, William Butler. Collected Plays. New York: Macmillan,
1952.

Young, Stark. Addio, Madretta & Other Plays. Chicago: C. S. Sergel and Company, 1912. Reprint edition, Great Neck, N. Y.:
Core Collection Books, 1976.

Zola, Emile. Oeuvres Completes: Théâtre I, II. Paris: François
Bernouard, 1927. Vols. 42-43.

A-A-America! and Stone, by Edward Bond. London: Methuen, 1976.

AC/DC & The Local Stigmatic, by Heathcote Williams. New York: Viking, 1973.

Acting Is Believing, by Charles J. McGaw. New York: Reinhart, 1955.

Actos, by Luis Valdez y El Teatro Campesino. San Juan Bautista, Calif.: Cucaracha Publications, 1971.

Addio, Madretta & Other Plays, by Stark Young. Chicago: C. S. Sergel and Company, 1912. Reprint edition, Great Neck, N. Y.: Core Collection Books, 1976.

African English Literature, edited by Anne Tibble. New York: October House, 1965.

Agee on Film, by James Agee. New York: McDowell, Obolensky, 1958, 1960. Vol. 2.

Aiiieeeee! An Anthology of Asian-American Writers, edited by Frank Chin and others. Washington, D. C.: Howard University Press, 1974.

Albert's Bridge and Other Plays, by Tom Stoppard. New York: Grove Press, 1977.

All the World's a Stage; Modern Plays for Young People, edited by Lowell Swortzell. New York: Delacorte Press, 1972.

Amedee; The New Tenant; Victims of Duty, by Eugene Ionesco. New York: Grove Press, 1958.

American Blues, by Tennessee Williams. New York: Dramatists Play Service, 1948.

The American Caravan: A Yearbook of American Literature, edited by Van Wyck Brooks, Lewis Mumford, Alfred Kreymborg, Paul Rosenfeld. New York: Macauly, 1927.

American Drama, edited by Alan Seymour Downer. New York: Crowell, 1960.

American Hurrah: Plays, by Jean-Claude Van Itallie. New York: Coward-McCann, 1967.

American Hurrah & Other Plays, by Jean-Claude Van Itallie. New York: Grove Press, 1978.

The American Writer and the Great Depression, edited by Harvey Swados. Indianapolis: Bobbs-Merrill, 1966.

Amphitryon: Three Plays in New Verse Translations, Together with a Comprehensive Account of the Evolution of the Legend and its Subsequent History on the Stage. Chapel Hill: University of North Carolina Press, 1974.

The Anthem Sprinters and Other Antics, by Ray Bradbury. New York: Dial Press, 1963.

Anthology of Danish Literature, edited by Frederick Julius Billeskov and P. M. Mitchell. Carbondale: Southern Illinois University Press, 1971.

Anthology of Japanese Literature, edited by Donald Keene. New York: Grove Press, 1955.

Anthology of the American Negro in the Theatre; a Critical Approach. New York: Association for the Study of Negro Life and History, 1967.

The Anxious Years: America in the 1930s; a Collection of Contemporary Writings, edited by Louis Filler. New York: Capricorn, 1963.

The Apartment and The Fortune Cookie, two screenplays by Billy Wilder and I. A. L. Diamond. New York: Praeger, 1970.

The Apprentice Fiction of F. Scott Fitzgerald, edited and introduced by John Kuehl. New Brunswick, N. J.: Rutgers University Press, 1965.

The Aquarium and Other Plays, by Stewart Conn. London: Calder and Boyars, 1973.

The Army Play by Play: Five One-Act Plays, with a foreword by John Golden. New York: Random House, 1943.

The Art of Modern Drama, compiled by R. F. Dietrich. New York: Holt, Rinehart and Winston, 1969.

Artist Descending a Staircase and Where Are They Now? Two Plays for Radio, by Tom Stoppard. London: Faber and Faber, 1973.

Artists' Theatre: Four Plays, edited by Herbert Manchiz. New York: Grove Press, 1960.

<u>Asif Currimbhoy's Plays</u>. New Delhi: Oxford and IBH Publishing
     Company, 1972.

<u>Atlantic Book of Modern Plays</u>, edited by Sterling Andrus Leonard.
     Boston: Little, Brown, 1921.

<u>Atlantic Harvest: Memoirs of the Atlantic</u>, compiled by Ellery Sedg-
     wick. Boston: Little, Brown, 1947.

<u>Australian Theatre Workshop</u>. Victoria: Heinemann Educational Aus-
     tralia, 1969-1975. Vols. 1-13.

<u>The Automobile Graveyard and The Two Executioners</u>, by Fernando
     Arrabal. New York: Grove Press, 1960.

<u>Ballada o Soldate</u>, edited by Laurence C. Thompson, Willis Konick,
     and Vladimir Gross. New York: Harcourt, Brace and World,
     1966.

<u>"Balls" and Other Plays</u>, by Paul Foster. London: Calder and Boy-
     ars, 1967.

<u>The Bankrupt and Other Plays</u>, by David Mercer. London: Eyre
     Methuen, 1974.

<u>Banner Anthology of One-Act Plays by American Authors</u>, compiled
     by Leslie H. Carter. San Francisco: Banner Plays Bureau,
     1969.

<u>Bell's British Theatre</u>, by John Bell. London: G. Cawthorn, 1797.
     34 vols.

<u>Bergman: Persona and Shame</u>, by Ingmar Bergman. New York:
     Grossman, 1972.

<u>Best American Plays</u>, edited by John Gassner. Third Series, 1945-
     1951. New York: Crown, 1952.

<u>Best American Plays</u>, edited by John Gassner. Fourth Series, 1952-
     1957. New York: Crown, 1958.

<u>Best American Plays</u>, edited by John Gassner. Fifth Series, 1958-
     1963. New York: Crown, 1963.

<u>Best American Plays</u>, edited by John Gassner. Sixth Series, 1963-
     1967. New York: Crown, 1971.

<u>Best American Plays</u>, edited by Clive Barnes. Seventh Series, 1967-
     1973. New York: Crown, 1974.

<u>Best American Plays</u>, edited by John Gassner. Supplementary Vol-
     ume, 1918-1958. New York: Crown, 1961.

Best Broadcasts of 1938-39; 1939-40, edited by Max Wylie. New
York: Whittlesey House, 1939, 1940. 2 vols.

Best Film Plays, 1945-1946, compiled by John Gassner and Dudley
Nichols. New York: Crown, 1946.

Best Mystery and Suspense Plays of the Modern Theatre, edited by
Stanley Richards. New York: Dodd, Mead, 1971.

The Best of Buster. The Classic Comedy Scenes Direct from the
Films of Buster Keaton. New York: Darien House, 1976.

The Best of Off-Off Broadway, edited by Michael Townsend Smith.
New York: Dutton, 1969.

Best One-Act Plays, selected by J.W. Marriott. London: Harrap,
1931-1959.

Best Pictures, 1939-40, edited by Jerry Wald and Richard Macaulay.
New York: Dodd, Mead, 1940.

Best Plays of the Early American Theatre from the Beginning to
1916, edited by John Gassner. New York: Crown, 1967.

Best Plays of the Modern American Theatre, edited by John Gassner.
Second Series, 1939-1946. New York: Crown, 1947.

Best Plays of the Sixties, edited by Stanley Richards. New York:
Doubleday, 1970.

Best Short Plays (formerly Best One-Act Plays), edited by Margaret
Mayorga. New York: Dodd, Mead, 1937-1967/68; edited by
Stanley Richards. New York: Chilton Book Co., 1968-1977.
10 Vols.

Best Short Plays of the Social Theatre, edited by William Kozlinko.
New York: Random House, 1939.

Best Short Plays of the World Theatre, 1958-1967, edited by Stanley
Richards. New York: Crown, 1968.

Best Short Plays of the World Theatre, 1968-1973, compiled and
edited, with an introduction and prefaces to the plays, by
Stanley Richards. New York: Crown, 1973.

Best Television Plays, edited by Gore Vidal. New York: Ballantine
Books, 1956.

Best Television Plays, 1957, edited by William I. Kaufman. New
York: Harcourt, 1957.

Best Television Plays of the Year, 1949, 1950-51, 1954, edited by
William I. Kaufman. New York: Merlin Press, 1950-1954.

Big Mother and Other Plays, by Charles Dizenzo. New York: Grove Press, 1970.

The Black Crook and Other 19th Century American Plays, edited by Myron Matlaw. New York: Dutton, 1967.

Black Drama Anthology, edited by Woodie King and Ron Milner. New York: Columbia University Press, 1972.

Black Fire: An Anthology of Afro-American Writing, edited by Le Roi Jones and Larry Neal. New York: William Morrow, 1968.

Black Insights: Significant Literature by Black Americans, 1760 to the Present. Waltham, Mass.: Xerox College Publishing, 1971.

The Black President and Other Plays, by James Erwin Schevill. Denver, Col.: A. Swallow, 1965.

A Black Quartet; Four New Black Plays. New York: New American Library, 1970.

The Black Teacher and the Dramatic Arts, by William R. Reardon and Thomas D. Painley. Westport, Conn.: Negro University Press, 1970.

Black Theater, edited by Lindsay Patterson. New York: Dodd, Mead, 1971.

Black Theater, USA: 45 Plays by Black Americans, 1847-1974, edited by James V. Hatch. New York: Free Press, 1974.

Black Voices from Prison, by Etheridge Knight. New York: Pathfinder Press, 1970.

Black Writers of America: A Comprehensive Anthology, edited by Richard Barksdale and Kenneth Kinnamon. New York: Macmillan, 1972.

Blackamerican Literature 1760-Present, edited by Ruth Miller. Beverly Hills, Calif.: Glencoe Press, 1971.

The Blue Dahlia; a screenplay by Raymond Chandler, with a memoir by John Houseman, edited by Matthew H. Bruccoli. Carbondale: Southern Illinois University Press, 1976.

Boccaccio's Untold Tale, by Harry Kemp. New York: Brentano's, 1924.

The Bodley Head Bernard Shaw, Collected Plays with Their Prefaces. London: The Bodley Head, 1970-1974. 7 vols.

The Bonnie and Clyde Book, by David Newman. New York: Simon and Schuster, 1972.

A Book of Short Plays XV-XX Centuries. London: English Association, Oxford University Press, 1940.

The Book of the Goons, by Terrence Allan ("Spike") Milligan. New York: St. Martin's Press, 1974.

The Box and Quotations from Chairman Mao Tse-tung, by Edward Albee. New York: Atheneum, 1969.

Brains and Other One-Act Plays, by Martin Flavin. New York: Samuel French, 1926.

Bread Loaf Book of Plays, edited by Hortense Moore. Middlebury, Vt.: Middlebury College Press, 1941.

Break Out! In Search of New Theatrical Environments, edited by James Schevill. Chicago: Swallow Press, 1973.

British Plays from the Restoration to 1820, edited by Montrose J. Moses. Boston: Little, Brown, 1929. 2 vols.

British Plays of the 19th Century, edited by James Osler Bailey. New York: Odyssey Press, 1966.

Broadway's Beautiful Losers, edited by Marilyn Stasio. New York: Delacorte Press, 1972.

Buddha, Confucius, Christ: Three Prophetic Plays, edited by Harry Lawton and George Knox. New York: Herder, 1971.

Burlesque Plays of the 18th Century, edited by Simon Trussler. New York: Oxford University Press, 1969.

By Women: An Anthology of Literature, edited by Marcia McClintock Folsom and Linda Heinlein Kirschner. Boston: Houghton Mifflin, 1976.

Caligula and Three Other Plays, by Albert Camus. New York: Alfred A. Knopf, 1958.

Camille and Other Plays, edited by Stephen S. Stanton. New York: Hill and Wang, 1957.

Canada on Stage, edited by Stanley Richards. Toronto: Clarke, Irwin, 1960.

The Card Index and Other Plays, by Tadeusz Rozewicz. New York: Grove Press, 1970.

Carolina Folk-Plays, edited by Frederick Henry Koch. New York: Holt, 1922.

Casablanca, Script and Legend, by Howard Koch. Woodstock, N. Y.:
    Overlook Press, 1973.

Cavalcade: Negro American Writing from 1760 to the Present, edi-
    ted by Arthur P. Davis and Saunders Redding. Boston: Hough-
    ton Mifflin, 1971.

The Challengers; a Series of Plays for Yorkshire Television, by Ed-
    mund Ward. London: Elek, 1972.

The Chamber Plays, by August Strindberg, translated by Evert Sprin-
    chorn, Seabury Quinn, Jr., and Kenneth Petersen. New York:
    Dutton, 1962.

Change and Other Plays, by Wolfgang Bauer. New York: Hill and
    Wang, 1973.

A Change of Hearts: Plays, Films, and Other Dramatic Works, by
    Kenneth Koch. New York: Random House, 1973.

Cheep Theatricks, by Robert Patrick. Winter Repertory no. 5. New
    York: Winter House, 1972.

A Chelsea Trilogy, by Kenneth Jupp. London: Calder and Boyars, 1969.

The Chicago Review Anthology, edited by David Ray. Chicago: Uni-
    versity of Chicago Press, 1959.

Chief European Dramatists, edited by Brander Matthews. Boston:
    Houghton Mifflin, 1916.

Chief French Plays of the 19th Century, edited by Eliott Mansfield
    Grant. New York: Harper, 1934.

Chief Plays of Corneille, translated by Lacy Lockert. Princeton,
    N. J.: Princeton University Press, 1957.

The Chief Rivals of Corneille and Racine, edited by Lacy Lockert.
    Nashville, Tenn.: Vanderbilt University Press, 1956.

Christie in Love and Other Plays, by Howard Brenton. London:
    Methuen, 1970.

The Citizen Kane Book: Raising Kane, by Pauline Kael; shooting
    script by Herman J. Mankiewicz and Orson Welles. Boston:
    Little, Brown, 1971.

The City and the Court: Five 17th Century Comedies of London Life.
    San Francisco: Chandler Publishing Company, 1968.

Clásicos Castellanos. Madrid: Espasa-Calpe, 1947-1975. 207 vols:
    Vols. 2-3, 15, 20, 23, 32, 35, 37, 39, 50, 57-60, 65, 69-70,
    74, 89, 92, 96, 106-107, 127, 131-32, 137-38, 141-42, 146-47,
    152-53, 156-57, 159, 162, 171, 180-83, 200-01, 204, 206.

The Classic Theatre, edited by Eric Russell Bentley. Garden City,
     N. Y.: Doubleday, 1958-1961. 4 vols.

I Clowns, a Cura di Renzo Renzi. Rome: Cappelli Editore, 1970.

Cockade; Three One-Act Plays, by Charles Wood. New York: Grove
     Press, 1967.

The Collected Books of Jack Spicer, edited and with a commentary
     by Robin Blaser. Los Angeles: Black Sparrow Press, 1975.

Collected Plays, by Jean Anouilh. London: Methuen, 1966-67. 2 vols.

Collected Plays, by Bertolt Brecht, edited by Ralph Manheim and
     John Willitt. New York: Random House, 1971-1974. Vols.
     1, 5, 7, 9.

The Collected Plays of Albert Camus. London: Hamish Hamilton,
     1965.

Collected Plays, by Austin Clarke. Dublin: Dolmen Press, 1963.

Collected Plays of Clemence Dane, by Winfred Ashton. London:
     Heinemann, 1961. Vol. 1.

Collected Plays, by John Drinkwater. London: Sidgwick and Jack-
     son, 1925. 2 vols.

The Collected Plays of Lady Gregory, by Isabella Augusta Persse,
     Lady Gregory. Edited, with a foreword, by Ann Saddlemyer.
     Gerrards Cross, Buckinghamshire: Smythe, Colin, 1970. 4
     vols.

The Collected Plays, by Lillian Hellman. Boston: Little, Brown,
     1972.

Collected Plays, by William Somerset Maugham. London: Heinemann,
     1952. 3 vols.

Collected Plays, by Arthur Miller. New York: Viking Press, 1957.

Collected Plays, by Sean O'Casey. London: Macmillan, 1949-51.
     4 vols.

Collected Plays, by Terence Rattigan. London: H. Hamilton, 1953.
     3 vols.

Collected Plays, by Wole Soyinka. London: Oxford University Press,
     1973.

The Collected Plays of John Whiting. New York: Theatre Arts
     Books, 1969. 2 vols.

Collected Plays, by Charles Williams. London: Oxford University
    Press, 1963.

Collected Plays, by Emlyn Williams. New York: Random House,
    1961. Vol. 1.

Collected Plays, by Heathcote Williams. London: Calder and Boy-
    ars, 1977. Vol. 1.

Collected Plays, by William Butler Yeats. New York: Macmillan,
    1952.

The Collected Tales and Plays, by Nikolai Gogol, edited by L. J.
    Kent. New York: Modern Library, 1969.

Collected Works, by Ambrose Bierce. New York: Neale Publishing
    Company, 1909-1912. Vol. 12.

Collected Works, by Oliver Goldsmith, edited by Arthur Friedman.
    Oxford: Clarendon Press, 1966. Vol. 5.

Collected Works, by William Morris. New York: Russell and Rus-
    sell, 1966. Vol. 9.

Collected Works, by John Millington Synge. London: Oxford Uni-
    versity Press, 1968.

Collected Works, Vol. 3: Plays, by Paul Valéry. New York: Pan-
    theon, 1960.

A Collection of Canadian Plays, edited by Rolf Kalman. Toronto:
    Simon and Pierre Publishing Company, 1976. Vols. 1-3.

A Collection of Old English Plays, edited by Arthur Henry Bullen.
    New York: Benjamin Blom, 1964. 7 vols. in 4.

A Collection of the Most Esteemed Farces and Entertainments Per-
    formed on the British Stage. Edinburgh: S. Doig, 1792.
    6 vols.

Collision Course, edited by Edward Parone. New York: Random
    House, 1968.

Colonel Wotherspoon and Other Plays, by James Bridie, pseudonym
    for Osborne Henry Mavor. London: Constable, 1934.

Comanche Cafe/Domino Courts, by William Hauptman. New York:
    Samuel French, 1977.

Comedies & Tragedies, by Thomas Killigrew. New York: Benjamin
    Blom, 1967.

Comédies et Commentaires. Paris: Gallimard, 1959.

The Comedies of Ariosto, translated and edited by Edmond M. Beame and Leonard G. Sbrocchi. Chicago: University of Chicago Press, 1975.

Comedies of Words and Other Plays, by Arthur Schnitzler, Englished from the German by Pierre Loving. Cincinnati: Stewart Kidd Company, 1917.

The Comedy of Neil Simon. New York: Random House, 1971.

The Complete Greed of Erich von Stroheim, compiled by Herman G. Weinberg. New York: Dutton, 1973.

The Complete Greek Drama, edited by Whitney Jennings Oates. New York: Random House, 1938.

Complete Plays, by William Congreve, edited by Herbert Davis. Chicago: University of Chicago Press, 1967.

Complete Plays, by Thomas Stearns Eliot. New York: Harcourt, Brace and World, 1967.

Complete Plays, by William Dean Howells, edited by Walter J. Meserve. New York: New York University Press, 1960.

Complete Plays, by Henry James, edited by Leon Edel. London: Rupert Hart-Davis, 1949.

Complete Plays, by David Herbert Lawrence. London: Heinemann, 1965.

Complete Plays, by Christopher Marlowe, edited by Irving Ribner. New York: Odyssey Press, 1963.

Complete Plays, by Joe Orton. London: Methuen, 1976.

Complete Plays, by Jean Baptiste Racine, translated by Samuel Solomon. New York: Random House, 1967.

Complete Plays, by William Wycherley, edited by Gerald Weales. New York: New York University Press, 1967.

The Complete Plays of Gilbert and Sullivan. New York: Modern Library, 1936.

The Complete Roman Drama, edited by George Eckel Duckworth. New York: Random House, 1942.

Complete Works, by George Farquhar, edited by Charles Stonehill. New York: Gordian Press, 1967. 2 vols.

Complete Works, by John Keats. New York: AMS Press, 1970.

The Complete Works, by Akira Kurosawa, in Japanese and English.
Tokyo: Kinema Jumop Sha, 1970-71.   Vols. 4, 6, 9.

Complete Works: One & Two, by Harold Pinter.   New York: Grove
Press, 1977.

Complete Works, by Thomas Shadwell.   London: Fortune Press,
1927. 5 vols.

Complete Works, by Percy Bysshe Shelley.   London: Oxford University Press, 1933.

Complete Works, by Algernon Charles Swinburne, edited by Edmund
Gosse and T. J. Wise.   London: William Heinemann, 1926.
Vols. 7-10.

Complete Works, by John Webster, edited by F. L. Lucas.   London:
Chatto and Windus, 1927.   4 vols.

Complete Works, by William Wycherley, edited by Montague Summers.
New York: Russell and Russell, 1964.   Vols. 1-2.

Complete Writings, by Alfred de Musset.   New York: J. L. Perkins
Company, 1908.   Vols. 2-5, 10.

Contact with Drama, by David L. Hay and James F. Howell.   Chicago: Science Research Associates, 1974.

Contemporary Black Drama, edited by C. F. Oliver.   New York:
Scribner's, 1971.

Contemporary Canadian Drama, edited by Joseph L. Shaver.   Ottawa:
Ottawa Press, Borealis Press, 1974.

Contemporary Chicano Theatre, edited by Roberto J. Garza.   Notre
Dame, Ind.:   University of Notre Dame Press, 1976.

Contemporary Drama: 13 Plays, edited by Stanley Clayes and David
Spencer.   New York: Scribner's, 2nd edition 1970.

The Contemporary French Theater, edited by Bettina Knapp.   New
York: Avon, Equinox Books, 1973.

The Contemporary German Theater, edited by Michael Roloff.   New
York: Avon, Equinox Books, 1972.

Contemporary One-Act Plays, edited by Benjamin Roland Lewis.   New
York: Scribner's, 1922.

Contemporary Russian Drama, translated by F. D. Reeve.   New York:
Pegasus, 1968.

The Cookie Jar and Other Plays, edited by Linda Walsh Jenkins.
Minneapolis: University of Minnesota Press, 1975.

Cop Out, Muzeeka, Home Fires, by John Guare.   New York: Grove
     Press, 1971.

Copperfield '70, by George Curry.   New York: Ballantine Books,
     1970.

Counting Sheep; the Log and the Complete Play: "Sheep on the Run-
     way, " by Art Buchwald.   New York: Putnam, 1970.

Crimes of Passion, by Joe Orton.   London: Methuen, 1967.

The Crucificado: Two Plays, by Edgar White.   New York: William
     Morrow, 1973.

Crystal and Fox and The Mundy Scheme, by Brian Friel.   New
     York: Farrar, Straus and Giroux, 1970.

Cumberland's British Theatre, edited by George Daniel.   London:
     John Cumberland, 1825-1855.   45 vols.

Curtain Calls, by Noël Coward.   New York: Garden City Publishing
     Company, 1940.

A Day in October and Other Plays, by Georg Kaiser.   London: Cal-
     der and Boyars, 1977.

The Day the Whores Came Out to Play Tennis and Other Plays, by
     Arthur L. Kopit.   New York: Hill and Wang, 1965.

De L'Autre Cote du Mur Suivi de Cinq Courtes Pieces, by Marcel
     Dubé.   Ottawa: Lemeac, 1973.

The Delinquent, the Hipster, the Square, and the Sandpile Series.
     St. Louis: Cooperative Publishing Association, Bethany Press,
     1962.

Das Deutsche Drama, 1880-1933.   New York: W. W. Norton Com-
     pany, 1938.   2 vols.

Deux Films Français: Les Visiteurs du Soir and Le Feu Follet,
     edited by Robert M. Hammond and Marguerite Hammond.
     New York: Harcourt, Brace and World, 1965.

Deux Pièces, by Michel Tremblay.   Ottawa: Lemeac, 1970.

The Devil and the Good Lord and Two Other Plays, by Jean-Paul
     Sartre.   New York: Vintage, 1960.

Das Dichterische Werk: 1, Die Dramen, by Ernst Barlach.   Mün-
     chen: R. Piper, 1956.

Dichtungen und Schriften: 2, Prosa und Dramen, by Georg Heym.
     Hamburg: Verlag Heinrich Ellermann, 1962.

<u>Diminutive Dramas,</u> by Maurice Baring.   Boston: Houghton Mifflin, 1911.

<u>Dinny and the Witches: Two Plays,</u> by William Gibson.   New York: Atheneum, 1960.

<u>Dirty Linen and New-Found Land,</u> by Tom Stoppard.   London: Faber and Faber, 1976.

<u>The Disinherited: Plays,</u> by Abe C. Ravitz.   Encino, Calif.:   Dickenson Publishing Company, 1974.

<u>Disputed Plays of William Shakespeare,</u> edited by William Kozlenko. New York: Hawthorn Books, 1974.

<u>12 Obras en Un Acto,</u> edited by Wilberto Cantón.   Mexico: Ecuador 0° 0'0", 1967.

<u>The Doctor and the Devil and Other Scripts,</u> by Dylan Thomas.   New York: New Directions, 1966.

<u>Dogs; or, The Paris Comedy,</u> by William Saroyan.   New York: Phaedra, 1969.

<u>The Drama: Its History, Literature and Influence on Civilization,</u> edited by Alfred Bates.   London: The Athenian Society, 1903. 22 vols.

<u>Dramas,</u> by Victor Hugo.   Boston: Dana Estes, 1900.   4 vols.

<u>Dramas by Present Day Writers,</u> edited by Raymond Woodbury Pence. New York: Scribner's, 1927.

<u>Dramas, Discourses, and Other Pieces,</u> by James A. Hillhouse. New York: Benjamin Blom, 1967.   2 vols. in 1.

<u>Dramas from the American Theatre, 1762-1909,</u> edited by Richard Moody.   Cleveland: World Publishing Company, 1966.

<u>Dramas of Modernism and Their Forerunners,</u> edited by Montrose J. Moses.   Boston: Little, Brown, 1931.

<u>Dramatic Works,</u> by Richard Brome.   New York: AMS Press, 1966. 3 vols.

<u>Dramatic Works,</u> by Sir Aston Cokayne.   New York: Benjamin Blom, 1967.

<u>Dramatic Works,</u> by John Crowne.   New York: Benjamin Blom, 1967.

<u>Dramatic Works,</u> by Sir William D'Avenant.   Edinburgh: W. Paterson, 1872-1874.   5 vols.

Dramatic Works, by Thomas Dekker. Cambridge University Press,
1953. 4 vols.

Dramatic Works, by John Dryden. New York: Gordian Press, 1968.
6 vols.

Dramatic Works, by Samuel Foote. New York: Benjamin Blom,
1968. 2 vols.

Dramatic Works, by David Garrick. London: A. Millar, Strand,
1798; reprint edition, Farnborough, England: Gregg International Publishers, 1969. 3 vols.

The Dramatic Works of John Lacy, 1875. New York: Benjamin
Blom, 1967.

Dramatic Works, by Shakerly Marmion. New York: Benjamin Blom,
1967.

Dramatic Works, by Richard Brinsley Sheridan. Oxford: Clarendon
Press, 1973. 2 vols.

Dramatic Works, by John Tatham. New York: Benjamin Blom,
1967.

Dramatic Works, by John Wilson. New York: Benjamin Blom, 1967.

Dramatic Works & Poems, by James Shirley. New York: Russell
and Russell, 1966. 6 vols.

Dramen, by Alfred Brust. Hrsg. von Horst Denkler. München: W.
Fink, 1971.

Dramen, by Fritz Hochwälder. Wiesbaden, Germany: Styria Graz
Wien Köln, 1975. 2 vols.

Dramen, by Hugo von Hofmannsthal. Frankfurt am Main: S. Fischer Verlag, 1950. 4 vols.

Dramen, by Hans Henny Jahnn. Frankfurt am Main: Europäische
Verlagsanstalt, 1965. 2 vols.

Dramen, by Karl Kraus. München, Wien: Albert Langen, 1967.

Dramen, by Fritz von Unruh. Nürnberg: Verlag Hans Carl, 1960.

Dream on Monkey Mountain & Other Plays, by Derek Walcott. New
York: Farrar, Straus and Giroux, 1970.

Early Black American Prose, edited by William H. Robinson, Jr.
Dubuque, Iowa: William C. Brown Company, 1971.

The Early Plays, by Mikhail Bulgakov, edited by Ellendea Proffer.
Bloomington: Indiana University Press, 1972.

Early Plays, by Harold Pinter. New York: Grove Press, 1969.

Early Plays from the Italian, compiled by Richard Warwick Bond.
    New York: Benjamin Blom, 1967.

Early Screenplays, by Federico Fellini. New York: Grossman, 1971.

East and Other Plays, by Steven Berkoff. London: Calder and Boy-
    ars, 1977.

Easy Money and Two Other Plays, by Alexandr Nikolaevich Ostrov-
    skii, translated by David Magarshack. Westport, Conn.:
    Greenwood Press, 1970.

The Ecstasy of Rita Joe and Other Plays, by George Ryga. New
    Drama 1. Toronto: New Press, 1971.

Edwardian Plays, edited by Gerald Clifford Weales. New York: Hill
    and Wang, 1962.

Eight American Ethnic Plays, edited by Francis Griffith and Joseph
    Mersand. New York: Charles Scribner's Sons, 1974.

Eight European Plays, compiled by Winifred Katzin, with a preface
    by Barrett H. Clark. New York: Brentano's, 1927.

Eight Expressionist Plays, by August Strindberg. New York: New
    York University Press, 1972.

Eight Plays, by Dietrich Eckart. Houston, Texas: William Gilles-
    pie, 1977. 35mm microfilm.

Eight Plays from Off-Off Broadway, edited by Nick Orzel and Mi-
    chael Smith. Indianapolis: Bobbs-Merrill, 1966.

Eighteenth Century Drama: Afterpieces, edited by R. W. Bevis.
    London: Oxford University Press, 1970.

Eighteenth Century Tragedy, edited by M. R. Booth. London: Ox-
    ford University Press, 1965.

Electronic Drama: Television Plays of the Sixties, selected by
    Richard Averson and David Manning White. Boston: Beacon
    Press, 1971.

Eleven Plays, by Henrik Ibsen. New York: Modern Library, 1935.

Eleven Short Plays, by William Inge. New York: Dramatists Play
    Service, 1962.

Eleven Verse Plays, by Maxwell Anderson. New York: Harcourt,
    Brace, 1940.

647   Title List of Anthologies

Elizabeth I and Other Plays, by Paul Foster. London: Calder and Boyars, 1973.

The Empress of Morocco and Its Critics: Settle, Dryden, Shadwell, Crowne, Duffet; with an introduction by Maximillian E. Novak. Augustan Reprint Society. Los Angeles: University of California Press, 1968.

Enclosure: A Collection of Plays, edited by Robert James Nelson. New York: D. McKay Company, 1975.

The End of Me Old Cigar and Jill and Jack, by John Osborne. London: Faber and Faber, 1975.

Ends and Odds: Eight New Dramatic Pieces, by Samuel Beckett. New York: Grove Press, 1976.

English One-Act Plays of Today, compiled by Donald Fitz John. London: Oxford University Press, 1962.

English Plays of the 19th Century, edited by Michael R. Booth. London: Oxford University Press, 1969-1973. 4 vols.

Epic and Folk Plays of the Yiddish Theatre, translated and edited by David S. Lifson. London: Associated University Presses, 1975.

Fables & Vaudevilles & Plays. Theatre More-or-Less at Random, by Norman D. Dietz. Richmond, Va.: John Knox Press, 1966.

The Factory Lab Anthology, edited by Connie Brissenden. Vancouver: Talonbooks, 1974.

Falling Sickness: A Book of Plays, by Russell Edson. New York: New Directions, 1975.

Famous Chinese Plays, translated by L. C. Arlington and Harold Action. New York: Russell and Russell, 1963.

Famous Plays of Today: 1929-39, 1953-54. London: Gollancz. 16 vols.

Fate of a Cockroach: Four Plays of Freedom, by Tewfik Al-Hakim. London: Heinemann, 1973.

Favorite American Plays of the Nineteenth Century, edited by Barret H. Clark. Princeton, N.J.: Princeton University Press, 1943.

Federal Theatre Plays, edited by Pierre De Rohan. New York: Random House, 1938. New York: Da Capo Press Reprint, 1973.

<u>Feminine Wiles,</u> by Jane Bowles, with an introduction by Tennessee Williams.   Santa Barbara, Calif.:   Black Sparrow Press, 1976.

<u>15 American One-Act Plays,</u> edited by Paul Kozelka.   New York: Washington Square Press, 1961.

<u>50 Best Plays of the American Theatre,</u> selected and introduced by Clive Barnes and John Gassner. New York: Crown, 1969. 4 vols.

<u>50 Contemporary One-Act Plays,</u> edited by Frank Shay.   Cincinnati: Stewart Kidd and Company, 1920.

<u>50 More Contemporary One-Act Plays,</u> edited by Frank Shay. New York: Appleton, 1928.

<u>Film: Book 1-2.</u> New York: Grove Press, 1959, 1962.

<u>A Film by H. G. Wells: The Man Who Could Work Miracles.</u> New York: Macmillan Co. , 1936.

<u>The Film Classics Library,</u> edited by Richard J. Anobile.   New York: Universe Books, 1974-75.   8 vols.

<u>Film Language; a Semiotics of the Cinema,</u> by Christian Metz.   New York: Oxford University Press, 1974.

<u>Film Scripts One, Two, Three and Four,</u> compiled by George P. Garrett. New York: Appleton-Century-Crofts, 1972.   4 vols.

<u>A Film Trilogy,</u> by Ingmar Bergman. New York: Orion Press, 1967.

<u>The Firesign Theatre's Big Book of Plays,</u> by Firesign Theatre Performing Group. Radio plays. San Francisco: Straight Arrow Books, 1972.

<u>First Love and Other Shorts,</u> by Samuel Beckett. New York: Grove Press, 1974.

<u>Five Chinese Communist Plays,</u> edited by Martin Ebon. New York: John Day, 1975.

<u>Five Comedies,</u> by Aristophanes, translated by B. B. Rogers. New York: Doubleday, 1955.

<u>Five Comedies of Medieval France,</u> edited by Oscar Mandel. New York: Dutton, 1970.

<u>Five Heroic Plays,</u> edited by Bonamy Dobrée. London: Oxford University Press, 1960.

Five Modern No Plays, by Mishima Yukio, pseudonym.   New York:
    Knopf, 1957.

Five Modern Scandinavian Plays.   New York: Twayne, 1971.

Five Modern Yugoslav Plays, edited by Branko Mikasinovich.   New
    York: Cyrco Press, 1977.

Five One-Act Plays, by Wolf Mankowitz.   Boston: Baker's Plays,
    1965.

Five One-Act Plays, by Murray Schisgal.   New York: Dramatists
    Play Service, 1968.

Five Plays, by Jean Cocteau.   New York: Hill and Wang, 1961.

Five Plays, by Georg Kaiser.   London: Calder and Boyars, 1971.

Five Plays, by John Mortimer.   London: Methuen, 1970.

Five Plays, by Kaj Harald Leininger Munk, translated by R. P. Keig-
    wim.   New York: American-Scandinavian Foundation, 1953.

Five Plays, by John O'Hara.   New York: Random House, 1961.

Five Plays, by Aleksandr Nikolaevich Ostrovskii, translated by E. K.
    Bristow.   New York: Pegasus, 1969.

Five Plays, by Jean Racine.   New York: Hill and Wang, 1960.

Five Plays, by Sam Shepard.   Indianapolis, Bobbs-Merrill, 1967.

Five Plays, by Peter Ustinov.   Boston: Little, Brown, 1965.

Five Plays, by Edmund Wilson.   New York: Farrar, Straus and
    Young, 1954.

Five Plays from the Children's Theatre Company of Minneapolis,
    edited by John Clark Donahue and Linda Walsh Jenkins.   Minne-
    apolis: University of Minnesota Press, 1975.

Five Plays from the Other Side.   London: Samuel French, 192-?

Five Restoration Adaptations of Shakespeare.   Urbana: University of
    Illinois Press, 1965.

Five Restoration Tragedies, edited by Bonamy Dobree.   London:
    Oxford University Press, 1928.

Five Screenplays, by Harold Pinter.   New York: Viking Press, 1973.

Five Three-Act Plays, with a foreword, by W. G. Fay.   London:
    Rich and Cowan, 1933.

Force Majeure, The Dispossessed, and Hasta Luego, by Errol John. London: Faber and Faber, 1967.

Foremost Films of 1938, edited by Frank Vreeland.   New York: Pitman, 1939.

Four Black Revolutionary Plays, by Le Roi Jones.   Indianapolis: Bobbs-Merrill, 1969.

4 by Truffaut: The Adventures of Antoine Doinel, by François Truffaut.   New York: Simon and Schuster, 1972.

Four Comedies, by Aristophanes, new English version by Dudley Fitts.   New York: Harcourt, Brace and World, 1962.

Four Comedies, by Charles Macklin, edited by J. O. Bartley.   London: Sidgwick and Jackson.   Hamden, Conn.:   Archon Books, 1968.

Four Continental Plays, edited by John Piers Allen.   London: Heinemann, 1964.

Four Dynamite Plays, by Ed Bullins.   New York: William Morrow, 1972.

Four Farces, by Georges Feydeau.   Chicago: University of Chicago Press, 1970.

Four Favorite Plays, by William Robertson Davies.   Toronto: Clarke, Irwin, 1949.

Four Major Plays, by Monzaemon Chikamatsu.   New York: Columbia University Press, 1961.

4 Modern French Comedies, introduced by Wallace Fowlie.   New York: Putnam, 1960.

Four Modern Verse Plays, edited by Elliott Martin Browne.   Harmondsworth, Middlesex: Penguin Books, 1958.

Four New Yale Playwrights, edited by John Gassner.   New York: Crown, 1965.

Four Plays, by Serafin and Joaquin Alvarez Quintero, in English versions by Helen and Harley Granville-Barker.   Boston: Little, Brown, 1928.

Four Plays, by Enid Bagnold.   Boston: Little, Brown, 1970.

Four Plays, by Hjalmar Bergman.   Seattle, Wash.:   University of Washington Press, 1968.

Four Plays, by Allen Curnow.   Wellington, New Zealand: A. H. and A. W. Reed, 1972.

Four Plays, by Jean Giraudoux, adapted and with an introduction by
    Maurice Valency. New York: Hill and Wang, 1958.

Four Plays, by Günter Grass. New York: Harcourt, Brace and
    World, 1967.

Four Plays, by Ludvig von Holberg, translated by Henry Alexander.
    Princeton, N. J.: Princeton University Press, 1946.

Four Plays, by William Inge. New York: Random House, 1958.

Four Plays, by Eugene Ionesco. New York: Grove Press, 1958.

Four Plays, by John Osborne. New York: Dodd, Mead, 1973.

Four Plays for Four Women, by Alice Gerstenberg. New York:
    Brentano's, 1924.

Four Plays of the Free Theater, translated by Barrett H. Clark.
    Cincinnati: Stewart Kidd and Company, 1914.

Four Renaissance Tragedies, edited by Donald Stone, Jr. Cambridge,
    Mass.: Harvard University Press, 1966.

Four Screenplays, by Ingmar Bergman, translated by Lars Malm-
    strom and David Kushner. New York: Simon and Schuster,
    1960.

Four Screenplays, by René Clair. New York: Orion, 1970.

Four Screenplays, by Carl Theodor Dreyer. Bloomington: Indiana
    University Press, 1970.

Four Short Plays for Introducing Discussions, by Marjorie Shearer.
    New York: Seabury Press, 1963.

Four-Star Scripts, edited by Lorraine Noble. Garden City, N. Y.:
    Doubleday, Doran, 1936.

The French Theater Since 1930, edited by Oreste F. Pucciani. Wal-
    tham, Mass.: Blaisdell Publishing Company, 1954.

From Nineveh to Now; Three Dramatic Fantasies Based on the Old
    Testament, by Gordon C. Bennett. St. Louis, Mo.: The
    Bethany Press, 1973.

From the Modern Repertoire, edited by Eric Bentley. Series I,
    Denver: University of Denver Press, 1949. Series 2-3,
    Bloomington: University of Indiana Press, 1952, 1956.

The Frontiers of Farce, by Peter Barnes. London: Heinemann,
    1977.

Funeral Games and The Good and Faithful Servant, by Joe Orton.
    London: Methuen,   1970.

A Galaxy of Black Writing, edited by R. Baird Shuman.   Durham,
    N. C. :   Moore Publishing Company, 1970.

A Gathering of Ghetto Writers: Irish, Italian, Jewish, Black and
    Puerto Rican, edited by Wayne Charles Miller.   New York:
    New York University Press, 1972.

Generations: A Trilogy of Plays, by David Mercer.   London: Cal-
    der and Boyars, 1964.

The Genius of the Early English Theatre, edited by Sylvan Barnet.
    New York: New American Library, 1962.

The Genius of the French Theatre, edited by Albert Bermel.   New
    York: New American Library, 1961.

The Genius of the German Theatre, compiled by Martin Esslin.   New
    York: New American Library, 1968.

The Genius of the Irish Theatre, edited by Sylvan Barnet.   New
    York: New American Library, 1960.

The Genius of the Italian Theatre, edited by Eric Bentley.   New
    York: New American Library, 1964.

The Genius of the Later English Theatre, edited by Sylvan Barnet.
    New York: New American Library, 1962.

The Genius of the Oriental Theatre, edited by George Lincoln Ander-
    son.   New American Library, 1966.

The Genius of the Scandinavian Theatre, edited by Evert Sprinchorn.
    New York: New American Library, 1964.

German Drama Between the Wars, edited by George E. Wellwarth.
    New York: Dutton, 1972.

Gesammelte Scriften 4:   Theater, by Erich Kästner.   Zürich: Atri-
    um Verlag, 1959.

Gesammelte Werke, by Bjørnstjerne Bjørnson.   Berlin: S. Fischer,
    1911.   Vols. 4-5.

Gesammelte Werke, by Odon von Horvath.   Frankfurt am Main:
    Suhrkamp Verlag, 1972.   8 vols.

Gilbert Before Sullivan: Six Comic Plays, by W. S. Gilbert, edited
    by Jane W. Stedman.   Chicago: University of Chicago Press,
    1967.

"Godfrey Daniels!" Verbal and Visual Gems from the Short Films
of W. C. Fields, edited by Richard J. Anobile. New York:
Darien House, 1975.

Gods and Kings; Six Plays, by Lajos Biro. London: George Allen
and Unwin, 1945.

The Goon Show Scripts, by Terrence Allan ("Spike") Milligan. New
York: St. Martin's Press, 1972.

Grease, a new 50s Rock 'n' Roll musical. Music, book and lyrics
by Jim Jacobs and Warren Casey. Winter Repertory Special
Number. New York: Winter House, 1972.

The Great American Life Show: 9 Plays from the Avant-Garde Theatre, edited by John Lahr and Jonathan Price. New York:
Bantam Books, 1974.

The Great American Parade. New York: Doubleday, Doran, 1935.

Great English Plays, edited by Harold F. Rubenstein. New York:
Harper, 1928.

The Great Jewish Plays, edited by Joseph C. Landis. New York:
Horizon Press, 1972.

Great Sanskrit Plays, edited by P. Lal. New York: New Directions,
1959.

Great Television Plays, edited by William I. Kaufman. New York:
Dell Publishing Company, 1969.

Great Television Plays, Vol. 2, edited by Ned E. Hoopes and Patricia Neale Gordon. New York: Dell Publishing Company, 1975.

Grove Plays of the Bohemian Club. San Francisco: H. S. Crocker,
1918. 3 vols.

Guerilla Street Theater, edited by Henry Lesnick. New York: Avon
Books, 1973.

Guernica and Other Plays, by Fernando Arrabal. New York: Grove
Press, 1969.

Guthrie New Theatre, edited by Eugene Lion. New York: Grove
Press, 1975. Vol. 1.

Hamlet em Brasilia e Outras Pecas, by Ida Laura. São Paulo:
Editora Franciscana, 1966.

Handbook of Radio Production, by Erik Barnouw. Boston: Little,
Brown, 1949.

<u>Harrison Texas: Eight Television Plays</u>, by Horton Foote. New York: Harcourt, Brace, 1956.

<u>Harrison's British Classiks</u>. London: Harrison, 1785-1786? 8 vols.

<u>Hiss the Villain</u>, edited by Michael R. Booth. New York: Benjamin Blom, 1964.

<u>Histoires d'Amour</u>, by Marcel Achard. Paris: La Table Ronde, 1959.

<u>The Hole and Other Plays and Sketches</u>, by N. F. Simpson. London: Faber, 1946.

<u>Homecookin': Five Plays</u>, by Clay Goss. Washington, D. C.: Howard University Press, 1974.

<u>Hooray for Captain Spaulding!</u> Verbal and Visual Gems from "Animal Crackers, " edited by Richard J. Anobile. New York: Darien House, 1974.

<u>How to Write and Sell Film Stories</u>, by Frances Marion. New York: Covici, Friede, 1937.

<u>How to Write Photoplays</u>, by John Emerson and Anita Loos. Philadelphia: George W. Jacobs and Company, 1923.

<u>Hunger and Thirst and Other Plays</u>, by Eugene Ionesco. New York: Grove Press, 1968.

<u>I Love Her, That's Why!</u> An autobiography by George Burns, with Cynthia Hobart Lindsay and prologue by Jack Benny. New York: Simon and Schuster, 1955.

<u>In Making a Film;</u> the story of "Secret People, " chronicled and edited by Lindsay Anderson, with shooting script of the film by Thorold Dickinson and Wolfgang Wilhelm. London: George Allen and Unwin, 1952.

<u>The Ink Smeared Lady and Other Kyogen</u>, translated by Shio Sakanishi. Tokyo: Tuttle, 1960.

<u>The Innocent Party: Four Short Plays</u>, by John Hawkes. Preface by Herbert Blau. New York: J. Laughlin, New Directions Publishing Corporation, 1966.

<u>Internal Colloquies</u>, by I. A. Richards. New York: Harcourt Brace Jovanovich, 1971.

<u>Introduction to Literature: Plays</u>, edited by Lynn Altenbernd. New York: Macmillan, 1963.

The Invasion from Mars, by Hadley Cantril. A study in the psycho-
logy of panic, with the complete script of the famous Orson
Welles broadcast by Howard Hoch, based on "War of the
Worlds, " by H. G. Wells. Princeton, N. J.: Princeton University Press, 1940.

The Investigation and Hot Buttered Roll, by Rosalyn Drexler. London: Methuen, 1969.

Irish Stories and Plays, by Paul Vincent Carroll. New York: Devin-Adair, 1958.

Isma; ou, Ce Qui s'Appelle Rien, by Nathalie Sarrante. Paris: Gallimard, 1970.

The Italian Straw Hat and The Spelling Mistakes, by Eugene Labiche,
translated and adapted by Frederick Davies. New York:
Theatre Arts Books, 1967.

The Jewish Wife and Other Short Plays, by Bertolt Brecht. New
York: Grove Press, 1965.

Kabuki: Five Classic Plays, translated by James R. Brandon. Cambridge, Mass.: Harvard University Press, 1975.

The Karl Marx Play and Others, by Rochelle Owen. New York:
Drama Book Specialists, 1974.

Kaspar and Other Plays, by Peter Handke. New York: Farrar,
Straus and Giroux, 1969.

Kelly's Eye and Other Plays, by Henry Livings. New York: Hill
and Wang, 1964.

The Killer and Other Plays, by Eugene Ionesco. New York: Grove
Press, 1960.

The King of Nowhere and Other Plays, by Osborne Henry Mavor.
London: Constable, 1938.

Kuntu Drama; Plays of the African Continuum, collected by Paul
Carter-Harrison. New York: Grove Press, 1974.

Lacy's Acting Edition of Plays, Dramas, Farces, Extravaganzas, Etc.,
edited by Thomas Hailes Lacy. London: T. H. Lacy, 1850.

Lacy's Plays. London: T. H. Lacy, 1863?

The Land of the Palms & Other Plays, by David Cregan. London:
Methuen, 1973.

Landscape and Silence and Night, by Harold Pinter. New York:
Grove Press, 1970.

The Last of the Knights; The Regent; Earl Birger of Bjalbo, translated and introduced by Walter Johnson. Seattle: University of Washington Press, 1956.

The Last Plays of Maxim Gorki, adapted for the English Stage by Gobson-Cowan. New York: International Publishers, 1937.

Late Victorian Plays, 1890-1914, edited by George Rowell. London: Oxford University Press, 1968.

Life and Works, by George Peele, edited by Charles Tyler Prouty. New Haven, Conn.: Yale University Press, 1952-70. 3 vols.

Life as Theatre: Five Modern Plays, by Nikolai Evreinov. Ann Arbor, Mich.: Ardis, 1973.

The Life Work of Henri René Guy de Maupassant. Akron, Ohio: The St. Dunstan Society, 1903.

The Line of Least Existence and Other Plays, by Rosalyn Drexler. New York: Random House, 1967.

The Literature of American Jews, edited by Theodore L. Gross. New York: Free Press, 1973.

The Literature of 18th Century Russia, translated by Harold B. Segel. New York: Dutton, 1967. 2 vols.

Little Stories from the Screen, 1917, by William Addison Lathrop. Reprint, New York: Garland Publishing, Incorporated, 1977.

Living It Up; or, They Still Love Me in Altoona, by George Burns. New York: G. P. Putnam's Sons, 1976.

The London Stage. London: Sherwood and Company, 1824-27. 4 vols.

The Long Christmas Dinner and Other Plays, by Thornton Wilder. New York: Harper and Row, 1963.

Long Voyage Out of War, by Ian Curteis; Playscript 54. London: Calder and Boyars, 1971.

Lovers, by Brian Friel. New York: Farrar, Straus and Giroux; Noonday Plays, 1968.

The Lulu Plays and Other Sex Tragedies, by Frank Wedekind, translated by Stephen Spender. London: Calder and Boyars, 1972.

Lunch Hour and Other Plays, by John Mortimer. London: Methuen, 1960.

Luv and The Typist and The Tiger, by Murray Schisgal. New York: New American Library, 1967.

Mad Dog Blues and Other Plays, by Sam Shepard. Winter Repertory
no. 4. New York: Winter House, 1972.

The Madman and the Nun and Other Plays, by Stanislaw Ignacy Witkiewicz. Seattle: University of Washington Press, 1968.

Major Plays of Chikamatsu, by Chikamatsu Monzaemon. Cambridge,
Mass.: Harvard University Press, 1953.

Makers of the Modern Theatre, edited by Barry Ulanov. New York:
McGraw-Hill, 1961.

Making of "One Day in the Life of Ivan Denisovich." by Ronald Harwood. New York: Ballantine Books, 1971.

The Mandarin Coat and Five Other One-Act Plays for Little Theatres,
by Mrs. Alice Cushing (Donaldson) Riley. New York: Brentano's, 1925.

_Many Loves and Other Plays: The Collected Plays of William Carlos
Williams_. New York: New Directions Books, 1961.

Marcus Brutus and The Silver Queen, by Paul Foster. London: Calder and Boyars, 1977.

The Master of Santiago and Four Other Plays. New York: Knopf,
1951.

Masterpieces of the Modern Central European Theatre, edited by
Robert W. Corrigan. New York: Collier Books, 1967.

Masterpieces of the Modern English Theatre, edited by Robert W.
Corrigan. New York: Collier Books, 1967.

Masterpieces of the Modern French Theatre, edited by Robert W.
Corrigan. New York: Collier Books, 1967.

Masterpieces of the Modern German Theatre, edited by Robert W.
Corrigan. New York: Collier Books, 1967.

Masterpieces of the Modern Irish Theatre, edited by Robert W.
Corrigan. New York: Collier Books, 1967.

Masterpieces of the Modern Italian Theatre, edited by Robert W.
Corrigan. New York: Collier Books, 1967.

Masterpieces of the Modern Russian Theatre, edited by Robert W.
Corrigan. New York: Collier Books, 1967.

Masterpieces of the Modern Scandinavian Theatre, edited by Robert
W. Corrigan. New York: Collier Books, 1967.

Masterpieces of the Modern Spanish Theatre, edited by Robert W.
Corrigan. New York: Collier Books, 1967.

Masterpieces of the Russian Drama, edited by G. R. Noyes. New
    York: Dover, 1960. 2 vols.

Masterworks of the British Cinema, with an introduction by John
    Russell Taylor. New York: Harper and Row, 1974.

Masterworks of the French Cinema, with an introduction by John
    Weightman. New York: Harper and Row, 1974.

Masterworks of the German Cinema, with an introduction by Roger
    Manvell. New York: Harper and Row, 1973.

Masterworks of World Drama, compiled by Anthony Francis Caputi.
    Boston: Heath, 1968.

The Maugham Reader, by William Somerset Maugham. New York:
    Doubleday, 1950.

Medieval Church Music-Dramas; a Repertory of Complete Plays,
    transcribed and edited by Fletcher Collins, Jr. Charlottes-
    ville: University Press of Virginia, 1976.

Medieval French Plays, translated by Richard Axton and John Stevens.
    Oxford: Basil Blackwell, 1971.

The Mentor Book of Short Plays, edited by Richard H. Goldstone
    and Abraham H. Lass. New York: New American Library,
    1969.

Milton's Paradise Lost: Screenplay for Cinema of the Mind, by
    John Collier. New York: Alfred A. Knopf, Borzoi Books,
    1973.

The Mimic Stage, a Series of Dramas, Comedies, Burlesques, and
    Farces, for Public Exhibitions and Private Theatricals. Bos-
    ton: Lee and Shepard, 1869.

Minnesota Showcase: Four Plays. Minnesota Drama Editions, no.
    9, edited by Michael Langham. Minneapolis: University of
    Minnesota Press, 1975.

Minor Elizabethan Tragedies, edited by T. W. Craik. London: J. M.
    Dent & Sons, 1973.

A Miracle of Saint Anthony, by Maurice Maeterlinck. New York:
    Boni and Liveright, 1917.

Modern French Theatre, edited and translated by Michael Benedikt
    and George E. Wellwarth. New York: Dutton, 1964.

Modern Italian One-Act Plays, edited by C. A. Swanson. Boston:
    D. C. Heath, 1948.

Modern Japanese Literature, edited by Donald Keene. New York:
    Grove Press, 1960.

Modern Nordic Plays: Denmark. New York: Twayne, 1974.

Modern Nordic Plays: Finland. New York: Twayne, 1973.

Modern Nordic Plays: Iceland. New York: Twayne, 1974.

Modern Nordic Plays: Norway. New York: Twayne, 1974.

Modern Nordic Plays: Sweden. New York: Twayne, 1973.

Modern Occasions, edited by Philip Rahv. New York: Farrar,
    Straus and Giroux, 1966.

Modern One-Act Plays from the French, compiled by Virginia and
    Frank Vernon. New York: Samuel French, 1933.

Modern Plays, edited by Ernest Rys. London: Dent, 1937.

Modern Scandinavian Plays. New York: Liveright Publishing Com-
    pany, 1954.

Modern Short Comedies from Broadway and London, edited by Stan-
    ley Richards. New York: Random House, 1970.

The Modern Spanish Stage: Four Plays, edited by Marion Holt. New
    York: Hill and Wang, 1970.

Modern Spanish Theatre, edited by Michael Benedikt and George E.
    Wellwarth. New York: Dutton, 1968.

Modern Stage in Latin America: Six Plays, edited by George William
    Woodyard. New York: Dutton, 1971.

The Modern Theatre, edited by Eric Bentley. Garden City, N. Y.:
    Doubleday, 1955-1960. 6 vols.

Modern Theatre, edited by Robert Willoughby Corrigan. New York:
    Macmillan, 1964.

Modern Theatre, a Collection of Plays, 1811, compiled by Elizabeth
    Inchbald. New York: Benjamin Blom, 1968. 10 vols.

The Moderns: an Anthology of New Writing in America. New York:
    Corinth Books, 1963.

Le Monde de Marcel Dubé. Ottawa: Lemeac, No. 1-2, 1971, 1973.

Monte Cristo and Other Plays, edited by Jon Ben Russak. Prince-
    ton, N. J.: Princeton University Press, 1941.

<u>Moot Plays of Corneille,</u> translated by Lacy Lockert.   Nashville, Tenn.:   Vanderbilt University Press, 1959.

<u>Moral Plays,</u> by Osborne Henry Mavor.   London: Constable, 1936.

<u>More About All About Eve,</u> by Joseph L. Mankiewicz.   New York: Random House, 1972.

<u>More One-Act Plays by Modern Authors,</u> edited by Helen Louise Cohen.   New York: Harcourt, Brace, 1927.

<u>More Plays by Rivals of Corneille and Racine,</u> compiled by Lacy Lockert.   Translated into English blank verse with an introduction.   Nashville, Tenn.:   Vanderbilt University Press, 1968.

<u>More Plays from Off Off-Broadway,</u> edited by Michael Townsend Smith. Indianapolis: Bobbs-Merrill, 1972.

<u>The Moscow Art Theatre Series of Russian Plays,</u> edited by O. M. Sayler.   New York: Brentano's 1923.

<u>Motion Picture Continuities,</u> 1929, by Frances Patterson.   Reprint edition, New York: Garland Publishing, Incorporated, 1977.

<u>Murnau,</u> by Lotte H. Eisner.   Revised and enlarged edition.   Berkeley: University of California Press, 1973.

<u>The Musical Fantasies of L. Frank Baum,</u> by Alla T. Ford and Dick Martin, with three unpublished scenarios.   Hong Kong: Ford Press, 1969.

<u>The Negro Caravan;</u> writings by American Negroes, selected and edited by Sterling Allen Brown, Arthur P. Davis, and Ulysses Lee.   New York: Dryden Press, 1941; reprint, Arno Press, 1969.

<u>Neighbours and Other Plays,</u> by James Saunders.   London: Deutsch, 1968.

<u>New American Plays,</u> edited by Robert Willoughby Corrigan.   New York: Hill and Wang, 1965-1971.   4 vols.

<u>New Black Playwrights,</u> compiled by William Couch.   Baton Rouge: Louisiana State University Press, 1968.

<u>New British Drama,</u> edited by Henry Popkin.   New York: Grove Press, 1964.

<u>The New Caravan,</u> edited by Alfred Kreymborg, Lewis Mumford, Paul Rosenfeld.   New York: W. W. Norton, 1936.

<u>The New Consciousness: An Anthology of the New Literature,</u> by Albert J. La Valley.   Cambridge, Mass.:   Winthrop, 1972.

New Directions in Prose and Poetry. New York: New Directions, 1936-1975. Vols. 1-30. New York: Kraus Reprint, 1967.

New Drama One, edited by Lloyd Fernando. Oxford Asia Modern Authors. Melbourne, Australia: Oxford University Press, 1972.

New English Dramatists, edited by Elliott Martin Browne. Harmonds-worth, Middlesex, England: Penguin Books, 1959.

New Fields for the Writer, edited by Stephen Moore. New York: National Library Press, 1939.

New Generation Spanish Drama, edited by George E. Wellwarth. Montreal: Engendra Press, 1976.

The New Lafayette Theatre Presents; Plays with Aesthetic Comments by Six Black Playwrights, edited by Edward Bullins. New York: Doubleday, 1974.

The New Negro Renaissance: An Anthology, edited by Arthur P. Davis and Michael W. Peplow. New York: Holt, Rinehart and Winston, 1975.

New Plays for Women and Girls. Los Angeles: Samuel French, 1935.

New Short Plays. London: Methuen, 1968-72. Vols. 1-3.

New Theatre for Now, edited by Edward Parone. (Vol. 2 of "New Theatre in America. ") New York: Dell, 1970.

New Theatre in America, edited by Edward Parone. New York: Dell, 1965.

New Theatre of Europe, edited by Robert Willoughby Corrigan. New York: Dell Publishing Company, 1962-68, vols. 1-3; edited by Martin Esslin, 1970. Vol. 4.

The New Wave Spanish Drama, edited by George E. Wellwarth. New York: New York University Press, 1970.

New Writing from the Philippines, by Leonard Casper. New York: Syracuse University Press, 1966.

The New Writing in Russia, translated by Thomas P. Whitney. Ann Arbor: University of Michigan Press, 1964.

Night Club & Other Plays, by Kenneth Bernard. Winter Repertory no. 1. New York: Winter House, 1971.

Nine Modern American Plays, edited by Barrett Harper Clark. New York: Appleton-Century-Crofts, 1951.

19 Necromancers from Now, edited by Ishmael Reed. New York: Doubleday, 1970.

Nineteenth-Century Russian Plays, edited by F. D. Reeve. New York: Norton, 1961.

No Exit and Three Other Plays, by Jean-Paul Sartre. New York: Vintage, 1955.

Nobel Prize Library, published under the sponsorship of the Nobel Foundation and the Swedish Academy. William Faulkner, Eugene O'Neill, John Steinbeck. New York: Alexis Gregory, 1971.

Nose! Nose? No-se! and Other Plays, by Andrei Amalrik. New York: Harcourt Brace Jovanovich, 1973.

Nouveau Théâtre de Poche, by Jean Cocteau. Monaco: Editions du Rocher, 1960.

Nouvelle Pièces Noires, by Jean Anouilh. Paris: La Table Ronde, 1958.

The Novels and Plays of Saki, by Hector Hugh Munro. New York: Viking Press, 1933.

Obras Breves del Teatro Costarricense. Collecion la Propia. San Jose: Editorial Costa Rica, 1969, 1971. 2 vols.

Obras Completas, by Pio Baroja y Nessi. Madrid: Biblioteca Nueva, 1946.

Obras Completas, by Federico García Lorca. Madrid: Aguilar, 1963.

Obras Completas, by Manuel Ortiz Guerrero. Asuncion: Patronato de Leprosos del Paraguay.

Obras Completas, by Manuel Tamayo y Baus. Madrid: Ediciones Fax, 1947.

Obras Completas, by Alejandro Tapia y Rivera. San Juan de Puerto Rico: Instituto de Cultura Puertorriqueña, 1968. 2 vols.

Oeuvres, by Paul Valery. Paris: Gallimard, 1960. 2 vols.

Oeuvres Complétes, by Honoré de Balzac. Paris: Louis Conrad, 1929. Théâtre I, II, vols. 34, 35.

Oeuvres Complétes, by Jean Cocteau. Geneve?: Marguerat, 1946-1951. Vols. 5-8

Oeuvres Complétes, by Alfred Jarry. Geneve: Slatkine Reprints, 1975. Vols. 1, 4.

Oeuvres Complétes, by Alfred Victor Vigny. Paris: Gallimard,
1948. 2 vols.

Oeuvres Complétes: Théâtre I, II, by Emile Zola. Paris: François Bernouard, 1927. Vols. 42-43.

Oeuvres Poetiques, by Charles Pierre Peguy. Paris: Gallimard,
1957.

Oeuvres Poetiques Complétes, by Alphonse Lamartine. Paris: Gallimard, 1963.

Oeuvres Théâtrales, by Gustave Lamarche. Quebéc: Les Presses
de L'Université Laval, 1971. Vol. 1.

Oeuvres: Théâtre, by Paul Ernest Hervieu. Paris: Alphonse Le-
merre, 1900-1909. 4 vols.

Off-Broadway Plays. Harmondsworth, Middlesex, England: Penguin,
1970, 1972. 2 vols.

The Off Off-Broadway Book, by Albert Poland and Bruce Mailman.
Indianapolis: Bobbs-Merrill, 1972.

The Official Rocky Scrapbook, by Sylvester Stallone. New York:
Grosset & Dunlap, 1977.

The Old Lady Says "No!" and Other Plays, by Denis Johnston. Boston: Little, Brown, 1960.

The Old Pine Tree and Other Noh Plays, translated by Makoto Ueda.
Lincoln: University of Nebraska Press, 1962.

Old Plays. Philadelphia: Bradford and Inskeep, 1810.

On Making a Movie: "Brewster McCloud," by C. Kirk McClelland.
New York: New American Library, 1971.

On the Air: A Collection of Radio and TV Plays, edited by Sylvia
Z. Brodkin and Elizabeth J. Pearson. New York: Scribner's,
1977.

On the Air: Fifteen Plays for Broadcast and for Classroom Use,
collected and edited by Garrett H. Leverton. New York:
Samuel French, 1944.

On the Eve of Publication and Other Plays, by David Mercer. London: Methuen, 1970.

On the High Road, compiled by Henry Garland Bennett. New York:
American Book Company, 1935.

One Act, edited by Samuel Moon. New York: Grove Press, 1961.

One-Act Comedies of Molière, translated by Albert Bermel. 2nd edition, New York: Ungar, 1975.

One-Act Play Magazine Anthology, 1937/38. New York: Contemporary Play Publications.

One Act Plays, by Christopher Darlington Morley. Garden City, N. Y.: Doubleday, Page, 1924.

One-Act Plays, by Luigi Pirandello, translated by William Murray. New York: Funk and Wagnall's, 1970.

One-Act Plays by Modern Authors, edited by Helen Louise Cohen. New York: Harcourt, Brace, 1921.

One-Act Plays for Everybody, by Dan Totheroh. New York: Samuel French, 1931.

One-Act Plays for Stage and Study. New York: Samuel French, Series 1-10, 1925-1949.

One-Act Plays from the Yiddish, translated by Etta Block. Cincinnati: Stewart Kidd Company, 1923.

The One-Act Theatre. New York: Samuel French, 1936. 2 vols.

100 Non-Royalty Radio Plays, edited by William Kozlenko. New York: Greenberg, 1941.

The Ordeal of a Playwright: Robert E. Sherwood and the Challenge of War, by John Mason Brown. New York: Harper and Row, 1970.

The Orgy: Modern One-Act Plays from Latin America, edited and translated by Gerardo Luzuriaga and Robert S. Rudder. Los Angeles: University of California Press, 1974.

Otherwise Engaged and Other Plays, by Simon Gray. New York: Viking Press, 1976.

The Oxford Chekhov. London: Oxford University Press, 1964-68. Vols. 1-3.

The Oxford Ibsen, edited and translated by James Walter McFarlane and Graham Orton. London: Oxford University Press, 1960-1972. 7 vols.

Ozu, by Donald Richie. Berkeley, Calif.: University of California Press, 1974.

Palace Plays, by Lawrence Houseman. London: Cape, 1930.

The Parachute with Two More TV Plays, by David Mercer. London: Calder and Boyars, 1967.

Parker's Television Plays, by Kenneth T. Parker. Minneapolis, Minn.: The Northwestern Press, 1954.

Parodies: An Anthology from Chaucer to Beerbohm--and After, by Dwight MacDonald. New York: Modern Library, 1965.

Passages from James Joyce's "Finnegans Wake," a Film by Expanding Cinema, by James Joyce. New York: Expanding Cinema, 1965.

Patterns: Four Television Plays, by Rod Serling. New York: Simon and Schuster, 1957.

Philippine Harvest, edited by Maximo Ramos. Quezon City, Philippines: Phoenix Publishing House, 1964.

Pièces Brillantes, by Jean Anouilh. Paris: La Table Ronde, 1954.

Pièces Costumees, by Jean Anouilh. Paris: La Table Ronde, 1967.

Pièces en un Acte, by Jules Romaines. Paris: Gallimard, 1930.

Pièces Grincantes, by Jean Anouilh. Paris: La Table Ronde, 1956.

Pièces Noires, by Jean Anouilh. Paris: Calman-Levy, 1942.

Pièces Roses, by Jean Anouilh. Paris: Calman-Levy, 1942.

A Play and Two Poems, by Robert Kelly, Ron Loewinsohn, and Diane Wakoski. Los Angeles: Black Sparrow Press, 1968.

The Play Book, by Jean Carter and Jess Ogden. New York: Harcourt, Brace, 1937.

Play Parade, by Noël Coward. London: Heinemann, 1949-62. 6 vols.

Playbook: Five Plays for a New Theatre. New York: New Directions, 1956.

Plays, by Leonid Andreyeff. New York: Scribner's, 1915.

Plays, by Jean Anouilh. New York: Hill and Wang, 1972. 3 vols.

Plays, by Fernando Arrabal. London: Calder and Boyars, 1966-1971. 4 vols.

Plays, by James M. Barrie, edited by A. E. Wilson. New York: Scribner's, 1956.

Plays, by Clyde Fitch, edited by Montrose J. Moses and Virginia Gerson. Boston: Little, Brown, 1915.

Plays, by Christopher Fry. London: Oxford University Press, 1961.

Plays, by St. John Hankin. London: Martin Secker, 1923. 2 vols.

Plays, by Eugene Ionesco, translated by Donald Watson. London:
J. Calder, 1958-1976. 10 vols.

Plays, by Ben Jonson, introduced by F. E. Schelling. London: Dent,
Everyman's Library, 1910. 2 vols.

Plays, edited by Frances Kemble. London: Longman, Green, Longman, Roberts, and Green, 1863.

Plays, by Maurice Maeterlinck, translated by Richard Hovey. Chicago: Stone and Kimball, 1894-96. 2 vols.

Plays, by John Marston, edited by H. H. Wood. London: Oliver
and Boyd, 1934. 3 vols.

Plays, by Philip Massinger. New York: AMS Press, 1966.

Plays, by Georges Courteline, pseudonym for Georges Moinaux. New
York: Theatre Arts Books, 1961.

Plays, by Ferenc Molnar. New York: Vanguard Press, 1929.

Plays, by Rene de Obaldia. London: Calder and Boyars, 1966-1977.
4 vols.

Plays, by Eugene O'Neill. New York: Random House, 1951. 3 vols.

Plays, by Robert Pinget. New York: Hill and Wang, 1966-68. 2
vols.

Plays, by J. B. Priestley. London: Heinemann, 1950. 3 vols.

Plays, by Romain Rolland. London: Jarrolds, 1927.

Plays, by Richard Steele. Oxford: Clarendon Press, 1971.

Plays, by Lev Nikalawich Tolstoi, translated by Louise and Aylmer
Maude. London: Oxford University Press, 1928.

Plays, by Sir John Vanbrugh. London: C. Hitch and L. Hawes,
1759.

Plays, by Arnold Wesker. New York: Harper and Row, 1976. Vol.
1.

Plays, by Oscar Wilde. New York: A. and C. Boni, 1935.

Plays and Manifestoes, by Richard Foreman, edited by Kate Davy.
New York: New York University, 1976.

Plays and Pageants from the Life of the Negro, edited by Willis
Richardson. Washington, D. C.: Associated Publishers, 1930.

Plays and Poems, by George H. Boker. New York: AMS Press,
1967. 2 vols.

Plays and Poems, by William Cartwright. Madison: University of
Wisconsin Press, 1951.

Plays & Poems, by Robert Greene. Oxford: Clarendon Press, 1905.

Plays as Experience, edited by Irwin Zachar. New York: Odyssey
Press, 1944.

Plays By and About Women, edited by Victoria Sullivan and James
Hatch. New York: Random House, 1973.

Plays, 1st and 2nd series, by Bjørnstjerne Bjørnson. New York:
Charles Scribner's, 1913-1914. 2 vols.

Plays for a New Theatre: Playbook 2. New York: New Directions,
1966.

Plays for England, by John Osborne. New York: Grove Press, 1966.

Plays for Plain People, by James Bridie, pseudonym for Osborne
Henry Mavor. London: Constable, 1944.

Plays for Public Places, by Howard Brenton. London: Eyre Methuen, 1972.

Plays for Small Stages, by Mary Aldis. New York: Duffield and
Company, 1915. Reprint edition, Great Neck, N. Y.: Core
Collection Books, 1976.

Plays from Black Africa, edited by Frederic M. Litto. New York:
Hill and Wang, 1968.

Plays from Molière by English Dramatists, edited by Henry Morley.
London: G. Routledge, 1883.

Plays from Radio, edited by Abraham Harold Lass. Boston:
Houghton Mifflin, 1948.

Plays of Copi, translated by Anni Lee Taylor. London: John Calder, 1976. Vol. 1.

Plays of Honore de Balzac. New York: Howard Fertig, 1976.

The Plays of Ivan S. Turgenev, translated by M. S. Mandell. New
York: Macmillan, 1924. 2 vols.

The Plays of James Patrick Donleavy. New York: Dell Publishing
Company, Delta Books, 1972.

Plays of Menander, edited by Lionel Casson. New York: New York University Press, 1971.

Plays of Negro Life, edited by Alain Le Roy Locke. New York: Harper, 1927.

Plays of Old Japan, edited by Marie Carmichael Gates and Joji Sakurai. New York: Dutton, 1913.

Plays of Our Time, compiled by Bennett Cerf. New York: Random House, 1967.

Plays of Protest, by Upton Sinclair. New York: M. Kennedy, 1912.

The Plays of Roswitha, by Hrotsvit, of Candersheim. New York: Benjamin Blom, 1966.

Plays of the American West, by Robert Finch. New York: Greenberg, 1947.

Plays of the Italian Theatre, translated by Isaac Goldberg. Boston: J. W. Luce and Company, 1921. Reprint edition, Great Neck, N. Y.: Core Collection Books, 1976.

Plays of the Natural and the Supernatural, by Theodore Dreiser. London: John Lane, 1916.

Plays of the Restoration and Eighteenth Century as They Were Acted at the Théâtres-Royal by Their Majesties' Servants, edited by Dougald MacMillan. New York: Holt, 1959.

Plays of the Year, edited by J. C. Trewin. London: P. Elek, 1948- 1976. Vols. 1-45.

Plays of the Year Special: Television scripts of the two series "The Six Wives of Henry VIII" and "Elizabeth R." edited by J. C. Trewin. London: P. Elek, 1972. 2 vols.

Plays of Three Decades, by Robert Ardrey. New York: Atheneum, 1968.

Plays on Classic Themes, edited by Franz Frillparzer. New York: Random House, 1969.

Plays One, by James Hanley. London: Kaye and Ward, 1968.

The Play's the Thing: Four Original Television Dramas, edited by Tony Gifford. Toronto: Macmillan of Canada, 1976.

Plays: Tragedies, Comedies, edited by T. M. Parrott. New York: Russell and Russell, 1961. 4 vols.

Playwrights for Tomorrow: A Collection of Plays, edited by Arthur H. Ballet. Minneapolis: University of Minnesota Press, 1966- 1975. 13 vols.

Poems and Plays of Lord Byron. New York: T. Crowell, 1880.

Poems and Plays of Alfred Lord Tennyson. London: Oxford University Press, 1967.

Poems and Verse Plays, by Hugo von Hofmannsthal, edited and introduced by Michael Hamburger. New York: Pantheon Books, 1961.

Poems, Prose and Plays, by Alexander Pushkin. New York: Modern Library, 1964.

Poetical and Dramatic Works, by Thomas Randolph, collected and edited by W. Carew Hazlitt. New York: Benjamin Blom, 1968. 2 vols.

Poetical Works, by John Gay. London: Oxford University Press, 1926.

Poetical Works, by Henry Wadsworth Longfellow. New York: AMS Press, 1966. Vols. 1, 3, 5-6, 19.

Poets and Dreamers: Studies from the Irish, including nine plays by Douglas Hyde, with a foreword by T. R. Henn. New York: Oxford University Press, 1974. Lady Gregory's Collected Plays, vol. 4.

Poil de Carotte and Other Plays, by Jules Renard, edited by Stanley Hochman. New York: Frederick Ungar, 1977.

Polanski: 3 Filmscripts, by Roman Polanski. New York: Harper and Row, 1975.

Polite Satires, by Clifford Bax. London: The Medici Society, Limited, 1922. Reprint edition, Great Neck, N. Y.: Core Collection Books, 1976.

Poor Tom/Tina, by David Cregan. London: Methuen, 1976.

Port-Royal and Other Plays, edited by Richard Hayes. New York: Hill and Wang, 1962.

Postwar German Theatre, edited by Michael Benedikt and George E. Wellwarth. New York: Dutton, 1967.

Pre-Inferno Plays, by August Strindberg. Seattle: University of Washington Press, 1970.

Presences: Seven Dramatic Pieces, by Peter Taylor. Boston: Houghton Mifflin, 1973.

The Private Ear and The Public Eye, by Peter Shaffer. London: Hamilton, 1962.

Prize Plays of 1927-28. Philadelphia: Penn Publishing Company, 1930. 2 vols.

The Prize Plays of Television and Radio, 1956, with a foreword by Clifton Fadiman. New York: Random House, 1957.

Promenade & Other Plays, by Maria Irene Fornes. Winter Repertory no. 2. New York: Winter House, 1971.

Pulitzer Prize Plays, edited by Kathryn Coe Cordell. New York: Random House, 1935.

Quare Fellow and The Hostage, by Brendan Behan. New York: Grove Press, 1964.

Que Viva México!, by Sergei-Mikailovitch Eisenstein, with an introduction by Ernest Lindgren. London: Vision Press, 1952.

Queen Christina; Charles XII; Gustav II, by August Strindberg, translated by Walter Johnson. Seattle: University of Washington Press, 1955.

Radio Drama in Action, by Erik Barnouw. New York: Farrar and Reinhard, 1945.

Radio's Best Plays, edited by Joseph Liss. New York: Greenberg, 1947.

Readers Theatre Handbook, edited by Leslie Irene Coger and Melvin R. White. Revised edition, Glenville, Ill.: Scott, Foresman, 1973.

Reading Drama, by Fred Benjamin Millett. New York: Harper, 1950.

Red Bud Women: Four Dramatic Episodes, by Mark O'Dead. Cincinnati: Stewart Kidd Company, 1922. Reprint edition, Great Neck, N.Y.: Core Collection Books, 1976.

Religious Drama, selected and introduced by E. Martin Brown. New York: Meridian Books, 1957-1959. 3 vols.

A Repertory of Plays for a Company of Seven Players, by Charles Rann Kennedy. Chicago: University of Chicago Press, 1930.

A Repertory of Plays for a Company of Three Players, by Charles Rann Kennedy. Chicago: University of Chicago Press, 1927-40. 3 vols.

Representative American Dramas, National and Local, edited by Montrose J. Moses. Revised edition, Boston: Little, Brown, 1941.

Representative American Plays from 1767 to 1949, edited by A. H.
     Quinn.   7th edition, New York: Appleton-Century-Crofts,
     1953.

Representative British Dramas: Victorian and Modern, edited by
     Montrose J. Moses. Boston: Little, Brown, 1918.

Representative Continental Dramas, edited by Montrose J. Moses.
     Boston: Little, Brown, 1924.

Representative Medieval and Tudor Plays, edited by Roger Sherman
     Loomis. Freeport, N. Y.: Books for Libraries Press, 1970.

Representative One-Act Plays by British and Irish Authors, edited by
     Barrett Harper Clark. Boston: Little, Brown, 1921.

Representative Plays by American Dramatists, edited by Montrose J.
     Moses. New York: Dutton, 1918-1925.   3 vols.

Restoration Comedy, edited by A. Norman Jeffares. London: The
     Folio Press, 1974.   4 vols.

Revolution: A Collection of Plays, edited by Gerald Clifford Weales
     and Robert J. Nelson. New York: D. McKay, 1975.

The Ride Across Lake Constance and Other Plays, by Peter Handke.
     New York: Farrar, Straus and Giroux, 1976.

The Rimers of Eldritch and Other Plays, by Lanford Wilson.   New
     York: Hill and Wang, 1967.

The Ritz and Other Plays, by Terrence McNally. New York: Dodd,
     Mead & Co., 1976.

Romantic Comedies, by Ferenc Molnár. New York: Crown, 1952.

Russian Plays for Young Audiences: Five Contemporary Selections,
     translated and edited by Miriam Morton. Rowayton, Conn.:
     New Plays Books, 1977.

Russia's Lost Literature of the Absurd: A Literary Discovery, trans-
     lated by George Gibian.   Ithaca, N. Y.: Cornell University
     Press, 1971.

S. R. O.: The Most Successful Plays of the American Stage, edited
     by Bennett Cerf. New York: Blakiston, 1946.

Salt of the Earth: The Story of a Film, by Herbert Biberman.
     Boston: Beacon Press, 1965.

Sarah B. Divine & Other Plays, by Tom Eyen. Winter Repertory no.
     3. New York: Winter House, 1971.

Satan, Socialites and Solly Gold, three new plays from England. New
    York: Coward McCann, 1961.

Savages and Shakespeare Wallah, two films, by James Ivory. Lon-
    don: Plexus Publishers, 1973.

Scenes from the Heroic Life of the Middle Classes: 5 Plays, by
    Carl Sternheim. London: Calder and Boyars, 1970.

Screenplays, by Michelangelo Antonioni. New York: Orion, 1963.

The Screenplays of Lina Wertmüller. New York: Quadrangle/New
    York Times Book Company, 1977.

Scrittori d'Italia, compiled by Natalino Sapego. Firenze: La Nuova
    Italia, 1964-1965. 3 vols. in 4.

A Search for Awareness, by John H. Bens. New York: Holt, Rine-
    hart and Winston, 1966.

The Season to Be Wary, by Rod Serling. Boston: Little, Brown,
    1967.

The Seeking Years: Six Television Plays from CBS-TV Series, Look
    Up and Live, edited by John M. Gunn. St. Louis, Mo.: The
    Bethany Press, 1959.

Sei Film, by Michelangelo Antonioni. Torino: Einaudi, 1964.

A Select Collection of Old English Plays, edited by Robert Dodsley.
    New York: Benjamin Blom, 1964. 15 vols. in 7.

A Select Collection of Old Plays, 1703-1764, edited by Robert Dods-
    ley. London: Prowell, 1825-1827.

Selected Plays, by Mrs. Clare (Beecher) Kummer. New York:
    Samuel French, 1934.

Selected Plays and Libretti, by Hugo von Hofmannsthal, edited and
    introduced by Michael Hamburger. New York: Pantheon
    Books, 1963.

Selected Tragedies, by Aleksandr Petrovich Sumarokov, translated
    by Richard and Raymond Fortune, with an introduction by
    John Fizer. Evanston, Ill.: Northwestern University Press,
    1970.

Selected Works, by Alfred Jarry. Edited by Roger Shattuck and Si-
    mon Watson Taylor. New York: Grove Press, 1965.

Seven Comedies, by Pierre Carlet de Chamblain de Marivaux. Itha-
    ca, N.Y.: Cornell University Press, 1968.

Seven Expressionist Plays: Kokoschka to Barlach, translated from the German by J. M. Ritchie and H. F. Garten. London: Calder and Boyars, 1968.

Seven Irish Plays, 1946-1964, edited by Robert Hogan. Minneapolis: University of Minnesota Press, 1967.

Seven One-Act Plays, by Ludvig von Holberg, translated by Henry Alexander. Princeton, N. J.: Princeton University Press, 1950.

Seven Plays, by Bertolt Brecht. New York: Grove Press, 1961.

Seven Plays, by Michel de Ghelderode, with an introduction by George Hauger. New York: Hill and Wang, 1960, 1964. 2 vols.

Seven Plays, by Elmer L. Rice. New York: Viking Press, 1950.

Seven Plays, by Ernst Toller. London: John Lane of the Bodley Head, 1935.

7 Plays and How to Produce Them, by Moyne Rice Smith. New York: Walck, 1968.

Seven Plays of Maxim Gorky. New Haven, Conn.: Yale University Press, 1945.

Seven Plays of the Modern Theatre, with an introduction by Harold Clurman. New York: Grove Press, 1962.

Seven Soviet Plays, with introductions by H. W. L. Dana. New York: Macmillan, 1946.

Shakespeare Adaptations, with notes by Montague Summers. New York: Benjamin Blom, 1966.

Shakuntala and Other Writings, by Kalidasa. New York: Dutton, 1959.

Short Plays by Representative Authors, edited by Alice Mary Smith. New York: Macmillan, 1920.

Showcase I, by John Lahr. New York: Grove Press, 1969.

Shyvers and X, by Barry Reckford. London: Calder and Boyars, 1977.

The Silver Foxes Are Dead and Other Plays, by Jakov Lind. New York: Hill and Wang, 1965.

Six American Plays for Today, edited by Bennett Cerf. New York: Modern Library, 1961.

Six Caroline Plays, edited by A. S. Knowland.   London: Oxford University Press, 1962.

Six Comedies, by William Somerset Maugham.   New York: Doubleday, 1937.

Six Early American Plays, compiled by William Coyle.   Columbus, Ohio: Merrill, 1968.

Six Kabuki Plays, edited by Donald Richie.   Tokyo: Hokuseido Press, 1963.

Six One-Act Plays, by Rachel Crothers.   Boston: Walter H. Baker Company, 1925.

Six Plays.   London: William Heinemann, 1934.

Six Plays, by David Belasco.   Boston: Little, Brown, 1928.

Six Plays, by Rachel Field.   New York: Scribners, 1924.

Six Plays, by Lillian Hellman.   New York: Modern Library, 1960.

Six Plays, by Slawomir Mrozek, translated by Nicholas Bethell. New York: Grove Press, 1962.

Six Plays, by Clifford Odets.   New York: Modern Library, 1939.

6 Plays, by Richard Rodgers and Oscar Hammerstein II.   New York: Modern Library, 1959.

Six Plays for a Negro Theatre, by Randolph Edmonds.   Boston: Walter H. Baker Company, 1934.

Six Plays for Children, by Aurand Harris, with a biography and play analyses by Coleman A. Jennings.   Austin: University of Texas Press, 1977.

Six Sanskrit Plays, edited by Henry W. Wells.   New York: Asia Publishing House, 1964.

Six Science Fiction Plays, edited by Roger Elwood.   New York: Pocket Books, 1976.

Six Soviet Plays, edited by Eugene Lyons.   Boston: Houghton Mifflin, 1934.

Six Television Plays, by Reginald Rose.   New York: Simon and Schuster, 1956.

Six Yüan Plays, translated by Liu Jung-en.   Harmondsworth, Middlesex, England: Penguin Books, 1972.

16 Famous American Plays, edited by Bennett Cerf.   New York:
         Modern Library, 1941.

16 Famous British Plays, edited by Bennett Cerf.   Garden City, N. Y. :
         Garden City Publishing Company, 1942.

16 Famous European Plays, edited by Bennett Cerf.   Garden City,
         N. Y. :   Garden City Publishing Company, 1943.

A Sleeping Clergyman and Other Plays, by Osborne Henry Mavor.
         London: Constable, 1934.

Social Plays, by Arthur Wing Pinero, edited by Clayton Hamilton.
         New York: Dutton, 1917-22.   4 vols.

Soldier, Soldier and Other Plays, by John Arden.   London: Methuen,
         1967.

The Sorrows of Frederick/Holy Ghosts, by Romulus Linney.   New
         York: Harcourt Brace Jovanovich, 1977.

South of the Navel, by Simi Horwitz.   New York: Crowell, 1973.

Soviet Scene: Six Plays of Russian Life, translated by Alexander
         Bakshy.   Freeport, N. Y. :   Books for Libraries Press, 1970.

Soviet One-Act Plays, edited by Herbert Marshall.   London: Pilot
         Press, 1944.

Spellbound in Darkness; a History of the Silent Film by George C.
         Pratt.   Revised edition, Greenwich, Conn. :   New York Gra-
         phic Society, 1973.

Spontaneous Combustion: Eight New American Plays, edited by Ro-
         chelle Owens.   The Winter Repertory 6.   New York: Winter
         House, 1972.

Sri Harsa's Plays, by Harsavardhana, King of Thanesar and Kanauj,
         translated by Bak Kun Bae; both Sanskrit and English texts
         are given.   New Delhi: Indian Council for Cultural Relations;
         New York: Asia House, 1964.

The Stage Works of Charles MacArthur.   Tallahassee: Florida State
         University, 1974.

Statements; two workshop productions   by Athol Fugard and others.
         London: Oxford University Press, 1974.

States of Grace: Eight Plays, by Philip Barry, edited by Brendan
         Gill.   New York: Harcourt Brace Jovanovich, 1975.

Stop, You're Killing Me, by James Leo Herlihy.   New York: Simon
         and Schuster, 1970.

Stories and Plays, by Flann O'Brien, pseudonym for Brian O'Nolan. London: Hart-Davis, MacGibbon, 1973.

The Storm and Other Russian Plays, translated by David Magarshack. New York: Hill and Wang, 1960.

Storm Song and A Bride for the Unicorn, by Denis Johnston. London: J. Cape, 1935.

Story, the Yearbook of Discovery, 1968-1971. New York: Four Winds Press. 4 vols.

Stripwell and Claw, by Howard Barker. London: Calder and Boyars, 1977.

A Stroll in the Air, by Eugene Ionesco. New York: Grove Press, 1965.

Stücke, by Max Frisch. Frankfurt am Main: Suhrkamp Verlag, 1962. 2 vols.

Stücke Erzahlungen Aufsatze Gedichte, by Georg Kaiser. Berlin: Kiepenheuer and Witsch, 1966.

The Sty of the Blind Pig and Other Plays, by Phillip Hayes Dean. Indianapolis: Bobbs-Merrill Company, 1973.

Suite in Three Keys, by Noël Coward. New York: Doubleday, 1967.

Susannah and the Elders and Other Plays, by Osborne Henry Mavor. London: Constable, 1940.

The Tale of the Tales, by Rumer Godden. London: Frederick Warne, 1971.

Talking to a Stranger: Four Television Plays, by John Richard Hopkins. Harmondsworth, Middlesex, England: Penguin, 1967.

Teatro, by Arthur Adamov. Buenos Aires: Editorial Losada, 1961. 2 vols.

Teatro, by Vitaliano Brancati. Milano: Bompiani, 1957.

Teatro, by Aldo Cavet. Rio de Janeiro: Graf. do Livro, 1968.

Teatro, by Georg Kaiser. Buenos Aires: Editorial Losada, 1959.

Il Teatro, by Sabatino Lopez. Torino: R. Streglio, 1905.

Teatro, by Rene Marques. Rio Piedras, Puerto Rico: Editorial Cultural, 1971. Vol. 2-3.

Teatro, by Alejandro Rodriguez Alvarez. Buenos Aires: Editorial Losada, 1951-1965. 2 vols.

Teatro, by Lope de Rueda.   Madrid: Espasa-Calde, 1949.

Teatro, by Armand Salacrou.   Buenos Aires: Editorial Losada, 1955.

Teatro, by Tennessee Williams, traduccion de Manuel Barberá. Buenos Aires: Editorial Losada, 1966.   2 vols.

El Teatro Actual Latinoamericano, edited by Carlos Solorzano.   México, D. F.:   Ediciones de Andrea, 1972.

Teatro Alemán Contemporáneo.   Madrid: Aguilar, 1965.

Teatro Argentino Contemporáneo.   Madrid: Aguilar, 1962.

Teatro Belga Contemporáneo.   Madrid: Aguilar, 1965.

Teatro Boliviano, edited by Raúl Salmon.   La Paz, Bolivia: Los Amigos del Libro, 1969.

Teatro Breve Hispanoamericano Contemporáneo.   Madrid: Aguilar, 1969.

Teatro Chileño Contemporáneo.   México, D. F.:   Aguilar, 1970.

Teatro Cómico Moderno, Ossia Raccolta di Alcune Commedie Italiane, by Luigi Sforzosi.   Parigi: Truchy, 1836.

Teatro Cómico Soviético.   Madrid: Aguilar, 1968.

Teatro Completo, by Rudolfo Usigli.   México, D. F.:   Fondo de Cultura Económica, 1963, 1966.   2 vols.

Teatro Contemporáneo Hispanoamericano: prologo, seleccion y notas de Orlando Rodriguez-Sardinas y Carlos Miguel Suarez Radillo. Madrid: Escelicer, 1971.   Tomo I-II.

Teatro Cubano Contemporáneo.   Madrid: Aguilar, 1959.

Teatro Danes Contemporáneo.   Madrid: Aguilar, 1962.

Teatro de Florencio Sánchez.   2nd edition, Buenos Aires: Editorial Sopena Argentina, 1942.

El Teatro de Hoy en Costa Rica, edited by Anita Herzfeld and Teresa Cajiao Salas.   San Jose, Costa Rica: Editorial Costa Rica, 1974.

El Teatro de la Esperanza, an Anthology of Chicano Drama, edited by Jorge A. Huerta.   Goleta, Calif.:   El Tcatro de la Esperanza, Incorporated, 1973.

El Teatro del Uruguayo, by Florencio Sanchez.   Barcelona: Editorial Cervantes, 1926.

Teatro di Giovanni Verga. Milano: Fratelli Treves, 1912.

Teatro Ecuatoriano Contemporáneo. Guayaquil, Ecuador: Casa de la Cultura Ecuatoriana, 1971. Vol. 2.

Teatro Español. Madrid: Aguilar, 1949/50-1973/74. 26 vols.

Teatro Flamenco Contemporáneo. México, D. F. : Aguilar, 1962.

Teatro Frances de Vanguardia. Madrid: Aguilar, 1967.

Teatro Guatemalteco Contemporáneo. Madrid: Aguilar, 1964.

El Teatro Hispanoamericano Contemporáneo, edited by Carlos Solorzano. México, D. F. : Fonda de Cultura Economica, 1964. 2 vols.

Teatro Inglés Contemporáneo. Madrid: Aguilar, 1965.

Teatro Inquieto Español. Madrid: Aguilar, 1967.

Teatro Irlandes Contemporáneo. Madrid: Aguilar, 1963.

Teatro Italiano Contemporáneo. Madrid: Aguilar, 1961.

Teatro Japonés Contemporáneo. Madrid: Aguilar, 1964.

Teatro: Maschere Nude, by Luigi Pirandello. Milano: A. Mondadori, 1930. 10 vols.

Teatro Méxicano. Madrid: Aguilar, 1958/59, 1963/64. 4 vols.

Teatro Méxicano Contemporáneo. Madrid: Aguilar, 1962.

Teatro Méxicano del Siglo XIX, prologo y notas de Antonio Magana-Esquivel. México, D. F. : Fonda de Cultura Economica, 1972. Vol. 1.

Teatro Méxicano del Siglo XX, seleccion, prologo y notas de Antonio Magana-Esquivel. México, D. F. : Fonda de Cultura Economica, 1956-70. Vol. 1-5.

Teatro Neerlands Contemporáneo. Madrid: Aguilar, 1959.

Teatro Norteamericano Contemporáneo. Madrid: Aguilar, 1968.

Teatro Noruego Contemporáneo. México: Aguilar, 1960.

Teatro 1, by Miguel Angel Asturias. Buenos Aires: Editorial Losada, 1964.

Teatro Peruano Contemporáneo. Madrid: Aguilar, 1959.

Teatro: Piezas Rosas, by Jean Anouilh. Buenos Aires: Editorial Losada, 1959.

Teatro Popular: Uma Experiencia, by Maria Helena Kühner. Rio de Janeiro: F. Alves, 1975.

Teatro Portugés Contemporáneo. Madrid: Aguilar, 1961.

Teatro Puertorriqueño: Octavo Festival. San Juan de Puerto Rico: Instituto de Cultura Puertorriqueña, 1966.

Teatro Puertorriqueño: Quinto Festival. San Juan de Puerto Rico: Instituto de Cultura Puertorriqueña, 1963.

Teatro Selecto, by Serafin y Joaquin Alvarez Quintero. Madrid: Escelicer, 1971.

Teatro Selecto, by Antonio Buero Vallejo. Madrid: Escelicer, 1966.

Teatro Selecto, by Jose Lopez Rubio. Madrid: Escelicer, 1969.

Teatro Selecto de Alejandro Casona, pseudonym for Alejandro Rodriguez Alvarez. Madrid: Escelicer, 1972.

Teatro Selecto de Alfonso Paso. Madrid: Escelicer, 1971.

Teatro Selecto de Alfonso Sastre. Madrid: Escelicer, 1966.

Teatro Selecto de Edgar Neville. Madrid: Escelicer, 1968.

Teatro Selecto de Enrique Jardiel Poncela. Madrid: Escelicer, 1968.

Teatro Selecto de Jose Maria Peman. Madrid: Escelicer, 1968.

Teatro Selecto de Miguel Mihura. Madrid: Escelicer, 1967.

Teatro Selecto de Victor Ruiz Iriarte. Madrid: Escelicer, 1967.

Teatro Sueco Contemporáneo. Madrid: Aguilar, 1967.

Teatro Uruguayo Contemporáneo. Madrid: Aguilar, 1960.

The Television Dramatist, edited by Robert Muller. London: Paul Elek, 1973.

Television Plays, by Paddy Chayefsky. New York: Simon and Schuster, 1955.

Television Plays for Writers, by Abraham Saul Burack. Boston: The Writer, 1957.

Television Playwright: 10 Plays for BBC, British Broadcasting Corporation. New York: Hill and Wang, 1960.

Ten Canadian Short Plays, edited by John Stevens.   New York: Dell Publishing Company, 1975.

10 Classic Mystery and Suspense Plays of the Modern Theatre, edited by Stanley Richards. New York: Dodd, Mead, 1973.

Ten Famous Plays, by John Galsworthy.   London: Duckworth, 1941.

Ten Fantasies for Stage and Study, by Theodore Johnson.   Boston: Walter H. Baker Company, 1932.

Ten Great Musicals of the American Theatre, edited by Stanley Richards. Radnor, Pa.:   Chilton, 1973, 1976.   2 vols.

Ten "Lost" Plays, by Eugene O'Neill.   New York: Random House, 1964.

Ten Minutes by the Clock and Three Other Plays for Out-Door and In-Door Production, by Mrs. Alice C. D. Riley.   New York: George H. Doran Company, 1923.

Ten One-Act Plays, by Alice Gerstenberg.   New York: Brentano's, 1921.

10 Short Plays, edited by M. Jerry Weiss.   New York: Dell Publishing Company, 1963.

Theaterstücke, by Arthur Schnitzler.   Berlin: S. Fischer Verlag, 1922.   4 vols.

Théâtre, by Denys Amiel.   Paris: Etablissements Pusson, 1938.

Théâtre, by Fernando Arrabal.   Paris: Christian Bourgois, 1968-1972.   9 vols.

Théâtre, by Jacques Audiberti.   Paris: Gallimard, 1948-1962.   5 vols.

Théâtre, by Enid Bagnold.   New York: Doubleday, 1951.

Théâtre, by Marie Joseph Blaise Chénier.   Paris: Foulon, 1818. 3 vols.

Théâtre, by Paul Claudel.   Paris: Gallimard, 1956.   2 vols.

Théâtre, by Alphonse Daudet.   Paris: Bibliotheque-Charpentier, 1896-1906.   4 vols.

Théâtre, by Maurice Donnay.   Paris: E. Fasquelle, 1908-1912.

Théâtre, by Jean Giraudoux.   Paris: Editions Bernard Grasset, 1958, 1959.   4 vols.

Théâtre, by Eugene Ionesco.   Paris: Gallimard, 1954.   4 vols.

Théâtre, by André Laurendeau.   Montréal: Editions HMH, Collection l'Arbre, 1970.

Théâtre, by Maurice Maeterlinck, edited by Eugene Fasquelle.   Paris: Bibliotheque-Charpentier, 1925.   3 vols.

Théâtre, by Henry de Montherlant.   Paris: Gallimard, 1972.

Théâtre, by Armand Salacrou.   Paris: Gallimard, 1943.   5 vols.

Théâtre, by Boris Vian.   Paris: Jean-Jacques Pauvert, 1972.

Théâtre, by Charles Vildrac.   Paris: Gallimard, 1943.   2 vols.

Théâtre Choisi, by Jean Rotrou.   Paris: Garnier Frères, 1928.

Théâtre Comique, by Gabriel Marcel.   Paris: A. Michel, 1947.

Théâtre Complet, by Henri Becque.   Paris: Bibliotheque-Charpentier, 1922.   2 vols.

Théâtre Complet, by Edouard Bourdet.   Paris: Librairie Stock, 1959.   5 vols.

Théâtre Complet, by Pierre Corneille.   Paris: Editions Garnier Frères, 1960.   3 vols.

Théâtre Complet, by Prosper Jolyot de Crébillon.   Paris: Garnier Frères, 1923.

Théâtre Complet, by François de Curel.   Paris: G. Crès et Cie., 1919.   5 vols.

Théâtre Complet, by Alexandre Dumas (Fils).   Paris: Michel Lévy, 1870-99.   8 vols.

Théâtre Complet, by Georges Feydeau.   Paris: Le Belier, 1949. 9 vols.

Théâtre Complet, by Victor Hugo.   Paris: Gallimard, 1969.   2 vols.

Théâtre Complet, by Eugene Marin Labiche.   Paris: Calmann Levy, 1881-1882.   10 vols.

Théâtre Complet, by H. R. Lenormand.   Paris: G. Crès, 1921-1924. 3 vols.

Théâtre Complet, by Pierre Carlet de Chamblain de Marivaux. Paris: Aux Editions du Seuil, 1964.

Théâtre Complet, by Georges Courteline, pseudonym for Georges Moinaux.   Paris: Flammarion, 1961.

Théâtre Complet, by Alfred de Musset. Paris: Gallimard, 1958.

Théâtre Complet, by Jules Renard. Paris: Gallimard, 1959.

Théâtre Complet de Beaumarchais. Geneve: Statkine Reprints, 1967.
4 vols.

Théâtre d'Amour, by Georges de Porto-Riche. Paris: Ollendorff,
1922. 2 vols.

Le Théâtre d'Aujourd'hui, compiled by Georges Pillement. Paris:
Le Belier, 1970.

Théâtre de Clara Gazul, by Prosper Mérimée. Paris: Calmann-
Lévy, 1925.

Théâtre du Chateau, by Jean Mace. Paris: J. Hetzel, 1861.

Théâtre du XVIIe Siècle, edited by Jacques Scherer. Paris: Gallimard, 1975. Vol. 1.

Théâtre du XVIIIe Siècle, edited by Jacques Truchet. Paris: Gallimard, 1972. 2 vols.

Le Théâtre et la Danse en Iran, by Medjid Rezvani. Paris: Maisonneuve et Larose, 1962.

Theatre Experiment, compiled by Michael Benedikt. Garden City,
N. Y.: Doubleday, 1967.

Theatre Guild Anthology. The Theatre Guild. New York: Random
House, 1936.

Théâtre Inedit, by Boris Vian. Paris: Christian Bourgois, 1970.

The Theatre of Don Juan: A Collection of Plays and Views, 1630-
1963, edited by Oscar Mandel. Lincoln: University of Nebraska Press, 1963.

The Theatre of Tennessee Williams. New York: New Directions,
1971-76. 5 vols.

Theatre 1-4. New York: International Institute of the United States,
1969-1972. 4 vols.

Theatre Wagon Plays of Place and Any Place, edited by Margaret
Collins. Charlottesville: University of Virginia Press, 1973.

Theatre: Works, by Sacha Guitry. Paris: Librairie Academique
Perrin, 1962. Vol. 12.

Theatrical Recorder, 1805, edited by Thomas Holcroft. New York:
Burt Franklin, 1968. 2 vols.

Theatricals, by Henry James. New York: Harper, 1894-95. 2 vols.

The Theme Is Blackness: The Corner and Other Plays, by Ed Bullins. New York: W. Morrow, 1972.

Themes of Drama: An Anthology, edited by George E. Wellwarth. New York: Crowell, 1973.

13 Famous Plays of Crime and Detection, edited by Van Henry Cartmell and Bennett Cerf. New York: Blakiston, 1946.

30 Famous One-Act Plays, edited by Bennett Cerf. New York: Modern Library, 1943.

This Is My Best, edited by Whit Burnett. New York: Dial, 1942.

This Is My Best in the Third Quarter Century, edited by Whit Burnett. New York: Doubleday, 1970.

Three Anglo-Irish Plays, edited by Rudolph Stamm. Freeport, N. Y.: Books for Libraries, 1970.

Three Australian Plays, edited by Eunice Hanger. Minneapolis: University of Minnesota Press, 1968.

Three British Screenplays, edited by Roger Manvill. London: Methuen, 1950.

Three Burlesque Plays, by Thomas Duffet. Iowa City: University of Iowa Press, 1972.

Three Comedies, by Bjørnstjerne Bjørnson. London: J. M. Dent, 1925.

Three Comedies, by Ludvig von Holberg. English text and introduction by Reginald Spink. London: Heinemann, 1957.

Three Distinctive Plays About Abraham Lincoln, edited by Willard Swire. New York: Washington Square Press, 1961.

Three Dramas, by Bjørnstjerne Bjørnson. London: J. M. Dent, 1925?

Three East European Plays, edited by George Rowell. London: Penguin, 1970.

Three European Plays, edited by Elliott Martin Browne. Harmondsworth, Middlesex: Penguin Books, 1958.

3 Filipino Playwrights. Manila, Philippines: Educational Theater Association, 1968.

Three Films, by Sergei Mikailovich Eisenstein. New York: Harper, 1974.

Three Films, by Jean-Luc Godard. New York: Harper and Row, 1975.

Three French Farces, translated by Frederick Davies. Harmonds-worth, Middlesex: Penguin Books, 1973.

Three Gallant Plays, by Fernand Noziere, pseudonym for Fernand Weyl. New York: William Edwin Rudge, 1929.

Three Irish Plays, edited by Elliott Martin Browne. Baltimore, M. D. : Penguin Books, 1960.

Three Japanese Plays from the Traditional Theatre, edited by Earle Ernst. London: Oxford University Press, 1959.

Three John Golden Plays. New York: Samuel French, 1925.

Three Modern Japanese Plays, translated by Yozan T. Iwasaki and Glenn Hughes, with an introduction by Glenn Hughes. Cincinnati: Stewart Kidd Company, 1923.

Three Oriental Plays, edited by Frayne Williams. Los Angeles: J. A. Alles Company, 1921.

Three Plays, by Alan Ayckbourn. London: Chatto and Windus, 1977.

Three Plays, by Ernst Barlach, translated by Alex Page. Minneapolis: University of Minnesota Press, 1964.

Three Plays, by Ugo Betti. New York: Grove Press, 1956.

Three Plays, by Paul Vincent Carroll. London: Macmillan, 1943.

Three Plays, by J. P. Clark. London: Oxford University Press, 1964.

Three Plays, by Padraic Colum. Dublin: Allen Figgis, 1963.

Three Plays, by Joseph Conrad. London: Methuen, 1934.

Three Plays, by Rachel Crothers. New York: Brentano's, 1923.

Three Plays, by Rachel Crothers. New York: Brentano's, 1924.

Three Plays, by Euripides, translated by Paul Roche. New York: Norton, 1974.

Three Plays, by Euripides, translated by Philip Vellacott. Harmonds-worth, Middlesex, England: Penguin Books, 1968.

Three Plays, by Eduardo de Filippo. London: Hamish Hamilton, 1976.

Three Plays, by Horton Foote. New York: Harcourt, Brace and World, 1962.

Three Plays, by Max Frisch. New York: Hill and Wang, 1967.

Three Plays, by Max Frisch. London: Methuen, 1962.

Three Plays, by David Garrick, edited by Elizabeth P. Stein. New York: Benjamin Blom, 1967.

Three Plays, by Jean Giraudoux, translated by Phyllis La Farge and Peter H. Judd. New York: Hill and Wang, 1964. Vol. 2.

Three Plays, by Friedrich Hebbel, translated by Marion W. Sonnenfeld. Cranbury, N. J.: Associated University Press, 1974.

Three Plays, by H. R. Lenormand. London: Gollancz, 1928.

Three Plays, by Gabriel Marcel. New York: Hill and Wang, 1965.

Three Plays, by John Mortimer. New York: Grove Press, 1962.

Three Plays, by Slawomir Mrozek. New York: Grove Press, 1973.

Three Plays, by Eric Patrick Nicol. Vancouver: Talonbooks, 1975.

Three Plays, by Andre Obey, translated from the French by Judith D. Suther and Earle D. Clowney. Fort Worth: Texas Christian University Press, 1972.

Three Plays, by Emmanuel Roblès. Carbondale: Southern Illinois University Press, 1977.

Three Plays, by Ramon Sartoris. Washington, D. C.: The Black Sun Press, 1944.

Three Plays, by Peter Shaffer. London: Penguin Books, 1976.

Three Plays, by Gore Vidal. London: Heinemann, 1962.

Three Plays, by Thornton Wilder. New York: Harper and Row, 1957.

Three Plays, by Yuzo Yamamoto. Tokyo: Hokuseido Press, 1957.

Three Plays About Ancient Hawaii, by Jean Charlot. Honolulu: University Press of Hawaii, 1963.

Three Plays from the Yale School of Drama, edited by John Gassner. New York: Dutton, 1964.

Three Plays on Justice, by Ugo Betti.   San Francisco: Chandler
Publishing Company, 1964.

Three Plays Without Words, by Elmer L. Rice.   New York: Samuel French, 1934.

Three Popular French Comedies, translated by Albert Bermel.   New
York: Frederick Ungar, 1975.

Three Port Elizabeth Plays, by Athol Fugard.   New York: Viking
Press, 1974.

Three Questor Plays, by Dannie Abse.   Lowestoft, Suffolk, England:
Scorpion Press, 1967.

Three Screenplays, by Luis Buñuel.   New York: Orion, 1969.

Three Screenplays, by Jean Cocteau.   New York: Grossman, 1970.

Three Screenplays, by Robert Rossen.   New York: Doubleday, 1972.

Three Screenplays, by Lucino Visconti.   New York: Orion, 1970.

Three Sentimental Comedies, by Colley Cibber.   New Haven, Conn. :
Yale University Press, 1973.

Three Short Plays, by Wole Soyinka.   London: Three Crowns Books,
Oxford University Press, 1969.

Three Spanish Sacramental Plays, edited by R. G. Barnes.   San
Francisco: Chandler Publishing Company, 1969.

Three Suitors: One Husband & Until Further Notice, by Guillaume
Oyono-Mbia.   London: Methuen, 1974.

Three Times Three, by William Saroyan.   Los Angeles: Conference
Press, 1936.

Three TV Comedies, by David Mercer.   London: Calder and Boyars,
1966.

Three TV Plays, by Alun Owen.   New York: Hill and Wang, 1963.

Three Works by The Open Theater, edited by Karen Malpede.   New
York: Drama Book Specialists, 1974.

Tojuro's Love and Four Other Plays, by Hiroshi Kikuchi.   Tokyo:
Hokuseido Press, 1925.

The Tolkien Reader, by J. R. R. Tolkien.   New York: Ballantine
Books, 1966.

Tonight at 8:30, by Noël Coward.   New York: Sun Dial Press, 1936.

Top TV Shows of the Year, 1954-55, edited by Irving Settel. New
York: Hastings House, 1955.

El Topo, a Book of the Film, by Alexandro Jodorowsky. New York:
Douglas Publishing Company, 1972.

Traditional Asian Plays, compiled by James R. Brandon. New York:
Hill and Wang, 1972.

Tragedie, by Vittorio Alfieri. Firenze: Salani Editore, 1964.
3 vols.

Tragedy: Texts and Commentary, compiled by Morris Freedman.
New York: Scribners, 1969.

Tragoedier, by A. G. Oehlenschläger. Kjøbenhavn: Selskabet til
udgivelse af Oehlenschlägers skrifter, 1879. 4 vols. in 2.

Transcending and The Dancers, by David Cregan. London: Methuen,
1967.

A Treasury of Ben Hecht. New York: Crown, 1959.

A Treasury of Classic Russian Literature, edited by John Cournos.
New York: Capricorn Books, 1962.

Tres Dramas Romanticos. Freeport, N. Y.: Books of Libraries
Press, 1970.

Trilogy, by Truman Capote and Eleanor and Frank Perry. New
York: Macmillan, 1969.

The Trilogy, by Alexander Sukhovo-Kobylin, translated by H. B. Segel. New York: Dutton, 1969.

Tropical Madness: Four Plays, by Stanislaw Ignacy Witkiewicz.
The Winter Repertory 7. New York: Winter House, 1972.

The Turkish Theatre, edited by Nicholas N. Martinovitch. New
York: Theatre Arts, 1933.

Twentieth Century American Writing, edited by William T. Stafford.
New York: Odyssey Press, 1965.

Twentieth Century Plays, edited by Frank W. Chandler and Richard
A. Cordell. New York: Nelson, 1934.

Twentieth-Century Polish Avant-Garde Drama, edited with an introduction by Daniel Gerould. Ithaca, N. Y.: Cornell University Press, 1977.

Twentieth Century Russian Plays: an Anthology, edited and translated by F. D. Reeve. New York: Norton, 1963.

PN
6112
.639

20 Best European Plays on the American Stage, edited by John Gassner. New York: Crown, 1957.

20 Best Film Plays, edited by John Gassner. New York: Crown,
1943.

20 Best Plays of the Modern American Theatre, 1930-1939, edited
by John Gassner. New York: Crown, 1939.

25 Best Plays of the Modern American Theatre: Early Series, 1916-
1929, edited by John Gassner. New York: Crown, 1949.

24 Favorite One-Act Plays, edited by Bennett Cerf. Garden City,
N. Y. : Doubleday, 1958.

24 One-Act Plays, edited by John Hampden. London: Dent, 1954.

27 Wagons Full of Cotton, by Tennessee Williams. Norfolk, Conn. :
New Directions, 1953.

26 Short and Amusing Plays for Private Theatricals, by Clarence J.
Howard. Being Howard's "Drawing-Room Theatricals" and
Hudson's "Private Theatricals for Home Performance" com-
bined in one volume. New York: Dick and Fitzgerald, 1871.

Two Comedies, by Thomas D'Urfey, edited by Jack A. Vaughn.
Cranbury, N. J. : Associated University Presses, 1976.

Two Great Belgian Plays About Love, translated from the French by
Marnix Gijsen. New York: Heinemann, 1966.

Two Great Plays by W. H. Auden and Christopher Isherwood. New
York: Modern Library, 1959.

Two Hawaiian Plays, by Jean Charlot. Honolulu: University Press
of Hawaii, 1976.

Two Miracles, edited by Nigel Wilkins. New York: Barnes and
Noble, 1973.

2 Musicals, by Tom Jones and Harvey Schmidt. New York: Drama
Book Specialists, 1973.

Two Plays, by Arthur Adamov. London: John Calder, 1962.

Two Plays, by Charles Bertin. Minnesota Drama Editions, no. 6.
Minneapolis: University of Minnesota Press, 1970.

Two Plays, by Eugene Labiche. English version by Emanuel Wax.
New York: Dramatist Play Service, 1962.

Two Plays, by Anthony Powell. Boston: Little, Brown, 1972.

Two Plays, by Peter Shaffer. New York: Atheneum, 1974.

Two Plays, by Rudolfo Usigli, translated by Thomas Bledsoe. Carbondale: Southern Illinois University Press, 1971.

Two Plays for Television: Through the Night and Such Impossibilities, by Trevor Griffiths. London: Faber and Faber, 1977.

Two Plays from Ancient India, translated by J. A. B. van Buitenen. New York: Columbia University Press, 1968.

Two Russian Film Classics. Classic Film Scripts Series. New York: Simon and Schuster, 1973.

Two Screenplays, by Jean Cocteau. New York: Penguin, 1968.

Types of Modern Dramatic Composition: An Anthology of One-Act Plays for Schools and Colleges, selected and edited by LeRoy Phillips and Theodore Johnson. Boston: Ginn, 1927.

The Ubu Plays, by Alfred Jarry. Edited with an introduction by Simon Watson Taylor. New York: Grove Press, 1969.

Underground: 4 Plays, by Edgar White. New York: Morrow, 1970.

The Unseen Hand and Other Plays, by Sam Shepard. Indianapolis: Bobbs-Merrill, 1972.

Victor and Other Plays, by Roger Vitrac. London: Calder and Boyars, 1977.

Victorian Melodramas: Seven English, French and American Melodramas, edited and introduced by James L. Smith. London: J. M. Dent, 1976.

Vision and Aftermath: Four Expressionist War Plays, translated from the German by J. M. Ritchie and J. D. Stowell. London: Calder and Boyars, 1969.

Visit to a Small Planet and Other Television Plays, by Gore Vidal. Boston: Little, Brown, 1956.

Voices of Change in the Spanish American Theatre, compiled by William Irving Oliver. Austin: University of Texas Press, 1971.

W. C. Fields by Himself, with commentary by Ronald J. Fields. Englewood Cliffs, N. J.: Prentice-Hall, 1973.

War and Four Other Plays, by Jean-Claude Van Itallie. New York: Dramatists Play Service, 1967.

The War Trilogy, by Roberto Rossellini, translated by Judith Green. New York: Grossman, 1973.

Werke, by Georg Kaiser. Frankfurt: Verlag Ullstein Gmbh, 1972.
6 vols.

Werke: Dramen, Essays, Dialoge, by Christoph Martin Wieland.
Munchen: Carl Hanser Verlag, 1967, Vol. 3.

Werke: Dramen und Prosa, by Friedrich Hebbel. Hamburg: Hoffmann und Campe Verlag, 1958?

Werke in Zwei Bänden, by Hans Sachs. Berlin: Aufbau, 1966. 2
vols.

The Wesker Trilogy, by Arnold Wesker. New York: Random House,
1960.

Wheelchair Willie and Other Plays, by Alan Brown. London: Calder and Boyars, 1977.

The White Steed and Coggerers, by Paul Vincent Carroll. New York:
Random House, 1939.

Whitest Elephant and Four Other Heroic Comedies, by Alan Sims.
London: French, 1950.

Who Is My Neighbour? and How Bitter the Bread, by Anne Ridler.
London: Faber and Faber, 1963.

The William Carlos Williams Reader, edited by M. L. Rosenthal.
New York: New Directions Books, 1966.

The William Saroyan Reader. New York: George Braziller, 1958.

Winnetou, Film-Bildbuch, by Rialto-Film Preben Phillipsen & Jad-
ran-Film. Hrsg. von Peter Korn. Bern: Phoenix Verlag,
1964-1966. 3 vols.

With Eisenstein in Hollywood, by Ivor Montagu. New York: International Publishers, 1969.

The Wonderful Ice Cream Suit and Other Plays, by Ray Bradbury.
New York: Bantam, 1972.

Woody Allen's "Play It Again, Sam, " screenplay and frame enlarge-
ments by Richard Anobile. New York: Grosset and Dunlap,
1977.

Works, by Honoré de Balzac. London: The Chesterfield Society,
1901. Vols. 33-36.

Works, by Francis Beaumont and John Fletcher. London: Cambridge University Press, 1905-12. 10 vols.

Works, by Aphra Behn. New York: Benjamin Blom, 1967. 6 vols.

Works, by Robert Browning. New York: AMS Press, 1966. Vols.
1-4, 10.

Works, by Alphonse Daudet. Boston: Little, Brown, 1899. Vols.
12, 15.

Works, by Charles Dickens. New York: Bigelo, Brown, 19--.
Vol. 18.

Works, by Henry Fielding, edited by James P. Brown. London:
Bickers, 1902. Vols. 2-4.

Works, by Henrik Ibsen. New York: Scribner's, 1911-12. 13 vols.

Works, by Hugh Kelly. London: T. Cadell, 1778; reprint edition,
Hildesheim, N. Y.: Georg Olms Verlag, 1973.

Works, by Thomas Kyd. Oxford: Clarendon Press, 1955.

Works, by Nathaniel Lee. Edited with introduction and notes by
Thomas B. Stroup and Arthur L. Cooke. Metuchen, N. J.:
Scarecrow Reprint Corporation, 1968. 2 vols.

Works, by Thomas Middleton, edited by A. H. Bullen. London: J.
C. Nimmo, 1885-86. 8 vols.

Works, by Jean Baptiste Poquelin Molière. New York: Benjamin
Blom, 1967. 6 vols. in 3.

Works, by Arthur Murphy. London: T. Cadell, 1786. Vols. 1-4.

Works: Dramatic Works, by François Marie Arouet de Voltaire.
New York: St. Hubert Guild, 1901. Vols. 8-10.

World Drama, edited by Barrett H. Clark. New York: Appleton,
1933. 2 vols.

World Historical Plays, by August Strindberg, translated by Arvid
Paulson with an introduction by Gunnar Ollen. New York:
Twayne, 1970.

Writing for Television, by Gilbert Vivian Seldes. Garden City,
N. Y.: Doubleday, 1952.

Writing for Television, by Max Wylie. New York: Cowles, 1970.

The Young American Writers, edited by Richard Kostelanetz. New
York: Funk and Wagnalls, 1967.

Zoo Story and Other Plays, by Edward Albee. London: J. Cape,
1962.

Ace Books, New York.
Arabic Translation Series of the Journal of Arabic Literature, E. J. Brill, Leiden.
Art of the Film Series, New American Library, New York.
Avon Books, New York.
Ballantine Books, New York.
Bantam Books Screenplays, New York.
Black Sparrow Press, Santa Barbara, Calif.
Borzoi Books Screenplays, Alfred A. Knopf, New York.
Calder & Boyars Playscripts Series, London.
Calder & Boyars Scottish Library Series, London.
Cape Goliard Press, London.
Cape Plays, Jonathan Cape, London.
Classic Film Scripts Series, Simon & Schuster, New York.
Classics of Drama in English Translation Series, Manchester University Press, N. Y.
Collection les Beaux Texts, Editions Lemeac, Ottawa.
Collection Théâtre Canadien, Lemeac, Ottawa.
Contemporary Drama Service, Downers Grove, Ill.
Dal Soggetto al Film, Cappelli, Bologna.
Dal Soggetto al Film Retrospettiva Series, Cappelli, Bologna.
Dell Books, New York.

Delta Screenplays, Dell Publishing Co., New York.
Dent-Aldine Press Film Scripts, London.
Dial Press, New York.
Dickenson Literature and Film Series: From Fiction to Film, Dickinson Publishing Co., Encino, Calif.
Dramatic Publishing Co., Chicago.
Dramatists Play Service, New York.
Editions de Minuit Ciné, Paris.
Evergreen Black Cat Playscripts, Grove Press, New York.
Evergreen Filmscripts, Grove Press, New York.
Evergreen Original Playscripts, Grove Press, New York.
Faber & Faber Plays, London.
Farrar, Straus & Giroux, New York.
Garland Classics of Film Literature Series, Garland Publishing Co., New York.
Garzanti Filmscripts, Milano.
Gribaudi Piero Filmscripts, Torino.
Grossman Library of Film Classics Series, New York.
Grove Press, New York.
Heinemann Drama Library, London.
Hill & Wang Spotlight Dramabook Series, New York.
Irish Drama Series, De Paul University, Chicago.
Jonathan Cape Plays, London.
Jonathan Cape Screenplays, London.
Lancer Books, New York.

Longman's Players Prompt
Book Play Series, New York.
Lorrimer Screenplay Series,
London.
The "Lost Play" Series. Pros-
cenius Press, Dixon, Calif.
M G M Library of Filmscripts
Series, Viking Press, New
York.
McGraw-Hill, New York.
Methuen Young Drama Series,
London.
Methuen's Modern Plays Series,
London.
Methuen's New Theatrescripts,
London.
Methuen's Theatre Classics,
London.
Minnesota Drama Editions, Uni-
versity of Minnesota Press,
Minneapolis.
Modern Film Scripts Series,
Simon & Schuster, New York.
National Theatre Plays, Heine-
mann, London.
New American Library, New
York.
New Drama. Oxford in Asia
Modern Authors, Oxford Uni-
versity Press, London.
New Drama Series, New Press,
Toronto.
Noonday Original Plays and
Screenplays, Farrar, Straus
& Giroux, New York.
Oxford Three Crowns Books,
London.

Pantheon Books Screenplays,
New York.
Paperback Library Original
Screenplays, New York.
Penguin Modern Playwrights
Series, Harmondsworth,
England.
Penguin Plays, London.
Phaedra Plays and Filmscripts,
Gannon, San Francisco.
Pocket Books, New York.
Random House Plays and
Screenplays, New York.
Samuel French's Tandem
Library Series of Transla-
tions Scripts, New York.
Scottish Repertory Plays, Go-
wans & Gray, London.
Signet Film Series, New Amer-
ican Library, New York.
Simon & Schuster, New York.
Stein & Day's Play Series,
New York.
Talonplays Series, Talonbooks,
Vancouver.
Teatro del Volador Serie, Joa-
quin Mortiz, Mexico, D. F.
Théâtre de la Table Ronde,
Paris.
Viking/Compass Book Screen-
plays, New York.
Women Write for the Theatre
Series, Playwrights Co-op,
Toronto.
Winter House Repertory, Win-
ter House, New York.

Americas; a Quarterly Review
of Inter-American Cultural
History, Academy of Amer-
ican Franciscan History,
Washington, D. C.
Anglo Saxon Review, London.
Arion, University of Texas,
Austin.
Asia and the Americas, New
York.
Atlantic Monthly, Boston.
Atlas, New York.
L'Avant-Scène Cinéma, Paris.
L'Avant-Scène Opéra, Paris.
L'Avant-Scène Théâtre, Paris.
The Benin Review, Ethiope Pub-
lishing Corporation, Benin
City, Nigeria.
Bookman, New York.
Boston University Journal.
Cahiers du Cinéma, Paris.
Canadian Fiction Magazine,
Prince George, British Co-
lumbia.
Canadian Theatre Review,
Downsville, Ontario.
Chicago Review.
Chinese Literature, Peking.
Cinema, Beverly Hills, Calif.
Commentary, National Jewish
Committee, New York.
Cosmopolitan, New York.
Dial, New York.
Dimension: Contemporary Ger-
man Arts and Letters, Dept.
of Germanic Languages, Uni-
versity of Texas at Austin.
Direction, New Directions Pub-
lishing Corp. , New York.
Divaldo/Theatre, Prague.
Drama, Chicago.
Drama and Theatre, Fredonia,
N. Y.

Drama at Calgary, University
of Calgary, Alberta.
The Drama Review, School of
the Arts, New York Univer-
sity.
Drama Survey, Minneapolis.
Educational Theatre Journal,
Columbia, Mo.
Encounter, London.
Esquire, Chicago.
Evergreen Review, New York.
Everybody's Magazine, New
York.
Fireweed, Columbus, Ohio.
First Stage, Lafayette, Ind.
Fortnightly, London.
Forum, Philadelphia.
Gambit: International Theatre
Review, Calder & Boyars,
London.
Golden Book, New York.
Harper's Magazine, New York.
Harvard Journal of Asiatic
Studies, Harvard-Yenching
Institute, Cambridge.
Horizon, New York.
Indian Writing Today, Nirmala
Sadanand Publishers, Bom-
bay.
Italian Theatre Review, Rome.
Journal of Beckett Studies,
London.
Journal of Irish Literature,
Newark, Delaware.
Kenyon Review, Gambier, Ohio.
The Knickerbocker: or, New
York Monthly Magazine.
Landfall: A New Zealand
Quarterly, Christchurch.
Life, Chicago.
Literary Review, Teaneck,
N. J.
Little Review, Chicago.

Living Age, Boston.
London Magazine.
Mademoiselle, New York.
Magazine of History, William
    Abbatt, New York.
Malahat Review, University of
    Victoria, British Columbia.
Massachusetts Review, Amherst.
Modern Drama, University of
    Toronto, Ontario.
Modern International Drama,
    University Park, Pa.
Modern Language Notes, Balti-
    more.
Ms. , New York.
Mundus Artium, Dept. of Eng-
    lish, University of Ohio,
    Columbus.
Music and Letters, London.
Negro History Bulletin, Wash-
    ington, D. C.
New Plays, TQ Publications,
    London.
New Republic, Washington,
    D. C.
The New Review, London.
New Statesman, London.
New Theatre Magazine, Dept.
    of Drama, University of
    Bristol.
New Yorker.
North American Review (n. s.),
    Mount Vernon, Iowa.
Ohio Review, Athens.
Paris Review
Partisan Review, New York.
Performance, New York.
Performing Arts in Canada,
    Toronto.
Performing Arts Journal, New
    York.
La Petite Illustration Théâtre,
    Paris.
Plaisie de France, Supplement
    Théâtral, Paris.
Playboy, Chicago.
Players Magazine, De Kalb,
    Ill.
Plays and Players, London.
Poet Lore, Boston.
Poetry, Chicago.
Quarterly Review of Literature,
    Princeton, N. J.

Ramparts, Menlo Park, Calif.
Religious Theatre, Wichita
    State University, Kansas.
Review of English Literature,
    Oxford University.
Revista de Teatro, Rio de
    Janeiro.
Russian Literature Triquarterly,
    Ardis Publishers, Ann Ar-
    bor, Mich.
Saturday Evening Post, Phila-
    delphia.
Saturday Review, New York.
Scribner's Magazine, New York.
Scripts, New York.
Seven Arts, New York.
Sewanee Review, Sewanee, Tenn.
Show, Hollywood.
Show, New York.
Sipario, Rome.
Soundings, Stony Brook, N. Y.
Southwest Review, Southern
    Methodist University, Dallas.
Sports Illustrated, Chicago.
Stage, New York.
TDR/The Drama Review, New
    York University.
Theater Arts, New York.
Theater: Chronik und Bilanz
    des Bühenjahares, Theater
    Heute, Hanover.
Theater der Zeit, Berlin.
Theater Heute, Velber bei,
    Hanover.
Transition, Paris.
Tulane Drama Review, Tulane
    University, New Orleans.
Unmuzzled Ox, Kingston, On-
    tario.
Virginia Quarterly Review,
    Charlottesville.
Vogue, New York.
Yale Literature Magazine, Yale
    University, New Haven,
    Conn.
Yale Review: A National
    Quarterly, Yale University,
    New Haven, Conn.
Yale/Theatre, Yale School of
    Drama, Yale University,
    New Haven, Conn.
Zuka, Journal of East African
    Creative Writing, East African
    Literature Bureau, Nairobi.

V. 2